There's something here for almost everyone.
Mac Home Journal

...one of the best guides to using System 7.
CompuServe

è un buon libro che vuol rappresentara una guida alternativa alla manualistica.
MacWorld di Boston

I recommend it to anyone with a Macintosh.
Diablo Valley MUG

I emphatically and gladly urge you to get this book.
appleJAC Digest

...takes readers by the hand and never lets them lose their way.
The Australian

Concisely written for the layman user...two thumbs up on this one!
Gulf Coast Computing

If you're considering the purchase of only one book to meet all your System 7 needs, this is the book for you.
Fordham University Mac User Group

As quick and exciting as a thriller! Craig Danuloff superbly unravels the great mysteries of System 7.
Diskette Gazette

The System 7.5 Book

The System 7.5 Book

Getting the most from your Macintosh operating system

Third Edition
through System 7.5

Craig Danuloff

VENTANA
PRESS

The System 7.5 Book: Getting the Most From Your Macintosh Operating System, Third Edition through System 7.5
Copyright © 1994 by Craig Danuloff

All rights reserved. This book may not be duplicated in any way without the expressed written consent of the publisher, except in the form of brief excerpts or quotations for the purposes of review. The information contained herein is for the personal use of the reader and may not be incorporated in any commercial programs, other books, databases or any kind of software without written consent of the publisher or author. Making copies of this book or any portion for any purpose other than your own is a violation of United States copyright laws.

Library of Congress Cataloging-in-Publication Data

Danuloff, Craig, 1963-
    System 7.5 book : getting the most from your Macintosh operating system / Craig Danuloff. — 3rd ed.
       p.   cm.
    Includes index.
    ISBN 1-56604-129-5
    1. Operating systems (Computers) 2. System 7. 3. Macintosh (Computer)— Programming. I. Title.
QA76.76.063D3485 1994
005.4'469—dc20   94-28998
                                                                     CIP

Book design: Marcia Webb, Karen Wysocki
Cover design: Nancy Frame, Nancy Frame Design; adaptation: Dawne Sherman
Cover illustration: Katherine Mahoney
Third Edition System 7.5 text & figure updates: Barrie Sosinsky
Index service: Mark Kmetzko
Technical review: Brian J. Little, Imagination Workshops
Editorial staff: Angela Anderson, Walter R. Bruce, III, Philip Orr, Pam Richardson, Jessica Ryan
Production staff: Patrick Berry, Cheri Collins, John Cotterman, Dan Koeller, Dawne Sherman, Marcia Webb, Mike Webster

Third Edition 9 8 7 6 5 4 3 2 1
Printed in the United States of America

For information about our audio products, write us at Newbridge Book Clubs, 3000 Cindel Drive, Delran, NJ 08375

Ventana Press, Inc.
P.O. Box 2468
Chapel Hill, NC 27515
919/942-0220
FAX 919/942-1140

Limits of Liability and Disclaimer of Warranty

The author and publisher of this book have used their best efforts in preparing the book and the programs contained in it. These efforts include the development, research and testing of the theories and programs to determine their effectiveness. The author and publisher make no warranty of any kind, expressed or implied, with regard to these programs or the documentation contained in this book.

The author and publisher shall not be liable in the event of incidental or consequential damages in connection with, or arising out of, the furnishing, performance or use of the programs, associated instructions and/or claims of productivity gains.

Dedication

Charles and Lillian Danuloff
Louis and Lillian Reisman

Trademarks

Trademarked names appear throughout this book. Rather than list the names and entities that own the trademarks or insert a trademark symbol with each mention of the trademarked name, the publisher states that it is using the names only for editorial purposes and to the benefit of the trademark owner with no intention of infringing upon that trademark.

Other Books by Craig Danuloff

Encyclopedia Macintosh*
Encyclopedia Macintosh Instant Software Reference*
Up & Running with PageMaker on the Macintosh
The PageMaker Companion*
Mastering Aldus Freehand*
Expert Advisor: Harvard Graphics
Desktop Publishing Type & Graphics*

*Coauthor Deke McClelland

Table of Contents

Introduction .... **xix**

Chapter 1 System Software Basics **1**
    What Does System Software Do? 2
    Parts of the System Software 4
    Using System Software 9
    Basic Macintosh Operations 11
        The Graphical User Interface • Files & Folders
        • Floppy Disks • Macintosh Utilities
    Data Transfer Methods 30
        Cut & Paste: Using the Clipboard & the Scrapbook
        • Macintosh Drag and Drop

Chapter 2 The Finder **41**
    New Finder Menus 44
    Finder Windows 53
        The Views Control Panel • The View Menu
        • Hierarchical Views • Navigating From the Keyboard
        • Dragging Files Between Windows • Working With
        Multiple Files • Title Bar Pop-Up Menu • Improved
        Zooming • Cleaning Up Windows & Icons
    The Help Menu 82
        Apple Guide • Balloon Help • Balloon Help
        Limitations • Additional Help
    Trash & Empty Trash 90
        Trash Tips
    The Get Info Dialog Box 93
        Get Info for the Trash • Get Info for Alias Icons

Chapter 3   Managing Your Hard Drive 101

Aliasing 102
   Basic Aliasing Concepts • Creating & Using Aliases
   • Advanced Aliasing Concepts • Aliasing Folders or
   Volumes • Using Aliases • Aliasing Summary
The Find Command 121
   Using the Find Command • The Find Dialog Box
   • The Find Item Dialog Box • Finding in System 7.5
   • Find Command Tips
Labels 136
   Configuring the Label Menu • Comments

Chapter 4   The System Folder 143

The System 7.5 System Folder 145
   The Apple Menu Folder • The Control Panels Folder
   • The Extensions Folder • The Fonts Folder • The
   Preferences Folder • The Startup Items Folder
The System File 159
   System File Access • Modifying the System Folder
   • Adding Files to the System Folder • Deleting Files
   From the System Folder

Chapter 5   System 7.5 & Your Software 169

System 7.5 Compatibility 170
   What Is Compatibility?
Launching 176
   Launching Methods • Macintosh Easy Open
   • The Launcher
Stationery Pads 186
   Creating a Stationery Pad • Using Stationery
   • Stationery Pad Tips
The Desktop Level 193
   Dialog Box Keyboard Equivalents
Desk Accessories 198

Chapter 6 **Power Macintosh & PowerBook System Software ... 203**

The Same Old Interface 205
RISC vs. CISC Chip Architecture 209
The PowerPC Series 214
Emulation vs. Native Routines 218
    The Mixed Mode Manager · Improving Application Performance
Power Macintosh-Specific Software 224
PowerBook Issues 226
    Power/Performance Management · Display Management · Connections, Remounting & Remote Access · The PowerBook Control Strip · File Synchronization

Chapter 7 **Working With Multiple Applications 247**

What Is Multitasking? 249
MultiFinder in System 6.0.x 251
Multitasking in System 7.5 253
Working With Multiple Applications 256
    Foreground & Background Applications · Background Processing · Background Printing · Copying Files in the Background · Hiding Applications · Hiding the Finder
Multitasking Tips 272
The Memory Implications of Multitasking 275

Chapter 8 **Memory Management 279**

Memory vs. Storage 280
    RAM & You
The Memory Control Panel 281
    Disk Cache · Virtual Memory · Enabling Virtual Memory · Virtual Memory Performance · Disabling Virtual Memory · 32-Bit Addressing · The Modern Memory Manager · Memory Control Panel Tips

Controlling Memory 294
    About This Macintosh • An About This Macintosh Tip
The Get Info Dialog Box 298
    Get Info in Version 7.0 • Get Info in Version 7.1 & Later • Setting Memory Options

Chapter 9   QuickDraw GX & Fonts 307

What Is QuickDraw? 308
About QuickDraw GX 311
Sophisticated Graphics Primitives 313
Fonts on the Macintosh 314
    PostScript Fonts • PostScript Font Challenges • Printing PostScript Fonts
Adobe Type Manager 325
    Using ATM
Installing Fonts 330
    Font Changes in System 7.1 • Printer Fonts in System 7 • Removing Fonts
TrueType 336
    TrueType GX • TrueType & PostScript • TrueType Technology • A Mixed World • Picking Your Font Standard
Advanced Typography 345
    Text Effects • Unicode, WorldScript & Localization • QuickDraw GX & Printing • Printing • The Print Dialog Box • The Print Spooler • Printing Extensions
Portable Digital Documents 359
ColorSync & Color Matching 361

Chapter 10   Inter-Application Communication & OpenDoc 367

The Edition Manager 368
    How Publish/Subscribe Works
Publish/Subscribe Commands 373
    The Create Publisher Command • The Subscribe To Command • The Publisher Options Command • The Subscriber Options Command • The Show Borders Command

Table of Contents

Editing Subscribers 383
Edition Files at the Finder 384
    Edition File Links • Unavailable Edition Files • Edition Files & Your Network
Edition Manager Tips 389
Inter-Application Communication 394
    Understanding AppleEvents • AppleEvents & Program Linking
OpenDoc 401
    What Is OpenDoc? • Documents & Parts • Apple's OpenDoc vs. Microsoft's OLE

Chapter 11 AppleScript 413

What Is AppleScript? 414
The AppleScript Architecture 418
Scripting Basics 420
The Script Editor 425
    Recording a Script • Saving a Script • Running a Script • Modifying a Script
Scripting Applications 435
The Scriptable Finder 437
The Useful Scripts Folder 438
Learning More About AppleScript 441

Chapter 12 An Introduction to File Sharing 443

What Is File Sharing? 445
    The Limits of File Sharing • A File Sharing Quick Tour
Preparing for File Sharing 450
Starting File Sharing 452
Registering Users & Groups 457
    Creating New Users • Configuring User Preferences • Creating & Working With Groups • Configuring Guest Preferences • Configuring Owner Preferences
Sharing Folders or Volumes 467
    Icons of Shared Items • Unsharing

Access Privileges 474
    Access Privilege Strategies
Monitoring File Sharing 484

Chapter 13 Working on a Network 487

Accessing Network Volumes 487
    Connecting With the Chooser • Selecting Specific Volumes • Connecting With PowerTalk • Remote Volumes & Access Privileges • A Volume Access Shortcut • Disconnecting From Remote Volumes • Accessing Your Hard Drive Remotely
Program Linking 500
Networks With Macs Running System 6.0.x 503
    Updating LaserWriter Drivers • Accessing File Sharing Volumes From System 6.0.x

Chapter 14 The AOCE—Apple Open Collaboration Environment. 509

About AOCE & Groupware 510
PowerTalk 515
Setting Up PowerTalk & PowerShare Servers 520
    Services & Addresses • Catalogs & Information Cards • Sending & Receiving Mail or Files • Remote Connections • AppleMail • DigiSign

Chapter 15 Apple's System 7 Extensions 543

MODE 32 545
PC Exchange 545
Macintosh Easy Open 550
At Ease 552
QuickTime 555
    QuickTime Movies • QuickTime & Data Compression • Using QuickTime • QuickTime 2.0
PlainTalk 563

Chapter 16 **Third-Party Utilities** 569
    Apple Menu Utilities 570
    Trash Utilities 573
    Alias Utilities 575
    Font Managers 578
    System Software Selectors 581
    File Sharing Utilities 583
    Extension Managers 584
    Printer Extensions 587
    Finder Performance Boosters 589
    Utility Collections 593

Appendix A **Installing or Updating System 7.5** 603
    Hardware Requirements 604
    Replacing System 6.x With System 7 605
        Back Up Your Hard Drive • Prepare Your Hard Drive
        • Run Apple's Compatibility Checker or Safe Install
        • Delete Existing System Software • Run the Installer
        • Install QuickDraw GX & PowerTalk • Configure the
        System 7 System Folder
    Updating System 7 623

Appendix B **A Brief History of System 7** 625
    The Many Faces of System 7 625
        System 7.0 • System 7.0.1 • System 7 Tune-Up
        • System 7.1 • System 7.1 Hardware System Update
        1.0 • System 7.0.1P, System 7.1P • System 7 Pro
        • Hardware System Update 3.0 • System 7.5 • Which
        Version Should I Use ? • Enablers • System Software/
        Hardware Compatibility Table • Macintosh Memory
        Configurations

Glossary 651

Index 659

Introduction

Once upon a time, there was a computer that was incredibly easy to use: Macintosh. It was full of youthful innocence, simple elegance and a kind of conservation of motion that made it impossible to describe any of its operations as complex.

Today, the Macintosh is grown up. It has traded innocence for experience, simplicity for sophistication and singularity for an incredible flexibility. Not surprisingly, the software at the core of the Macintosh has grown up, too.

System 7.5 provides powerful new features, extensive additional hardware and network support, and an expanded array of core technologies for software applications. Overall, it redefines the way the Macintosh is used, but it does so within the same intuitive framework of previous system software versions.

In *The System 7.5 Book*, you'll explore every aspect of System 7.5, learning how you can use each feature to be more efficient and productive.

What's New in System 7?

Any great product improvement keeps the existing product's solid familiar features, adds exciting new breakthrough features and throws in subtle enhancements for good measure. System 7.5 is no exception. As a result, booting up with System 7.5 will give even the most sophisticated Macintosh user a renewed sense of power and possibility, and that satisfying "out-of-box" experience.

Broadly speaking, System 7 features fall into three categories:

- **Enhanced ease-of-use.** The basic metaphors that make the Mac so friendly, such as point-and-click operation of mouse and icons, have been extended, so that even more complex tasks—like exchanging data, moving fonts and changing control panels—are now more intuitive. The result is a Macintosh environment that is more intuitive and easier to use and customize.

- **Support for recent hardware advances.** Almost every aspect of Macintosh hardware and peripherals has evolved and improved by several orders of magnitude since the January 1984 introduction of the 128k Macintosh; but until now, the system software has never received the overhaul it needed to fully support this equipment. System 7 was a completely new system software, designed for the technology of the '90s. System 7.5 extends this progression to the new generation of Macintosh computers based on a different family of microprocessors.

- **Inter-application communication.** The Macintosh has always allowed data to be shared between separate applications, using the Clipboard or the Scrapbook. In System 7, the interaction between applications moved forward light years, not only improving data-sharing between programs, but also making it possible for applications to communicate with and control one another.

It would take a whole book to describe everything new in System 7 and newer still in System 7.5 (hey, there's an idea); but just to whet your appetite, here's a brief listing of specific ways System 7 improved the Macintosh over System 6:

- Allows file sharing between AppleTalk-connected Macs.
- Displays hierarchical outline-format views of nested files and folders.
- Replaces the Control Panel.
- Eliminates the Font/DA Mover.
- Enhances MultiFinder and Background Printing functions.
- Expands application launching options.
- Expands file-finding capabilities.
- Improves font display and typographic support with TrueType.
- Introduces the ability to store files in more than one place.
- Introduces live Copy-and-Paste of data between applications.
- Provides additional file information in Finder windows.
- Adds QuickTime video support.
- Supports full-color icons.
- Supports virtual memory for increased RAM availability.
- Adds support for PowerBooks and RISC-based Power Macintosh computers.

What's New in System 7.5?

 System 7.5 adds over 50 major capabilities to system software. Some of these were part of separate AppleSoft products; some appeared in the System 7 Pro release; and others are new. Most notably System 7.5:

- Adds Macintosh Drag and Drop to move information, start processes or place clippings on your desktop.

- Adds hierarchical submenus: automated tasks, recent files, applications and server connections, etc. to the Apple menu.

- Includes an underlying macro language, AppleScript; a scriptable Finder; and a set of automation macros.

- Installs a new context-sensitive active online help system called Apple Guide.

- Improves the print architecture, making it more powerful, easier and extensible; eliminates the Print Monitor.

- Supports advanced typographical features and a portable document format with QuickDraw GX.

- Better supports virtual memory for increased RAM availability.

- Lets you create "Mac" notes, the electronic equivalent of the "post-it" note.

- Adds PowerTalk, a powerful electronic mail system to your computer.

- Provides both cross-platform and interapplication file translation.

- Improves overall speed while maintaining compatibility over the wide range of Macintosh models.

- Adds additional networking capability through MacTCP, making connections to the Internet easier.

System 7.5 continues in the Macintosh tradition of providing intuitive features while preserving the "look and feel" of the Macintosh desktop. But despite the range and depth of these improvements, a deliberate effort has been made to retain the Macintosh spirit, in commands and design elements. You may not even notice the improvements when you first use System 7.5–everything seems like the familiar Macintosh environment you're used to. But closer inspection will show you signs of change almost everywhere.

Who Should Read This Book?

The System 7.5 Book was written for both the experienced Macintosh user who is upgrading to System 7.5 from previous versions of System 7 or from System 6, and the new Macintosh user who is learning the Mac and System 7.5 simultaneously. The information provided in this book will suit users of every Macintosh model (since System 7.5 is compatible with nearly every Mac) and applies equally to the casual and the habitual user. *The System 7.5 Book* addresses the features, capabilities and requirements that the release of a new generation of Macintosh computers, PowerBooks and Power Macintosh, have imposed on the system software. In summary, if you use a Mac, this book is for you.

Experienced System 7 Users

If you have experience with System 7.0 or 7.1, this book will

- **Describe each new feature in System 7.5.** You won't have to play the trial-and-error guessing game in order to fully understand the system software upgrade.

- **Provide specific tips on using System 7.5.** We'll go beyond the basics and look at ways you can take advantage of the new System 7.5 abilities to improve your productivity and enhance your computing power.

- **Explain ways that System 7.5 will alter the way you use the Mac.** There are a number of areas where System 7.5's new abilities will alter the way you do things. To help you make the most of these changes, I'll give you real-world situations that show the results of these features in your work.

- **Clarify how the Power Macintosh and PowerBooks are accommodated in system software.** System 7.5 provides features that make them both easier to use and more powerful. For PowerBook users, System 7.5 helps you improve battery lifetimes between recharges, remotely access other computers and do file management. System 7.5 also installs on the new RISC-based Power Macintosh computers to provide the same familiar desktop you used previously. Support for PowerBooks first appeared in System 7.0.1; support for Power Macintosh computers were first part of System 7.1.2.

New Macintosh Users

If you're new to the Macintosh, pay special attention to Chapter 1, "System Software Basics." Much of the information in this chapter describes general Macintosh operations, setting the stage for System 7.5 features covered in later chapters.

You could also consult other resources focused more on introductory topics, including the reference manuals that came with your Macintosh and *The Little Mac Book, 2nd Edition,* by Robin Williams (published by Peachpit Press). For more information, see "Other Sources of System 7 Information," later in the Introduction.

System 6 Users Who Are Considering Upgrading

If you're a Macintosh user who has not yet upgraded to System 7, this book will

- **Explain all the new System 7.5 features.** I'll discuss what's new in a way you can understand even without hands-on experience with previous versions of System 7.

- **Give you a clear picture of System 7.5's benefits.** And a few of its drawbacks. You'll be able to make an informed decision about whether to upgrade now.

- **Clarify System 7.5's hardware requirements.** A few System 7.5 features are supported only by specific Macintosh hardware configurations. I'll identify those that may require you to upgrade your hardware.

- **Wait patiently on your bookshelf for the day you do upgrade.** At that time, *The System 7.5 Book* will provide all the details you need in order to quickly set up and operate your Mac using System 7.5.

Apple's System Software Strategy

Apple plans to introduce major versions of system software every year, migrating the technology to one that is portable across a wide range of hardware. This is accomplished by creating a core set of technologies in a microkernel architecture, building a hardware adaption layer (HAL) to translate operating system functions to different computer types. Important features to come include: memory protection, better multitasking — the ability to run several processes at the same time, and an improved graphical user interface.

System 7 Pro was the first major upgrade of System 7, adding major new capabilities to the operating system. Its highlights were:

- PowerTalk, and the Apple Open Collaboration Environment or AOCE: a groupware enabling toolkit.

- AppleScript, a high-level macro language with both system and third-party application specific support.

- PlainTalk, Apple's voice recognition technology (the result of the Casper project).

- QuickTime 1.6, an upgrade of Apple's video technology with extensions and player support on Microsoft Windows.

- DOS file input and output (I/O), disk mounting and file translation.

AppleSoft, a new software publishing unit of Apple, released a catalog of separate products based on system software. You can purchase Apple Remote Access, QuickTime Starter Kit, AppleScript, Macintosh PC Exchange, PowerBook/DOS Companion, PowerBook File Assistant, At Ease and At Ease for Workgroups, the Apple Font Pack, PhotoFlash, AppleShare and others as stand-alone packages from Apple. These products are described in appropriate places in this book.

System 7.5 began the composer series of system software releases, with 7.5 being the result of the "Mozart" project. In addition to technologies that were part of System 7.5 and other previously released software, the major new technologies in System 7.5 are:

- Improved multithreading, the ability to retain the context of several processes in memory at the same time.
- Macintosh Drag and Drop.
- QuickDraw GX, advanced graphics and typography, and portable documents.
- Intelligent help, Apple Guide, which was the result of the Reno project.
- Scriptable Finder, making the desktop AppleScript enabled.
- MacTCP network support, part of Apple's Open Transport network protocols.
- File synchronization capability.
- Telephony architecture and the Telephone Manager that lets you integrate a telephone and a Macintosh.
- Both 680x0 (commonly called 68k Macintosh) and Power Macintosh support.

Perhaps the single most important achievement of System 7.5 was the extension of the system software to RISC-based Macintosh computers, while maintaining compatibility with earlier 68k Macs and the library of Macintosh software. This feature appeared first in System 7.1.2, but System 7.5 included more system software routines written specifically for, or "native to," the Power Macintosh computers.

About 15 to 20 percent of the Macintosh Toolbox has been rewritten in native PowerPC code, yielding about 80 percent of the expected speed enhancement. You should expect to see native applications run at two to three times the speed of previous software on a PowerPC 601 computer. The next generation 620 chip promises a ten-fold increase. In emulation, programs written for 68k Macs should run at about the speed of a Quadra 700 on a 601 Power Macintosh.

Future versions of system software will continue this transition. Chapter 6 details these features more fully.

Apple's system software strategy identifies four major areas of transition for upgrades over the next three years:

- **User interface.** The current passive graphical user interface (or GUI) will be gradually replaced by an intelligent interface that offers active assistance. Apple Guide is an expression of this trend. Agents will collect mail, harvest information, automate tasks and do other tasks.

- **Microprocessor.** Apple will continue to migrate the installed hardware and software base from CISC to RISC computers. System software will seem to get somewhat faster in future revisions.

- **Networking.** PowerTalk and the Apple Open Collaboration Environment will become part of system software and find expression in advanced conferencing and groupware applications.

- **Application architecture.** You will see a transition from large monolithic applications to component software. With OpenDoc, compound documents will be easier to create using smaller modular applications.

Apple's new motto for its system software strategy is: "Fitting in while standing out." Fitting in embraces providing solutions for multiple platforms like DOS, Windows and UNIX, extending cross-platform compatibilities, improving network interoperability by ascribing to the Open Transport Communications Architecture and implementing OpenDoc as an open industry document technology.

To stand out, Apple cites its transition to the RISC computer architecture, deployment of the OpenDoc standard and the development of the Open Scripting Architecture (of which AppleScript is a part), inclusion of PowerTalk, and Apple Guide. All of these new technologies are discussed in the chapters to come.

The next major system software release is nicknamed "Copeland," and is scheduled for release in 1995. Copeland will probably be System 8, although it is unnamed at the present. Among its most important technologies will be:

- Microkernel architecture.

- Memory protection.

- Improved and extended I/O architecture, with new bus technologies.

- OpenDoc, a component-based application technology.

- More active assistance technology.

- Improved networking.

Efforts for Copeland are well underway. *The System 7.5 Book* details the expectations for OpenDoc in Chapter 10, with other core technologies described throughout the book. You can also expect to see Apple's system software appear on several other major hardware platforms over the next two years.

Further out in time is Apple's "Gershwin" project, with an expected release in 1996. If Apple retains its current numbering scheme, Gershwin will be System 9. On the drawing board for Gershwin are:

- Preemptive multitasking, the ability to run several processes at the same time.

- HAL, the hardware adaption layer that mediates between the microkernel and various types of computers.

- Intelligent assistance.

- Advanced graphics.

- A new Graphical User Interface or GUI, the reworking of the Macintosh desktop.

More substantive details on Gershwin are, as you would expect, hard to come by at this date.

A Word About Versions & Hardware Requirements

Since its initial release, System 7 has been enhanced, extended and updated several times. System 7.5 is a unified release for all models of Macintosh, and it ships with a single "universal" Enabler file to support all models of Macintosh. System 7.5 replaces System 7 Pro and System 7.1, and all of the versions of System 7 that came before it. You can buy System 7.5 from Apple on floppy disk, CD-ROM or pre-loaded onto the hard drive of a new Macintosh.

You may have encountered versions 7.0, 7.0.1 and 7.1, 7.1.1 or 7.1.2, three different bug-fix/performance improvement extensions (Tune Up 1.0, 1.11 and Macintosh Hardware System Update 1.0), two special versions (7.01P and 7.1P, for the Macintosh Performa line) and a slew of system enablers. System 7.5 replaces all of these previous versions. With the exception of requiring more RAM to run, System 7.5 will run on all models of Macintosh that run other versions of System 7. The recommendation for minimum requirements to run System 7.5 are: 4mb RAM for 68k Macs — 8mb when running QuickDraw GX and PowerTalk. For Power Macintosh models, use 8mb for 7.5, and 16mb to use QuickDraw GX and PowerTalk.

This book covers all versions of System 7. Any time the reference "System 7" is used, the features being described are common to all versions listed above. Whenever a feature unique to one version of System 7 is being described, the software is referred to by its specific version name, such as "Version 7.5," "Version 7.0.1"or "Version 7.1P."

A detailed description of the differences between the various System 7 versions, explanations of the tune-ups and enablers and information on selecting the correct version for you is presented in Appendix B.

What's Inside?

The System 7.5 Book is made up of 16 chapters, two appendixes, a glossary and an index.

Chapter 1: System Software Basics

In order to provide a context for discussing System 7's enhancements and additions, Chapter 1 summarizes basic concepts about the system software and the way it functions on the Macintosh. This information can be used as a review for those who need it and an introduction for first-time Mac users. Macintosh Drag and Drop (new in 7.5) is described in this chapter.

Chapter 2: The Finder

The Finder gives you tools for organizing and manipulating your disks and files. System 7's Finder greatly expands these capabilities with new menu commands, more ways to view and manipulate files in Finder windows, additional onscreen help and Apple Guide, improved Get Info dialog boxes and more. Several improvements from 7.5 are introduced here.

Chapter 3: Managing Your Hard Drive

Several System 7 features can help you organize your hard drive more efficiently and access your stored data quicker and more conveniently. These features include "aliases," a Find command (enhanced in System 7.5), the Label menu and improved support for comments. This chapter shows you how all these features help you control your hard drive and other storage media.

Chapter 4: The System Folder

The System Folder remains a unique and important part of your Macintosh in System 7, but many changes have been made to the way you use the System Folder and its files. You'll learn about the new System Folder organization and many of the files and folders found there. You'll also learn how to modify and customize the System file.

Chapter 5: System 7.5 & Your Software

The introduction of System 7 had a direct impact on every software application you use on your Macintosh; this chapter shows you how and why. First, the important issue of System 7.5 compatibility and the requirements for the new "System 7.5-Savvy" status are discussed. Then we'll look at some new features System 7.5 provides to all applications, including ways to launch applications using Stationery Pads, the Desktop level and the new status of desk accessories.

Chapter 6: Power Macintosh & PowerBook System Software

Power Macintosh RISC computers have necessitated a rewrite of Apple's system software. Although the system software still "looks" the same, it operates differently internally. These differences introduce a new language, affect the way you buy and install software, and may change your upgrade plans. In this chapter we look at how Power Macs were integrated into the Macintosh family of computers. Also, Chapter 6 looks at the special requirements of portable computing, and at PowerBook computers, in particular. System 7.5 includes a number of convenient utilities like the Control Strip, file synchronization, remote access, and network and desktop mounting.

Chapter 7: Working With Multiple Applications

System 7 allowed you to open and use as many different programs as your Macintosh's available memory can accommodate. This chapter introduces the concepts and capabilities of multitasking, providing examples of how multitasking helps you work more efficiently. Included are discussions of the Hiding commands and the memory implications of using multiple applications. You can now "hide the Finder" so that you no longer lose your place in an application when you click on the desktop.

Chapter 8: Memory Management

Additional system software features, together with today's more sophisticated Macintosh hardware and software, put more demands than ever on your Macintosh's memory. This chapter documents two System 7 features that expand the amount of memory you can make available to your Mac, and focuses on overall concepts of memory management that relate to System 7's built-in multitasking.

Chapter 9: QuickDraw GX & Fonts

System 7.5 introduces a more powerful graphics engine to the Macintosh, called QuickDraw GX. With QuickDraw GX comes improved and extensible printing capabilities, a new font technology, color matching through ColorSync and portable documents. Through the Layout Manager, a number of exciting new text effects are possible. QuickDraw GX supports WorldScript and language localization. One area where System 7 presented dramatic changes from past system software is font management. The Font/DA Mover is no longer used in System 7, and fonts reside instead directly in the System file (Version 7.0) or in the new Fonts folder (Version 7.1 and above). This chapter examines all aspects of font management, reviewing bitmapped fonts, PostScript fonts and TrueType, and the new QuickDraw GX font technology.

Chapter 10: Inter-Application Communication & OpenDoc

Inter-Application Communication (IAC) and OpenDoc are two brand-new System 7 features that make a significant contribution to data-sharing between applications. Inter-Application Communication provides a framework that software developers will use to facilitate automatic data-sharing and communication between programs. This chapter looks ahead to OpenDoc, Apple's new compound document technology, and describes its implementation and the effect it will have on your computing style.

Chapter 11: AppleScript

You can save time by capturing common tasks as an automated program, and reduce errors that occur due to manual entry. Prior to System 7 you were forced to seek third party solutions. Chapter 11 describes AppleScript, System 7.5's macro language. It provides a rich high-level language connection between the Finder and other applications. You will learn how to write and run scripts, and apply them to common problems.

Chapter 12: An Introduction to File Sharing

When you're running System 7, you can share any folder or volume from your hard drive with any other computer on your Macintosh network. This chapter looks at the many advantages of the File Sharing feature, including granting others access to your shared files, controlling access privileges to those files and folders, and monitoring the use of your shared data by other network users.

Chapter 13: Working on a Network

This chapter looks at the other side of the File Sharing coin—ways you can access data from other Macintoshes on your network. Included is information on using AppleShare file servers and logging onto your own Mac hard drive from another network computer. The IAC feature of Program Linking is reviewed, and issues involved in working on a network that includes Macintoshes still using system software 6.0x are also covered.

Chapter 14: AOCE—The Apple Open Collaboration Environment

AOCE is enabling technology for a variety of collaborative services or groupware. Its first implementation is PowerTalk. PowerTalk installs a "universal desktop mailbox" that serves as an interface to send and receive fax, voice and email. Third-party gateways let PowerTalk mail agents harvest information sources and communicate automatically. PowerTalk comes with AppleMail, a letter and messaging application that can connect with Microsoft's Enterprise Messaging System on Windows. Additionally, PowerTalk provides DigiSign digital signatures, encryption and password protection.

Chapter 15: Apple's System 7 Extensions

Another important change that has arrived with System 7 is Apple's ability to update the system software without waiting for the next major upgrade release. Bug fixes, new features and other modifications can all be released in the form of extensions, and users who don't want to take advantage of the new features don't have to. This chapter examines some of Apple's special extensions—like QuickTime, PlainTalk, the Telephone Manager and Printer Extensions—that add significant power and performance to your Mac.

Chapter 16: Third-Party Utilities

While Apple has eventually provided—in the form of extensions—some of the features System 7 was lacking, there are still dozens of little things about the Mac and the way it works that most people would like to see improved upon. Fortunately, an army of third-party software developers and shareware authors are working to provide Mac users with the features and capabilities that System 7.5 lacks. This chapter looks at some of the best third-party System 7.5 utilities and helps you find software that picks up where System 7 leaves off.

Appendix A: Installing or Updating System 7.5

Unless you were fortunate enough to have Apple or your computer dealer install System 7.5 on your hard drive, the first thing you must do to get running is use the System 7.5 Installer. Appendix A explains how to use Apple's Compatibility Checker utility, and helps you understand the options and intricacies of the System 7.5 Installer. Also included is information on using the Installer on an AppleTalk network to install System 7.5 from a remote Macintosh.

Appendix B: A Brief History of System 7

Apple has exploited a major strength of System 7 in releasing special customized versions of it to different groups of specialized users. This allows Performa, PowerBook, Quadra and Power Macintosh owners to have system software tailored to their machines and address their particular needs. Appendix B examines the release histories and different versions of System 7 that have evolved since its initial introduction.

Book Conventions

7.5 This book uses a few graphic elements to highlight new or important information in the book. They're used sparingly. One you've encountered already. It's the System 7.5 icon. Whenever a section deals with new technology introduced in System 7.5 you'll see this icon. Small tips on System 7.5 will not always be marked with this icon, but will be described in the text.

? Using Apple Guide, the System 7.5 manual has shrunk to 75 pages by referencing tutorial information in that system. *The System 7.5 Book* also references Apple Guide assistance so that you can try the techniques you learned about in this book. Any time you see the Apple Guide icon, the text tells you what general topic in Apple Guide to look in for help.

Finally, system software is meant to protect you from yourself so that you can't make unrecoverable mistakes. Apple even writes that principle into its developer guidelines. Still, there are ways to go wrong. You'll find a "Caution" note wherever one of those special "gotchas" is to be found.

Other Sources of System 7 Information

There are many other sources of Macintosh information you may want to use as well:

- **Other books.** There are many fine books that serve as an introduction to Macintosh computers. In addition to *The Little Macintosh Book, 2nd Edition*, by Robin Williams (Peachpit Press), *Mac for Dummies*, by David Pogue (IDG Press) and *The Macintosh Companion*, by Sharon Zardetto Aker (Addison-Wesley) and *Mac, Word & Excel Desktop Companion*, by Tom Lichty (Ventana Press) are also recommended for novice users. The three best books at a somewhat higher level are: *Everything You*

Wanted to Know About the Mac, 2nd Edition, Hayden Press, *Macworld Complete Mac Handbook, 2nd Edition*, by Jim Heid (IDG Books) and *The Apple Macintosh Book, 4th Edition*, by Cary Lu (Microsoft Press). For tips, tricks and traps books, you can do no better than the cult classic *The Macintosh Bible, 4th Edition*, by Arthur Naiman et al. (Peachpit Press), *Voodoo Mac*, by Kay Nelson (Ventana Press), *Macworld Macintosh Secrets*, by David Pogue and Joel Schorr (IDG Press), or *Dr. Macintosh*, by Bob Levitus (Addison-Wesley).

- **Magazines.** Popular informative periodicals, such as *Macworld, MacUser, MacWEEK* and the *Mac Home Journal*, provide the latest news on Macintosh hardware and software, including issues that relate to using System 7 on your Mac.

- **User groups.** It's a great idea to visit your local Macintosh user group. User groups provide local support on virtually every Macintosh topic. The introduction of System 7.5 will undoubtedly be the topic of many user-group meetings. You can find a group near you by calling the Apple Computer at 800-538-9696, extension 500.

- **Bulletin board systems.** If you have a modem, check out the many Macintosh-related areas on America Online or the CompuServe Information Service. They provide you and your Mac direct access to thousands of other Mac users and to many software and hardware developers. Spending a little time online is often the best way to get a Macintosh related question answered; you can also browse through detailed information on almost any Macintosh topic and even download useful software utilities or upgrades.

Apple provides a service to developers and the technical community called AppleLink that is available for outside subscription. In 1994 Apple launched eWorld, an online service similar to America Online with a graphical iconic interface. eWorld contains special services for Macintosh users, and particularly those who own Apple Newton personal data assistants (PDAs). Call 408-996-1010 for information on eWorld or AppleLink; 800-227-6364 for America Online; and 800-848-8990 to inquire about CompuServe.

Craig Danuloff
CompuServe: 76566,1722
AppleLink: ICat.Craig
Fax: 206/623-0477

Ventana Press
PO Box 2468
Chapel Hill, NC 27515
America Online: Ventana500
Internet: Ventana500@aol.com
CompuServe: 70524,3216
919/942-0220
Fax: 919/942-1140

Chapter 1

System Software Basics

Why is the Macintosh so popular? Is it the "graphic user interface?" Maybe it's that all Macintosh applications use similar menus and commands. Or is it because configuring hardware and peripherals on the Mac is so easy?

The answer, as everyone knows, is "all of the above." But while you probably know how easy a Macintosh is to use—it's friendly, consistent and expandable—you may not know *why*. The reason is because the system software that controls the computer also gives it all of these qualities.

The release of System 7 gave Macintosh system software new prominence; the topic was rarely discussed in the past. And though this emphasis is largely due to Apple's marketing agenda, anyone who uses a Macintosh ought to understand the role of the system software and its capabilities, including how to use it most effectively.

This chapter introduces and defines the functions of the Macintosh system software. It also offers a quick tour of Macintosh basics, using some of the more common commands and features the system software provides.

This tour is designed for those who are using a Macintosh for the first time, and people who'd like a little review before diving into the details of System 7.5's features. If you're comfortable using your Macintosh, you can probably skip the "Basic Macintosh Operations" section of this chapter and skim "What Does System Software Do?" and "Using System Software" before moving on to Chapter 2, "The Finder."

What Does System Software Do?

What makes the Macintosh smile when you turn it on? Why does the disk icon appear on the desktop when you insert a floppy disk? How are fonts shared among all your applications? The answer to each of these questions is the same: the system software does it.

System software (or an *operating system* as it is known on other computer platforms) has three main responsibilities: it controls the hardware built into your Macintosh (and any peripherals you have connected), provides common elements and features to all your software applications and lets you manage your disks, files and directories. Let's briefly look at each of these areas.

- **Hardware control.** In order for your Mac to work, its RAM, disk drives, video monitor, keyboard, mouse, printer and scanner (or other peripherals), must be individually controlled and collectively managed. Saving files to disk, drawing images on the screen and printing are examples of hardware control managed by the system software.

- **Common software elements.** Every Macintosh software application has common elements, such as menus, dialog boxes and support for fonts. These common elements are delivered to software applications from a "software toolbox" in the system software. Apple assures consistency among applications and spares software developers the difficult task of programming these elements by centrally providing these elements and including conventions for their use as part of the system software.

- **Disk and file management.** The Finder, which is a part of the system software, provides the ability to format disks, lets you find, copy, move, rename and delete files, and displays icon and text-based information about disks and files. The Finder also allows you to launch other applications, and acts as a "home base" when you start up or after you quit other programs.

System software performs this magic by analyzing the model of Macintosh you have to determine what instructions are "hard-wired" into your computer, and what additional instructions are needed. Thus it appears as if software running on the lowliest Macs operates much like the software on the fastest Power Macintosh, although with much less speed and in some cases with certain missing higher functionality.

Even with the new generation of RISC-microprocessors (Reduced Instruction Set Computing) in the Power Macintosh computers, Apple system software can run the library of software written previously for CISC-microprocessor (Complex Instruction Set Computing—CISC-based Macs are also called 68k Macs after the 680x0 series of Motorola microprocessors), albeit more slowly than software specially written for the Power Macintosh. Even the system software itself has only been about 15 to 20 percent translated into native code to run on the PowerPC microprocessor.

Without system software, each application would have to provide its own self-contained operating features for running the hardware and managing your disks and files. There would be no continuity from one application to the next, and software programs would be far more complex, as well as time-consuming and costly to develop.

Fortunately, Apple's system software performs all these tasks well, allowing developers to focus on unique and sophisticated programs, while leaving the rest to Apple.

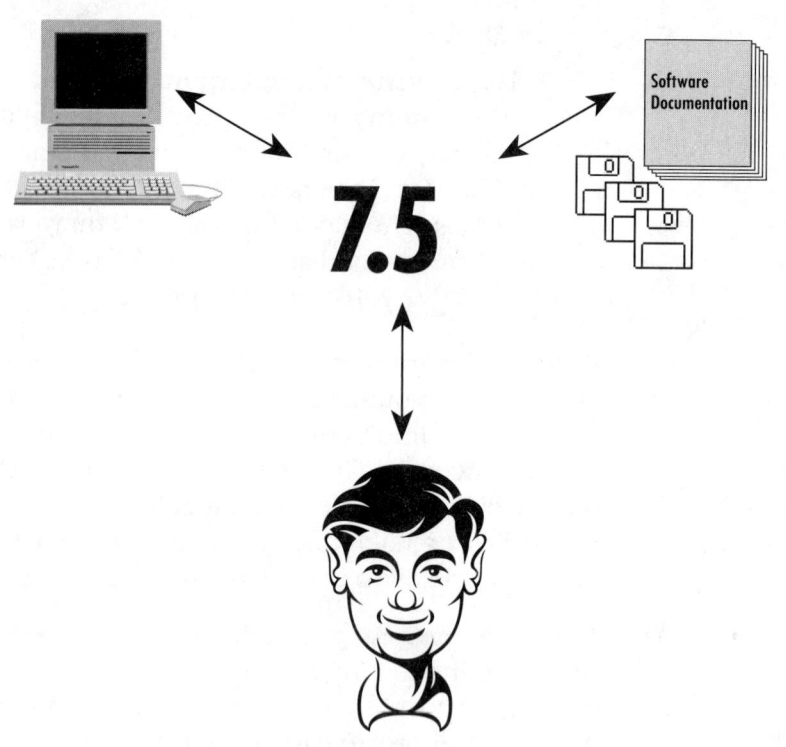

Figure 1-1: System software provides the link between you, your Macintosh and your software.

Parts of the System Software

The most prominent files that make up the Macintosh system software are the System file and the Finder, but printer and network drivers, control panel devices, extensions and resources (fonts, desk accessories, sounds, function keys) are also part of the system software. All system files are found in the System folder, which is described more fully in Chapter 3, "Managing Your Hard Drive." The list below summarizes the functions of these components:

- **System file.** The System file is involved in the most important and most frequently used aspects of the system software. It also acts as a framework that other parts of the system software can connect to. The System file helps the Mac start up and provides many of the dialog boxes and menu bars, commonly used icons and code that help applications manage memory and other hardware resources.

- **Resources.** Resource files also add capabilities to the Macintosh. Resources, including fonts, sounds or keyboard layouts can exist as stand-alone files or can be placed into the System file itself. (Note that fonts are best placed in the Fonts folder within the System folder, or managed by a resource manager like Suitcase II or MasterJuggler.)

- **Finder.** The Finder is a program designed to help you control your disks, drives and files. It provides many utility features such as formatting disks, printing disk catalogs and deleting files; it's also a "home base" for sorting and working with files and launching other applications.

- **ROM.** Portions of the Macintosh operating system are stored in Read-Only Memory (ROM) chips on the computer's logic board. These are not technically considered part of the system software, but they're vital to its operation. ROM-based software handles startup and many basic aspects of Mac hardware control. System software looks at your computer's ROM and adds or updates missing system code so that what loads in memory is the latest and greatest system software.

- **Printer drivers.** Printer drivers are small conversion programs that change data from its original format into a format the printer can digest and output. Printer drivers are selected in the Chooser and "run" with the Print command. QuickDraw GX significantly changes and improves the Macintosh print architecture, making it extensible through third-party programs, and making printer drivers easier to write for developers. This new feature is described in Chapter 9, "QuickDraw GX & Fonts."

  Apple provides printer drivers for most Macintosh printers and output devices, but other vendors offer printer drivers that allow the Macintosh to be used with output devices that Apple drivers don't necessarily support. If you are having printing difficulties, check with your printer vendor to determine if you have the latest version of a printer driver that is compatible with System 7.5.

- **Network drivers.** Network drivers are also accessed using the Chooser control panel. They help your Macintosh communicate with network file servers, print service, remote modems and other network devices. Apple provides network drivers for AppleTalk, Ethernet Token Ring and MacTCP (new to System 7.5–TCP/IP provides Internet support) network communications. Many other network drivers are provided along with third-party Macintosh network hardware. Network drivers are found in the Extensions folder and are often classified as extensions. The network drivers described above are part of Apple system software—other drivers are distributed by third-party software and hardware vendors.

- **Extensions.** Because Macintosh system software is modular, it can be enhanced, modified or extended by small files that temporarily become part of the system software when loaded at startup. These files are called extensions. (Note: They were called INITs in previous

Chapter 1: System Software Basics 7

versions of the system software.) The icons for most extensions appear across the bottom of your screen at startup.

7.5 Examples of important Apple system software extensions in System 7.5 are: Apple Guide, AppleScript, AppleShare, AppleTalk, Catalogs, File Sharing, Find File, LaserWriter, PowerTalk, QuickDraw GX, QuickTime, StyleWriter, Sound Manager, SCSI Manager, among others. Most specialized peripheral devices (for example, printers, monitors [like the Quadra AV], CD-ROM players and networks) normally come with an extension(s) file.

Extensions are the way Apple "extends" the system software without having to release a major new system software upgrade. Thus when QuickTime was first released in 1990, it appeared as an extension. As extensions are improved over time and stabilized, often they are added directly to system software with their functional code being added to the System or Finder file. Finally, when system software code becomes routine and standardized, what initially started out as an extension may eventually end up encoded in ROM in later models of Macintosh.

Extensions sometimes conflict with one another, with your regular applications and with system software. You can control which extensions load at startup, and the order that they load as a means of circumventing extension conflicts. The new System 7.5 Extension Manager control panel provides a means for doing this. This is described in more detail in "The System Folder," in Chapter 4.

Several extensions are provided with the system software, but most are created independently by third parties. Most extensions add some new feature or capabilities to the system software. Examples include DiskDoubler, which lets you compress your files to save drive space; Suitcase II, which makes using fonts, sounds and FKEYs more convenient; or SAM Intercept and other virus detection utilities.

- **Control panels.** These are mini-applications that provide preference or general control over some aspect of the system software, an extension utility or a hardware peripheral. Control panels, provided along with the system software, control your Mac's memory, its internal clock, colors, file sharing and many other system attributes. At the system level, control panels work much like extensions, but they feature an interface that offers the user control over certain variables in the device's function. In some cases a function will ship with both an extension and a control panel.

  You might ask: What is the difference between extensions and control panels? In reality, not much. Often these two types of files do many of the same things. Developers use control panels when they want to allow you to make changes; otherwise they use extensions. Settings you make to your system with control panels are stored until changed again. Therefore, if you remove those control panels from your System folder the settings can't be changed.

- **Desk accessories.** These are also independent files, and in all versions of System 7 they operate just like normal applications. (In previous versions of the system software, desk accessories were special files run in their own single layer of memory and accessed only from the Apple Menu.) Desk accessories (DAs) provide utility functions not built into the system software. DAs provided as part of the system software include the Chooser, Alarm Clock, Calculator and Key Caps, to name but a few.

Using System Software

System software is used almost constantly from the moment you turn on your Macintosh. To further help you understand its role, let's take a look at a few of the tasks it controls or assists:

- **Startup.** From just a moment after the power is turned on, your Macintosh's system software controls the startup process, running any available extensions, verifying that your hardware is functioning properly and loading the Finder.

Only the System, Finder and Enabler files are mandatory for your Macintosh to start up. The additional components are important, but not required. You can prepare an emergency disk with just those three components, and use that disk should your computer not start up properly. You can then copy over additional components from disk as required.

- **File management.** When you work on the Finder desktop, manipulating windows and icons, your actions are translated from the onscreen graphic display into actual changes to the files on disk. But files aren't stored on disk as cute little icons; they're simply strings of magnetic 1's and 0's. It's the system software that turns them into meaningful text, beautiful graphics, stirring sounds and moving images.

- **Application launching.** When you run a software program, the system software accesses the computer and sees to it that the correct portions of the file are read from disk, that the available memory is properly managed and that data files (and sometimes temporary work files) are created and maintained on disk.

- **Font usage.** Every time a font is used on the Macintosh, whether it's a bitmapped, PostScript, TrueType or QuickDraw GX outline font, character information, including the way it should look in any particular size and style, is provided by the system software.

- **Dialog boxes.** System software provides the basic format of almost every dialog box used on the Macintosh. For Open... and Save As... dialogs, the system software also supports the scrolling file listing and reading or writing files.

- **Printing.** An application must pass its data through one of the system software's printer drivers so it can be converted into a format the printer can understand. After this, the system software communicates the file to the printer, and in some cases receives feedback from the printer during output.

- **Screen display.** System software is responsible for producing the display that appears on your Macintosh screen. Applications communicate the display information to the system software in a format called QuickDraw; then the ROM-based portions of the system software convert this information and use it to draw the screen.

- **Networking.** Nearly every aspect of communication between the Mac and its peripherals is controlled by the system software. This includes data transfer from the disk to the AppleTalk port (and other ports); the timing of operating network communications while other software is being run onscreen; cabling; and two-way communications with sophisticated printers, modems and storage drives.

So as you can see, almost any task you perform on your Macintosh—from the smallest mouse click to the largest data transfer—relies on the system software. Fortunately, you don't need to understand the technical intricacies of how system software does its tasks in order to use your Macintosh. But it is useful to have an appreciation for the range and depth of the system software's functions.

Basic Macintosh Operations

From the technical descriptions of the system software provided above, we'll now turn to the easiest and most fundamental aspects of using the Macintosh. This section looks at the things you need to know in order to use the Macintosh efficiently. It also defines terms you'll encounter throughout the book.

This information is intended primarily for those who are using System 7.5 in their first experience on the Macintosh. If you've been working with the Macintosh under system software 6.0x, you'll probably want to skip this section and move ahead to Chapter 2, "The Finder."

The Graphical User Interface

The first and most fundamental requirement for using the Mac is understanding its graphical user interface. Instead of communicating your commands in words, you select pictures—or icons—that represent words. These icons, along with windows and menus, represent Macintosh hardware and software functions and features. And you use the mouse cursor to communicate with the Macintosh. (Yes, you'll use the keyboard too, but we'll assume you've already mastered that device.)

Let's look at each of these elements individually:

- **Icons.** These are small graphics (drawings) of things that appear on the Macintosh screen and represent items such as disks and folders (the icon actually looks like a disk or folder, as shown in Figure 1-2).

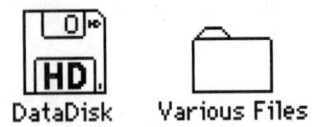

Figure 1-2: Disk and folder icons.

Various versions of icons are used to represent files stored on your disks. The particular version of a file's icon tells you what kind of file it is. The standard application file icon and the standard document file icon are shown in Figure 1-3. But many application and document files use custom icons. A collection of custom application and document file icons appears in Figure 1-4.

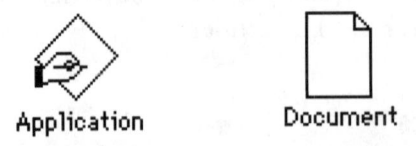

Figure 1-3: Standard application and document file icons.

Figure 1-4: Custom application and document file icons.

- **Windows.** When a Macintosh file is opened, its contents are displayed in a window. The most common type of window looks like the one shown in Figure 1-5: it includes a *title bar* at the top and scroll bars on its right and bottom edges. You can move a window around (by dragging its title bar), close a window (by clicking the close box in its upper left corner) and change the size of a window (by dragging the size box in its lower right corner).

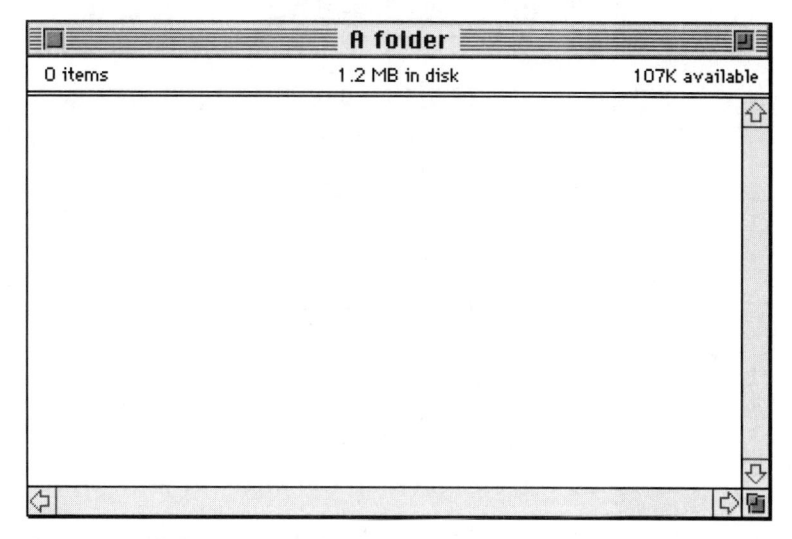

Figure 1-5: A sample Finder window.

However, there are other types of windows, including *dialog boxes*. A sample dialog box is shown in Figure 1-6. These small specialized windows usually present a set of options that allow you to customize a command or activity.

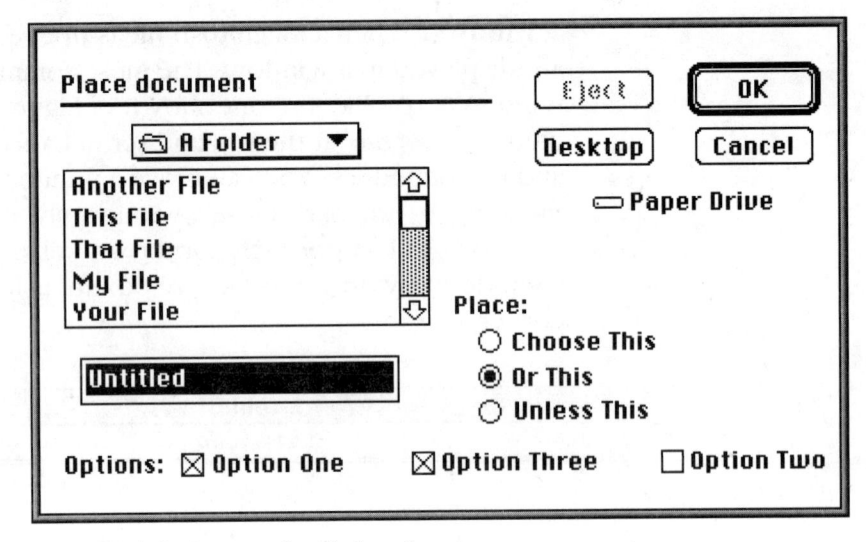

Figure 1-6: A sample dialog box.

There are four common kinds of dialog box options. Small round *radio buttons* present a set of mutually exclusive choices. Small square *check boxes* present a set of choices you can select in any combination. An *option box* is a small area where you type in your choice. Some options provide a set of alternatives in a *pop-up menu*; you can click on the one you want with the mouse.

Some dialog boxes don't present options but simply provide information. Usually this information is feedback concerning a command or action you're engaged in, or a message from one of your hardware devices. These are called *alert dialog boxes*, or simply alerts; a sample is displayed in Figure 1-7.

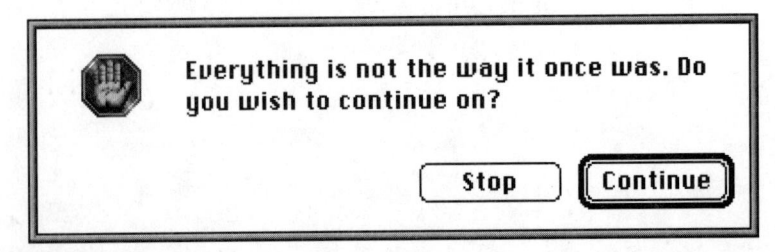

Figure 1-7: An Alert dialog box.

Another type of window used in some software applications is called a *palette*. A palette is a small "floating" window, so called because you can move it around easily. Unlike an ordinary dialog box, which disappears after you've selected options or dismissed it, palettes may remain open for the duration of a work session. A palette presents a set of icons that represent tools you can work with; or sometimes it presents a text list of commands or options you can choose from.

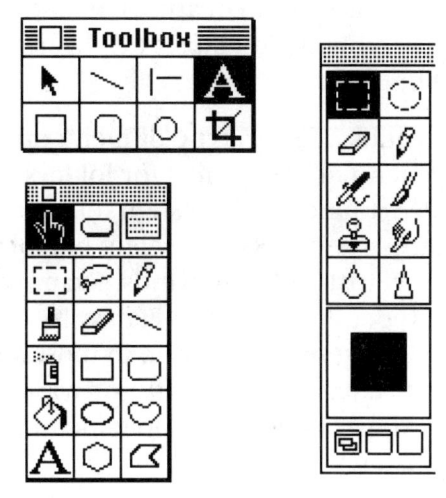

Figure 1-8: Sample palettes.

- **Menus.** Most commands in Macintosh applications are presented in menus displayed along the menu bar at the top of the screen. Commands are usually grouped logically, with logical names that provide clues about what they're used for. The menu bar is the most distinctive element of the Macintosh. The now familiar Chicago font was specifically designed for the purpose of attractive screen display on the original Macintosh.

  Menus drop down when the mouse is clicked on the menu name; they remain visible for as long as the mouse button is pressed. This behavior is commonly referred to as pull-down menus, but the action feels more like pop-down menus. As you drag the mouse down, each command highlights as it's selected. Releasing the mouse while the command is selected executes that command, with the feedback of having the selection command flash two or three times. (More about using the mouse later in this chapter.)

There are four basic types of menu commands. Some commands execute as soon as they're selected. Others toggle the status of some features on and off. Command names that end with an ellipsis (...) bring up a dialog box of related options.

7.5 ▶ System 7.5 adds a fourth type of menu option, a hierarchical submenu of commands for folders in the Apple Menu folder (found in the System folder). Holding the mouse button down lets you select one of these normal, toggling or ellipsis subcommands. Examples of all four command types are shown in Figure 1-9. Hierarchical menus have long been common in most Macintosh applications, but required third-party software for system software. (More about your Apple menu's hierarchical submenus later.)

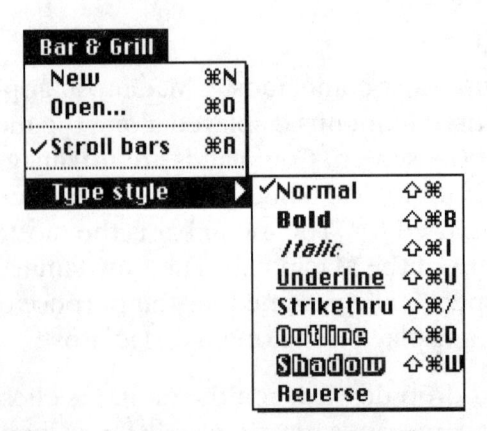

Figure 1-9: Four command types.

Chapter 1: System Software Basics

All these graphic elements interact with your Macintosh via mouse manipulation. Operating the mouse is simple enough: you move the mouse on your desk and the mouse cursor moves onscreen accordingly. Only the motion of the mouse on your desktop produces a change in cursor position, making the mouse a *relative* pointing device. (Some devices like graphics tablets are *absolute* pointing devices as each point on their surface maps to a point on your screen.) The type of cursor that appears at any given time depends on the item being pointed to, the software being used, the commands chosen and the keys pressed on the keyboard. When working in the Finder, the mouse cursor will be the left facing arrow.

Arrow cursors appear whenever you're pointing to the menu bar, regardless of the application being used. Macintosh applications also use the arrow cursor to select and manipulate objects. Other common cursors are shown in Figure 1-10.

Figure 1-10: Common cursors.

There are five common actions you can make with the cursor. These actions manipulate icons, invoke Macintosh commands and control application tools:

- **Pointing.** Positioning the cursor over a particular icon or other object or window element. If the cursor is an arrow, the arrow's tip marks the specific point. Other cursors have their own "hot spots," or specific points of action.

- **Clicking.** Quickly pressing and releasing the mouse button. In most cases, the click executes when the button is fully released, not while it's depressed. Mouse clicks select objects, including icons, buttons and dialog box options.

- **Double-clicking.** Pressing and releasing the mouse button twice in rapid succession. Most beginners don't double-click fast enough to prevent the Macintosh from interpreting them as two single clicks instead of one double-click. Double-clicking controls many Macintosh actions, like opening icons to display their windows. The sensitivity of double-clicking can be changed using the Mouse control panel.

- **Pressing.** Holding down the mouse button while a command or action is completed. For example, the mouse button must be held down for menus—they're visible onscreen only while the mouse button is down.

- **Dragging.** Moving the mouse—and therefore the cursor—while the mouse button is pressed (held down). This action usually moves an item or causes the current cursor tool to be used while the mouse button is down (such as drawing a line with a pencil tool).

Files & Folders

Once you understand icons and windows, and you're comfortable working your mouse, you're ready to put all that knowledge and skill to work. One of the most important tasks will be manipulating files on the desktop.

There are many different types of files—including applications, data documents, system software files, utilities, fonts and dictionaries. To keep all these files organized, you'll put them into *folders*. You can create new folders to hold any type of file whenever you like, using the File Menu's New Folder command. You can also create folders inside other folders, establishing a hierarchical arrangement of files and folders, as shown in Figure 1-11. If you've worked on other types of computer systems, folders are directly analogous to directories or subdirectories.

> See the "Files & Disks" topic of Apple Guide for related information.

To reposition files or folders—adding them to a folder, or copying them to another disk or hard drive—point to the icon of the file or folder you want to manipulate, click and hold the mouse button, drag the file onto the destination icon and release the mouse button. If you drag files to a different folder on the same disk, the files are *moved* (they now appear only in the new location, not in the old location). If you drag files to a different disk, or to a folder on a different disk, they're *copied* (they appear—and exist—in their new location and in the old location).

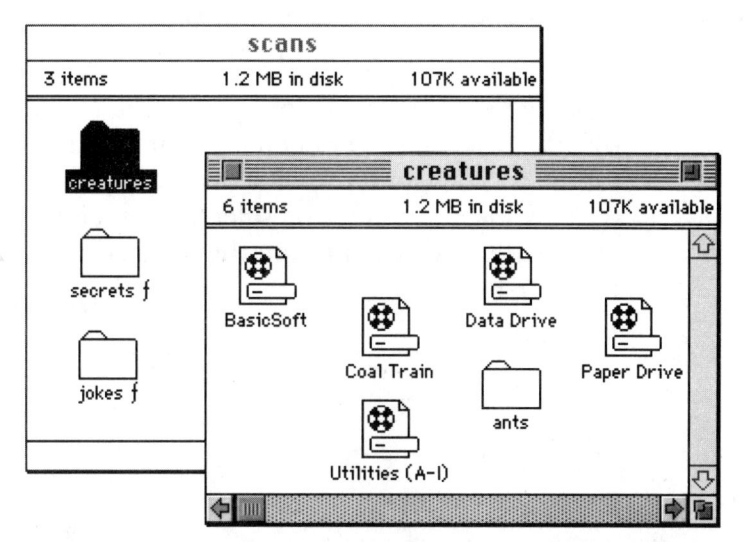

Figure 1-11: In this example, the "ants" folder is inside the "creatures" folder which is inside the "scans" folder.

Floppy Disks

Two types of floppy disks are supported by the Macintosh: *800k* floppies, (sometimes known as "regular" or "double-density" or "DD") and *1.44mb* floppies (sometimes called "high-density" or "HD"). Most Macs can use either disk type, but some (the 128, 512, XL, Mac Plus, Mac II and older Macintosh SEs) can use 800k disks only. You can tell the difference between the two by the number of small windows at the top of the floppy disk: 800k floppies have one window, 1.44mb have two. High-density disks usually have a distinctive "HD" logo stamped on the lower left, near the shutter. As older Macintosh models recede into history, 800k floppy disks are used less often.

Before using a floppy disk for the first time, it must be *formatted.* This erases the disk and prepares it for use. (If the disk has been used before, formatting erases whatever is on it, making the data unrecoverable.) Formatting delineates cylindrical sections (with magnetic lines), and writes a directory or table of contents for the disk thus lowering somewhat the actual capacity of the floppy disk.

When you insert a new floppy disk, the Macintosh can tell that the disk has never been used, and asks if you want to format it. You can reformat a disk at any time, deleting all its files, by inserting the disk, selecting its icon and choosing the Erase Disk... command from the Special Menu, as shown in Figure 1-12.

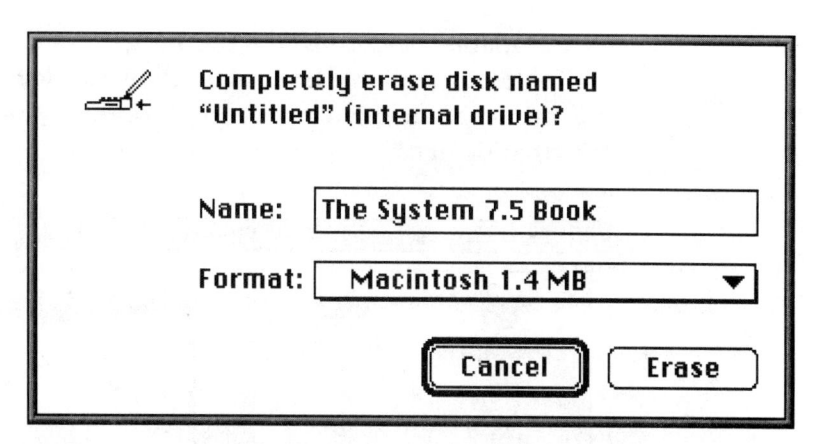

Figure 1-12: The Erase Disk dialog box.

> See the topic "Using DOS Files & Disks" for additional information.

With System 7.5 installed you are given the additional options (enabled by the File System Extension) of formatting your floppy disk for an IBM PC or PC clone as a "DOS" disk, or as a Pro-DOS disk for Apple II family computers. A DOS disk appears on your desktop in System 7.5 with the letters PC in the disk icon. It will operate correctly in an IBM PC computer. Be careful to format the floppy disk as you intend, as it's easy to forget and use your previous format setting.

Macintosh Utilities

There are several built-in utilities you use frequently when you're working on the Macintosh:

- **The Chooser.** This desk accessory is an electronic switchbox that lets you select from printers, networks and file servers your Macintosh is connected to. The Chooser appears, as shown in Figure 1-13, when its name is chosen from the Apple Menu. On the left side of the Chooser are icons representing the devices that may be available. Selecting an icon brings up a list, in the right side of the dialog box, of available devices. Selecting the name of the device you want connects your Macintosh to that device.

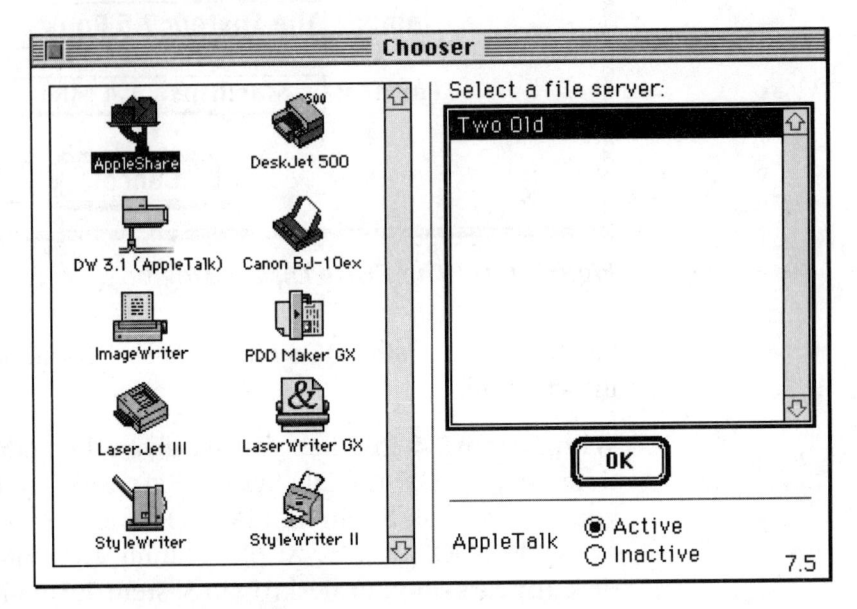

Figure 1-13: The Chooser.

- **Control Panels.** Several of the control panels in the Control Panels folder, accessed via the Apple Menu, are used to specify basic settings and preferences for your Macintosh. System 7.5 reworks several of the control panels, separating out functions that were previously grouped together and adding new functionality.

Use the "Setting Options" topic for information on Control Panels and the Chooser.

The *General Controls control panel* is used to change a number of desktop behavior characteristics. The number of times a menu command blinks when selected, and the frequency an insertion point blinks were previously

Chapter 1: System Software Basics 23

found in this control panel. All of the remaining functions are new to System 7.5. New functions include: showing the desktop when in another application, viewing the Launcher at startup, an improper shut down warning, system and application folder protection, and the location a new document is saved to are found here. Many of these functions are described more fully in the next three chapters. The General Controls control panel is shown in Figure 1-14.

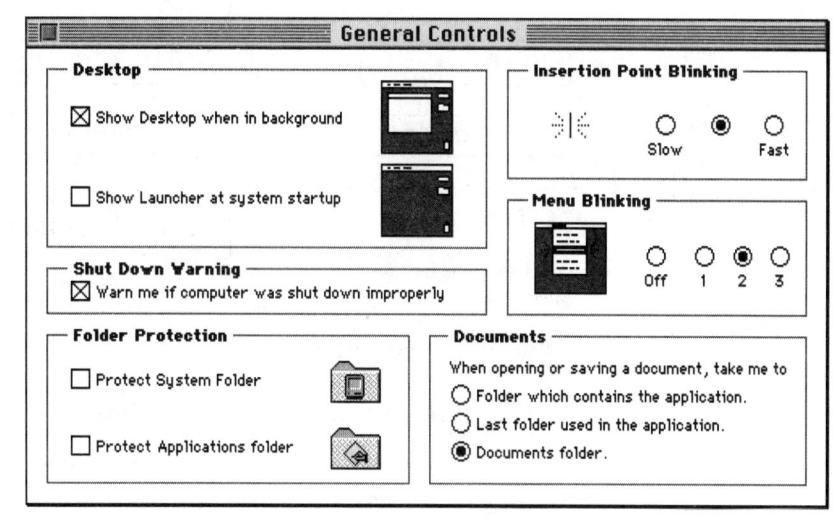

Figure 1-14: The General Controls control panel.

The *Date & Time control panel* is used to set the system date and time of your computer, as well as the time zone. This is the date and time that appears in your menu bar (optionally set here), and is used to time stamp file creation or modification times. It is also used by many applications to do maintenance and updates: for example, to find "today" in a calendar program. The Date & Time control panel, added to versions 7.1 and later, is shown in Figure 1-15.

Dates and times are a central function of your computer's bookkeeping. You normally set these parameters once, then an internal battery runs the clock under its own power. If you are seeing erratic time behavior, it could be that your battery has run down. When the battery isn't at fault, it portends a more serious hardware problem.

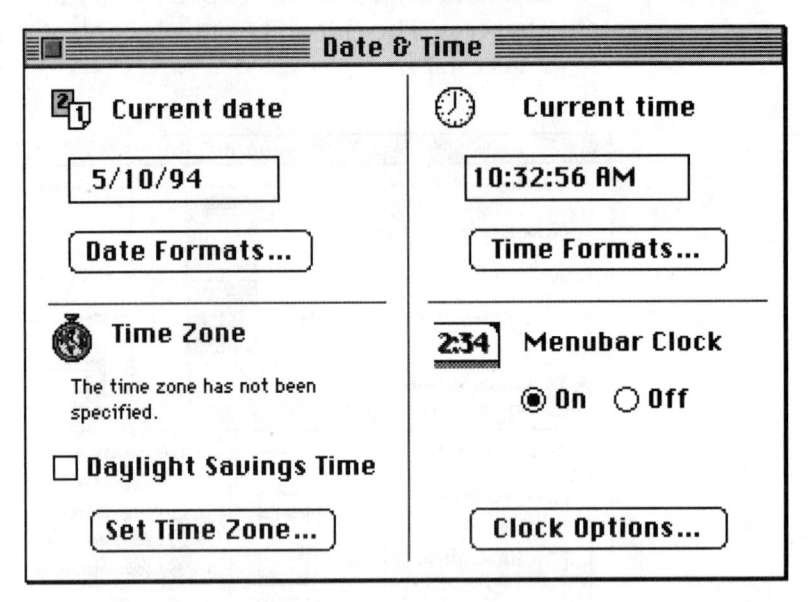

Figure 1-15: The Date & Time control panel.

The *Desktop Pattern control panel* is used to choose the color and pattern of your desktop. System 7.5 adds an extended set of 56 patterns, some of which were previously found in the Performa series. These new patterns are sure to please you, they are what discriminating desktops are wearing these days. The only omission from the Desktop Pattern control panel were suitable names for each pattern. The Desktop Pattern control panel is shown in Figure 1-16. Patterns prior to version 7.5 were set in the General control panel.

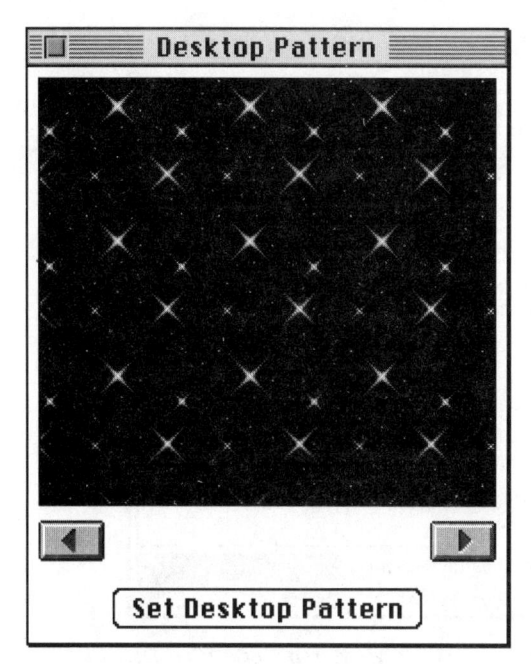

Figure 1-16: The Desktop Pattern control panel.

The *Monitors control panel* is used to define your monitor's display of colors or gray values. It also lets you set the relative position of each monitor, if you have more than one connected to your Macintosh. The Monitors control panel is shown in Figure 1-17.

Refer to the "Video & Monitors" topic for related information.

Prior to System 7.5 changes made in the Monitors control panel required restarting your computer to effect. In this new version, changes can occur as soon as you close the control panel. Another new feature that PowerBook owners are sure to appreciate is the ability of Power-Books with external monitors (such as the 160, 180 and 500 series) to be put to sleep with the external monitor attached.

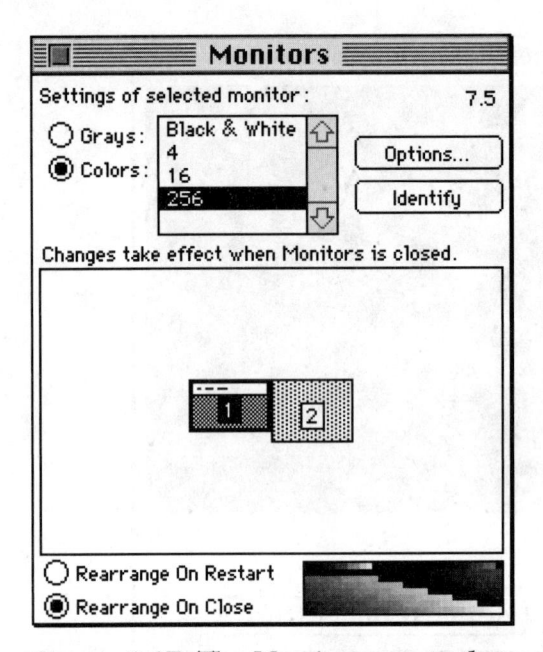

Figure 1-17: The Monitors control panel.

The *Mouse control panel* is used to define the speed of your onscreen cursor relative to how fast you move the mouse, and the amount of delay between clicks, which will be interpreted as two separate mouse clicks instead of one double-click. A PowerBook-specific feature (new in 7.5) called Mouse Tracks leaves a trail as you move the mouse, making it easier to see the mouse's location on a PowerBook screen (particularly useful for passive matrix LCD screens). The Mouse control panel is shown in Figure 1-18.

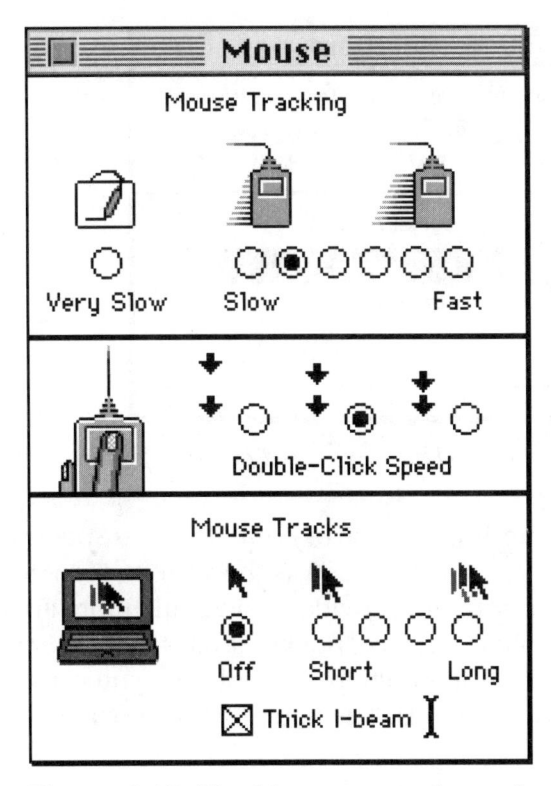

Figure 1-18: The Mouse control panel, as seen on a PowerBook (the Mouse Tracks feature will not appear on desktop Macs).

The *Keyboard control panel* lets you set the character set of your keyboard. You can also use this panel to control the repeat rate for keystrokes. The Keyboard control panel is shown in Figure 1-19.

28 The System 7.5 Book

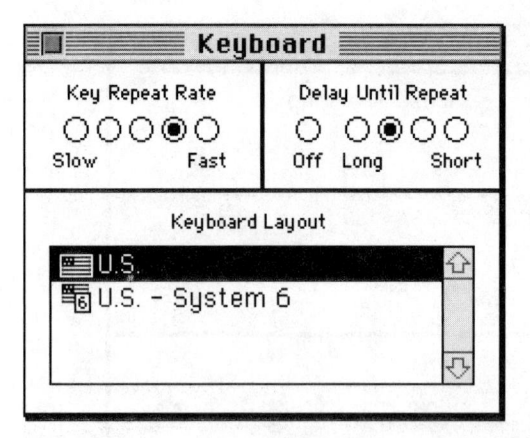

Figure 1-19: The Keyboard control panel.

The *Sound control panel* lets you specify the volume and type of sound used as the system beep. Several sound options are provided, and many more are available from online services, bulletin boards and user groups. If your Mac has a built-in microphone, you can even create your own sounds. The Sound control panel is shown in Figure 1-20.

Refer to the "Sound & Speech" topic of Apple Guide.

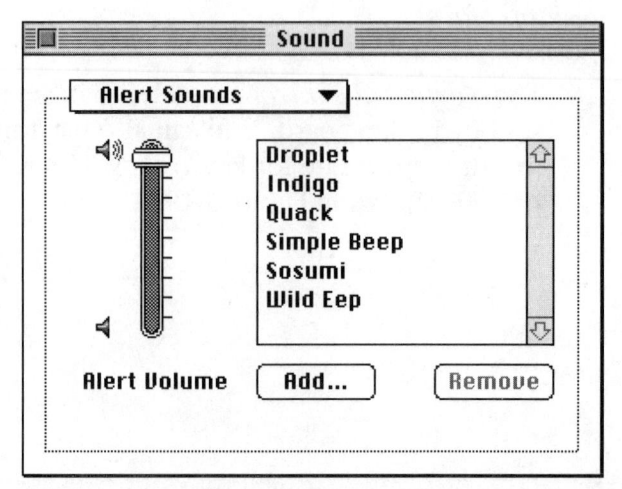

Figure 1-20: The Sound control panel.

Two new control panels appeared in System 7.5 to support foreign language text and number formats, called the Text and Numbers control panels, respectively. A new text editor SimpleText replaces the old TeachText application from previous system software. SimpleText supports stylized text, graphics and various language scripting that are enabled with settings you make in the Text and Numbers control panel.

- The *Text control panel* offers two simple options: Script and Behavior. A script is a method of writing characters: such as left to right for the Latin or Roman language, or right to left for Hebrew or Arabic; as well as what constitutes a word (delimiting characters). Behavior specifies the character set which is often, but not always, country dependent. In the United States we use ASCII, England uses a different character set, and so on. Behavior affects sort order and letter case. The Text control panel is shown in Figure 1-21.

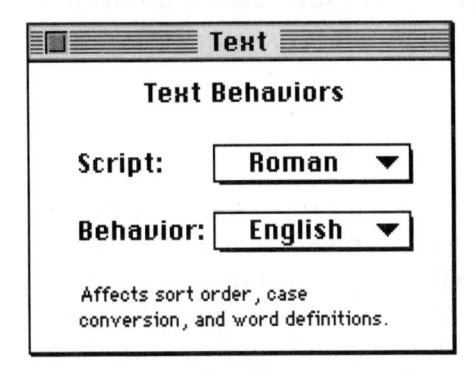

Figure 1-21: The Text control panel.

- The *Numbers control panel* lets you specify a format by country. You can also set separators and currency symbols. The Numbers control panel is shown in Figure 1-22.

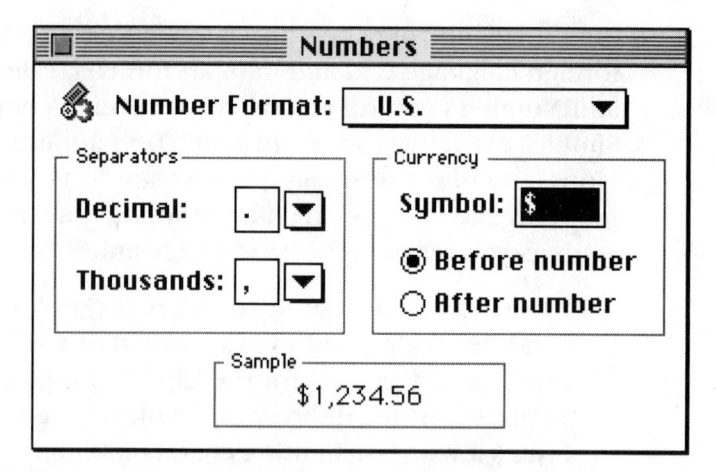

Figure 1-22: The Numbers control panel.

Three important Apple system control panels that affect what you see on your desktop are covered in other sections. They are Finder function options. Specifically, the Apple Menu Options, Views and Labels are described in Chapter 2, "The Finder."

Data Transfer Methods

The Macintosh system software provides a simple built-in method for transferring text, sounds, graphic elements and even movies from one location to another—the Clipboard. You can use the Clipboard to move items within a document or from one document to another—even if the documents were created by different software applications. The metaphor is described well by the commands used to manipulate the Clipboard found on the Edit menu: Cut, Copy and Paste.

7.5 Since you never see the information being transferred, it's easy to make mistakes with Clipboard operations. Even when you're careful and check the contents of the Clipboard using the Show Clipboard command common to most applications, Clipboard transfers are at least a two-step operation; checking adds a third step. System 7.5 adds another more direct method for moving information about: Macintosh Drag and Drop. With Drag and Drop you click and drag information about. Most users will find Drag and Drop to be one of the best major new features of System 7.5, a real convenience. It's probably the one you'll think about least, but that will save you the most time. In its way it's every bit as important a metaphor as Cut and Paste.

Drag and Drop can even move data as objects to the desktop: text as Text Clippings, graphics as Picture Clippings, sound as Sound Clippings and video as Video Clippings. A special Clipping extension manages their actions. Clippings are available to be used by any other file—just drag and drop it. Drag and Drop capability is being added to applications upgraded to take advantage of System 7.5. In system software, the Clipboard, Note Pad, Find File and SimpleText take advantage of Drag and Drop. Drag and Drop also starts processes like printing (drag and drop a file to a printer icon—enabled by QuickDraw GX) or opening files (drag and drop a file onto an application icon). We'll pay particular attention to Macintosh Drag and Drop as we proceed through the book, repaying your reading with tremendous time savings.

Sticky Memos, a small application that resides in your System 7.5 Apple Menu is another application that can take advantage of Macintosh Drag and Drop. Sticky Memos puts electronic post-it notes on your desktop for use as reminders, or for transferring information (although that is not its primary purpose). Sticky Memos is really a small application, so to use Sticky Notes you have to switch to that program by clicking on a sticky note or choosing that program from the Apple or Application menus.

Another metaphor for transferring information is called Publish & Subscribe, a form of interapplication communication. You can think of Publish & Subscribe as a special form of live copy and paste in which the information that is pasted retains a link to the source of the data. That link can be automatically updated or manually updated. Publish & Subscribe is the subject of Chapter 10, "Inter-Application Communication and OpenDoc."

Future versions of Macintosh system software will come with a modular system for working with data called OpenDoc. The metaphor of OpenDoc is called parts, and system software will mediate between parts of the same ilk (movie parts, for example) to enable small applications, or *applets*, as they've been dubbed, to exchange information. OpenDoc is described at the end of Chapter 10.

Cut & Paste: Using the Clipboard & the Scrapbook

You never access the Clipboard directly; instead, you manipulate the contents of the Clipboard using the Cut, Copy and Paste commands. These commands are used so commonly that it's a good idea to remember their keystroke equivalents: Command-X for Cut, Command-C for Copy and Command-V for Paste.

- The Cut command removes the selected objects from their current location and places them on the Clipboard, replacing the previous Clipboard contents. (The Clipboard can contain only the result of the last Cut or Copy command.)

- The Copy command places the selected objects on the Clipboard, but leaves them in their current location as well. The objects that are copied replace the previous contents of the Clipboard.

- The Paste command places a copy of the objects currently on the Clipboard into the current document at the cursor location. Using the Paste command does not remove items from the Clipboard; you can paste the same item repeatedly.

There are many ways to use the Clipboard. The most common is to move an element—like a paragraph or graphic item—from one place to another in the same document. To do this, you select the element, choose the Cut command, position the cursor at the new location and choose the Paste command.

The Clipboard is also used to move elements between different documents, even ones created by different applications. For example, to move a chart from a file you created with your spreadsheet into a word processor file:

- Open the spreadsheet and choose the chart. Use the Copy command, since you want to leave the chart in the spreadsheet even after it has been moved to the word processor.

- Open the word processor, or switch to it if it's already open. Open the document that will receive the copied chart. You can quit the spreadsheet, but it's not necessary. (Details on opening and switching between several applications are presented in Chapter 7, "Working With Multiple Applications.")

- Position the cursor in the word processor file where you want the chart placed. Choose the Paste command.

Chances are that if you can select some information, you can copy it to the Clipboard and move it about. In addition to simple text, the Clipboard supports stylized text and various graphics formats. The Clipboard even supports sound and QuickTime video.

If you want to remove selected items without affecting the Clipboard, use the Clear command or the Delete key. Since the Clipboard can hold only one item and is not saved out to a file, whenever it is modified it is overwritten. Sometimes when you have a large selection on the Clipboard you can tie up Macintosh memory you need for other programs. To free up that memory, clear the Clipboard or copy a single character to it.

It's easy to forget the contents of your Clipboard. Most applications have a command called Show Clipboard as a menu item. Its placement varies. In the Finder this command is found in the Edit menu, Microsoft Word places it in the Window menu, other programs place it on a View menu. In the Finder the Show Clipboard command is enabled by the Clipboard file placed at the top level of the System folder. Selecting this command opens a window that lets you view the Clipboard's contents and tells you what kind of data it contains. Figure 1-23 shows an example.

```
Clipboard
Clipboard contents: text

<para>It's easy to forget what you have on the Clipboard. Most applications have a
command called Show Clipboard command as a menu item. It's placement varies. In
the Finder this command is found in the Edit menu, Microsoft Word places it in the
Windows menu, other programs place it on a View menu. In the Finder the Show
Clipboard command is enabled by the Clipboard file placed at the top level of the
System folder. Selecting this command opens a window that lets you view the
Clipboard's contents, and tells you what kind of data it contains. Figure 1-23 shows
an example.
<88 Inline Graphic>
<fcap>Figure 1-23: The Show Clipboard window.
```

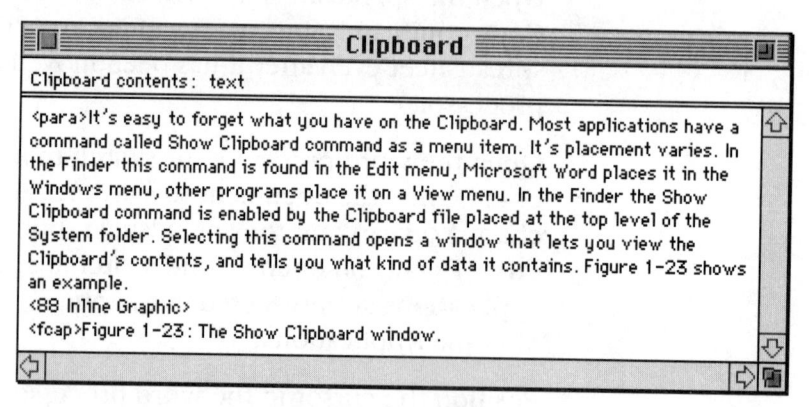

Figure 1-23: The Clipboard window.

Another related Macintosh tool is the Scrapbook, a desk accessory found on the Apple menu that can hold a catalog of text and graphic elements you use frequently or need to move from one document to another. The Scrapbook saves data to a file, and so represents permanent storage (until you modify the data). Elements are moved into or out of the Scrapbook via the Clipboard and the Cut, Copy and Paste commands previously described. A Scrapbook displaying a single element is shown in Figure 1-24.

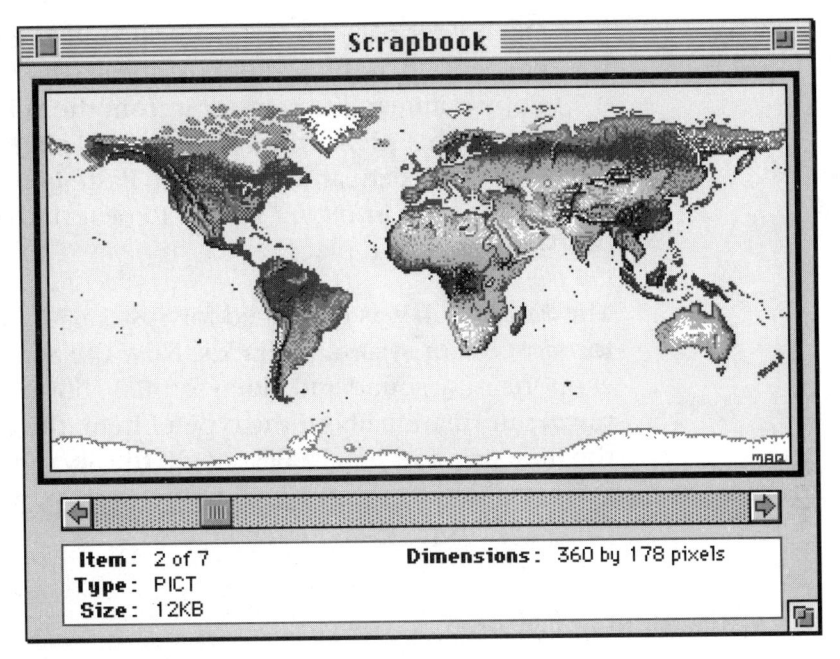

Figure 1-24: The Scrapbook.

For example, if you needed to use a set of icons throughout a magazine layout you were creating, you could transfer them all into the Scrapbook and access them from there as needed. To do this, you would:

- Open the file containing the icons. Select one icon, and choose the Copy command to move it to the Clipboard.

- Open the Scrapbook, and choose the Paste command to move the icon on the Clipboard into the Scrapbook. The Scrapbook automatically creates a new page each time you paste in a new element.

- Go back to the file containing the icons, select another icon and again use the Copy command to move it to the Clipboard. Access the Scrapbook again, and paste in the new icon. Repeat this process until the Scrapbook contains all the needed icons.

- Open your page layout program, and as each icon is needed, open the Scrapbook, locate the icon and use the Copy command to transfer it from the Scrapbook onto the Clipboard. Set the cursor at the location where the icon is needed, and choose the Paste command to transfer the icon into your layout. Repeat this procedure until all icons are in place.

The Scrapbook was enhanced for System 7.5, as it has been for most major system upgrades. Now the Scrapbook not only supports new sound and video formats, but it gives you additional information about the type of item, the size in bytes and the dimension in pixels. Best of all, the Scrapbook is Drag and Drop enabled. Let's now look at this great new feature: the Drag and Drop.

Macintosh Drag and Drop

Drag and Drop is a technique for direct manipulation of data in documents, files and applications. Various aspects of drag and drop behavior have been around for some time now. In previous versions of System 7 you could drag a file icon onto an application, and if the application could open that file and translate it, it would. For example, when Macintosh Drag and Drop was used with the System 7 Pro Finder and Macintosh Easy Open (a system software extension), any file dragged onto an application could be automatically translated and opened provided that the capability was set up beforehand.

System 7.5 extends Drag and Drop so that you can print files by dragging them to a printer icon in your desktop (a feature of QuickDraw GX covered in Chapter 9). The most important extension of Drag and Drop is the property of transferring data within a file, between files, and even to the Macintosh desktop. Drag and Drop is monitored by a new Drag Manager in the system software.

Macintosh Drag and Drop is a terrific method for data exchange because it is intuitive. If you've used drag and drop in other applications (like Microsoft Word 5.x), then you are familiar with the basics. Select the data and drag it to a new location. It moves an outline of your selected data to the new location and completes the data move when you release the mouse button. An example of moving text within a document is shown in Figure 1-25 using Apple's new text editor SimpleText.

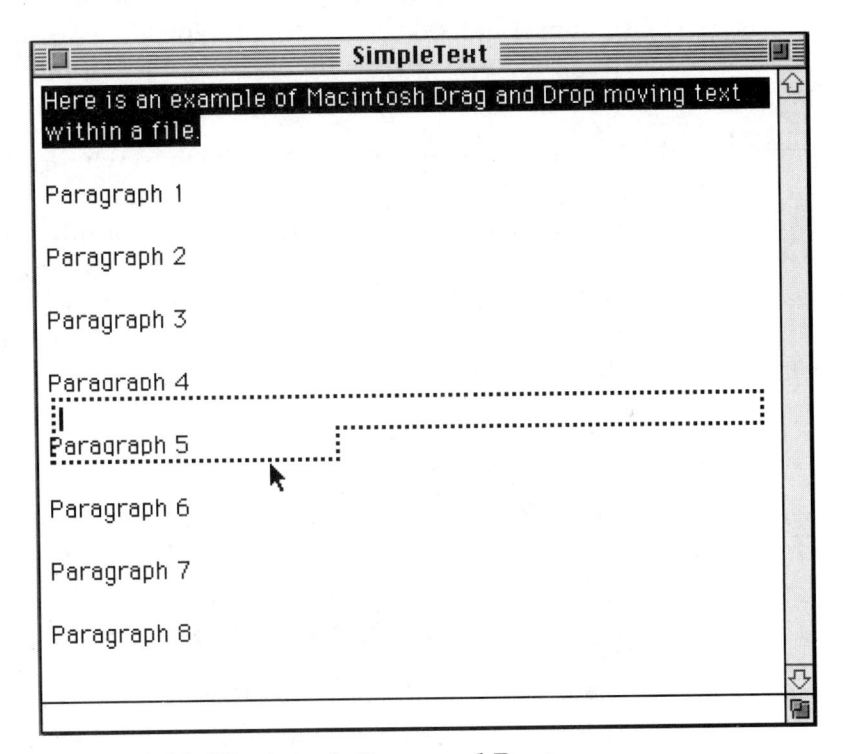

Figure 1-25: Macintosh Drag and Drop.

SimpleText is a text editor that opens files containing simple text, stylized text and graphics. It replaces TeachText and expands upon it by allowing basic text editing, as well. You could think of SimpleText as a basic word processor; it even records and plays sounds and speech. SimpleText will open the Read Me files that often accompany new software. These files tell you about late-breaking information that couldn't be included in the manual. Whenever you are trying to open an unknown file on your Macintosh, try SimpleText first.

One very nice new feature of System 7.5 is the ability to Drag and Drop selections to the Macintosh desktop. The resulting objects are called "clippings," and are given a default file name such as text clipping to indicate the data type. You can edit the file name using standard Macintosh editing techniques. Click on the file name, type a new name and press the Return key to change the name. Some clippings are shown in Figure 1-26.

To use clippings, simply drag them to where you want them in another file. Clippings are a convenient way to add logos or headers to documents, glossary items or other items you might have stored in your Scrapbook. Clippings are tracked and managed by the new Clippings Extension. You may want to consolidate your clippings within a single folder on your desktop to reduce clutter.

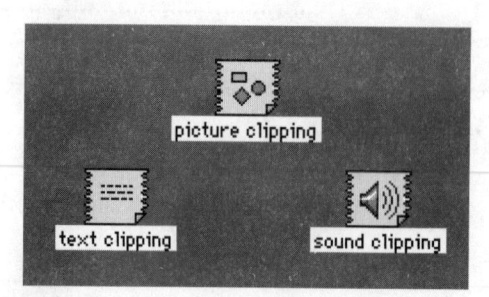

Figure 1-26: Desktop clippings.

7.5 System 7.5 introduces a desk accessory that you can find on the Apple menu called Sticky Memos. An example is shown in Figure 1-27. With Sticky Memos you can create windows of text that float on your desktop like post-it notes. You can scroll the text using the Arrow keys and collapse the windows to a single bar.

Sticky Memos supports cut, copy and paste, and can import and export text; it even supports drag and drop. Sticky Notes can be different colors, any rectangular size down to a single line, and when you're done with a note, close the note and save it to a file or simply delete it.

Another older desk accessory called Note Pad can place a single window on your desktop. You can move from page to page by clicking on the dog-ear of the notepad. Note Pad has been part of Apple system software from its inception. Note Pad is shown in Figure 1-28.

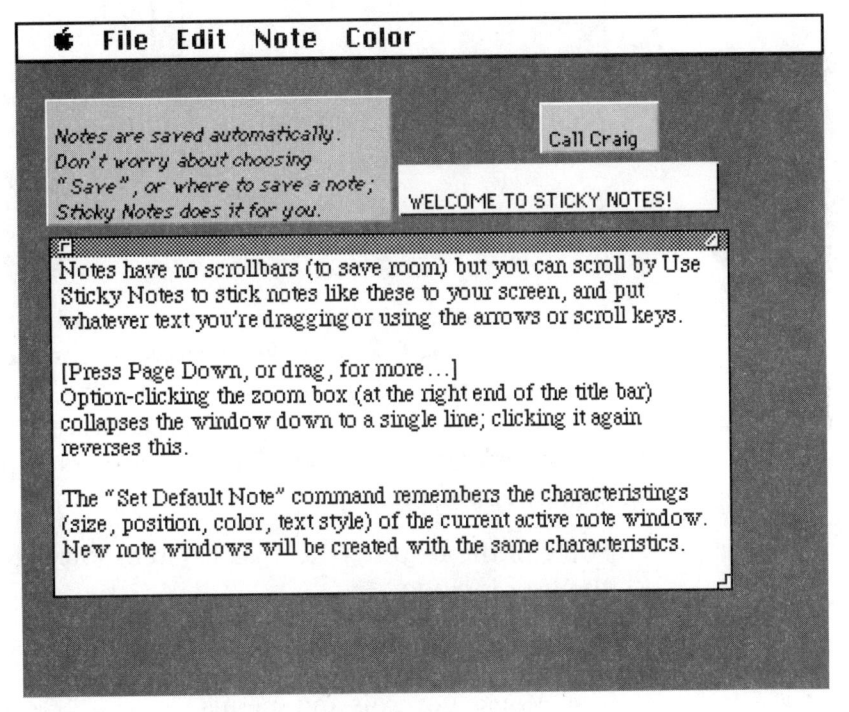

Figure 1-27: A Sticky Memo.

Figure 1-28: Note Pad.

Moving On

System software is the core of what we think of as the Macintosh. System software makes it possible for the computer to interact with other programs. It also helps in controlling Mac hardware and peripherals. System software standardizes the Macintosh and allows software developers to produce high-quality applications.

Some of the features the Mac's system software provides to the user include

- Icons, windows and dialog boxes
- Mouse controls and menus
- Windows and palettes
- The Clipboard and the Scrapbook

In Chapter 2 we'll examine another important aspect of system software, the Finder, which provides tools that help control the disks and files you use on the Macintosh.

Chapter 2

The Finder

Most people don't think of the Finder as a software application, but it really is—just like your word processor, spreadsheet or graphics program. But while each of those other applications is dedicated to the creation and manipulation of one specific type of data, the unfortunately named Finder focuses on helping you manage your disks and files.

It does this by providing you with the well-known Macintosh desktop, with icons for each disk, drive, folder and file—plus the Finder menus and the Trash. The Finder lets you view and modify the contents of your disks and drives in many different ways and allows you to launch other applications or control panels. Most people think of the desktop as the Finder, but the desktop is really a window you use to view into the Finder.

System 7 introduced many enhancements to the Finder, providing more information about your disks and files, more consistency in commands and features and additional customizing capabilities. Fortunately these benefits came without a change in the Finder's familiar interface—if you were comfortable working in Finder 6.0, you'll have no problem adjusting to the new Finder and taking advantage of its expanded capabilities.

This chapter starts by examining the Finder's menu commands and then looks at the important topic of Finder windows. Other changes in System 7's Finder such as Apple Guide (new in 7.5), Balloon Help, the Trash and the Get Info dialog box are also covered.

This chapter is not, however, the only place in this book where you'll read about new Finder capabilities. Many Finder features are introduced in this chapter and then elaborated on in later chapters in more appropriate contexts. For example, aliasing, the Find command and the Label menu are discussed in Chapter 3, "Managing Your Hard Drive." The About This Macintosh... command is described in detail in Chapter 8, "Memory Management." The Sharing command is explained in Chapter 12, "An Introduction to File Sharing." Catalogs and the PowerTalk Key Chain are described in Chapter 14, "AOCE–The Apple Open Collaboration Environment," where AOCE and PowerTalk are described. You'll be referenced to more detailed discussions throughout this chapter.

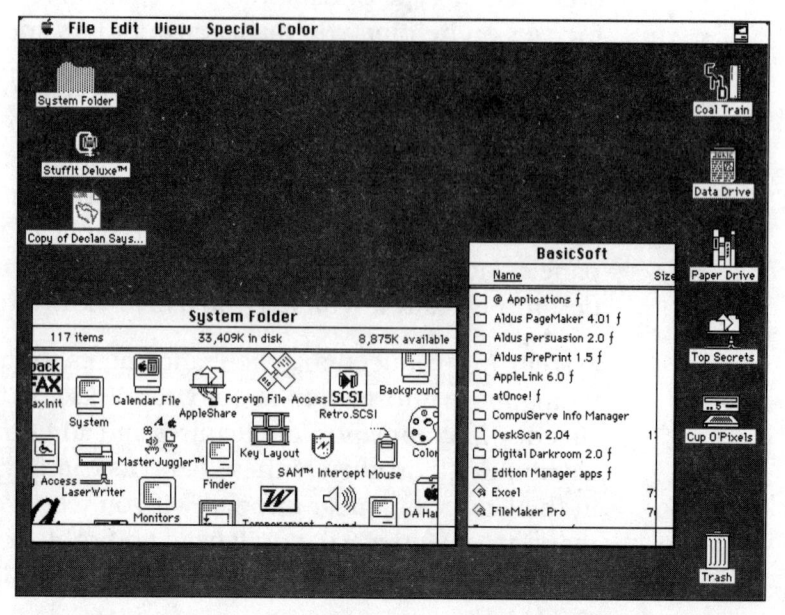

Figure 2-1: The Finder desktop in system software 6.0.x.

Chapter 2: The Finder **43**

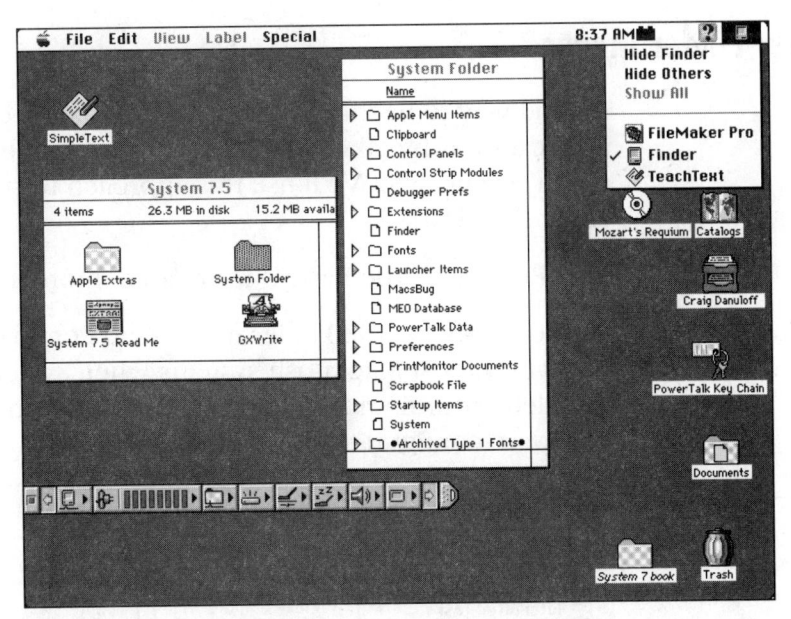

Figure 2-2: The Finder desktop in system software 7.5 for a series 160 PowerBook.

What you see on your desktop after installation of System 7.5 depends on what model of Macintosh you're using. New components such as Catalogs, the PowerTalk Key Chain and the Mailbox are part of PowerTalk and are installed on most Macintosh computers as part of the Easy Install option. With a PowerBook model, installation puts the new Apple Control Strip floating palette on your desktop. The Control Strip is described more fully in Chapter 6, "Power Macintosh & PowerBook System Software."

Additional new desktop elements you may notice are a menu bar clock and a Documents folder. The Documents folder is an option turned on in the General control panel that saves new documents by default to this location. Turning on the menu bar clock and setting up the Documents folder in the General Controls control panel were briefly described in the previous chapter.

New Finder Menus

A good way to become familiar with any new or upgraded application is by taking a quick tour through its menu bar and menu commands. We'll use this approach to start learning about the Finder.

See "Reviewing the Basics" for related information.

Figure 2-3 shows the Finder menus and commands as they appear on most Macintosh systems when System 7.5 is first installed. Your menus may vary slightly, depending on your hardware configuration and option settings.

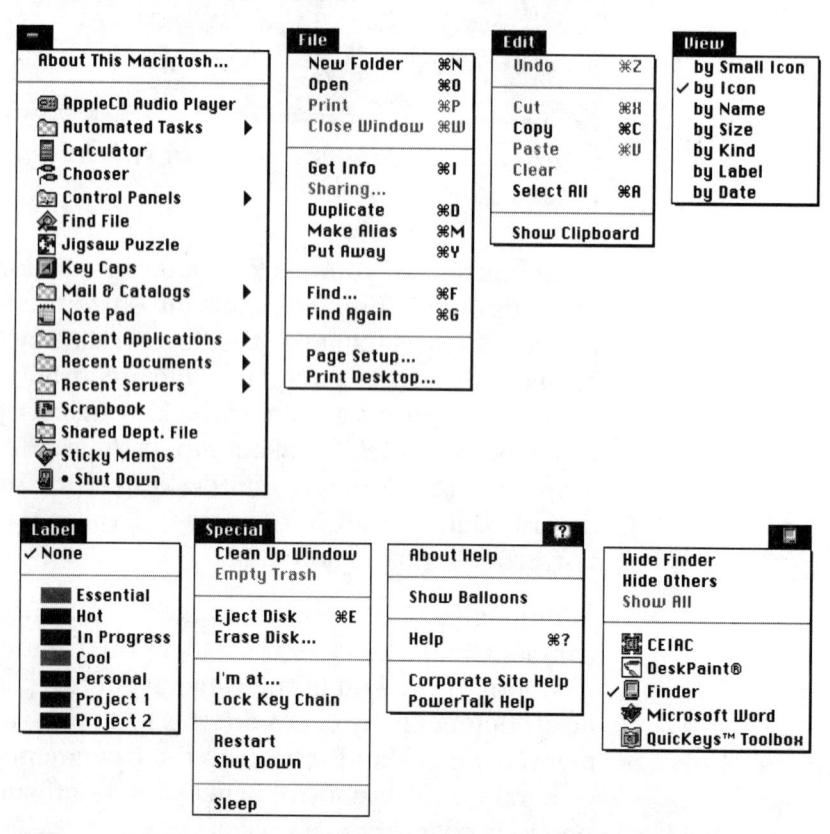

Figure 2-3: The default Finder menus in System 7.5. The Sleep command in the Special menu only appears for PowerBook Macintosh computers.

More than half the Finder commands are unchanged in name or position from version 6, and most work the same today as they did previously. To save space (and avoid boring you), this section discusses only commands new to System 7's Finder or previous commands that have been improved or upgraded.

7.5 You may notice that the System 7.5 Apple menu folders now display submenus (a hierarchical menu system) when you click on them. These menu items have right-facing arrows next to them. Of the hierarchical menu items found in the Apple menu, the Control Panel is a familiar item, but the Recent Applications, Recent Documents, Recent Servers and Useful Scripts are new to System 7.5. You won't see the Recent... Folders until you access at least one file, application or server. Then your system software creates the new folder and places an alias to the file, application or server into that folder.

The Control Panel folder and the three Recent... Folders are described more fully in Chapter 4, "The System Folder." Information about using the AppleScripts found in the Useful Scripts folder is deferred to the discussion on "The Useful Scripts Folder" found in Chapter 11, "AppleScript."

The new commands are listed on the following pages in the order they appear in the menus, from left to right on the menu bar.

- **About This Macintosh...** (Apple Menu). The dialog box this command brings up now displays more information about your Macintosh, such as available memory and open applications. (More information about this dialog box appears in Chapter 8.)

See "Files & Disks" for help.

- **Recent Documents, Recent Applications and Recent Servers submenus** (Apple Menu). Selecting one of these commands displays a list of your last used files, applications and servers, allowing you to launch a file or application, or mount a server. This is a tremendous time saver, one you are likely to use frequently in your daily work. This function is found in numerous third-party products like SuperBoomerang (part of the Now Utilities) and HAM, both of which are described in Chapter 16, "Third-Party Utilities."

    The submenus are controlled by the new Apple Menu Options control panel shown in Figure 2-4. Using this panel you can turn submenus on and off, and set the number of recent files, applications and servers that your Macintosh remembers. Your most recently used item replaces your least recently used item in the list. In computer jargon, it's "last in, first out." If you use an item more than once, the date of last use determines its position in the stack.

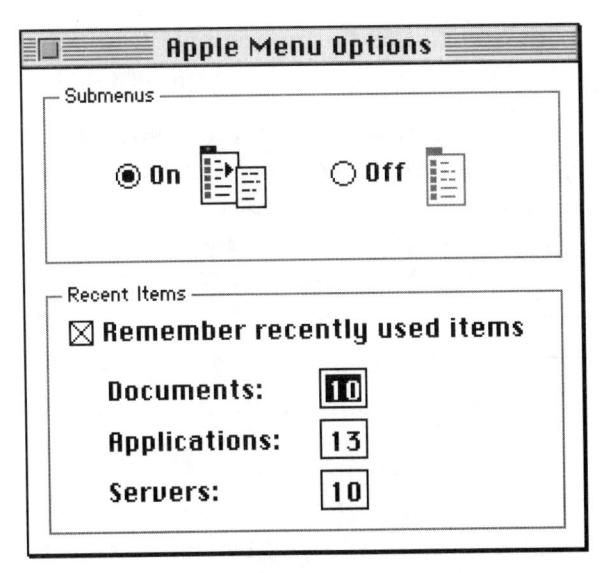

Figure 2-4: The Apple Menu Options control panel.

- **Sharing...** (File menu). This command controls access privileges you grant other users on your AppleTalk network. You can allow or disallow sharing of your Macintosh files and determine which users can read and write particular folders and volumes of shared files.

  The Sharing command does not appear unless File Sharing has been installed; it remains dimmed until File Sharing is turned on. (A complete discussion of File Sharing and other System 7.5 networking features appears in Chapter 12.)

- **Make Alias** (File menu). Make Alias creates a duplicate icon for a file or folder without duplicating the file or folder itself. This duplicate icon, called an alias, can be freely positioned on any volume or folder and used as if it were the original file or folder. You can think of an alias as a "pointer" to the original icon. The benefits of creating and using an alias rather than a copy are that an alias takes up almost no space on your hard drive, the alias remains linked to the original file and any changes made to the alias are reflected in the original and vice versa.

The Make Alias command lets you store a file or folders in two places at once—in fact, in any number of places at once, since you can create many aliases for a single file or folder. (More about aliasing in Chapter 3.) In System 7.5 you can now use the Command-M keystroke to invoke the Make Alias command.

- **Find...** (File menu). The Find command replaces the Find File desk accessory of previous system software versions. The Find command can search for files by file name, size, creation date, label, etc., and when files matching your search criteria are located, the Finder opens a window containing the file (or files) and selects the file's icon. Using the Find Again command (Command-G), you can repeat the last search, locating and displaying the next file matching the current search criteria.

Finding a number of items that match the search criteria with System 7 prior to 7.5 was a time-consuming procedure with Find and Find Again (and Find Again...). In System 7.5 the Find dialog box ends a search by displaying the Found Items dialog box showing *all* of the documents, applications or disks that match the search criteria (see Figure 2-5). Just double-click on the name to go to the location of your selection. Finding items is covered in much greater detail in Chapter 3.

Note that the Found Items dialog box is Macintosh Drag and Drop enabled, so that you can drag a file onto your desktop or into a window to move it, onto an application icon to open it, to a printer icon (with QuickDraw GX installed) to print it, and so on.

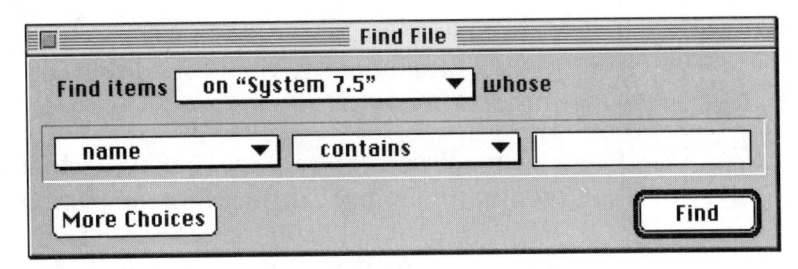

Figure 2-5: The simple Find dialog box.

- **Label menu.** The new Label menu is in some ways similar to the Colors menu used in system software 6.0x: it allows you to specify colors for file and folder icons. A few important improvements have been added to this colorization process. You can now color-code your files by specifying a classification title for each color (see Figure 2-6). In addition, color labels are supported by the View menu and Find command, so you can use label categories as part of your hard-disk organization and management strategy. (You'll find more on the Label menu in Chapter 3.)

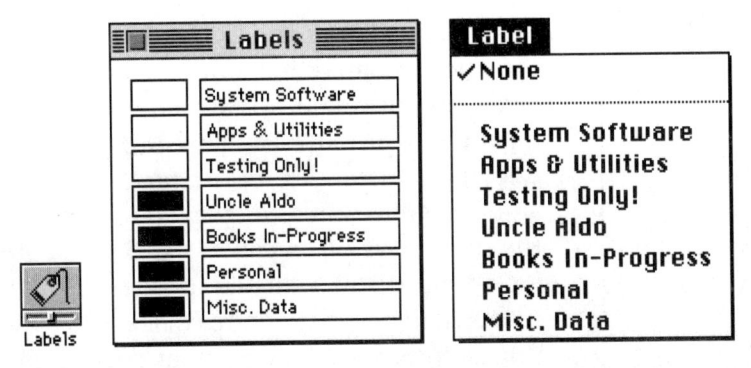

Figure 2-6: The Label control panel icon (left), Label control panel (center) and a customized Label menu (right).

- **Clean Up** (Special menu). The new Clean Up command is an enhanced version of its old counterpart used to rearrange icons on the desktop or in Finder windows. (You'll find more information on this command later in this chapter.)

- **Empty Trash** (Special menu). This is an improved version of the Empty Trash command from previous versions. In System 7's Finder, files and folders remain in the trash until the Empty Trash command is selected; they're not deleted when applications are run, when your Macintosh is shut down or at any other time. (More information on this command is presented later in this chapter.)

- **Menu Bar Clock.** By default a menu bar clock appears just to the left of the Help menu. This feature can be disabled by turning it off in the General Controls control panel. The time you see is what is set in the Date & Time control panel. Clicking on the clock changes the display to the current date, which is also set in the Date & Time control panel (clicking again on the clock changes it back to a time display. Both control panels were described in the previous chapter. The new clock is a detuned version of the shareware classic SuperClock.

- **Help menu.** Near the right edge of the menu bar, under the question mark icon and inside a yellow square, is the new and improved Apple Help menu. The new icon is meant to symbolize the new Apple Guide system introduced in System 7.5. In the previous versions of System 7 a question mark was displayed inside a picture tube, and the menu was often called the Balloon Help menu. Balloon Help is still available in System 7.5, but the more useful active Apple Guide (discussed toward the end of this chapter) is the prominent command on this menu.

Both Apple Guide and Balloon Help are available at all times in your applications, not just in the Finder. The quality and quantity of help you get in either help system is determined by whether and how well the developer of your software chose to implement it.

The Show Balloons command turns on context-sensitive help balloons that pop up as you point to menu commands, dialog box options, icons and other Macintosh screen elements. To turn balloons off, select the Hide Balloons command. (More on the Help menu is presented later in this chapter.) Beginners seem to like Balloon Help, whereas more advanced users hate it.

In System 7.5 Apple Guide has become the de facto standard help system. Simply select the Help command or press the Command-Shift-? keystroke to open Apple Guide. (Don't forget to hold down the Shift key to type a question mark character.) Apple Guide can also be customized. You may see additional Help systems listed in the Apple Help menu, as was the case for Figure 2-2 where a Corporate Help and a PowerTalk Help system were listed.

- **Applications menu.** This is the last addition to the menu bar; it's located in the upper-right corner. This new feature lets System 7.5 open multiple applications simultaneously, so you can quickly switch from one open application to another. It's available at all times, not just when you're using the Finder. The Applications menu is shown in Figure 2-7.

See "Working With Programs" for assistance.

The name of every open application will automatically appear in this menu. To switch from one application to another, select the name you want from the Application menu, and that application and its windows immediately appear.

```
Hide PageMaker 4.0
Hide Others
Show All
-----------------
   📄 FileMaker Pro
   📃 Finder
   💿 HyperCard
   📘 Microsoft Word
 ✓ 📄 PageMaker 4.0
   📊 Persuasion 2.0
```

Figure 2-7: The Applications menu.

Note that in most cases only your current application, the one selected with a check mark in the Applications menu, is actually running and processing. There are some processes like printing and communications that can run in the background, but in System 7.5 most do not.

The Macintosh saves the state of your other applications and processes in memory so that it can return to them, a feature called multithreading. Moving between applications (and threads) is called context switching. Running applications sessions concurrently, called multitasking, is being written into system software gradually. We'll have more to say about this in subsequent chapters, particularly in Chapter 5, "System 7.5 & Your Software," and Chapter 8.

Using the various Hide... commands, the Applications menu also lets you temporarily hide all windows from the current application or all windows except those of the current application, thus reducing the onscreen clutter that can result from running multiple applications at once. (See Chapter 5.)

Caution: If you've lost your place on the desktop and menus have changed, check the Applications menu to see what program is active in the foreground. This is a common beginner's mistake: clicking on the desktop and switching to the Finder.

7.5 System 7.5 allows you to "hide the Finder," a feature enabled in the General Controls control panel. The default condition is to show the desktop in the background. Just click off the checkbox "Show desktop when in background" (found in the desktop section) to hide the Finder and prevent losing your place when working in an application. When the Finder is hidden, you do not see any icons like the Trash, disk or drive icons, or folders that were on the desktop.

Finder Windows

As a disk and file management tool, the Finder's menu commands play only a small part. Most of the time you move, copy, delete, arrange and open files by using the mouse to directly manipulate icons on the desktop and in Finder windows. In System 7, your ability to see and manipulate files and folders in windows was dramatically improved.

See "Reviewing the Basics" for help with windows and views.

The basic attributes of Finder windows, however, have not changed:

- Windows are created each time a volume or folder is opened.

- Each window has a title bar, zoom box and close box.

- Windows can be freely positioned by dragging their title bars.

- Windows can be resized by dragging on the resize box.

- Windows display the files and folders contained in a single volume or folder.
- The window display is controlled via the View menu.

The improvements to the Finder in System 7, however, gave you more control over windows, a more consistent user interface and a wider range of display options:

- The font, icon size and information displayed in Finder windows are customizable.
- Keyboard commands let you navigate windows and select files without using the mouse.
- Smart zooming opens windows only enough to display their content.
- The contents of any folder or subfolder can be displayed in hierarchical format in any window.
- Hierarchical levels allow files in different folders to be manipulated simultaneously.

7.5 It's easy to get lost when you have a number of windows open on your screen. Most applications have a Window menu for just such occasions, but the Finder does not. It's particularly a problem on a small PowerBook or Mac Classic display. You can add a window management tool to system software using shareware. The control panel AppleWindow will put hierarchical submenus in the Application menu displaying open windows.

Finally, system software offers some help with window clutter. System 7.5 includes a version of WindowShade, formerly a shareware program. Using WindowShade is easy; just click twice on the Title bar to reduce the window to its Title bar only. Double-click again on the "minimized" window's Title bar to return the window to its full size. An example of a minimized window created by WindowShade is shown in Figure 2-8.

Figure 2-8: A minimized window.

The WindowShade control panel is shown in Figure 2-9. There are a few options in this control panel—a setting for the number of clicks (one or two) to minimize the window and a setting to determine which key (Command, Option or Control) will act as a modifier to enable WindowShade. You can also click the checkbox to enable the Windowshade sound effect. However, the most important feature of the control panel is the Off button, because WindowShade is left *off* as a default upon installation. You need to manually turn it on to use this feature.

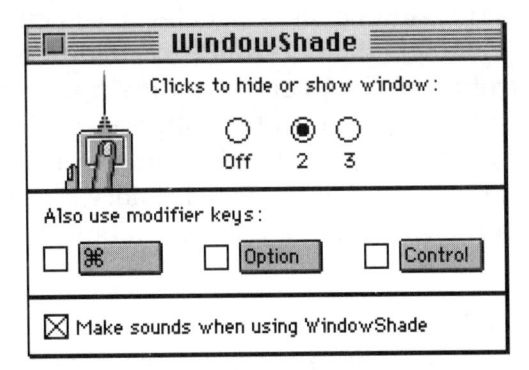

Figure 2-9: The WindowShade control panel.

These and other new features and improvements to the operation of Finder windows are discussed in detail later in this chapter.

The Views Control Panel

In previous Finder versions, the presentation of text and icons in Finder windows was preset and could not be modified. Text was always listed in Geneva 9 point, and icons appeared in preset sizes in each icon view. In System 7, the Views control panel provides a variety of options that let you control the information and the way it's displayed in Finder windows.

It should be noted that control panels are the System 7 evolution of the cdevs (control devices) that appeared in the System 6.0x Control Panel desk accessory. In System 7, a control panel is a small independent application launched by double-clicking on its icon, just like other applications. The only distinction between a control panel and a regular application is that the control panel is implemented in a single window and provides no menus. Control panels are stored in the Control Panels folder, which is stored inside the System Folder.

See "Setting Options" for help on control panels.

To access the Views control panel, you can either open the System Folder and the Control Panels folder, or you can select the Control Panel command from the Apple Menu. (Although the Control Panel command initially appears in the Apple Menu, it may not appear there if your system has been customized.) Once the Control Panels folder is open, double-click on the Views icon to open the Views control panel (shown in Figure 2-10).

Changes in Finder windows register instantly as you modify the options in the Views control panel. You don't need to close the Views dialog box to see the effect of your selections. When you're satisfied, close the Views control panel by clicking the close box in the upper-left corner of its title bar.

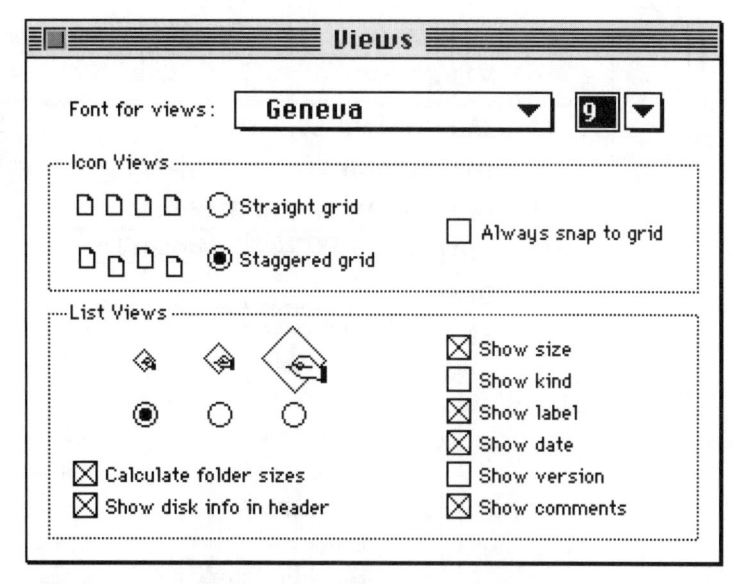

Figure 2-10: The Views control panel.

The Views control panel options are grouped in three sets. The first is the Font for views, a typeface and type size option that controls the display of text in all Finder windows. A font pop-up menu presents the names of all installed fonts; you may select the one you want for all Finder windows. Use the size pop-up menu to select the point size for the text display. If you want to use a point size not available in the pop-up menu, type the size you want directly into the Size option box.

Caution: *Although it's appealing to be able to choose from such a wide range of fonts and sizes, you may want to stick with the default, Geneva 9-point. While it doesn't look very good in print, it provides the most legible font for onscreen display purposes.*

58 The System 7.5 Book

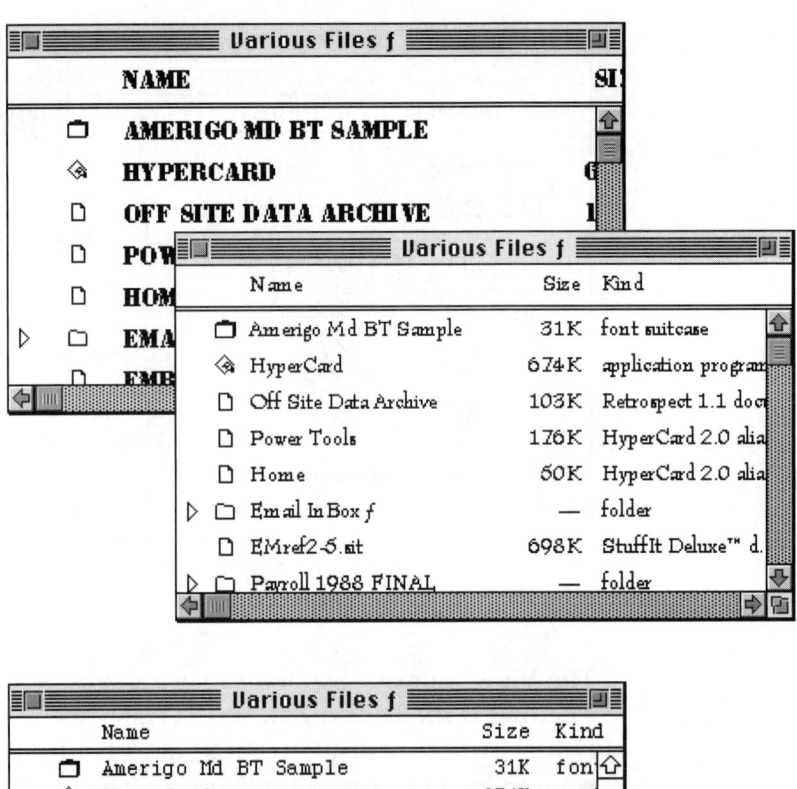

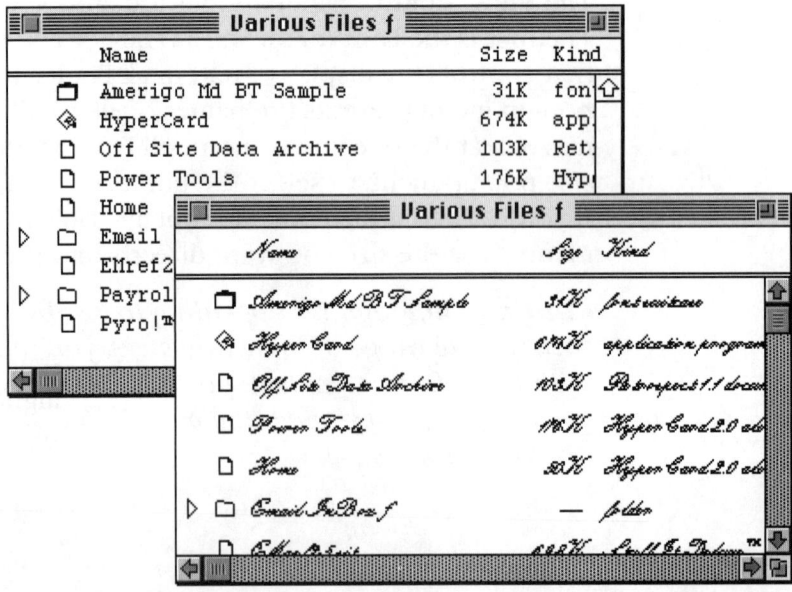

Figure 2-11: Finder windows in various fonts.

The second set of Views dialog box options is grouped under Icon Views. These options affect the way icons are positioned when the By Icon and By Small Icon commands from the View menu are selected. The Straight grid and Staggered grid options determine whether icons are arranged on a common or an irregular baseline. All versions before System 7 have arranged icons on a straight grid, which can sometimes force file names to overlap, leaving them illegible, as shown in Figure 2-12. The Staggered option positions icons so their names cannot overlap.

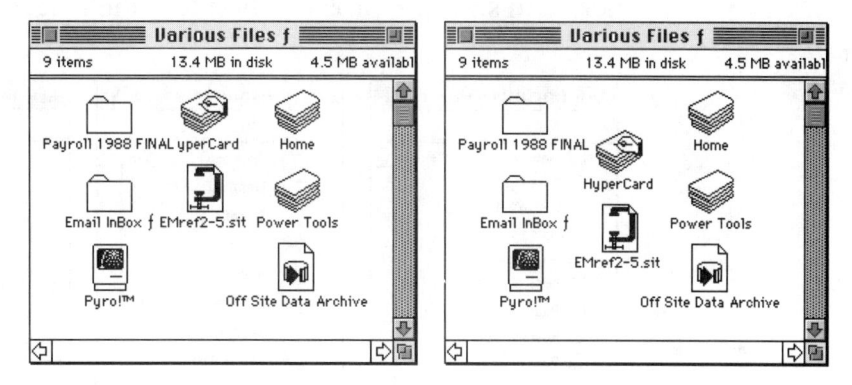

Figure 2-12: Examples of Finder windows using the Straight grid and Staggered grid options.

The Always snap to grid option forces any repositioned icons to automatically snap to the nearest point on an invisible grid. This is the same invisible grid used by the Clean Up command, and will result in either normal or staggered baseline alignment, depending on whether the Straight grid or the Staggered grid option is chosen. The concept of keeping files always grid-aligned in this way may sound appealing, but it can be disconcerting when the Finder grabs and relocates files while you're trying to position them. In most cases, it's probably better to leave this option off and use the Clean Up command to correct any icon alignment problems in Finder windows.

List Views is the final set of Views dialog box options. These options apply to the display for all windows except those using the By Icon or By Small Icon commands from the View menu (by Name, Date, Size, etc.). This set of options includes three groups: one specifying icon size, one offering additional information in Finder windows and the last controlling the window columns and View menu commands.

The icon display size is chosen by using the three different icon size radio buttons. The result of each option is shown in Figure 2-13. As with the Font for views option discussed earlier, icon sizes are probably best left unchanged.

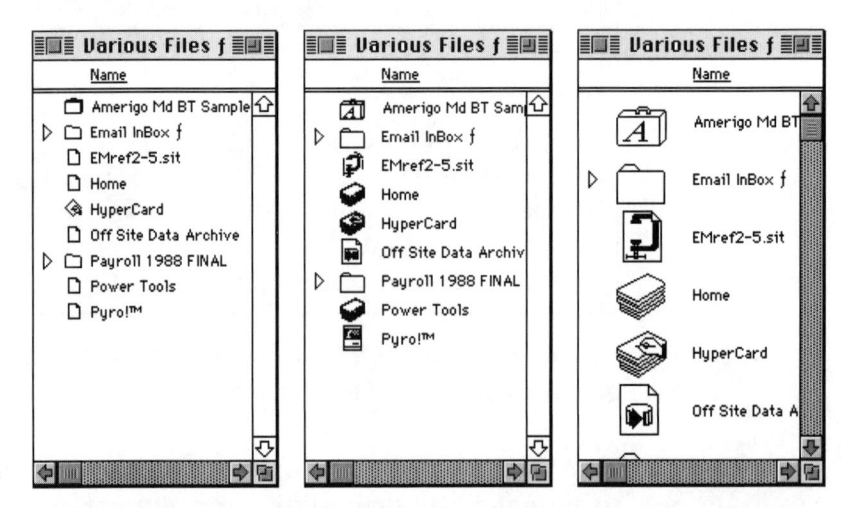

Figure 2-13: Finder windows using the small, medium and large icons corresponding to the Views control panel options.

Below the icon size radio buttons are two check box options: Calculate folder sizes and Show disk info in header. These options add additional information to that already provided in Finder windows.

- **Calculate folder sizes.** It would be difficult to determine the "one little thing" that most bothered users in previous Finder versions, but the fact that folder sizes were not displayed in Finder windows was high on many users' pet peeves list. The Calculate folder sizes option lets you add the size of a folder's contents to all text view displays.

    Caution: Calculate folder sizes, unfortunately, causes a perceptible and at times annoying slowdown in the display of some windows, particularly when the windows contain numerous large folders. You'll have to decide whether the slower display speed is a fair price to pay for the additional information and turn this option off or on accordingly. My recommendation is to leave it off. When it's turned off, an alternate way to determine the size of a folder is to select the folder and choose the Get Info command from the Finder's File menu.

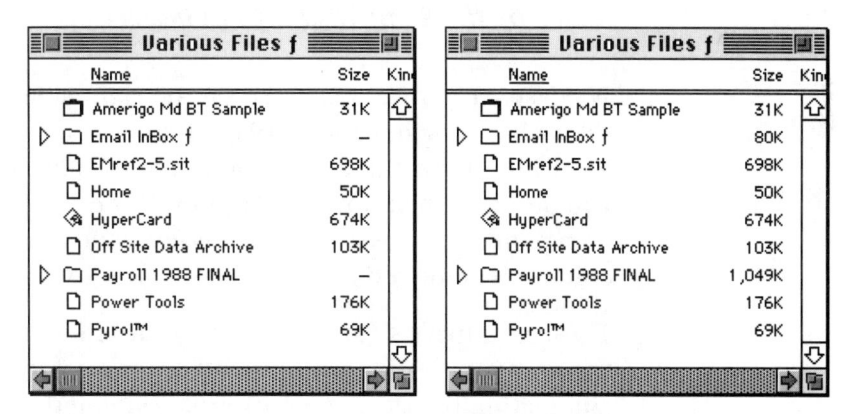

Figure 2-14: The same Finder window with and without folder sizes displayed.

- **Show disk info in header.** Selecting this option adds three pieces of information to the upper section of each window: the number of items contained, the total space consumed by files on the disk and the amount of free space on the current volume. This information fits discreetly in the window header, as shown in Figure 2-15.

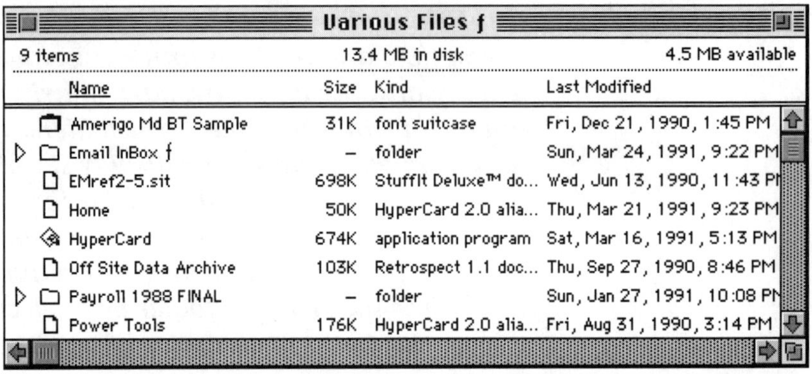

Various Files f				
9 items		13.4 MB in disk		4.5 MB available
Name		Size	Kind	Last Modified
	Amerigo Md BT Sample	31K	font suitcase	Fri, Dec 21, 1990, 1:45 PM
▷	Email InBox f	—	folder	Sun, Mar 24, 1991, 9:22 PM
	EMref2-5.sit	698K	StuffIt Deluxe™ do...	Wed, Jun 13, 1990, 11:43 PM
	Home	50K	HyperCard 2.0 alia...	Thu, Mar 21, 1991, 9:23 PM
	HyperCard	674K	application program	Sat, Mar 16, 1991, 5:13 PM
	Off Site Data Archive	103K	Retrospect 1.1 doc...	Thu, Sep 27, 1990, 8:46 PM
▷	Payroll 1988 FINAL	—	folder	Sun, Jan 27, 1991, 10:08 PM
	Power Tools	176K	HyperCard 2.0 alia...	Fri, Aug 31, 1990, 3:14 PM

Figure 2-15: A Finder window including the information added by the Show disk info in header option.

The last set of options, listed on the right side of the List Views box, toggles the display of commands in the Finder's View menu and the display of columns in Finder windows. If you deselect the Show date option, for example, the By Date command is removed from the View menu, and the Date column is removed from all Finder windows.

These commands can customize your Finder windows to suit the way you work with files and organize your hard drive, eliminating the display of information you don't find useful and reducing the onscreen clutter of windows with too much information. For example, if you're not using the Label menu to apply meaningful labels to your files, then the Show label option should be deselected. Similarly, if you won't be entering extensive comments into the Get Info dialog boxes of your files, the Show comments option can be deselected. (The Get Info dialog box and comments are discussed more thoroughly later in this chapter.)

Figures 2-16 and 2-17 show the Finder window resulting from two different option settings.

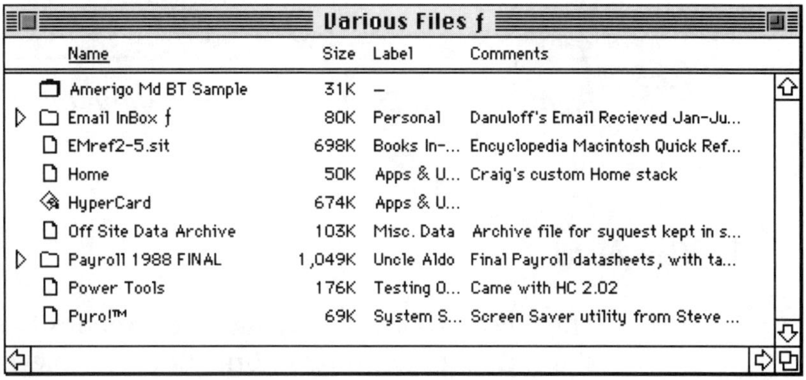

Name	Size	Label	Comments
Amerigo Md BT Sample	31K	—	
▷ Email InBox ƒ	80K	Personal	Danuloff's Email Recieved Jan-Ju...
EMref2-5.sit	698K	Books In-...	Encyclopedia Macintosh Quick Ref...
Home	50K	Apps & U...	Craig's custom Home stack
HyperCard	674K	Apps & U...	
Off Site Data Archive	103K	Misc. Data	Archive file for syquest kept in s...
▷ Payroll 1988 FINAL	1,049K	Uncle Aldo	Final Payroll datasheets, with ta...
Power Tools	176K	Testing O...	Came with HC 2.02
Pyro!™	69K	System S...	Screen Saver utility from Steve ...

Figure 2-16: A Finder window as it appears when the Show kind, Show date and Show version options are deselected in the Views control panel.

	Various Files ƒ			
Name		Size	Kind	Last Modified
📄 Amerigo Md BT Sample		31K	font suitcase	Fri, Dec 21, 1990, 1:45 PM
▷ 📁 Email InBox ƒ		80K	folder	Sun, Mar 24, 1991, 9:22 PM
📄 EMref2-5.sit		698K	StuffIt Deluxe™ do...	Wed, Jun 13, 1990, 11:43 PM
📄 Home		50K	HyperCard 2.0 alia...	Thu, Mar 21, 1991, 9:23 PM
📄 HyperCard		674K	application program	Sat, Mar 16, 1991, 5:13 PM
📄 Off Site Data Archive		103K	Retrospect 1.1 doc...	Thu, Sep 27, 1990, 8:46 PM
▷ 📁 Payroll 1988 FINAL		1,049K	folder	Sun, Jan 27, 1991, 10:08 PM
📄 Power Tools		176K	HyperCard 2.0 alia...	Fri, Aug 31, 1990, 3:14 PM
📄 Pyro!™		69K	control panel	Thu, Nov 29, 1990, 11:44 PM

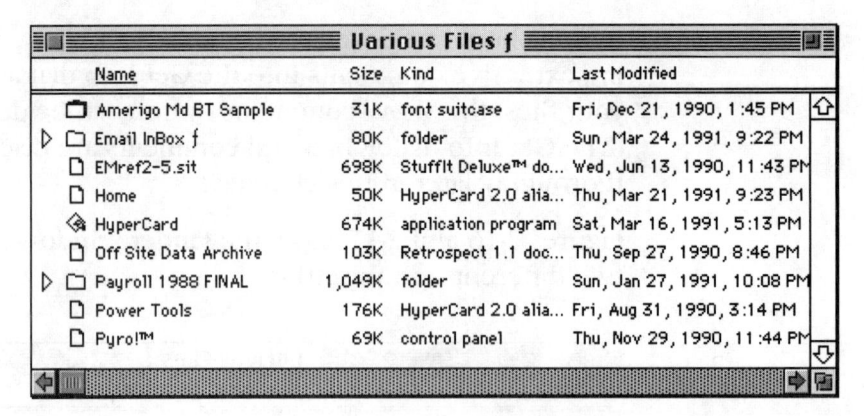

Figure 2-17: A Finder window without label, version or comments.

The View Menu

The Finder's View menu, like View menus in past Finder versions, determines how information is displayed in the current active window. Previous versions of the View menu let you display files and folders by icon, small icon, name, date, size, kind and color. In System 7, the View menu provides all these view methods except for color but adds View by label, version and comment.

Each time you apply a View menu command to a particular window, that window's display is arranged according to the selected format (by icon, by small icon, etc.), and it retains that view format until a different View menu command is applied to it. When a window is closed and later reopened, it always appears in the same display view it had before it was closed. There's no way, unfortunately, to change the View option for all open or closed windows, since the View menu controls each window independently.

Choosing the By Icon or By Small Icon commands causes only the file icon and file name to be displayed. The other view commands display a small icon, the file name and additional columns of data as specified in the Views control panel described above. The particular view command that's selected determines the order in which files in the window are sorted:

- **By Size.** This command sorts files in descending size order. If you've selected the Show folder sizes option in the Views control panel, folders are also sorted in this list according to their size. Otherwise, folders are grouped alphabetically at the end of the list.

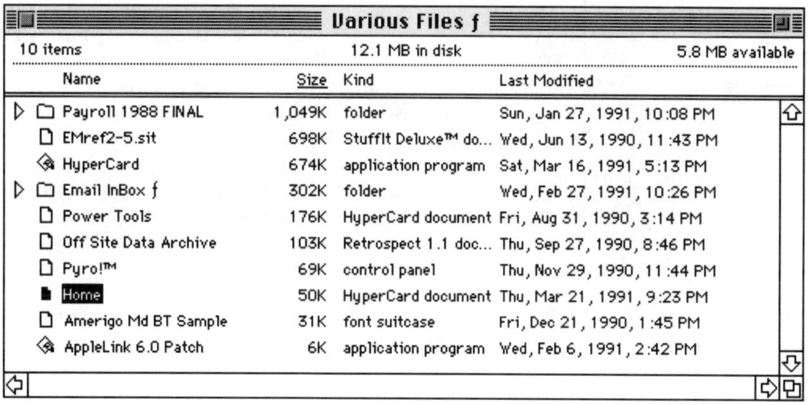
Various Files ƒ
10 items
12.1 MB in disk
5.8 MB available
Name
Size
Kind
Last Modified
Payroll 1988 FINAL 1,049K folder Sun, Jan 27, 1991, 10:08 PM
EMref2-5.sit 698K StuffIt Deluxe™ do... Wed, Jun 13, 1990, 11:43 PM
HyperCard 674K application program Sat, Mar 16, 1991, 5:13 PM
Email InBox ƒ 302K folder Wed, Feb 27, 1991, 10:26 PM
Power Tools 176K HyperCard document Fri, Aug 31, 1990, 3:14 PM
Off Site Data Archive 103K Retrospect 1.1 doc... Thu, Sep 27, 1990, 8:46 PM
Pyro!™ 69K control panel Thu, Nov 29, 1990, 11:44 PM
Home 50K HyperCard document Thu, Mar 21, 1991, 9:23 PM
Amerigo Md BT Sample 31K font suitcase Fri, Dec 21, 1990, 1:45 PM
AppleLink 6.0 Patch 6K application program Wed, Feb 6, 1991, 2:42 PM

Figure 2-18: A Finder window viewed By Size.

Commonly, the By Size command is used to find files known to be either very large or very small, or to locate large files that could be deleted to free up space.

- **By Kind.** This command sorts files alphabetically by a short description based on the file type, a four-letter code assigned by the developer or application creator. Document files associated with a particular application program include the name of their application, using "Word 5.1 document" or "HyperCard 2.2 document," for example, as the kind.

Common file kinds include Alias, Application Program, Chooser Extension, Database Extension, Desk Accessory, Document file, Folder and System Extension. Viewing files by kind is useful if you know the kind of file you're looking for and if the window containing that file has many different files in it.

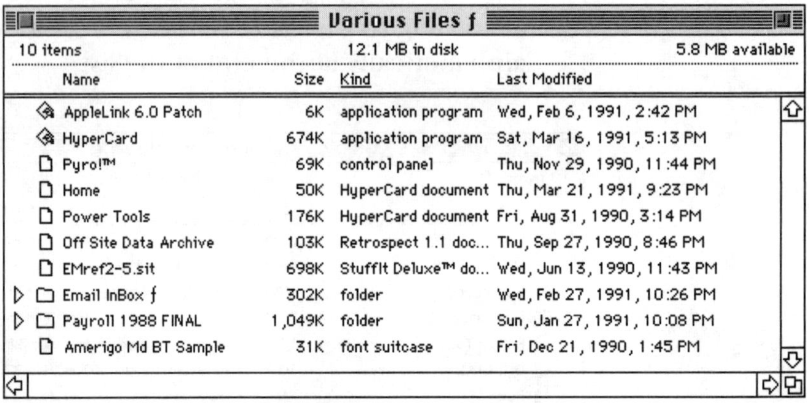
Various Files ƒ
10 items
12.1 MB in disk
5.8 MB available
Name
Size
Kind
Last Modified
AppleLink 6.0 Patch 6K application program Wed, Feb 6, 1991, 2:42 PM
HyperCard 674K application program Sat, Mar 16, 1991, 5:13 PM
Pyro!™ 69K control panel Thu, Nov 29, 1990, 11:44 PM
Home 50K HyperCard document Thu, Mar 21, 1991, 9:23 PM
Power Tools 176K HyperCard document Fri, Aug 31, 1990, 3:14 PM
Off Site Data Archive 103K Retrospect 1.1 doc... Thu, Sep 27, 1990, 8:46 PM
EMref2-5.sit 698K StuffIt Deluxe™ do... Wed, Jun 13, 1990, 11:43 PM
Email InBox ƒ 302K folder Wed, Feb 27, 1991, 10:26 PM
Payroll 1988 FINAL 1,049K folder Sun, Jan 27, 1991, 10:08 PM
Amerigo Md BT Sample 31K font suitcase Fri, Dec 21, 1990, 1:45 PM

Figure 2-19: A Finder window as it appears using the View menu's By Kind command.

- **By Label.** This command sorts by the label name given to the file with the Label command. (See Figure 2-20.) Labels, as discussed in Chapter 3, "Managing Your Hard Drive," group files according to some user-defined scheme. For example, you might have a group of files that all relate to personal (non-business) issues, a group relating to one project you're working on, etc.

  In any case, this command lets you sort the files in the current window according to labels previously applied. Files are arranged as they appear in the Label menu. Unlabeled files appear at the bottom of the listing.

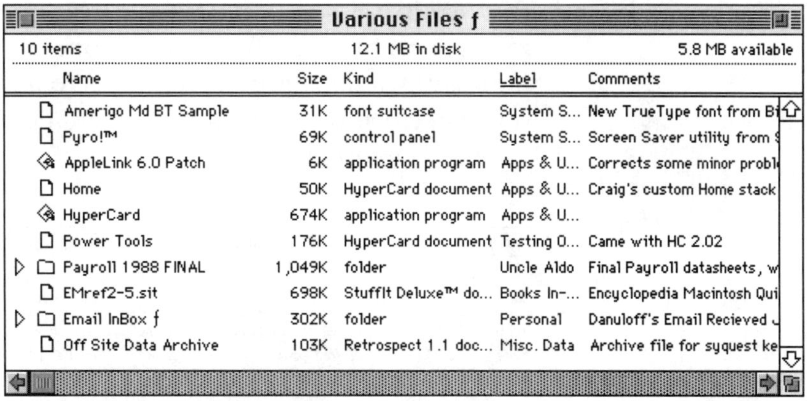

Chapter 2: The Finder

```
┌─────────────────── Various Files ƒ ───────────────────┐
│ 10 items              12.1 MB in disk      5.8 MB available │
├───────────────────────────────────────────────────────┤
│   Name                    Size  Kind           Label        Comments                          │
│ 🗎 Amerigo Md BT Sample    31K  font suitcase  System S...  New TrueType font from Bi         │
│ 🗎 Pyro!™                  69K  control panel  System S...  Screen Saver utility from §       │
│ ❖ AppleLink 6.0 Patch      6K  application program  Apps & U...  Corrects some minor probl   │
│ 🗎 Home                    50K  HyperCard document   Apps & U...  Craig's custom Home stack   │
│ ❖ HyperCard              674K  application program  Apps & U...                              │
│ 🗎 Power Tools            176K  HyperCard document   Testing O...  Came with HC 2.02          │
│ ▷ 🗀 Payroll 1988 FINAL  1,049K folder          Uncle Aldo   Final Payroll datasheets, w     │
│ 🗎 EMref2-5.sit           698K  Stuffit Deluxe™ do...  Books In-...  Encyclopedia Macintosh Qui│
│ ▷ 🗀 Email InBox ƒ        302K  folder          Personal     Danuloff's Email Recieved       │
│ 🗎 Off Site Data Archive  103K  Retrospect 1.1 doc...  Misc. Data  Archive file for syquest ke│
└───────────────────────────────────────────────────────┘
```

Figure 2-20: A Finder window as it appears using the View menu's By Label command.

- **By Date.** This command sorts files by the date they were modified, with the most recently updated files at the top of the list. This view is useful when you're looking for files that are much older or much newer than most of the other files in a certain folder.

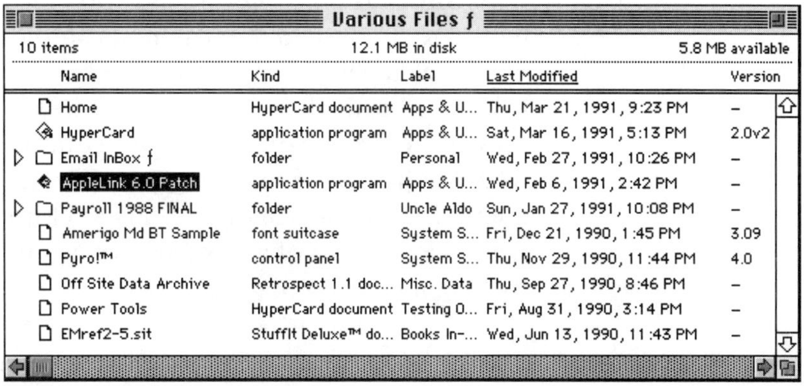

```
┌─────────────────── Various Files ƒ ───────────────────┐
│ 10 items              12.1 MB in disk      5.8 MB available │
├───────────────────────────────────────────────────────┤
│   Name                     Kind           Label        Last Modified              Version │
│ 🗎 Home                     HyperCard document  Apps & U...  Thu, Mar 21, 1991, 9:23 PM      –    │
│ ❖ HyperCard                application program  Apps & U...  Sat, Mar 16, 1991, 5:13 PM     2.0v2 │
│ ▷ 🗀 Email InBox ƒ          folder          Personal     Wed, Feb 27, 1991, 10:26 PM         –    │
│ ❖ AppleLink 6.0 Patch      application program  Apps & U...  Wed, Feb 6, 1991, 2:42 PM      –    │
│ ▷ 🗀 Payroll 1988 FINAL    folder          Uncle Aldo   Sun, Jan 27, 1991, 10:08 PM          –    │
│ 🗎 Amerigo Md BT Sample     font suitcase   System S...  Fri, Dec 21, 1990, 1:45 PM         3.09  │
│ 🗎 Pyro!™                   control panel   System S...  Thu, Nov 29, 1990, 11:44 PM        4.0   │
│ 🗎 Off Site Data Archive    Retrospect 1.1 doc...  Misc. Data  Thu, Sep 27, 1990, 8:46 PM    –    │
│ 🗎 Power Tools              HyperCard document  Testing O...  Fri, Aug 31, 1990, 3:14 PM     –    │
│ 🗎 EMref2-5.sit             Stuffit Deluxe™ do...  Books In-...  Wed, Jun 13, 1990, 11:43 PM –    │
└───────────────────────────────────────────────────────┘
```

Figure 2-21: A Finder window as it appears using the View menu's By Date command.

- **By Version.** Useful only for application files, this command sorts by the software developer's assigned version number. Ancillary application files (e.g., dictionaries and references) and data files you create do not have this type of version number.

Name	Kind	Label	Last Modified	Version
HyperCard	application program	Apps & U...	Sat, Mar 16, 1991, 5:13 PM	2.0v2
Amerigo Md BT Sample	font suitcase	System S...	Fri, Dec 21, 1990, 1:45 PM	3.09
Pyro!™	control panel	System S...	Thu, Nov 29, 1990, 11:44 PM	4.0
AppleLink 6.0 Patch	application program	Apps & U...	Wed, Feb 6, 1991, 2:42 PM	–
▷ Email InBox f	folder	Personal	Wed, Feb 27, 1991, 10:26 PM	–
EMref2-5.sit	StuffIt Deluxe™ do...	Books In-...	Wed, Jun 13, 1990, 11:43 PM	–
Home	HyperCard document	Apps & U...	Thu, Mar 21, 1991, 9:23 PM	–
Off Site Data Archive	Retrospect 1.1 doc...	Misc. Data	Thu, Sep 27, 1990, 8:46 PM	–
▷ Payroll 1988 FINAL	folder	Uncle Aldo	Sun, Jan 27, 1991, 10:08 PM	–
Power Tools	HyperCard document	Testing O...	Fri, Aug 31, 1990, 3:14 PM	–

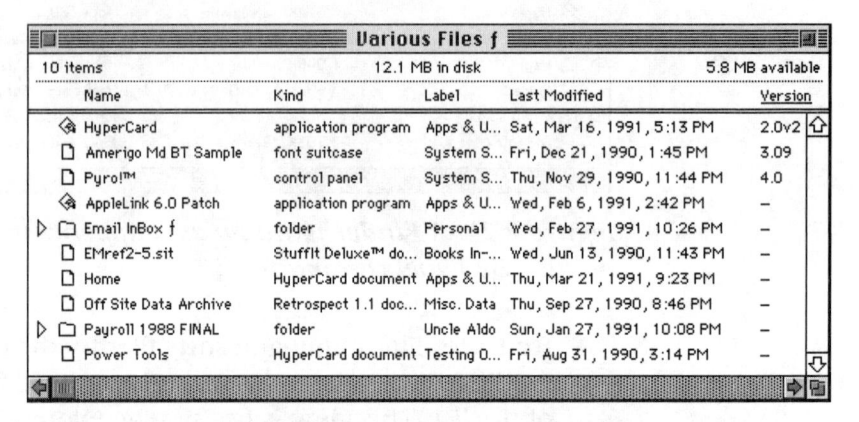

Figure 2-22: A Finder window as it appears using the View menu's By Version command.

- **By Comment.** This command sorts files alphabetically by the text contained in their Get Info dialog box comment fields. Displaying comment text in Finder windows is a major new file management feature, but it's useful only if the first characters of the comment are significant, or if you just want to separate all files that have comments from those that don't. Files without comments are placed at the top of any windows using the View menu's By Comment command.

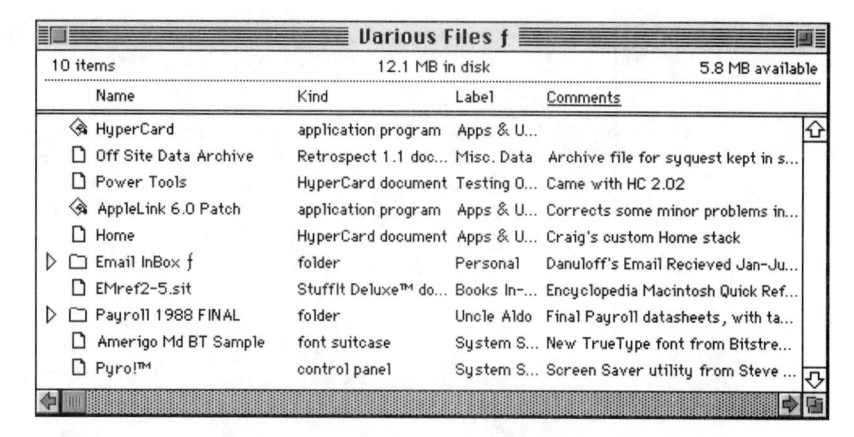

```
                    Various Files f
10 items              12.1 MB in disk              5.8 MB available
    Name             Kind              Label      Comments
   HyperCard         application program  Apps & U...
   Off Site Data Archive  Retrospect 1.1 doc...  Misc. Data  Archive file for syquest kept in s...
   Power Tools       HyperCard document  Testing O...  Came with HC 2.02
   AppleLink 6.0 Patch  application program  Apps & U...  Corrects some minor problems in...
   Home              HyperCard document  Apps & U...  Craig's custom Home stack
 ▷ Email InBox f     folder            Personal   Danuloff's Email Recieved Jan-Ju...
   EMref2-5.sit      StuffIt Deluxe™ do...  Books In-...  Encyclopedia Macintosh Quick Ref...
 ▷ Payroll 1988 FINAL  folder          Uncle Aldo  Final Payroll datasheets, with ta...
   Amerigo Md BT Sample  font suitcase  System S...  New TrueType font from Bitstre...
   Pyro!™            control panel     System S...  Screen Saver utility from Steve ...
```

Figure 2-23: A Finder window as it appears using the By Comment command.

Hierarchical Views

This important feature displays the contents of any folder without opening a new folder window. In previous versions, the only way to view and manipulate folder contents was to open the folder, thereby creating a new window. In System 7, you can display any folder contents by clicking on the small triangle that appears to the left of the folder icon. The contents then appear, indented slightly beneath the folder icon, as shown in Figure 2-24.

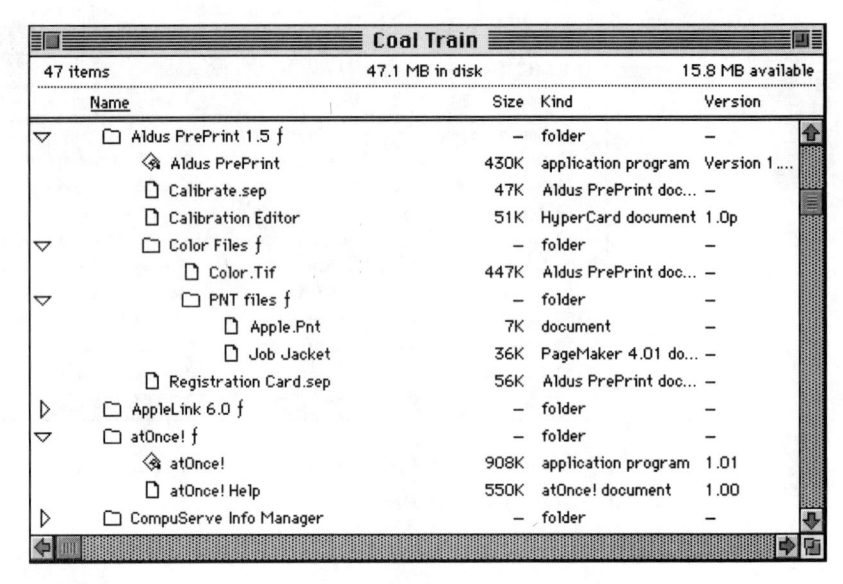

	Coal Train			
47 items	47.1 MB in disk		15.8 MB available	
Name	Size	Kind	Version	
▽ 📁 Aldus PrePrint 1.5 ƒ	—	folder	—	
Aldus PrePrint	430K	application program	Version 1....	
Calibrate.sep	47K	Aldus PrePrint doc...	—	
Calibration Editor	51K	HyperCard document	1.0p	
▽ 📁 Color Files ƒ	—	folder	—	
Color.Tif	447K	Aldus PrePrint doc...	—	
▽ 📁 PNT files ƒ	—	folder	—	
Apple.Pnt	7K	document	—	
Job Jacket	36K	PageMaker 4.01 do...	—	
Registration Card.sep	56K	Aldus PrePrint doc...	—	
▷ 📁 AppleLink 6.0 ƒ	—	folder	—	
▽ 📁 atOnce! ƒ	—	folder	—	
atOnce!	908K	application program	1.01	
atOnce! Help	550K	atOnce! document	1.00	
▷ 📁 CompuServe Info Manager	—	folder	—	

Figure: 2-24: A Finder window with hierarchical display.

This display is a hierarchical view because it allows you to see the contents of several levels of nested folders (folders inside of folders) at one time simply by clicking on the triangle next to the appropriate folder. (Alias folder icons, which are discussed in Chapter 3, appear without a triangle and cannot be displayed hierarchically.) Figure 2-25 shows a window in which aliased folders are not displayed hierarchically.

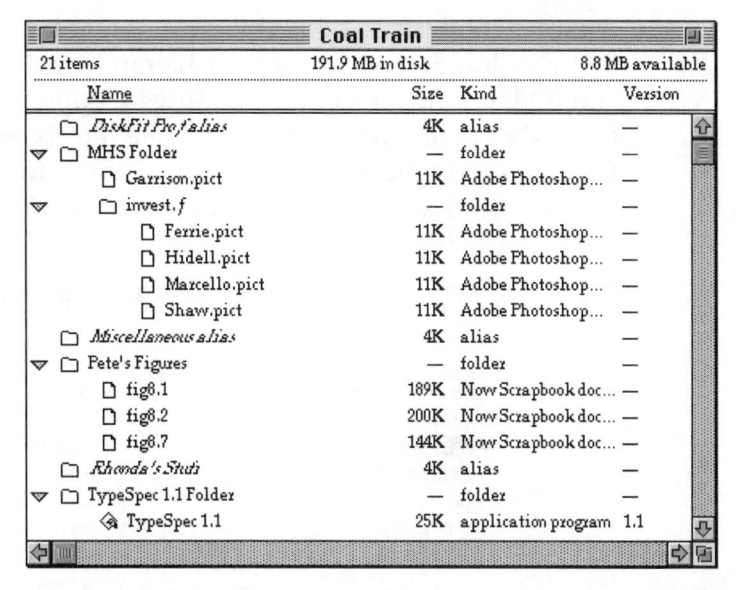

Figure 2-25: Finder window with hierarchical folders open.

You can drag hierarchically displayed files and folders from one location to another just as if they appeared in separate windows. In Figure 2-24 on page 70, you could move the file "Job Jacket" to the "AppleLink 6.0 ƒ" folder by dragging its file icon into that folder. You can also drag files or folders to other volumes (copying the files), to other open Finder windows (moving the files), to the desktop or to the Trash. In short, you can take advantage of the new hierarchical view to do everything you need.

The primary benefit of hierarchical views is the elimination of desktop clutter, since there's no need to open a new Finder window for every folder you want to open. In addition, hierarchical views allow you to select and manipulate files and folders from different hierarchical levels at the same time, which was not possible in previous Finder versions because each time you clicked the mouse in a new window the selection in the previous window was released.

Figure 2-26 illustrates this ability, showing four different files and a folder, each on a different hierarchical level. The files and folder in this selection can now be copied, moved, trashed or manipulated like any single file. To select files and folders at multiple levels of the hierarchy at the same time, hold the Shift key while selecting the file names.

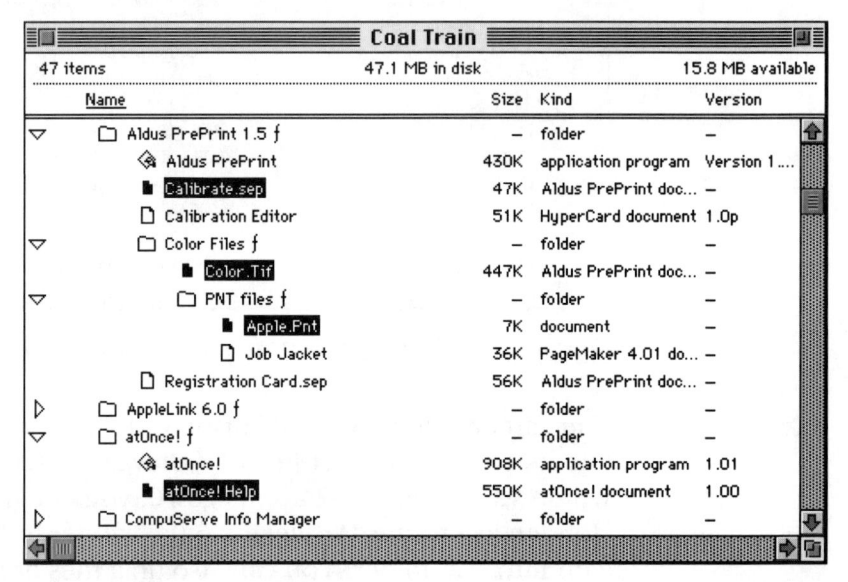

```
┌─────────────────────────── Coal Train ───────────────────────────┐
│ 47 items              47.1 MB in disk           15.8 MB available │
│   Name                              Size  Kind           Version  │
│ ▽  📁 Aldus PrePrint 1.5 ƒ            —   folder            —     │
│       📦 Aldus PrePrint              430K application program Version 1... │
│       ▪ Calibrate.sep                 47K Aldus PrePrint doc... — │
│       📄 Calibration Editor           51K HyperCard document 1.0p │
│ ▽     📁 Color Files ƒ                 —  folder            —     │
│         ▪ Color.Tif                 447K  Aldus PrePrint doc... — │
│ ▽       📁 PNT files ƒ                 —  folder            —     │
│           ▪ Apple.Pnt                  7K document          —     │
│           📄 Job Jacket               36K PageMaker 4.01 do... — │
│       📄 Registration Card.sep       56K Aldus PrePrint doc... — │
│ ▷  📁 AppleLink 6.0 ƒ                  —  folder            —     │
│ ▽  📁 atOnce! ƒ                        —  folder            —     │
│       📦 atOnce!                    908K application program 1.01 │
│       ▪ atOnce! Help                550K atOnce! document   1.00  │
│ ▷  📁 CompuServe Info Manager          —  folder            —     │
└──────────────────────────────────────────────────────────────────┘
```

Figure 2-26: Finder window showing multiple open nested folders with four files selected.

To collapse a folder's hierarchical display, click the downward pointing triangle next to the folder icon again; the enclosed files and folder listing disappear. When you close a window, the hierarchical display settings are remembered and will reappear the next time the window is opened.

Of course, you can still open a new window for any folder, rather than display its contents hierarchically. Simply doubleclick on the folder icon rather than the triangle. Or select the folder icon and then the Open command from the File menu.

Navigating From the Keyboard

Even though the Macintosh relies primarily on its graphic interface and the mouse, there are many times when you need keyboard control. A variety of keyboard shortcuts can now be used to select files, move between file windows and manipulate icons. The keyboard commands that follow are available in all Finder windows and on the desktop:

- **Jump to file name.** Typing the first few letters in a file name selects that file. For example, if you want to select a file named "Budget," when you type "B," the first file name starting with a "B" is selected. When the "u" is typed, the selection will be the first file name starting with "Bu," etc. You must not pause between letters, or the Mac will interpret each additional letter as the first letter of a new search.

    If you don't know an exact file name, type an "A" to cause the display to scroll to the top of the list, an "L" to scroll to the middle or a "Z" to scroll to the end.

- **Select next alphabetical file name.** This is done by pressing the Tab key. All files visible in the current window, including those displayed in hierarchically open folders, are included in this selection.

- **Select previous alphabetical file name.** Press Shift-Tab. This is useful when you press the Tab key one time too many and need to back up one step in reverse alphabetical order.

- **Select next file.** Down, Left and Right Arrow keys select the next file or folder icon in the respective direction.

- **Open selected folder.** Command-Down Arrow opens the selected file or folder, unless the selected file or folder is already open, in which case this key combination brings its window to the front.

- **Open selected file or folder and close current window.** Press Command-Option-Down Arrow. If the selected file or folder is already open, this key combination brings its window to the front and closes the current folder or volume window.

- **Open parent folder window.** Press Command-Up Arrow. If the selected file or folder is already open, this key combination brings its window to the front.

- **Open parent folder window, close current window.** Pressing Command-Option-Up Arrow closes the current window.

- **Edit file name.** Press Return. (File names can also be opened for editing by clicking the cursor on the text of the file name.) You can tell the name has been selected for editing when its display is inverted and a box is drawn around the file name.

  Once open for editing, the backspace key deletes characters, the Right and Left Arrow keys position the cursor. To complete the renaming, pressing Return again saves the file-name changes and returns the name to an inverted display.

- **Make Desktop active.** Command-Shift-Up Arrow makes the current window inactive and the Finder Desktop active.

The following keyboard commands are available only when working in Finder windows using text views (By Name, Size, Kind, Version, Label or Comment):

- **Expand hierarchical display.** Command-Right Arrow hierarchically displays the folder contents.

- **Expand all hierarchical display.** Command-Option-Right Arrow hierarchically displays the contents of the current folder and all enclosed folders.

Chapter 2: The Finder   75

- **Collapse hierarchical display.** Command-Left Arrow collapses the hierarchical display of the current folder.

- **Collapse all hierarchical display.** Command-Option-Left Arrow collapses the hierarchical display of the current folder and all enclosed folders.

Dragging Files Between Windows

Another new feature lets you select and move a file from an inactive window. In previous Finder versions, as soon as an icon was selected, the window containing that icon became the active window and brought the window forward. This created a problem when that window overlapped and obscured other folder icons. In the Finder, any visible icon in any window can be selected and dragged to a new location without the source-file window becoming active.

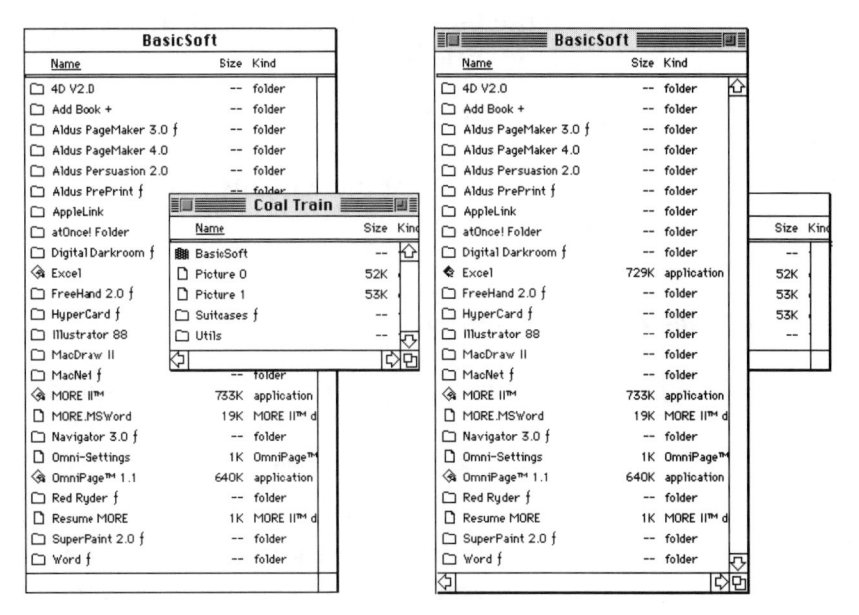

Figure 2-27: Dragging files between overlapping windows.

This feature is more clearly described by an example. Suppose we want to drag a file or folder from the "BasicSoft" window into a folder on the "Coal Train" drive. This would be impossible in previous Finder versions without repositioning the Coal Train window; as soon as the BasicSoft file was selected the BasicSoft window covered the Coal Train window, as shown at the right of Figure 2-27.

In System 7's Finder, however, we can simply point the mouse to the item to be moved from the BasicSoft window and hold the mouse button down while dragging the icon into the Coal Train window. As long as the mouse button is not released, the BasicSoft window won't be selected and therefore won't overlap the Coal Train window.

However, this method cannot be used to move more than one file at a time. To move multiple files from BasicSoft to Coal Train, the Coal Train window would have to be repositioned. To move a Finder window without making it active, hold down the Command key while dragging the inactive window's title bar.

In order to give the user more feedback, starting in System 7.1 and System 7 Pro, when you drag items over and into a window, the inside of the window that will contain the item becomes outlined.

Working With Multiple Files

To perform any operation on one or more files, first select that file or group of files. Most aspects of selecting files in System 7.5 are the same as in System 6.0x, but there are some changes and new features:

- **Immediate marquee selection.** The marquee (selection rectangle), created by clicking the mouse button and dragging with the button pressed, now selects files as soon as any part of the file name or icon is inside the selection rectangle. In previous versions, files were not selected until the mouse button was released, and only files completely contained in the selection rectangle were selected.

- **Marquee selection in text views.** Previously, the marquee could be used only in By Icon or By Small Icon views or on the desktop. In System 7.5 marquee selection is supported in all Finder windows; for example, you can drag-select in the By Name or By Date views.

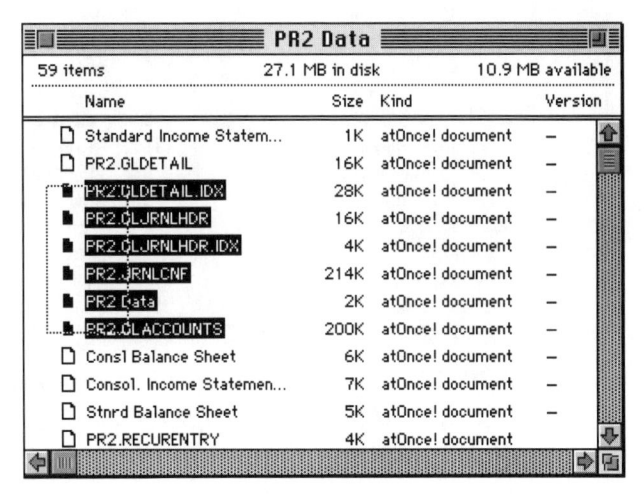

Figure 2-28: Multiple files can be selected using the marquee, even when files are listed by name.

- **Shift select.** Using the Shift key, the marquee can select non-contiguous sections of any Finder window.

- **File dragging.** It's still possible to drag files by clicking on their names. To open a file name for editing, click on a file name and wait a few seconds for a box to appear around the file name.

- **Finder scrolling.** When dragging with a marquee, the Finder window scrolls automatically as soon as the cursor hits one of its edges, as shown in Figure 2-29. This is very useful when selecting in Finder windows displaying icons.

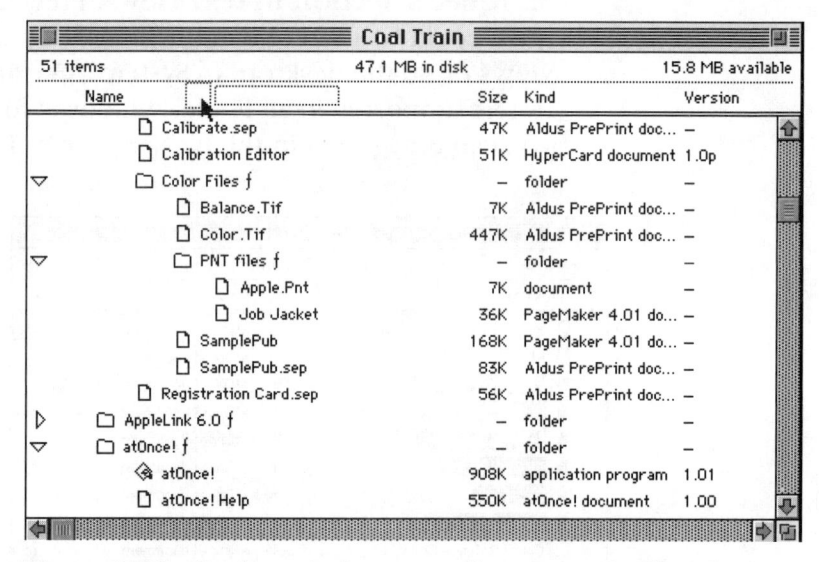

Figure 2-29: Finder windows scroll automatically when items are dragged past their edges.

Title Bar Pop-Up Menu

While hierarchical window views make it easy to move down the folder hierarchy, there's also a new way to move up the folder hierarchy—via a pop-up menu that appears in the title bar of any window when you hold down the Command key and click on the folder's name.

Figure 2-30 shows the pop-up menu for a folder named "System 7 Letters *f*," which is inside the "Technology Topics *f*" folder, which is inside the "Email Inbox *f*" folder, on the "Data Drive" disk. This pop-up menu displays the current folder's parent folder names and the volume on which the current folder is located. (In this case, since the "System 7 Letters ƒ" folder is inside the "Technology Topics ƒ" folder, "Technology Topics ƒ" is the parent folder and "System 7 Letters ƒ" is the child.)

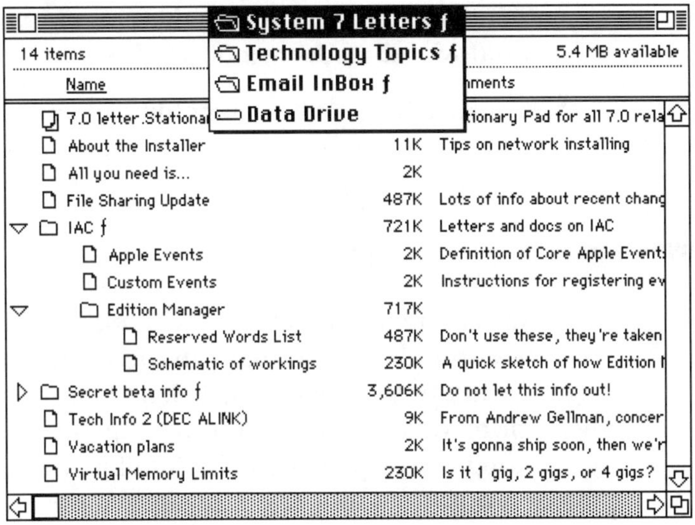

Figure 2-30: Title bar pop-up menu, and graphic of hard drive arrangement producing this menu.

Selecting a folder or volume name from this pop-up menu opens a new Finder window that displays the folder or volume contents. If a window for the selected folder or volume was already open, that window is brought forward and made active. This feature is a real time saver when hunting files down in the Finder.

Holding down the Option and Command keys while selecting a folder or volume name from the Title bar pop-up menu causes the current window to be closed as the new folder or volume is opened, helping you avoid a cluttered desktop by automating the process of closing windows that aren't being used.

Holding down the Option key also closes windows in several other situations:

- **Folders.** While opening a folder by double-clicking on its icon at the Finder, the current folder will close as the new one is opened.

- **Windows.** While clicking the close box in any Finder window, all Finder windows close.

- **Applications.** While launching an application, the window in which the application appears closes.

Improved Zooming

To resize an open window, you can either drag the size box in the lower-right corner or click in the zoom box in the upper-right corner of the window title bar. The zoom box operation was improved in System 7: it now expands the window size just enough to display the complete file list or all file and folder icons; it no longer opens the window to the full size of the current monitor unless that size is necessary.

Cleaning Up Windows & Icons

As in previous system software versions, the Clean Up command rearranges icons in Finder windows or on the desktop to make them more orderly and visible. Several new Clean Up options were added in System 7, however, to help arrange icons in specific situations or to create custom icon arrangements. These options appear in place of the standard Clean Up command, depending on the current selection and whether you're using the Shift, Option or Command key:

- **Clean Up Desktop.** When you're working with icons on the desktop (not in a Finder window), the Clean Up command normally reads Clean Up Desktop, and will align icons to the nearest grid position.

- **Clean Up All.** Holding down the Option key, however, changes the command to Clean Up All, which returns all disks, folders and volume icons to neat rows at the right edge of your primary monitor. (Again, this command is available only on the desktop, not in Finder windows.)

- **Clean Up Window.** When you're working in a Finder window, the Clean Up command is dimmed when the View command is set to anything other than By Icon or By Small Icon. When By Icon or By Small Icon is selected, the Clean Up Window command appears and arranges all icons in the current window into either aligned or staggered rows, depending on the settings in the Views control panel (as discussed earlier).

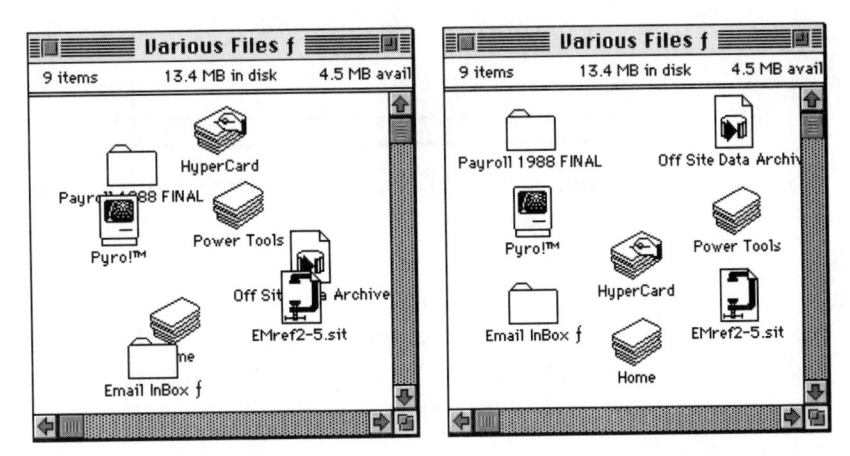

Figure 2-31: A Finder window before and after using Clean Up Window.

- **Clean Up By Name (By Size, etc.).** Holding down the Option key while selecting a Finder window lets you arrange icons by file name, size, date, comment, label or version. The specific option presented is the one selected in the View menu before the By Icon or By Small Icon command was chosen.

To arrange icons by size, for example, select the respective windows for the icons you want to affect, choose By Size from the View menu, choose By Icon (or By Small Icon) from the View menu, then hold down the Option key while choosing Clean Up By Size.

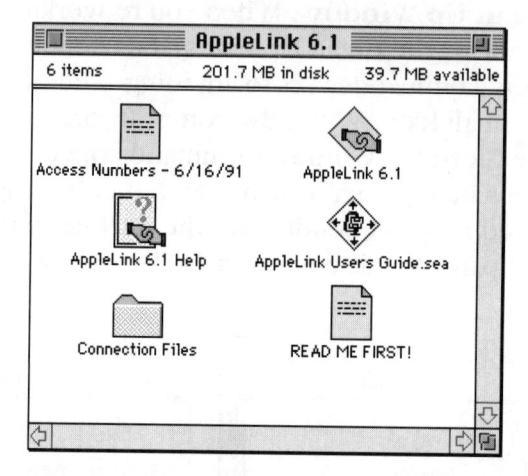

Figure 2-32: A Finder window with icons arranged alphabetically.

- **Clean Up Selection.** While a specific file or group of files is selected, holding down the Shift key activates Clean Up Selection, which will reposition only the selected files.

The Help Menu

When System 7 was introduced, it included several features that were often touted by Apple as primary benefits of their new system software but which have in fact turned out to be either impractical, poorly implemented or just plain useless. The new Help menu and Balloon Help, for example, were major disappointments. While some novice users seem to actually like Balloon Help, the great majority of Macintosh users actively hate it.

Balloons are passive and don't lead you through complex task assistance. Apple took so much heat on Balloon Help that they rethought the entire issue. In System 7.5 Apple's solution to increasingly difficult software is Apple Guide, an active context-sensitive help system that is the result of several years of work. The sections that follow explain both help systems.

Apple Guide

7.5 Apple Guide opens in its own window at the lower-left corner of the screen when you select the Macintosh Guide command (Command-Shift-? keystroke) from the Help menu. Arranged by topic, it provides interactive help to common questions. Onscreen visual devices lead through an established procedure: menu commands are flagged in red, radio buttons and check boxes are circled with coach marks, and so on. All the while Apple Guide instructs you on the next step. Apple Guide will even scroll windows to guide you to a feature. Figure 2-33 provides an example. If you make a mistake, Apple Guide tells you so and instructs you on how to correct it. Pretty cool, huh?

See the Apple Guide tutorial for help on Apple Guide.

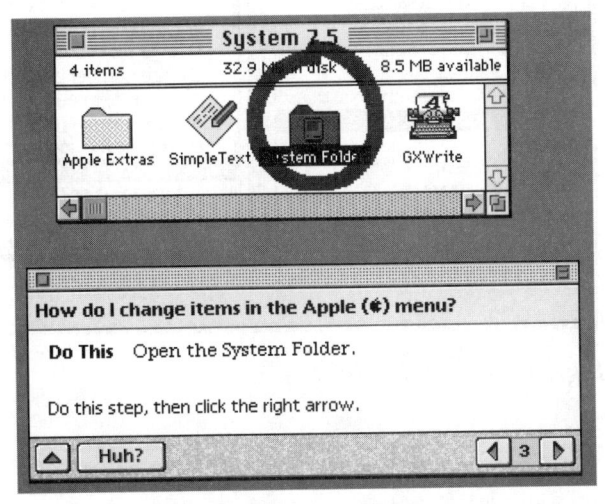

Figure 2-33: An Apple Guide instruction and coach mark.

Apple is confident enough in Apple Guide to use it to "write down" the System 7.5 manual to just 75 pages. Instead of giving you step-by-step instructions in the manual, you are sent to the topic and question giving the required procedure. Since Apple Guide is implemented as a developers' toolkit, it will undoubtedly improve in content and operation over time. Most developers will add Apple Guide to their programs over the next year or two. In this book you may have noticed an Apple Guide icon leading you to the important topics of interest in appropriate sections.

With the Apple Guide window open, click the Topics button to see a list of areas covered in Apple Guide. Topics are general categories. Clicking a topic brings up a list of common task-oriented questions in the right-hand scroll box, as shown in Figure 2-34. Double-click on a question to begin the active help process.

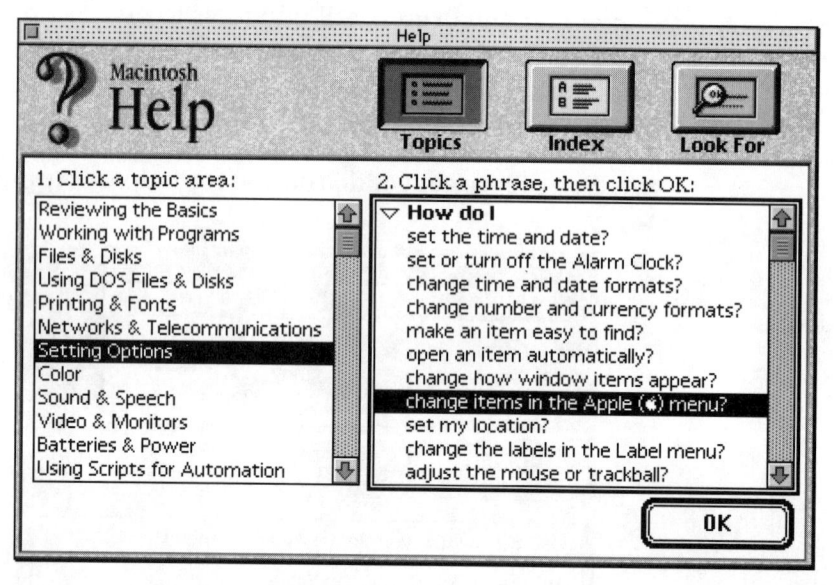

Figure 2-34: A Topics list.

If you know what you want but don't see the right question, there are a couple of other ways to get into Apple Guide. You can see a list of keywords by clicking the Index button. The third button, Look For, lets you search Apple Guide for a keyword without having to browse the list of keywords or questions. What you see in Apple Guide depends upon the application that is active at the moment. For a while after System 7.5 is released, most applications will not ship with enabled Apple Guide systems.

Once a task is selected the window opens up to display information and show you the first step in the task. An example is shown in Figure 2-35. The selected question appears at the top of the window, information appears in the center and arrow buttons lead you forward and backward in the process. Sometimes you will see the Huh? button; clicking it shows you information related to the task. To return to the Topics list, click the Up Arrow button.

Figure 2-35: A task step.

Once a step is completed, click the Next button (the Right Arrow button) to proceed to the next step. You will get an error message if you made a mistake. Arrows dim when there is no next or previous step in the process.

The Guide window is a special kind of floating window that is always available at the top of your screen. Chances are that you will want to recover the real estate to see other items, while keeping Apple Guide around for additional help. You can move the Apple Guide window by dragging its Title bar. To minimize the window (shown in Figure 2-36), click the minimizer box in the upper-right corner of the Title bar. You can restore the window to full size by clicking on the minimizer box again. Or, click on the Right Arrow button to open the window fully and go to the next step. Apple Guide can be closed by clicking the Close box at the upper-left corner of the Title bar.

Figure 2-36: A minimized Apple Guide window.

Apple Guide and AppleScript form a powerful combination. You can embed AppleScript functionality in an Apple Guide help system to actively assist users. For example, if you are supplying a FileMaker Pro database system to a client, you can place buttons in the Apple Guide window that open files or perform other operations. The button launches an AppleScript macro, and commands FileMaker through AppleEvents to perform the task. Even the Finder in System 7.5 is scriptable, and susceptible to being managed through an Apple Guide help system. We'll have more to say about AppleScript in Chapter 11.

Balloon Help

Balloon Help gives Macintosh software applications the ability to provide onscreen context-sensitive information. It works by providing the Show Balloons command, which, when selected, causes a help balloon to be displayed when the arrow cursor is positioned over any menu command, window element, dialog box option, tool or icon. This help balloon provides a brief description of that command, element or icon function.

The System 7 Finder and control panels supply extensive help balloons, some of which are shown in Figure 2-37.

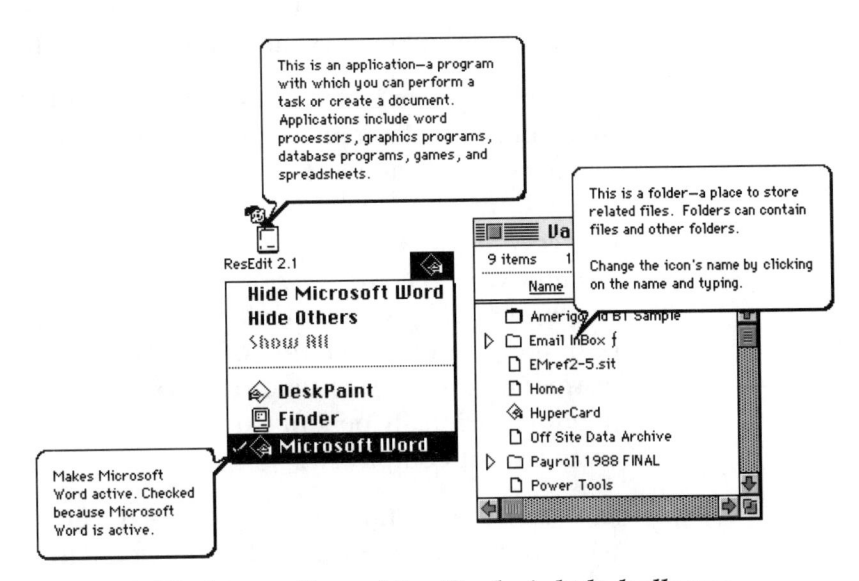

Figure 2-37: A sampling of the Finder's help balloons.

After the Show Balloons command has been chosen, it changes to the Hide Balloons command, which can be used to turn off the display of help balloons.

Balloon Help Limitations

In theory, Balloon Help makes it easier to learn new applications and refresh your memory when accessing infrequently used commands or dialog box options. However, these balloons can appear only in applications that have been written or upgraded specifically for System 7 and in which Balloon Help has been specifically implemented. More than three years after the introduction of System 7, only a limited number of programs fully support Balloon Help.

In those programs that do offer Balloon Help, the information provided is usually too limited or too generic to be truly helpful. This appears to be caused by the limited amount of space available for balloon text and limited efforts from developers.

A bigger problem is the annoying way that help balloons pop up from every element your cursor points to once the Show Balloons command has been chosen. Someone wishing to take advantage of Balloon Help is unlikely to need assistance on every single object, command and element—but instead would like to read the one or two help balloons relevant to a single, specific problem. Unfortunately, Apple's current "all-or-nothing" implementation of Balloon Help leads to a very distracting display that tends to encourage many users who might occasionally benefit from Balloon Help to instead stay away from it completely.

A better implementation would display help balloons only when the cursor has pointed to a specific item for more than a few seconds or only if a modifier key was held down. One shareware program, Helium, works in just this way. Several other third-party developers offer extensions that modify the way Balloon Help works, making it more pleasant and practical. These are described in Chapter 16, "Third-Party Utilities." However, with Apple Guide here, Balloon Help is probably on its way out in future system software releases.

Additional Help

Optionally, in addition to Balloon Help, applications may add additional commands to the Help menu, usually to provide access to more in-depth online Help systems. In each application, check the Help menu for additional commands and online Help systems.

The Finder provides an example of this additional help with the Finder Shortcuts command and dialog box found in previous versions of System 7. This dialog box is shown in Figure 2-38. In System 7.5 Finder Shortcuts has been replaced by the Shortcuts command, a special Apple Guide help system for working with the Finder. Figure 2-39 shows the introductory screen to the new Shortcuts command, which works as previously described in the Apple Guide section you just read.

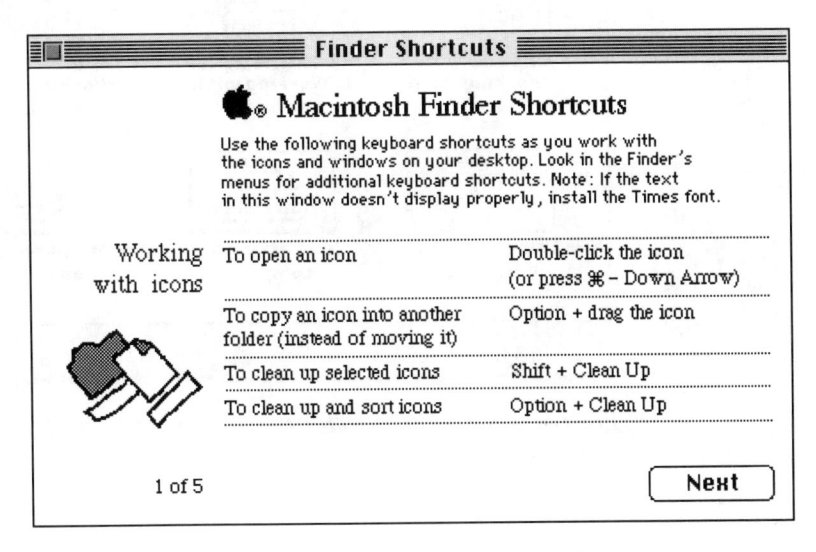

Figure 2-38: The Finder Shortcuts dialog box.

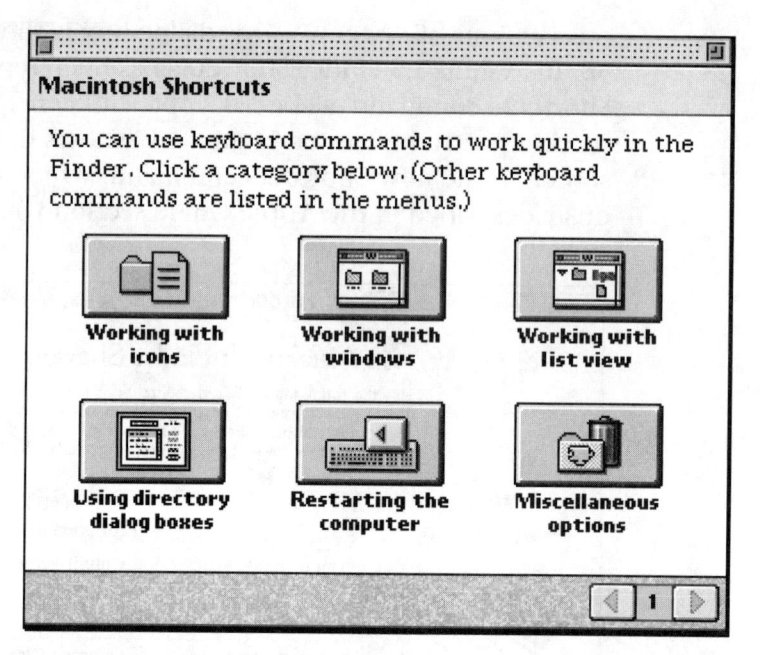

Figure 2-39: The Shortcuts Apple Guide help system for the System 7.5 Finder.

Trash & Empty Trash

The big news in System 7 was that the garbage collector no longer came without being invited—the Trash is emptied only when the Empty Trash command is chosen from the Special menu. In previous versions of the system software, the Trash was automatically emptied when any application was launched, or when the Macintosh Restart or Shut Down commands were selected. Now, items remain in the Trash until Empty Trash is selected, even if the Mac is shut down.

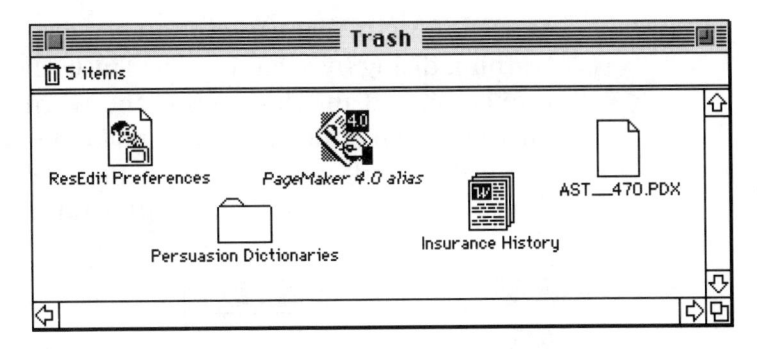

Figure 2-40: The Trash window displays files currently in the trash.

When the Empty Trash command is accessed, a dialog box appears asking you to confirm that you want to delete the current Trash files. This dialog box appears regardless of what files the Trash contains and informs you how much disk space will be freed by emptying the Trash.

Figure 2-41: The Empty Trash? dialog box.

Trash Tips

While the basic use of the Trash is straightforward, there are several less-obvious aspects you'll want to know about:

- **Avoid Trash warnings.** If you hold down the Option key while choosing Empty Trash, the confirmation dialog box will not appear and the Trash will be emptied immediately.

- **Disable Trash Warnings.** You can also disable the warning dialog by selecting the Trash, choosing the Get Info command and deselecting the Warn before emptying option. Of course, this will make it easier to delete application and system software files accidentally, so this option should be deselected with caution.

Figure 2-42: The Trash Info dialog box.

- **Retrieving Trashed Items.** Any time before the Empty Trash command is chosen, items inside the Trash may be recovered and saved from deletion. This is done by double-clicking on the Trash icon and dragging the file icons you want to recover out of the Trash window and back onto the desktop, or onto any volume or folder icon.

- **Freeing disk space.** Only when the trash has been emptied and this command is chosen is disk space released. In previous systems, dragging items to the Trash alone was sufficient to cause disk space to be freed—although not always immediately.

- **Repositioning the Trash.** In System 7.5, you can reposition the Trash on your desktop and it will stay there even if you reboot. It's no longer automatically returned to the lower-right desktop corner each time you reboot.

This is helpful if you use a large monitor or multiple monitors.

Caution: Don't be in too much of a hurry emptying the trash. Do it every so often when you need to recover disk space but give yourself a chance to retrieve mistakenly trashed items first. Once the Trash is emptied, deleted files can still often be recovered. You will need to use one of several third-party undelete utilities such as: Symantec Utilities for the Macintosh, Norton Utilities or Central Point Software's Mac Tools, among others.

The Get Info Dialog Box

As in previous Finder versions, selecting any file, folder or drive icon and choosing the Get Info command from the File menu brings up an Info dialog box (usually called a Get Info dialog box) that displays basic information and related options. The basic System 7.5 Get Info dialog box, as shown in Figure 2-43, is only slightly different from those in previous Finder versions.

Figure 2-43: The Get Info dialog box for files.

There are now five different versions of the Get Info dialog box—one each for files, folders, applications, volumes and alias icons. Options may differ among versions, but the basic information each provides is the same:

- **File name.** The exact file name that appears on the desktop, which cannot be changed from within this dialog box.

- **Icon.** This appears to the left of the file name, providing a visual reference for the file.

  You can customize the icon of almost any data file, application or volume by pasting a new icon on top of the existing icon here in the Get Info dialog box. To change an icon, copy any MacPaint or PICT graphic onto the Clipboard, select the icon you want to replace in the Get Info dialog box (a box will appear around the icon, indicating its selection) and choose the Paste command from the Edit menu. If the picture is too large to fit into the icon frame, it is scaled down. Close the Get Info dialog box and the new icon will appear in the Finder window or on the desktop. Likewise, you can copy and paste any icons from between Get Info boxes.

- **Kind.** Provides a brief description of the selected file. For data files, this usually includes the name of the application that created the file.

- **Size.** The amount of disk space that the file consumes.

- **Where.** The location of the selected file, including all folders enclosing it and the volume it's on.

- **Created.** The date and time when the file was created. This date is reset when a file is copied from one volume to another or if a new copy is created by holding down the Option key while moving a file into a new folder.

- **Modified.** The date and time the contents of the file were last changed.

- **Version.** Lists the software application's version number. No information on data files, folders or volumes is provided.

- **Comments.** Although it isn't obvious here, System 7 vastly improved its support for adding comments to this Get Info dialog box field. In System 7.5 comments can be displayed in Finder windows and you can use the new Find command to locate files by the comment text. A complete discussion of comments is provided in Chapter 3, "Managing Your Hard Drive."

   Unfortunately, comments are still erased whenever the Finder's invisible desktop file is recreated, a bug that persists despite long-standing promises to remedy it.

Several other options appear in some Get Info dialog boxes:

- **Locked.** Makes it impossible to change or delete the selected file. The Locked option appears for data files, applications and aliases. Locking ensures that unwanted changes are not accidentally made to data files that should not be altered. Locked data files can be opened, in most applications; but changes cannot be saved unless you use Save As... to create a new file.

   Locked files are also spared accidental deletion, since they must be unlocked before they can be emptied from the Trash. If you try to delete a locked file, the dialog box shown in Figure 2-44 appears. It's important to note, however, that locked files will be deleted from the Trash without notice or warning if you hold down the Option key while you choose Empty Trash from the Finder's Special menu.

Figure 2-44: The warning that appears when locked items are placed in the Trash.

- **Memory.** These options appear only for application files and include Suggested size, Minimum size and Preferred size. Suggested size specifies the application developer's recommendations for the amount of memory to be allocated to the program when it's opened. The Minimum size is the least amount of RAM that the application requires to be opened, and the Preferred size indicates the amount of RAM the user wishes to allot the application. (A discussion of these options is presented in Chapter 8, "Memory Management.")

- **Stationery Pad.** Available for data files only, this turns the selected document into a template. (A template is a master document on which new documents are based.) With this option, each time the selected document is opened, a copy of the file is created, and any changes or customizations are made to this copy, leaving the original Stationery Pad document available as a master at all times. (A complete discussion of Stationery Pads is provided in Chapter 5.)

Get Info for the Trash

The Trash's Info dialog box, shown in Figure 2-45, contains two important pieces of information and one useful option. The dialog box lists the number of files and the amount of disk space they consume, which lets you know how much space will be freed by the Empty Trash command. It also lists the date when the most recent item was placed in the Trash.

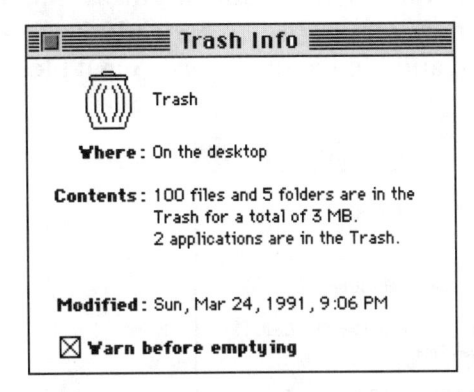

Figure 2-45: The Trash's Info dialog box.

The Warn before emptying option, which is a default, causes a confirmation dialog box to display when the Empty Trash command is selected (shown in Figure 2-46). If you don't want the dialog box to display each time the Empty Trash command is chosen, deselect the Warn before emptying option. But without this warning dialog box, you increase the risk of permanently deleting files you may want later.

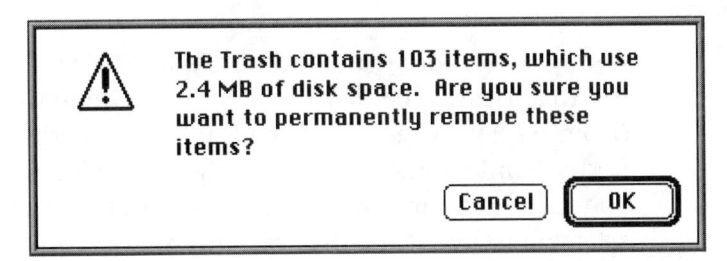

Figure 2-46: The Empty Trash confirmation dialog box.

Get Info for Alias Icons

The Get Info dialog box for alias icons is different in several ways from the one used by standard files. First, the version information normally displayed beneath the dates is replaced with the path and file name of the original file.

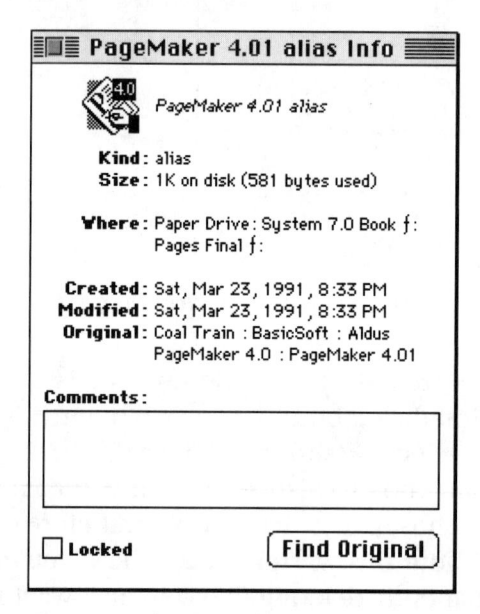

Figure 2-47: The Get Info dialog box for an alias icon.

Also, the Get Info dialog box includes the Find Original button that locates the disk or folder containing the original file (from which the alias was made). It can open the disk or folder window and select the original file icon. If the disk or volume containing the original file is not available, a dialog asks you to insert the disk containing the original file, or, in the case of a network volume, the volume will be mounted.

Comments and Locked are available for aliases, behaving exactly as they do for any other files. The "Stationery Pad" option, however, is not available for alias icons.

Moving On

The Finder is the most visible part of the Macintosh system software; as we've seen in this chapter, it gives you powerful and intuitive tools to manage the disks and files you're using with your Macintosh:

- The new Finder menus.
- The many ways you can see and manipulate data in Finder windows.
- The Help menu and Balloon Help.
- The Trash and Empty Trash command.
- The Get Info dialog box, in its many forms.

From general disk and file management tools, we move into Chapter 3, "Managing Your Hard Drive," where four new System 7 features—and their System 7.5 modifications—will be documented in detail. Aliasing, the Find... command, labels and comments—all used at the Finder—are vital for control and productivity on your Macintosh.

Chapter 3

Managing Your Hard Drive

As we've seen already, the Finder provides a comprehensive set of commands and features that help you manage disks and files. The new Finder does not, however, require you to organize your electronic files in any particular way; it's still up to you to decide the best way to arrange your files.

For related information, see "Files & Disks."

File management is an interesting challenge; you must balance your available storage space with the quantity and size of files you need to keep available, and you must design a logical arrangement that will allow you to quickly locate the files you need.

Fortunately, System 7.5 provides several file-management tools, including the Make Alias command, the Find command and the Label menu. These commands will affect the way you store files on your hard disk—and on floppy disks, removable cartridges, network file servers or any other storage devices. In this chapter, we'll take a look at these new features and how they can help you organize your hard drive.

Aliasing

Wouldn't it be nice to be in several places at one time? Imagine, for example, that while you were hard at work earning your paycheck, you could also be lying on a beach enjoying the sun. And if being in two places at once sounds appealing, how would you like to be in any number of places at one time? For example, you could be at work earning a living, at the beach getting a tan, at the library reading a book and on a plane bound for an exotic destination—all at the same time.

System 7 extended this convenience to your electronic files through a feature called *aliasing*. Aliasing is perhaps the most significant improvement System 7 offered the average Macintosh user, because it removes the single largest constraint—space limitation—from the task of organizing files and thereby makes it easier to take full advantage of your software applications and data files.

Basic Aliasing Concepts

In simple terms, an *alias* is a special kind of copy of a file, folder or volume. Unlike copies you might create with the Duplicate command or other traditional methods, an alias is only a copy of the file, folder or volume *icon*.

To understand this distinction, think of a file icon as a door; the file that the icon represents is the room behind the door. As you would expect, each room normally has just one door (each file has one icon), and opening that door (the icon) is the only way to enter the room.

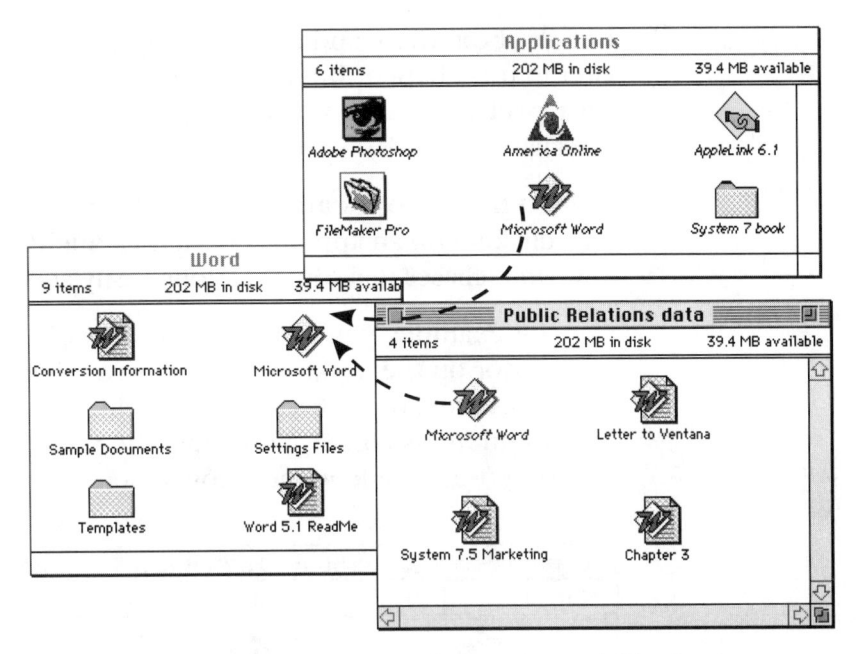

Figure 3-1: Each alias points to the original file that was used to create it.

Creating an alias is like adding an additional door to a room; it presents another entrance, usually in a location different from the existing entrance. Just as you wouldn't have two doors to the same room right next to each other, you won't usually have two icons for the same file (the original and an alias) in the same location. This is the first important feature of an alias: it can be moved to any folder on any volume without affecting the relationship between the alias and its original file. In fact, the link between an alias and its original file is maintained even if both files are moved.

Another key feature of an alias is that it requires only about 1k or 2k of disk space, regardless of the size of the original file. That's because the alias is a copy of the icon, not a copy of the file itself. The alias's small size is an important attribute, since it consumes very little storage space.

Details about these and other aspects of aliases are provided later in this chapter, but before getting too far into the technical aspects, let's take a quick look at a few practical ways to use aliases:

- **To make applications easier to launch.** Since double-clicking on an application's alias launches that application, aliases make applications easily accessible.

    For example, you can keep one alias of your word processor on the desktop, another in a folder full of word processing data files and yet another alias in the Apple Menu Items Folder. You could then launch this application using the icon most convenient at the moment.

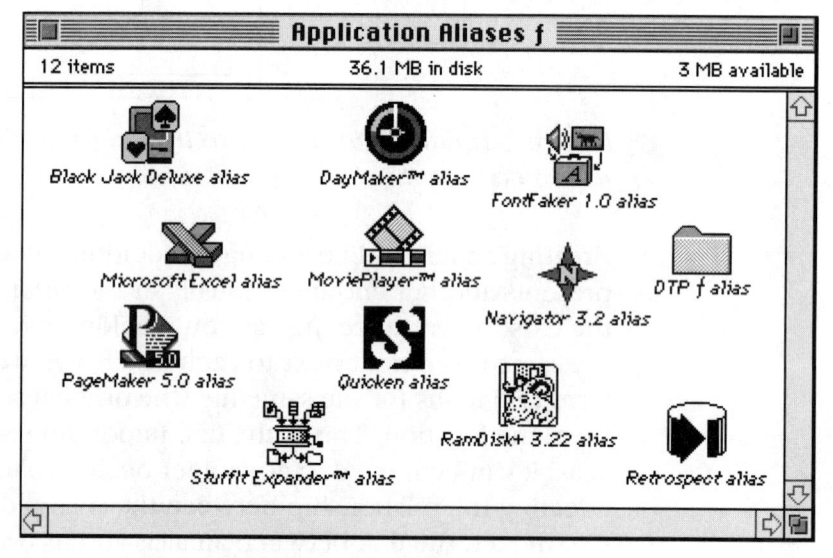

Figure 3-2: Aliasing an application makes it more convenient to launch.

- **To organize data files more logically.** You can keep alias copies of data files in as many folders as they logically belong in.

If you keep a spreadsheet file with information on your income taxes, for example, in a folder along with all the spreadsheets you've created during that year, you could also keep an alias copy of that same spreadsheet in a personal-finances folder, in another tax-file folder and in a general-accounting folder.

Storing alias copies in multiple locations has several benefits. First, it lets you quickly locate the file you're looking for, because there are several places to find it. It's also easier to find files because they can be stored along with other files they're logically connected with. Finally, archival storage lets you move the originals off the hard drive, saving disk space while still allowing access to the file via aliases.

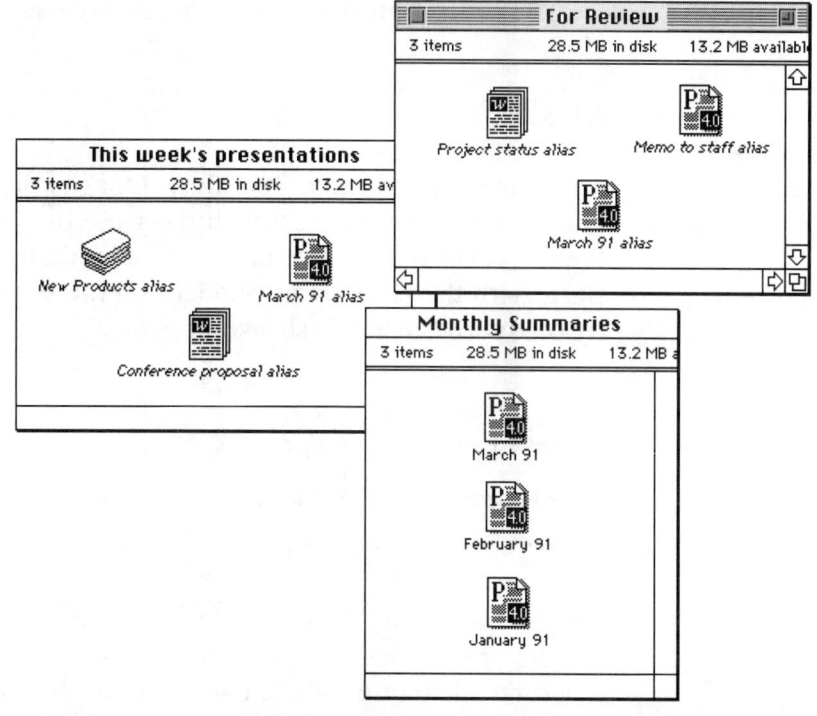

Figure 3-3: Aliasing data files allows them to be stored in multiple logical locations.

- **To simplify access to files stored on removable media.** Keeping aliases from floppy disks, removable hard drives, CD-ROMs and other removable storage media on your local hard drive lets you locate those files quickly and easily.

  When an alias of a file stored on removable media is opened, the Macintosh prompts you to insert the disk (or cartridge) that contains the original file.

- **To simplify access to files stored on network servers**. Placing aliases of files from network file servers on your local hard drive is another way to quickly and easily locate the files no matter where they're stored.

  When an alias of a file stored on the network server is opened, the Macintosh automatically connects to the server, prompting you for necessary passwords.

Creating & Using Aliases

To create an alias, select the file, folder or volume icon and choose the Make Alias command (or use the Command-M keystrokes) from the File menu. An alias icon will then appear, with the same name and icon as the original, followed by the word "alias," as shown in Figure 3-4.

/DTP Forum   /DTP Forum alias

Figure 3-4: An original file and an alias of that file.

For the most part, alias icons look and act just like other files, folders or volumes. You can change the file name of an alias at any time; changing the file name doesn't break the link between the alias and its original file. Changing a file name is like changing the sign on a door; it doesn't change the contents of the room behind the door.

Figure 3-5: An original file and an alias of the file that's been renamed.

You've probably noticed that alias file names appear in italic type. This is always true, even when they're listed in dialog boxes (*except* when aliases are listed under the Apple Menu). The italic type helps you distinguish the alias files from the original files.

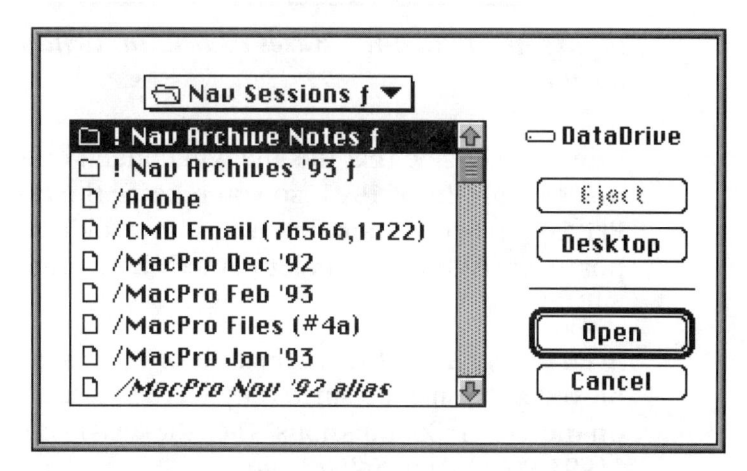

Figure 3-6: Alias file names appear in italics in dialog boxes.

As mentioned earlier, alias icons can be moved to any available folder or volume without losing the link they maintain to the original file. This is the magic of aliases and the key to their utility. No matter how files are moved, the links are maintained.

Original files can also be moved, as long as they remain on the same volume; and they can be renamed without breaking the link with their aliases. When the alias icon is opened, the Macintosh finds and opens the original file.

To illustrate how this automatic linkage is maintained, assume you have a file called "1991 Commission Schedule," which is stored in a folder named "Corporate Spreadsheets." You created an alias of this file, moved the alias into a folder called "1991 Personal Accounting" and renamed the alias "1991 Commissions" (see Figure 3-7).

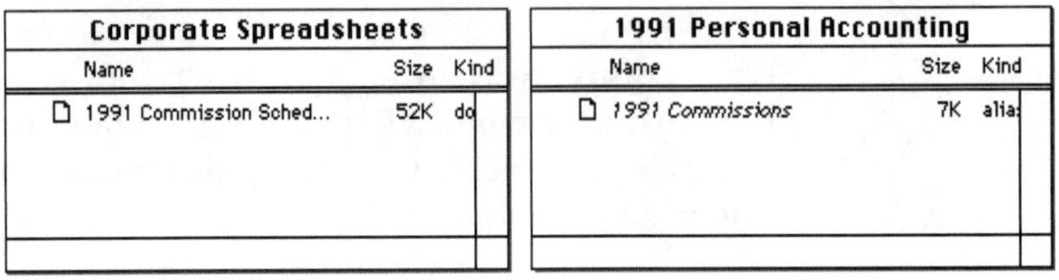

Corporate Spreadsheets		
Name	Size	Kind
1991 Commission Sched...	52K	do

1991 Personal Accounting		
Name	Size	Kind
1991 Commissions	7K	alia

Figure 3-7: Files and aliases as originally named and positioned.

Later, you decide that this file will contain only data for the first six months of 1991, so you rename the original file "1991 Pt1 Comm Sched," and put it in a new folder inside the "Corporate Spreadsheets" folder named "Jan-June Stuff" (see Figure 3-8).

Even though both the original file and the alias have been moved and renamed since they were created, double-clicking on the "1991 Commissions" file (the alias) will open the "1991 Pt1 Comm. Sched" file.

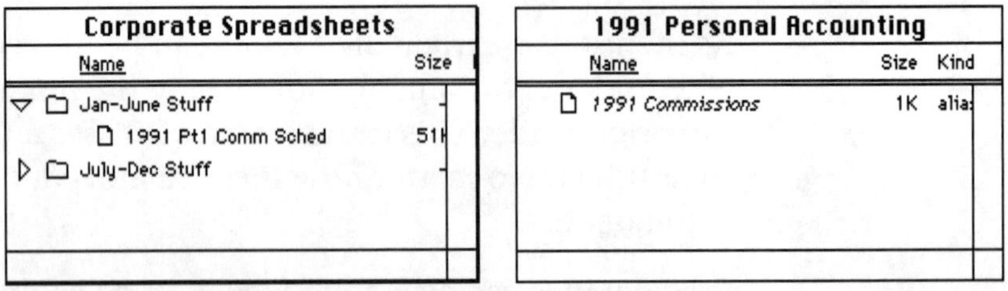

Corporate Spreadsheets	
Name	Size
▽ ▢ Jan-June Stuff	
1991 Pt1 Comm Sched	51
▷ ▢ July-Dec Stuff	

1991 Personal Accounting		
Name	Size	Kind
1991 Commissions	1K	alia

Figure 3-8: Files and aliases after being moved and renamed.

Advanced Aliasing Concepts

Once you understand the basic concepts of aliases and begin using them, you may have questions, such as: How many aliases can one file have? Is it possible to alias an alias? What happens when an alias's original file is deleted? The answers to these and other questions follow.

- **Multiple aliases.** There is no limit to the number of aliases you can create from a single file, folder or volume.

    When creating multiple aliases, alias names are designated by numbers, to distinguish them from existing alias names. The first alias of a file named "Rejection Letter" is named "Rejection Letter Alias"; the second, "Rejection Letter Alias 1"; and the third, "Rejection Letter Alias 2"—and so on until the earlier aliases are renamed or moved to different locations. These alias numbers have no significance beyond serving to avoid file-name duplication.

- **Aliasing aliases.** You can create an alias of an alias, but this causes a chain of pointing references: the second alias points to the first, which points to the original. In most cases, it's better to create an alias directly from the original file.

    If you do create a chain and any one of the aliases in the chain is deleted, all subsequent aliases will no longer be linked to the original file. To illustrate this problem, assume an alias named "New Specs Alias" was created from an original file named "New Specs," then "New Specs Alias 2" was created from "New Specs Alias" (see Figure 3-9).

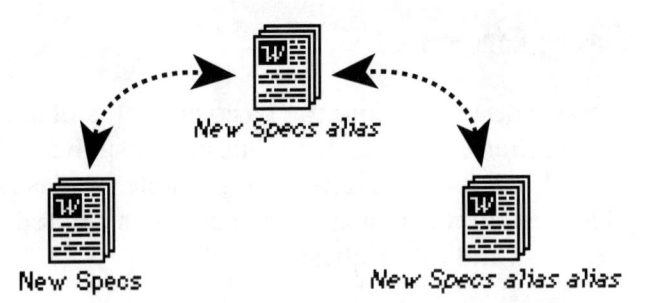

Figure 3-9: Creating an alias of an alias causes a chain that can be broken if one alias is deleted.

At that point, each of these files can be repositioned and renamed and the alias links will be automatically maintained. However, if the "New Specs alias" file is deleted, "New Specs alias alias" will no longer be linked to "New Specs." There's no way to reestablish the link should a break occur.

- **Deleting aliases.** Deleting an alias has no effect on the original file, folder or volume. It simply means that in order to access the item that the alias represented, you'll have to access the original item or another alias.

  You can delete aliases in any of the ways you delete normal files: drag the alias to the Trash, then choose the Empty Trash command, or delete the alias using some other file deletion utility.

- **Moving original files.** The link between an alias and its original file is maintained regardless of how the original is moved on one volume; but links are not maintained when you copy the original file to a new volume and then delete the original file. In other words, there's no way to transfer the alias link from an original file to a copy of that original file.

  If you're going to move a file from which aliases have been created from one volume to another, and you must delete the original file, all existing aliases will be unlinked and therefore useless. You could create new aliases from the original file in its new location and replace the existing aliases with the new ones, but you'd have to perform this process manually.

- **Deleting original files.** Deleting a file from which aliases have been made has no immediate effect; no warning is posted when the file is deleted. But when an attempt is made to open an alias of a file that's been deleted, a dialog box appears informing you that the original file cannot be found. There's no way to salvage a deleted file to relink with this alias, so in most cases you'll want to delete the orphaned alias.

   The exception to this rule is when the original file is still in the Trash. In this case, if you try to open an alias, a dialog box will inform you that the file cannot be opened because it's in the Trash. If you drag the original from the Trash, it's again available to the alias.

- **Finding original files.** Although an alias is in many ways a perfect proxy for a file, there are times when you'll need to locate the alias's original file—for example, if you want to delete the original file or copy the original onto a floppy disk.

   To locate the original file for any alias, simply select the alias icon in the Finder and choose Get Info (Command-I) from the Finder's File menu. This brings up a special Get Info dialog box (shown in Figure 3-10) that displays basic information about the alias icon, the path information for the original file and the Find Original button.

   When the Find Original button is clicked, the original file, folder or volume is selected and displayed on the desktop. If the original file is located on a removable volume that's not currently available, a dialog box appears prompting you to insert the disk or cartridge containing that file. If the original file is located on a network file server, the Macintosh attempts to log onto the server to locate the file, prompting for any required passwords.

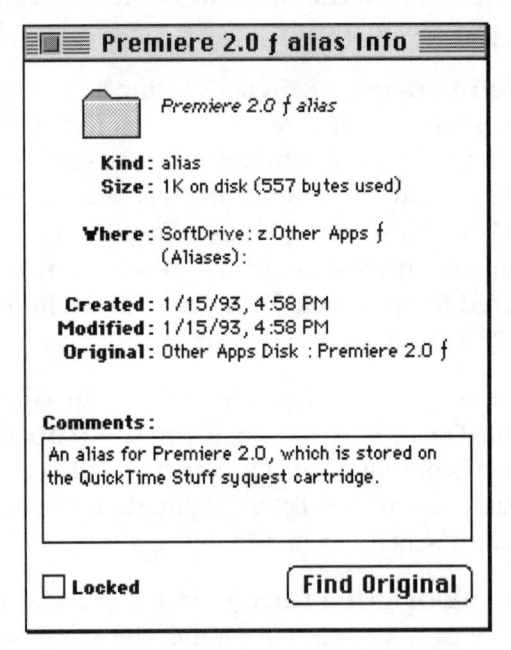

Figure 3-10: The Get Info dialog box for an alias.

If the current alias is an alias of an alias, clicking the Find Original button will find the original file, not the alias used to create the current alias. If the alias file has been accessed via File Sharing, the Find Original button will usually be unable to locate the original file, although its location is accurately documented in the original text of the Get Info dialog box.

- **Replacing alias icons.** As introduced in Chapter 2, "The Finder," new icons can be pasted into the Get Info dialog box for any file. This is also true of alias icons. Replacing the icon of any alias has no effect on the icon of the original file.

Aliasing Folders or Volumes

So far, most of this section has focused on aliasing in relation to application and data files. But almost without exception, aliasing works the same way for folders and volumes. Folder aliases are created, renamed, repositioned, deleted and linked to their originals in exactly the same way as the file aliases previously described:

- Aliasing a folder creates a new folder icon with the same name as the original, plus the word "alias."

- The name of an alias folder appears in italics on the desktop or in dialog box listings.

- Folder aliases can be renamed at any time. Of course, an alias cannot have the same name as an original or another alias while in the same location.

- Folder aliases can be moved inside any other folder or folder alias or to any volume.

- When an alias folder is opened, the window of the original folder is opened. Aliasing a folder does not alias the folder's content. For this reason, the original folder must be available anytime the folder alias is opened. If the original folder is on a volume that's not currently mounted, you'll be prompted to insert the volume, or the Macintosh will attempt to mount the volume if it's on the network.

- Deleting a folder alias does not delete the original folder or any of its contents.

But there are some unique aspects of folder aliases:

- When a folder alias is displayed hierarchically in a Finder window, it cannot be opened hierarchically (no triangle appears to its left) because the folder alias has no contents, strictly speaking. You can open the folder alias by double-clicking on it to open a new Finder window.

- Folder aliases appear in standard file dialog boxes, and the contents of the original folder can be revealed from within these dialog boxes.

- Anything put into a folder alias is actually placed into the original folder, including files, folders and other aliases. The folder alias has no real contents; it's just another "door" to the original folder.

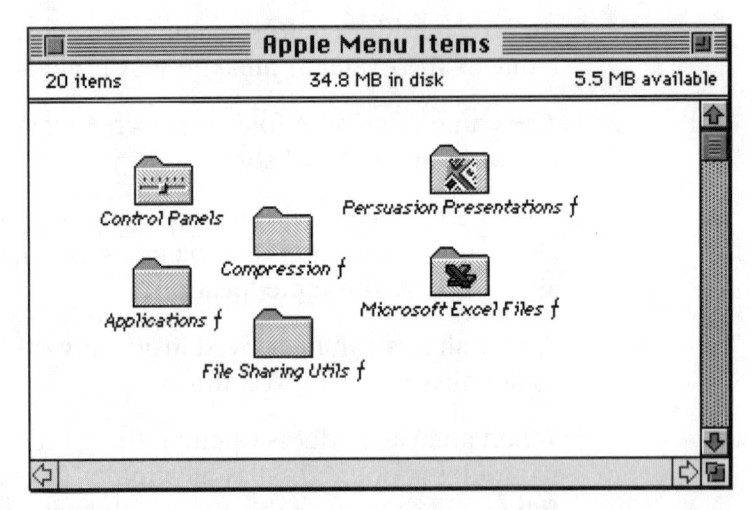

Figure 3-11: Alias folders are commonly used in the Apple Menu.

Volume aliases are similar to file aliases but have some of the same characteristics as folder aliases:

- Opening a volume alias mounts the original volume if it's not already available. If the original volume is not currently mounted, you'll be prompted to insert the volume, or the Macintosh will attempt to mount the volume if it's on the network.

- Opening a volume alias displays the Finder window of the actual volume and the contents of this window.

Chapter 3: Managing Your Hard Drive **115**

- Aliasing a volume does not alias the volume contents, just the icon of the volume itself.

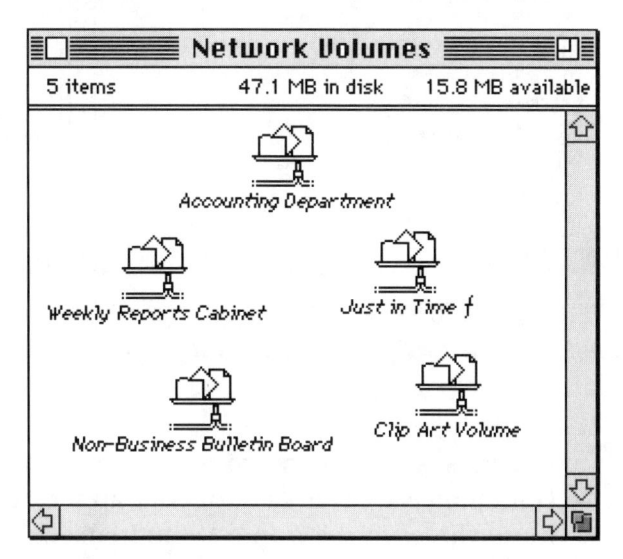

Figure 3-12: Alias volumes, stored in a folder.

Using Aliases

Aliases have a multitude of uses. Following are some of the more interesting possibilities:

- **Alias applications.** The easiest way to launch an application is to double-click on its icon. But many of today's applications are stored in folders containing a morass of ancillary files—dictionaries, color palettes, Help files, printer descriptions and so on. Amid all this clutter, it's hard to locate the application icon in order to launch it. Aliasing allows easier access.

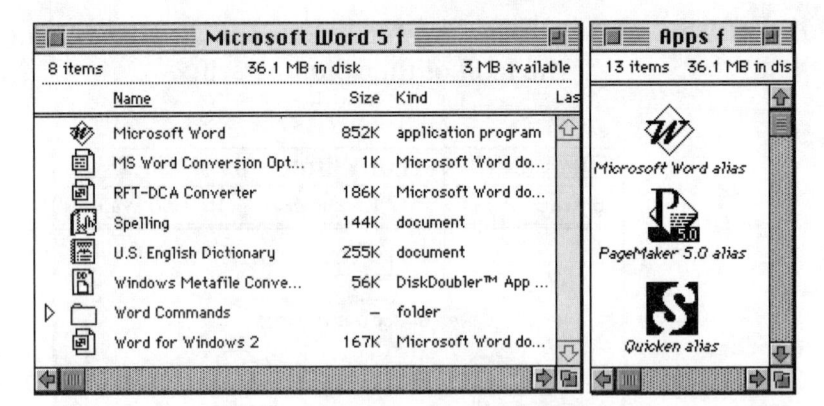

Figure 3-13: Microsoft Word, along with its ancillary files (left), and an alias of Word in a folder with other application aliases (right).

The most straightforward way to simplify application launching is to alias each of your applications and place these aliases in the Apple Menu Items Folder of your System Folder. You can then launch the applications by simply choosing their names from the Apple Menu. Keep in mind that the new System 7.5 Recent Applications folder may make this a less practical approach than in previous versions of system software.

Or, instead, you might group your application aliases into folders, then alias these folders and place them in the Apple Menu. Doing it this way takes two steps instead of one, but this method leaves room in your Apple Menu for other folder, volume and file aliases. Of course, you could leave a few applications that you use extensively directly in the Apple Menu, but since System 7.5 shows hierarchical menus for any folder in the Apple Menu folder the former approach is preferable.

You can also put application aliases, along with groups of documents created with the application, on your desktop. But since double-clicking on any document will launch the application anyway, this is not really very useful.

- **Multiple data-file aliases.** To avoid having to remember all the places where a frequently used file is stored every time you want to use it, you can use aliases to store each data file in as many places as it logically fits—anywhere you might look for the file when you need it later.

   Suppose, for example, you write a letter to your boss about a new idea for serving your company's big client, Clampdown, Inc. Depending on your personal scheme, you might store this letter, along with other general business correspondence, in a folder pertaining to Clampdown, Inc., or you might even have a file where you keep everything that has to do with your boss. Using aliases, you can store the file in all these locations and in a folder containing all work you've done in the current week.

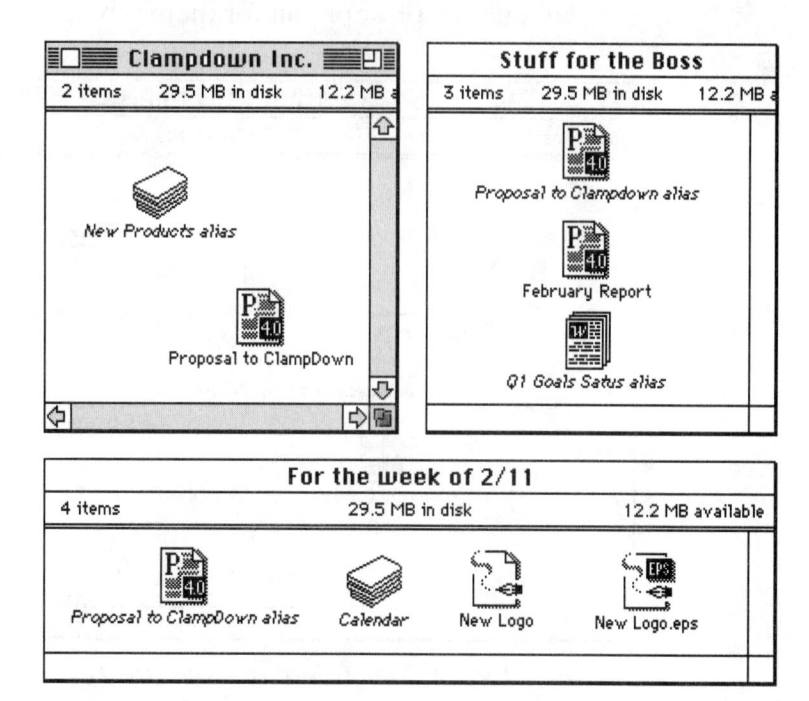

Figure 3-14: Aliasing a file into multiple locations.

- **Aliases of data files from remote or removable volumes.** You can store hundreds of megabytes worth of files on your hard drive, regardless of how big it is, by using aliases. Keeping aliases of all the files you normally store on removable disks or drives and all the files from network file servers that you occasionally need to utilize lets you locate and open the files by simply searching your hard drive (at the Finder, in dialog boxes or using a search utility) without the cost of hard-drive space.

  This is perfect for storing libraries of clip-art files, downloadable fonts, corporate templates or other infrequently used file groups. Storing these aliased files on your hard drive lets you browse through them whenever necessary. The hard drive will automatically mount the required volumes or prompt you for them when they're needed.

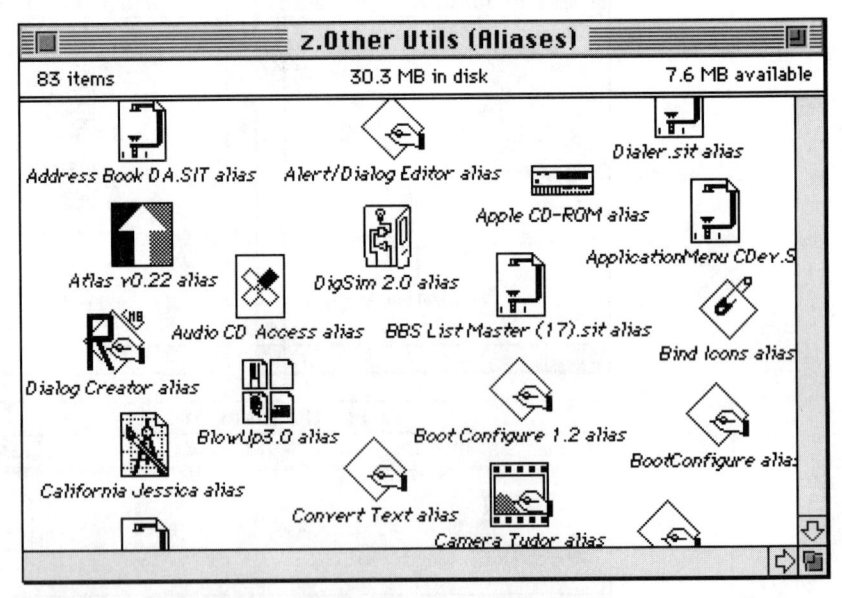

Figure 3-15: A folder full of aliased utility files stored on a removable volume.

- **Trash alias.** You can alias the Finder's Trash and store copies of it in any folder. Dragging folder files to the Trash alias is the same as dragging them to the actual Trash. Files trashed in this way will not be removed until you choose Empty Trash from the Special menu, and they can be retrieved by simply opening the Trash (or an alias of it) and dragging the file back onto a volume or folder.

- **Removable cartridge maps.** Create a folder for each removable cartridge, drive or floppy disk. Alias the entire contents of these volumes and store the aliases in the volume's folder. Then you can "browse" these volumes without mounting them. You may also want to keep other aliases of files from these volumes in other locations on your drive.

- **Network file-server volume maps.** Create a folder called "Network" and place an alias of each remote volume inside that folder. You can then log onto any remote volume by simply double-clicking on the volume alias. This eliminates the need to access the Chooser, locate the file server and locate the volume every time you want to use the volume. Of course, you'll be prompted for any required passwords.

- **Hard-drive alias.** If you work on a large AppleTalk network, put an alias icon of your hard drive on a floppy disk and carry it with you. If you need to access your hard drive from another location, all you have to do is insert the floppy disk containing your hard drive alias into any Macintosh on the network, double-click on the alias icon and your hard drive will be mounted via AppleTalk.

Aliasing Summary

- You can alias any file, folder, volume icon or the Trash.

- To create an alias, select the desired icon and choose Make Alias from the Finder's Special menu.

- An alias initially takes the same name as its original file with the word "alias" appended.

- Alias names always appear in italics, except in the Apple Menu.

- Aliases can be renamed at any time. The standard Macintosh 32-character name limit applies.

- Aliases can be moved to any location on the current volume or any other volume.

- An alias is initially given the same icon as its original. The icon can be changed in the Get Info dialog box.

- Most alias icons require only 1k or 2k of storage space.

- The link between an alias and its original is maintained even when the files are renamed or repositioned.

- Deleting an alias icon has no effect on its original file, folder or volume.

- Copying an alias to a new location on the current drive (hold down Option key while dragging) is the same as creating a new alias of the original file—it does not create an alias of an alias.

- Use the Get Info command to locate an alias's original.

- Opening a folder alias opens the window of the original.

- Opening a volume alias opens the window of the original volume.

The Find Command

Regardless of how well organized your electronic filing system is, it's impossible to always remember where specific files are located.

To solve this problem in the past, Apple provided the Find File desk accessory (DA) to let you search for files—by file name—on any currently mounted volume. Find File locates the files and lists them in a section of its window. Once a file is found, selecting the file name reveals the path of the located file, along with other basic file information, as shown in Figure 3-16. Using this information, you can then quit the Find File DA and locate the file yourself, or Find File can move the file to the desktop where it's easy to access.

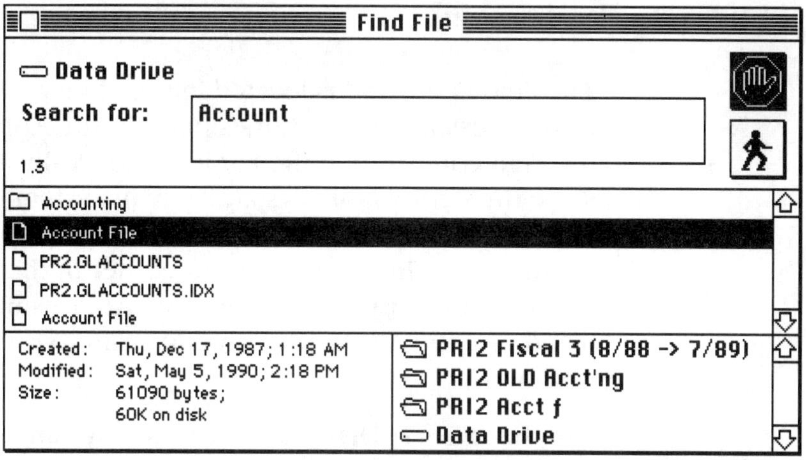

Figure 3-16: The Find File desk accessory.

Beyond Find File, other file-finding utilities have also been available for quite some time. Most of them let you search for files not only by file name but also by creation date, file type, creator, date modified, file size and other file attributes and combinations of attributes—PrairieSoft's DiskTop is one example. Like Find File, most of these utilities locate matching files, display the path information and let you return to the Finder and use or modify the file as required. (There are also a class of utilities that search inside files to find matches to text strings, such as Retrieve It!, GOFer and OnLocation to name but a few.)

7.5 In System 7, a new Find... command was added to the Finder. This command and its companion command, Find Again, significantly improve on the Find File desk accessory. System 7.5 significantly improves on the Find command by returning all matches to a search in a new Found Items dialog box, thereby eliminating repetitive Find Again searches. Because these new commands are built into the Finder, they offer important advantages over other file-finding utilities.

Using the Find Command

The Find command is located in the Finder's File menu, while desk accessory-based utilities put it in the Apple Menu. Having the Find command in the Finder is not really a disadvantage, since the Finder is always available in System 7. (To access the Find command while using another application, use the Applications menu in the upper-right corner of the menu bar to bring the Finder to the foreground. After using the Find command, use the Applications menu again to return to your application.)

Use the "Files & Disks" topic for help finding files.

When the Find command (Command-F) is selected in System 7.0 – 7 Pro, the very simple Find dialog box appears. This dialog box, shown in Figure 3-17, can search files only by name, much like Find File. Additional search criteria are accessed by clicking the More Choices button, which brings up an additional criterion to search by, as shown in Figure 3-18.

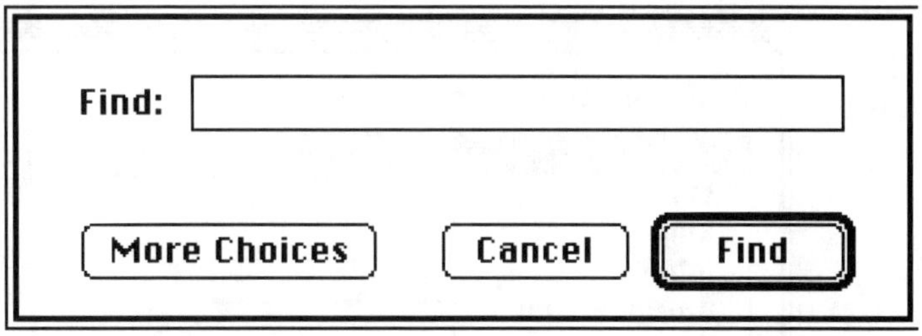

Figure 3-17: The Find dialog box.

Let's start with the simple Find dialog box; later in this section, you'll look at the other options available with the Find Item dialog box. In both sections, you'll evaluate the Find command's capabilities in finding files, but it should be noted that the Find command will also locate folders matching the selected search criteria.

The Find Dialog Box

Using the basic Find dialog box to locate files by name, you can enter the complete file name or only the first portion of the file name.

- **Enter a complete file name.** If you know the complete file name you're looking for, enter it into the Find option box. In most cases, only the correct file will be found, but if you make even a slight error in spelling the file name, the correct file will not be found. This is not the most efficient way to execute a file search.

- **Enter only the first portion of a file name.** Entering the first few characters of the file name is the most commonly used and usually the most efficient file name search method. This locates all file names that begin with the characters you've specified. The exact number of characters you should enter will depend on the circumstances; the goal is to enter enough characters to narrow the search down but not so many that you risk a spelling mistake and therefore a chance of missing the file.

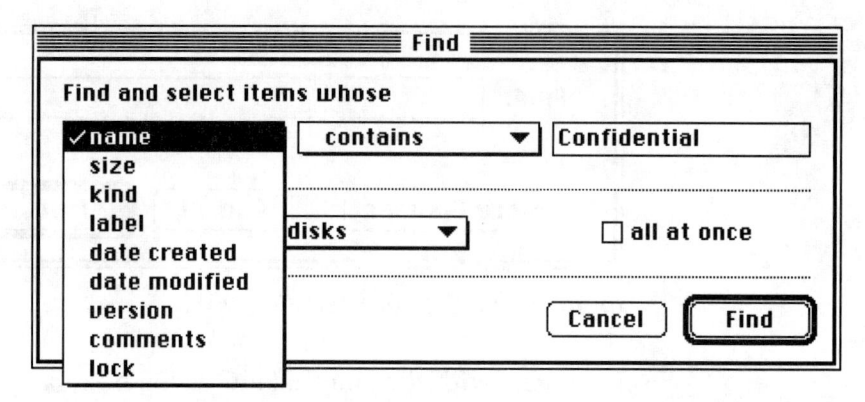

Figure 3-18: The full Find dialog box prior to System 7.5.

As an example, if the file you wanted to locate was "Archaeology Report," specifying only the letter "A" would yield a huge number of files to sort through. On the other hand, entering six or seven characters could allow files with spelling errors, such as "Archio" or "Arhcae," to escape the search. Decide on the number of characters according to how common the first few characters are among your files and how well you remember the file name. In this example, searching for files starting with "Arc" would probably be the best strategy.

After specifying the search criteria, click the Find button to start the search. The search starts at the startup drive and proceeds to all mounted volumes. If the search will take more than a few seconds, a Progress dialog box appears. In versions of the system software prior to System 7.5, when a file matching the search criteria is located, a window is opened, and the file is displayed.

At this point, you can use or modify the file as required. If the selected file is not the one you wanted, or if after modifying the selected file you want to continue searching for the next file that matches the search criteria, choose the Find Again command from the File menu or press Command-G. As each matching file is located, you can use or modify it (or simply ignore it), then repeat the process to proceed to the next matching file.

The Find Item Dialog Box

Clicking the More Choices button in the Find dialog box brings up the Find Item dialog box (see Figure 3-19), which has several advantages over the standard Find dialog box:

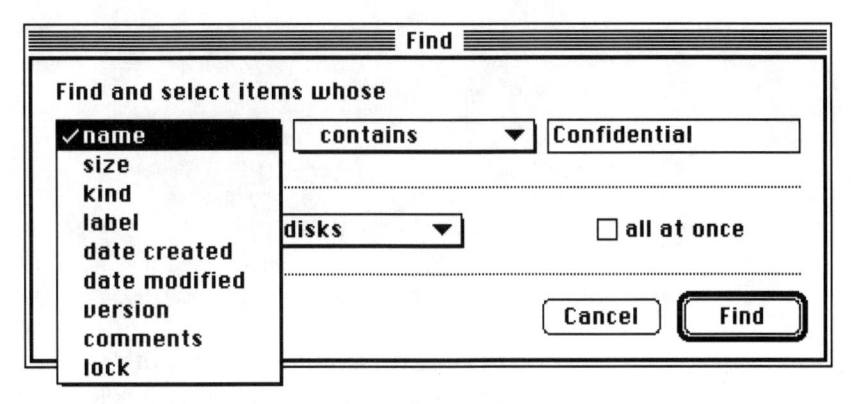

Figure 3-19: The Find Item dialog box.

- **More search criteria.** While the basic Find dialog can search only for file names, the Find Item dialog can search with the additional criteria shown in Figure 3-18. You can also limit your search location to specific volumes or selections.

- **More range control.** For each search parameter, the Find Item dialog box lists specific search constraints (see Table 3-1).

- **More result control.** The all at once option lets you look at a group of files matching the specified criteria all together.

Table 3-1: The available search criteria and their respective constraints and ranges.

Search by	Constraint	Range
Comments (for versions prior to 7.5)	contains/does not contain	any text
Creator	four letter application code	any four alphanumeric
Date created	is/is before/is after/is not	any date
Date modified	is/is before/is after/is not	any date
File Type	four letter file format	any four alphanumeric
Folder Attribute	label used	any label
Label Attribute	is/is not	any label/none
Lock	is	locked/unlocked
Kind	is/is not	alias/application/clipping file/document/folder/letter/stationery
Name	contains/starts with/ends with/is/is not/doesn't contain	any text
Size	is less than/is greater than	any # k
Version	is/is before/is after/is not	any number

To specify your criteria, select an option from the first pop-up menu. Depending on the option you select, the second or third part of the Find specification will become either a pop-up menu, an option box or a date. Enter your search specification. (To change a date, click on the month, year or day and then use the arrows to reset that portion of the date.) Several sample criteria are shown in Figure 3-20.

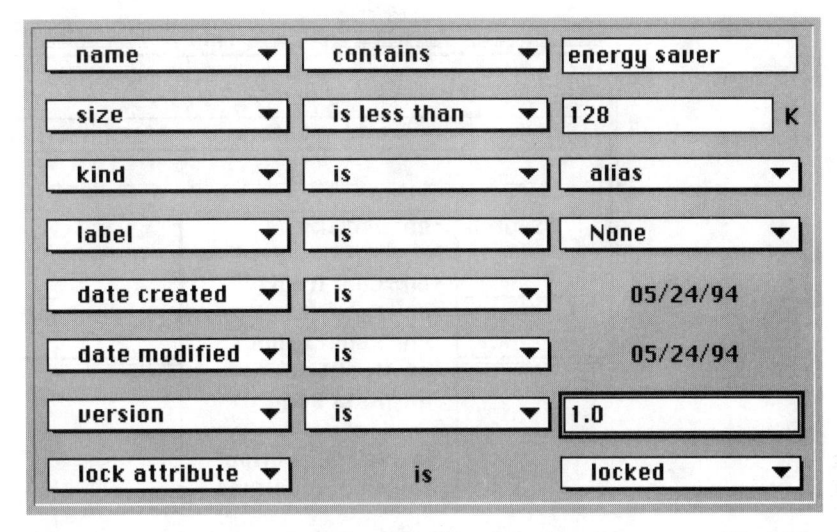

name ▼	contains ▼	energy saver
size ▼	is less than ▼	128 K
kind ▼	is ▼	alias ▼
label ▼	is ▼	None ▼
date created ▼	is ▼	05/24/94
date modified ▼	is ▼	05/24/94
version ▼	is ▼	1.0
lock attribute ▼	is	locked ▼

Figure 3-20: Several different search criteria as specified in the File Search dialog box.

You can also specify the search range using the Search pop-up menu (or, in System 7.5, the Find Item pop-up menu), shown in Figure 3-21.

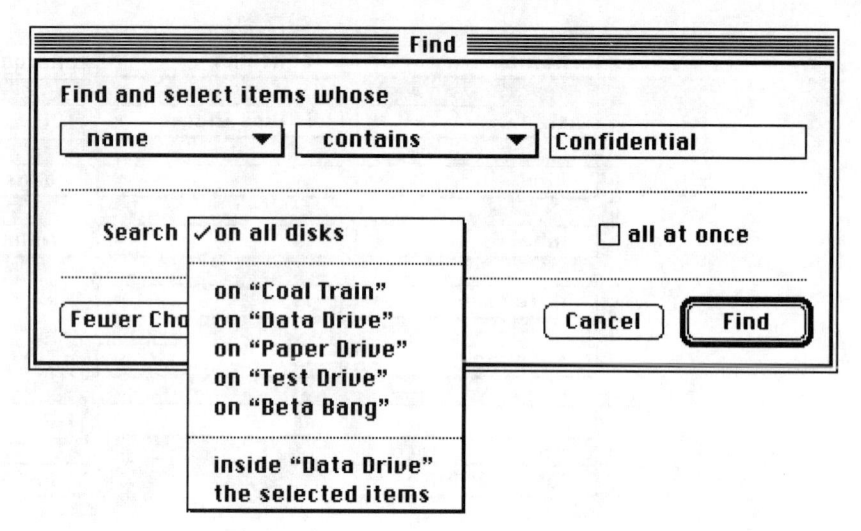

Figure 3-21: The Search pop-up menu. (In System 7.5, this menu is redesignated the Find Item pop-up menu.)

The Search options are:

- **On all disks.** This will search all mounted volumes, including all folders and items appearing on the Finder desktop. With this option, the all at once option isn't available.

- **On <any one currently mounted volume>.** Limits the search to one particular volume. System 7.5 differentiates this criteria to be either: "On local disks" or "On mounted servers." Local disks are part of your SCSI chain. Mounted servers are network connected volumes. All these volumes show up as their volume names. For example, you might see "Macintosh HD" as a listing.

- **Inside <the current selection>/on the desktop.** Limits the search to the currently selected volume or folder. If no volume or folder is selected, the option becomes on the desktop, which searches all mounted volumes.

- **The selected items.** Confines the search to those items currently selected. This is often used to further limit the results from a previous search yielding a multiple-criteria search.

  For example, suppose you need to free some space on your hard drive, so you search for all files larger than 250k, using the all at once option, which will give you an open Finder window with all 250k or larger files selected. To locate only those larger than 250k that have not been changed in more than one month, choose the Find command again and search the selected items for all files modified prior to 30 days ago. You can now back up and delete these files.

The all at once option determines whether files matching your search criteria are presented individually or all together. A single window for the volume or window being searched is displayed, and all files matching the search criteria are selected in that window. Files located in subfolders are displayed hierarchically. This option cannot be used when the on all disks search-range option is selected.

If the all at once option is not selected, clicking the Find button locates the first file in the specified search range that matches the search criteria; the file window is opened and the file is selected. If the selected file is not the one you want, or if you want to find the next matching file after modifying the selected file, choose the Find Again command from the File Menu (Command-G) and the search will continue, using the same search criteria and range. Again, you can continue using the Find Again command as required.

After completing all the required options in the Find Item dialog box, click the Find button to execute the search. If the search is going to be prolonged, a progress dialog box will appear indicating the percentage of range already searched.

When a matching file is located,

- The progress dialog box, if visible, disappears.

- A window opens for the folder or volume containing the matching file.

- If the all at once option was selected, a window listing all files matching the specified criteria appears, as shown in Figure 3-22.

- If the all at once option was not selected, the matching file's icon is selected, as shown in Figure 3-23.

Any time you're working in the Find Item dialog box, you can click the Fewer Choices button to return to the Find dialog box, described above.

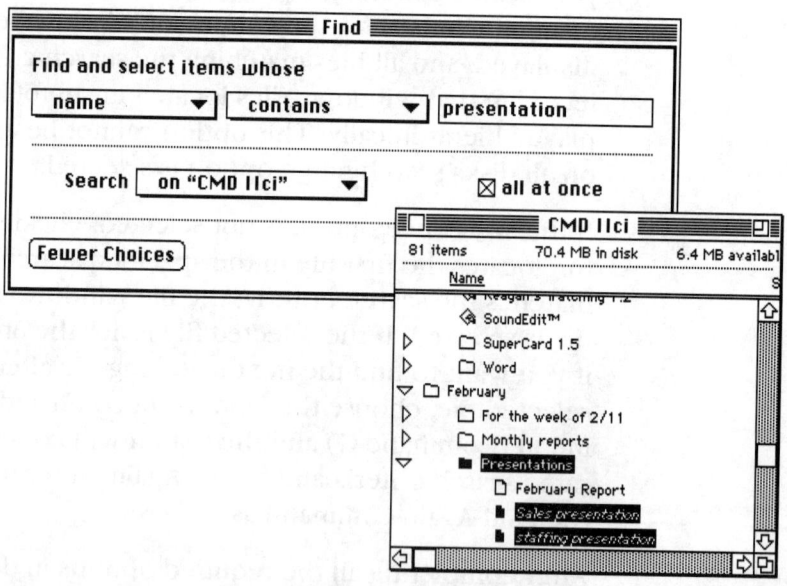

Figure 3-22: A group of files located by the Find command.

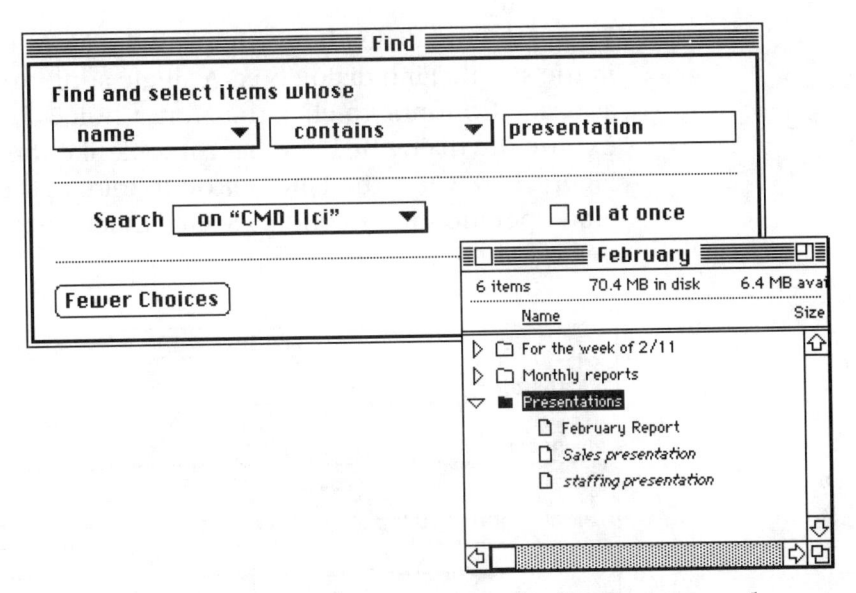

Figure 3-23: A single file located by the Find command.

Finding in System 7.5

7.5 ▶ System 7.5 provides many new capabilities to the file search function of system software. It does this while retaining the flavor of the Find command you have already learned. You will note that System 7.5 adds find commands to the File menu, and adds an alias of the extension to the Apple menu.

You initiate a search in System 7.5 by using the Find command on the File menu, or by pressing Command-F. For a previous search in a session, use the Find Again command, or Command-G from the File menu.

The full Find dialog box of System 7.5 shown in Figure 3-24 contains all of the same choices described previously (some new to 7.5). The most notable and important exception is that you can now search by more than one criterion at a time, a major improvement. Also, superficially the Find dialog box has the embossed 3D look that seems to be an industry standard.

To see the full dialog box, you click the More Choices button in the simple Find dialog box. A single additional criterion appears. Continue to click the More Choices buttons to fully expose the dialog box and have it look like the one shown in Figure 3-24. Click the Find button to initiate the search. The Find operation in System 7.5 seems much faster than its previous versions.

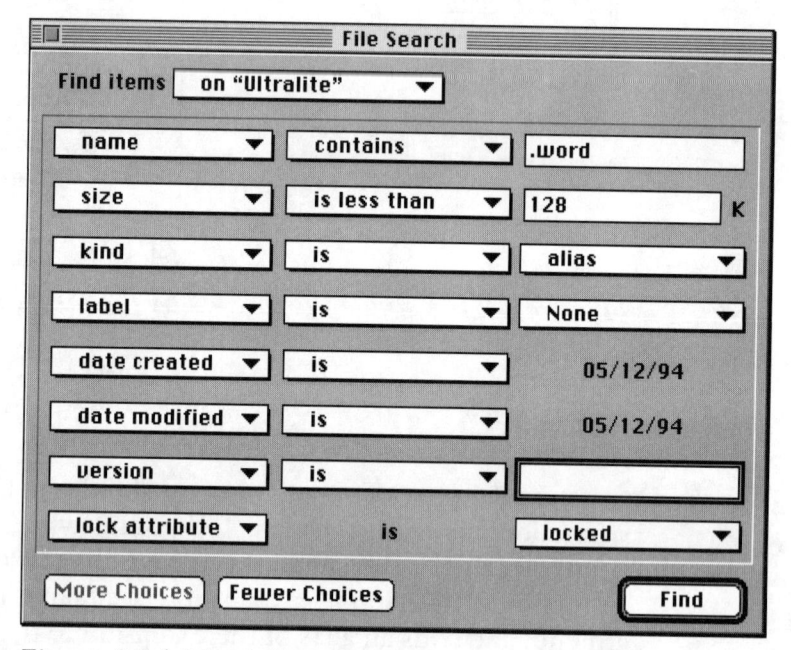

Figure 3-24: The full Find dialog box of System 7.5.

System 7.5 also substantially improves on the items returned in a Find by posting the new Found Items dialog box shown in Figure 3-25. All matching items appear in the scrolling window. When you select an item from the scrolling list, the window immediately below the list shows a hierarchical diagram of the folder or file's position, starting with the drive it's on, and running through each successive folder until you reach the item itself. You can do a number of things using Macintosh Drag and Drop with selections in the Found Items dialog box. You can:

- **Open that item's window.** Hit Command-E to open the item's enclosing folder, or select the "Open Enclosing Folder" command from the File menu.

- **Move the file.** Drag the file or folder name to a new location. The item moves to where you drag it. When you drag the item to another disk, it is copied.

- **Open the file.** Double-clicking on a folder, or typing Command-O with a folder selected, will open the folder. The same actions will open a selected file if the application that created the file is available. You can also drag the file name to an application. If the application can open that file type, it launches (if necessary) and opens the file—translating the file, if needed.

- **Print the file.** Drag the file onto a QuickDraw GX printer icon on the Finder.

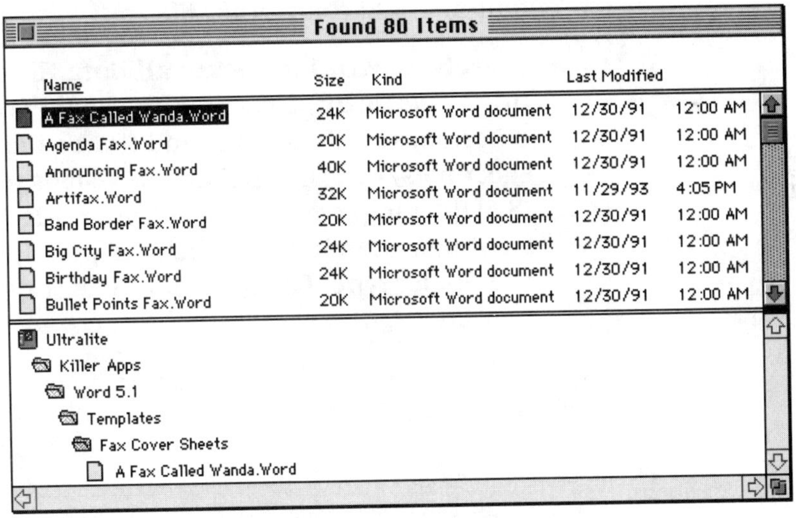

Figure 3-25: The Found Items dialog box.

Once you close the new Found Items dialog box, the criteria of your search are forgotten.

Find Command Tips

- **Find does not look inside the System file.** Items like fonts or sounds that have been placed inside the System file will not be located by the Find command.

- **Find locates aliases as well.** Any alias that matches the specified search criteria can be found just like regular files. Aliases will appear in italic text in the Found Items dialog box.

- **The Find Again command (Command-G) can be used at any time.** The search parameters entered in the Find or Find Item dialog box remain until the Mac is restarted or the parameters are changed. You can always repeat the last search using the Find Again command.

- **Find also locates folders and volumes.** Any folder or volume matching the specified search criteria will be found, just like any other file.

- **Search By Kind to locate all data files created by one specific application.** To use the by kind search criterion, specify the file kind (for example, all spreadsheet files) that the application assigns to its data files. (See the sample file kinds in Figure 3-26.) To see these additional search types, click the pop-up menu. Items like Folder type, File type and Creator type appear at the bottom.

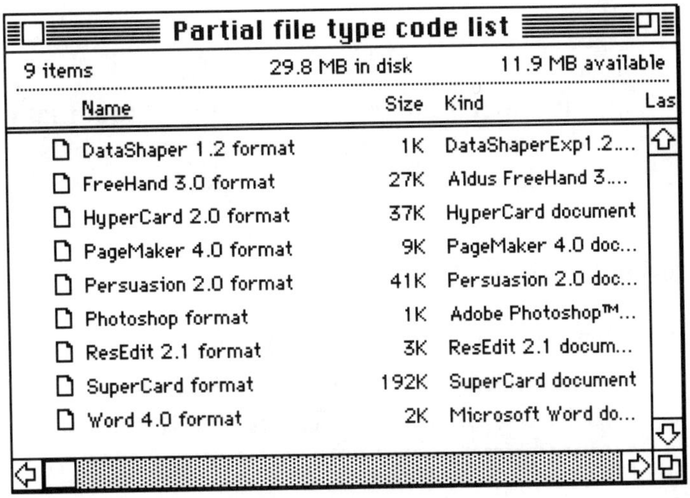

Partial file type code list		
9 items	29.8 MB in disk	11.9 MB available

Name	Size	Kind
DataShaper 1.2 format	1K	DataShaperExp1.2....
FreeHand 3.0 format	27K	Aldus FreeHand 3....
HyperCard 2.0 format	37K	HyperCard document
PageMaker 4.0 format	9K	PageMaker 4.0 doc...
Persuasion 2.0 format	41K	Persuasion 2.0 doc...
Photoshop format	1K	Adobe Photoshop™...
ResEdit 2.1 format	3K	ResEdit 2.1 docum...
SuperCard format	192K	SuperCard document
Word 4.0 format	2K	Microsoft Word do...

Figure 3-26: The Kind column displays the name of the application that created the file.

- **Use Find to do quick backups.** After you've used the Find command to locate all files on a volume modified after a certain date, you can drag those files to a removable volume for a "quick and dirty" backup. Of course, this procedure shouldn't replace a good backup utility—but you can never have too many backups.

- **Use the selected items search range to perform multiple-criteria searches.** For example, the Find command will locate all file names beginning with S that are less than 32k in size and have the Microsoft Word creator type (or any other set of multiple criteria). The first criterion is searched for using the on <any one volume> range; then you search for each additional criterion using the selected items range.

Labels

The Label menu is a great System 7 tool that helps you categorize your files, identify certain types of files, locate these files and, in some cases, manipulate them as a group.

Configuring the Label Menu

The Label menu is in the Finder menu bar; it's configured using the Labels control panel. Figure 3-27 displays the open Labels control panel. The text and color of your labels are configured in this control panel.

To set label text, click in each label text block and enter the name of the label category you want to define. In label assignments, form must follow function; there's no advantage in having label assignments that don't help you use and manipulate your data more efficiently.

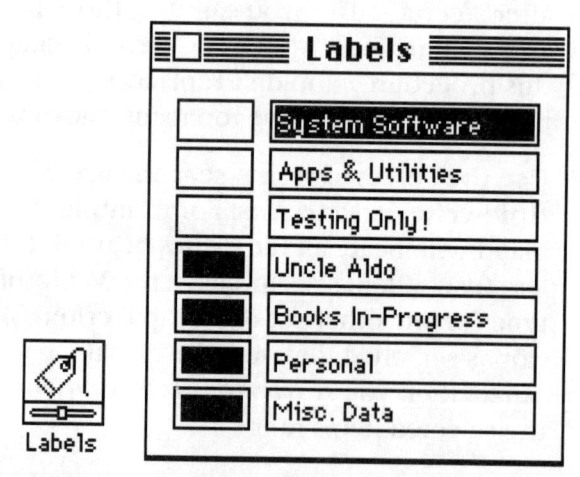

Figure 3-27: The Labels control panel.

There are several ways to use labels:

- **To categorize files.** Labels provide an additional level of categorization for files. Files are already categorized by type, creation and modification dates and related folders, but—using aliases—you can also classify them by topic, importance or any other way you choose.

- **For visual distinction.** Color-coding icons helps you quickly distinguish one type of file from another on a color monitor. For example, all applications can be red, making them easier to spot in a folder full of dictionaries, Help instructions and other files. You can also use the Labels column in Finder windows, which lists label names next to file names.

- **To facilitate data backup.** You can find all files assigned to a specific label, then copy them to another disk or volume for backup purposes.

- **To indicate security requirements.** When using File Sharing, you can create labels that remind you of the security level of specific folders, files and volumes.

There are many ways to use the available label categories:

- **Categories for logical subdivisions of data files.** If your work is project-based, you can specify large projects by individual labels and use one miscellaneous label for smaller projects. You could also have Long-Term Projects, Short-Term Projects and Permanent Projects labels.

- **Categories for software applications.** You can differentiate launchable applications or label both applications and their ancillary files. You might want a separate label for utility programs, including third-party extensions, control panels, desk accessories and utilities that are launchable applications.

- **Specify security levels.** If special security is required in your work environment, label one or two folders to identify them as secure. You can then use encryption utilities to safeguard these files; use them carefully with File Sharing or apply third-party security utilities to protect them.

To change colors, see "Colors" in Apple Guide.

Once labels are defined, you can alter label colors (available only on color Macs). To do this, click on any color in the Labels control panel to bring up the color wheel dialog box, shown in Figure 3-28. Specify the color you want for the label. Because label colors are applied over existing icon colors, weaker colors with lower hue and saturation values (found toward the middle of the wheel) work best.

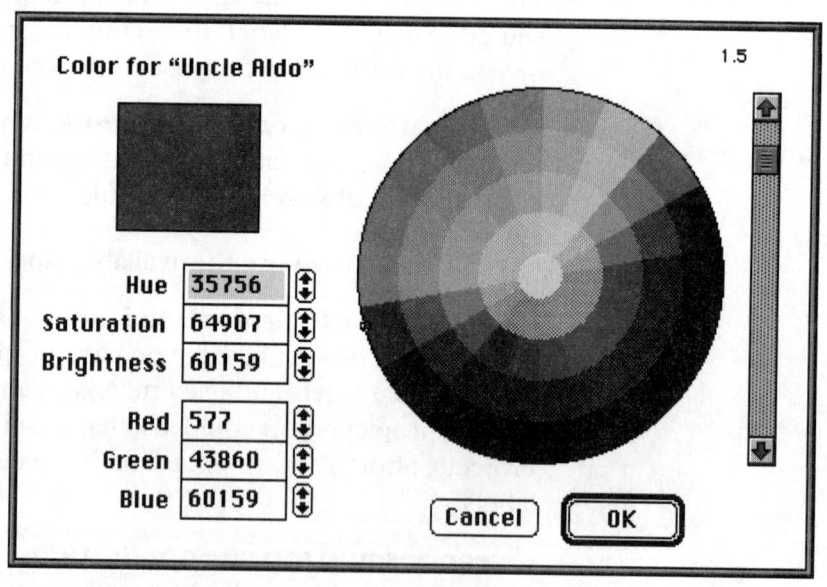

Figure 3-28: The Apple color wheel.

After you've modified the label names and colors, close the Labels control panel. The Label menu and any files or folders affected are then updated. You can reopen the Labels control panel any time you need to reset the text or colors.

Comments

In the past, adding lengthy comments to Macintosh files has been unsatisfactory, to say the least. The main problem was that the comments were likely to disappear every time the invisible desktop file was replaced or rebuilt (unfortunately, this problem still persists under System 7.5). Most people stopped using comments when they discovered that they could never be sure how long they'd last. Plus, comments could only be seen by opening the Get Info dialog box, so they were inconvenient to use.

System 7 attempted to breathe new life into file comments, correcting some of their former shortcomings and adding some interesting possibilities that could make comments an important part of working with your Macintosh files.

In the Finder, comments have been improved in two important ways:

- **Visibility.** You can now see comments in Finder windows. When the Show comments option in the Views control panel is selected (as detailed in the previous chapter), comments will display in Finder windows. This makes them practical to use.

- **Searchability.** The Find command (prior to System 7.5) lets you search for text in file comments, making it possible to locate files by comment entries.

People will find other productive ways to use these new comment features. One idea is to use comments as cues: keywords or phrases can provide information not already included in the file name, date, kind or other file information. Client names, project titles, related and document names are a few examples. This additional information would be displayed in Finder windows via the Find command.

Unfortunately, as mentioned earlier, Finder comments are still lost when the desktop file is rebuilt. (The "desktop file" is actually a pair of invisible files that the Finder maintains on each disk or drive you use with your Mac.) The desktop file is sometimes automatically rebuilt by the system software when minor disk problems are detected. Or, you can force the desktop to be rebuilt by holding down the Command and Option keys during startup.

Figure 3-29 shows some files with comments added. Complete comments make it easy to see at a glance what these files contain when browsing Finder windows; it also makes the files easy to retrieve with the Find command.

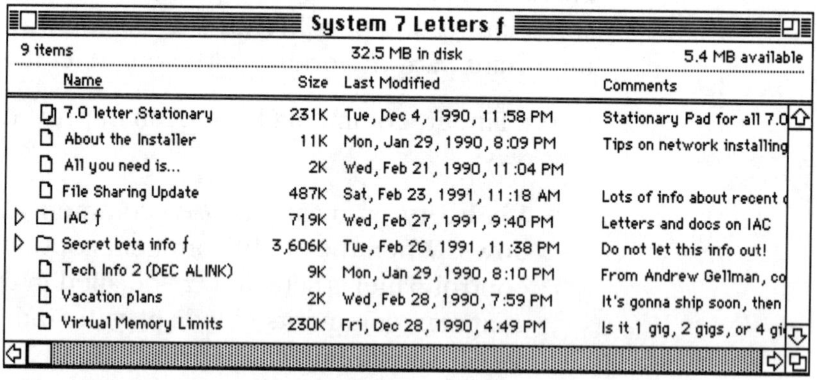

Figure 3-29: A Finder window as it appears when using the Show comments option.

Moving On

The power and importance of the capabilities introduced in this chapter cannot be overestimated. As you become more familiar with System 7 or System 7.5, you'll use these features frequently:

- Aliases help you locate and launch files and access network data quickly and easily.

- The Find command will solve your "where is that file?" problem.

- Labels make it easier to keep important files organized.

- Comments remind you of details about particular file or folder content.

Next, in Chapter 4, we'll examine the most important folder on your hard drive, the System Folder. In System 7.5 the System Folder is still the home of your system software, but it's organized a little differently. Innovations include automatic file placement, and a new way of working with fonts and other resources used by the System file.

Chapter 4

The System Folder

There's one folder on every Macintosh hard drive that's distinct from all others—the System Folder, home of the Macintosh system software and many other important files. The System Folder is given special treatment by the system software, by other software applications and by you as a Macintosh user.

While you can arrange files on your hard drive (and all other volumes) to suit your personal needs, you can only change the organization of the System Folder in certain ways. That's because of the fundamental role software in the System Folder plays in the operation of your Macintosh.

In January 1984, when Version 1.0 of the system software was released with the Macintosh 128k, the System Folder contained 22 items that consumed only 225k of disk space. Using System 6 on a Mac with a normal assortment of applications and utilities could easily result in a System Folder containing 100 files or more, and the total size of the System Folder can easily soar above one megabyte. In System 7 you can barely fit just the System and Finder files and an Enabler file on a single 1.44mb floppy disk. A well-endowed System Folder can now run between 10mb and 20mb in size.

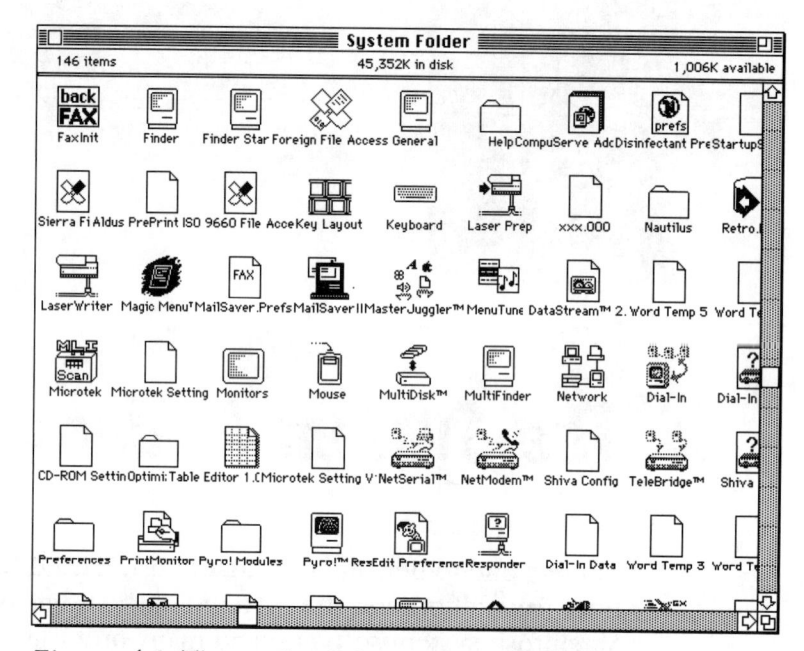

Figure 4-1: The author's large, messy System 6.0x System Folder.

The main problem with such a large System Folder is the resulting lack of organization, as shown in Figure 4-1. A crowded System Folder is slow to open at the desktop, and finding what you want in the maze of files is a slow and tedious process.

Increasing complexity has been partially responsible for the growth of the system software, but a more direct cause has been the growing number of non-system software files that reside in the System Folder. These include third-party fonts, sounds, desk accessories, FKEYs, control panels and extensions. Adding these files place obvious demands on disk space, and has also resulted in chaotic System Folder organization and some measure of system instability.

System 7 does little to reduce the pace of System Folder growth, but it does provide new methods of maintaining System Folder organization. It also introduces a few basic means of avoiding the instability caused by the old System Folder organization.

In this chapter, we'll look at the new System Folder organization and offer some suggestions to help you effectively manage this important resource.

The System 7.5 System Folder

In System 7.5, the System Folder includes a number of pre-defined subfolders, each of which is designed to hold a specific type of file. This new organizational system is created by the System 7.5 Installer when System 7.5 is installed, and greatly reduces the potential for clutter.

This new organization uses folder designations and file arrangements based on the same logic you use in organizing your hard drive. Subfolders include the Apple Menu Items folder, Control Panels folder, Extensions folder, Fonts folder, Launcher Items folder, PowerTalk Data folder, Preferences folder, PrintMonitor Documents folder and Startup Items folder.

In System 7.5, the Installer places all unknown extensions and control panels into a "May Not Work with 7.5" folder until you can check them out. This is done to be certain that you can sucessfully boot up after a System 7.5 installation regardless of what you had on your hard drive. Additionally, when you use the Extension Manager control panel to turn extensions, control panels or other System Folder items off you will see the folders: Control Panel (Disabled), System Extensions (Disabled) or Extensions (Disabled), depending upon what you turned off. Other folders that appear include: the Control Strip Modules folder for PowerBook installations, an

• Archived Type 1 Fonts • folder (if any were installed) and some others.

A display of the most basic parts of the System 7.5 System Folder is shown in Figure 4-2.

In some ways, the new System Folder is more complex than the old. Fortunately, as we'll see, Apple has built in an "invisible hand" to help make sure that System Folder files are always located correctly.

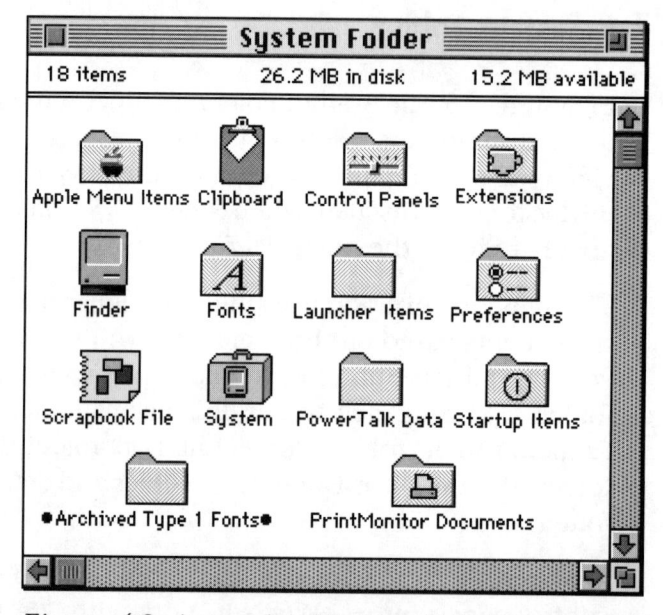

Figure 4-2: A standard System 7.5 System Folder.

Because the new System Folder and subfolders are so important to the operation of your Macintosh, it's important to understand what type of files should be placed in each folder. This section describes the folders and provides some basic tips for organizing and using them.

The Apple Menu Folder

One of the best things about desk accessories was their accessibility, via the Apple Menu, from inside any application. In System 7, the convenience of the Apple Menu was extended beyond desk accessories to include applications, documents, folders and even volumes. And best of all, this powerful new Apple Menu was completely customizable.

When System 7.5 is installed, the AppleCD Audio Player, Calculator, Chooser, Key Caps, Find File, Jigsaw Puzzle, Key Chain, Note Pad, Scrapbook, Sticky Memos and •Shutdown desk accessories appear in the Apple Menu. Additionally, the Mail and Catalogs folder, Control Panels folder alias, Recent Applications folder, Recent Document folder, Recent Server folders and Useful Scripts folder alias appear in the Apple Menu. If you open the Apple Menu Items folder inside the System Folder, these are exactly the files you find inside, as shown in Figure 4-3.

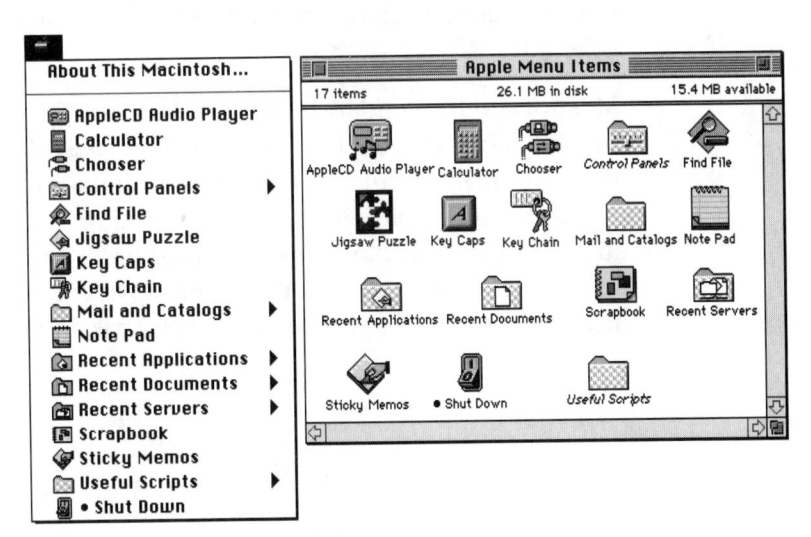

Figure 4-3: The System 7.5 Apple Menu and Apple Menu Items folder (as configured by the Installer).

Longtime Macintosh users will note the loss of the venerable Alarm Clock desk accessory from the Apple menu in System 7.5. It's been replaced by the Date & Time control panel, now easily accessible from the Control Panels submenu. The Alarm Clock was the preferred method for changing the system date and time in several whole number versions of system software. Prior to 7.5 you could also change the date and time from within the General control panel.

To modify the contents of the Apple Menu, add or remove files and aliases. The Apple Menu is updated immediately and displays the first 50 items (alphabetically) contained in the Apple Menu Items folder.

The four types of files (or aliases) you'll probably want to place in the Apple Menu Items folder are applications, documents, folders and volumes. Each is much easier to access from the Apple Menu than by using traditional double-click methods. Choosing an item from the Apple Menu is equivalent to double-clicking on the item's icon: the selected DA or control panel is run, or the selected folder or volume is opened.

Most of the files added to the Apple Menu Items folder should be alias icons rather than original files, to avoid moving the file, folder or volume icon from its original location. In the Apple Menu Items folder, the file name remains displayed in italics but the file name appears in standard roman font in the Apple Menu—you can't tell by looking at the Apple Menu that the file in the Apple Menu Items folder is an alias.

🗋	(space bar)	🗋	. (.)	🗋	œ (Op-Q)	🗋	¶ (Op-7)	🗋	º (Op-9)
🗋	! (Sh-1)	🗋	/ (/)	🗋	w (W)	🗋	ß (Op-S)	🗋	ª (Op-0)
🗋	" (Op-[)	🗋	= (=)	🗋	z (Z)	🗋	® (Op-R)	🗋	Ω (Op-Z)
🗋	" (Op-])	🗋	? (Sh-/)	🗋	[([)	🗋	© (Op-C)	🗋	¿ (Sh-Op-/)
🗋	# (Sh-3)	🗋	@ (Sh-2)	🗋	] (])	🗋	™ (Op-2)	🗋	i (Op-1)
🗋	$ (Sh-4)	🗋	å (Op-A)	🗋	^ (Sh-6)	🗋	≠ (Op-=)	🗋	¬ (Op-L)
🗋	% (Sh-5)	🗋	A (Sh-A)	🗋	` (`)	🗋	∞ (Op-5)	🗋	√ (Op-V)
🗋	& (Sh-7)	🗋	æ (Op-')	🗋	{ (Sh-[)	🗋	≤ (Op-,)	🗋	ƒ (Op-F)
🗋	' (Op-])	🗋	B (Sh-B)	🗋	} (Sh-])	🗋	≥ (Op-x)	🗋	≈ (Op-X)
🗋	' (Sh-Op-])	🗋	c (c)	🗋	~ (Sh-`)	🗋	¥ (Op-Y)	🗋	Δ (Op-J)
🗋	((Sh-9)	🗋	ç (Op-c)	🗋	† (Op-T)	🗋	µ (Op-M)	🗋	... (Op-;)
🗋	) (Sh-0)	🗋	E (Sh-E)	🗋	¢ (Op-4)	🗋	∂ (Op-D)	🗋	- (0--)
🗋	* (Sh-8)	🗋	f (f)	🗋	£ (Op-3)	🗋	Σ (Op-W)	🗋	— (Sh-Op--)
🗋	+ (Sh-=)	🗋	G (SH-G)	🗋	§ (Op-6)	🗋	π (Op-P)	🗋	÷ (Op-/)
🗋	- (-)	🗋	ø (Op-O)	🗋	• (Op-8)	🗋	∫ (Op-B)		

Figure 4-4: The list above demonstrates, from top to bottom, left to right, the special characters that can be used to alphabetize files in the Apple Menu, and the keys you press to access them.

Because the Apple Menu displays files alphabetically, you can reorder the menu items by modifying their names with numerical or alphabetical prefixes. A list of the prefixes available appears in Figure 4-4. The result of using some of these is shown in the Apple Menu pictured in Figure 4-5, in which applications, folders, desk accessories, control panels, documents and volumes are ordered separately.

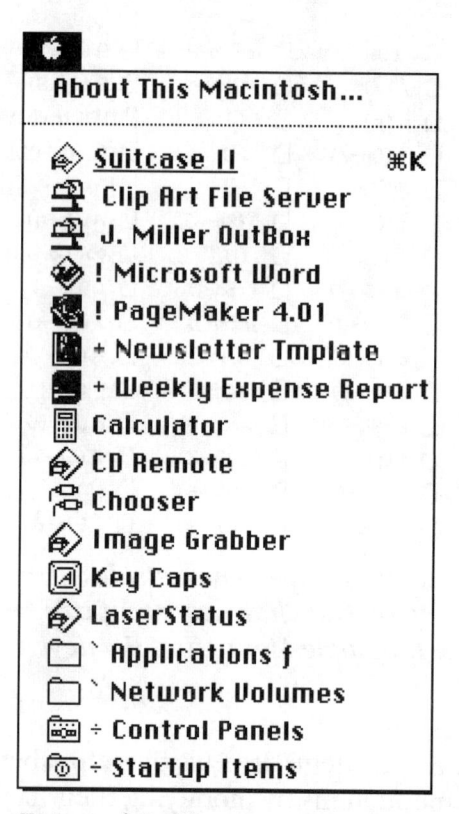

```
  About This Macintosh...
..........................................
  Suitcase II                    ⌘K
  Clip Art File Server
  J. Miller OutBox
  ! Microsoft Word
  ! PageMaker 4.01
  + Newsletter Tmplate
  + Weekly Expense Report
  Calculator
  CD Remote
  Chooser
  Image Grabber
  Key Caps
  LaserStatus
  ` Applications ƒ
  ` Network Volumes
  ÷ Control Panels
  ÷ Startup Items
```

Figure 4-5: Files are arranged in this Apple Menu using file name prefixes.

To some extent the inclusion of the Recent Applications, Recent Documents and Recent Servers folders in the Apple menu obviates the need to add commonly used items to the Apple menu. However, if you find that a favorite item disappears every now and then from the submenu in one of these folders, by all means add its alias to the Apple Menu folder for permanent inclusion.

The Control Panels Folder

Control panels are the evolution of control devices (cdevs) that used to appear in the System 6.0x Control Panel desk accessory. In System 7, a control panel is a small, independent application launched by double-clicking on its icon. The only difference between a control panel and a regular application is that the control panel is implemented in a single window and provides no menus.

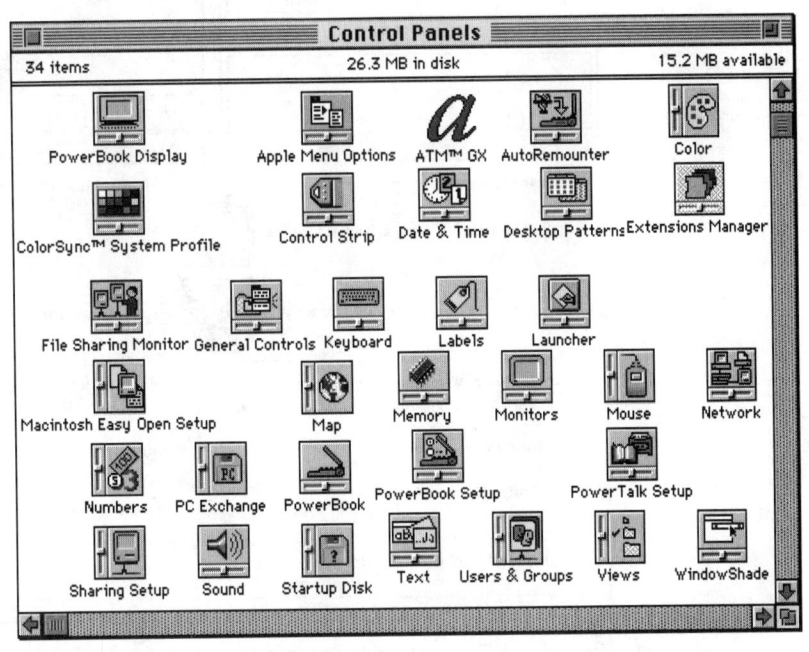

Figure 4-6: The Control Panels folder as installed on a PowerBook.

Control panels are stored in the Control Panels folder, which itself is stored inside the System Folder—mainly because control panels often contain special resources (like extensions) that must be run during startup. If the extension portion of the control panel isn't loaded at startup, the control panel may not function properly.

If you want to keep a copy of any control panel in another location, create an alias and move the alias to your preferred location. You could, for example, store aliases of frequently used control panels in the Apple Menu Items folder or in a folder containing other utility applications.

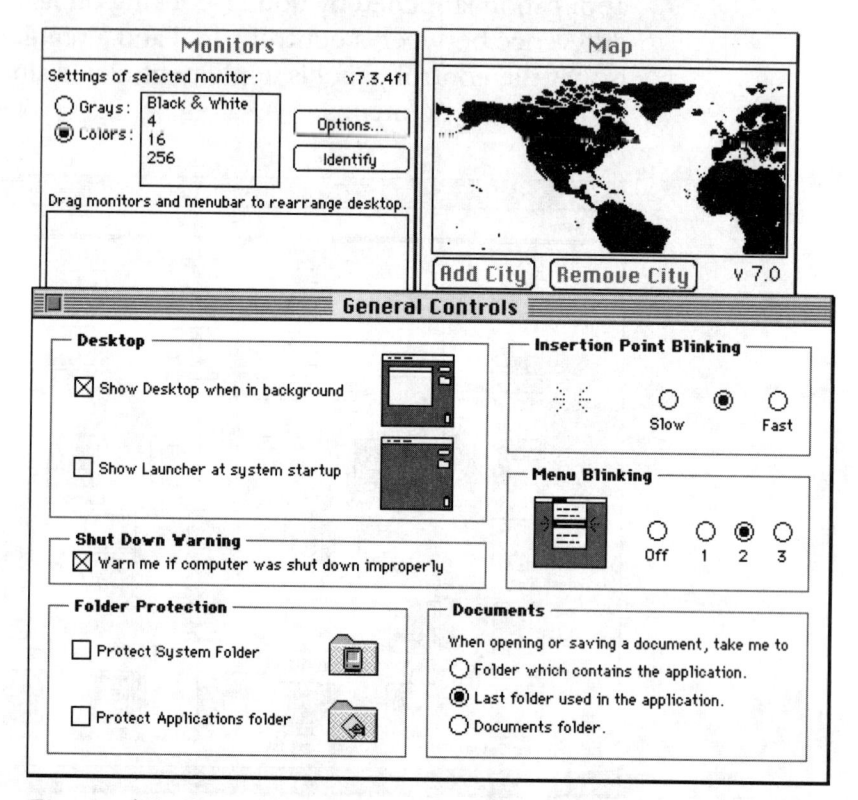

Figure 4-7: Control Panels appear in independent windows.

The Extensions Folder

As mentioned previously, INITs (now called extensions), printer drivers and network drivers are major contributors to System Folder overcrowding. In System 7, these files, which have invaded System Folders in epidemic proportions since the introduction of System 6.0, have a home in the Extensions folder. Your Extensions folder may become quite crowded, as exemplified by Figure 4-8, but at least you can find your more important system files without having to wade through all of your extensions.

For help related to extensions, see "Setting Options."

Most INITs add features to the Mac's system software, hence the name "extensions." Drivers extend system software capabilities in a less dramatic but important way.

During startup, the system software looks in the Extensions folder and executes the code found there. These files can also be accessed during startup from the Control Panels folder, but separation of files between these two folders should be maintained. Extensions and control panels that aren't stored in the Extensions or Control Panels folders won't execute at startup and won't operate properly until they're correctly positioned and the Macintosh is restarted. Some, but not all, extensions will appear as icons at the bottom of your startup screen; as will some control panels.

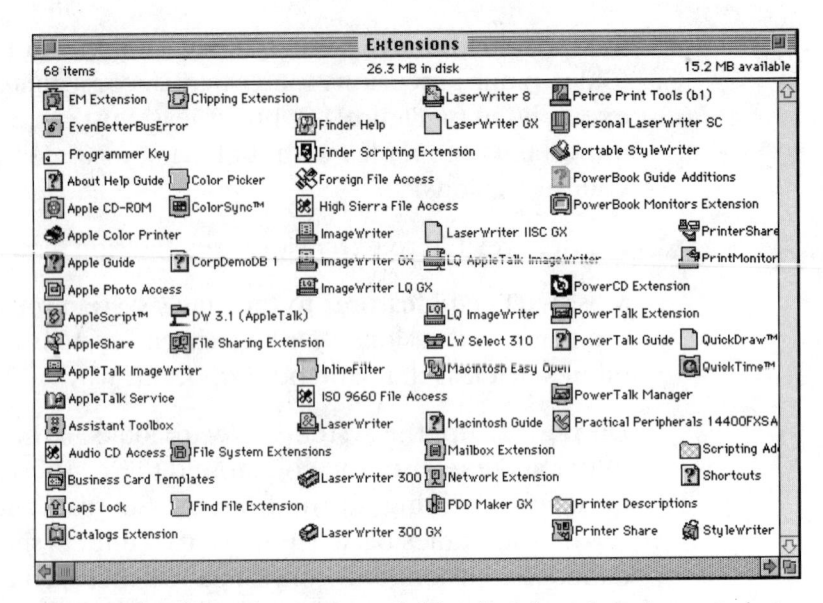

Figure 4-8: The Extensions folder holds extensions, printer drivers and network drivers. It can become quite crowded in System 7.5, inviting the View By Name view.

Because extensions and control panels modify or enhance the system software at startup, a new extension or control panel may cause your Macintosh to crash if the item is incompatible with the system software, some other extension, another control panel or a certain combination of extensions and control panels or even applications that you use. The range of problems you can encounter is the stuff of legend.

If you experience a compatibility problem, suspect an extension conflict first. To test the theory try turning off your extensions. Hold down the Shift key while restarting your Macintosh. This will disable all extensions and allow you to remove the incompatible file from the System Folder.

When you restart or start up with the Shift key held down, the words "Extensions Off" will appear under the "Welcome to Macintosh" message, as shown in Figure 4-9. As soon as these words appear, you can release the Shift key, and the Macintosh will start up without executing any of the items in the Extensions folder or the Control Panels folder.

```
                    Welcome to Macintosh.
                    Extensions off.
```

Figure 4-9: The Welcome to Macintosh dialog box as it appears when the Shift key is pressed at startup.

In the good old days of System 6 you could resolve extension conflicts by adding or removing extensions one at a time from your System Folder until the offending extension (or combination) was found. Often you could avoid conflicts by changing the loading order, just by simply renaming the extension: for example, changing ATM to ~ATM. Various third-party utilities were introduced to automate the process of turning extensions on and off, changing the loading order or creating extension worksets.

7.5 In System 7.5 extension proliferation has become so overwhelming that Apple felt compelled to introduce the Extension Manager control panel shown in Figure 4-10. Click the check mark off to remove an extension, system extension (one found in the Extensions folder), or control panel. Disabled items are placed into the Extensions (Disabled), System Extensions (Disabled) or Control Panel (Disabled) folders. You will still need to reboot your Macintosh to effect the new system configuration.

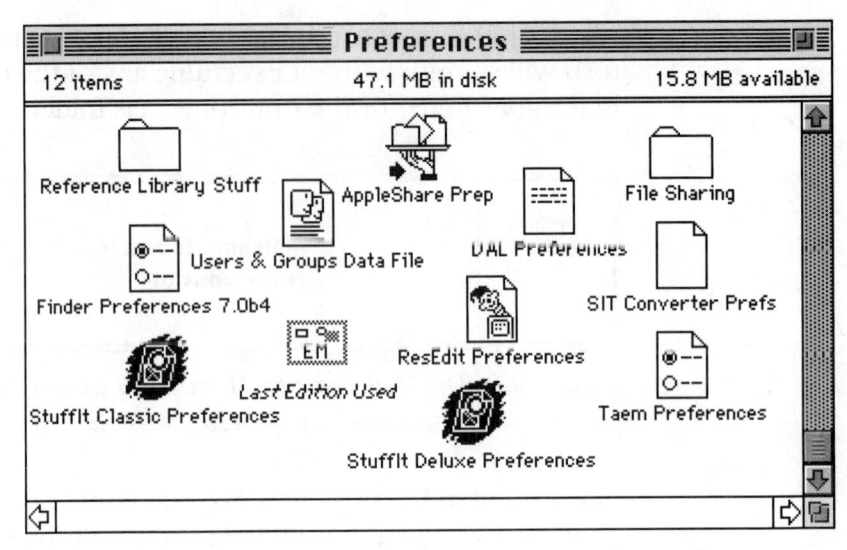

Figure 4-10: The Extensions Manager control panel.

A final word about positioning extensions: Although System 7 was designed to house startup items in the Extensions folder or in the Control Panels folder, extensions located directly in the System Folder *will* execute during startup. This is necessary because some older INITs and cdevs don't operate properly when nested in System Folder subfolders. New versions of these items have since been made compatible with the new System Folder structure; but if you find an item that doesn't load properly from the appropriate subfolder, try placing it directly in the System Folder.

The Fonts Folder

Support for a wide range of typefaces has always been an important characteristic of the Macintosh, but it's surprising that eight years after the first Macintosh, Apple is still trying to figure out an elegant way of handling fonts in its system software. But it's true. System 7.0 brought major changes to the way fonts were handled, and System 7.1 brought additional changes.

See "Printing & Fonts" for help.

The Fonts folder, introduced in System 7.1, holds PostScript screen fonts and printer fonts, as well as TrueType and QuickDraw GX fonts. After screen fonts or TrueType fonts are added to the Fonts folder, they become available in all subsequently launched applications. Fonts moved out of the Fonts folder, or into subfolders of the Fonts folder, are no longer available to applications.

All aspects of working with Fonts in System 7.0, 7.1 and 7.5, including the Fonts folder, are described in detail in Chapter 9, "QuickDraw GX & Fonts."

The Preferences Folder

Preferences files created by application programs and utilities also became important contributors to System Folder growth under System 6.0x. In System 7, these files are stored in the Preferences folder.

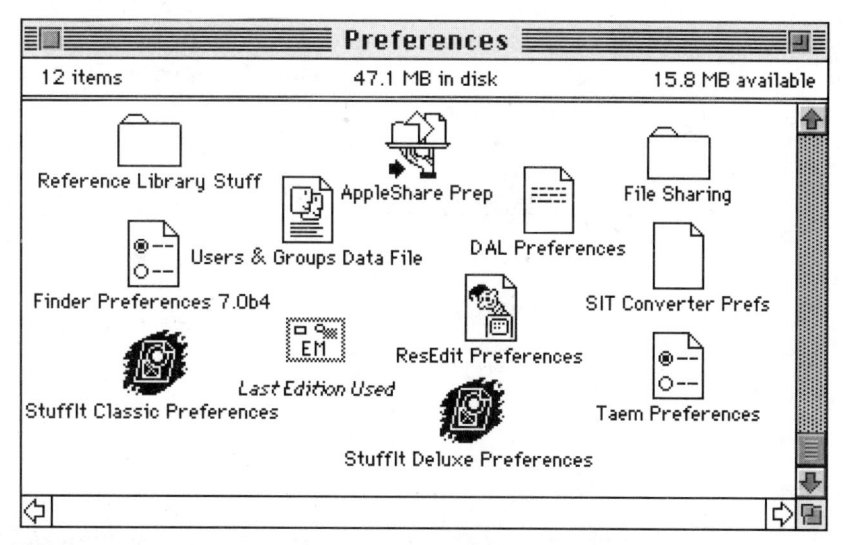

Figure 4-11: The Preferences folder.

As a user, you shouldn't have to do anything to the Preferences folder or its files. Your application programs should create and maintain these files automatically. However, you might want to check this folder occasionally and delete the preferences files of unwanted applications or utilities that you've deleted from your drives.

If you want to go back to the default condition you had when you first installed an application, you can try removing the preference file from the System folder (but don't delete the file until you're sure you haven't lost any important settings). You can also try locking a preference file to save a favored application configuration. This works in certain but not all circumstances.

The Startup Items Folder

Applications, documents, folders and volumes in the Startup Items folder automatically run (or open) each time your Macintosh is started or restarted. This folder takes the place of the Set Startup... command found in the Special menu of previous system software versions. As with the Apple Menu Items folder, most of the icons in the Startup Items folder will probably be aliases.

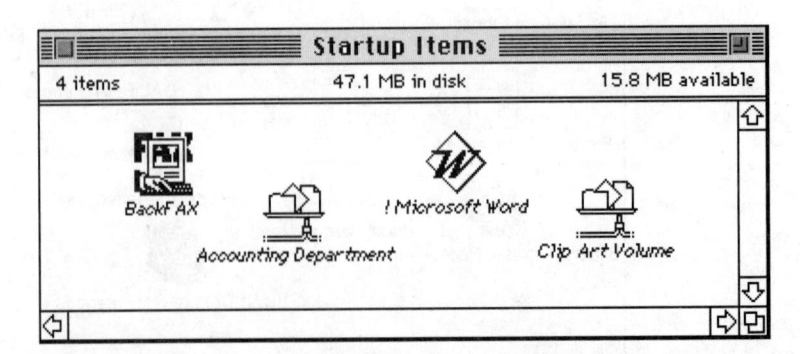

Figure 4-12: The Startup Items folder with alias icons that will be launched or mounted at startup.

While the Startup Items folder's main purpose is to open applications and documents, it's also a good place to put folder and volume icon aliases. These aliases will be opened, or mounted, at startup—a simple but useful function. (Of course, before mounting any networked volumes, any required passwords will be requested.) Mounting networked services automatically is one of the functions handled by PowerTalk, described more fully in Chapter 14.

The System File

The System file remains the centerpiece of Macintosh system software, overseeing all basic Macintosh activities and assisting every application and utility that runs on the Macintosh. As a user, you can remain blissfully ignorant of most of the work performed by the System file. You should understand, however, the System file's traditional role as home to fonts, desk accessories, FKEYs, sounds and keyboard resources.

When stuffed with these items, a single System file in the days before System 7 could grow to 600k or larger—often much larger. This overload often resulted in an unstable System file that would easily and frequently become corrupt, making the annoying and time-consuming effort of deleting and rebuilding the System file necessary.

The release of System 7 provided some relief to bulging System files by providing the Apple Menu Items folder (described earlier in this chapter) as the new default home for desk accessories, and by allowing DAs to be converted into stand-alone applications that can be stored anywhere on your hard disk (as described in Chapter 5, "System 7.5 & Your Software"). As a result of these two changes, DAs are no longer stored inside the System file.

Fonts, on the other hand, remain in the System file in System 7.0, although in System 7.1 and later they have moved instead to the new Fonts folder, as described above. (For more information about fonts, see Chapter 9.)

System File Access

Before System 7, the only way to add or remove fonts, desk accessories, FKEYs or sounds was to use specialized utilities such as the Font/DA Mover or ResEdit. In System 7, the System file's contents can be manipulated directly: you can open the System file by double-clicking on it as if it were a folder. A window opens, displaying icons for all fonts, sounds and keyboard configurations it currently contains. More often than not you will see only sound and keyboard icons in System 7.5, as fonts reside in the Fonts folder.

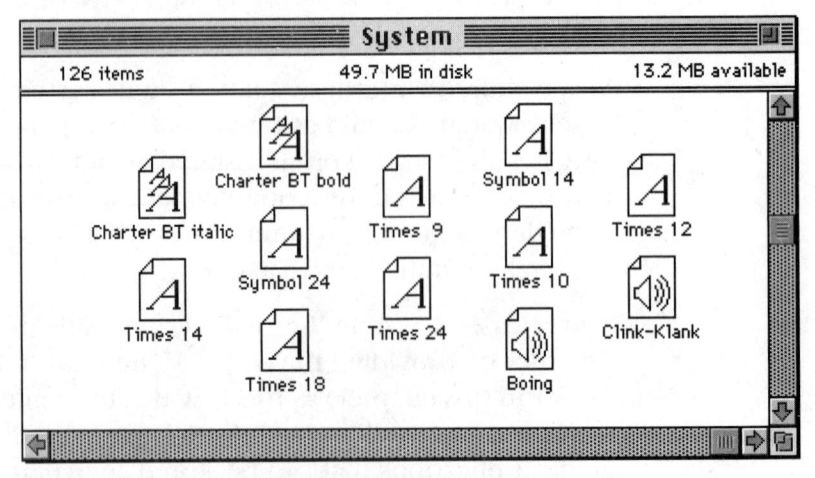

Figure 4-13: An open System file window.

While the System file is open, any font, sound and keyboard files will appear with unique individual icons. Double-clicking on any of these icons will open the resource file, displaying a font sample or playing the sound. (See Figure 4-14.)

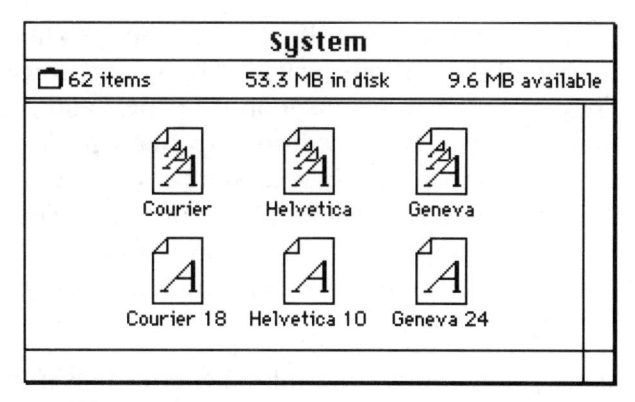

Figure 4-14: Both bitmapped and TrueType fonts can be installed in the System file in System 7.

Fonts, sounds and keyboard files can be added to the System file by simply dragging their icons into the System file window, the same way files are dragged in or out of any normal Mac folder. (All other applications must be closed before adding to the System file.) To remove fonts or sounds, drag their icons out of the open System Folder window and into another folder or volume, or directly into the Trash.

Modifying the System Folder

The System Folder and its subfolders are created by the Installer when you first install System 7.5, and at that time, all system software files are placed into their proper locations. The System Folder is constantly modified, however, as you install other software applications or perform other common tasks on your Macintosh.

There are several types of files added to the System Folder after the initial installation: fonts and sounds, system extensions (which add functions to the system software), and miscellaneous files that enable other software applications to function properly.

System extensions modify the way the system software works or extend the options provided by system software features. They include extensions, control panels and printer or network drivers. There are hundreds of examples of extensions and drivers that modify your system software. SuperClock, Pyro, Vaccine, AppleShare, DOS Mounter, NetModem, MailSaver, Autographix, PageSaver and After Dark are a few of the most popular. You've probably added files of this type to your System Folder.

Many applications store miscellaneous files in the System Folder which don't interact directly with the system software. They're placed in the System Folder for other reasons:

- **Safety.** The System Folder is the only "common ground" on a Mac hard drive that applications can rely on in every configuration.

- **Simplicity.** The Macintosh operating system can easily find the System Folder, regardless of what it's called and where it's located. This allows applications quick access to files stored in the System Folder.

- **Security.** The System Folder is a safe place for applications to add files because most users are not likely to disturb files in their System Folder.

To improve further upon the safety factor of placing files in your System folder, you can enable the Protect System folder option found in the General Controls control panel shown in Figure 4-7. This feature essentially locks the folder from changes. If you create a folder called the Application Folder, then you can use the Protect Application Folder option in the same control panel. Files in a protected folder cannot be removed or renamed. Changes to files (such as preference files) can occur, however—so the files are not locked in these folders.

Some of the many application-related files (or folders) that use your System Folder as a safe storage place are Microsoft Word's Word Temp files (later versions of Word store temp files in the Word folder), the PageMaker and FreeHand Aldus folder, and StuffIt's Encryptors, Translators and Viewers.

Printer font files are also in this category. Printer fonts are placed in the System Folder so they are available when needed for automatic downloading to a PostScript printer, and so they can be found by Adobe Type Manager. Usually, these are the most space-consuming files in the System Folder—30k to 50k each. Although utilities like Suitcase II and MasterJuggler make it possible to store printer and screen fonts in other locations, many people choose to keep them in the System Folder anyway. It's the preferred location when you have a static set of fonts that you normally work with.

Adding Files to the System Folder

There are several ways that files may be added to the System Folder after its creation:

- **By the Apple Installer.** To add additional printer drivers, network drivers or keyboards, you can rerun the Apple Installer application at any time. The Installer adds the selected files to your System Folder, placing them into the proper subfolders.

  You don't have to use the Installer to add drivers or files from the system software disks; you can drag-copy files directly from these disks into your System Folder.

- **By application software installers.** Many software applications use installation programs that copy the software and its associated files to your hard drive. Installers that have been specifically written or updated for compatibility with System 7.5 can place files correctly into the System 7.5 System Folder or subfolders.

Older installer applications often place all files directly in the System Folder, ignoring the subfolder structure. In these cases, the application may require that the files remain as positioned by the installer. However, most extensions should be moved to the Extensions folder, and control panels should be moved to the Control Panels folder—regardless of how they were originally positioned. (Although all extensions should be placed in the Extensions folder or Control Panels folder, most items of this nature located directly in the System Folder will be executed at startup.)

- **By software applications.** Historically, many software applications read and write temporary and preferences files to the System Folder. Others use the System Folder for dictionaries and other ancillary files. Applications updated for System 7 should properly read and write files in the System Folder and its subfolders.

    Older applications not rewritten for System 7 may not use the subfolders, but files placed directly in the System Folder will be accessed properly and won't cause any problems for your system software or other programs. New program releases will address subfolder location, in the interest of further System Folder simplification.

- **By you—the Macintosh user.** Since some programs and utilities don't use installer applications, many files must be placed into the System Folder manually. These files can be dragged onto the System Folder icon or dragged into an open System Folder window.

    When files are dragged onto the System Folder icon, the Macintosh automatically positions them in the correct System Folder or subfolder. This Helping Hand helps you manually add files to the System Folder correctly, even if you know nothing about the System Folder structure.

Before positioning files, the Helping Hand informs you it's at work and tells you how it's positioning your files, as shown in Figure 4-15. The Helping Hand works only when files are dragged onto the System Folder icon.

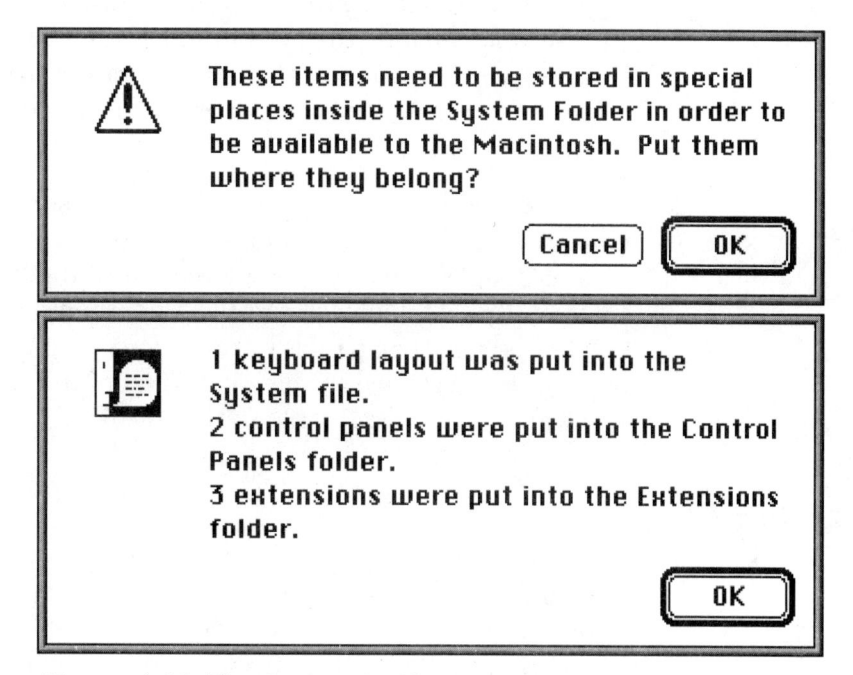

> ⚠ **These items need to be stored in special places inside the System Folder in order to be available to the Macintosh. Put them where they belong?**
>
> [Cancel] [OK]

> 1 keyboard layout was put into the System file.
> 2 control panels were put into the Control Panels folder.
> 3 extensions were put into the Extensions folder.
>
> [OK]

Figure 4-15: The System Folder's Helping Hand makes sure files are positioned properly.

Of course, once files are in the System Folder, you can reposition them freely. The Helping Hand will not affect the movement of files within the System Folder.

You can also avoid the action of the Helping Hand by dragging files directly into an open System Folder window. When you drag files this way, you can place files into any System Folder subfolder, or into the System Folder itself, without interference.

Deleting Files From the System Folder

For the most part, files in the System Folder can be deleted just like any other file, by dragging them into the Trash. However, some files cannot be deleted because they're "in use." "In use" files include the System file; the Finder; any extensions or control panels with code that ran at startup; open control panels; and any temporary or preferences files used by open applications.

To delete the System file or Finder, you must restart the Macintosh using another boot disk. To delete an "in use" extension or control panel, move the file out of the Extensions or Control Panels folders, restart the Mac, then delete the file. To delete open control panels or temporary or preferences files of open applications, simply close the control panel or open application and drag the file to the Trash.

Moving On

Working in the System Folder used to be like playing with a house of cards, but as we've seen, System 7 brought new order and stability to this important part of your hard drive. The new subfolders are especially useful:

- The Apple Menu Items folder lets you customize your Apple Menu.

- The Extensions folder contains all the extensions and drivers that add features to your Mac and the system software.

- The Control Panels folder holds special "mini-applications" that set preferences for system software features, utilities and even hardware peripherals.

- The Startup Items folder lets you determine which files and applications are opened each time your Mac is turned on.

In the next chapter, we turn our attention to the effects this new system software has on software applications used on the Mac—from new ways of accessing your software to a new document type that makes it easier for you to create frequently used files. We'll also look at the enhanced dialog boxes you will encounter whenever you open or save files with System 7. System 7.5 adds new meaning to the words "compatible" and "savvy". There are also now new ways to launch files and applications, and mount servers.

Chapter 5

System 7.5 & Your Software

Thus far, the System 7.5 features we have discussed are those that change the way you organize and manipulate data files on your Macintosh. But as important as file management is, it's not the reason you use a Macintosh. You use the Mac because its software applications—word processors, spreadsheets, databases, graphics programs and the rest—help you accomplish your work productively.

In this chapter, we'll look at some of the ways System 7.5 affects software applications, beginning with the important issue of compatibility. Then we'll see the expanded launching methods, new Stationery Pads and desktop-level enhancements System 7.5 provides. Other major enhancements that affect software applications, including data sharing, program-to-program communication and support for TrueType fonts, are discussed in Chapter 10, "Inter-Application Communications & OpenDoc," and in Chapter 9, "QuickDraw GX & Fonts."

System 7.5 Compatibility

It's always exciting to get a new software upgrade—it means more features, better performance and an easier-to-use interface. But as seasoned computer users know, along with improvements and solutions, software upgrades often introduce bugs and incompatibilities.

System software is particularly susceptible to upgrade compatibility problems because every Macintosh application is so heavily dependent on the system software. Each application must be fine-tuned and coordinated to work together smoothly with the system. The relationship between system software and an application is like that of two juggling partners, each throwing balls into the air that the other is expected to catch. Upgrading system software replaces a familiar partner with a new one, without changing the routine or allowing time to practice, while still expecting each toss and catch to occur precisely.

During development of System 7, Apple worked hard to ensure that it was compatible with as many existing applications as possible. (The beta in development was distributed to many thousands of people using a variety of applications and Macintosh models.) In fact, Apple claimed that any application running under System 6.0.x would operate under System 7 without alteration, as long as the application was programmed according to System 7's widely published programming rules. For the most part, this claim was apparently true.

The majority of major applications were compatible with System 7's initial release, and a great many utility programs were compatible too. Naturally, many utility programs whose functions were to modify or extend the system software itself were not initially compatible.

Now—two years after the introduction of System 7—it's almost impossible to find an application or utility that isn't System 7-compatible. Every program written or updated in that time period has been created or modified with System 7 in mind. System 7.5 continues in this tradition of extending system software capabilities, while maintaining high compatibility with the existing third-party software library.

The introduction of System 7.5 brings additional changes to the system software and more capabilities, yielding yet another set of potential problems. Very few programs—again, usually utilities that modify or extend the system—have proven incompatible, however. More likely, you will find that the new capabilities of system software make obsolete many programs you currently use in your working environment.

What Is Compatibility?

Generally speaking, to be considered System 7-compatible, an application must run under System 7 and provide the same features, with the same degree of reliability, that it did under System 6.0.x. But System 7 compatibility is not black and white—it can exist in varying degrees in different applications. Most compatible applications will launch and provide basic operations under System 7 and operate correctly in System 7's multitasking environment; but problems with 32-bit memory and File Sharing were more common in early releases of System 7-compatible software.

Applications written before System 7 was released, which are not System 7-compatible, will have to be upgraded by their developers in order to be System 7-compatible. Nearly all have been by now. If you have an application that doesn't operate properly in System 7, contact the software developer to obtain a System 7-compatible upgrade.

If a System 7-compatible application is (more or less) no better under System 7 than it was under System 6.0.x, compatibility is obviously not the ultimate accomplishment. Such applications have been dubbed "System 7-Aware." The ultimate goal is to take full advantage of all new System 7 features, a status that Apple calls "System 7-Savvy." To be System 7-Savvy, an application must be specifically written, or updated, for technical compatibility with System 7 and provide support for its new features.

In other words, applications that are System 7-compatible will survive, but applications that are System 7-Savvy will thrive. To be considered System 7-Savvy, applications must do the following:

- **Support multitasking.** System 7 lets your Mac open multiple applications and process data simultaneously. Applications should be able to operate in both the foreground and the background, and should support background processing to the greatest degree possible. (More information on multitasking and background processing appears later in this chapter.)

- **Be 32-bit clean.** When the "32-Bit Addressing" option is turned on in the Memory control panel, certain Macintosh models can access large amounts of memory (see Chapter 8, "Memory Management"). Applications should operate correctly when this option is used.

- **Support the Edition Manager's Publish and Subscribe features.** The Edition Manager, described in Chapter 10, "Inter-Application Communications & OpenDoc," allows data to be transferred from one application to another while maintaining a link to the original file. Applications must include the basic Publish and Subscribe commands.

- **Support AppleEvents and Core events.** System 7's Inter-Application Communication (IAC), also described in

Chapter 10, "Inter-Application Communication & OpenDoc," defines a basic set of AppleEvents that allow one application to communicate with another.

- **Impose no limit on font sizes.** Applications should support all font sizes, from 1 to 32,000 in single-point increments. (See Chapter 9, "QuickDraw GX & Fonts.")

- **Provide help balloons.** As described in Chapter 2, "The Finder," Balloon Help offers quick pop-up summaries of an application's menu commands, dialog box options and graphic elements.

- **Be AppleShare-compliant.** System 7 allows any user to access files shared on AppleShare servers or files from other System 7 Macintoshes using File Sharing. Applications should operate correctly when launched over an AppleTalk network, or when reading or writing data stored on File Sharing or AppleShare volumes (see Chapter 12, "Introduction to File Sharing").

- **Support Stationery Pads.** Applications should be able to take full advantage of Stationery Pads, a new type of document template featured in System 7. (See the "Stationery Pads" discussion later in this chapter.)

Most of the Macintosh software that is being sold today includes a sticker on the box that designates the program as either System 7-Compatible or System 7-Savvy. Many mail-order catalogs also distinguish between incompatible, compatible and savvy software.

System 7.5 introduces some new technologies that "savvy" applications should enable in order to be truly in the know. These technologies include the following:

- **AppleScript.** Two levels of AppleScript awareness are recognized. An application is called "scriptable" if it can be controlled by an external AppleScript. A scriptable application contains a dictionary of AppleScript programming verbs and objects that are supported. Scriptable is savvy.

The second level of AppleScript awareness is called "recordable." A recordable application allows the user to record actions and compose a script reflecting that action using the AppleScript recorder function. Recordable is a lower level of compatibility, more like being "aware." Refer to Chapter 11, "AppleScript," for a discussion of AppleScript.

- **Macintosh Drag and Drop.** Drag-and-drop actions can be data transfer within a file, between files and to the desktop as clippings. Additional drag-and-drop techniques let the user initiate processes such as opening a file, printing data and others. No standard for "full" support exists, but programs such as SimpleText, the Scrapbook, Find File and other system software come closest. Applications may implement any subset of these features.

- **QuickDraw GX implementation.** QuickDraw GX is a portfolio of graphics, fonts, color and printing routines with broad requirements and upgrade opportunities. Again, no current standard exists for what features a program must include for it to be deemed "QuickDraw GX-savvy." At the minimum, most developers would agree that QuickDraw GX font support is a basic requirement because it enables both advanced typographical features and the portable digital document standard that is central to workgroup collaboration technologies.

  Other important QuickDraw technologies are color matching through the ColorSync System Profile control panel and advanced printing and peripheral I/O device driver architecture. Extensions and control panels are QuickDraw GX-savvy when they support desktop printer icons and enable advanced printing features such as multisided, multijob print processes. Because extensions are system software, most applications should achieve a rapid level of QuickDraw GX awareness by allowing these advanced print options in their respective print dialog boxes. QuickDraw GX is described more fully in Chapter 9, "QuickDraw GX & Fonts."

Some other features are important for System 7.5 compatibility, but they're not as fundamental as the three just described. These other features are as follows:

- **PowerTalk support.** Programs are "PowerTalk-savvy" when they implement the AppleMail mailing feature from within a document. Networks and network operating systems are PowerTalk-savvy when they support the universal mailbox, pass messages transparently and otherwise support the "Open Transport" model that Apple has subscribed to. Many of these technologies are still developing, so the definition of what's "savvy" is likely to change over time. Refer to Chapter 14, "AOCE—The Apple Open Collaboration Environment," for more information on this subject.

- **Apple Guide support.** The ability to work with a customized Apple Guide help system is universal for Macintosh applications. Therefore, all Macintosh applications are intrinsically "Apple Guide-aware." Apple Guide support is therefore really a function of whether developers have added this technology to their products.

Whew! That's quite a list. Of course, you have to be careful not to take the "savvy" label too seriously. Many great applications have been upgraded to take full advantage of System 7.5 but cannot be officially categorized as "savvy." The usual reason is that the programs' developers intentionally decided to not implement one or more of the required items because such features were either unimportant or inapplicable for that application. Sometimes developers are using a different programming and interface model in their work.

For instance, many applications don't support Balloon Help or the Edition Manager. Some vendors such as Microsoft will undoubtedly choose to promote their own online help system in place of Apple Guide. Microsoft is also implementing OLE, a compound document technology that competes with Publish and Subscribe. Finally, some of the core system software technologies are complex, multifaceted, and are still developing—which will make their adoption slow in coming.

Launching

Double-click, double-click, double-click. That's how most Macintosh users launch their software applications. Two clicks to open the drive or volume, two to open the application folder and a double-click on the application icon to launch the software.

See "Files & Disks" for help launching files with the Launcher.

This method can quickly grow wearisome when it means clicking through many volumes and folder layers to reach an icon. As alternatives, a wide range of application launching utilities—including OnCue, NowMenus, SuperBoomerang, DiskTop and MasterJuggler—have appeared in recent years. With these utilities, you can launch by selecting application names from a list, instead of searching through folders for icons.

Applications could still be launched in System 7 by double-clicking icons, but more icons were made available, including aliases and stationery documents. It also became possible to launch applications or documents from the Apple menu or by dragging a document onto an application icon.

7.5 System 7.5 introduces three new ways to launch files or applications. You can now use the Recent Documents or Recent Applications submenu off the Apple menu (discussed in previous chapters). With the Macintosh Easy Open control panel, applications can do transparent file translation, enabling a drag-and-drop type process. Lastly, out of the positive experience that Apple has had with Performas and the At Ease interface has come the Launcher control panel. Any object that can have an alias—files, applications, AppleScripts, servers, and so on—can be added to the Launcher window. Opening that object or starting the process is then just a click away in the Launcher window. We'll look at Macintosh Easy Open and the Launcher in more detail in this section.

In fact, you can now launch applications in all the following ways:

- **Double-click an application icon.** You can double-click an application icon, or the alias of an application icon, to launch that application.

- **Double-click a document icon or its alias.** If the application that created a document is unavailable, the Application Not Found dialog box, shown in Figure 5-1, will appear. To open a document that presents this dialog box, you must either locate the original application or use another application that's capable of opening that type of document.

    For example, suppose a MacWrite II file displays the Application Not Found dialog box when double-clicked. You could open Microsoft Word and then access the file using the Open... command under Word's File menu. Similarly, SuperPaint can open MacPaint files, and many applications can open TIFF or EPS files. Most applications can open documents of several different file types. The new System 7.5 Macintosh Easy Open control panel, which is discussed later in this chapter, addresses this problem.

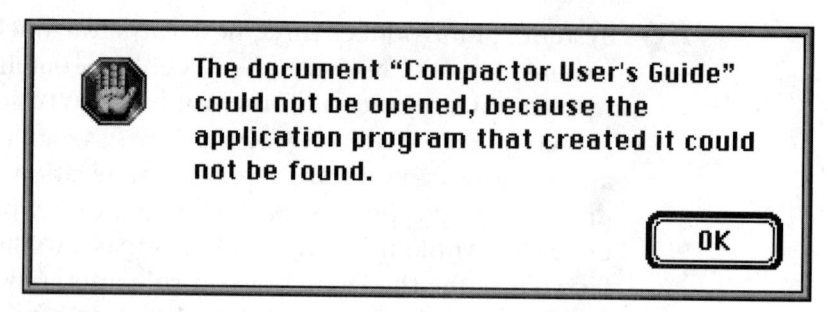

> ⛔ The document "Compactor User's Guide" could not be opened, because the application program that created it could not be found.
>
> [OK]

Figure 5-1: The Application Not Found dialog box.

- **Double-click a Stationery Pad document or its alias.** Stationery Pad documents are template documents that create untitled new documents automatically when opened. (More about Stationery Pads appears later in this chapter.)

- **Drag a document icon onto an application icon.** This method of launching will work only when the document is dragged onto the icon of the application that created it.

    If an application will launch, the application icon highlights when the document icon is above it. Application icons will highlight only when appropriate documents are positioned above them, as shown in Figure 5-2.

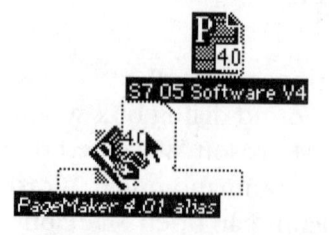

Figure 5-2: Application icons highlight when you drag onto them documents that they can launch.

- **Add applications or documents to the Startup Items folder inside the System Folder.** To automatically launch an application or open a document and its application at startup, add the application or document icon or an alias of one of these icons to the Startup Items folder inside the System Folder. This action will cause the application or document to be launched automatically at startup. (See Chapter 4, "The System Folder," for more information on using the Startup Items folder.)

- **Choose an application or document name from the Apple menu.** By placing an application or document in the Apple Menu Items folder inside the System Folder, the application or document name will then appear in the Apple menu and can be launched by choosing the application or document name. (Information on configuring the Apple menu is found in Chapter 4, "The System Folder.")

- **Choose an application or document name from the Recent Document or Recent Application submenus of the Apple menu.** If you've enabled this option in the Apple Menu Options control panel (it's on by default) in System 7.5, a variable number of your most recently accessed files or applications are added to these submenus. Items are replaced on a last used, first out basis. This feature was described in Chapter 2, "The Finder." Select the name of the document or application you want as you would any other command name.

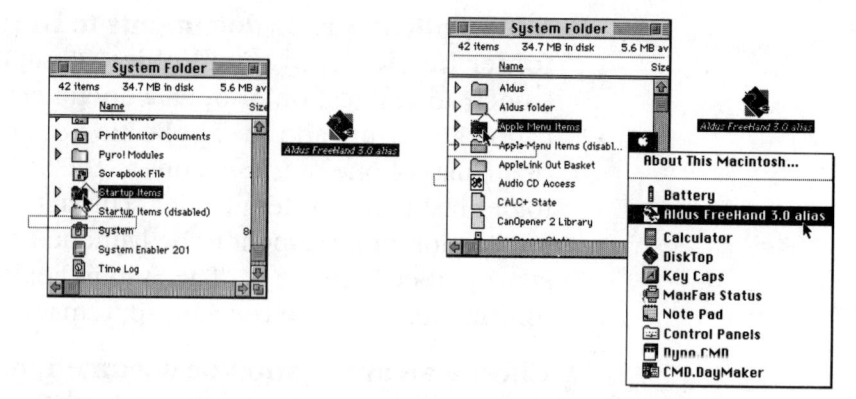

Figure 5-3: Items are launched at startup when you add them to the Startup Items folder (left), or when you select them from the Apple menu.

Launching Methods

There's no one best way to launch applications. You'll probably find that a combination of methods is the most efficient. Keep the following launching tips in mind:

- **The Apple menu.** Add the applications and documents you use most frequently to the Apple menu. (Chapter 4, "The System Folder," has more on the Apple menu.) If you use a document or program daily, it will probably stay in the Recent Applications or Recent Documents submenu, so you may not need to put it in the Apple menu. Use your judgment on the best method of organizing your own Apple menu.

- **Alias folders.** Assemble groups of application aliases into folders according to application type; add aliases of frequently used folders to the Apple menu.

    You can select the folder name from the Apple menu to open the folder and double-click the application you want to launch. Hold down the Option key while you double-click the application icon to close the open folder window automatically during the launch.

Figure 5-4 shows an Apple menu configured using this method. An @ character has been added before the name of each folder alias, which forces these folders to group near the top of the Apple menu.

```
About This Macintosh...
-------------------------
 @ Application alias ƒ
 @ Utilities alias ƒ
 Calculator
 DiskTop
 Key Caps
 MaxFax Status
 Note Pad
 Control Panels
 CMD.DayMaker
```

Figure 5-4: Adding folders full of application icons to the Apple menu makes them easy to access.

This method, while appropriate to system software versions prior to System 7.5, is now less convenient than relying on the Recent Applications submenu or the Launcher window. There's virtually no setup time involved in configuring the Recent Applications submenu, and it's just as convenient. For the same amount of work as adding a folder of aliases, you can configure the Launcher. In fact, if you have already created a folder of aliases or added aliases to the Apple menu, just copy those aliases over to the Launcher Items folder found in your System Folder.

- **Double-click icons.** When you're browsing in Finder windows to locate specific files, use the tried-and-true double-click method to launch applications, aliases, documents or stationery icons.

- **Drag icons onto applications.** If you store documents and applications or their aliases in the same folder, or if you place application icons or aliases on the desktop, dragging icons onto applications (or drop-launching, as it's called) may prove useful, although double-clicking the document is often easier.

Macintosh Easy Open

Did you ever open a document created by another program and get an alert box with the message "Can't open document. Application busy or missing"? Macintosh Easy Open cures this problem. And guess what?! It's easy! Macintosh Easy Open is a translator utility that you can configure from the Macintosh Easy Open Setup control panel shown in Figure 5-5.

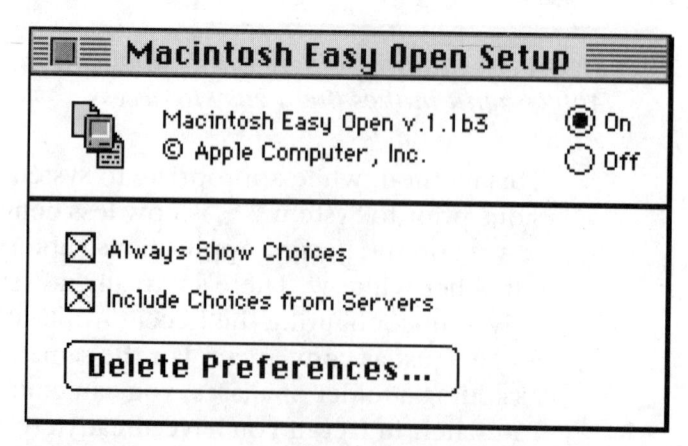

Figure 5-5: Macintosh Easy Open Setup control panel.

7.5 By default, Easy Open is turned on upon installation of System 7.5. You can turn it off by clicking the Off radio button. Macintosh Easy Open offers only two options. Select the Always Show Choices check box to choose from a list of other applications that will open the document. When you turn off this option, your Macintosh will automatically open a document in the application of its choice. Enabling the Include Choices from Server option allows Macintosh Easy Open to launch applications on a network server. The program-linking choice in File Sharing must be turned on for this option to work properly. Both options are on by default.

The Launcher

System 7.5 adds the Launcher control panel as a means of enabling novice users to launch files, applications, or any other item for which you can create an alias in the Finder. If you've ever worked with Apple's At Ease utility (standard on Macintosh Performas), then you will recognize this feature. It's a great time saver and an absolute boon for novice users and small children.

When you combine the Launcher with the option not to "Show Desktop When in Background," (found in the General Controls control panel) you can lock out users from switching inadvertently to the Finder with a misplaced click. This can be very confusing to novice users. The combination works well, but it is incomplete in shielding the novice user from the Finder because the Launcher itself will show the Macintosh Desktop when it is in the background. For more complete protection, check out AppleSoft's At Ease and At Ease for Workgroups, which are described more fully in Chapter 15, "Apple's System 7 Extensions."

To open the Launcher, double-click on the Launcher control panel or choose its name from the Control Panel submenu under the Apple menu. You can choose to always show the Launcher upon startup by turning on that option in the Desktop section of the General Controls control panel, as shown in Figure 5-6. In this same section, you can turn on "Finder hiding."

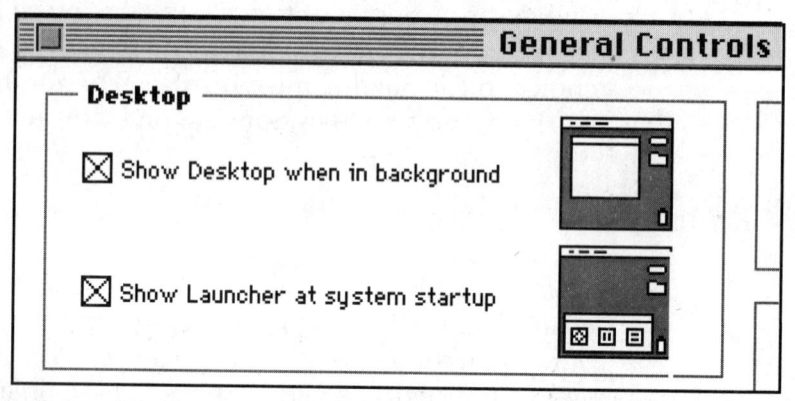

Figure 5-6: The Desktop section of the General Controls control panel.

You add items to the Launcher by copying or moving aliases of files, applications, AppleScripts, servers, control panels, folders, the QuickDraw GX printer—literally anything you can alias in the Finder—to the Launcher Items folder. This folder is normally located at the top level of your System Folder.

You delete items from the Launcher by removing their aliases from that folder. If you have a folder of aliases for applications or have added aliases to your Apple Menu Items folder, you may want to copy or move those aliases to the Launcher Items folder to get started (see Figure 5-7).

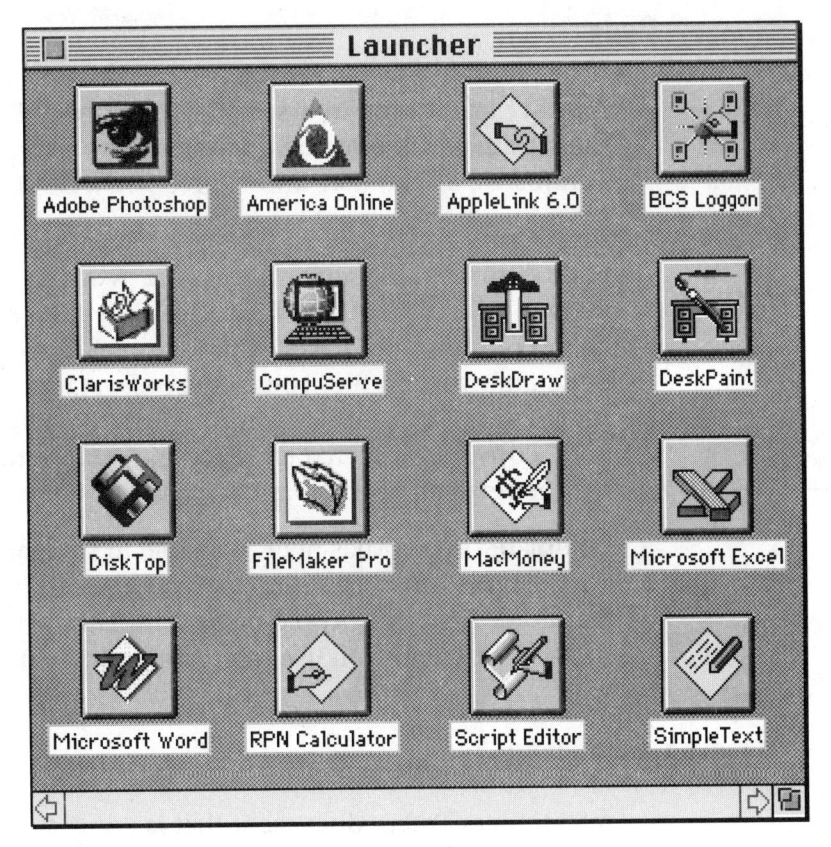

Figure 5-7: A well-stocked Launcher.

There isn't much to the Launcher, but it is a tremendous time saver. Click once on an icon to open the object or start the process. The current Launcher is not Macintosh Drag and Drop enabled; that is, you can't drag a document onto an application icon in the Launcher. However, future versions of the Launcher may be more savvy. Remember, you can use the WindowShade control panel to minimize the Launcher window when it's not in use.

Stationery Pads

Another innovation in System 7 is Stationery Pads. You use them to make an existing document into a template quickly. Templates, as you may know, give you a head start in creating new documents.

For example, the documents in your word processor probably fall into a handful of specific formats—letters, reports, memos, chapters and so on. Rather than start each document with a new, unformatted file, you can use the stationery document for a letter, for example, that provides the date, salutation, body copy, closing character and paragraph formatting, correct margins and other basic formatting.

Template support has been available in several Macintosh applications for some time, but by adding the Stationery Pad feature to System 7, Apple made templates available in every software package you use to create documents.

Creating a Stationery Pad

A Stationery Pad (a document that is going to be stationery) is usually created in three steps:

- First, you find an existing typical example of a document you commonly create.

- Then you modify the typical document to make it a good generic representation and save it to disk.

- Finally, select the "Stationery pad" option in the file's Get Info dialog box.

As an example, to create a memo Stationery Pad, open an existing representative document, like the one shown in Figure 5-8. Although this memo is typical, it does have one unusual element—the embedded graphic. We remove that element because most of the memos we create do not call for such graphic elements. The remaining memo elements are left to serve as placeholders.

Figure 5-8: A letter that will become a Stationery Pad.

Before you save the memo Stationery Pad, it's a good idea to edit the text in all placeholders so that they're appropriate to use in final documents. Replace placeholder text with nonsensical data ("greeking"), which helps ensure that no placeholder elements are accidentally used in finished documents. For the memo date, for example, use 0/0/00, and the memo address can read To: Recipient.

You might overlook a date such as 7/15/91 and use it instead of the current date each time you use the Stationery Pad. You're almost certain to notice the 0/0/00 date, on the other hand when you proofread the document. Figure 5-9 shows our sample memo with generic placeholders inserted.

```
0/00/00


To: Recipient,

This is your lucky day! I am pleased to inform you that your
name has been selected in our weekly grand-prize drawing,
and you have won a new car and dream vacation valued at
$20,000.
In order to claim your prize, please stop by our store, and
complete a Prize Winner Registration form, available from
our Store Manager, Ms. Juni Enrich. You will then be
allowed to select your automobile and vacation from the
prize-winner catalog.
Once you receive your prizes, our contest photographer will
contact you to arrange to have promotional pictures taken of
you and your prizes. (You agreed to such photo's in your
signed entry form.)

Sincerely,


Robert Scrunge
Store Manager
```

Figure 5-9: After being edited, the document contains placeholders.

After you edit the memo, use the Save As... command to save the template document to disk. Use names that are easily identified in Finder windows and dialog box listings: for example, add the letters "STNY" to the end of each document name. You're not required to use naming conventions; you'll be able to distinguish Stationery Pads by their icons alone, but using distinct file names gives you an extra advantage. See Figure 5-10.

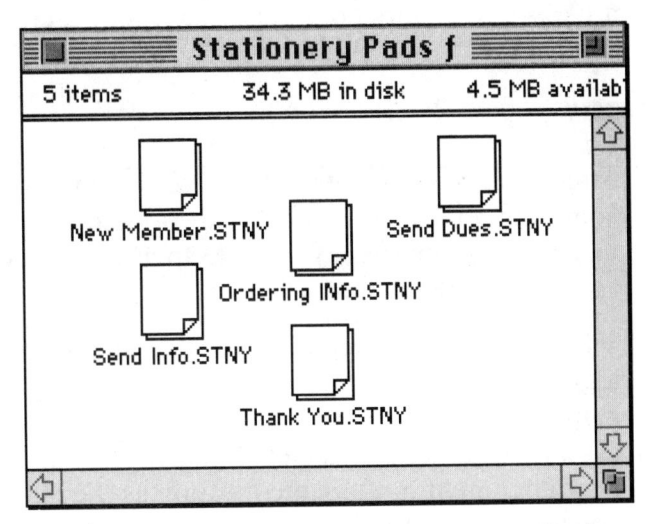

Figure 5-10: A folder full of Stationery Pads.

There's one final but critical step in creating a Stationery document. After you've edited and saved your document, go to the Finder and select its icon. Then choose the Get Info command from the File menu. Click in the Stationery Pad check box in the lower-right corner of the Get Info dialog box. Notice that the icon inside the Get Info dialog box changes to show that the document is now a Stationery Pad. After you close the Get Info dialog box, the conversion is complete.

Note: Some applications, such as Simple Text and Microsoft Word, give you the option of saving your documents in Stationery Pad format. Saving this way may be simpler than digging up the Get Info box, particularly if your document is buried several folders deep on your drive.

The document's icon at the Finder will also be updated to reflect its new status, but the icon that appears depends on the application you used to create the document. These icons are discussed more completely later in this chapter.

Using Stationery

After you've created Stationery Pad documents, you can either launch them from the desktop by double-clicking their icons, or you can open them with the Open command in an application's File menu.

When you launch a Stationery Pad from the desktop, the dialog box shown in Figure 5-11 appears, prompting you to name and save the new document being created. After entering a new name, you can click the OK button and save the new document in the same location as the Stationery Pad, or you can use the Save In... button to save the file in a new location before it's opened. Some applications choose to open stationery documents as "Untitled", behavior that differs from the Apple guidelines.

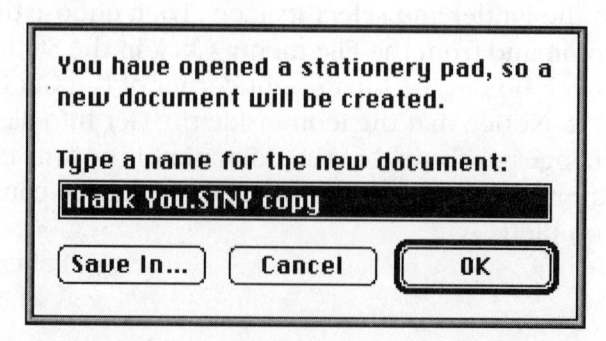

Figure 5-11: The Open Stationery Pad dialog box.

Because the Stationery Pad file is duplicated and renamed before it's opened, if you later decide you don't need this new document, you'll have to manually delete it from your disk.

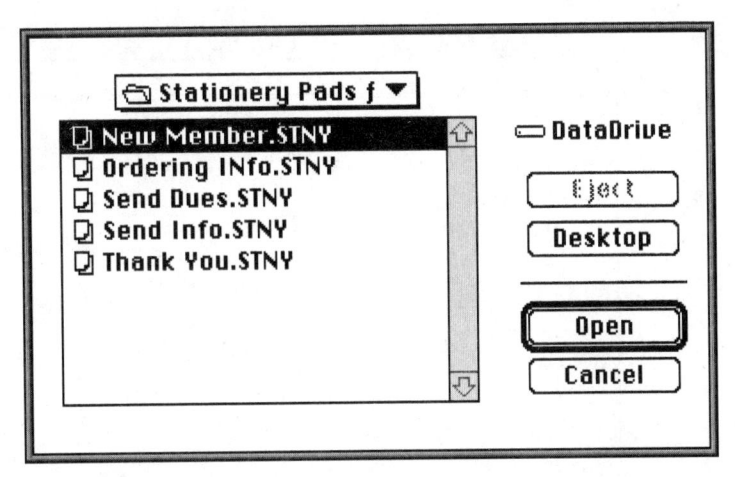

Figure 5-12: An Open dialog box with Stationery Pads visible.

Once you've opened a copy of a Stationery Pad document, you can customize it as required. Be sure to edit all placeholders that you set when creating the Stationery Pad document. You can delete unnecessary elements, add new ones and edit the document in any other way you choose.

Stationery Pad Tips

- **Stationery Pad aliases.** Whether they were created before or after the "Stationery Pad" option was set, aliases of Stationery Pad documents access the Stationery Pad normally. The alias icon displays the Stationery Pad icon.

- **Stationery Pad folder.** Create a Stationery or Templates folder and keep aliases of all your Stationery Pad documents in this folder. Keep the original documents organized as they were originally. This way, it is easy to access Stationery Pads when you need them. If you use them frequently, you can also put an alias of this folder in your Apple Menu Items folder. See Figure 5-13.

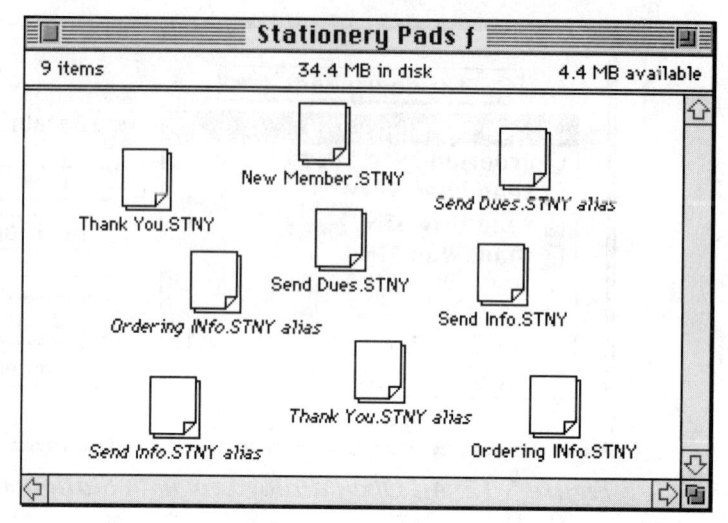

Figure 5-13: A folder containing Stationery Pads and Stationery Pad aliases.

- **Application support for multiple documents.** If an application does not support more than one open document at a time, opening a Stationery Pad from the Finder when the application and a document are already open may not work. In this case, close the open document and then reopen the Stationery Pad using the Open command.

- **Opening Stationery using the Open command.** Opening a Stationery Pad document from inside an application that isn't "Stationery Pad aware" may cause problems. An application may open the Stationery Pad itself rather than create a new Untitled copy. When you open Stationery Pads using the Open command, be sure to use a new file name and the Save As command so that you don't accidentally overwrite your Stationery Pad document.

- **Editing Stationery Pads.** Deselecting the "Stationery Pad" option in the Get Info dialog box will turn any Stationery Pad document back into a "normal" document—it will lose its Stationery Pad properties. You can then edit the Stationery Pad document, making changes to your master. After editing and saving this document, reselect the "Stationery Pad" option in the Get Info dialog box to turn the file back into a Stationery Pad.

The Desktop Level

It is impossible to work on the Macintosh and not hear—and use—the word "desktop." In Macintosh terminology, the word "desktop" usually refers to the Finder desktop, which is the onscreen area where volume icons, windows and the Trash appear. Also, files and folders can be dragged from any mounted volume or folder and placed directly on the desktop.

In previous system software versions, the Finder desktop was ignored by the Open and Save dialog boxes. In these dialog boxes, each mounted volume was discrete, and all files were on disks or in folders. See Figure 5-14.

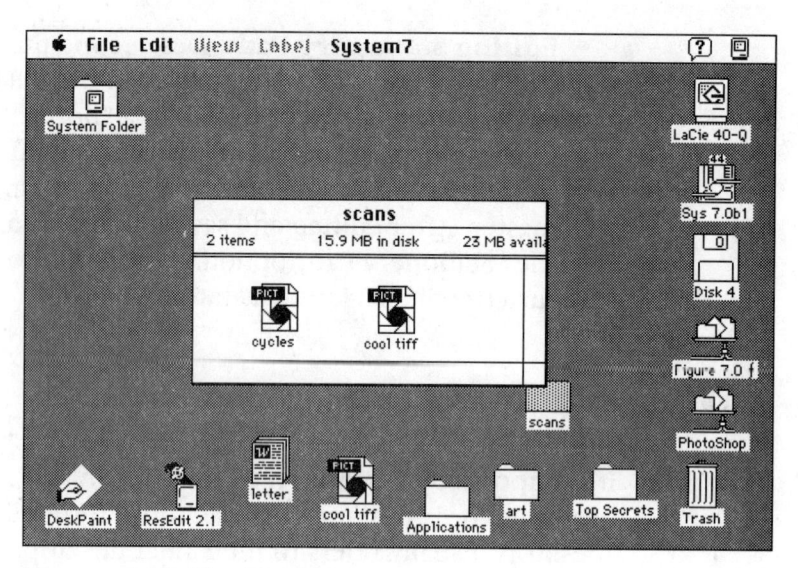

Figure 5-14: The Finder desktop.

In System 7, dialog boxes provide access to the Finder desktop and all volumes, files and folders that reside there. In fact, the Drive button has been replaced with a Desktop button that causes a new desktop view to appear in the scrolling file listing. This desktop view displays the name and icon of each volume, file and folder that exist on the Finder desktop. In Figure 5-15 you can see the Open File dialog boxes of Systems 6 and 7. Figure 5-16 offers you a view of the desktop level in an iconic representation.

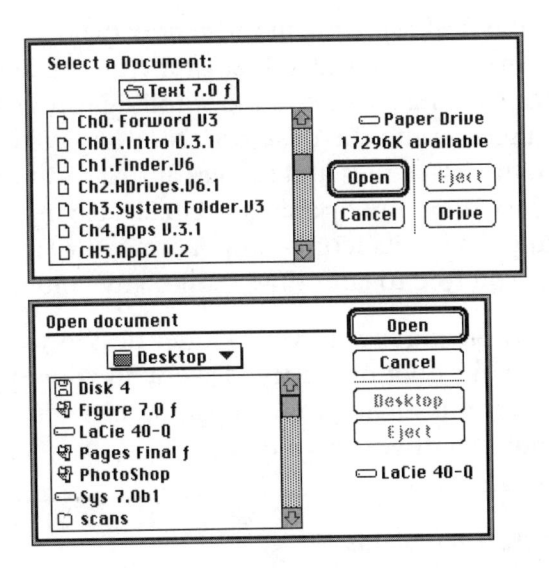

Figure 5-15: A sample dialog box from System 6.0.x (top) and one from System 7 (bottom).

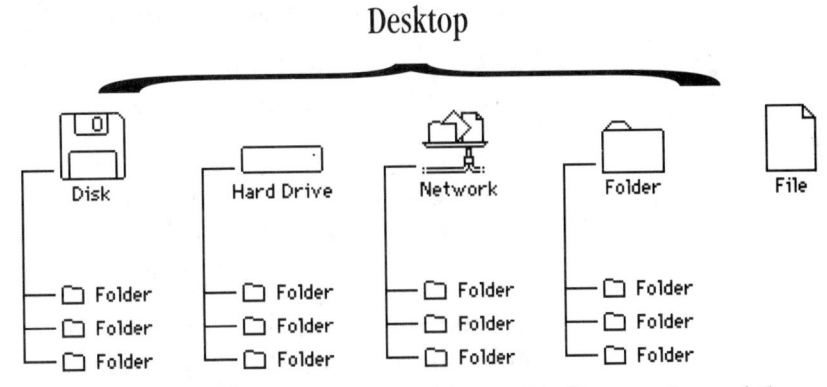

Figure 5-16: The desktop level offers a bird's-eye view of the available volumes, files and folders.

From the desktop view in these new dialog boxes, you can move into any volume, folder or file on the desktop by double-clicking a name in the scrolling list, or you can save files directly onto the desktop. Once any volume or folder is open, the list of files and folders at that location is displayed, and the dialog box operates normally. Saving a file onto the desktop causes its icon to appear on your Finder desktop and leaves you free to later drag it onto any volume or folder.

Caution: Saving files to your Finder desktop writes the actual data to your boot drive (the drive with your System Folder on it). Be careful—saving to the desktop can get confusing if you use multiple drives or volumes.

Dialog Box Keyboard Equivalents

In addition to the new Desktop button, all Open and Save dialog boxes now support a number of keyboard equivalents that make it faster and easier to find and create files:

- **Desktop express.** Pressing Command-D is the equivalent of clicking the Desktop button.

- **Next or previous volume or drive.** To cycle through available volumes (formerly done by the Drive button), press Command-Right arrow. You can now also cycle backward by pressing Command-Left arrow.

- **File listing / File name options.** In Save As dialog boxes, pressing the Tab key toggles back and forth between the scrolling file listing and the file name option. You can tell which is activated by the presence of an extra black border, and you can also control the active window from the keyboard. (In earlier versions of the system software, pressing the Tab key was the equivalent of pressing the Drive button.)

When the file name option is active, you can control the cursor position with the arrow keys and, of course, enter any valid file name. When the scrolling file listing is active, use the following keyboard equivalents to locate, select and manipulate files and folders. See Figure 5-17.

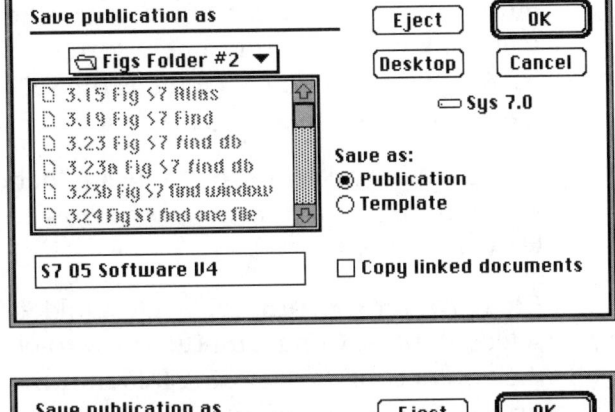

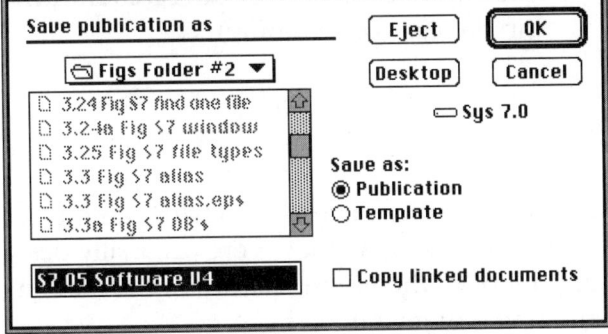

Figure 5-17: A dialog box with the scrolling list active (top) and with the Name option box active (bottom).

The following keyboard equivalents are available in the scrolling file listing of either Open or Save As dialog boxes:

- **Jump alphabetically.** Typing any single letter causes the first file name starting with that letter, or the letter closest to it, to be selected.

- **Jump alphabetically and then some.** If you quickly type more than one letter, the Mac will continue to narrow down the available file names accordingly. In other words, typing only the letter F will jump you to the first file name that starts with an F; typing FUL will pass by the file "Finder 7 Facts" and select the file "Fulfillment Info." When typing multiple characters to find files, you must not pause between characters; otherwise, the Mac will think you're starting a new search—instead of interpreting your second character as the second letter of a file name, it will treat it as the first letter of a new search.

- **Open folder or volume.** While a folder (or volume) is selected, press Command-Down arrow to open it and view its contents.

- **Close folder or volume.** While a folder (or volume) is selected, press Command-Up arrow to close it and view the contents of its enclosing folder or the Finder desktop (in the case of a volume).

Desk Accessories

Desk accessories have always had a fond place in the hearts of Macintosh users. As they were originally designed, DAs came to symbolize the unique nature of the Mac—its customizability and much of its fun.

The main benefit of using desk accessories was being able to run an additional application (even if it was a small one) without quitting the main application—you could open a calculator or delete files from your disk without leaving your word processor, for example. With system software 5.0, MultiFinder became an inherent feature of the system software, giving users the ability to run multiple large and small applications.

The introduction of MultiFinder meant that desk accessories' days were numbered. System 7 pounds the last nail into the coffin, but not before assuring them an afterlife. The cause of death is System 7's inability to launch or install desk accessory files from the DA suitcase format. The resurrection is provided by System 7's ability to easily turn these old desk accessories into new double-clickable stand-alone applications.

Existing desk accessories appear at the Finder with their familiar suitcase icons, as shown in Figure 5-18. In previous system software versions, these suitcases were opened and installed into the System file using the Font/DA Mover, or attached to the System file via utilities such as Suitcase II and MasterJuggler. In System 7, however, these DA suitcases are relics whose only purpose is to store desk accessories until they're converted for use in System 7.

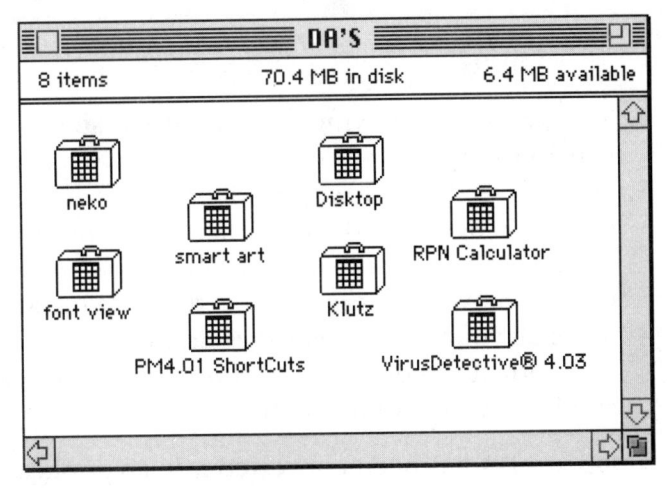

Figure 5-18: DA icons.

To convert desk accessories into System 7-compatible applications, double-click the suitcase icon, and a window will open, as shown in Figure 5-19. This window displays each desk accessory in the suitcase, with its own Application icon. At this point, you may run the DA by simply double-clicking it, or you can permanently convert the DA into an application by dragging it out of the suitcase and into any other folder or volume. As you copy the DA into a new folder or volume, it's transformed into a stand-alone application. From this point forward, it functions as an application, although it's still listed in the Finder's Kind information as a desk accessory.

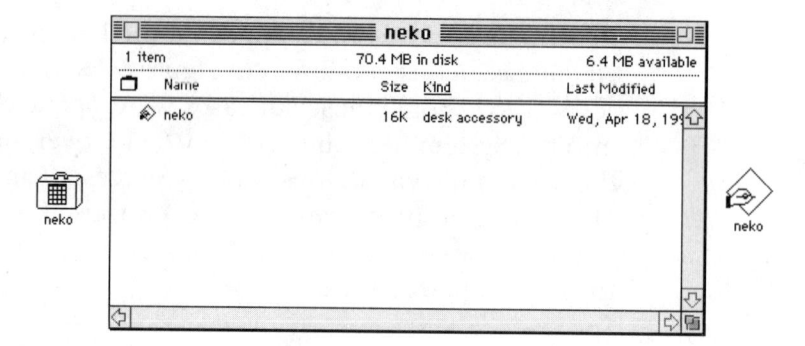

Figure 5-19: A DA icon, open DA window and DA application.

This process (removing DAs from their suitcases) is the only way to use DAs in System 7. Once they're "converted" into System 7-compatible applications, you can't use them as applications in System 6.0.x or earlier. If you try to launch a converted desk accessory into earlier system software, the Name dialog box will appear. For this reason, you should keep copies of all your desk accessories, in their original desk accessory format, on disk in case you ever need to use them with an older version of the system software.

Once a DA has been converted into an application, you can use it just like any application. You can store it in any folder, and you usually launch it by double-clicking its icon. Of course, you can launch the converted DA with any of the launching methods described earlier in this chapter. You'll also want to install the DA, or its alias, in the Apple Menu Items folder so that you can launch it from the Apple menu.

After opening a converted DA, you can either close it when you're finished, hide it with the Applications menu's Hide command, or bring another application to the foreground and leave the DA open in the background. You can close most converted DAs by clicking the close box in their window title bar, but you can also use the File menu's Quit command.

Moving On

Even the oldest Macintosh programs are improved by System 7, as we've seen throughout this chapter. Some improvements are dramatic and substantial, whereas others are more subtle or incidental:

- Now you have even more ways than ever to launch your applications and their document files.

- A new document type, the Stationery Pad, is provided by the system software to every application.

- The Desktop level is given official presence in all Open and Save dialog boxes.

- Desk accessories leave the shelter of the Apple menu and can now be used like normal applications.

Another important aspect of System 7 is the ability to open and use several applications simultaneously. Chapter 6, "Power Macintosh & PowerBook System Software," focuses on the special support that system software provides to the two newest classes of Macintosh computers. This support takes the form of essential services, necessary utilities, and useful enhancements meant to increase your efficiency while working. Chapter 6 contains an introduction to RISC computing and the PowerPC chip, and explains how RISC affects speed and software installation. PowerBook users need special screen and battery life extenders that are provided in System 7.5.

Chapter 6

Power Macintosh & PowerBook System Software

The Installer has always been smart enough to put just the right components for the Macintosh model you use into your System Folder. Up until System 7, there were few differences that really mattered, and you could install system software manually. Now the Installer checks your Macintosh model and installs some radically different code to support microprocessors other than the familiar Motorola 680x0 series.

The new 680x0 microprocessors introduced some incompatibilities that required minor patches here and there. A new monitor or printer required a new driver, and there were minor performance improvements (mostly hardware based). These changes are nothing compared to the fundamental changes in system software required by the introduction of the RISC-based Power Macintosh computer, or the support given to the PowerBook series.

The best part of System 7.5 (and 7.1.2) is the part you can't see: support for the RISC-based Power Macintosh computers. Internally, much of the programming used in system software has changed, although you will notice few operational changes. System 7 supports the library of programs written for 680x0 (called 68k) Macintosh computers in emulation, and it supports programs written for the new PowerPC-microprocessor series called *native mode programs*. System 7 can switch back and forth between these program types automatically.

PowerBook system software support began with System 7.0.1. A suite of simple utilities for controlling your PowerBook's basic functions—controlling screen display, measuring battery lifetimes, doing processor cycling and other tasks—were included in that software release. Sensing an opportunity, many vendors rushed in, substantially improving upon Apple's meager offerings with packages such as Claris's Power To Go, Connectix's CPU, Norton's Essentials for the PowerBook, Inline Design's PBTools and so on. Several million PowerBooks later, Apple substantially improved the support that PowerBook owners looked for elsewhere. Some of these features new to System 7.5, such as the Control Strip, will doubtless appeal to many people.

This chapter details the important hardware-specific support given these Power Macintosh and PowerBook series. Even though there are some differences in system software support for Performas, LCs, Quadras and so on, they are judged to be minor in comparison. These differences are noted where appropriate throughout the book.

The Same Old Interface

The first things you notice when you start up a Power Macintosh are a new "Welcome to Macintosh" message and a new, deep-throated start-up sound created with the help of jazz guitarist Stanley Jordan. From there on, few things in the Macintosh interface will look different to you. Underlying this familiarity are many changes, which we will get to presently. For the truly observant, you may notice the following new features:

- **The Get Info dialog box.** A Finder extension for Power Macintosh adds a note at the bottom of the Get Info dialog box noting whether an application is in native code.

- **The Memory control panel.** There is now a setting for the Modern Memory Manager, described in detail in Chapter 8. The Modern Memory Manager is a set of re-written routines and new algorithms for improved memory management. The new algorithms are said to be responsible for a 10 to 20 percent performance increase.

Support for the Power Macintosh series began with the short-lived System 7.1.2, a major upgrade with an interim version release number. System 7.1.2 embodied over 400 man-years of work and testing. Because 7.1.2 was meant for Power Macintosh computers only, those users were the first to see the components described below added to system software. Users upgrading their Quadras, Centris or LC III computers via board swaps and add-in cards also require system version 7.1.2 or later.

- **PC Exchange.** This utility for handling IBM PC-compatible floppies was finally added to system software in the 7.1.2 release.

- **Macintosh Easy Open** was also added to System 7.5. This utility translates between file formats.

- **QuickTime 1.6.2.** This version of QuickTime added native compressor-decompressors to Power Macs via a QuickTime PowerPlug extension that enabled improved QuickTime performance. QuickTime 2.0 will be added to system software late in 1994 after System 7.5 first ships.

- **Video Monitor 1.0.1.** Video Monitor captures still images from a video source; or with an AV card installed, it can be used as a virtual TV.

- **Apple HD Setup 7.3.** This formatting utility writes 68k Macintosh drivers on Apple hard drives.

SimpleText, Apple's new electronic browser DocViewer 1.1, and AppleScript 1.1 also appeared in System 7.1.2. AppleScript is described in Chapter 11. PC Exchange, Macintosh Easy Open, QuickTime and other system extensions are described in Chapter 15, "Apple's System 7 Extensions."

Also making their first appearance in 7.1.2 were the Energy Saver and AutoPower control panels, which are part of the Energy Star requirements. Both of these panels were replaced by a PowerOff control panel (see Figure 6-1) in System 7.5. PowerOff blanks a monitor or turns off your computer at times you specify. Options include turning off hardware after a certain idle time (15 minutes to 12 hours), at certain times of the day or on certain days. Options for not shutting down your computer are also available; they include having a busy serial port, a connection to a shared network disk, a watch cursor being present, or when sounds are being played. Not all models can use these features, but those that are "Energy Star-compliant" (a government specification) can.

Figure 6-1: The PowerOff control panel.

Mostly, what you will notice with a Power Macintosh is its speed. Menus pop open, windows scroll effortlessly, and applications launch significantly faster. To give you an idea of the speed of the Power Macintosh computers, several demo versions of native applications are placed on the Power Macintosh CD-ROM. One notable application is the Apple Graphing Calculator. This native application lets you graph 3D functions. Shown in Figure 6-2 is a solution to one sinusoidal algebraic function.

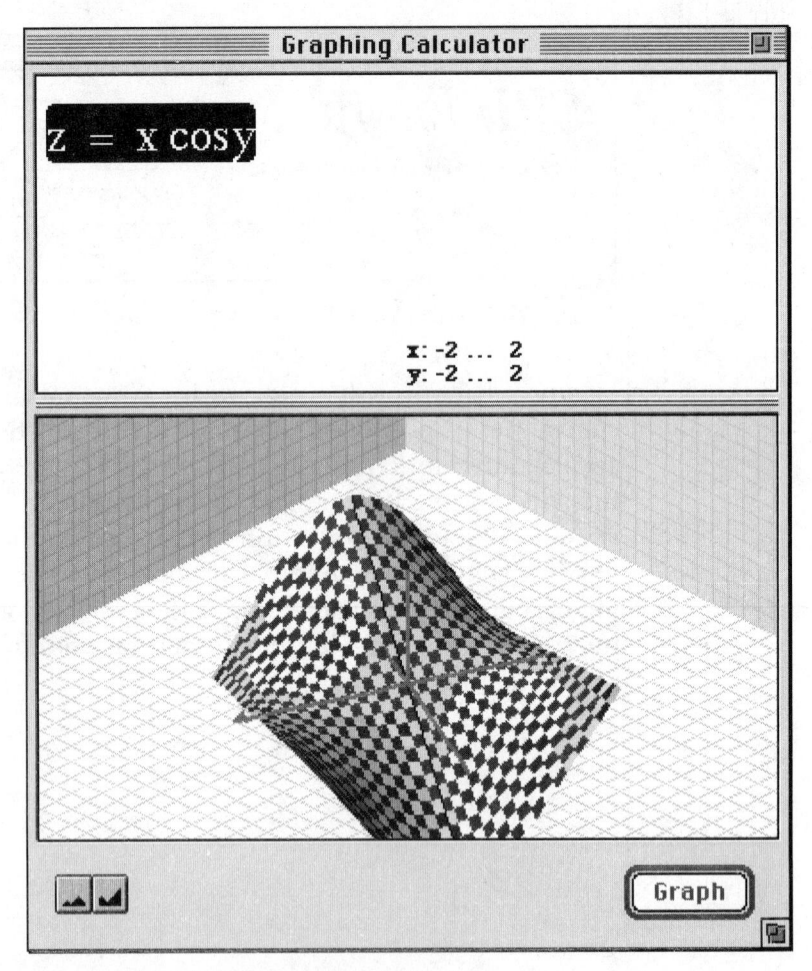

Figure 6-2: The Graphing Calculator.

And oh, yes, be prepared for a loud car-crash sound if your Power Macintosh has a start-up problem.

RISC vs. CISC Chip Architecture

Underlying all decisions about software design are the principles of execution of a computer's microprocessor. Decisions such as the number of instruction registers, how memory is accessed, using integer and/or floating point numbers, and other factors affect programming and performance. All microprocessors perform the following basic tasks in a processing cycle:

- **Fetch.** Instructions and data are read from memory.

- **Decode.** Instructions are translated (compiled) into a form that can be operated on and then "dispatched" to the processing unit. The compiler is where the really important performance gains can be made.

- **Execute.** An operation in Boolean logic (1's and 0's) is carried out.

- **Write.** Derived data or instructions from the microprocessor are sent back to memory or to storage; this process is also called *WriteBack*.

The Fetch, Decode, Execute, and Write events represent one processor cycle. The performance of the number of cycles per second is the clock speed, an intrinsic horsepower number. However, because there are often delays in getting instructions from disk, a processor waits until it's ready to process the next instruction. This delay is called a *wait state*, and it has the same effect that friction has on moving objects. Therefore, a more effective measure of a CPU's performance is the *execution time*, which is the number of cycles per instruction divided by the cycle time. An execution time is the number of instructions per second a system can achieve. This number is both hardware and software related.

No matter how fast your microprocessor is, it has a certain inefficiency due to the regularity of clock timing. A processor may be too fast, or the compiled instructions (microcode) waiting to be processed may be inefficiently received. Many systems therefore build wait states into their processing cycle.

Inefficiencies are also due to building the queue of compiled code waiting to be processed. It may take longer to complete one instruction than another, particularly when the instructions are of variable length. The art of building a queue of instructions has direct impact on performance. Microprocessors use a technique called *pipelining* to process several instructions at the same time and eliminate execution holes, or *pipeline stall*. A clocking scheme retrieves compiled instructions from each pipe, in turn, improving performance.

As you can see in Figure 6-3, perfect microcode dovetails one instruction after the next. There are no inefficiencies. Notice that when you use complex instructions of varying sizes, it's hard to avoid pipeline stalls. This is the case in current Macintosh computers. For a compiler that uses words of the same length, it's easier to get efficient performance. This is one reason that RISC (reduced instruction set computers) processors outperform CISC (complex instruction set computers) processors. But there are other reasons as well (as you'll see in the following pages).

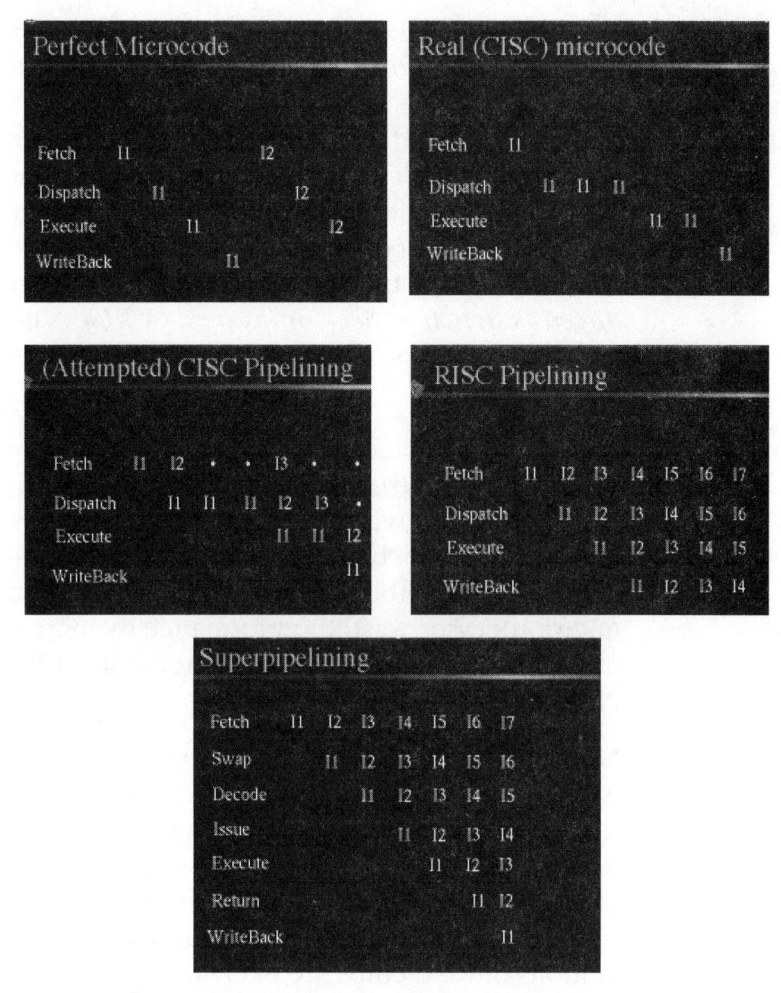

Figure 6-3: Principles of pipelining. (Source: Apple Computer.)

Advanced technologies employ *superscalar pipelining*, or multiple pipelines running at the same time. This technology requires more steps, and instructions can be sent back into the queue if needed for more efficient processing. Compilers do their best to optimize instructions sent to the pipeline, but there always is some pipeline stall intrinsic in any architecture.

The commands that a system issues to a microprocessor are called its *instruction set*. The simpler an instruction set is, the more instructions it needs to do a certain task, the larger its programming and memory requirements, and the faster and more efficiently it must operate. Smaller instructions also process more quickly. A rich, complex instruction set requires less instruction, less memory, and less programming. Microprocessors using small instruction sets are called *Reduced Instruction Set Computers*, or *RISC*, and those with large instruction sets are called *Complex Instruction Set Computers,* or *CISC*.

The Intel 80x86 and Motorola 680x0 microprocessors at the heart of most personal computers are CISC chips. CISC chips were developed when RAM was limited and expensive. Maximizing the instruction set meant minimizing the memory requirements. Although increasing the complexity of the microprocessor wasted performance by increasing system overhead (resulting in larger, hotter and harder-to-design chips), CISC made sense.

Much of what's in a complex instruction set isn't used often. About 20 percent of the instructions are used 80 percent of the time. Therefore, by simplifying the instruction set, combining simple instructions to create complex ones and running a RISC processor faster and more efficiently, you can see tremendous performance benefits. What's more, future generations of RISC chips are likely to get faster than a CISC architecture would, because of the reduction of programming and logic overhead.

A design principle in RISC is to use a fixed-length instruction size so that it is easier for the compiler to optimize instructions sent to the pipeline and to prevent pipeline stall. RISC chips are simpler to design, cheaper to create, and are smaller, less complex and cooler to run. These principles are at the heart of the decision to migrate the Macintosh to a RISC-based architecture.

Figure 6-4 shows Apple's projections for the two different architectures. In Table 6-1 the PowerPC 601 and Pentium chip, both operating near 66 MHz, are compared. The source of this information was an Apple white paper, compiled from the magazine studies shown. The relative sizes of the chips are somewhat misleading because the PPC chips use a large on-board cache to improve performance. The size of the logic components should be compared.

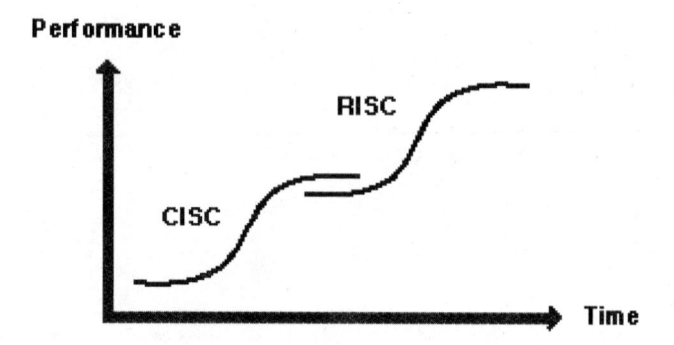

Figure 6-4: CISC vs. RISC performance over time (by Apple Computer).

Table 6-1: PowerPC vs. Pentium. (Source: Apple Computer.)

Feature	PowerPC 601	Pentium
Architecture	64-bit RISC	32-bit CISC
Age of architecture	3 years	15 to 20 years[1]
Primary operating system	32 bit[2]	16 bit[3]
Transistor count	2.8 million	3.1 million
Core logic transistor count	~1.2 million[4]	~2.3 million[4]
On-chip cache size	32K	16K
Die size	118.8 mm^2	262.4 mm^2
Heat dissipation at 66 MHz	9 watts	16 watts
Performance—integer at 66 MHz	>60 SPECint92	64.5 SPECint92
Performance—floating point at 66 MHz	>80 SPECfp92	56.9 SPECfp92
Estimated manufacturing cost[5]	$76	$483
Maximum instructions per cycle[6]	3	2
General-purpose registers	32 32-bit registers	8 32-bit registers
Floating-point registers	32 64-bit registers	8 80-bit registers

[1] Number of years depends on whether the 8080 or the 8086 is used as the starting point.
[2] System 7
[3] MS-DOS and Windows 3.1
[4] Total transistor count minus the number of transistors devoted to on-chip cache.
[5] Based on MicroDesign Research estimates published in *Microprocessor Report*, August 2, 1993.
[6] *BYTE*, August 1993, page 84.
* *Microprocessor Report*, August 2, 1993.
** *PC Week*, September 13, 1993, page 22.

The PowerPC Series

IBM developed a RISC architecture for its 801 and series RS/6000 workstations based on the Power chip set. When Apple decided to build RISC-based personal computers, they entered into a joint venture with IBM to create a chip called the PowerPC (PPC). That chip incorporates the core functions of the Power chip set into one large RISC chip. Motorola was chosen to be the third partner in the alliance, fabricating the chips. All three companies worked together on the project at the Somerset Design Center in Austin, Texas, where the chips were created.

In 1993, the 601 chip was the first PPC to be released. The 603 and 604 chips are due out in late 1994. The 603 is meant for lower power consumption (primarily PowerBooks), and the 604 for higher end applications. The 604 is expected to be two to three times faster than the 601 chip it will replace.

Also being designed is the 620 PowerPC chip, a 64-bit chip with full multiprocessing that is expected to be 10 times faster than a 601. The 620 should ship in mid- to late 1995. Add six months to a year to these dates and you'll get the dates you should expect to see the first Power Macintosh computers based on these chips.

Apple chose to call its computers Power Macintosh to emphasize that it uses the Power technology but still is a Macintosh. The same chip powers computers made by IBM and others. The Power Macintosh had a successful introduction, selling 250,000 units in its first quarter. Although that pace has slowed somewhat, it is expected to increase as Apple draws down its stock of older 68k Macintosh computers.

The PowerPC chip was designed to run both Intel- and Motorola-type software so that it could run any operating system a vendor might apply. To facilitate this capability, the PowerPC chip accommodates both *little endian* and *big endian* instructions. Little endian puts the least significant byte first and is used in the Intel 80x86 architecture. Big endian is the reverse and is used by Macintosh computers running the Motorola 680x0 series. It's completely analogous to writing a language right-to-left vs. left-to-right. PowerPC chips can do either.

Another goal of the PowerPC project is to create a new UNIX operating system called PowerOpen. This system would be based on IBM's AIX and Apple's A/UX operating systems. Taligent, the Apple/IBM programming alliance, is also expected to release an operating system in 1995.

The trade press devoted numerous pages to the performance of the PowerPC 601 Macintosh computers vs. Pentium-based PC systems. The comparision between the two is spurious as Motorola and Intel race to produce faster chips based on increased clock rates. Also, the Pentium is no longer a CISC-only chip, incorporating many RISC techniques in its architecture. Pentium has more chip overhead to support old 8088 code than the PowerPC chip, so versions of the PowerPC will likely get faster quicker. But both chips have reasonable futures and the selection of either chip is equally acceptable.

By now you may have seen a demonstration of a Power Macintosh at a store or trade show, or even worked on one. The experience is a pleasant one, and the speed enhancement is significant—but not, as one magazine said, "phenomenal." Running a 601 Power Macintosh with a native application at three times the speed of a Quadra 800 isn't going to change the *way* you use your computer. You'll have to wait a year or two until the second generation 620 chips arrive with a tenfold speed boost. Those computers should enable significant new technologies with rapid processing of rich data types (video, sound and so on).

Some perspective is in order. Consider QuickTime. A threefold system increase in speed can double the area of a window and improve the frame rates somewhat. A tenfold processor increase coupled with some expected improvements in the technology over the next year and a half could make full-screen full-motion video a reality. Similar improvements in speech and other audiovisual technologies are also possible, as are other more fundamental refinements.

A new 4mb ROM in the Power Macintosh accompanied System 7.1.2's release. It contains the small nanokernel of code for PowerPC support. The nanokernel is the core assembly language routines that can control the RISC microprocessor and perform Input/Output for higher level functions.

The nanokernel is the first part of the microkernel core scheduled for release in Copeland. The microkernel will enable the Macintosh operating system to be ported easily to other microprocessors, and make memory protection and preemptive scheduling or true multitasking possible. These features are discussed more fully in Chapter 8, "Memory Management." IBM also is developing a microkernel architecture, and they are somewhat ahead of Apple's development because the Power chip set was an IBM architecture.

The PowerPC microprocessor has hardwired support for just one system interrupt. Macintosh users have been spared the nonsense of understanding and working with interrupt levels, but they are the bane of PC users. Just ask one who has tried to install a sound board in a PC (although the new plug-and-play PC hardware-specification support in Windows 4 may help PC users in this respect). Interrupt levels provide the timing events necessary to make your system run. To recreate the behavior that Macintosh software and hardware expects, the nanokernel recreates in ROM and a custom chip the eight different Macintosh interrupts that drivers and system software require.

System 7.1.2 and 7.5 and the new Modern Memory Manager introduced a whole new set of conventions for loading code into memory, the location of data in memory, how functions call other functions or system routines, and more. The use of 32k code segments was at the heart of why desk accessories were created in the first place, and was responsible for a whole host of system software limitations. System and application code competed in this arrangement and sometimes clashed.

In the new software for Power Macs, this model is replaced by a dynamic scheme of loading code through the low-level Code Fragment Manager, regardless of the source of the code. The whole run-time programming environment for the Power Macintosh is different, although the old 68k Mac version is still supported. These differences may not be readily apparent to you as a user.

What you will notice is that with virtual memory enabled on a Power Macintosh, native-mode applications will require less memory when running. System software uses a system called *file mapping* that loads code fragments from your hard drive to memory without using an intermediate virtual memory swap file that was present in earlier system versions. Starting with System 7.1.2, it is recommended that you turn on virtual memory all the time.

System 7.1.2 introduced shared libraries of programming code managed by the Shared Library Manager. This system is similar to dynamic linked libraries (DLLs) used in Microsoft Windows. Only called procedures are loaded into memory for shared libraries, however, not the entire library. There's less programming overhead in system software now because of better memory management. File mapping and shared libraries are a central feature of the OpenDoc compound document architecture.

Emulation vs. Native Routines

One level above the nanokernel is the software that makes it possible to run Macintosh programs on a PowerPC chip: the 600x0 microprocessor emulator. An emulator is a translator program that interprets programming meant for one operating system by another: here translating between 68k and PPC native code. The price you pay for emulation is performance.

Any operating system can be emulated in software, even the Macintosh—provided you know what the internal routines are. Not knowing just makes the task of writing an emulator somewhat harder. This process of writing code to emulate software is called reverse-engineering. Compaq was the first to reverse-engineer the IBM PC BIOS, and others have reverse-engineered the Macintosh. You are, perhaps, familiar with Insignia Solutions's products: SoftPC and SoftWindows, emulators for Microsoft's popular operating system. When emulation is done using the "official" Microsoft library of Windows routines, as Insignia Solutions has done with SoftWindows, then compatibility is high.

SoftWindows even comes bundled with some Power Macintosh computers, and that's about the only way you are going to find it to be useful. In its original 7.1.2 incarnation, SoftWindows emulates Intel's 80286 and 80287 computers, appearing about as fast as a 25 MHz 486SX machine without some of the advanced memory management techniques of Windows 3.1 (extended memory). A true 486 emulator should be available by the time you read this book. To get more information, you can call Insignia Solutions at 415-694-7600.

The 580k emulator for the Power Macintosh was written by engineer Gary Davidian at Apple, and it represents a major Apple achievement. Because memory management was rewritten for PPC, and floating-point operations are also routed to the PPC, emulation is officially that of the original Mac II as a 68020 microprocessor. Memory management and floating-point operations were the major new features of the 68030 and 68040 microprocessors that were missing in the 68020. However, other 68040 routines are supported, and the new Modern Memory Manager (described in Chapter 8) was added. Therefore, Apple describes the 580k emulator as a 68LC040 emulator.

Macintosh software looks, feels and operates like Macintosh software because it calls a set of routines in the Macintosh toolbox. The toolbox is a set of standard system software services available to any program running on the Macintosh. Apple publishes these programming calls in its *Inside Macintosh* book series published by Addison-Wesley. System software began its transition from 68k code to native PowerPC code with the 7.1.2 release. About 10 percent of the code was translated in that release. In System 7.5, about 20 percent of the code has been rewritten.

The number of toolbox routines that run in native mode continues to grow over time. In the 7.1.2 release, the following routines were native: QuickDraw, DrawText, Memory Manager, Font Manager, TrueType scaler, integer math and floating point (SANE) routines, BlockMove, Component Manager and trap dispatching. In System 7.5, QuickDraw GX (see Chapter 9) and AOCE (see Chapter 14) were added to the list. Others soon to be upgraded past 7.5 are the Finder, icon drawing routines, PlainTalk, PowerTalk and the SCSI Manager 4.3. The File System routines will probably be among the last sets rewritten. You may see many of these changes appear as interim releases on online services; others will be part of future system software versions.

Because native code runs much faster on a Power Macintosh than emulated code runs, you would expect that having 80 percent of the code running in emulation would negate any speed advantage that the new RISC chips give you. In fact, an analysis of just which routines are called most often in the 68k instruction set suggested that rewriting just 15 percent of the code into native form would give 80 percent of the speed increase you'd expect from completely native code. This rule of emulation let Apple make an early introduction of PowerPC. System 7.5 on a Power Macintosh appears, in emulation, roughly as fast as a Quadra 700. A lot of variance is based on the actual piece of software used, however.

As all the system software is rewritten (a process that should be complete about the end of 1995), you will see system software get somewhat faster in emulation—not much faster than now, but somewhat faster. The full effect of PowerPC performance is best seen in native mode applications where only native code is used. Native software running on the 601 machines is about three times faster than the fastest Quadras—some routines are as much as five times faster.

The Mixed Mode Manager

At the heart of the emulator is a new set of operating system routines called the Mixed Mode Manager. This component analyzes toolbox calls and routes them to the PowerPC microprocessor if possible or the emulator if necessary. You can think of the Mixed Mode Manager as just a fancy kind of two-way switch. In order to improve performance, the Mixed Mode Manager has a "look-ahead" function that minimizes state changes.

Because of the way the Mixed Mode Manager is constructed, switching between sending instructions to the 68LC040 emulated toolbox and the PPC-native toolbox is a time-consuming task. Routines that force mode switching are called *fat traps*. These "mode switches" are programmatically transparent but require about 50 680x0 instructions, or about 15 microseconds. That's a long time for a speedy CPU and thus a considerable system drag.

Apple was able to rewrite many of the routines that force mixed mode switching, many of them very small precursors to larger routines. Because Apple left 68k and native routines in both toolboxes, you see a marked improvement in emulation performance because the mode will not switch over when it's faster to execute 68k code. However, fat traps also show up in some system extensions such as Adobe's Type Manager and Type Reunion, Berkeley Systems's After Dark,

Farallon's Timbuktu and Fifth Generation's Suitcase II. The solution to the problem with these programs is, unfortunately, to upgrade to newer Power Macintosh-compatible versions as they become available.

Figure 6-5 shows you the important components of a Power Macintosh System 7.5 installation as a block diagram.

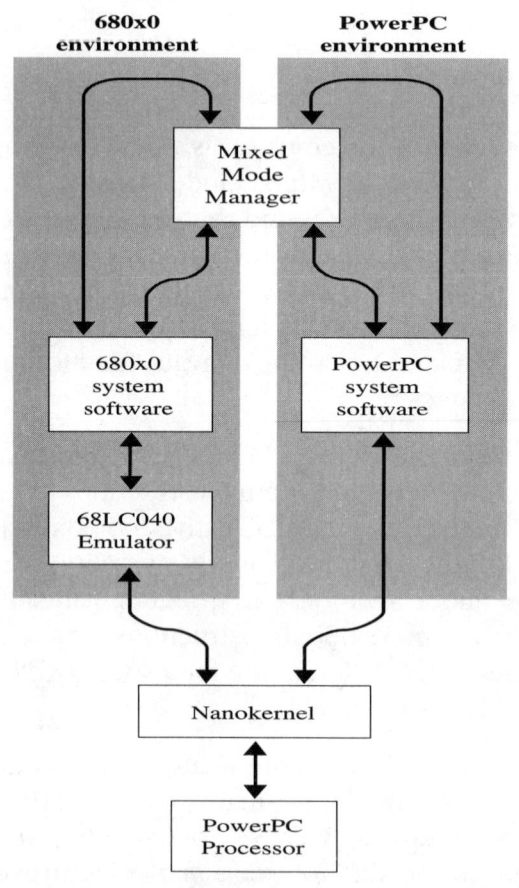

Figure 6-5: System 7.5 Power Macintosh implementation.

Improving Application Performance

The whole system of emulation, a Mixed Mode Manager, and native routines works surprisingly well. Early reviewers were surprised by the remarkable compatibility and stability that the Power Macintosh has shown with System 7.1.2. System 7.5 improves upon the dramatic performance. Chances are that you could go into your library of old Macintosh software and dig out a version of an application or game that no longer runs on a PowerBook, Centris or Quadra and have it run properly on your Power Macintosh. What few software problems you may encounter are most likely due to the factors noted in this section.

When 68k applications call for floating-point operations using the SANE (Standard Apple Numeric Environment) routines, those calls are trapped and rerouted to slower native-PPC integer routines, not the faster PPC 601 floating-point instructions, as you would expect. Applications of this type do extensive number crunching; they include spreadsheets, graphics, 3-D visualization applications and so on—just the kind of applications that you bought your Power Macintosh to run. Native applications run floating-point operations in native mode and are much faster.

Another issue is that the PowerPC chips don't include a math coprocessor. Applications that call on your math coprocessor for 68k Macintosh computers will freeze a Power Macintosh. You can get around this problem by using the shareware control panel Software FPU (use version 2.43 or later), but this solution is a kludge. Even with FPU on, programs running in emulation calling a math coprocessor will crawl compared to their performance on a Quadra.

Starting with the 68040 (Quadra series) chips, Motorola redesigned the on-board cache. Some programs could not run with the cache enabled. Caching is a major feature of the Power Macintosh series as well. To disable the 040 cache, use the Cache Switch control panel (see Figure 6-6) to turn it off. You may notice a slight performance decrease.

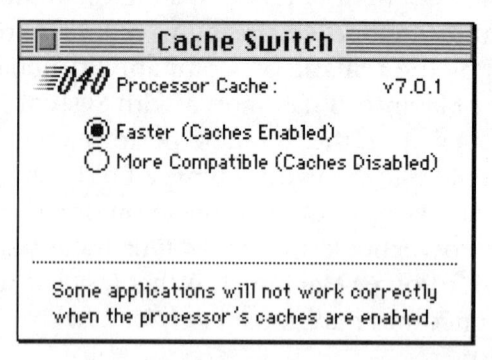

Figure 6-6: The 040 Cache Switch control panel.

The major upgrade from the 68020 to 68030 chip was the memory management unit. Few programs suffer from the lack of a paged memory management unit (PMMU); most problems relate to FPU or math coprocessor code. The only real relief to floating-point performance and math coprocessor calls is to upgrade to native applications when they become available. Most of the major applications have been or are probably close to being upgraded. Until then you may be better off running your critical processor-intensive applications on a Macintosh Quadra.

Power Macintosh-Specific Software

The process of converting software to PowerPC code can be easy or hard depending on the language that the software was originally written in. Software written in C or C++ ports well due to good language tools. Software written in Pascal (FileMaker Pro, for example) may require a major rewrite to produce a PowerPC version. The speed of conversion of software to PowerPC code is largely dependent on this major factor.

For older software requiring rewriting and not simple conversion, vendors have made the early investment in native applications when the performance benefit made a significant difference. Graphics programs such as Aldus Freehand and PageMaker, Adobe Illustrator and Premier, DeltaGraph Pro, Fractal Design Painter, Frame Technologies' FrameMaker, Ray Dream Designer, and Wolfram Research's Mathematica, among others, were early adopters. Programs such as ClarisWorks (originally written in C++) and WordPerfect got early translation. WordPerfect used its conversion as an advantage over Word 6.0, an entrenched competitor. About 50 major native applications shipped within 60 days of the Power Macintosh release (June 1994); by the end of the year, that number should be around 200 major applications.

What you pay for these software upgrades depends on the vendor: some will upgrade as part of their normal upgrade path; others will upgrade for nominal fees; and a few other vendors are treating the Power Macintosh as a brand new computer platform and sticking you for the full application price.

Software vendors can write programs that are either native, use emulation mode, or are a combination of the two called a *fat binary* (or just a *fat*) application. Having a fat binary application doesn't automatically mean that the application will be twice the size of one of the other types. Code segments made large by screen elements (windows, dialog boxes and other resources) can be shared between the two kinds of code. Fat applications are expected to be about 25 to 70 percent larger than other kinds, with a 50 percent increase being average.

As a rule of thumb, native applications are naturally about 20 percent larger than the same 68k-based applications. This increase is a result of RISC code requiring more instructions due to a reduced instruction set. Just how much size increase an application incurs in the port depends on the original language and the programming skills of the developer.

WordPerfect 2 was originally written in assembly language, small compact code close to machine (CPU) language, so it experienced a considerable size increase going to PPC, Version 3. FrameMaker 4 was written from code used on UNIX and suffered little size increase in translation.

However software vendors choose to write their programs, options are also available for installing applications. Vendors shipping native or emulation software can write an installer that installs just the right *files* into your model of Macintosh. For fat binary applications, some vendors will use smart installers. A smart installer will install just the right *code* that your Macintosh requires. Some applications (like Adobe's) will let you install the larger fat binary applications, if you choose. Doing so would allow you to use the software you install on any other Macintosh. You may find some differences in pricing based on these software options.

PowerBook Issues

The Apple PowerBook 100 series was the most successful introduction of any family of portable computers in history. The PowerBook replaced the ill-fated Portable, and Apple learned volumes from the experience. Millions of Macintosh users have not just supplemented their computing needs, but replaced their desktop machines as well. Minimal system software support for the PowerBook series began with System 7.0.1 but has grown stronger over the past three years.

PowerBook users have the following requirements:

- **Improved battery lifetime between recharges.** Various techniques to reduce power consumption are slowing down the processor, reducing screen brightness, spinning down hard drives, reducing hard disk input and output (I/O) using a RAM disk and going to system sleep. All these capabilities are supported in system software.

- **Easy connection.** PowerBook users require automatic remounting of hard drives and network servers upon wakeup, remote access, and other features for which there is now system support.

You can use the PowerBook Setup control panel shown in Figure 6-7 to connect your PowerBook to another Macintosh as if it were an external hard drive or another SCSI device.

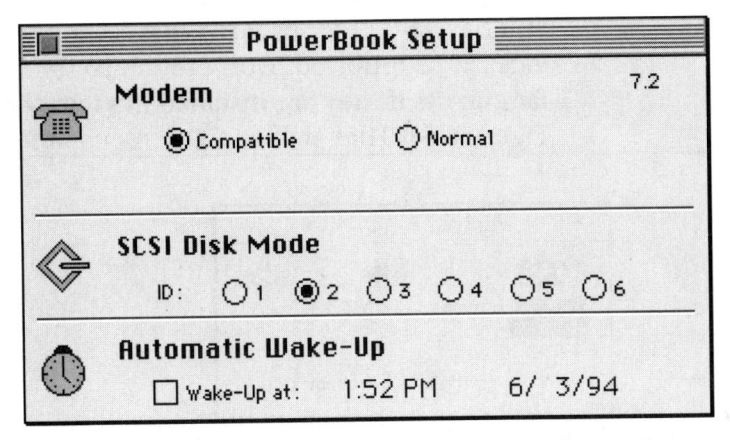

Figure 6-7: The PowerBook Setup control panel.

- **Presentation services.** PowerBooks manage external displays. Video-out is a feature of many models, as is video mirroring. These features are provided in an updated Monitors control panel.

- **Spooling of print documents for later printing.** You can store documents to a printer with a "Print Later" feature, which is enabled by the Assistant toolbox extension, and print them when you are connected to that printer. When you try to print to a printer that isn't connected, you will get a dialog box asking you if you want the document stored. Printing occurs automatically the next time you connect to that printer.

The Assistant toolbox, a component of System 7.5, supplements your PowerBook support. It adds features such as mouse tracks and fat cursors (in the Mouse panel), a keystroke for instant sleep or hard drive spin down, and some screen dimming. You can add this to earlier system versions by purchasing the PowerBook File Assistance package, which is meant primarily for file synchronization.

- **Peripheral support.** Keyboards, trackballs, trackpads (if you have a 500 series PowerBook) and other ADB devices are supported. Don't forget to try mouse tracks and fat cursors if they are installed in your system (shown in Figure 6-8). They make LCD screens much easier to use.

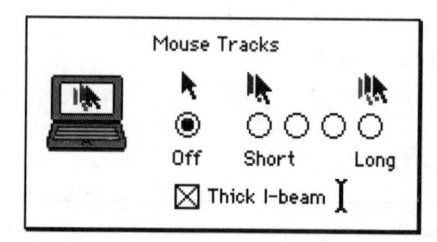

Figure 6-8: Mouse tracks and fat cursors in the Mouse control panel.

- **File synchronization.** In order to update files on a PowerBook with your other Macintosh computers, you can use the Macintosh File Assistant for this task.

System 7.5 adds a number of new features that PowerBook users will appreciate, notably a convenient Control Strip utility and the File Assistant. Most other PowerBook utilities have been reworked to a small extent in System 7.5.

There is much to know about PowerBooks, and not enough space in this book to cover it. Two books you might appreciate are *The PowerBook Companion*, Second Edition, by Sharon Zardetto Akker and Bruce Wolfson, 1993, Addison-

Wesley; and *PowerBook: The Digital Nomad's Guide*, by Andrew Gore and Mitch Radcliffe, 1993, Random House. Although both books are good, the Akker/Wolfson book is more up to date in a rapidly changing marketplace.

Power/Performance Management

The power consumption of PowerBooks is a major portability issue, particularly with models using NiCad batteries and color screens. System software employs a number of techniques to reduce power consumption through the PowerBook control panel in System 7.5. You can view this control panel in its Easy view as in Figure 6-9 or in the Custom view shown in Figure 6-10.

Figure 6-9: The PowerBook control panel in the Easy view.

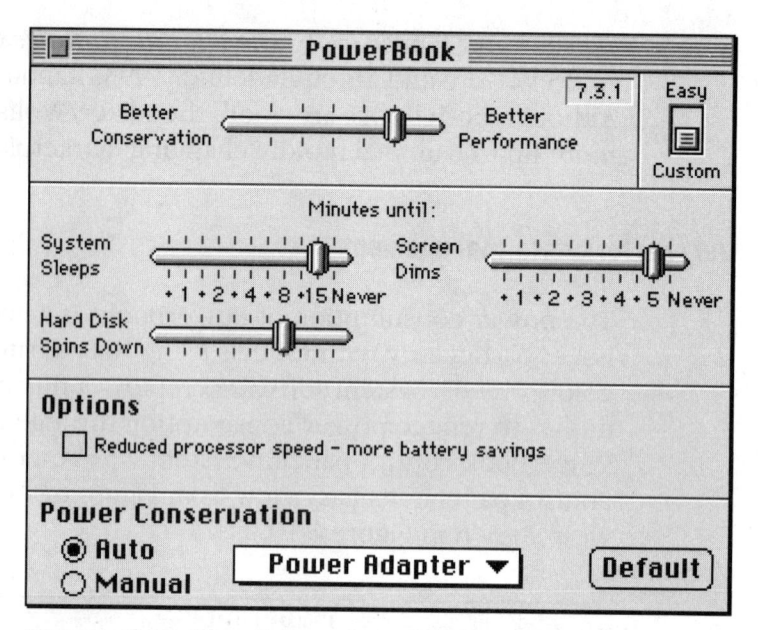

Figure 6-10: The Custom view of the PowerBook control panel.

You want easy? Move the Battery Conservation slider to the Better Conservation side of the slider to increase battery longevity. Use this setting when you aren't plugged in somewhere. Move the setting to Better Performance when you are plugged in. Your PowerBook translates your settings into the time it takes to dim your screen, spin down your hard drive and go to system sleep, among other things. As a rule of thumb, when you are on the road, use Better Conservation until you notice performance differences that bother you.

You can monitor your battery's performance by viewing the Battery desk accessory shown in Figure 6-11 (from System 7.1). This battery has eight bars that change color as a function of your battery's *voltage* level. When all eight bars are black, you are fully recharged. Bars go white from right to left as your battery depletes. You get two warnings about power depletion before your last warning, which is 10 seconds before your PowerBook is sent to sleep. In System 7.5, this desk accessory is replaced by the Battery Monitor in the Control Strip utility.

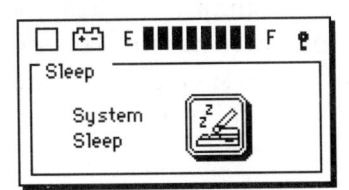

Figure 6-11: The System 7.1 Battery desk accessory shown fully charged and open.

This system of measuring voltage levels is accurate and reliable, as far as it goes. What voltage measurements don't tell you is how much time your battery has left. For that indicator, you need to know the lowest voltage level your battery will drop to, your instantaneous power consumption and the history of power consumption you have had. Anomalies such as which battery you are using, memory effects, unusual power consumption activities and other factors make learning your battery's life a difficult proposition. So the power warnings you get only tell you voltage levels, not how long you have left on a battery.

Battery life is such a valuable measurement that newer Blackbird 500 series PowerBooks have switched to batteries with microprocessors in them. These new batteries give more accurate measurements in the Battery Monitor section of the PowerBook Control Strip, and an estimated time is given in hours. For models with two batteries, you see a Control Strip like the one in Figure 6-15.

Surprisingly, your microprocessor is a major energy draw, at about 25 percent current used. The other major power draw is the display, which depending on its type can consume anywhere from 20 percent (black and white) to 50 percent (color) of your current. (Display issues are covered in the next section of this chapter.)

Most later model PowerBooks contain a microprocessor capable of lower energy consumption states. In one state, the CPU goes down to a lower clock rate. This feature is called *processor cycling*, and it can save energy when you use it. This state is different from the processor *sleep state,* in which only CPU memory is preserved.

To turn on processor cycling, use the Custom section of the PowerBook control panel, and click the Reduced processor speed check box in the Options section. (Refer to Figure 6-10.) Because your processor fires up instantaneously, processor cycling is a good feature to enable when you are on battery power. These and other power consumption routines are part of the Power Manager in the Macintosh toolbox that first appeared in System 6.

Sleep is the condition in which your hard drive is spun down, your screen powered off, and your microprocessor is put in a quiet comatose state. Each component can be put to sleep separately. Sleep is a perfectly safe condition for transporting your PowerBook and storing it for short periods. Depending on the model, your PowerBook can retain contents of memory for two weeks in this condition. A major factor in this equation is the amount of memory you have installed that needs to be refreshed.

You have several ways of putting your PowerBook to sleep in System 7.5:

- Choose the Sleep command from the Special menu.
- Press the Command-Shift-Zero keystroke (added by the Assistant toolbox).
- Click the Sleep portion of the Battery desk accessory in Systems 7.0.1 through 7.1.1.

- Set the period of inactivity for automatic sleep in the PowerBook control panel (Figure 6-7).
- Click the Sleep Now icon in the Control Strip (Figure 6-15).

Press any keystroke other than the Caps Lock to wake your Macintosh up from sleep.

Your hard drive is another source of power draw for a PowerBook. It's estimated to consume about 15 percent of your power, on average. You can do some things to improve the power consumption of this element:

- Use memory-resident (RAM) applications that don't require much I/O.
- Press the Command-Shift-Control-Zero keystroke to spin down your hard drive instantly (added by the Assistant toolbox).
- Set the period of inactivity for automatic hard drive spin down in the PowerBook control panel (Figure 6-7).
- Click the HD Spin Down icon in the PowerBook Control Strip (Figure 6-15) to spin down a drive instantly.
- Use a RAM disk to limit disk access. This feature is covered in Chapter 8, "Memory Management," and is part of the Memory control panel.

Don't get too carried away with keeping your hard drive spun down. The energy expended in spinning up a hard drive is equivalent to something like 30 seconds to a minute of the hard drive spinning at its rated speed. You need to be in situations in which you don't access the disk more than every two or three minutes at a time for this feature to be valuable.

Similarly, keeping AppleTalk active takes a minor amount of power. The serial port must be polled for activity. Using the AppleTalk serial switch accessed from the Control Panels or from the AppleTalk Serial icon of the PowerBook Control Strip (Figure 6-15), you can turn AppleTalk on and off. Another minor factor is File Sharing, which you can also turn on and off from the File Sharing icon in the Control Strip.

Display Management

You can achieve substantial battery savings by simply turning down your display screen. This savings is particularly true for color Macintosh computers for which the screen is the major power draw. The PowerBook control panel will blank your screen after some period of inactivity but not dim it. You can manually dim your screen using the slider or button on your PowerBook model. If you want finer control, then you need to purchase a third-party utility for that purpose. You may be surprised by the substantial amount of dimming that is possible in low-light conditions.

An external monitor is one of the nicest features of a PowerBook. Many PowerBooks have built-in video support and video-out ports, which are signified by the TV icon on the PowerBook. This is true of the 160, 180, 200 and 500 series PowerBooks. You can supplement other models to add video-out through external devices. (You can also buy adapters to run a monitor from your SCSI chain, with a somewhat lower performance quality.) A video adapter that will enable you to connect the video-out port to an external monitor is also supplied with your PowerBook.

You can plug in a monitor during sleep or at shutdown. When you start up your Macintosh, the external monitor is powered up. After the start-up icons appear on your PowerBook, the desktop should appear on the external monitor. If the desktop does not appear, open the Monitors control panel and drag the menu bar from the icon of your PowerBook screen to the icon of the external monitor.

7.5 In System 7.5, you can have changes to the external monitor take effect as soon as you shut the Monitors control panel. This behavior is enabled by the new Display Manager, which is part of System 7.5. For System 7.0.1 or 7.1, you may need to restart your Macintosh once again.

You cannot go into system sleep with your PowerBook when an external monitor is in use. For larger external displays, it is recommended that you leave processor cycling turned on so that your battery can recharge and so that your battery doesn't get too hot. External screen blanking will occur based on your setting in the PowerBook control panel. You can also turn down your PowerBook screen manually. Almost any activity will turn your screen back on.

When working in presentation mode, you may find it convenient to have the same display on your external monitor that appears on your PowerBook. This process is called video mirroring. To turn on video mirroring, use the PowerBook Display control panel, as shown in Figure 6-12.

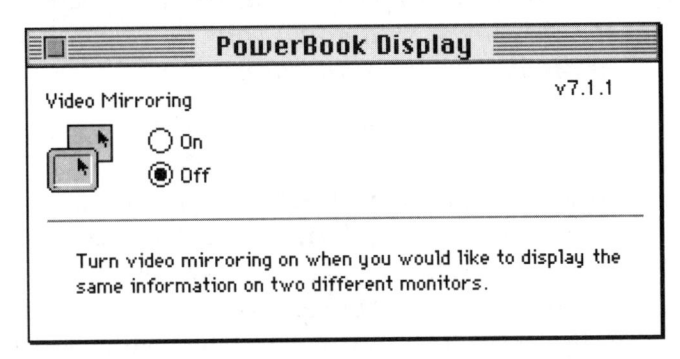

Figure 6-12: The PowerBook Display control panel.

Connections, Remounting & Remote Access

System software makes connecting your Macintosh to other drives, Macintosh computers, networks and phone lines easier. Some of these capabilities are there for you, right out of the box. The connection features that are different for PowerBooks are mentioned in this section.

The ability to mount a PowerBook as an external hard drive, the so-called *SCSI disk mode*, is a useful feature. You enable this mode using the PowerBook control panel shown in Figure 6-7. The original PowerBook 100 had this feature, and although it disappeared with the PowerBook 140 and 180, it reappeared for later models. A mounted PowerBook can be convenient for file synchronization because SCSI is a high-speed data bus. See "File Synchronization" later in this chapter.

Caution: *You need to pay special attention to SCSI termination for PowerBook chains; otherwise, you can run into trouble with the SCSI disk mode. Refer to your PowerBook manual or third-party books for more details. Also, you should always shut down your PowerBook before making or breaking SCSI connections.*

AutoRemounter is a control panel that performs a simple but necessary task (see Figure 6-13). When your PowerBook goes to sleep or disconnects from a network, normally servers and shared volumes are dismounted. AutoRemounter remembers these connections and can automatically remount disks when waking, or can require a password to be entered. Automatically asking for a password is safer when you are connected to a network and are leaving your PowerBook on.

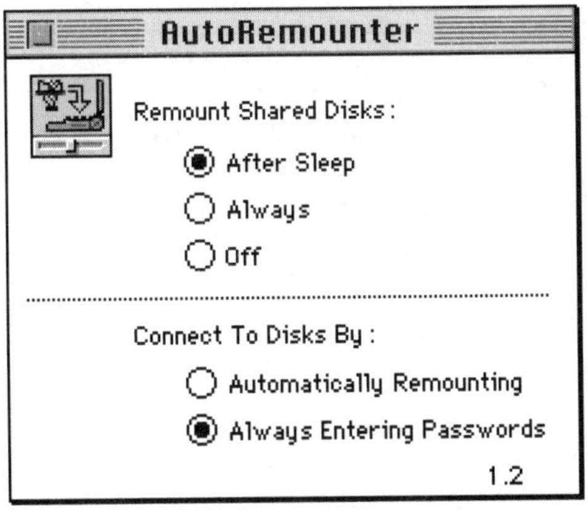

Figure 6-13: AutoRemounter.

AutoRemounter first shipped in System 7.1, and it does not work with early PowerBooks (100, 140, 145 and 170). Without AutoRemounter, you need to mount your volumes manually and reestablish network connections.

Unfortunately, one of the most useful adjuncts to system software for PowerBooks has not yet been included in the standard release. It is Apple Remote Access (ARA). It is mentioned here in passing because it is a terrific product that can connect you while you are on the road via modem to remote servers. Apple Remote Access is sold by AppleSoft in a client version (Figure 6-14) and various server configurations.

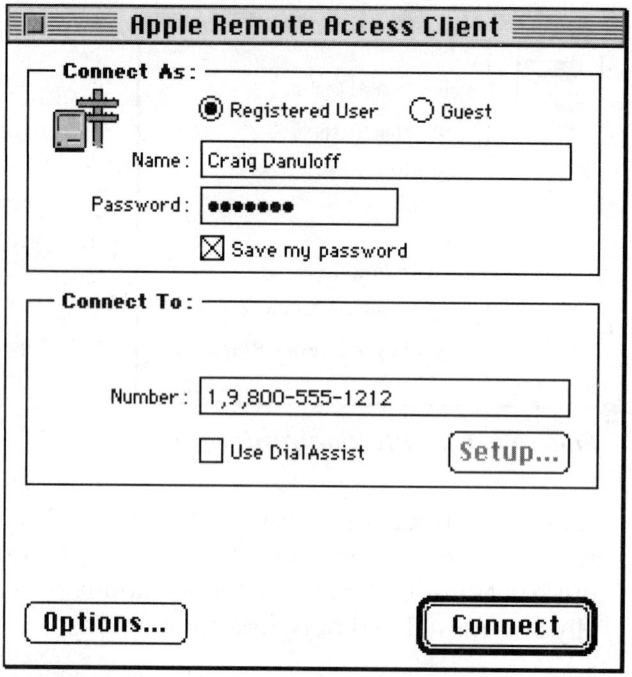

Figure 6-14: Apple Remote Access Client.

You can set up your desktop Macintosh to receive incoming calls and then dial in using ARA. Using the Apple Remote Access MultiPort Server, you can configure a Macintosh to accept several incoming ARA sessions. Some companies also sell dedicated multiline ARA servers that replace a Macintosh and a set of modems.

Once you supply a password or have ARA supply it, you are connected just as you would be in an office. Modem connections are a slow data exchange medium, so without fast modems ARA is best used as a message exchange medium. For high-speed modems (14,400 baud and above), you can use ARA to do large file exchanges using File Sharing, remote database work with serious data manipulation and other tasks. ARA can be a good place to try program linking.

The PowerBook Control Strip

7.5 ▶ Because third parties have expressed so much interest in PowerBook utilities and the class of application has been so popular, Apple decided to include an extensible PowerBook utility in System 7.5. It's called the Control Strip, and by default it's on your screen. (To turn off the Control Strip, use the Control Strip control panel shown in Figure 6-15.) The Control Strip (shown in Figure 6-16) is a floating palette that appears as the topmost window on your PowerBook screen, regardless of your current application. It's one of System 7.5's nicest small features.

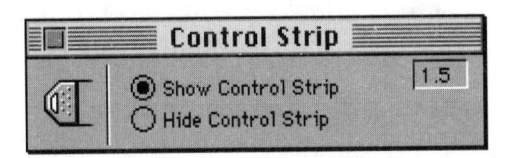

Figure 6-15: The PowerBook Control Slip control panel.

Figure 6-16: The PowerBook Control Strip shown for a PowerBook 500 series computer with dual intelligent batteries.

Each icon contains a pop-up menu that enables you to select from a set of options. Most are simple on and off settings, but more commands may be added over time. Some additional Control Strip modules may appear as third-party shareware because Apple has published the needed specifications.

The Control Strip has the following features (from left to right):

- **Close box.** Click to close the strip down to the Control Tab. To remove the Control Strip, use the Control Strip control panel shown in Figure 6-15.

- **Scroll arrows.** Use these arrows (on both ends of the strip) to view additional panels that may be hidden.

- **Battery monitor.** The monitor indicates both voltage and estimated battery lifetime. Icons indicate if the battery is full, discharging or charging.

- **AppleTalk switch.** By turning AppleTalk off, you can save power. This switch duplicates the function found in the Chooser.

- **File Sharing.** You can manually turn File Sharing on and off using this panel. You can also check to see who's connected. This panel duplicates functions found in the Sharing Setup and File Sharing Monitor control panels. Refer to Chapter 13, "Working on a Network," for more details.

- **HD Spin Down.** This feature spins down your drive.

- **Sleep Now.** This feature puts your computer into system sleep.

- **Sound volume.** Drag to the sound level you desire. This feature recreates the Sound slider in the Sound control panel.

- **Video mirroring.** Use this switch to turn on video mirroring without taking a trip to the PowerBook Display panel.

- **Tab.** Drag the Tab to resize the Control Strip. Click the Tab to shrink the strip to just the Tab. When you are viewing just the Tab, click the Tab to view the Control Strip again.

You will note some differences between Control Strips installed on different models of PowerBooks. For example, only intelligent batteries give time estimates, and only models with video-out capabilities support the video mirroring panel.

You can also remove modules from the Control Strip folder of the System Folder, as desired. To shorten the Control Strip, drag the Tab to the left. You can view modules in the shortened strip by clicking the left- and right-facing arrows at the end of the Control Strip. To collapse the Control Strip to just a Tab, click the close box at the left of the strip.

File Synchronization

When you use two or more computers for your work, tracking file changes can be tedious. You want to always work with the most current version of your work and not have to recreate changes. You can do this using a procedure called *file synchronization*. When you create or modify a file, it is time-stamped with the date and time of your system. Then you can replace older files with newer ones, adding new files to folders that didn't contain them.

If you had to track all these changes manually, you probably wouldn't do this important task. Therefore, you can use the PowerBook File Assistant for this important task. With this utility (part of System 7.5, or purchased separately), you can designate files and folders that you want updated. The utility is basic and easy to learn. You only need to connect your two computers directly via a network or with modems to use the File Assistant.

In the PowerBook File Assistant Setup dialog box (see Figure 6-17) that you see when you launch the program, you can simply drag and drop (for System 7.1 and later) files and folders that you want synchronized. You link pairs of items on either side of the arrow into linked sets. For earlier system versions, you need to use the Select An Item to Synchronize (Command-E) from the File menu and make selections in a standard File dialog box. You can create as many pairs as you wish, and scroll the window to review them. Using the Preferences command from the File menu, you can also link nonmatching named folders.

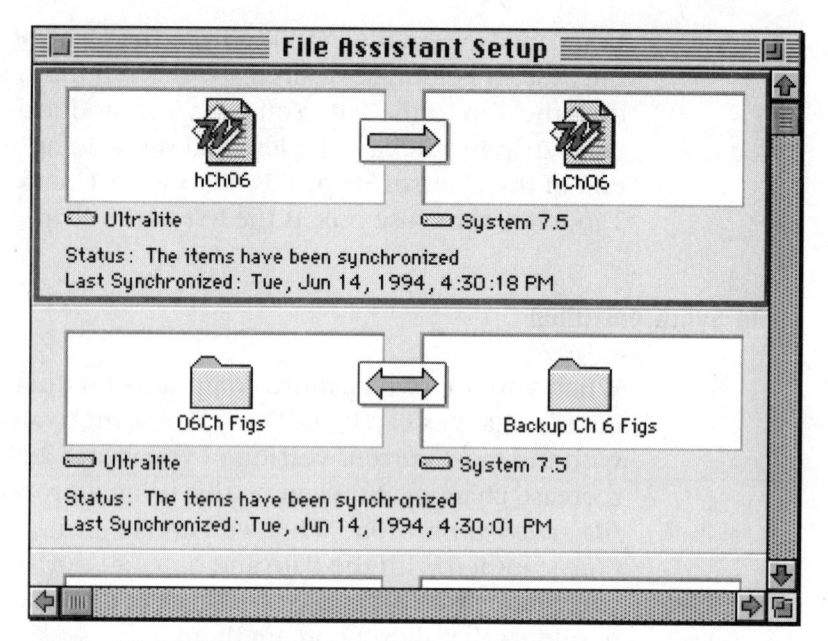

Figure 6-17: The PowerBook File Assistant Setup dialog box.

You can specify whether Synchronization is manual or automatic via commands on the Synchronize menu shown in Figure 6-18. Other choices allow you to choose the direction of the updating that you wish to occur. A double-headed arrow will update either file when there are changes. Single-head arrows are most useful when you wish to use the server to update a file on your hard disk.

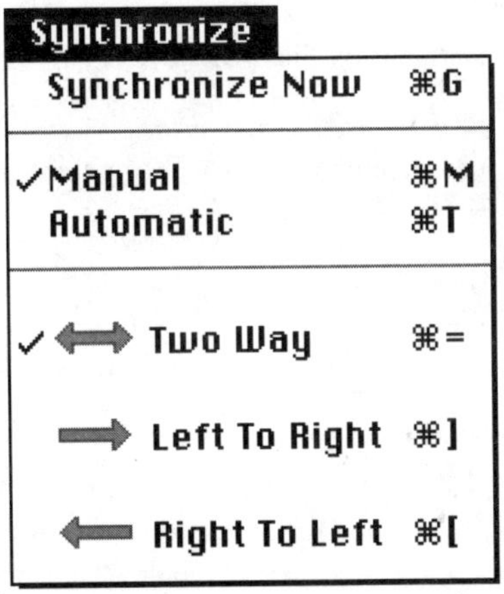

Figure 6-18: The PowerBook File Assistant Synchronize menu.

After you have set up the PowerBook File Assistant, you only need to connect the two computers and run the PowerBook File Assistant. The Synchronize Now command (Command-G) begins the process. If you select a manual synchronization, you will need to click the arrow outline to synchronize each pair. For automatic synchronization, you can use AutoRemounter to reconnect shared disks and then place the File Assistant in your start-up disk. Whenever you mount your drives and File Assistant is running, your files are automatically updated.

Three types of actions are monitored by the File Assistant: modifications of files and folders, deletions of missing and moved files and folders, and the replacement of a file with another of the same name. Table 6-2 summarizes the results based on your settings.

Table 6.2 Actions monitored by File Assistant

Left File	Right File	Result
Changes	Doesn't Change	The right file is updated.
Doesn't Change	Changes	For a two-way update, the left file is updated. For a left-to-right update, there are no changes.
Doesn't Change	Deleted	For a two-way update, you get a message asking you whether you want to delete the left file. For a left-to-right update, the right file is updated.
Deleted	Unchanged	You get a message asking you whether you wish to delete the right file.

Moving On

System 7.5 makes working on a Power Macintosh possible. It also makes working on a PowerBook easier. Support for both series of computers is unique in many respects that were described in this chapter. Using built-in system utilities, you can make your Power Macintosh or PowerBook perform better. In this chapter, you learned

- RISC computing offers some compelling advantages for future technology advances.

- The difference between emulation of programs written for 680x0 computers and those that are in native code for the PowerPC chip.

- How native applications are going to be built, bought and installed.

- How to make your PowerBook last longer on a battery charge.

- How to connect your PowerBook locally or remotely, how to connect an external monitor and how to synchronize files and folders.

Another important aspect of System 7 is the ability to open and use several applications simultaneously. Chapter 7, "Working With Multiple Applications," focuses on multitasking, describing the commands and features it supports and looking at the ways you can use multitasking to work more productively.

Chapter 7

Working With Multiple Applications

One "exciting new feature" of System 7 is actually an exciting old feature that some Macintosh users have been using for more than five years. Known as MultiFinder in previous system software versions, this feature lets you do the following:

- Run multiple applications at once.
- Switch between open applications as necessary.
- Leave one program working while you switch to another.

MultiFinder was a separate utility file, kept in the System Folder of previous system software versions. Because Multi-Finder's features have been incorporated into System 7, the MultiFinder utility is no longer used. As you'll see, System 7 provides all the features of MultiFinder, plus some new ones.

Because the MultiFinder utility file is no longer used, the name "MultiFinder" is no longer appropriate. In this book, the set of features that allows you to open multiple applications simultaneously will be called the multitasking features of System 7. Other people and publications may continue to refer to them as MultiFinder features, or you may also hear them described as the "Process Manager." Some may avoid using any specific name, simply referring to the features as part of the system software or the Finder.

Technically speaking, there are two kinds of multitasking: cooperative and preemptive. System 7 provides cooperative multitasking, which means that all open applications have equal access to the Macintosh's computing power. In cooperative multitasking, applications are responsible for "letting go" of the microprocessor, whereas in preemptive multitasking, system software assigns a "time slice" to each application and shuttles processing between each running application. Time slices occur so frequently that each application appears to be running in real time.

Some purists consider preemptive multitasking, which ascribes priority to specific applications or tasks, to be the only "real" multitasking. Because, in preemptive multitasking, the system software switches between running applications, such a system gives the user some protection from program crashes or hangs. You find preemptive multitasking in more "robust" operating systems such as UNIX, where each computer supports multiple users. Apple is slowly migrating the system software towards full multitasking and memory protection.

The distinctions between cooperative and preemptive multitasking are unimportant—and probably uninteresting—to most Macintosh users. Faster hardware and more memory make running multiple applications much more practical, however. For convenience, we'll use the term "multitasking" to describe the Mac's ability to open and operate multiple applications simultaneously.

What Is Multitasking?

Multitasking allows several programs to be opened and used simultaneously. You can have your word processor, page layout software and graphics package all running at the same time, and you can switch between them freely. It's even possible for an application to continue processing information while you're using another application. Figure 7-1 shows Adobe Illustrator, Microsoft Word, and Aldus PageMaker open simultaneously on the Macintosh.

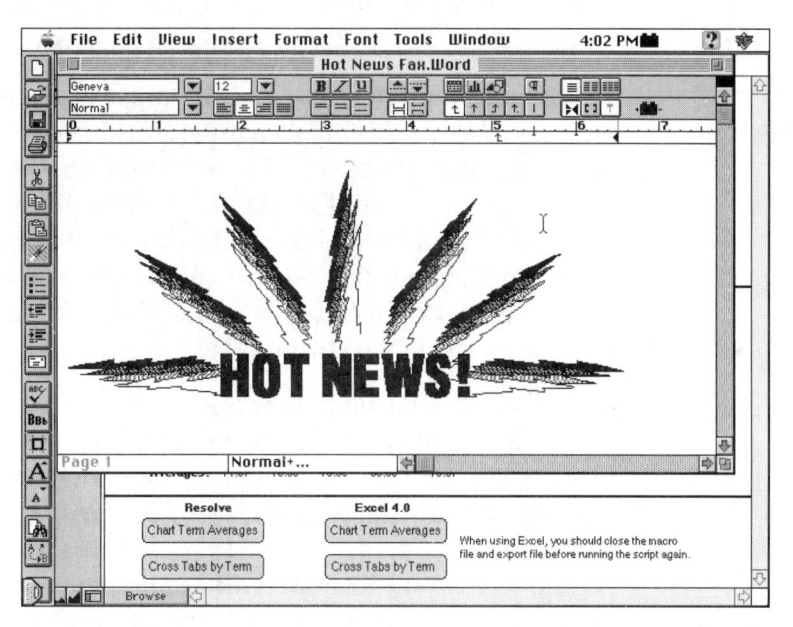

Figure 7-1: A Mac as it appears with several open applications.

Multitasking is a fantastic productivity booster, allowing you to use time and resources with maximum efficiency. For example, you're working in your word processor when you receive a telephone call from your mother. She wants to know whether she'd be better off investing the $10,000 she just won playing bingo in a 7-year CD paying 8.25 percent, or if she should sink it into T-bills paying 6.15 percent tax-free. To help dear old Mom out of her dilemma, you need access to a spreadsheet. So you quit your word processor, launch your spreadsheet, perform the necessary calculations, offer your advice, quit the spreadsheet, launch the word processor, reload your file and say good-bye to Mom.

Following this approach is fine—of course you want to help your mother—but all the time it took to quit your word processor, launch the spreadsheet, quit the spreadsheet, relaunch the word processor and reload your file could have been avoided. Multitasking would have allowed you to run your spreadsheet without quitting your word processor.

This example points to one of the most obvious benefits of multitasking—the ability to handle interruptions with minimum loss of productivity. For most people, interruptions are an unavoidable part of working, and whether they're in the form of a ringing telephone, a knock on the door, an urgent email message or your own memory lapses (you forgot to print that report and drop it in the mail), the least disruption possible is the key to productivity.

The second major benefit of multitasking is its ability to use two or more applications together to complete a single project. To prepare a mail merge, for example, you can export data from your database manager, prepare the merge lists and then execute the merge. In most cases, the raw data exported from your database will require some cleaning up before it's ready to be merged; and often you'll encounter a minor data formatting problem that requires you to repeat the whole export and data cleanup process. But by using multitasking, you avoid the delay and frustration of quitting the word processor to return to the database and then quitting the database to return to the word processor.

As other examples, you may need to read reports and view database or spreadsheet data while preparing presentation graphics; update graphic illustrations in a drawing package before importing them into a page layout; or use an optical character recognition package to read in articles for storage in a database. In these and many other cases, quickly switching from one application to another and using the Mac's Cut, Copy and Paste commands to transfer data between these open applications allow transfer of information between applications that can't otherwise share data.

The third benefit of multitasking is the most exciting—and certainly the one yielding the largest productivity gains: multitasking supports background processing. Therefore, an open application can continue to process data even when you switch away from that application to work in another. Any task that ties up your computer, forcing you to wait for it to finish, can probably benefit from background processing. Common examples are printing, transferring files to or from bulletin boards, making large spreadsheet calculations and generating database reports. Examples of background processing and ways you can take advantage of this tremendous capability are discussed later in this chapter.

MultiFinder in System 6.0.x

If you're familiar with MultiFinder from earlier versions of the system software, you'll find only a few differences between MultiFinder and the multitasking features of System 7. The most notable difference is that multitasking is always available and, unlike MultiFinder, cannot be turned off.

If you didn't use MultiFinder in previous versions of the system software, it was probably for one of the following reasons:

- **Insufficient memory.** MultiFinder required two megabytes of RAM (at a minimum) and four or more megabytes of RAM to be useful. The same is true of the multitasking capabilities in System 7, although the recent lowering of RAM prices and the addition of virtual memory in System 7 make having insufficient memory less of an issue than in the past. (System 7 memory requirements are discussed later in this chapter, and in Chapter 8, "Memory Management.")

    As the system software has continued to grow, so too has System 7's memory appetite. In System 7.5, the current recommended minimum RAM for basic system software is 4mb in a 68k Mac, and 8mb in a Power Macintosh. (Double these minimums when you're using PowerTalk and QuickDraw GX.) This increase is more associated with additions of numerous features (extensions, control panels, and the like) than it is with the memory management requirements of multitasking.

- **Reputation.** MultiFinder had a reputation for instability. Many people believed that using MultiFinder made the Macintosh prone to frequent crashes. As often happens with software and hardware, this reputation was undeserved—the rumors of crashes were not based on the real facts.

    When MultiFinder was first released, many applications crashed when they were launched under MultiFinder. Crashing was not the fault of MultiFinder; it was usually because the application had not been written according to Apple's programming rules. Once these incompatible applications were made MultiFinder-compatible, almost all problems vanished.

    Another problem—again not MultiFinder's fault—was the increasing use of start-up programs, which caused a memory conflict in the System Heap (an area of RAM used by the operating system), often resulting in crashes when using MultiFinder. This problem was easily cured with utilities such as HeapFix or HeapTool, which are freely available from user groups and bulletin boards. In any case, this type of problem is not apparent in System 7.

- **Complexity.** MultiFinder was considered too complex by many novice Macintosh users. This perception was understandable—after all, MultiFinder was offered as a virtually undocumented utility program. A Macintosh user had to be somewhat adventurous just to turn it on and learn how to use it. For the majority of users who don't spend their free time attending user groups, browsing on CompuServe or reading about the Macintosh, MultiFinder seemed intimidating and too risky.

In System 7, multitasking is seamlessly integrated into the system software, making the simultaneous use of multiple applications a fundamental part of the working routine. Everyone who uses the Macintosh should take the time to learn, understand and benefit from this powerful tool.

Multitasking in System 7.5

The ability to keep multiple programs in memory and recall them from the background to the foreground has been part of Macintosh system software since before MultiFinder. (The MultiFinder evolved from the Switcher utility written by Andy Hertzfeld, who was part of the original Macintosh team and is now a vice president with General Magic.) This kind of behavior is called context switching. An application in the background is suspended at its last point of execution. Context switching is not multitasking, because only one process is running at a time. In technical parlance, your Macintosh stores the different threads of execution—but only a single thread in one application can execute.

Starting in System 6, and continuing into System 7, has been the appearance of background processing. Many lower-level I/O (input/output) functions have been enabled, allowing you to print, communicate and display data in the background while a single application runs in the foreground. This is the beginning of multitasking: your Macintosh can run multiple processes, but it limits which types of processes can be concurrent. In this manner, the Macintosh is single-threaded because only one thread operates for the foreground and any background running processes. That is, only one process is running at a time and your Macintosh CPU cycles between foreground and background tasks. This is commonly referred to as "time slicing."

System 7.5 introduces the Thread Manager (compatible with all versions of System 7), whose icon is shown in Figure 7-2. The Thread Manager is a system extension that allows for multithreading within a single application. On 68k Macs, both cooperative multitasking and preemptive multitasking through the Thread Manager are possible; Power Macintoshes permit only preemptive multitasking. This is still lightweight, concurrent processing, but it's another step along the way toward a fully multitasked system.

With the Thread Manager, you can now work in your database, word processor, or spreadsheet while calculating other functions in the same application. It's up to application developers to implement the programming necessary to take advantage of the Thread Manager, but the capability is ignored by applications that don't choose to implement it. Therefore, no compatibility problems are expected.

Figure 7-2: The Thread Manager extension.

One example of apparent multitasking to come is to be found in the OpenDoc compound document architecture. In OpenDoc, the architecture creates a document frame and manages parts within the document. When you add a part, the Part Handler checks to see whether the applet (text, sound, video and so on) is open, and if not, opens it. As you work in a text part, clocks, animation parts, movie parts, or a live video feed can be running concurrently. It looks like multitasking, but it's really more a form of multithreading within a single application à la the Thread Manager.

OpenDoc is so seamless that it's likely to be a very large part of the Macintosh's future. It will be released as a system extension in early 1995 and eventually will be written into the Macintosh system software. However, we'll defer discussion of OpenDoc until Chapter 10, "Inter-Applications Communication & OpenDoc."

Currently, full multitasking is being written into the Macintosh operating system. It's slated to be phased in over the next two major releases of the system software: Copeland and Gershwin (see the "Introduction" for more details). In Copeland, Apple is building the core of its next operating system into a very small, fast and portable core of code called the microkernel. The microkernel will allow Apple to run the operating system on a variety of microprocessors.

More importantly for this discussion, the microkernel comes with true memory protection. Memory protection isolates programs' threads in their own "containers" so that one thread cannot call for memory used by any other thread. A thread can crash and burn, but it does not bring your system to a halt. Memory protection is the single most important difference between the Macintosh and the high-price spreads. It will allow real-time multiuser transaction processing, the kind that banks use to run ATM machines and airlines use for reservations, to run on a Macintosh.

That kind of processing, along with better security protection, is the primary reason that Apple uses A/UX on its WorkGroup Servers. A/UX is Apple's "kinder and gentler" UNIX, although few users will rate it as having many points of light. UNIX is built on a microkernel architecture, and as such provided both memory protection and more stringent security measures. Running several processes in UNIX is like running several "virtual computers" inside the same microprocessor. They run independently of one another.

Gershwin is where full multitasking is slated to be introduced. Apple has taken a lot of heat over the years from industry pundits for not having multitasking built into the Macintosh operating system. Although memory protection is important, a veritable "Fanfare for the Common Man," just how important is true multitasking anyway? In reality, not very important. You know how fast (or how slow) your applications run now. Multitasking divides the speed by however many applications are running at the time—not an exact division, but in general. So a multitasked Macintosh would crawl. By the time Gershwin appears, the Power Macintoshes should be running at speeds where multitasking won't have you humming "Rhapsody in Blue."

Working With Multiple Applications

System 7 allows you to open multiple applications automatically, without any special configuration or initiation. In fact, when you launch your first application from the Finder, you'll immediately notice the effect: the Finder desktop (the volume icons, Trash and so on) does not disappear as the new application is launched, as was the case in previous versions of the system software. The Finder remains visible in System 7 because both your new application and the Finder now run simultaneously. (See Figure 7-3.)

See "Working With Programs" for related information.

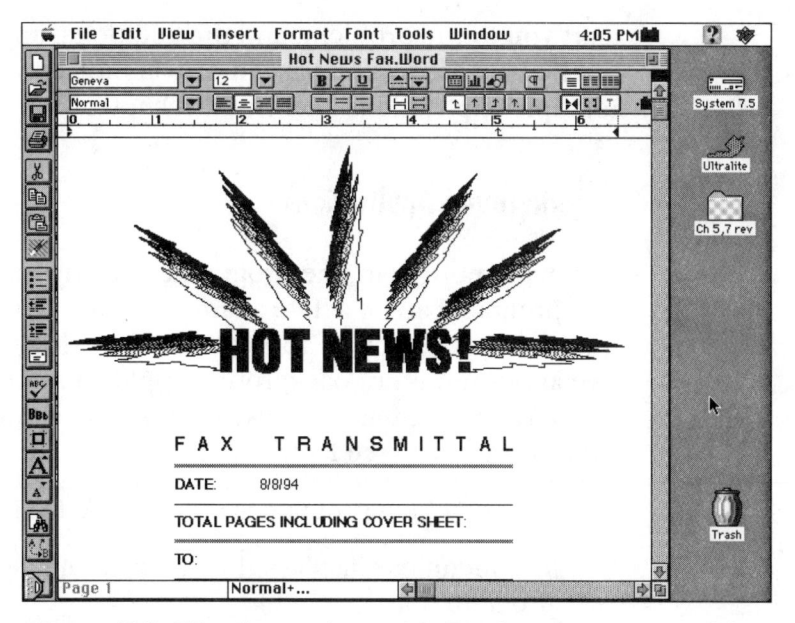

Figure 7-3: Word running with Finder elements visible.

Note that in System 7.0.1P, 7.1P and 7.5 an option allows you to "hide the Finder." In that case, the Finder icons will disappear when you switch to another application. See "Hiding the Finder" later in this chapter for more details.

When you launch additional applications, you continue to see the capabilities of multitasking. As each additional program opens, its menu bar and windows are displayed, and other open applications are unaffected.

When you first start using multiple applications simultaneously, the sight of several windows open at the same time may be a little disconcerting. As you learn to arrange and manipulate these windows and enjoy the benefits of multiple open applications, you'll soon find yourself wondering how you ever got along using just one program at a time.

The number of applications you can launch simultaneously is limited only by the amount of memory you have available. If your launch will exceed available memory, a dialog box will alert you to the problem, and the additional application will not be launched. (You learn more on memory and running multiple applications later in this chapter.)

Foreground & Background Applications

Although more than one program can be open at once, only one program can be active at any one time. The active program is the foreground application, and other open but inactive applications are background applications, even if you can see portions of their windows or if they're simultaneously processing tasks (see Figure 7-4).

You can tell which program is currently active in several ways:

- The menu bar displays the menu commands of the active program only.

- The active program's icon appears at the top of the Applications menu.

- The active program name is checked in the Applications menu.

- The Apple menu's About This Macintosh... command lists the active program name.

- Active program windows overlap other visible windows or elements.

- Active program windows display a highlighted title bar, which includes horizontal lines, the close box and the zoom box.

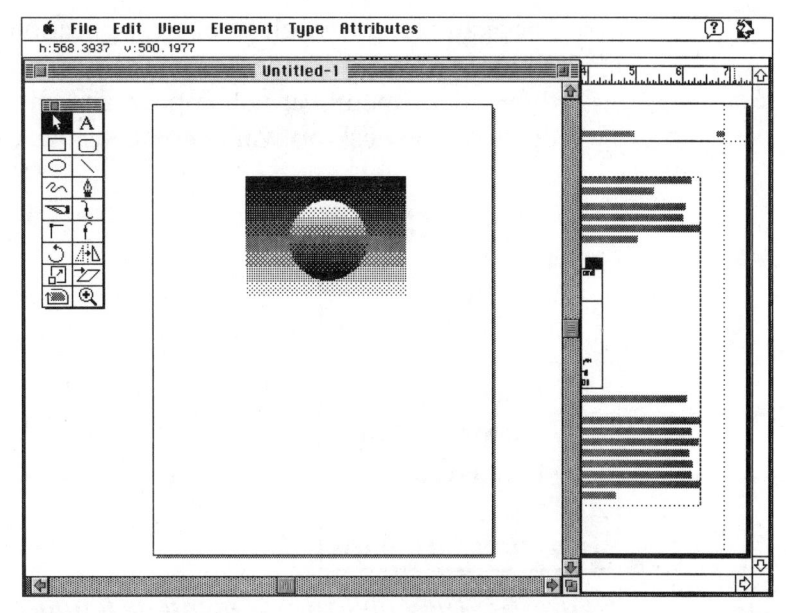

Figure 7-4: Aldus FreeHand is the active program in this window; PageMaker is in the background.

In contrast, a background application's menu bar does not appear, its icon is not checked in the Applications menu, none of its windows are highlighted, and some or all of its windows may be hidden or obscured.

Because only one program can be in the foreground, it's important to be able to switch quickly and easily from one foreground program to another. Switching between applications is commonly referred to as "sending to the back" and "bringing to the front."

You can switch between open applications in two ways:

- Use the Applications menu. Located in the upper-right corner of the menu bar, the Applications menu lists the names of all applications currently running. Choose the name of the application you want to switch to, and that program will bring its menu bar and windows to the front.

For example, to switch from an application to the Finder, choose the word "Finder" from the Applications menu: the Finder's menu bar will appear, and any icons and windows on the desktop will become visible. (See Figure 7-5.)

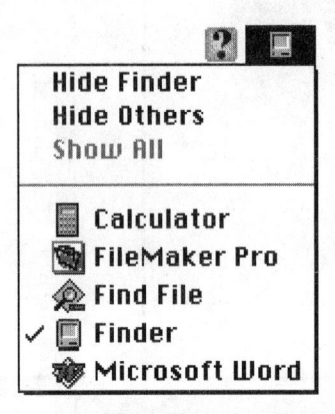

```
Hide Finder
Hide Others
Show All

   Calculator
   FileMaker Pro
   Find File
✓  Finder
   Microsoft Word
```

Figure 7-5: The Applications menu as it appears with numerous open applications.

- Click any visible window. Clicking any visible element on the screen brings the application owning that element to the front. For example, while working in your word processor, if you can still see the icons on the Finder desktop, clicking one of these icons will bring the Finder to the front, making it the current application. After working in the Finder, return to the word processor by clicking its window.

Background Processing

You can bring any application to the foreground, sending any other to the background, at any time except when dialog boxes are open. You can even send most applications to the background while they're processing data—they'll continue to calculate or process in the background. Background processing adds an entirely new dimension to using multiple open applications simultaneously.

If you could use multiple open applications only sequentially, one after the other, productivity increases would be limited to the time you saved by avoiding repeated opening and quitting of applications. Background processing, however, lets you print a newsletter, calculate a spreadsheet and dial up a remote bulletin board at the same time. This capability is the ultimate in computer productivity.

Background processing is easy. Start by doing a lengthy process, such as a spreadsheet calculation or a telecommunication session; then bring another open application to the foreground. The background task continues processing while you use the computer for another task in another application. Because foreground and background applications are sharing the hardware resources (there's only one central processing unit in the Macintosh), you may notice a slowdown or jerky motion in the foreground application. The severity of this effect will depend on your Macintosh's power and the number and requirements of the background tasks being performed; but there should be no detrimental effect on your foreground application.

Periodically, you may need to attend to a task left running in the background, or you may be given notice when it completes its task. If so, an Alert dialog box will be displayed, a diamond will appear before the application's name in the Applications menu, or the Application menu icon will flash alternately with the alerting application's icon.

Background Printing

The first background processing most people use is printing. Background printing is not quite the same as using two applications at once, but it's similar.

Without multitasking, you have to wait for the entire file to be printed—because of the time it takes for the printer to mechanically do the job. In background printing, files are printed to disk as fast as the application and printer driver can handle them. Then a utility called a print spooler sends the print file from the disk to the printer. The advantage is that the print spooler takes over the task of feeding the pages to the printer and waits as the printer performs its slow mechanical tasks while you continue working in your main application or even use another software application.

Background PostScript printing support is built into System 7 and controlled via the Chooser's Background Printing option. By default, Background Printing is turned on, but you can turn it off at any time by clicking the Off radio button, as shown in Figure 7-6.

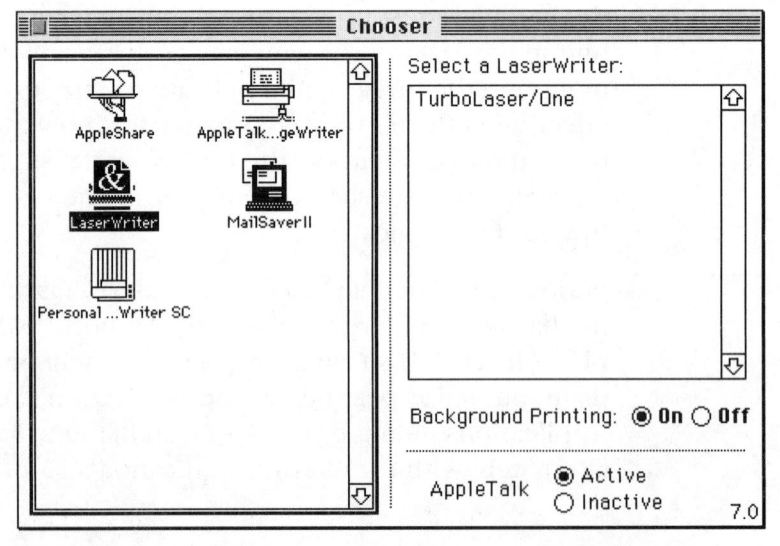

Figure 7-6: Chooser and Background Printing option.

With Background Printing turned on, files printed using the LaserWriter driver are spooled to your hard drive. At the same time, the PrintMonitor utility, automatically running in the background, begins printing the spooled file to the selected PostScript printer. While PrintMonitor is printing, you can bring it to the foreground by selecting its name from the Applications menu. (See Figure 7-7.)

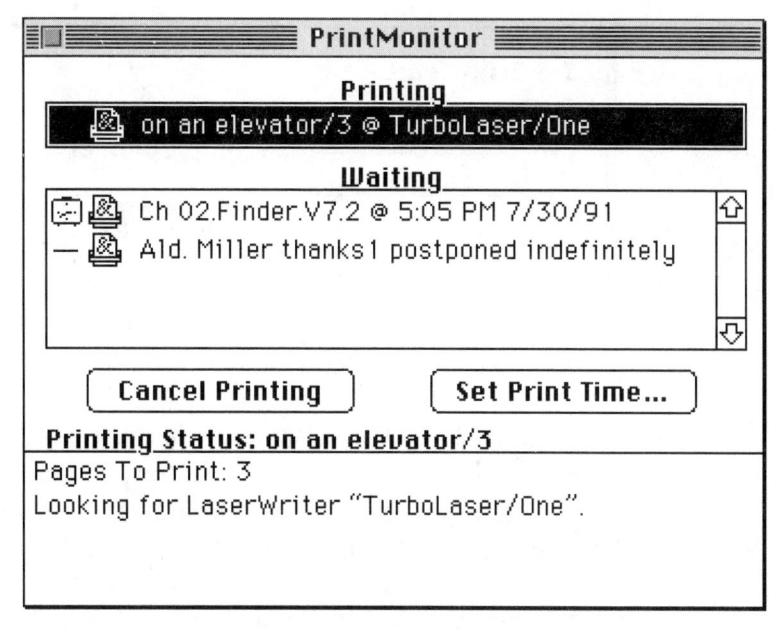

Figure 7-7: The PrintMonitor dialog box.

PrintMonitor provides several options: you can delay the printing of any spooled file for a specific or indefinite period of time; you can rearrange the printing order if several files have been spooled; and you can cancel the printing of a spooled file. You also can use PrintMonitor simply to monitor the status of background printing as it occurs.

To delay or postpone the printing of any spooled file, click its file name and then click the Set Print Time... button, as shown in Figure 7-8. When the Set Print Time dialog box appears, select the portion of the time or date you want to change and then click the up or down arrow next to that time or date to reset it. Click the Postpone Indefinitely radio button if you're not sure when you want to print the file but wish to save it so it can be printed later. After completing these settings, click the OK button to return to the PrintMonitor dialog box.

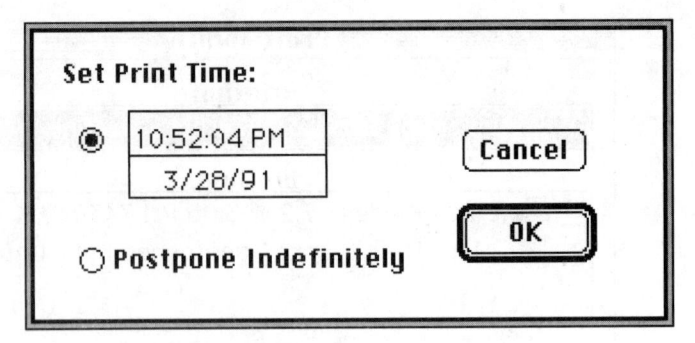

Figure 7-8: The Set Print Time dialog box.

To cancel after printing has begun, click the Cancel Printing button. It will take a few seconds for printing to stop, at which time the file name will be removed from the Printing message area at the top of the PrintMonitor dialog box. To cancel printing a file waiting in the print queue, select the file name from the Waiting area and then click the Remove From List button.

Normally, PrintMonitor completes its job invisibly in the background. If your Macintosh happens to crash, or be shut off, while PrintMonitor is handling a print job, PrintMonitor will run automatically when your Macintosh is restarted and advise you (by flashing its icon at the top of the Applications menu) that an error has occurred. Bring the PrintMonitor to the foreground, and it will tell you which file it was unable to finish printing, and ask if you want to re-attempt printing that file.

QuickDraw GX, part of System 7.5, supports a different model of background printing: one that is both simpler and more powerful. It replaces the execrable PrintMonitor and frequent trips back to the Chooser. You see the new System 7.5 background printer files in your Extensions folder; they're the Printer Share and PrinterShare GX extensions. QuickDraw GX printers can now appear as icons on your desktop when you select that printer from the Chooser and click the Create button. You can place multiple GX printer icons on your desktop. Icons represent real printers (or other output devices like plotters), just as a hard disk icon represents a real hard disk.

To print to a printer, you can drag and drop a file to that printer's icons. Some QuickDraw GX icons are shown in Figure 7-9. Even serial printers connected via a network (such as an AppleTalk ImageWriter) and personal printers can be mounted as printer icons on your desktop. You can send a document to any printer that you see on your desktop, and you do not have to go back to the Chooser to reselect printers repeatedly. QuickDraw GX also allows you to select printers from within an application's Print dialog box—provided that the application is coded to take advantage of that option.

StyleWriter GX   ImageWriter GX

LaserWriter 300 GX   ImageWriter LQ GX

LaserWriter GX   LaserWriter IISC GX

Figure 7-9: QuickDraw GX printer icons.

Each QuickDraw GX printer manages its own print queue, just as each Macintosh on a network now does. When you double-click a printer icon, its print queue status window appears. You can reorder, delete or postpone a print job. You can also drag a print job to another QuickDraw GX printer. Print jobs are in the new, portable digital document format, and each printer does the appropriate translation. Each print queue is spooled, and background processing prints each printer job in turn. Figure 7-10 shows a typical QuickDraw GX printer queue. Refer to Chapter 9 for further discussion of QuickDraw GX.

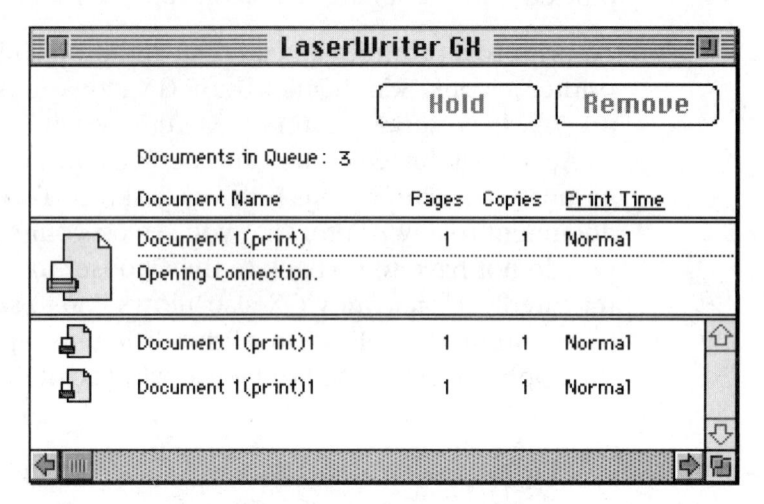

Figure 7-10: A QuickDraw GX printer queue.

Copying Files in the Background

Copying files from one location to another is a basic capability the Finder has always provided, but through the successive Finder versions, the activity has continued to evolve.

Early versions of the Finder provided only a simple dialog box during file copying. Later, a counter of files being copied was added. Then names of copied files were added, and finally the progress bar became a part of this dialog box. Despite these improvements, which seemed to make time pass more quickly, you were still forced to wait while files were copied.

In System 7, the process of copying files takes a huge step forward: the wait has been eliminated altogether. You can now work in any open application while the Finder copies a file in the background. To use this feature, follow these steps:

- Open the application you want to use while the Finder is copying.

- Switch to the Finder using the Applications menu or by clicking the Finder desktop.

- Start the copy process in the normal way by dragging the desired files from their source location to the icon of the destination folder or volume. The copying process will begin, and the copying dialog box will appear.

- Then select the Applications menu with the stopwatch cursor and choose the name of the open application you want to use while the file copy is in progress. This application will come to the foreground and is ready for you to use, while the Finder continues its copy operation in the background.

- Switch back to the Finder any time you like, using the Applications menu or clicking the Finder desktop.

Hiding Applications

Running several applications concurrently can result in an on-screen clutter of windows displayed by open applications. To alleviate this problem, System 7 lets you "hide" open application windows, thus removing them from the screen without changing their status or the background work they're doing. You can hide an application at the time you leave it to switch to another application, or while it's running in the background. (See Figures 7-11 and 7-12.)

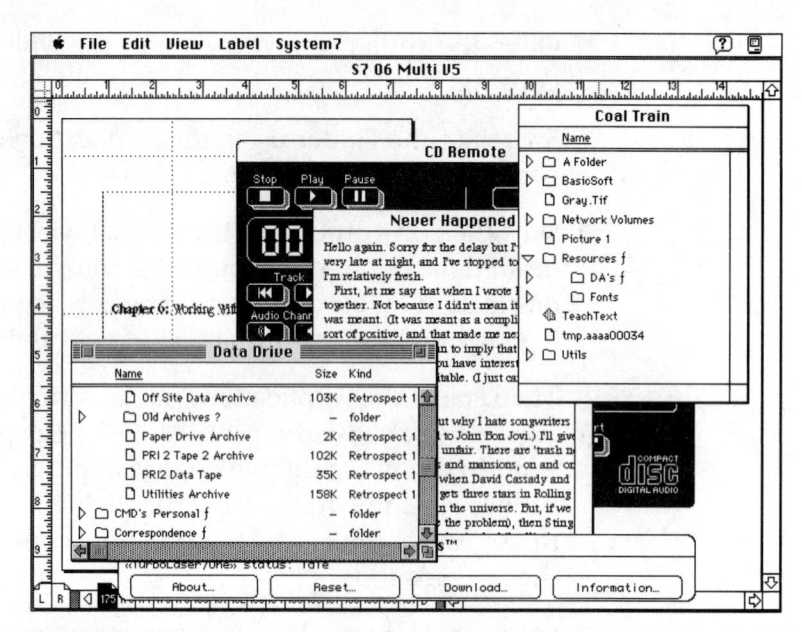

Figure 7-11: Running multiple applications without hiding can result in a crowded display.

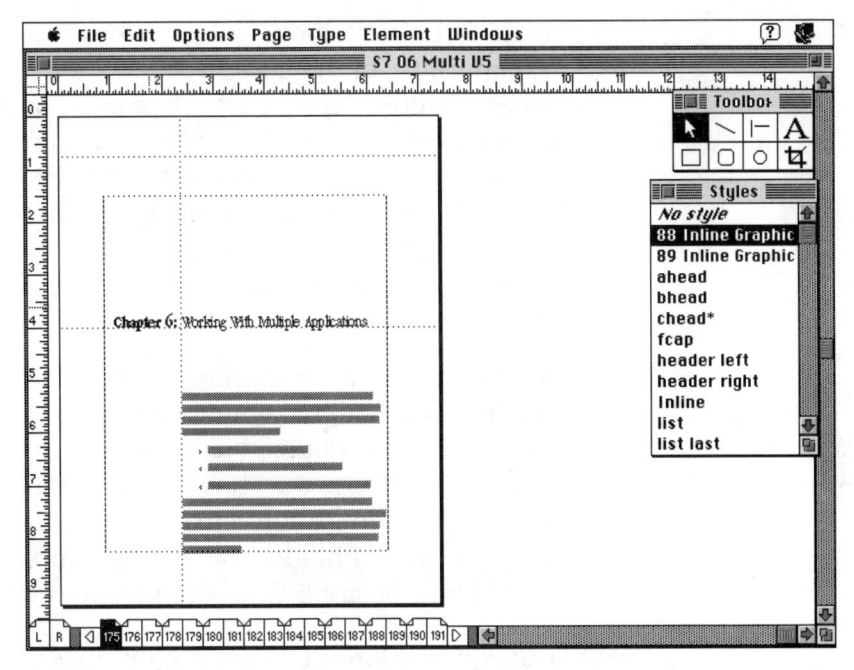

Figure 7-12: Using hiding, the same open applications result in a clear display.

The Applications menu provides three Hide commands: Hide Current Application (Current Application being the name of the current foreground application), Hide Others and Show All.

- **Hide Current Application.** Removes all windows of the current application from the screen and brings another window of an open application to the foreground. Usually, the Finder is brought to the foreground; but if the Finder itself has been hidden, the next application in the Applications menu is brought forward instead.

  A hidden application's icon is dimmed in the Applications menu to signify that it's hidden. To unhide the application, either select its name from the Applications menu, which will bring it to the foreground, or choose the Show All command.

- **Hide Others.** Removes all windows from the screen except those of the current application. This is useful when onscreen clutter is bothersome, or if you're accidentally clicking windows of background applications and bringing them forward. After the Hide Others command has been used, all open applications icons, except those of the foreground application, are dimmed in the Applications menu, as a visual reminder that these applications are hidden.

- **Show All.** Makes all current applications visible (not hidden). You can tell which applications are currently hidden by their dimmed icons in the Applications menu. When you choose the Show All command, the current foreground application remains in the foreground, and the windows of hidden background applications become visible but the applications remain in the background.

While an application is hidden, it continues to operate exactly the same as it would if it were running as a background application and not hidden. If an application can normally perform tasks in the background, it will still perform these tasks in the background while it's hidden. In fact, because of the effort saved by not having to upgrade the screen display, some tasks operate faster in the background when their application is hidden.

You can also hide the current foreground application when you send it to the background, by holding down the Option key while bringing another application forward (either by choosing its name from the Applications menu or by clicking the mouse on its window). You can retrieve applications hidden in this manner by using the Show All command or by selecting their dimmed icons from the Applications menu.

Hiding the Finder

7.5 There's a potential problem for novices working with multiple applications at the same time. If you inadvertently click the Finder desktop, you switch into the Finder and out of your current program. Suddenly, you've lost your place, and the menus have changed. Because the Performa series was built for the home market (and novices), Apple included a feature called "Finder hiding" into System 7.0.1P and 7.1P that prevents you from switching to the Finder by inadvertently clicking on the desktop.

Voluntary Finder hiding has appeared finally in System 7.5. With Finder hiding, when you switch into an application other than the Finder, the desktop disappears (rather like the way things worked before System 7, with the difference that this hiding is by choice). You can't click the background and switch out of your application. You turn on Finder hiding by disabling the "Show Desktop when in background" check box in the General Controls control panel. So if you're working in an application and you can't see your hard disk, Trash, or file and folder icons where they should appear, Finder hiding is the cause. Figure 7-13 shows an example of Word running with the Finder hidden.

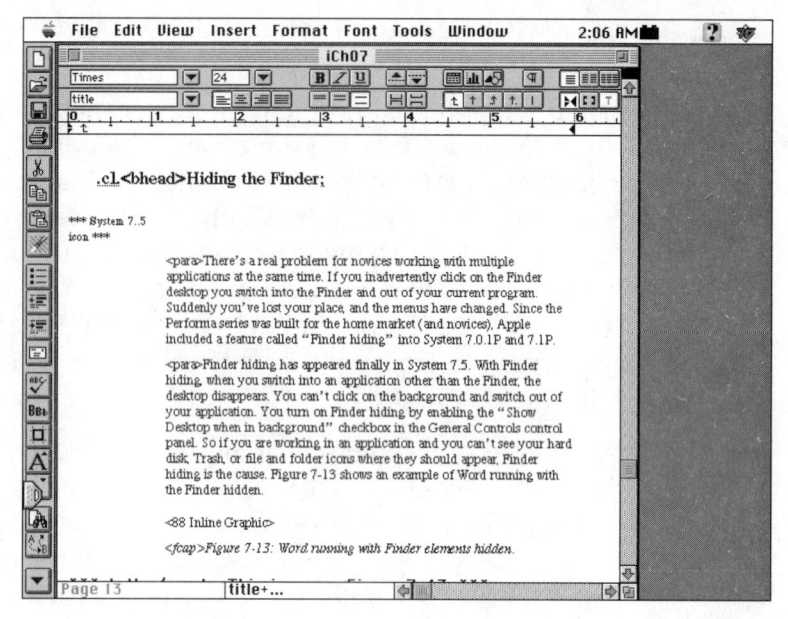

Figure 7-13: Word running with Finder elements hidden on a Macintosh PowerBook.

Multitasking Tips

Once you start using the Hide commands to reduce screen clutter, you should be comfortable working with multiple open applications. The following tips can help:

- **Saving before switching.** Before bringing another application to the foreground, save your work in the application you're leaving so that if your Mac crashes or is turned off accidentally, you won't lose your work.

- **Resuming after crashing.** If an application crashes in System 7, you can usually force the Mac to close that application and regain access to your other applications by pressing Command-Option-Escape. (See Figure 7-14.)

Note that after resuming from this kind of a crash, your system may be unstable and prone to additional crashes. Using this option is a bit like driving a nail with a sledgehammer—it works but is likely to do some damage. You should save any unsaved work in other open applications, and you may want to restart your Macintosh, just to be safe.

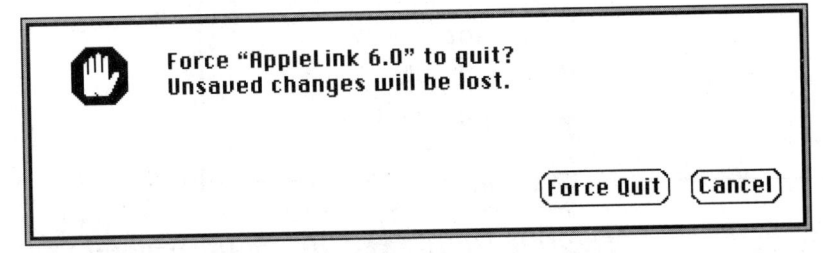

Figure 7-14: The Force Quit dialog box.

- **Shutting down or restarting.** Selecting the Shut Down or Restart commands from the Finder's Special menu while multiple applications are open will cause all open applications to be quit. If any open documents contain changes that haven't been saved, the application containing the document will be brought to the foreground, and you'll be asked whether you want to save those changes (see Figure 7-15). Click Yes to save, No to discard the changes or Cancel to abort the Shut Down or Restart operation.

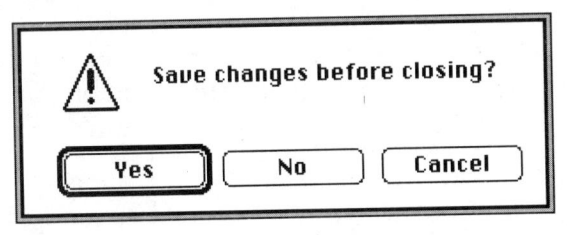

Figure 7-15: Save Changes dialog box.

> **7.5** ■ In System 7.5, the Shut Down command has been added to the bottom of the Apple menu (see Figure 7-16). You can now shut down without switching to the Finder by selecting "• Shut Down"—a minor convenience.

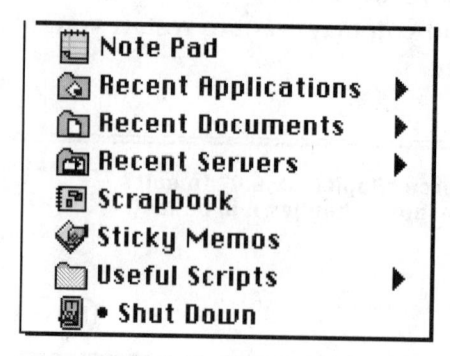

```
📝 Note Pad
📇 Recent Applications    ▶
📑 Recent Documents       ▶
📁 Recent Servers         ▶
📖 Scrapbook
📝 Sticky Memos
📁 Useful Scripts         ▶
🖥 • Shut Down
```

Figure 7-16: The System 7.5 Apple menu Shut Down command.

■ **Maintaining efficiency for background applications.** Applications in the background often run more efficiently if hidden with one of the Hide commands from the Applications menu. This is true because often the onscreen display can't keep up with the application's processing rate; as a result, the application has to wait for the screen to be drawn. The extent of this delay depends on your computer system and video display. Using the Hide command eliminates all video-related delay.

■ **Switching and hiding.** To hide an application while switching to another open application, hold down the Option key while clicking the open application's window, or while selecting the name of another open application from the Applications menu.

The Memory Implications of Multitasking

Everything has its price. Macintosh users know this well (especially experienced Macintosh users). Multitasking is no exception—its price is memory.

Put simply, you can run only as many applications at once as your available Macintosh memory can handle. A predefined amount of memory must be dedicated to the application while it's open. Running multiple applications simultaneously requires enough memory to satisfy the cumulative amounts of those applications. Your total amount of System 7 available memory includes what's supplied by the RAM chips installed on your computer's logic board or on NuBus cards, plus any virtual memory created with the Memory control panel. (See Chapter 8, "Memory Management," for more information about virtual memory.)

When you first turn on Macintosh System 7, some of your memory is taken up immediately by the system software and the Finder. This amount varies depending on how many fonts and sounds you've installed, your disk cache setting, the extensions you're using and whether you're using File Sharing. As many as three or four megabytes of memory can be consumed by the system software itself in some circumstances. Your Macintosh's memory usage is documented in the About This Macintosh dialog box, shown in Figure 7-17. If you would like to reduce the amount of memory your system software consumes, remove unused fonts or sounds, reduce the size of your RAM Disk and turn off File Sharing.

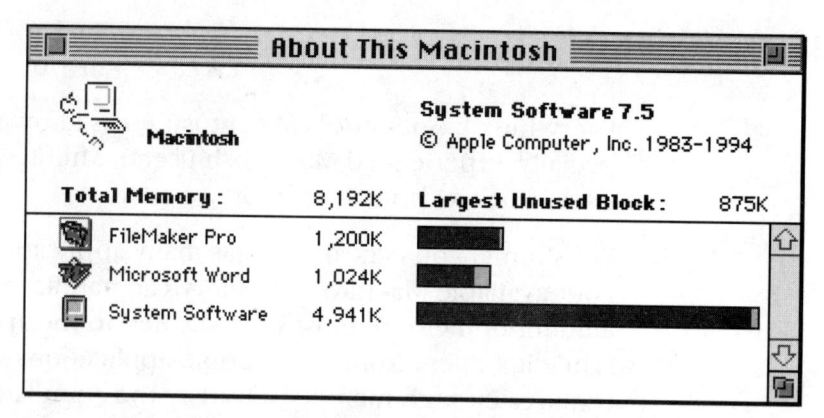

Figure 7-17: The About This Macintosh dialog box.

Each time you launch an application, it requests the amount of memory that it needs in order to run. If enough memory is available, the application is launched. If enough memory isn't available, one of three dialog boxes will appear. The first, shown in Figure 7-18, informs you there's not enough memory available to launch the selected application. The second, shown in Figure 7-19, tells you the same thing but it also gives you the option of launching the application in the amount of RAM that is available. Lastly, a dialog box appears which tells you that an application with no open windows is open in memory and asks if you'd like to close it. Normally, launching the application under these circumstances will allow you to use the application without incident.

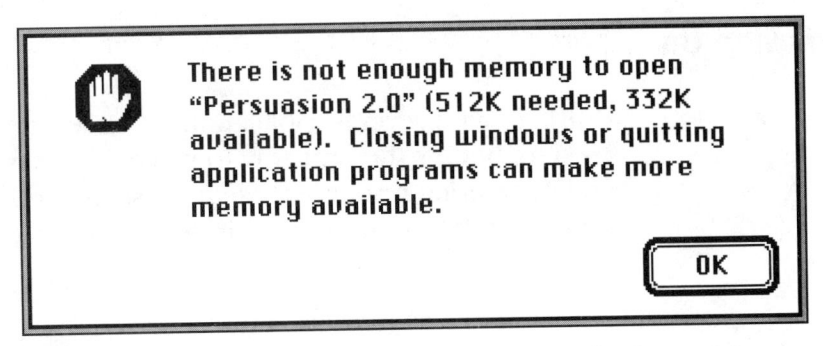

> ⛔ There is not enough memory to open "Persuasion 2.0" (512K needed, 332K available). Closing windows or quitting application programs can make more memory available.
>
> [OK]

Figure 7-18: This dialog appears when you're launching an application with limited memory available.

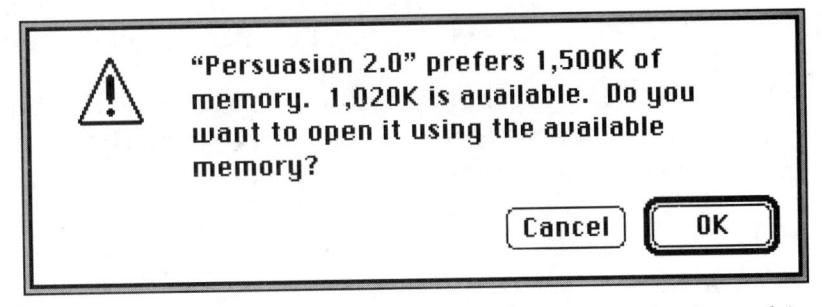

> ⚠ "Persuasion 2.0" prefers 1,500K of memory. 1,020K is available. Do you want to open it using the available memory?
>
> [Cancel] [OK]

Figure 7-19: This dialog box appears when you're launching an application with almost enough memory available.

If available memory is insufficient to launch an application, quit one or more applications currently open to free up additional memory. Then try again to launch the application you want. If these steps aren't enough, quit additional open applications and retry the launch until you're successful.

For more information on your Mac's memory, including ways you can expand available memory, tips on reducing the amount of memory each application consumes and more about using the About This Macintosh dialog box, see Chapter 8, "Memory Management."

Moving On

Working with several applications at once takes some getting used to, but it's the best way to make the most of your time and computing resources. As we've seen in this chapter, System 7's multitasking support is impressive:

- You can launch as many different applications as your available memory permits.

- Many applications can continue to process data while they're running in the background.

- "Hiding" open applications reduces onscreen clutter without affecting the operation of the applications.

Like many other System 7 features, multitasking is available to every System 7-compatible program. Next, Chapter 8 introduces memory management concepts.

Chapter 8

Memory Management

When someone asks you about your Macintosh, you probably say something like, "I've got a Quadra 650 with 8 megs of memory and a 230-meg hard drive." It's no accident that the three variables you use to describe your computer are its model name, the amount of installed memory, or Random-Access Memory (RAM) and its hard disk size. These are the factors that determine what you can do—the speed and range of activities you can perform—with your computer.

With System 7.5, the amount of RAM installed in your Mac is still important, but it's no longer the total measure of memory or the only important memory issue. In this chapter, we look at the overall picture of Macintosh memory, including the new Memory control panel options, the About This Macintosh... dialog box and ways you can configure applications to use memory most efficiently.

Memory vs. Storage

Before we jump into the new memory options and implications of System 7.5, let's clarify the difference between memory (RAM) and storage (disk space). This distinction may be clear to experienced Macintosh users, but if you're not certain you understand the difference, please read this section carefully.

In the simplest terms, memory consists of the chips in your computer where data is temporarily stored while it is being used by the Macintosh. This is in contrast to your hard disk, floppy disks and other storage devices where data is permanently stored when it is not being used by your Macintosh.

The differences between RAM and storage (hard drives, floppies and other media) are very important. Both RAM and storage hold data—application programs, system software and data files—but the similarities end there. RAM stores data electronically on a set of chips, and as a result, these chips "forget" their contents as soon as the power is turned off or the Mac is restarted. Storage devices like hard drives and floppy disks operate magnetically, or by optical technology, and only lose information if it is intentionally erased.

More importantly, the Macintosh can only work with data stored in RAM; it cannot directly manipulate data on any storage device. In order to open an application or file, it must be read from storage and written into memory. Once in memory, the application can be executed or the file can be modified, but to make these changes permanent, the information in RAM must be written back out to the storage device—this is what happens when you choose the Save command.

RAM & You

If we compare the way your Mac uses memory and storage with the way you work and think, perhaps the difference will become more apparent and easier to remember. In this analogy the computer (and it's processor) plays the part of the human brain, memory (RAM) is equated with our own memory, and floppy and hard disk storage is equated with written or typed notes.

As you know, no information can gain access to your brain without also entering your memory; regardless of whether information originates from your eyes, ears or other senses, it is immediately put into memory (RAM) so that your brain (the Macintosh processor) can access it. But what do we do with information that we want to use in the future? We transfer it to some storage medium, like paper (disk). This way we know that when this information is needed in the future we can transfer it back into memory by reading it. Of course, the fact that humans have both short-term and long-term memory weakens this analogy, but it is generally a useful way to make the distinction between memory and storage.

The Memory Control Panel

One of the realities Macintosh users have to confront is the finite amount of memory available in their computers. Today's software seems to have an insatiable appetite for RAM, and new technologies—like multitasking, 24-bit color and sound, and particularly RISC-based microprocessors like those in the Power Macintosh—intensify the problem. The crusade for additional memory has traditionally encountered certain roadblocks: the operating system's limited ability to address the need for large amounts of memory, the computer's physical limitations and the high price of memory chips.

System 7 began the process of breaking down these barriers, or at least temporarily pushed them back. The Memory control panel was one of System 7's new memory-related features. This control panel offers virtual memory, 32-bit addressing and RAM disk options, as well as the disk cache option, which is System 7's version of the RAM cache found in the General control panel of earlier systems. All of these elements undergo continual improvement as system software develops. Even when the outward appearance of the Memory control panel remains unchanged, you can detect speed enhancements due to underlying changes—particularly in System 7.5.

The Memory control panel does not provide all of these options on all Macintosh models, however. When a certain Mac model doesn't support an option, it doesn't appear in the control panel. Each of these options and their compatibility details are described in detail below.

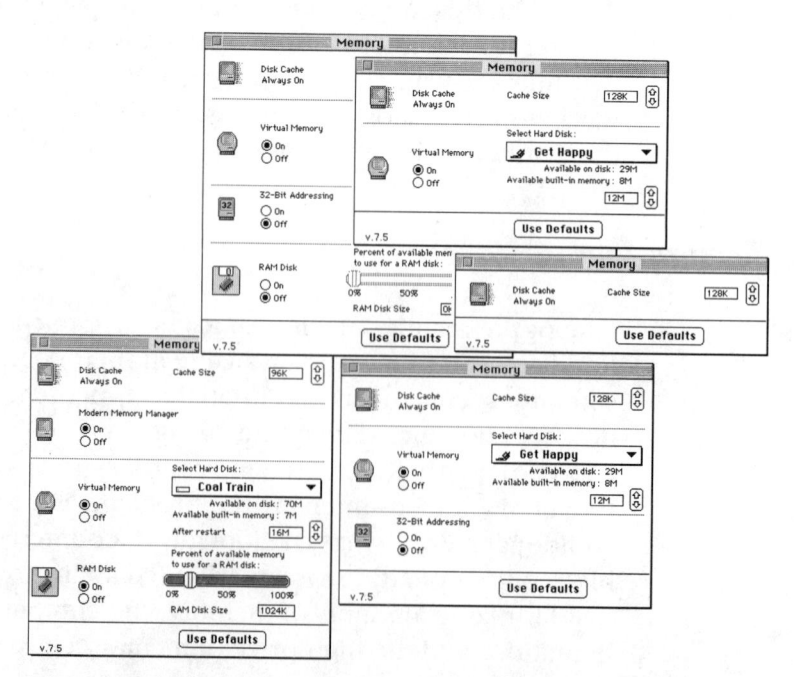

Figure 8-1: The five versions of the Memory control panel that appear on Macintosh models.

Disk Cache

A disk cache is a small section of Macintosh RAM set aside to store a copy of the most recent data read from disk (or volume) into memory. Storing this copy makes the data readily available when it's needed again. Reaccessing data via the RAM-based cache, rather than having to reread it from disk, saves considerable time.

By default, your Macintosh uses 32k of cache for every one megabyte of RAM installed in your Mac. If you have 4 megabytes of RAM, for example, 128k would be the default cache setting. Using the arrows, you can increase or decrease your disk cache size as required.

For most users, settings between 96k and 256k are sufficient. Unless you have specific memory limitations, you shouldn't reduce the cache below its default setting, since the small amount of memory the cache consumes significantly improves your Macintosh's performance. In most cases, you should not increase the size of your cache too much either, as there is a distinct point of diminishing returns after which more disk cache will actually slow down your Macintosh.

Settings over 384k or perhaps 512k should be used only in very specific situations. In situations where large cache allocations aid performance, normally your software's documentation will mention this. For example, Adobe's Type Manager can use large cache allocations when it is rendering several fonts for a document. The "built" fonts can be stored in memory, and the larger cache is helpful in that circumstance. Most applications use their own internal memory cacheing scheme, and don't rely on the system software's cache for performance enhancement.

The perfect disk cache size is a matter of great debate even among the most technically knowledgeable Macintosh users. Your Macintosh hardware and software configuration, and the way you use your Mac has a big effect on your optimal setting, so trial and error is really the only way to find what works best for you.

7.5 ▶ The disk cache is one of the few elements of memory handling that has been reworked in System 7.5–although you wouldn't know it to look at the Memory control panel. A new file system cache scheme extends the current file system cache into temporary memory (RAM) when possible. This is of particular benefit to users with a large amount of physical RAM installed. Also, menus are now better cached so that the next time a menu is pulled down it is drawn immediately. Menu performance varies as a function of the CPU speed, but will be most apparent to users with slower machines.

Virtual Memory

Virtual memory is a software trick. It uses space on your hard drive to "fool" the Macintosh into thinking there's more available memory than there really is. Using virtual memory, a Macintosh with only 2 or 4mb of actual RAM can act like it has 12mb or more. In fact, in conjunction with 32-bit addressing (discussed later in this chapter), virtual memory can provide your Macintosh up to 1 gigabyte (1000mb) of memory. This number is one half of the addressable disk space in System Version 7.1. System 7.5 has a 4gb addressable disk space, half of which is addressable as virtual memory (double the amount of potential virtual memory from earlier versions). In reality you will address only a small fraction of that virtual limit.

Virtual memory substitutes hard disk space for RAM. One benefit of using this device is that hard drive space is generally much less expensive than actual RAM. In addition, with 32-bit addressing, virtual memory can provide access to more memory than is possible with RAM chips alone.

However, using virtual memory has two main drawbacks. First, performance is slower than with real RAM, since the mechanical actions required of your hard drive are no match for the electronic speed of RAM chips. Second, virtual memory appropriates hard disk space normally available for other activities. You'll notice a striking difference in hard drive speed on virtual memory when you upgrade to a new drive. An on-board hard drive disk cache (installed RAM) can improve virtual memory performance.

In order to use virtual memory, your Macintosh must be equipped with a 68030 or better processor, such as the Macintosh SE/30, Macintosh IIci, IIsi or IIfx. Virtual memory can also be used with a 68020 Macintosh II, with a PMMU chip installed. At this point you may have difficulty locating a PMMU chip for installation in a Mac II. Virtual memory cannot be used with the Macintosh Plus, Classic, SE, LC or Portable.

Without 32-bit addressing, virtual memory provides the following amounts of memory to your Macintosh:

- Macintosh Plus, Classic, SE, Portable, LC, II, PowerBook 100 — None

- Mac IIx, IIcx, SE/30 or II w/PMMU — 14mb less 1mb per installed NuBus card

- Other Macintoshes — 14mb less 1mb per installed NuBus card

With 32-bit addressing, the virtual memory option provides these amounts of memory:

- Macintosh Plus, Classic, SE,   None
  Portable, LC, II, PowerBook 100

- Mac IIx, IIcx, SE/30   14mb less 1mb per
  or II w/PMMU   installed NuBus card

- Other Macintoshes   2gb
  w/68030, 68040,
  or 601 microprocessors

Enabling Virtual Memory

If your Macintosh supports virtual memory, go to the Memory control panel to activate this feature. After clicking the On button, the Select Hard Disk option becomes available. From the pop-up menu, select the hard disk volume on which the virtual memory storage file will be created and stored.

The amount of available space on the selected hard disk is displayed below the hard disk pop-up menu. The amount of free space available determines the amount of virtual memory that can be configured. A virtual memory storage file, equal to the total amount of memory available while using virtual memory, will be placed on the selected disk. In other words, if your Macintosh has 4mb of actual RAM, and you wish to reach 12mb by using 8mb of virtual memory, a 12mb virtual memory storage file must be created on the selected volume.

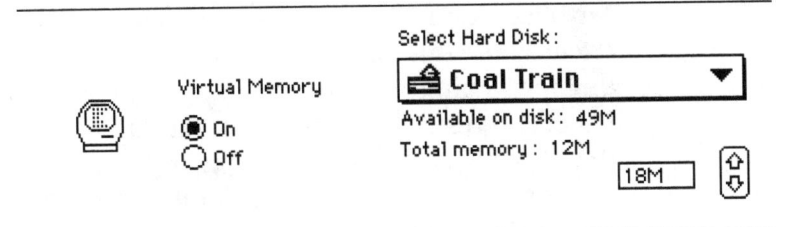

```
                              Select Hard Disk:
         Virtual Memory        [ Coal Train    ▼ ]
            ● On              Available on disk: 49M
            ○ Off             Total memory: 12M
                                              [ 18M ]  ↕
```

Figure 8-2: The virtual memory option in the Memory control panel determines the size and location of the virtual memory file.

Appearing below the Available on disk option is the total amount of memory currently available. The After restart option indicates the amount of memory specified, including actual RAM and virtual memory. Click on the arrows to modify this specification. If the After restart option is not visible, click one of the arrows until it appears.

The amount of memory you can specify depends on your hardware configuration and the 32-bit Addressing option setting. Without 32-bit addressing, you can specify up to 14mb of memory minus one megabyte for each NuBus card installed in your Macintosh. If 32-bit addressing is turned on, up to 1gb of memory can be specified, depending on which Mac you have and on the free space available on the selected hard disk.

Any changes made to the virtual memory option will not take effect until your Macintosh is restarted. When you finish setting the Memory control panel options, close the control panel and restart. To verify that virtual memory is on, choose the About This Macintosh command to display the current memory status. (More information on the About This Macintosh dialog box later in this chapter.)

Virtual Memory Performance

Virtual memory works by moving information between a disk-based swap file and the RAM inside the computer; even when virtual memory is being used, the Macintosh communicates only with the real RAM. This movement of data between hard disk and RAM, technically known as paging, causes the Macintosh to perform slower than it does when using actual RAM alone.

The amount of paging slowdown depends on how much actual RAM is available and how virtual memory is being used. The more available RAM, the less paging interference. The type of activity called for also affects paging; working on multi-megabyte data files and frequent switching between open applications are examples of activities that usually require more paging and therefore decrease performance. Problems with virtual memory show up as poor performance in animation, video and sound. Games and multimedia content that require large data manipulation are the first to suffer. Virtual memory is a prime energy drain in PowerBook computers.

A good rule of thumb in determining your own RAM/virtual memory mix is that you should have enough actual RAM to cover your normal memory needs and enough supplemental virtual memory to handle occasional abnormally large requirements. If you find that approximately 4mb of RAM let you work comfortably in the three or four open applications you use regularly, but you occasionally need 8mb to open additional applications or work with large data files, then 4mb of real RAM and a combined total of 10mb of RAM and virtual memory would probably be adequate. Trying to get by with just 2mb of real RAM and 10mb of virtual memory would result in prohibitively slow performance and the potential for crashes caused by the heavy paging.

Exactly what ratios of real to virtual memory Macintosh users should set has long been the subject of speculation and, finally, some technical study. With 2mb of real RAM, virtual memory is practically useless as you need to free up nearly all of your system heap by turning off all extensions and control panels. With System 7 Pro and later, 4mb is the minimum requirement for the system to run. For 4mb RAM try a setting between 4mb and 10mb virtual memory. With 8mb RAM a setting as high as 20mb is possible (remember to turn on 32-bit addressing first). For 16mb of RAM, 50mb of virtual memory are practical; and with 32mb or more of RAM there is no real practical limit to the amount of virtual memory you can use.

Disabling Virtual Memory

Virtual memory can be turned off by clicking on the Off button in the virtual memory area of the Memory control panel and restarting your Macintosh. After disabling virtual memory, the virtual memory storage file is usually deleted from your hard drive automatically. If it isn't, you can remove it by dragging it to the Trash.

32-Bit Addressing

In the past, 8mb was the maximum amount of RAM that could be installed (or used) on the Macintosh. This limitation was posed by the way the available memory chips were addressed by the Macintosh system software, including those parts that reside on the ROM chips on the computer's logic board. When used on Macintosh computers containing newer versions of the ROM chips, System 7 breaks the 8mb barrier, allowing up to 1gb of RAM.

This extended ability to use memory is called 32-bit addressing, referring to the number of digits used in the new memory-addressing scheme. The Mac's older memory scheme is 24-bit addressing, since only 24 digits are used. Twenty-four–bit addressing is still used on most Macintosh models, and is also supported by System 7.5. Power Macintosh computers have 32-bit addressing built in, and cannot have it turned off. Therefore, you don't see a 32-bit Addressing section on a Power Macintosh Memory control panel.

The ROM chips required for 32-bit addressing are 32-bit clean ROMs, and are currently included in all shipping Macintoshes except the Macintosh Classic and the PowerBook 100. Certain "older" models, specifically, the Plus, Classic, SE, SE/30, Portable, II, IIx, IIcx and LC, do not have 32-bit clean ROMs and therefore can't normally use 32-bit addressing. The SE/30 and Macintosh II, IIx and IIcx can be upgraded to 32-bit clean capacity using an extension called MODE32, or the 32-bit Addressing system enabler, both of which are available without charge from user groups and online services. Apple used to distribute and support MODE32, but no longer does so. Support for this function is built into later versions of the system software.

When used on a 32-bit compatible Mac, the Memory control panel includes the 32-bit Addressing option, as shown in Figure 8-3. When the option is set to Off, the Macintosh uses 24-bit addressing and only 8mb of RAM can be used (or up to 14mb of virtual memory). When set to On, the Mac uses 32-bit addressing, and all installed RAM (within the limits discussed below) becomes available to the system software. Changes to this option take effect only after restarting the Macintosh. The 32-bit Addressing option does not appear on Macs which are not 32-bit compatible.

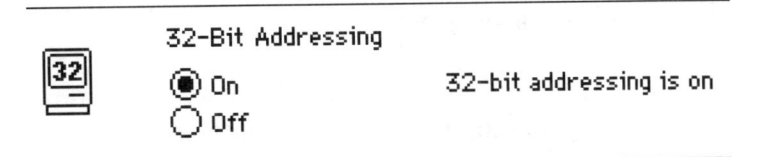

Figure 8-3: The 32-bit Addressing option.

Most Macs using 32-bit addressing can access up to 128mb of real RAM and up to 1gb of virtual memory, or 2gb with System 7.5 (as described earlier in this chapter). Some older software applications written and released before the introduction of System 7 are not compatible with 32-bit addressing, and so you will have to turn 32-bit addressing off to use them. These incompatible applications are fairly rare, but if you notice unpredictable behavior on your Mac, or frequent crashes, and you're using one or more older applications, utilities or extensions, try turning 32-bit addressing off to see if the problems are related to 32-bit addressing incompatibility. There are few commercial applications that now function improperly under 32-bit addressing. Mostly you will run into these problems with older applications or with shareware or freeware programs.

In some cases, launching an application that's not compatible with 32-bit addressing will cause a dialog box to appear, warning you that you must restart your Macintosh with 32-bit addressing turned off. Most of the time, however, this dialog box will not appear and you'll have to find this out the hard way, by experiencing a system crash or unpredictable behavior.

If your Mac has more than 8mb of RAM installed, or you want to use more than 16mb of virtual memory, you should activate 32-bit addressing. If more than 8mb of RAM is installed and you don't turn 32-bit addressing on, the About This Macintosh dialog box will report that your system software is consuming all of your RAM over 8mb. (This dialog box is discussed more fully later in this chapter.) If you have 8mb of RAM or less and don't need to use 16mb of virtual memory or more, you should leave the 32-bit addressing disabled.

The Modern Memory Manager

Caution: If you own a Power Macintosh computer, you will note that its control panel contains a new section called the Modern Memory Manager, as shown in Figure 8-4. When you turn on the Modern Memory Manager option (first introduced in System 7.1.2) you are enabling a new memory processing scheme specially written for the Power PC chip and native applications. RISC-based microprocessors load so much more of the instruction set into RAM than CISC-based microprocessors that virtual memory, paging, and other memory operations were among the first that were ported into native PPC code.

The Modern Memory Manager contains new algorithms that improve memory performance: not only when you are using native PPC programs, but even when you are using older programs operating in 680x0 emulation mode. Just as the introduction of 32-bit addressing caused compatibility problems early on, so too does the Modern Memory Manager. So far, it is the single biggest cause of compatibility problems with the Power Macintosh series. Turn the Modern Memory Manager off if you are experiencing problems with programs running on your Power Macintosh.

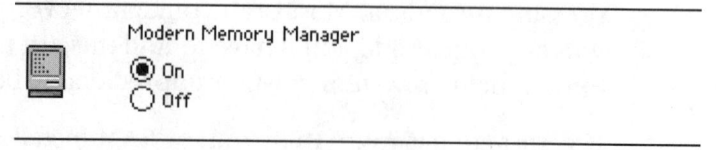

Modern Memory Manager
● On
○ Off

Figure 8-4: The Modern Memory Manager option.

Memory Control Panel Tips

- Use at least the minimum recommended disk cache. The disk cache speeds up operation, so you should leave it set to at least 32k for every megabyte of RAM installed in your Mac. (That means 64k for 2mb, 128k for 4mb and 256k for 8mb.)

- Install enough real RAM in your Macintosh. Real RAM chips should provide enough memory to cover your normal daily memory needs—at least 4mb and in some cases up to 8mb. Although virtual memory can provide inexpensive additional memory, 80 percent of your memory needs should be covered by real RAM. The performance drawbacks of relying too heavily on virtual memory don't justify the relatively small amount of money saved.

- Extend your available memory with virtual memory. Once you've installed enough RAM to satisfy your everyday needs, use the virtual memory to give yourself extra memory to cover special occasional situations, such as working with large color images, animation or more than the usual number of simultaneously open programs.

- If you have 4mb of real RAM in your Mac, 8 to 10mb use supplemental virtual memory; at 8mb real RAM, 12 to 20mb virtual memory; at 16mb RAM, 20 MB to 50mb virtual memory; and at 32mb RAM and above, use as much as you desire. Users with 32-bit-addressing compatible Macs can go beyond the 14mb limit up to 1gb, although amounts of 20 to 30mb will usually suffice for most applications except image processing applications.

    Caution: Turn off virtual memory when you see performance problems. Some programs like games and graphics programs do considerable data input/output. Virtual memory can degrade performance, and rapid paging can also lead to system crashes. Turn virtual memory off if you are experiencing these conditions.

- Use 32-bit addressing carefully. Although most old applications and nearly every new application is compatible with 32-bit addressing, there are a few programs out there that still don't run well (or at all) with 32-bit addressing activated. When using a program for the first time after turning on 32-bit addressing, save your data frequently until you're sure the program is working properly. Leave 32-bit addressing turned off if you don't need to use it.

Controlling Memory

Once you've determined how much memory you need and made it available to System 7.5 (by installing RAM and by using virtual memory and 32-bit addressing), you'll want to manage that memory wisely and use it economically. Managing your Mac's memory allows you to make sure that each application has enough RAM to operate properly, and that enough total memory is available to open as many different applications as necessary.

System 7.5 provides two excellent tools for memory management—the About This Macintosh dialog box and the Get Info dialog box. We'll look at both of these tools in this section.

About This Macintosh

In System 7.5, the familiar About The Finder command has been changed to About This Macintosh, and the dialog box associated with it has been improved. The About This Macintosh dialog box provides information about the Macintosh being used, the system software version, installed and available memory, and the amount of memory used by each open application.

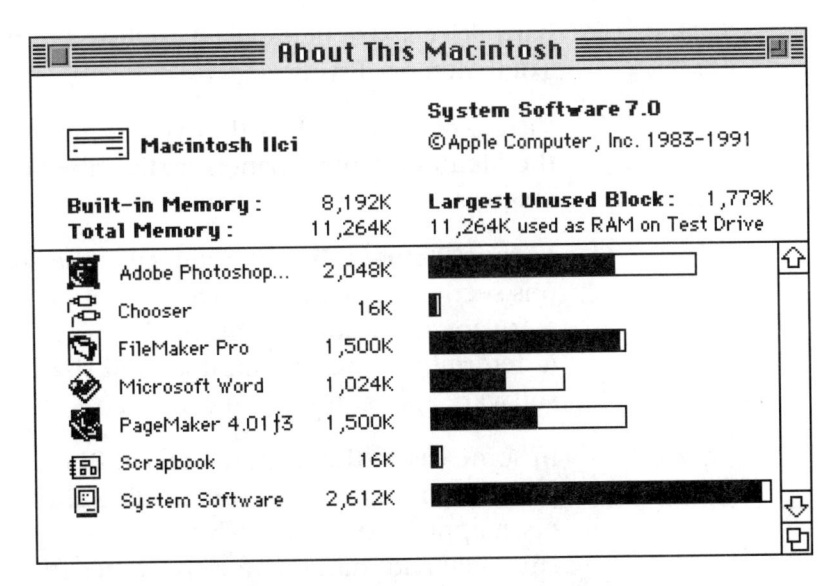

```
╔══════════════ About This Macintosh ══════════════╗
                        System Software 7.0
    ▭ Macintosh IIci    ©Apple Computer, Inc. 1983-1991

    Built-in Memory:   8,192K   Largest Unused Block:  1,779K
    Total Memory:     11,264K   11,264K used as RAM on Test Drive

    [icon] Adobe Photoshop...  2,048K   [████████████████]
    [icon] Chooser                16K   [▌               ]
    [icon] FileMaker Pro       1,500K   [████████████    ]
    [icon] Microsoft Word      1,024K   [████            ]
    [icon] PageMaker 4.01 ƒ3   1,500K   [███████████     ]
    [icon] Scrapbook              16K   [▌               ]
    [icon] System Software     2,612K   [███████████████ ]
```

Figure 8-5: The About This Macintosh dialog box.

The upper section of the dialog box gives the icon and name for your Macintosh, the version of system software currently in use and the following data related to the memory available in your Mac:

- **Built-in Memory.** Displays the amount of actual RAM installed in your Macintosh, not including virtual memory. This listing does not appear on Macintoshes that don't support virtual memory, such as the Plus, Classic, Mac II (without a PMMU), Portable, and LC, or on any Mac with virtual memory turned off. All models of Performas, LC II and LC III, Centris, Quadras, PowerBooks, and Power Macintosh computer show this heading, provided virtual memory is on.

- **Total Memory.** Documents the total memory available in your Macintosh, including installed RAM plus available virtual memory. If virtual memory is being used, the name of the hard disk storing that file and the amount of hard drive space being used are listed to the right of the Total Memory listing.

Virtual memory and hard drive designations are set via the Memory control panel, as described earlier in this chapter.

- **Largest Unused Block.** Calculates the largest contiguous section of memory currently not being used by open software applications. This number is important because it determines both the number and size of additional software applications you can open.

In some cases, the Largest Unused Block will not equal the amount of total memory available, less the size of all open applications. That's because as applications are launched and quit, memory becomes fragmented—gaps are created between sections of memory that are used and those that are available. To defragment your memory and create larger unused blocks, quit all open applications and then relaunch them. As they're relaunched, applications will use available memory sequentially, leaving the largest possible unused block.

Caution: If you get an out-of-memory alert box and there should be plenty of memory left, you have a fragmented memory situation. This occurs when you launch and quit programs repeatedly. Try and "unlearn" techniques of the past by leaving programs you will use later open and in memory. If you have a fragmented memory problem, try first quitting programs in the reverse order they were opened. If that doesn't do the trick, you will have to restart to flush your Macintosh's memory.

Each software application requires a particular amount of memory in order to be opened successfully. The amount of memory is documented, and can be controlled, in the Get Info dialog box, as described later in this chapter. When a program is launched, if its memory requirement is larger than the largest unused block, it can't be opened. So you need to know approximately how much memory an application needs.

The lower portion of the About This Macintosh dialog box displays information about each open application, including its name, icon and amount of memory allocated and used.

- **Application name and icon.** Each open application is listed in alphabetical order along with a small version of its icon.

- **Amount of memory allocated.** Just to the right of the application name, the total amount of memory that was allocated to that program when it was opened is displayed, along with a bar graph showing this amount in relation to amounts used by other open applications. The total bar represents total allocated memory; the filled portion of the bar represents the portion of that allocated memory currently in use.

- **Amount of memory used.** In most cases when an application is opened, only a portion of its total allocated memory is used immediately. Usually, some of the memory is used by the application itself, some is used to hold open document files and some is left over for use by the software's commands and features. Only the memory currently being used appears as the filled-in percentage of the memory allocation bar.

An About This Macintosh Tip

- A secret dialog box. Holding down the option key changes the About This Macintosh command into the About The Finder command, which brings up a copyright screen that first appeared in Finder 1.0 in 1984 (waiting a bit will get you a history of the Finder's programmers, scrolling across the screen).

Figure 8-6: The About The Finder dialog box.

The Get Info Dialog Box

The Get Info dialog box allows you to use the information provided in the About This Macintosh dialog box to take charge of your Macintosh's memory use. You do this by adjusting the amount of memory each program uses, to minimize problems related to memory shortages or better allocate your available RAM to the different applications you want to open simultaneously.

The memory-related options of the Get Info dialog box are different in System 7 Version 7.0 and Version 7.1, so we will examine each of these separately.

Get Info in Version 7.0

The Get Info dialog box's Memory option is shown as it appears in version 7.0 in Figure 8-7. The Memory option has two parts: Suggested Size and Current Size.

- **Suggested Size.** Displays the amount of RAM the developer recommends to properly run the application. You can't change this option, but it's very valuable as a reminder of the original Current Size setting.

- **Current Size.** Specifies the actual amount of RAM that the application will request when it's launched. (By default, the Current Size is equal to the Suggested Size.) You can change the amount of memory that will be allocated by entering a new value in this option, then closing the Get Info dialog box.

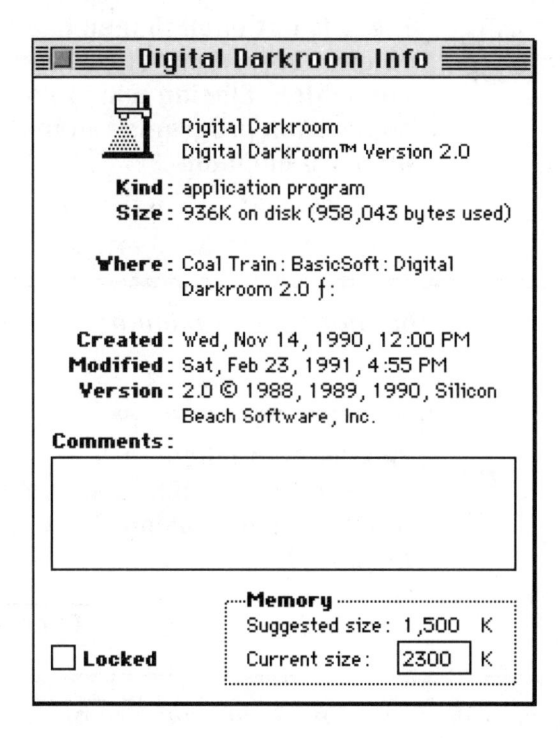

Figure 8-7: An application's Get Info dialog box in System 7.0.

When an application is launched, the program requests the amount of memory specified in the "Current Size" option. If this amount is available in an unused block, the memory is allocated and the program is opened. You can check the size of the largest available block in the About This Macintosh dialog box, as described earlier.

If the amount of memory requested is larger than the largest available unused block, a dialog box will appear, stating that not enough memory is available (shown in Figure 8-8), asking if you want to try to run the application using less memory (shown in Figure 8-9), or suggesting that you quit an open application to create enough free memory (see Figure 8-10).

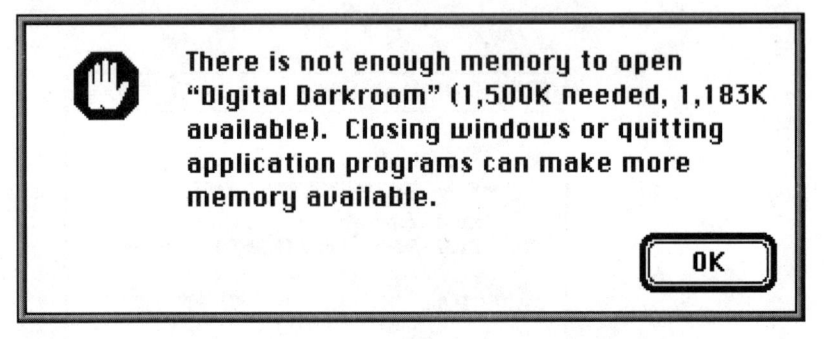

> There is not enough memory to open "Digital Darkroom" (1,500K needed, 1,183K available). Closing windows or quitting application programs can make more memory available.
>
> [OK]

Figure 8-8: The "not enough memory" dialog box.

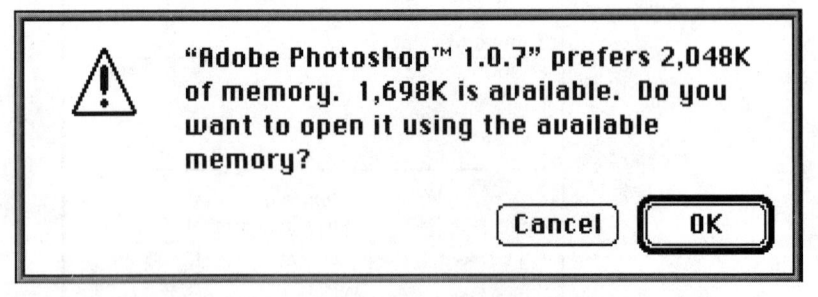

> "Adobe Photoshop™ 1.0.7" prefers 2,048K of memory. 1,698K is available. Do you want to open it using the available memory?
>
> [Cancel] [OK]

Figure 8-9: The "almost enough memory" dialog box.

> **There is not enough memory to open "FileMaker Pro" (3,530K needed, 3,523K available).**
>
> To make more memory available, try quitting "Adobe Photoshop® 2.0.1".
>
> [OK]

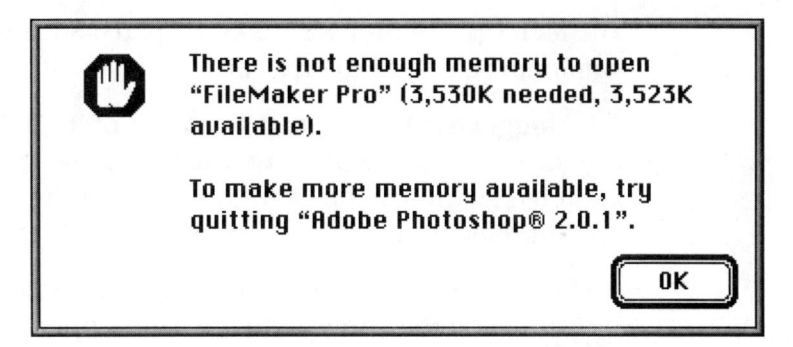

Figure 8-10: The "enough memory if you quit" dialog box.

Get Info in Version 7.1 & Later

In System 7 Version 7.1 and later, the Get Info dialog box's options eliminate the need to change settings for different memory situations by allowing you to set options that determine the amount of memory that will be used depending on the amount of memory available at launch time.

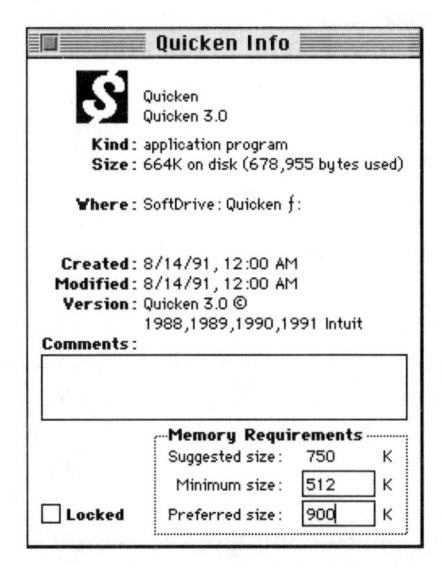

Figure 8-11: An application's Get Info dialog box in system software Versions 7.1–7.5.

The Memory option here has three parts: Suggested Size, Minimum Size and Preferred Size.

- **Suggested Size.** Lists the amount of RAM the developer recommends to properly run the application. You can't change this option—it's a reminder of the memory requirements as set by the application developer.

- **Minimum Size.** Designates the smallest amount of RAM in which the application will run properly. You can change this option by entering a new value.

- **Virtual Memory.** Lists the amount of virtual memory available on your Power Macintosh. This option appears in the Get Info of Power Macintosh models only.

- **Preferred Size.** Specifies the actual amount of RAM that the application will request when it's launched. You can change the amount of memory that will be allocated by entering a new value in this option, then closing the Get Info dialog box.

When an application is launched, the program requests the amount of memory specified in the Preferred Size option. If this amount is available in an unused block, the memory is allocated and the program is opened. You can check the size of the largest available block in the About This Macintosh dialog box, as described earlier.

If the amount of memory requested by the Preferred Size option is not available, but more memory is available than the Minimum Size option, the application will launch using all available memory. If the amount of RAM specified in the Minimum Size option is unavailable, one of two dialog boxes will appear: one offers to quit an open application that has no open files in order to free enough memory to complete the launch (see Figure 8-12); the other one states that not enough memory is available to complete the launch (see Figure 8-13).

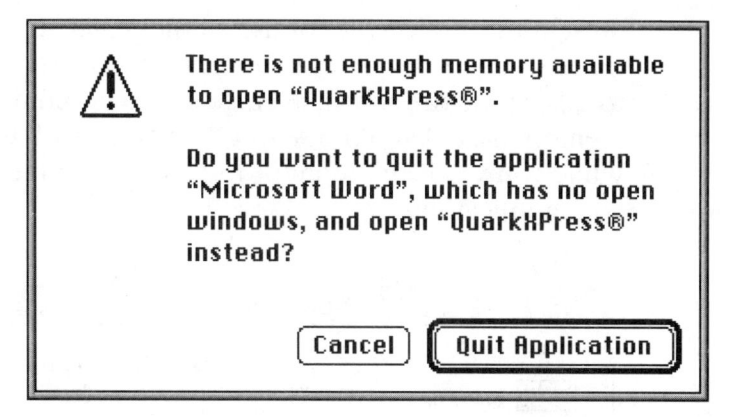

> [!WARNING]
> There is not enough memory available to open "QuarkXPress®".
>
> Do you want to quit the application "Microsoft Word", which has no open windows, and open "QuarkXPress®" instead?
>
> [Cancel] [[Quit Application]]

Figure 8-12: The "not enough memory unless you quit another application" dialog box.

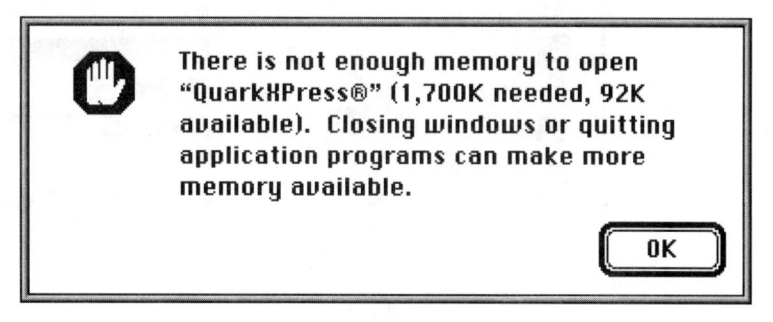

> ✋ There is not enough memory to open "QuarkXPress®" (1,700K needed, 92K available). Closing windows or quitting application programs can make more memory available.
>
> [[OK]]

Figure 8-13: The "not enough memory" dialog box.

Setting Memory Options

Optimally, 15 to 25 percent of the space in the memory allocation bar displayed next to an application name in the About This Macintosh dialog box should remain open, or unused, while the application is running. (As explained earlier, the bar graph displays total allocated RAM in white and the portion of memory actually being used in black.)

Most applications will not use all their allocated memory at all times—usage will vary as commands and features are used. So to determine the actual, average and maximum amount of memory used, keep the About This Macintosh window open while you work and monitor the changes in memory use by your applications.

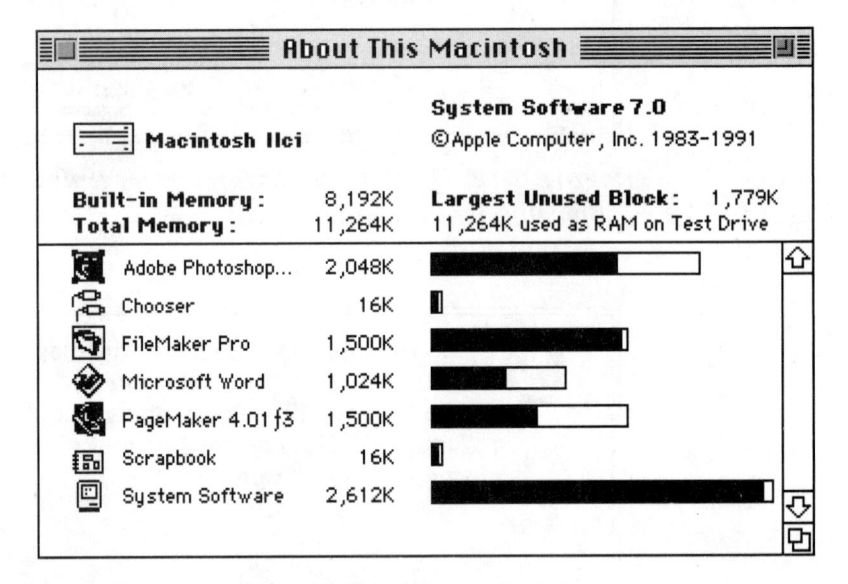

Figure 8-14: Application memory use is documented in the About This Macintosh dialog box.

Given that 15 to 25 percent unused space is the goal, watching the amount of actual memory used will show if the current memory allocation is too low, too high or about right. As a result, you may need to increase a program's memory allocation, or you may be able to decrease it. Either of these modifications is done with the Current Size (Version 7.0) or Preferred Size (Versions 7.1–7.5) options.

Increasing memory allocation provides additional memory that can in many cases improve application performance, allow larger and more complete document files to be opened and reduce or eliminate the possibility of memory-related crashes. These effects are hardly surprising, when you consider how an application uses its allocated memory: it must control and manage its own code, data from any open document files and all data manipulations performed by its commands and features. And it must do all this with an allocated memory that's less than the total size of the application program and its data files, let alone what it needs to manipulate its data. As a result, software must constantly shift parts of its own code and data from open documents back and forth between disk-storage memory and real memory. Providing additional memory minimizes this activity and allows the program to concentrate on operating efficiently.

For most programs, increasing the Current Size or Preferred Size option by 20 to 25 percent is optimal, but if you experience frequent "out of memory" errors in any software application, continue increasing until these errors are eliminated.

Decreasing memory allocation allows you to successfully launch applications with less memory, thereby running more programs simultaneously. This is not generally a recommended practice, but in many cases software will operate successfully using less RAM than the developer suggested.

There is no easy way to determine what the true Minimum Size should be, although it will rarely be more than 20 percent smaller than the Suggested Size. Don't be afraid to try it—just be sure to test the application in this configuration before working on important data and save frequently once you begin working. Start by reducing the Current or Minimum Size by just 5 to 10 percent; if you find the About This Macintosh dialog box shows large amounts of unused space, you may be able to reduce the allocation even more.

With the advent of virtual memory support, the need for most Macintosh users to reduce these sizes should become less common. Even if you have only 2mb of RAM installed, using virtual memory is preferable to reducing the Current or Minimum Size options. You're less likely to experience crashes or loss of data using virtual memory than with a reduced Current Size. (See the discussion of virtual memory earlier in this chapter.)

Of course, the best long-range solution is to add enough RAM to your Macintosh so you won't have to depend on either virtual memory or Memory Requirements reductions.

Moving On

The amount of memory available on your Macintosh determines, in large measure, what you can do with your computer. As we've seen in this chapter, System 7.5 has fine-tuned changes made in System 7 designed to give you much more control over memory availability and how that memory is utilized.

- Virtual memory lets you "create" memory by using space on your hard drive as if it were RAM.

- 32-bit addressing makes it possible to access a vast amount of memory.

- The Get Info dialog box helps you control the amount of memory an application uses.

- The About This Macintosh dialog box provides constant feedback about what's happening with your Mac's memory.

System 7.1, 7.5 and later support Apple's new advanced graphics module, QuickDraw GX. Printing, font handling, color matching and a number of other related technologies are made both more powerful and easier to use with QuickDraw GX. In the next chapter we examine graphics and font handling supported by system software.

Chapter 9

QuickDraw GX & Fonts

A great measure of the success that the Macintosh has achieved has been due to its capabilities in the graphics and publishing arena. Desktop publishing is the Macintosh's heritage. System 7 makes major changes in this technology, introducing sophisticated graphics, outline fonts, advanced typography, color matching, a new print architecture, a portable document format and improved localization for international software. Many of these new changes are due to the release of QuickDraw GX in System 7.5. QuickDraw GX is Apple's extension to its graphics programming routines and page description language.

Fonts are both the blessing and curse of the Macintosh. No other computer offers such a variety of fonts or typographic capabilities; but because of technical problems and corporate politics, no other aspect of the Mac has caused so many headaches for so many people.

System 7 has extended Macintosh font technology, simplifying font installation, improving the appearance of fonts onscreen and introducing two new font formats called

TrueType and TrueType GX. System 7.5 offers some relief for "font hell," and some additional complexity. Unfortunately, many legitimate font issues remain unresolved.

In this chapter, we'll look at each of the technologies supported by QuickDraw GX, paying special attention to fonts and type issues. Here you'll find out what's practical and what's possible.

What Is QuickDraw?

Of all the sets of routines or managers in the Macintosh toolbox, few are as recognized and recognizable as QuickDraw. QuickDraw was there in 1984 when the first Macintosh shipped. MacPaint and MacDraw, and a generation of Macintosh programs that followed, use QuickDraw for most of their capabilities. Anything you see drawn within a window on your Macintosh screen is due to QuickDraw.

You use the QuickDraw programming language to create images. Put another way, QuickDraw is an imaging model. These images are then sent to your monitor, to your printer and to any other output device whose device driver supports QuickDraw. As such, QuickDraw is really a page description language (or PDL) in the same way that PostScript is.

QuickDraw is responsible for lines and shapes you draw, their patterns and fills, properties such as transparency or opacity, colors, color models, and color selection, fonts, and even less intuitively, what you see in a print dialog box.

Printers are QuickDraw printers when they take QuickDraw output and rasterize it to print its image. Similarly, PostScript printers rasterize PostScript output. QuickDraw can be printed on PostScript printers because QuickDraw is translated to PostScript in your Macintosh when it is output to a PostScript device.

QuickDraw was never designed to meet the demands of high-quality output. Apple created QuickDraw to simplify and codify screen display at 72 dpi in black and white (which were the screen characteristics of the classic Macintosh series) and to draw to simple printers such as the ImageWriter. For higher quality printing needs, Apple cut a co-marketing deal in 1985 with a small graphics programming company called Adobe and licensed the sophisticated PostScript language. Apple would sell Cannon's laser printing xerographic engine run by a PostScript controller, and QuickDraw would be converted to PostScript in the operating system of the Macintosh. The rest is, as they say, history.

One of the first QuickDraw upgrades came in 1988 when the Macintosh II was introduced. In its original release, only eight QuickDraw colors were supported. Color QuickDraw was added to system software with the addition of System 5, adding a 32-bit color modeling capability. Soon thereafter with the introduction of the Mac IIx, Color QuickDraw was written into the new ROMs.

By 1989, high-quality type and graphics had become big business and a central technology on the personal computer. PostScript fonts were encrypted and proprietary, although the rest of the language was published. Therefore, Adobe had created a lock on the type business for the Macintosh, and it had control over essential system software and applications.

Adobe, responding to the needs of their customers, specked out an advanced version of PostScript, called PostScript Level 2. PostScript had problems with complexity, file size and particularly performance. These problems could be solved by adding a new memory model, compression technology and new methods for drawing (rasterizing) a page. Other needed improvements would include better color support for printed (CYMK) color, color matching, advanced printing support and several other technologies. QuickDraw always suffered in comparison to PostScript; PostScript Level 2 threatened to make QuickDraw an anachronism.

With System 7, Apple decided to make the break. Along with Microsoft, which was developing Windows 3.1, Apple decided to introduce an open outline font type standard called TrueType and a page description language called TrueImage. Apple set about addressing the other deficiencies in QuickDraw by revising the language and adding new technologies through a language extension.

Because the TrueType font technology was ready to go in 1991, it was released with System 7.0. Some other components in the original System 7 list–the LineLayout Manager and the New Print Architecture–were not. Those two new features became part of a larger package, QuickDraw GX, meant to support the needs of color publishing. QuickDraw GX would fix problems handling color, text layout, typography, printing and so on. Because these problems are industry-wide, it's not surprising that both QuickDraw GX and PostScript Level 2 address similar issues. After nearly four years in development and testing, QuickDraw GX ships with System 7.5. Both QuickDraw and QuickDraw GX have been translated to native code to run on the Power Macintosh. Figure 9-1 shows a diagram of the QuickDraw GX architecture and its relation to system software.

QuickDraw	ColorSync	QuickDraw GX Type	QuickDraw GX Graphics
	QuickDraw GX Printing Architecture		
	System 7.1		

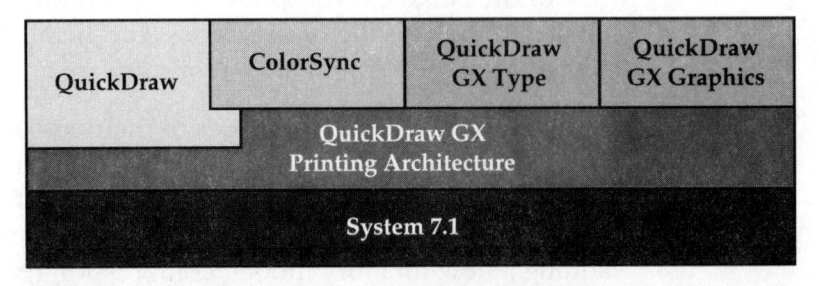

Figure 9-1: The QuickDraw GX architecture.

About QuickDraw GX

QuickDraw GX is a system extension that supplements the capabilities of QuickDraw now present in your system. If an application is QuickDraw GX-aware or -savvy, it can use the new capabilities. If not, they are ignored. As you upgrade your applications, fonts and printer drivers, you will begin to notice the new capabilities that QuickDraw GX provides. Until then, you can continue to work in the way you've become accustomed to. (See the QuickDraw GX icon in Figure 9-2.)

Figure 9-2: The QuickDraw GX icon.

QuickDraw GX has the following important capabilities:

- **Higher level graphics routines.** More complex shapes and transformations are supported. Applications that are QuickDraw-savvy can use these system routines; they require less memory to operate and less storage space. The following section, "Sophisticated Graphics Primitives," describes these changes.

- **New print architecture.** You will first notice QuickDraw GX's effect in printing because current applications and hardware can take advantage of it. A new, more powerful, simplified print dialog box also appears in System 7.5. You can create virtual printers on your desktop as icons, drag and drop files to them, and have better control over your printers and spooled documents anywhere on a network.

All printer types that you now use are supported. For example, System 7.5 ships with a new set of Apple PostScript printer drivers. Other vendors are expected to provide timely upgrades. For more information on this topic, see "QuickDraw GX & Printing" later in this chapter.

- **Advanced typography.** QuickDraw GX uses special TrueType GX fonts to create advanced type effects such as automatic kerning and justification, and special character support based on context. You can continue to use your current font collection, bitmaps or outline fonts, converted PostScript Type 1 fonts (with a System 7.5 utility), or you can upgrade to TrueType GX to take advantage of the new capabilities.

- **Advanced layout.** The LineLayout Manager provides support for international text such as Kanji, Hindi, Hebrew, Arabic or any character set. You can mix right-to-left, left-to-right or vertical arrangements of letterforms within a document, a paragraph or a line. To use these capabilities, an application must be QuickDraw-savvy, and you must install QuickDraw GX fonts. TrueType GX fonts are aware of their relative character positioning and can change shapes appropriately. The "Advanced Typography" sections describe both the new type effects and the LineLayout Manager.

- **Improved localization.** WorldScript provides a system for Macintosh developers to transform applications from one language and character set to another. QuickDraw GX performs the display and handling of fonts and supports character sets based on the Unicode standard. "Unicode, WorldScript & Localization" describes these new capabilities.

- **Portable digital documents.** QuickDraw GX supports a new "universal" file format known as a portable digital document (PDD). A PDD created by an application can be opened, viewed and printed by any other user who has QuickDraw GX on his or her computer, whether or not the user has the creator application and typefaces.

- **Custom print functions.** Because fonts, printing and other objects can be controlled by QuickDraw GX, developers can more easily create custom printer drivers, printer extensions and solutions for specific markets.

- **Color matching.** QuickDraw GX incorporates ColorSync, Apple's color management technology. Because QuickDraw can profile device characteristics, colors can be reproduced as closely and as accurately as the device allows. ColorSync was released about the time System 7.1 appeared. See "ColorSync & Color Matching" later in this chapter for further discussion.

QuickDraw GX comes as part of System 7.5 but requires separate installation. It requires a minimum of 5mb of RAM; it requires 8mb of RAM when used with PowerTalk. These figures are for the Roman character set on a 68k Macintosh. For use on a Power Macintosh, you should double those figures. Any Macintosh running System 7.1 or later can use QuickDraw GX. Other than the disk storage space required, no other additional hardware demands are made.

Sophisticated Graphics Primitives

QuickDraw GX greatly extends the range of graphics primitives, or shapes, in QuickDraw. Beyond simple line movements that produce the basic shapes—lines, curves, rectangles, polygons, paths and so on—QuickDraw GX adds more advanced attributes. In this regard, outline type is a just another shape, with both the same attributes and range of possibilities. Drawn or vector shapes are resolution-independent and scale to any size correctly.

QuickDraw GX recognizes three different attributes:

- **Style.** Style describes the pen thickness (line or stroke), line end cap (pointed, rounded or flat), whether the line is drawn inside or outside a shape, line dashes and patterns, and line joins and corners. Text style includes font, size and other attributes such as bold, italic, etc.

- **Transform.** A range of shape transformations is supported, including scaling, rotation, perspective, skew and clipping.

- **Ink.** The ink attributes are the descriptions of the color properties of a shape: data on the selection in a color space, transfer information (opacity, transparency or mixing), and the description of how to view and display a selected color on a device.

These three words—style, transform and ink—will enter the vocabulary of any application that uses QuickDraw GX to draw, manipulate type, work with color and so on. Seasoned Macintosh users have worked with these concepts in their applications for years, but these capabilities were part of an application, not system software. These capabilities are also part of the PostScript vocabulary. Adding them to QuickDraw makes them available to all QuickDraw applications, resulting in a wider range of possibilities in Macintosh applications with less development time.

Fonts on the Macintosh

The introduction of the Macintosh in 1984 brought with it many innovations, but one of the most important was the way Macintosh enhanced the appearance of text. Whereas earlier personal computers reduced all communication to the drab, mechanical and impersonal look of pica-12 (the original dot-matrix font), the Macintosh produced text in a wide range of typefaces, both onscreen and on the printed page. Typography—long an important part of printed communication—became a part of personal computing.

> For related information, see "Printing & Fonts."

The original Macintosh fonts (New York, Monaco, Geneva and Chicago) were bitmapped fonts, which means that each character in each font was predefined by the series of dots necessary to create that character at a specific point size. Most bitmapped fonts were produced at sizes of 9-, 10-, 12- and 14-point. Chicago 12-point is the system font.

These original bitmapped fonts, and the many bitmapped fonts that soon joined them, were optimized for display on the Macintosh screen and for printing on the Apple ImageWriter (which was the only printer available at the time). There were, however, limitations to working with these bitmapped fonts:

- **Dot-matrix bitmapped quality was unacceptable for most business uses.** Although typeface variety was certainly a welcome improvement, most people still considered ImageWriter output quality unacceptable for business use regardless of the fonts.

- **Font variety was limited.** Although bitmapped fonts proliferated, almost all were "novelty" faces with little value beyond advertisements, invitations and entertainment.

- **The 400k system disks could hold only a limited selection of fonts.** Because hard drives were not generally available at that time, it was necessary to boot the Macintosh from a 400k floppy disk. After you squeezed the System Folder plus an application or two onto a floppy, only a small amount of room was left for font styles and sizes.

- **Macintosh applications could support only a limited number of fonts at one time.** When too many fonts were installed in the System file, applications acted strangely, often providing only a random subset of the installed fonts.

These problems were solved, after some time, with new releases of system software, application software and third-party utility programs. The next big change in the Macintosh font world was not based on software, but on the introduction of the Apple LaserWriter printer with its built-in support for the PostScript page description language.

PostScript Fonts

The introduction of the Apple LaserWriter printer brought a new type of font to the Macintosh: the PostScript font. These fonts were required in documents created for output to the LaserWriter (and all later PostScript printers) in order for type to be printed at high resolution. Bitmapped fonts were inadequate for these new printers. Eventually, PostScript fonts came to be known by a variety of names, including laser fonts, outline fonts and Type 1 fonts.

Each PostScript font consists of two files: a screen font file and a printer font file. (See Figure 9-3.) The screen font file for a PostScript font is nearly identical to the font file of bitmapped fonts, providing bitmapped versions of the font at specific sizes optimized for onscreen use. There are other similarities too:

- Both appear with a suitcase icon.
- Both are provided in different styles and sizes.
- Both were installed with the Font/DA Mover until the release of System 7.
- Both appear in the font menu or dialog box in all applications.

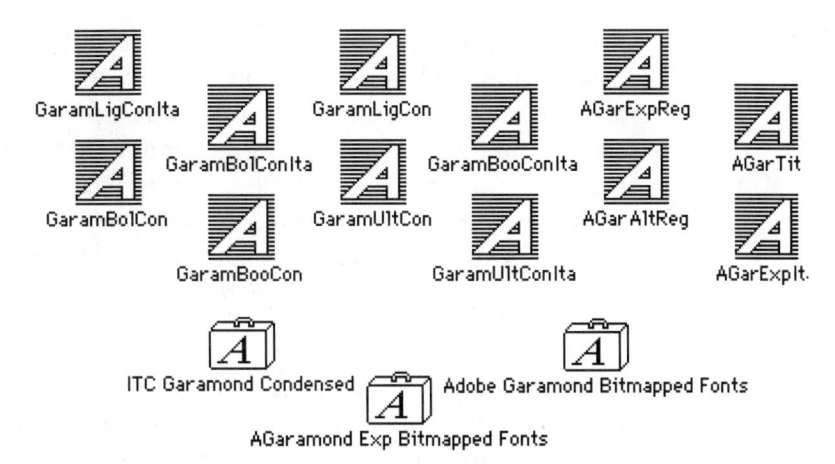

Figure 9-3: Icons for some popular screen font files (below) and printer font files (above).

The difference between PostScript screen fonts and bitmapped screen fonts is that each PostScript screen font has a corresponding PostScript printer font. (See Figure 9-4.) This printer font provides the PostScript printer with a mathematical description of each character in the font, as well as other information it needs to create and produce high-resolution output. When you're printing PostScript fonts, the screen font is used only as a pointer to the printer fonts. Your Macintosh works with the printer font descriptions to create text output.

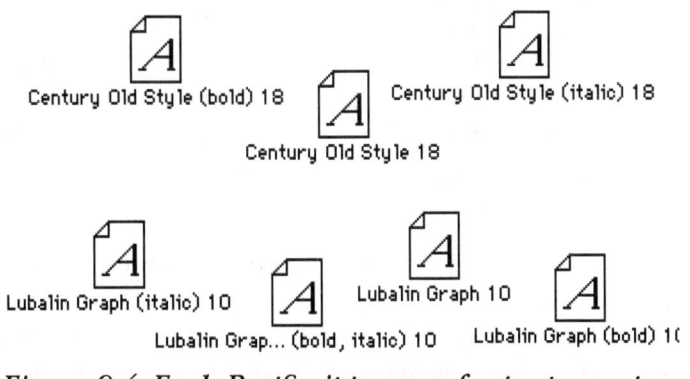

Figure 9-4: Each PostScript screen font represents a single font, size and style.

Printer font files often display an icon that looks like the LaserWriter, but depending on the way the printer font was created, another icon may appear. Each printer font is usually around 50k in size but can range from a minimum of 10k to a maximum of 75k. In most cases, there is a one-to-one correspondence between screen fonts and printer fonts (there's a unique printer font file for each unique screen font name). In some cases, however, printer fonts outnumber screen fonts, and vice versa.

Regardless of whether all screen fonts and printer fonts are matched, you don't always have to use all the available screen fonts, but you must always use all printer fonts. In other words, you can create Helvetica Bold without installing the Helvetica Bold screen font (by using the Helvetica font and the Bold type style), but you cannot print Helvetica Bold without the Helvetica Bold printer font.

For a PostScript font to be printed correctly, the printer font file must be "available" to the PostScript printer when it appears in a file being printed. A font is available when it is built into the printer's ROM chips, stored on a printer's hard disk, or kept on the Macintosh hard disk and manually or automatically downloaded to the printer.

When you install QuickDraw GX, the PostScript Type 1 fonts in your System Folder are converted to a form that works with QuickDraw GX. The original Type 1 fonts are placed in a folder called "•Archived Type 1 Fonts•" in your System Folder. Any Type 1 fonts that you install after you've installed QuickDraw GX must be manually converted using the Type 1 Enabler utility that is located on the QuickDraw GX installation disks.

To install the Type 1 Enabler on your hard drive, do a Custom Installation of QuickDraw GX and select the QuickDraw GX Utilities option. Several utility applications will be installed. To modify PostScript Type 1 fonts, open the Type 1 Enabler by double-clicking its icon, shown in Figure 9-5. In the standard dialog box, select the font or folder containing fonts that you wish to modify; then click the Select button. The fonts are then converted.

Figure 9-5: The Type 1 Enabler application.

PostScript Font Challenges

For a variety of reasons, using PostScript fonts in the real-world Macintosh environment has never been easy. The main problem is that the software and hardware environment in which PostScript fonts are used and the PostScript fonts themselves have been in a constant state of evolution. Most of these problems have been overcome through system software upgrades, new font-management utilities or "work-around" methods that have become well known and commonly accepted as necessary for font survival.

The following list describes many of the challenges PostScript font users have faced, along with the corresponding solutions, resolutions or workarounds:

- **PostScript fonts vs. non-PostScript fonts.** Because PostScript screen fonts are not noticeably different from non-PostScript screen fonts, it is difficult for inexperienced users to distinguish between them when creating documents that will be output on high-resolution PostScript printers.

    This problem has been solved, at least partially, by PostScript's dominance in the Macintosh world; most Macintosh users now have access to PostScript printers.

And PostScript fonts are now the rule rather than the exception. Apple and Adobe should have provided a better solution, forcing PostScript screen fonts to indicate their PostScript status—perhaps a symbol character displayed before or after their font names. This solution would simplify determining which fonts can be used to prepare documents to be output on PostScript printers.

- **Screen font availability.** After a document is created, there's generally no easy way to determine which fonts it contains, in order to be sure all necessary screen and printer fonts are available at print time—especially if the person printing the file is not the one who created it.

  Over time, individual software vendors have developed schemes to help identify screen fonts used in a document. PageMaker displays the dimmed names of used but not currently available fonts in its font menu, and both PageMaker and QuarkXPress produce a list of fonts used, for example. Only Adobe has addressed the problem of screen font availability, allowing Illustrator to print files correctly even if the screen fonts used to create the file aren't available at the time the file is printed. Unfortunately, this solution hasn't caught on with other vendors. (It's possible that Adobe's proprietary font knowledge allows them this advantage.)

  Some applications have a font-substitution capability. PageMaker 4.2 and 5.0 use Checklist, both also have a "Display Pub Info" addition that checks for font availability. FreeHand 4.0 checks for and substitutes fonts. Quark has a font-missing alert and can substitute fonts with a built-in utility.

- **Printer font availability.** The most fundamental requirement of PostScript fonts is that for each screen font used in a document, a corresponding printer font must be available at print time. This requirement has caused tremendous difficulty for Mac users because there's no automated way to track the screen font/printer font correspondence.

The advent of large font-storage printer hard drives, the Suitcase II and MasterJuggler font-management utilities, the ability to download screen fonts and the NFNT font resource have made the "Font Not Found: Substituting Courier" messages less common. But unfortunately, the only real solution to this problem lies with users and service bureau operators.

- **Too many font names in the font menus.** For non-PostScript screen fonts, a single font is provided in several different sizes, but you must create bold and italic versions using the Style command. PostScript fonts, on the other hand, provide a separate screen font for each size and style. As a result, font menus are very long. For example, Helvetica includes four entries (B Helvetica Bold, I Helvetica Italic, Helvetica and BI Helvetica Bold Italic). Times has four as well, and so on.

  Some applications such as ClarisWorks build a unified font menu when they launch; most others such as Microsoft Word 5.1 do not. Figure 9-6 shows the difference between the two behaviors.

  Utilities such as Suitcase's Font Harmony and Adobe's Type Reunion combine these font styles into a single font menu entry, reducing the four different Helvetica entries to one, providing a drop-down submenu for selecting variants of the font (bold, italic, bold italic and so on) and using the Style command for additional font styles. But sometimes, during the process, the ID numbers that the System file uses to keep track of fonts internally are altered, resulting in fonts being "lost" when you move documents from one Mac to another.

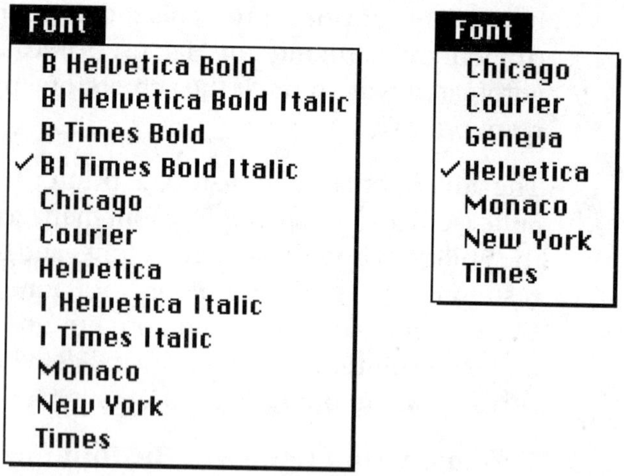

```
Font
  B Helvetica Bold
  BI Helvetica Bold Italic
  B Times Bold
✓ BI Times Bold Italic
  Chicago
  Courier
  Helvetica
  I Helvetica Italic
  I Times Italic
  Monaco
  New York
  Times
```

```
Font
  Chicago
  Courier
  Geneva
✓ Helvetica
  Monaco
  New York
  Times
```

Figure 9-6: Each style of a font is listed separately (left) when fonts are not harmonized, but not when they are harmonized (right).

- **Font ID conflicts.** The original Macintosh system was designed to handle only a small number of fonts. With the font explosion that followed PostScript's introduction, there were soon more fonts than available Font ID numbers. The Apple Font/DA Mover resolved Font ID conflicts as new fonts were added to the System file, but unfortunately, the Font/DA Mover did so by randomly renumbering the fonts. Renumbering fonts caused problems because some applications tracked fonts by Font ID number, and as a result, the same font would have different ID numbers on different Macintoshes.

  Because many applications used the Font ID numbers to keep track of font assignments within documents, Font ID instability caused documents to "forget" which fonts were used to create them when they were transferred from one Macintosh to another. Working with a wide range of fonts on the Macintosh became like playing a low-stakes game of Russian roulette.

This problem was partially solved with the release of system software 6.0, which added more complete support for a Macintosh resource called NFNT (pronounced N-Font). NFNT offered a font-numbering scheme capable of handling over 32,000 different fonts. Of course, implementing the new system meant that millions of non-NFNT fonts already in use had to be replaced with new NFNT versions, and that a master set of new NFNT fonts had to be distributed for use in this replacement.

To make matters worse, Apple and Adobe used the same uneven, unplanned and unprofessional distribution methods for the new font ID system that they used for Apple system software and shareware updates—user groups, bulletin boards and friendly file sharing. Therefore, the problem was only partially solved.

To further complicate the introduction of NFNT fonts, Apple and Adobe chose not to "harmonize" the NFNT fonts by allowing only a single font menu entry to appear for each font (as discussed previously). So it was left to users to perform this harmonization with their own utilities, which results in a non-universal set of fonts.

- **Different fonts with the same names.** As more vendors produced more PostScript fonts, another problem appeared: different versions of the same fonts released by different vendors.

This proliferation of fonts not only caused Macintoshes to become "confused" about which screen fonts and printer fonts were used in documents, but it also made it hard for service bureaus to know if the Garamond specified in a document was the Adobe, Bitstream or other font vendor version of the typeface. This point was crucial because font substitutions wouldn't work. And, even if they did, character width differences would play havoc with the output.

- **The Type 1 font secret.** Because Adobe Systems had developed PostScript, they kept the specifics of the optimized format known as "Type 1" for themselves. The Type 1 font format provided fonts with "hints" embedded in the font outline that made them look better when output in small type sizes on 300 dpi laser printers.

  The Type 1 format was also the only format compatible with Adobe's TypeAlign and Adobe Type Manager (ATM) utilities. This restriction excluded all other vendors' PostScript fonts from using these utilities because all non-Adobe PostScript fonts were in the "Type 3" format.

  Because Adobe fonts were compressed and encrypted, other vendors had to reverse-engineer the Type 1 font hinting scheme to optimize their type. Bitstream and others were successful in "cloning" PostScript. So, after the political turmoil surrounding the announcement of TrueType and successful cloning of PostScript Type 1 fonts, Adobe released the specification for the Type 1 font format. There was little reason left for them not to do so. Today most other font vendors have upgraded their fonts to the Type 1 format.

Printing PostScript Fonts

When a document containing PostScript fonts is printed to a PostScript printer, the LaserWriter printer driver queries the PostScript printer to determine whether the printer fonts that the document requires are resident in the printer. These fonts may be built into a printer's ROM chips, or they may have been previously downloaded into the printer's RAM or onto the printer's hard disk. If the fonts are resident, the document is sent to the printer for output. If the fonts are not resident, the printer driver checks to see whether the printer font files are available on the Macintosh hard disk. If they are, they're downloaded into the printer's RAM temporarily. If they aren't, an error message in the Print Status dialog box alerts you that specific fonts are unavailable (this message usually states that Courier is being substituted for the missing font, and your document is then printed with that substitution).

When the document is printed, the PostScript printer uses the printer font information to create each character. The information from the PostScript screen font is translated into new printer font characters. Screen fonts are only placeholders onscreen. The process of creating the printed characters is called rasterization—the most complex part of the PostScript printing process. During rasterization, PostScript uses the PostScript printer font file's mathematical character descriptions to select the output device pixels necessary to produce the requested character at the highest possible resolution.

When a document containing PostScript fonts is printed to a non-PostScript printer, such as a QuickDraw or dot-matrix printer, screen font information is transferred directly to the printer and is the only source used to produce the printed characters. None of the advantages of PostScript are used. On a QuickDraw or dot-matrix printer, there is no difference between the use of a PostScript font and a non-PostScript font (except when ATM is being used, in which case PostScript fonts are superior).

Adobe Type Manager

Not long after Apple's announcement of System 7 and TrueType, Adobe Systems released Adobe Type Manager (ATM), a utility (rasterizer) that allows PostScript fonts to be drawn more smoothly at any resolution onscreen or on any non-PostScript output device. ATM incorporates the elements of display PostScript that Apple chose not to license. This development eliminated the biggest advantages that TrueType fonts initially had over PostScript fonts. It also proved that competition is often good for the consumer.

Adobe Type Manager is an extension that allows you to view PostScript printer font data onscreen. When ATM is installed, PostScript fonts display at the best possible resolution onscreen at any point size, for any font whose screen and printer fonts are installed. ATM also improves the output quality of PostScript fonts on non-PostScript printers. With ATM, almost any PostScript font can be printed successfully at any size on any dot-matrix, ink-jet or QuickDraw laser printer. The effect of ATM on PostScript Type 1 type is shown in Figure 9-7.

Jagged Smooth

Figure 9-7: Without ATM (left), fonts appear jagged onscreen at most point sizes. With ATM (right), the same fonts are smooth at any size.

ATM quickly became a huge success, and most people who worked with more than a few PostScript fonts either purchased the utility or received it in a bundle with some other software application or application upgrade. It was estimated that by the time System 7 shipped, over 80 percent of the installed base of Macintosh users were using ATM.

Some time after the initial shipment of System 7, Apple began offering ATM to anyone who purchased System 7 or a System 7 upgrade package. But Apple did not add ATM to the System 7 install disks, making it necessary to order the "free" copy of ATM from a toll free number (800/521-1976 ext. 4400) for a shipping and handling charge of $7.50. This practice stops with System 7.5, where ATM Version 3.7 is installed directly as system software.

The primary drawback of ATM is that you must keep a printer font corresponding to each installed screen font on your hard drive. Doing so requires more space and increases the cost of working with lots of fonts. You can obtain screen fonts without charge from service bureaus or online sources, but you must purchase most printer fonts at costs ranging from a few dollars to a few hundred dollars per type family.

Using ATM

ATM consists of two files, an ATM control panel and a file called ~ATM 68020/030, which must be in your System Folder. (See Figure 9-8.) The ~ATM 68020/030 file is absent in System 7.5 installations. To use ATM, you must also have the printer font files for any PostScript files you want ATM to work with. Several of the fonts provided with System 7 are PostScript screen fonts, but the printer font portions are missing; Times, Helvetica, Courier and Symbol are examples. You must obtain or purchase these printer fonts separately.

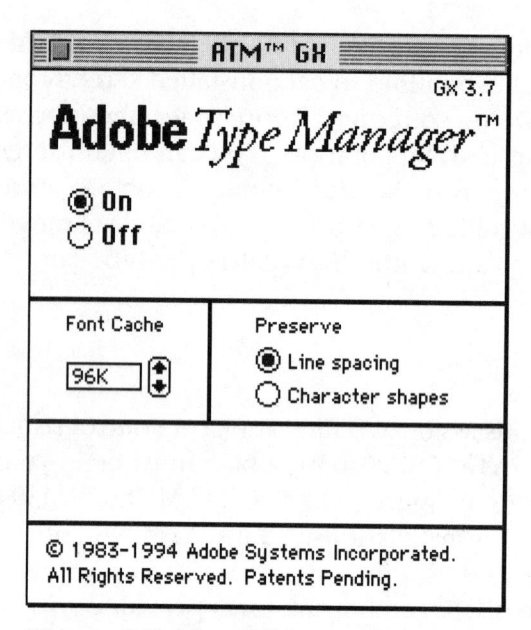

Figure 9-8: The ATM control panel.

Several versions of ATM are in circulation, and each has different System 7 considerations:

- **ATM Version 2.0.** This version is System 7-compatible but not 32-bit clean. (It will cause crashes if 32-bit addressing is turned on.) Printer fonts must reside in the System Folder itself, even though printer fonts dragged to the System Folder icon will be automatically placed in the Extensions folder (if this happens, you need to manually drag them back into the System Folder itself.) It is not recommended that you use this version with System 7.

- **ATM Version 2.02.** This version is System 7-compatible and 32-bit clean, but it does not recognize printer fonts in the Extensions folder or Fonts folder—they must reside in the System Folder itself.

- **ATM Version 2.03.** This version is System 7-compatible, 32-bit clean, and it recognizes the printer fonts in the Extensions folder but not in the Fonts folder. It is a safe version to use with System 7 Version 7.0 or Version 7.01, but it's not recommended for Version 7.1.

- **ATM Version 3.0.** This version is fully compatible with—and recommended for—System 7 Versions 7.0, 7.01 or 7.1. In addition to adding support for System 7.1's Fonts folder, ATM 3.0 supports Adobe's Multiple Master font technology.

- **Super ATM Version 3.5.** This version of ATM not only supports Multiple Master fonts, but it also takes advantage of them to construct fonts when you open or print documents containing missing fonts. It is fully compatible with System 7 Versions 7.0, 7.01 and 7.1.

- **Super ATM Version 3.6.** Version 3.6 adds support for the Power Macintosh. It is fully compatible with System 7 Versions 7.0, 7.01 and 7.1.

- **ATM GX Version 3.7.** Version 3.7 adds support for TrueType GX fonts, Type 1 PostScript fonts that have been converted to GX format, and type effects native to the QuickDraw GX language.

- **ATM GX Version 3.8.** This version fixes the "fat traps" (see the discussion in Chapter 6, "Power Macintosh & PowerBook System Software") that result from crossover between 68k emulation and native PowerPC code in the Mixed Mode Manager. Fat traps lead to poor performance when you're using ATM on a Power Macintosh. You can use Versions 3.7 and 3.8 with System 7.1 and 7.5.

Installing Fonts

Before the release of System 7, you installed screen fonts using the Font/DA Mover, which transferred them between their font suitcases and the System file. Over the years, however, the Font/DA Mover became a scapegoat for many of the larger problems of how the Mac managed fonts. Because of this, and due to the fact that the Font/DA Mover's interface was seen as inconsistent with the drag-and-drop method by which other files were moved from one location to another, a new method of installing screen fonts was introduced in System 7 Version 7.0.

This new method requires no utility program—you simply drag fonts onto the System Folder icon or the icon of the System file. They are then placed into the System file automatically. This method works with all kinds of fonts (TrueType fonts, bitmapped fonts and PostScript screen fonts), and the only limitation is that fonts cannot be installed while any application other than the Finder is open. If you try to drag fonts into the System file or the System Folder while applications are open, the dialog box shown in Figure 9-9 appears.

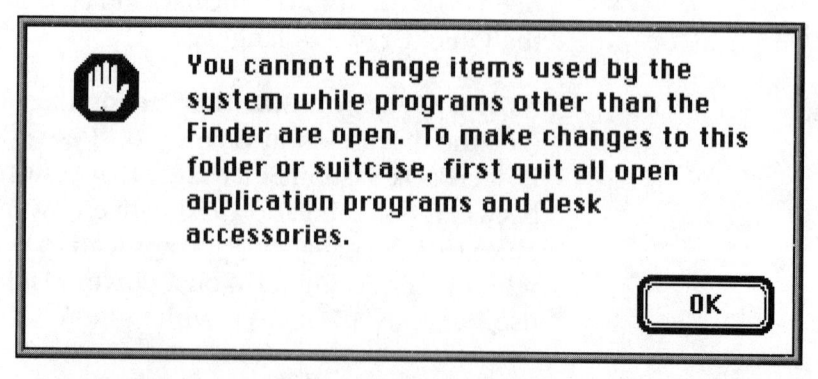

Figure 9-9: The System file "Cannot Change" Items dialog box.

Another change in System 7 is that you can open screen font suitcases directly from the Finder by double-clicking them as if they were folders. This action opens a suitcase window, displaying individual icons for each screen font in the folder. You can distinguish PostScript screen fonts or bitmapped fonts from ones in the new TrueType format by the icon they display. TrueType fonts use an icon with three A's, and PostScript screen fonts or bitmapped fonts use an icon with a single A, as shown in Figure 9-10.

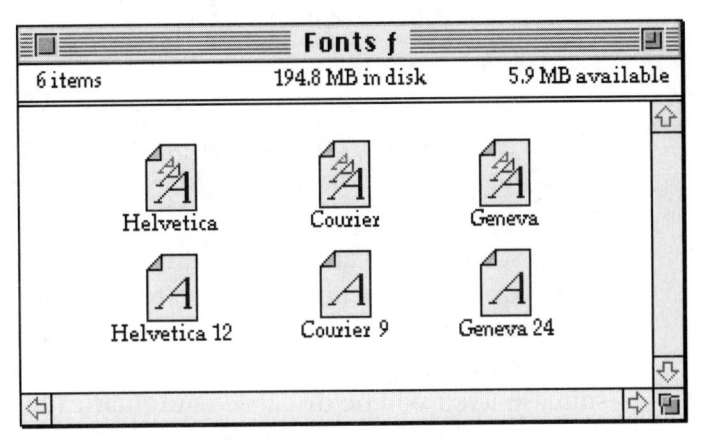

Figure 9-10: Font icons for TrueType and PostScript.

Double-clicking an individual screen font icon opens a window showing a brief sample of the font. For TrueType fonts, this sample shows the font at 9-, 12- and 18-point sizes. Non-TrueType fonts display only a single sample. Figure 9-11 shows two examples.

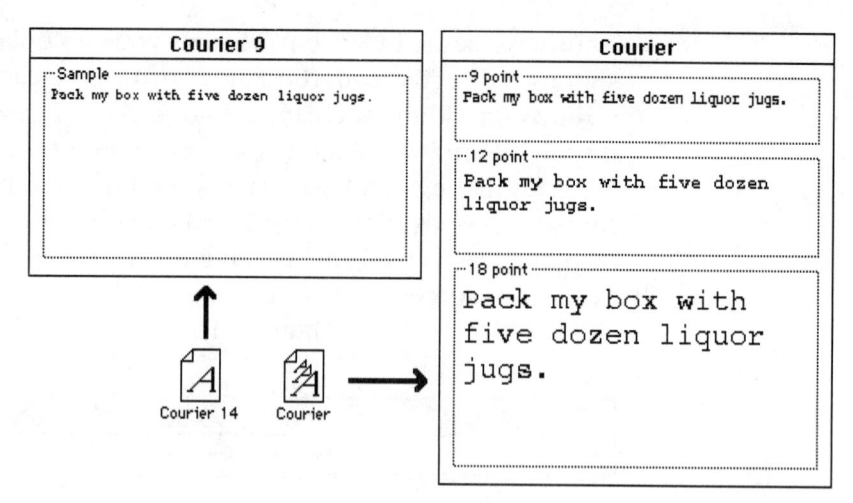

Figure 9-11: A non-TrueType sample window (left) and TrueType sample window (right).

When screen fonts are installed into the System file in System 7 Version 7.0, the suitcase is discarded and only the individual font file icons are added. If you install fonts by dragging the suitcase to the System Folder icon or onto the System file, the suitcase itself will be discarded automatically. You can also drag individual font icons from an open suitcase window to the System Folder icon, the System file icon, to an open System file window, or to another suitcase icon or open suitcase window.

In System 7.0, individual font icons must always be stored in a font suitcase or in the System file; they cannot be stored as files in any other folder. System 7 provides no easy way to create new empty font suitcases, so if you need a new suitcase to store your fonts, you'll have to duplicate an existing suitcase file and then discard the fonts contained in that duplicate. You can then copy any fonts you want into that suitcase and rename it as necessary. Shareware and commercial font-management utilities that can create empty suitcases are also available.

Font Changes in System 7.1

Although System 7 Version 7.0 eliminated the Font/DA Mover, it did little to correct the more fundamental problems of Macintosh font management. One of these fundamental problems was that installing fonts into the System file—when done by the system software or by some utility—resulted in large System files that tended to cause crashes. Sometimes these crashes were so severe that they required a complete system software reinstallation.

The release of System 7 Version 7.1 corrected this problem by adding a "Fonts" subfolder to the System Folder; all screen fonts and printer fonts now reside in this folder—they are no longer stored in the System file. Up to 128 screen font files or font suitcases (each containing any number of fonts) stored in the Fonts folder will be loaded at startup and become available in the font menu or dialog box of your applications.

You can add font suitcases or individual font files to the Fonts folder by dragging them there just as with any other folder. Or you can drag fonts onto the System Folder icon, and they will be placed into the Fonts folder automatically. If you open the Fonts folder window, you can merge the fonts from one font suitcase with another by dragging one suitcase onto another (see Figure 9-12).

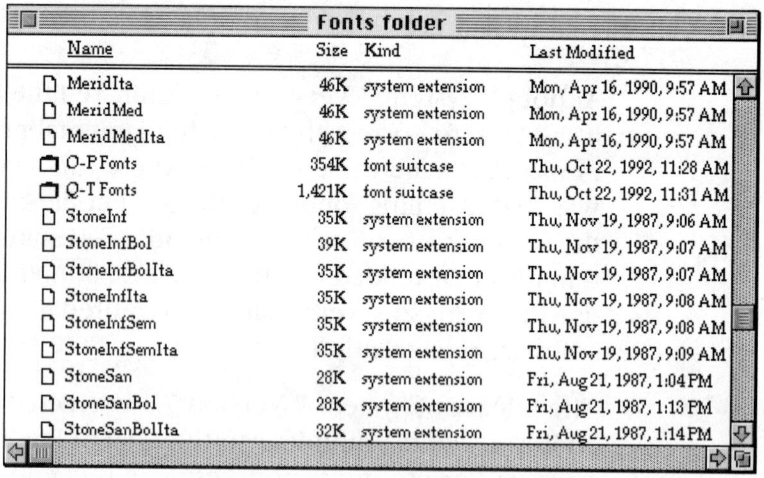

Name	Size	Kind	Last Modified
MeridIta	46K	system extension	Mon, Apr 16, 1990, 9:57 AM
MeridMed	46K	system extension	Mon, Apr 16, 1990, 9:57 AM
MeridMedIta	46K	system extension	Mon, Apr 16, 1990, 9:57 AM
O-P Fonts	354K	font suitcase	Thu, Oct 22, 1992, 11:28 AM
Q-T Fonts	1,421K	font suitcase	Thu, Oct 22, 1992, 11:31 AM
StoneInf	35K	system extension	Thu, Nov 19, 1987, 9:06 AM
StoneInfBol	39K	system extension	Thu, Nov 19, 1987, 9:07 AM
StoneInfBolIta	35K	system extension	Thu, Nov 19, 1987, 9:07 AM
StoneInfIta	35K	system extension	Thu, Nov 19, 1987, 9:08 AM
StoneInfSem	35K	system extension	Thu, Nov 19, 1987, 9:08 AM
StoneInfSemIta	35K	system extension	Thu, Nov 19, 1987, 9:09 AM
StoneSan	28K	system extension	Fri, Aug 21, 1987, 1:04 PM
StoneSanBol	28K	system extension	Fri, Aug 21, 1987, 1:13 PM
StoneSanBolIta	32K	system extension	Fri, Aug 21, 1987, 1:14 PM

Figure 9-12: An open fonts window viewed by name.

When you add fonts to the Fonts folder, they do not become available to any applications that are already open until you quit and relaunch those programs. Fonts or suitcases with the same names as existing fonts or suitcases cannot be added to the Fonts folder; you must first move the previously installed font to another folder or into the Trash. (See Figure 9-13.)

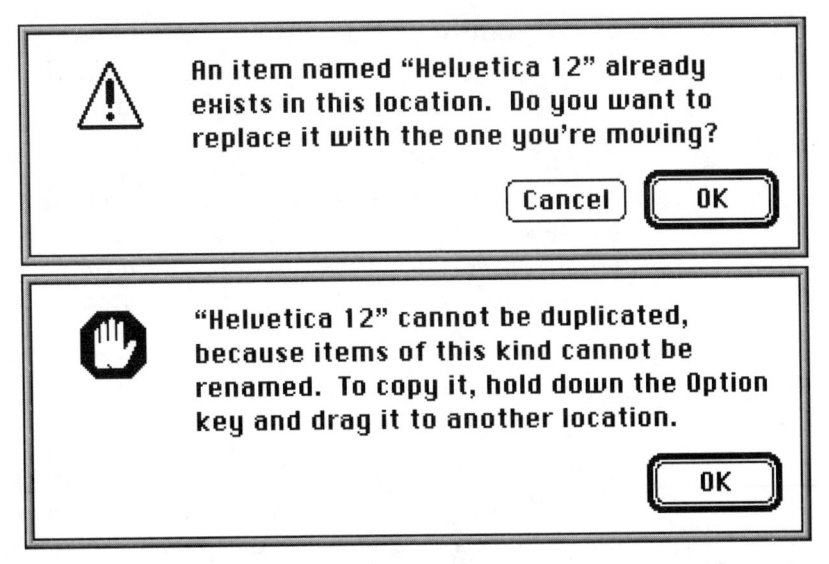

Figure 9-13: You'll see one of these error messages if you try to duplicate a font or replace it with a font of the same name.

You can use System 7 with QuickDraw GX, so it is also possible to work with TrueType GX fonts in that version. It makes little sense to do so, however. If your Macintosh fits the memory requirements of QuickDraw GX, then you are better served by upgrading to version 7.5. System 7.5 makes no additional changes to adding, locating or removing fonts to the procedures described for System 7.1.

Printer Fonts in System 7

Printer font files must be easily located by the system when they are needed for automatic downloading during a print job. In System 7 Version 7.0, they must reside in the Extensions folder or be loose in the System Folder itself. Under Version 7.1, they must reside on the main level of the Fonts folder, or in the Extensions folder or be loose in the System Folder itself.

Printer fonts dragged onto the System Folder icon in Version 7.0 are placed into the Extensions folder, whereas in Version 7.1, they are moved into the Fonts folder.

When you're using ATM versions prior to 2.0.3, printer fonts must reside in the System Folder itself because ATM cannot locate them if they are installed in the Extensions folder or the Fonts folder. For maximum compatibility, ATM Version 3.0 or later should be used with any version of System 7.

Removing Fonts

In System 7 Versions 7.0, 7.1 and 7.5, you remove fonts by a drag-and-drop method. In Version 7.0, double-click the System file to open a System file window and then drag the icons of any fonts you want to remove to another location or into the Trash. In Versions 7.1 and 7.5, simply open the Fonts folder and drag the icons of any fonts you want to remove to another location or into the Trash. In neither case can you remove fonts while applications other than the Finder are open.

TrueType

In addition to supporting the same bitmapped and PostScript fonts that Macintosh users have worked with for years, System 7 also introduces a new font format. TrueType fonts were designed to appear on the Macintosh screen at high resolution at any point size and to print at high resolution on virtually any output device.

TrueType is a fundamental shift from bitmapped fonts and PostScript fonts. Each TrueType font exists as a single file that does the work of both the screen font and the printer font. And when used along with System 7, TrueType fonts appear onscreen without "jaggies" at any point size, without the use of any extensions such as ATM. TrueType fonts can be printed at full resolution on any dot-matrix, QuickDraw, TrueType or PostScript printer.

TrueType is an open type format whose font specifications have been published for use by a wide variety of type vendors. It is supported by AGFA Compugraphic, Bitstream, International Typeface Corporation, Monotype and others. Future versions of Windows and OS/2 will continue to support the TrueType standard, providing for strong cross-platform compatibility. You can buy TrueType font packages from most vendors, with the notable exception of Adobe—at least to this point. Both Apple (through AppleSoft) and Microsoft now sell repackaged typeface packages.

TrueType GX

TrueType GX is an extension of the TrueType specification. It takes advantage of the new capabilities found in QuickDraw GX. You buy QuickDraw GX fonts—as you would any other font format—as software bundles. For example, Bitstream and the International Typeface Corporation have announced a set of 26 GX fonts, and Linotype-Hell has also announced their intention to sell GX fonts. Although TrueType and converted PostScript Type 1 fonts are compatible with QuickDraw GX, they are not upgradeable.

QuickDraw GX will be notable for its handling of complex character sets and pictographic languages, and it should help make the Macintosh more attractive to the users of non-Roman languages. It also introduces advanced typographical capabilities for fine control over letterforms and intelligent handling of characters in a layout. Apple describes GX fonts as "smart fonts" for their added intelligence.

TrueType GX and PostScript Type 1 fonts that follow the QuickDraw GX data structure can store information about justification, optical alignment, optical scaling, hanging punctuation, tracking and kerning. Additional intelligence can add ligatures or fractions based on the context of the character.

Just like Adobe's Multiple Master technology, TrueType GX can create precise styling: bold, italic, expanded or condensed along two, three or four variation axes. Apple defines these axes as weight, width, slant and optical size (optimal shape at a size). Figure 9-14 shows an example using the width and weight axes and Skia font. Using the slider bar(s) within an application lets you apply the amount of width, weight, slant or optical size you desire. Some applications will offer you a choice of font weights from a pop-up menu, as shown in Figure 9-15.

Skia - Variations in 2-axes
The System 7.5 Book (Regular)
The System 7.5 Book (Extended)
The System 7.5 Book (Condensed)
The System 7.5 Book (Light)
The System 7.5 Book (Black)
The System 7.5 Book (Bold)

Figure 9-14: Font variation along two axes.

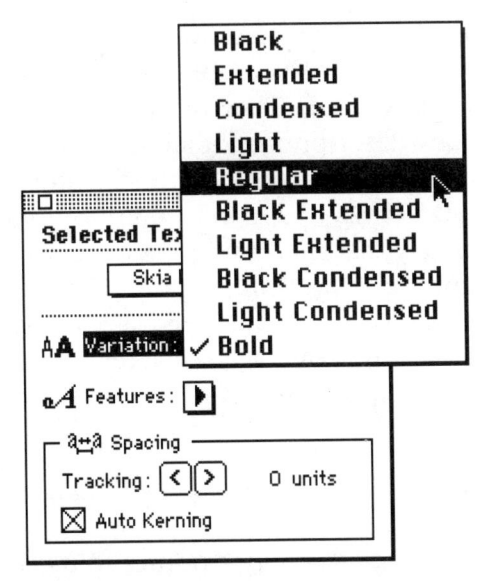

Figure 9-15: GX Font styles.

Because you can adjust letter size and spacing, you can use one TrueType GX font in place of another without changing line and page breaks. QuickDraw GX supplies the conversion that lets you make this substitution. TrueType GX fonts are the "ink" that Apple's new portable document format uses. See "Portable Digital Documents" later in this chapter.

TrueType & PostScript

TrueType is an alternative to PostScript, not a replacement for it; PostScript is fully supported in System 7, as described previously in this chapter. Neither is necessarily better than the other; they're just different. Later in this chapter, we'll examine the realities of working in a world of mixed PostScript and TrueType fonts, and offer some suggestions on the best ways to organize and utilize these font technologies on your system.

Although TrueType is in many ways a competitor for PostScript fonts, it's not a competitor for the complete PostScript language. TrueType printers use TrueType for fonts but QuickDraw descriptions for all other page elements. QuickDraw has proven itself on the Macintosh screen, but its use in QuickDraw GX as a high-resolution printing model is new. It's unlikely that the PostScript standard will be replaced in the near future; it has firm support from developers of high-end software, hardware developers, service bureaus and end users. The PostScript language will likely continue to dominate personal computer printing.

TrueType Technology

TrueType fonts, like PostScript printer fonts, are outline fonts, which means that each character is described mathematically, as opposed to the bit-by-bit description used by existing screen fonts. TrueType mathematical descriptions are based on quadratic Bézier curve equations rather than PostScript's standard Bézier curve equations. The difference between these equations is in the number of points used to determine the position of the lines and curves that make up each character. Apple claims TrueType's method creates better-looking characters at a wider range of output and display resolutions.

Because TrueType uses mathematical descriptions for onscreen and printer font versions, a single file can serve both the display and any output devices. As mentioned previously in this chapter, PostScript requires two files, a screen font file and a printer font file, to print or display at full resolution. Although it's easier to manage one font file than two, Adobe claims that putting its screen fonts and printer fonts in separate files is an asset because either can be updated or enhanced independently at any time without affecting existing documents or printer configurations.

When a document containing TrueType fonts is printed, the sequence of events depends on the type of printer used:

- **Dot-matrix printers.** When a document containing TrueType fonts is printed to a dot-matrix printer, the characters are reproduced in their natural contours, just as they appear on the screen. The output images are the results of the onscreen rasterization process, not the TrueType outlines. Therefore, dot-matrix output can only provide a more exact representation of the Mac's onscreen display.

- **QuickDraw printers.** When a document containing TrueType fonts is printed to a QuickDraw printer such as the LaserWriter II SC, the same process as described for dot-matrix printers occurs—information from the onscreen rasterization process is sent to the printer.

- **68000-based PostScript printers with 2mb of RAM.** When a document containing TrueType fonts is sent to a PostScript printer or output device using a Motorola 68000 CPU and at least 2mb of RAM (such as the LaserWriter IINT and most of today's imagesetters), the printer driver queries the device to see whether the TrueType font scaler is available. The TrueType font scaler may be built into the printer's ROM, or it may have been previously downloaded onto the printer's hard disk or into printer RAM (using the LaserWriter Font Utility). If the TrueType font scaler is not available, it is automatically downloaded into the printer's RAM, where it will reside until the printer is reset. This font scaler will consume approximately 80k of printer memory.

  With the font scaler in place, the page is sent normally. Mathematical descriptions of any included TrueType fonts are sent to the printer and processed by the TrueType font scaler. The page is then output at full resolution, using any TrueType fonts rasterized by the font scaler software.

- **68000-based PostScript printers with less than 2mb of RAM, or RISC-based Adobe PostScript printers.** When a document containing TrueType fonts is printed to a PostScript printer or output device using a Motorola 68000 CPU and less than 2mb of RAM (such as the LaserWriter Plus) or to a RISC-based Adobe PostScript printer, TrueType fonts are encoded into PostScript Type 1 font format and sent to the printer where they're processed just like all other PostScript fonts. The encoded Type 1 fonts do not contain PostScript "hints."

- **Printers with built-in TrueType scaling.** When a document containing TrueType fonts is sent to a printer with a built-in TrueType (TrueImage) font scaler, such as the LaserMaster 400XL or MicroTek TrueLaser, the TrueType outline information is sent directly to the printer where the font is rasterized and imaged.

A Mixed World

In a laboratory environment, where some Macintoshes used only PostScript fonts and some used only TrueType fonts, where all documents using PostScript fonts were created only on the PostScript machines and those using TrueType fonts were created only on the TrueType machines, the daily use of these systems from a font-technology perspective would be very straightforward.

Unfortunately, none of us live or work in such a laboratory. Most Macintosh computers are more likely to be configured with PostScript fonts, TrueType fonts and non-PostScript non-TrueType bitmapped fonts. And most people will have some documents created with only PostScript fonts, some with only bitmapped fonts, some with only TrueType fonts and many documents with mixes of TrueType, PostScript and bitmapped fonts. So how can all this jumble work in the real world?

It depends—on the way you install fonts in your System file, the printer(s) you use and how software developers implement fonts in their updated System 7-compatible applications.

Picking Your Font Standard

When you install System 7, the Installer adds both the PostScript and TrueType versions of many default fonts, including Helvetica, Times and Geneva. Over time, you will add additional fonts to your system, some PostScript, some TrueType, and sometimes you will add both PostScript and TrueType versions of the same fonts.

Once you've installed these fonts, their names will appear in the font menus or dialog boxes of all applications, but you will have no easy way to distinguish the TrueType fonts from the PostScript fonts, or those for which both versions have been installed: you cannot tell which formats are installed by looking at a name in a font menu. (Again, it's a shame Apple didn't make these distinctions visible.)

As you use fonts in your documents, when you choose a font that is installed in both PostScript and TrueType formats, the Macintosh will decide whether to use the PostScript screen font or a scaled TrueType font for each occurrence, depending on the point size at which the font is used. Assume, for example, that you have the PostScript screen fonts for Helvetica, Helvetica Bold, Helvetica Italic and Helvetica Bold Italic installed in your System file, each in 10-, 12- and 14-point sizes. Also assume that the TrueType Helvetica, Helvetica Bold, Helvetica Italic and Helvetica Bold Italic files are also installed. In this case, most applications would use the PostScript versions of Helvetica for any instances of 10-, 12- or 14-point type, and the TrueType version in all other cases. In other words, PostScript screen fonts are used when they're available at the size specified, and TrueType fonts are used for all other sizes.

Of course, when no TrueType font has been installed, PostScript versions are used at all sizes, just as they were before TrueType. If ATM is installed, ATM will scale the onscreen font display to provide smooth character representations. PostScript outlines will be used at print time to produce smooth type at the resolution of the output device (assuming the output device is equipped with a PostScript interpreter).

Caution: *This process of alternating PostScript screen fonts and TrueType fonts is controlled by each application. Some software developers choose to use TrueType fonts even when PostScript screen fonts of the exact size requested are available. There's no way to tell whether TrueType or PostScript fonts are being used until the document is printed, so consult your application manuals for more information.*

This situation is clearly confusing. It gets worse if you consider the possibility that some older documents on your hard drive were created using only PostScript fonts, and when you now open them, you may be instead using TrueType versions of those same fonts. These old documents will then be forced to use TrueType fonts, and extensive text repositioning may occur as a result. The same thing will happen if you're using an application that ignores PostScript screen fonts and uses the TrueType fonts in all situations.

Text repositioning occurs because character widths for TrueType fonts will not always exactly match PostScript font character widths, even in the same font and family. The width of a 14-point Helvetica Bold H may be slightly different in TrueType than it was in PostScript. The cumulative result of the character width accommodations in your document will be text repositioning.

Because using both PostScript and TrueType versions of the same font at the same time makes it impossible to determine which version is being used at any one time, it is best not to install both PostScript and TrueType versions of the same fonts. This is especially true for fonts you'll use in documents being prepared for high-resolution output that will be printed at a remote site, such as a service bureau.

If you use the default System 7 fonts (Times, Helvetica and so on) for high-resolution output, you may want to remove either the PostScript or the TrueType versions of them from your System file (Version 7.0) or Fonts folder (Version 7.1) so both are not installed. If you just use these fonts onscreen and from your local laser printer, however, it is probably not worth the trouble of removing one of them.

Advanced Typography

The development of computer-aided design tools has led to an explosion in type design and to a typographical revival. There never have been as many high-quality typefaces available as there are now, in almost any format you choose to buy. Several technical challenges remain to be overcome in typography: contextual use of letterforms, international character sets and more flexible type handling. Using QuickDraw GX along with TrueType GX fonts may provide some solutions to these problems.

The contextual use of characters is a style issue. Characters are language elements, including letters, numbers, punctuation marks and other linguistic symbols that have a value or meaning in that language. QuickDraw GX introduces the concept of a glyph. A glyph is a representation of a character. Glyphs are what the characters looks like in that particular instance, but they don't contain any meaning beyond the characters they represent. An application specifies a character, and QuickDraw GX automatically draws the appropriate glyph of the right size, style and so on. Figure 9-16 shows an example.

The System 7.5 Book

The Syſtem 7.5 Book

Tʰᵉ ₛystem 7.5 ᴮᵒᵒᵏ

Figure 9-16: Same characters, different glyphs.

A TrueType GX font follows the Unicode specification for an international character set. It can contain up to 65,000 glyphs (called characters in other systems). This expansion of the character set and the LineLayout Manager's line layout capabilities make it easier to support digital type in non-Roman languages. Roman language users will benefit by additional characters being added to character sets: small caps, fractions, superior/inferior characters, ligatures, swashes, fleurons and borders being included in a single font. The LineLayout Manager creates these special characters in context based upon the intelligence built into the font.

In Roman languages, glyph substitution places ligatures where two or three characters make the text more readable and attractive. For example, "fl" is substituted for the letters "f" and "l", and "fi" for "f" and "i." Because these glyphs retain the original two character definitions, they spell check, search and replace, and substitute correctly. Ligatures can be made to appear inside or at the ends of words.

Whereas glyph substitution is a nice type style feature in Roman languages, it assumes added importance in text systems such as Arabic or Hindi in which characters change their shape based upon their positions in a word. QuickDraw GX makes the appropriate placement of glyphs, cutting down on data entry and character selection.

Glyph substitution also lets developers create animated fonts. The animation occurs between different glyphs of the same characters, in the same manner that cursors can be animated in Macintosh system software.

In System 7.5, as applications become QuickDraw GX-savvy, use glyphs, and apply glyph substitution, you will find that much of the work you do styling a document is now done for you automatically. You may also find that applications come with menus or dialog boxes that allow you to select which of these typographical features you wish to apply in a document. Figure 9-17 shows an example of one such menu.

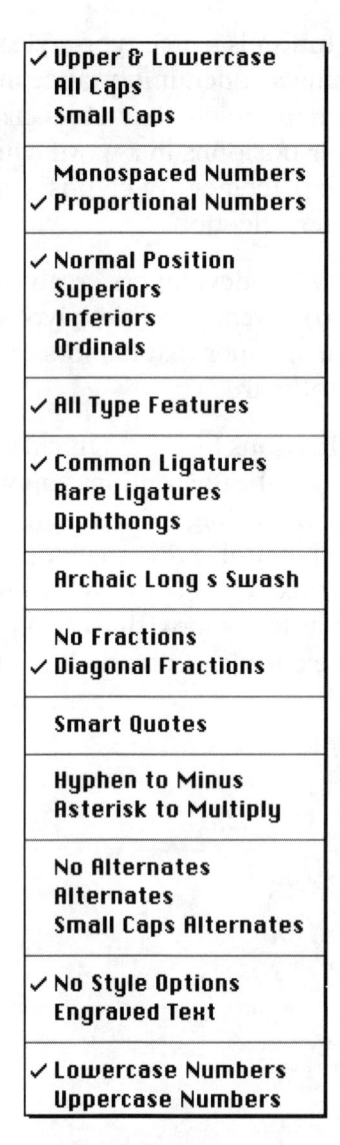

```
✓ Upper & Lowercase
  All Caps
  Small Caps

  Monospaced Numbers
✓ Proportional Numbers

✓ Normal Position
  Superiors
  Inferiors
  Ordinals

✓ All Type Features

✓ Common Ligatures
  Rare Ligatures
  Diphthongs

  Archaic Long s Swash

  No Fractions
✓ Diagonal Fractions

  Smart Quotes

  Hyphen to Minus
  Asterisk to Multiply

  No Alternates
  Alternates
  Small Caps Alternates

✓ No Style Options
  Engraved Text

✓ Lowercase Numbers
  Uppercase Numbers
```

Figure 9-17: Selecting advanced type effects in a QuickDraw GX-savvy application.

Text Effects

Because QuickDraw GX treats text as a shape, designers have the same latitude in applying special effects that illustrators do in creating artwork. Certain of the more tedious tasks that designers require have already been automated inside TrueType GX fonts, including optical scaling and alignment, glyphs, automatic kerning and tracking.

You can expect to see a proliferation of text effects. Some effects include applying transformations such as skew, rotation, mirroring and perspective to a line of text using text. The results of such transformations rival programs such as Adobe's TypeAlign, BroderBund's TypeStyler or other illustrators' tools. However, since these effects are now part of system software they will appear in many other (often smaller) programs. Other effects such as ductile type may be new to you. In ductile type, a character can expand or contract to provide script continuity.

Because written languages can be like English (read left-to-right), Hebrew (read right-to-left) and Japanese (read top-to-bottom), QuickDraw GX can mix a variety of scripts together—even on the same line.

For anyone who has traveled abroad—say to Japan, where Japanese and English are mixed on the same page—this capability is a boon. With ideographic languages (those using pictures for characters, such as Japanese, Chinese or Korean), QuickDraw GX can apply proportional vertical writing and automatic alignment to centered baselines. That line can be rotated to any angle or transformed like any shape. You also can mix different lines of text such as Kanji and Roman type and apply the baseline of your choice.

Typography is not the subject of this book, however; System 7.5 is. The typographical capabilities that QuickDraw GX gives Macintosh users are unique for any computer system—probably a landmark in the type and computer industries. For more information about the use of type, the following books are recommended to you: Type from the Desktop, by Clifford Burke, 1992, Ventana Press; The Macintosh Font Book, 2nd Edition, by Erfert Fenton, 1993, Peachpit Press; and TYPEStype, by Daniel Will-Harris, 1992, Peachpit Press.

Unicode, WorldScript & Localization

Computer vendors have long struggled with the task of translating software between languages and cultures. A version of software for another language or culture is called a localized version, and the process is called localization. The problem is compounded by several issues. Different languages use different character sets. Even when the languages are the same, as is the case for American and British English, the character sets may differ. Character sets can even be based on different alphabets, with different numbers of characters. Ideographic languages—Japanese Kanji, Chinese Han and Korean—have thousands of characters. These differences make translation difficult, they affect sort orders, and they slow down the spread of new innovative software worldwide.

Many standard character sets have been used locally throughout the years. The ACSII standard for American text is one such standard. A consortium of industry vendors has created and codified a system of 65,000 characters incorporating all the modern languages in the world, and some of the ancient languages as well. That system is called Unicode, and it has been adopted by Apple in System 7.5. Now there is a standard complete character set that localized versions can refer to.

See "Setting Options" for help.

Apple has developed a technology called WorldScript that manages a variety of localization issues such as date and time formats, sort orders and input methods. To change the text features for the script system on your Macintosh, open the

Text control panel and select the feature you want from the pop-up menu. The Text control panel was discussed briefly in Chapter 3, "Managing Your Hard Drive." Similarly, you can choose dates, times and numbers from the Date & Time and Numbers control panels.

Input methods are important in non-Roman languages such as Japanese or Chinese. For these languages, users enter phonetic values used in speech and the input method translates to a character. This way, with an ideographic language, you can use a standard keyboard for data entry. For example, Japanese users type Roman characters until the Kanji characters are recognized and substituted. WorldScript works by using a user-installed script, or onscreen instructions that make the appropriate character translations.

QuickDraw GX expands WorldScript's capabilities by providing the advanced typographical capabilities for text and characters that have been described previously. Now WorldScript can provide sophisticated scripting of text handing in any language. With these new tools, developers have a method for localizing software quickly. As evidence, System 7.5 shipped in ten localized versions within 30 days of its American release.

QuickDraw GX & Printing

QuickDraw GX introduces the new print architecture that was supposed to ship with the original version of System 7.0. A panoply of changes in System 7.5 make printing easier, more intuitive and more convenient. Among the most important new features, you will find the following:

- **Desktop printers.** Printers can appear on your desktop, virtual printers that output files to real printing devices. You can drag and drop files to a printer, manage its print queue and print to several printers without visiting the Chooser. Printers can be shared across a network via File Sharing.

- **New Print dialog boxes.** The new print architecture provides a redesigned Print dialog box. You now can select a printer within the Print dialog box of any application.

- **Better print spooling.** Each individual printer manages its own print queue. You can reorder and delete print jobs and drag and drop print jobs from one printer to another.

- **Improved background printing.** You'll notice less drag on your foreground application when you print in the background, due to the redesigned print architecture.

- **Expanded print options.** You can mix page formats in a document. You could, for example, print a document with both landscape and portrait pages. Also, you could print a letter, envelope and post card in a single print job. Multiple tray, double-sided and other options are supported. You can also print a document to any printer; QuickDraw GX makes the needed conversions so that the page prints correctly, even if the page size or printable area changes.

- **Printer extensions.** Developers can create specialized printer drivers called printer extensions that provide your printer with special capabilities. Writing printer drivers has also become easier because QuickDraw GX provides a ready-to-use toolbox for developers.

- **Portable digital documents.** You can print PDD files on any Macintosh with QuickDraw GX installed—whether or not you have the creator application and fonts. A PDD file can be created by any Macintosh application, whether it's QuickDraw GX-savvy or not.

These changes are major—more changes to the way you do printing than in any other system software version. Although a lot is new here, most of it will seem intuitive and much easier than what came before.

Printing

As you learned in Chapter 4, "The System Folder," you select printers using the Chooser, specifying the serial port or network connection. When you want to change printers, you must go back to the Chooser to make another selection. With Backgrounder installed, you can check the status of print jobs, delete print jobs from the queue, and suspend or resume printing using the Print Monitor. But that's about it.

With QuickDraw GX installed, you still need to select printers from the Chooser. Now, however, when you select a printer, you simply click the Create button and the printer's icon appears on your desktop as a virtual printing device. You can select several printers of different types and in different locations and then place them on your desktop. Figure 9-18 shows some examples. You only go to the Chooser once to mount your printers, a process that can be automated using AppleScripts or any other macro utility.

Figure 9-18: QuickDraw GX printer icons.

You can mount any output device, either a network printer or personal printer, on your desktop. Connections to shared devices are controlled through the standard File Sharing Users and Groups Setup dialog box and passwords schemes, which are described in Chapter 12, "An Introduction to File Sharing." Not only can you mount printers, but you also can mount film recorders, fax modems or any device that can currently be selected in the Chooser. With appropriate controls, only selected individuals can use only the devices you want them to, saving on wasted materials or inappropriate usage.

The Print Dialog Box

In the new system software, printing from within an application has been enhanced with a new Print dialog box, shown in Figures 9-19 and 9-20 in its abbreviated and full configuration, respectively. One of the first things you may notice is the new pop-up menu (shown in Figure 9-21) that lets you select your output device from within the Print dialog box. In its simple form, the Print dialog box asks you only the number of copies and the print range. Apple's studies found that users selected these options and no other 95 percent of the time. Click the More Choices button to see the expanded Print dialog box.

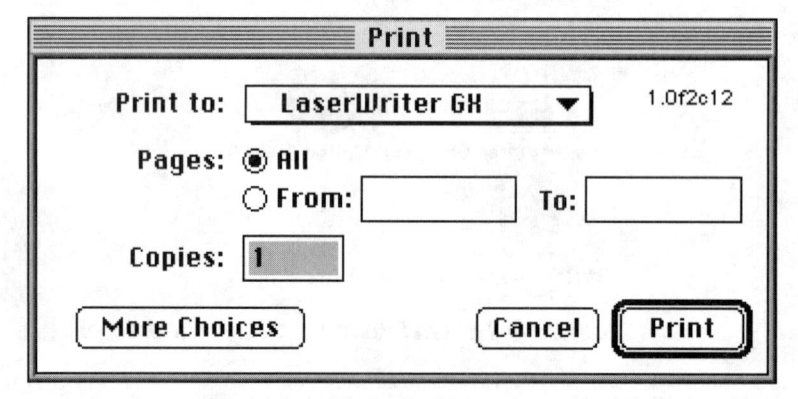

Figure 9-19: The simple QuickDraw GX Print dialog box.

Figure 9-20: The expanded QuickDraw GX Print dialog box.

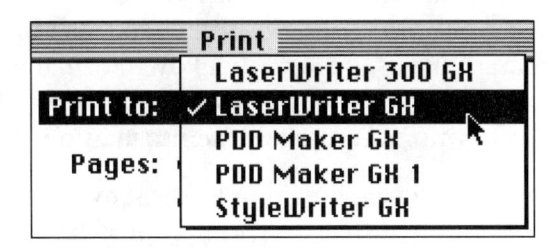

Figure 9-21: The printer pop-up menu.

Although many of the options in the Print dialog box will be familiar, over time you will see many new print options. Some of these, such as document formatting, are software specific; others, such as automatic printer functions, will be added as hardware and printer drivers are updated.

When you click the Print button in the Print dialog box, the document is spooled and sent to the printer of your choice. It's placed in a print queue, as discussed in the next section. If the printer is connected, the document is printed. If not, it prints when you connect to that printer again.

QuickDraw GX enables device-independent printing. You can format a document to print on a specific printer. Page formatting is preserved even when the size of the page or printable area changes. For extreme changes in size, in which the text would be unreadable or the quality of the page compromised, QuickDraw GX will apply user-selected defaults to tile, scale or clip the printed image. You can also select to format a print job for "Any Printer." You do so when sending a document to an unknown printer. In that case, the document's line and page breaks are preserved.

As it stands now, applications provide their own page definitions. QuickDraw GX provides standard definitions for page formatting that lets one application copy and paste pages to another without having to reformat the document. Because pages have uniform definitions, you can also break documents into separate pages, each with its own format and page setup. These options will appear as standard Print and Page Setup dialog box options across all Macintosh applications.

You could mix letters, mailing labels, envelopes, anything within a document that you print appropriately. Because you will have control over tray selection and other features, these capabilities will be practical in the near future. As you print to a standard printer with just one tray, you will be signaled when you need to feed odd-sized paper or envelopes manually into the printer for a print job. When you have multiple trays, the new print architecture automatically routes pages to the correct tray. You do not have to select a bin number; just feed your printer print stock.

The Print Spooler

These printers work like actual printers, and you can drag and drop files to them. When a printer has a queued document in its queue, you see a printer icon with a document on your desktop, as shown in Figure 9-22.

Figure 9-22: A QuickDraw GX printer with a document in the print queue.

Each printer manages its own print queue. (Figure 9-23 shows an example of a print queue.) In this regard, QuickDraw GX printers are print servers, in the same sense that you have network file servers. To manipulate the print queue, do the following:

- To open a print queue, double-click the printer icon.

- To reorder the queue, drag the document icon to a new position.

- To move a print job to another printer, drag the document icon to that printer icon.

- To delete a job, drag the document icon to the Trash.

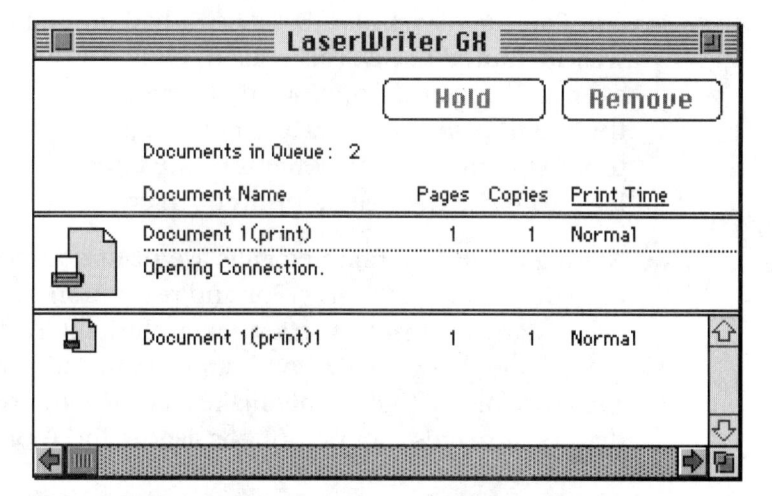

Figure 9-23: A QuickDraw GX printer print queue.

You'll notice several other changes apparent when you print using a print queue. Because of the new background printing architecture, there's less of a performance hit when you are working in the foreground. You'll notice this benefit more on slower, older Macintosh computers, but it's a welcome change. QuickDraw GX monitors the needs of the foreground application and allocates more resources to printing when that application is idle. Resources are returned to the foreground when activity increases.

The print queue is smarter, too. When your Macintosh crashes, you'll find after rebooting that your print job resumes from the point where it stopped, even if that point was in the middle of a job. Therefore, for a multipage print job, the last page prints again, followed by the next one. You no longer have to reprint the entire job or respecify the print job when you crash.

Printing Extensions

Creating printer drivers has been a major chore for developers. The slow start that IBM's OS/2 had in the marketplace was attributed to just this reason. QuickDraw GX provides over 100 standard functions that developers can use to create their own printer drivers and custom printer extensions. This toolbox eliminates 95 percent of the code that developers have to write to create a printer driver.

Among these programmed calls are print components; standard dialog boxes; font, color and resolution selectors—nearly every standard print function. Even difficult PostScript font management is provided with a program call. Having system calls to work with not only makes it easier to create printer drivers: it makes them more consistent and more capable.

QuickDraw GX device drivers can output to PostScript Level 1 and 2 printers, raster impact printers and even vector devices like plotters, doing any necessary data conversions between formats.

What you, the user, will see is a new class of printer, or driver, extensions that can create a custom solution base on the device you use. Printer extensions appear in a scrolling window at the left side of the Chooser. These driver extensions can add the following capabilities:

- Overprinting letters with marks such as confidential, top secret or shred.
- Printing watermarks.
- Activating printer functions through responses to dialog boxes.
- Securing access to devices through password protection.
- Creating and managing print jobs based on job numbers.
- Counting users' pages printed.

Some of these printer extensions are described in Chapter 16 in the section titled "Printer Extensions."

Portable Digital Documents

QuickDraw GX defines a new document format called a portable digital document, or PDD. You can create a PDD from within any application, even those that aren't QuickDraw GX-savvy. The option to do so appears in the Print dialog box when you have the PDDMaker utility mounted on your desktop, as shown in Figure 9-24. Click the Save button to create a PDD file. The icon of a PDD file is shown in Figure 9-25.

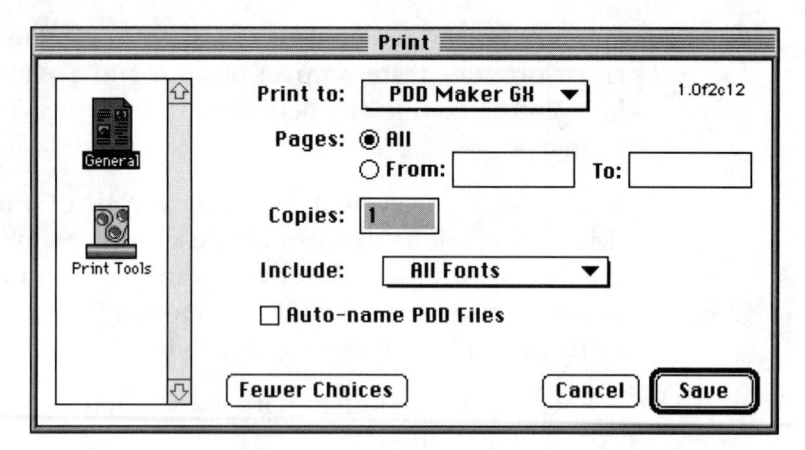

Figure 9-24: Creating a PPD file from the Print dialog box.

Figure 9-25: A PDD icon.

PDDMaker uses TrueType GX font information and QuickDraw GX page description to create a resolution-independent file format. Compression is applied to PDD files sent to Level 2 PostScript printers for improved print performance. You can choose which fonts to include in the PDD document.

When another user with QuickDraw GX installed receives a PDD file, he or she can open, view (the Portable Document viewing mode) and print that document. QuickDraw GX opens the PDD file in a SimpleText application window. The creator application or fonts are not required; even if the user had them on his or her computer, the receiving party could not change the document. Fonts are embedded in the PDD. Having embedded fonts makes it easy to distribute a PDD file in an electronic form to other users or to other members of a workgroup and thus preserve a version's history.

Because PDDs do not require a creator application or fonts, users are less likely to request their own unregistered copies. Since the receiver of the document is limited to displaying and printing data, the data in the document is locked from change. These two features of a PDD let you publish a PDD in a copyrighted form that others can use but not modify.

There's a lot of interest in portable document technology, and other vendors have introduced products in this area. Adobe's Acrobat Distiller is a universal writer, and the Adobe Acrobat Exchange is their universal reader. Acrobat uses Adobe's Multiple Masters PostScript fonts to create their Portable Document Format (PDF) for this purpose. Farallon's Replica is a similar product.

The uses for a portable document are legion. Suffice it to say that a portable document represents a new kind of electronic publishing medium. Much of the collaborative needs of a company, complex product manuals and other communications can be sent in this new form.

ColorSync & Color Matching

The Mac's proficiency and popularity as a publishing computer is well known. And in the past few years, advances in processing power, storage capacities, scanning and output technology have earned the Mac a significant place in even the most demanding high-quality color publishing situations. Publications from *The New Yorker* to *People* to *Playboy* are now produced fully or partially on the Macintosh.

Despite this acceptance, and the overall improvements in color publishing technology, one aspect of using Macs for color publishing has remained a challenge: matching colors that appear onscreen to those that are printed on color proofing devices and, finally, to the colors of the finished product, which are usually based on film output. Keeping colors consistent as they move from an onscreen display to different output devices has been difficult for two basic reasons.

First, computer monitors produce colors by adding together differing percentages of red, green and blue light. This method of mixing light from original sources is called additive color. Output devices, on the other hand, work by applying color to a page that will selectively absorb light waves when the document is illuminated via an external white light (such as light bulbs or the sun). This method of creating colors is called subtractive color. There are fundamental differences in the ranges of colors that additive and subtractive color can produce. For this reason, onscreen color (additive) offers bright, highly saturated colors that invariably appear darker when printed (subtractive) on paper or other materials.

Second, variations between different printers, monitors and presses make it impossible for them all to produce the exact same range and quality of colors. An inexpensive ink-jet printer is going to have one set of printable colors, a color laser printer another, a dye sublimation printer yet another, a web press another and a high-quality sheet-fed press another still.

Differences in the color models and technical characteristics of color devices result in each having its own specific gamut, or range of colors. The trick to achieving consistent color across different devices is to map colors from one device to another so that when a file is displayed or produced on each device, the differences between the devices' gamuts are accounted and compensated for, and the color remains as consistent as possible.

Apple's ColorSync extension performs this task exactly. When ColorSync is installed, colors are converted from their original definitions into a device-independent definition based on the international CIE XYZ color standard or color space. (A color space is the range of colors that are possible shown in a three-dimensional mapping.) This conversion is done using a device profile, which is a small file that tells ColorSync about the color characteristics and capabilities of the input device or monitor. Once a color is defined in CIE XYZ, it can then be translated using a set of color matching method (CMM) algorithms for output using the device profile of the output device.

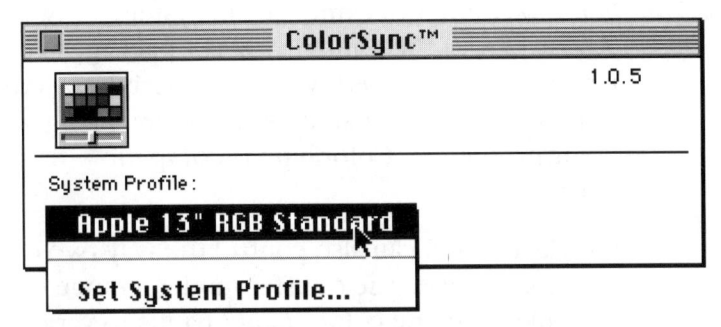

Figure 9-26: ColorSync.

Apple will provide device profiles for its own monitors, scanners and color printers, but the success of ColorSync will be dependent upon third-party developers producing and distributing their own device profiles for their scanners, monitors and printers. In order for you to use ColorSync effectively, you must have device profiles for the exact scanners, monitors and printers you are using (or intend to use) for any given project.

When ColorSync translates colors into or out of the CIE XYZ color model, it does so with the goal of providing the best possible match between the original color and the final color. Differences in devices do not always make an exact match possible, as explained earlier. The algorithm ColorSync uses to perform this translation was designed for optimum results, but it was also designed to use a small amount of memory and provide good performance. Other companies such as EFI and Kodak have developed other conversion methods—based on lookup tables rather than algorithms—which will produce superior results but require much more memory, information and expertise about each input and output device. These methods are compatible with ColorSync, however, and can be taken advantage of by anyone working in high-quality color who desires improved results.

ColorSync was released as a separate extension when System 7.1 appeared. It became part of system software in Version 7.5, as part of the QuickDraw GX package. You may find ColorSync distributed with color peripherals that you buy: scanners, printers, cameras and so on, along with the device's color profile file. ColorSync is compatible with System 7.1 and later.

QuickDraw GX can also control the way two or more colors are mixed, called the transfer mode. A range of behavior is possible from one color being opaque to various percentages of mixing, to transparent. When two colored shapes are overlaid, you can have any range of transfer from opacity through equal mixing, to replacement of one color by another, in any degree.

By providing an automated color-matching system, Apple has taken the uncertainty out of using color. What was once tedious work is now handled for you by hardware vendors and solutions providers. The quality of this translation will no doubt improve over time.

Moving On

QuickDraw GX brings to the Macintosh imaging capabilities that equal and in some areas exceed that of the Adobe PostScript page description language. You will see more powerful graphics, type descriptions, color handling and printing functions in your applications. These innovations should further the Macintosh's presence as the preeminent personal computer in the publishing and graphics market and Apple's role as a leader on the cutting edge.

Fonts continue to be an exciting part of the Macintosh, and as shown in this chapter, font technology remains a source of innovation and controversy. System 7 supports four different font formats: bitmapped, PostScript, TrueType, and TrueType GX. It supports five if you count Adobe's Multiple Masters font technology.

In this chapter, you learned about the following:

- **QuickDraw and QuickDraw GX.** Apple's system-level graphics and type page description language allows for easy development of sophisticated applications.

- **Fonts.** You learned how to select, install and work with fonts on the Macintosh. You also learned about TrueType GX fonts and their effect on foreign language applications.

- **The new print architecture.** System 7.5 introduces a new way of working with printers, print spoolers and printer extensions.

- **The portable document format.** QuickDraw GX defines a new "universal" file format that allows anyone to open, view and print a document he or she didn't create.

In Chapter 10, "Inter-Application Communication & OpenDoc," you'll learn how exchange data using the Publish & Subscribe metaphor. You can link data between programs, and have that data update either authomatically or manually. Also introduced in the next chapter is the soon to be released OpenDoc, a new compound document standard.

Chapter 10

Inter-Application Communication & OpenDoc

Launching several applications simultaneously can dramatically improve your productivity on the Macintosh, as you saw in Chapter 7, "Working With Multiple Applications." But System 7.5 makes it possible to integrate your applications more closely: text and graphic elements can be shared between documents; messages and commands can be passed from one application to another. These capabilities are made possible by the Edition Manager and Inter-Application Communication (IAC), respectively.

Although the power of the Edition Manager and IAC is provided by System 7, neither feature is automatically available to System 7-compatible applications. Each capability must be specifically added by software developers when their programs are updated for System 7. Support for the Edition Manager is widespread because it is one of the requirements for System 7-Savvy status. Basic support for IAC is also a part of being System 7-Savvy, but as you'll see, full support for IAC is much more complex and is therefore appearing in applications more slowly.

Taken to the extreme, the best way of mixing different data types and application capabilities is by using a compound document architecture. With this model, a document is the central construct, not an application. When you add data to a compound document or try to modify it, a small application capable of handling that part is called.

This architecture is what OpenDoc is about. OpenDoc provides a document framework using AppleEvents and the Open Scripting Architecture (which AppleScript subscribes to) to enable a new class of application and a new style of computing. Best yet, when you use OpenDoc, you are using concepts you already know (such as cut and paste) in a way you are already familiar with. Your Macintosh still feels like a Macintosh.

OpenDoc is intimately associated with the concepts described in this chapter. Because OpenDoc will appear as an interim release early in 1995 and in system software in the next major version (Copeland), it is described here now. Chances are that over time OpenDoc will bring about profound changes in the way Macintosh users buy applications and do their work.

The Edition Manager

Creating text and graphic elements within one application and using them in other applications has always been a hallmark of the Macintosh. Its legendary Cut and Paste commands are even being offered by other me-too graphical operating systems. But while others are matching the 1984 Macintosh's capabilities, System 7 raises the ante considerably for this type of feature with the introduction of the Edition Manager's Publish and Subscribe commands.

By using Publish and Subscribe in your System 7-Savvy applications, you can move elements between applications, and those elements can be manually or automatically updated as you modify them. In other words, when text, graphic, sound or video elements are moved from one document to another, original and duplicate elements remain linked. When the originals are changed, so are the duplicates.

The benefits are obvious:

- Charts created in spreadsheets or databases and used in word processors or page layout applications can be automatically updated any time the data changes.

- Legal disclaimers and other boilerplate text commonly used in documents can be automatically updated (such as dates on a copyright notice, for example).

- Illustrated publications can be created using preliminary versions of graphic images that are automatically updated as these graphics are completed.

And you can use Publish and Subscribe commands for more than simple "live copy and paste" between two applications on your own Macintosh. These commands support Macintosh networks (using System 7's File Sharing feature or other networking systems), so your documents can include components created, manipulated and stored by many people on many network file servers.

(Note: Although the term Edition Manager is the technical programming term for this set of capabilities, we'll use the term Publish/Subscribe for the remainder of this chapter to refer to the entire set of Edition Manager capabilities.)

How Publish/Subscribe Works

Although Publish/Subscribe is a powerful feature, its basic premise is simple: any elements—text, graphics, sound or video—or combinations of them can be transferred from one document to another using Publish/Subscribe. The transfer begins when elements to be shared are selected and then published to a new edition file. (See Figure 10-1.) This process is similar to the Cut or Copy process, except that instead of being transferred into memory, the selected elements are saved to the edition file on disk. At the time you publish these elements, you name the edition file and specify where on your hard drive it will be stored.

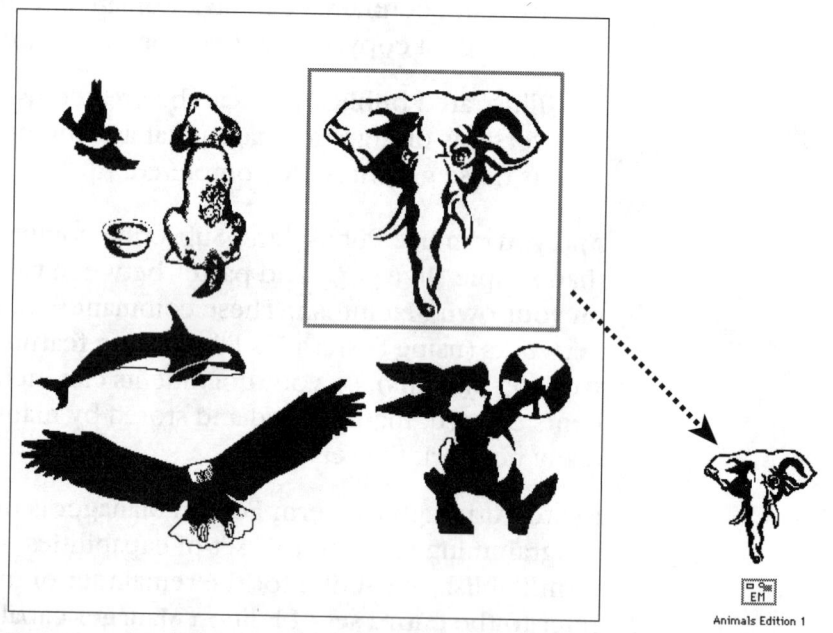

Figure 10-1: An element published from a document is stored in an edition file.

The section of your document used to create an edition is called the Publisher. A link is automatically maintained between an edition file and the document that created it. When changes are made in the Publisher, the edition file is updated to reflect these changes. (See Figure 10-2.) Updates can be made any time the original document is changed, or at any other time you initiate them.

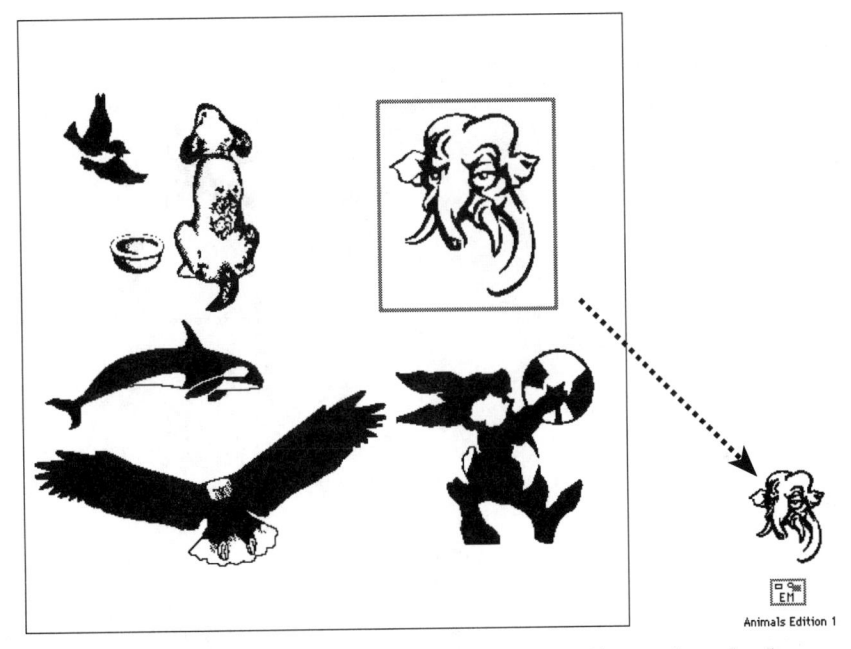

Figure 10-2: The edition file is automatically updated when the document changes.

To complete the transfer of elements between documents, the receiving document subscribes to the edition file by importing the edition file elements and establishing a link between the edition and the subscribing document. The document section imported from an edition becomes a Subscriber (to the edition). Figure 10-3 illustrates this process.

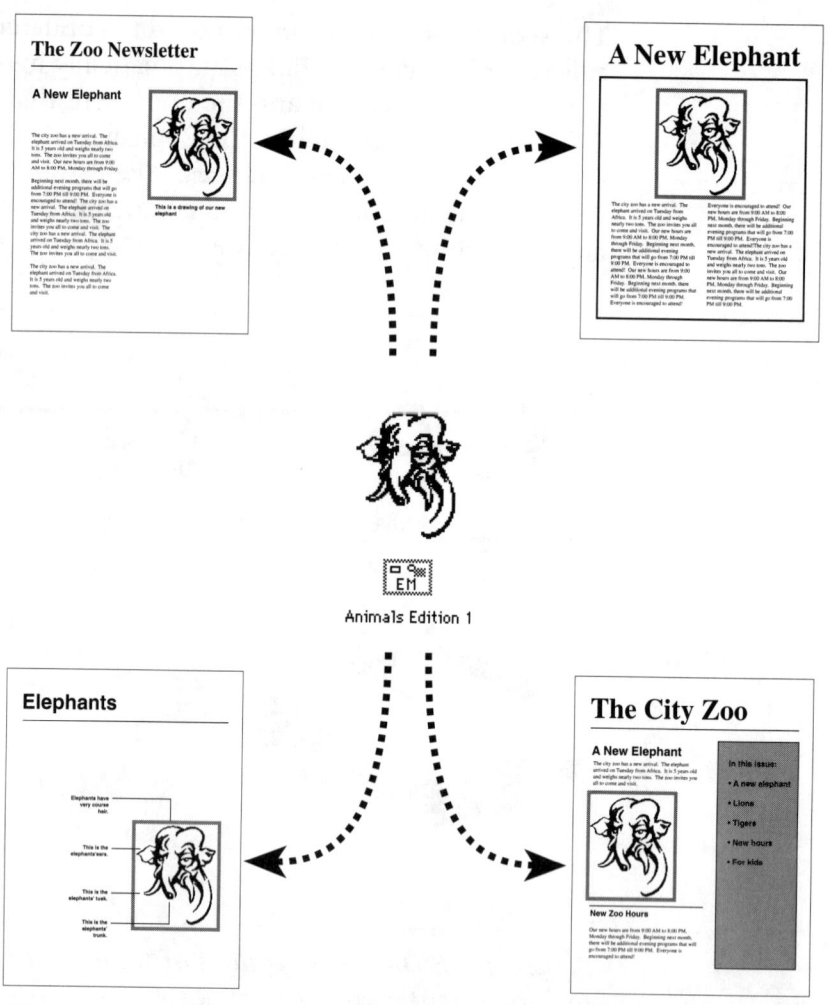

Figure 10-3: Edition files can be subscribed to by any number of other documents.

At this point, the edition file is an independent disk file, linked to the document that published it and any documents subscribing to it. (Any number of documents can subscribe to a single edition.) As elements in the publisher document change, the edition file is updated according to options set in that original document. As the edition file is updated, the edition data used by subscribers is also updated according to options set in the subscribing document. This entire process is shown in Figure 10-4.

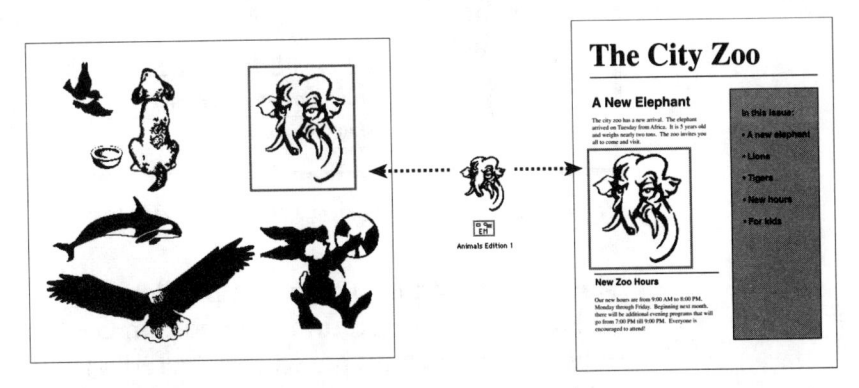

Figure 10-4: Both the publishing document and the subscribing document are linked to the edition file.

Publish/Subscribe Commands

In applications that support Publish/Subscribe, four new commands usually appear in the Edit menu: Create Publisher, Subscribe To, Publisher Options/Subscriber Options, and Show Borders. Some applications use other command names for these functions, but they should work essentially the same as those described in the following sections.

The Create Publisher Command

Create Publisher creates a new edition file, which you name and store in any desired location on any available volume. The edition file contains the text and graphic elements selected when you choose the command. To publish any elements, select the areas of the current document that you wish to share, and choose the Create Publisher command. The Create Publisher dialog box, shown in Figure 10-5, then appears.

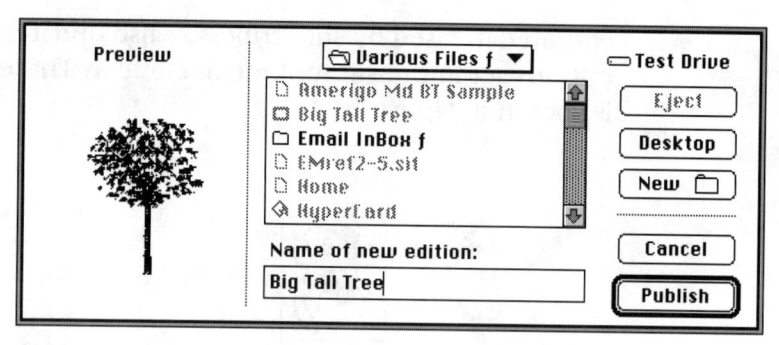

Figure 10-5: The Create Publisher dialog box.

The left side of this dialog box previews the elements that will be included in the edition. The edition contents depend not only on which elements were selected with the Create Publisher command, but also on the "Select how publisher decides what to publish option" setting. This option is described in the section on the Publisher Options dialog box.

To complete the creation of the edition, enter a name in the "Name of New Edition" option box, and select a destination to which the file will be saved. Then click the Publish button, which saves your new edition to disk.

There's now a new file on disk (separate from the document you're currently working in) that contains a copy of the elements you selected to publish. This file—this edition—will be placed into other documents and applications using the Subscribe To command. The edition will be updated to include any changes made to the elements it contains, according to the options set in the Publisher Options dialog box.

The Subscribe To Command

The Subscribe To command, the Publish/Subscribe equivalent of the Paste command, imports a copy of an edition file into the current document. When you choose this command, the Subscribe To dialog box appears, as shown in Figure 10-6.

The names of edition files appear in the scrolling list, and a preview of any edition appears when you select the file name. Select the edition you want, click the Subscribe button, and the chosen edition appears in your document.

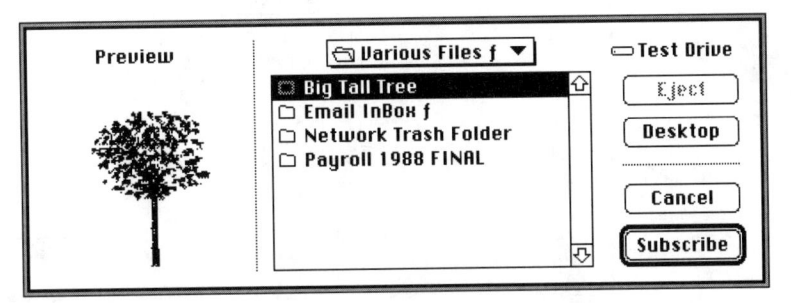

Figure 10-6: The Subscribe To dialog box.

When you're working in text-based applications, the edition appears at the place where the cursor was positioned when you chose the Subscribe To command. In graphics applications, the edition file usually appears in the current screen display area. Details on how to use these included editions follow.

The Publisher Options Command

The third Edition Manager command is either Publisher Options or Subscriber Options, depending on the current selection. The Publisher Options command, available only when you select the rectangle surrounding published elements, presents the dialog box shown in Figure 10-7.

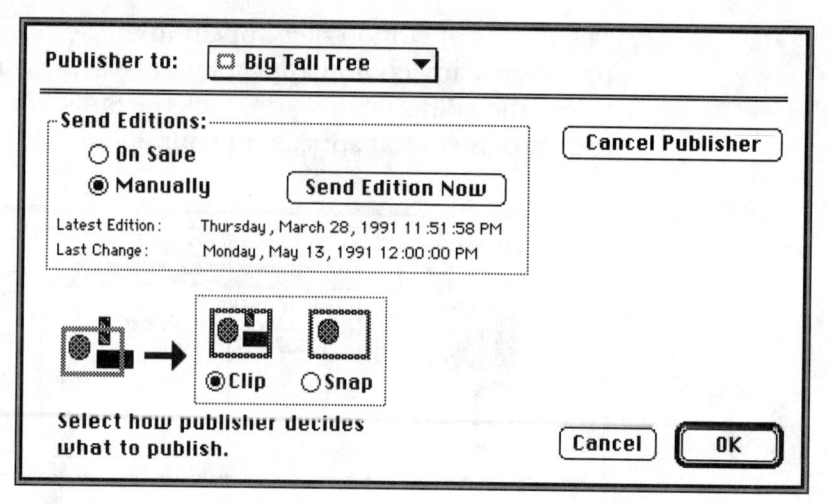

Figure 10-7: The Publisher Options dialog box.

You also can access the Publisher Options dialog box by double-clicking the border of any published elements.

This dialog box presents five important options:

- **Publisher to.** This menu is not really an option because it offers no alternatives; it simply shows you where the edition is stored and the path to that location. To see the storage location, click the Publisher to: pop-up menu.

- **Send Editions.** This option lets you choose when the file associated with the selected edition will be updated. If you choose On Save, the edition file is updated each time the current document is saved; if you choose Manually, you must click the Send Edition Now button to update the edition file.

  This option also displays the date and time the edition file was last updated. If On Save is selected, this information probably indicates the date and time the creating file was last saved. If Manually is selected, the time the elements included in the edition were last changed is also listed, letting you know how up to date the edition is in relation to the file's current status.

- **Send Edition Now.** Clicking this button updates the edition file to reflect the current status of the published elements. This button is normally used only when Send Editions Manually is selected.

- **Select how publisher decides what to publish.** As mentioned earlier, the light rectangle that appears after a publisher has been created defines the portions of the current document to be included in the edition. With this option, you decide if the edition will include only objects completely inside the box, or all elements (those partially enclosed as well as those fully enclosed).

  Select Clip if you want the edition to include all elements you select or partially select. Select Snap to include only fully enclosed elements. (See Figure 10-8.)

  Because the content of an edition is defined by a rectangle, you may notice some elements in the preview that were not selected when the Create Publisher command was selected. There's no way to exclude these elements, other than by altering the Select how publisher decides option.

Figure 10-8: Using the Snap option would exclude the whale from the edition created by the top example, and the eagle from the edition file created by the bottom example. The Clip option would include both animals in both examples.

- **Cancel Publisher.** The Cancel Publisher button removes the link between the published elements in the current application and the edition file. Canceling the publisher does not delete the edition file, so it doesn't directly affect any documents that subscribe to that edition.

  You can't re-establish the link to an edition once it's been canceled (although you can use the Create Publisher command to create a new edition with the same name, saved in the same location), so you should use the Cancel Publisher button only in certain circumstances. It would be better to use the Send Editions Manually option, to temporarily prevent editions from being updated.

  If you accidentally use the Cancel Publisher button, you may be able to undo it by exiting your document with the Close command, clicking the Don't Save button to avoid saving your changes and then re-opening the document with the Open command. (Of course, doing so means you lose any changes you've made.) The Revert command offered by some applications may also return your document to the state it was in before you canceled the publisher.

The Subscriber Options Command

The Subscriber Options command can be selected only when a subscribed edition is selected, as shown by the dark rectangle around the edition. When you select an edition, the Subscriber Options dialog box, shown in Figure 10-9, appears.

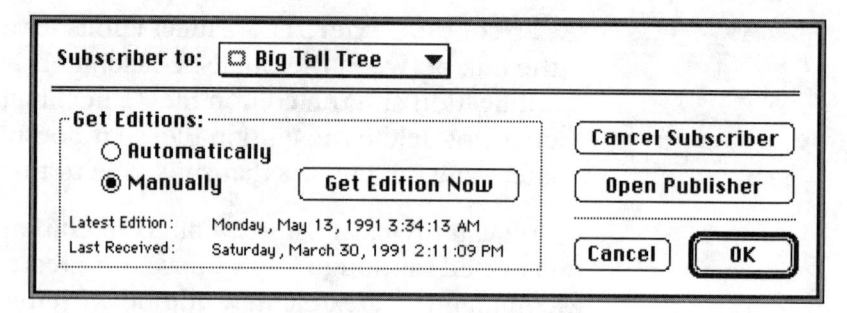

Figure 10-9: The Subscriber Options dialog box.

You also can access the Subscriber Options dialog box by double-clicking the subscribed elements.

This dialog box presents five options:

- **Subscriber to.** This menu offers no alternatives; it simply lets you see where the edition is stored and the path to that location. To see the storage location, click the Subscriber to: pop-up menu.

- **Get Editions.** This option lets you choose when the edition elements will be updated to reflect any changes made to the edition file. The Automatically option causes any changes to the edition file to be imported each time you open the document or whenever the edition file changes; the Manually option requires you to click the Get Edition Now button in order for changes to the edition to be reflected in your document.

  If you choose Automatically, your document will always have the latest version of the text or graphic elements contained in the edition file. If you choose Manual, your document may not always reflect updates to the edition file, but you can choose when those updates are made.

  The date and time the current edition was last changed by the application that created it are displayed below the Get Editions option. If you selected Manually, the date and time the edition was imported into the current document are also listed. If these dates and times are not the same, the edition data contained in the current document is not up to date with the current edition file.

If the dates and times are dimmed, the edition file can't be located: it's been deleted or moved to another volume. The link between the current document and the edition file has been broken. More information on re-establishing this link is provided later in this chapter.

- **Get Edition Now.** Clicking this button imports the current edition file contents into your document. It's normally used only when the Manually option is selected.

- **Cancel Subscriber.** The Cancel Subscriber button removes the link between the imported elements and the edition file. The imported elements remain in the current application, but future changes to the edition will not be reflected in the current publication.

    You cannot re-establish the link to an edition once it's been canceled (although you can use the Subscribe To command to create a new link to that same edition), so you should limit using the Cancel Subscriber button to particular circumstances. A better strategy would be to use the Get Editions Manually option to temporarily prevent editions from being updated in the subscribing document.

    If you accidentally use the Cancel Subscriber button, you may be able to undo it by exiting your document with the Close command, clicking the Don't Save button to avoid saving your changes and then re-opening the document with the Open command. (Of course, following these steps means you lose any changes you've made.) The Revert command offered by some applications may also return your document to the state it was in before you canceled the subscriber.

- **Open Publisher.** The Open Publisher button performs an impressive task indeed, launching the application that created the selected edition and opening the document from which the edition was published. This way, you can edit the contents of the edition using all the tools and capabilities of the application that originally created it.

    There is no difference between using the Open Publisher button to launch an application and open the document that created an edition and performing these same tasks using the Finder. But the Open Publisher button makes the process convenient. Changes you make to the open document will be reflected in the disk file and related edition files, depending on the settings you use in the Publisher Options dialog box and whether you use the Save command.

    You also can modify the edition file without changing the original document, using the following steps after launching the application with the Open Publisher button: (1) Set the Publisher options for the edition to Send Editions Manually; (2) Make the necessary changes to the text or graphic elements; (3) Click the Send Edition Now button in the Publisher Options dialog box; (4) Close the document or quit the application without saving your changes. The edition file will now be updated, but the original document and any other editions will remain unchanged.

The Show Borders Command

Rectangular borders distinguish elements in your document that have been published in an edition file from elements that are part of another edition file that's been subscribed to. The border around published elements is light (about a 50 percent screen); the border around subscribed elements is dark (about a 75 percent screen), as shown in Figure 10-10.

Figure 10-10: Borders surround published elements (right) and subscribed elements (left).

The Show Borders command toggles the display of these borders, allowing you to hide or display them as necessary. Regardless of the Show Borders command setting, borders always appear when a publisher or subscriber is selected. Borders never appear on printed versions of your documents—they're for onscreen use only.

Editing Subscribers

Because the contents of a subscriber are provided by an edition file and are usually updated periodically (according to the setting in the Subscriber Options dialog box), there are limits to manipulating a subscriber within any document. In general, you can't make any changes that would be lost when a new version of the edition becomes available.

Following are some of the limitations in editing subscribers:

- **Text subscribers.** With subscribers that include only text, you can't edit the text when subscribing to the edition. The only exception is that you can set the font, type size or type style of the text, as long as the change applies to the entire subscriber text. You can't make one word in the edition bold or set one sentence in a different font.

- **Graphic subscribers.** When using subscribers that include graphics, you can reposition the editions you've subscribed to, but in most cases you can't resize them. (If you are permitted to resize the subscriber, graphic handles appear on the corners of the subscriber border.)

- **Text in graphic subscribers.** The text in a graphic subscriber cannot be modified in any way. In the subscriber, the text is considered a part of the graphic element.

The correct way to edit a subscriber is to reopen the document that published the edition, make changes in that document, then save those changes or use the Send Edition Now button to update the edition. You can quickly access the original document for any edition by clicking the Open Publisher button in the Subscriber Options dialog box.

Edition Files at the Finder

The edition files created with the Create Publisher command look just like any other files on your disks. They use a small shaded rectangle icon like the one surrounding editions in publishing or subscribing applications; you can add comments to them using the Get Info command.

Double-clicking an edition file in the Finder opens a window (shown in Figure 10-11) that contains the edition contents, the edition type (PICT and so on) and the Open Publisher button. The Open Publisher button launches the application that created the document from which the edition file was created and opens that document.

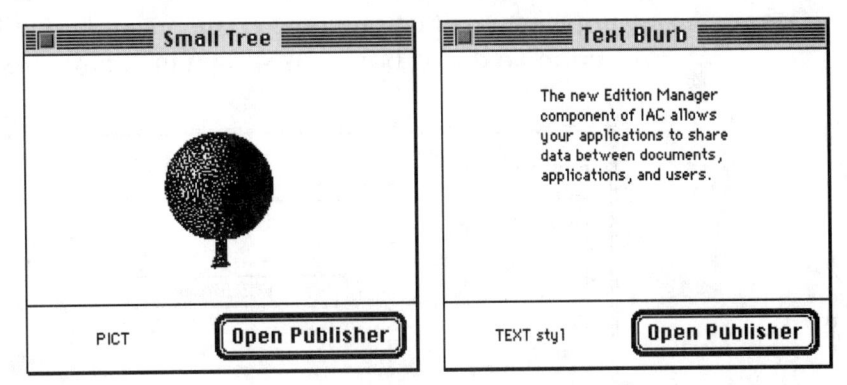

Figure 10-11: These windows are opened by clicking edition files.

You work only on the document that created the edition, not on the edition file. Any changes made to the edition elements are then updated to the edition file (based on the options in the Publisher Options dialog box). Therefore, deleting a file that has published editions makes it impossible to ever modify or update those editions again—the data in the editions cannot be accessed from either the edition file or the subscriber document.

Edition File Links

The link between edition files and their publishers and subscribers is automatically maintained, even if you rename or move these documents to new locations on the current volume. If you move an edition file, publishing document or subscribing document to a new volume and delete the copy on the original volume, the links to and from the file will be broken.

When links to or from an edition file are broken, it's impossible to automatically or manually update the edition file or the version of that edition file used in any subscribing documents. You can tell that a link is broken by the grayed-out appearance of certain type elements in the Publish To or Subscribe To dialog boxes, as shown in Figure 10-12.

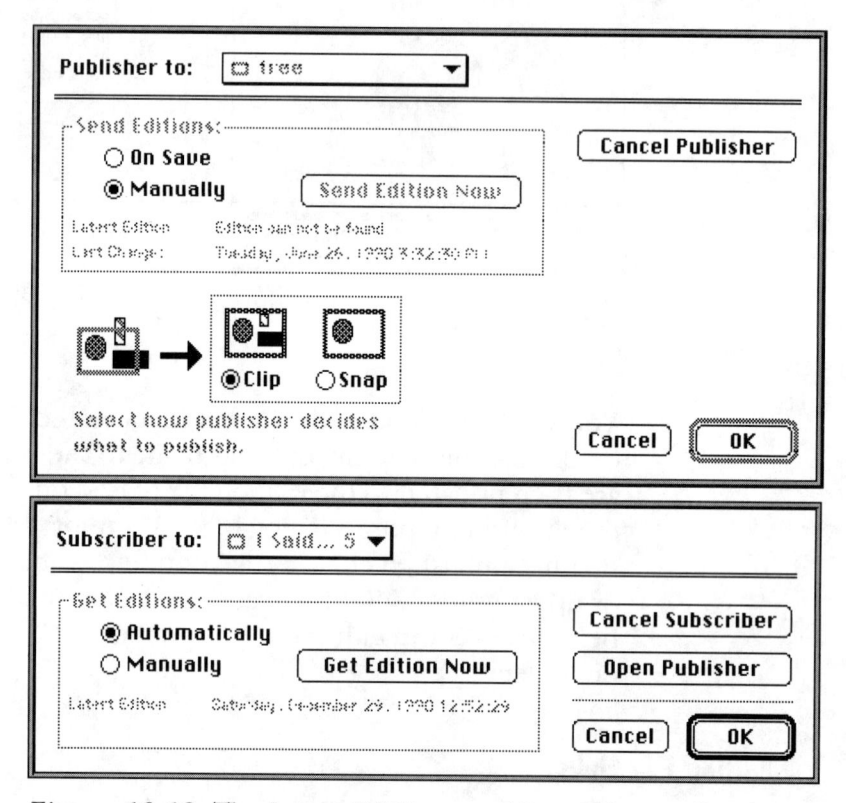

Figure 10-12: The Latest Edition and Last Change lines are dimmed when the edition has been deleted or moved to another volume.

Although there's no direct way to "reconnect" a broken Publisher or Subscriber link, you can recreate a link between an application and an edition published from it:

- Open the application and select the border surrounding the previously created edition. Even though the link has been broken, the border will still be visible.

- Select the Create Publisher command, and save the edition with the same name as the previous edition, to the same location as the previous edition, overwriting the unlinked copy that remains there.

- Any Subscribers using this edition will now update, according to their option settings, using the information in this new version of the edition.

To recreate a link between an edition and a subscribing application:

- Open the subscribing application and select the element that was imported as a subscribed edition.

- Select the Subscribe To command and locate the edition file to which you want to recreate a link. Then click the Subscribe button.

- The data from the edition file as it now exists will appear in your document, replacing the older version that was selected. This edition is now linked to the edition file on disk and will update according to the settings of the Publisher and Subscriber options.

Unavailable Edition Files

When you open a document containing subscribers, the Macintosh attempts to locate edition files linked to each subscriber. If any of these edition files reside on unmounted floppy disks or removable volumes, you'll be prompted to insert the disks or volumes. Then the document will open normally, and the links between the subscribers and their edition files will be maintained.

If you don't wish to insert the requested disks or volumes, click the Cancel button in the Please Insert the Disk... dialog box. The subscriber elements will still appear in the document, but the Subscriber Options dialog boxes will display an Edition is Missing dialog box. (See Figure 10-13.) To establish a link to the edition, insert the correct disk; then click the Get Edition Now button.

Figure 10-13: The Edition is Missing dialog box.

Edition Files & Your Network

Edition files can be published to or subscribed from any available network or File Sharing volume. There's no real difference in the way they operate on network/File Sharing volumes, except that documents containing publishers and subscribers must access the editions over the network in order to keep all files updated properly.

To expedite sharing editions via a network, you can create aliases of editions stored on network volumes that you access frequently. You can then browse these aliases on your local hard drive (from the Subscribe To dialog box) and when the editions are used, the aliases will automatically connect to the appropriate network volumes and access the edition files.

To subscribe directly to editions on network volumes, aliases will also mount automatically when you open documents subscribing to the editions.

Figure 10-14 shows one sample network: in this case, edition files could be stored on the AppleShare file server or on either File Sharing Mac, and be used either directly or through aliases, by any network user.

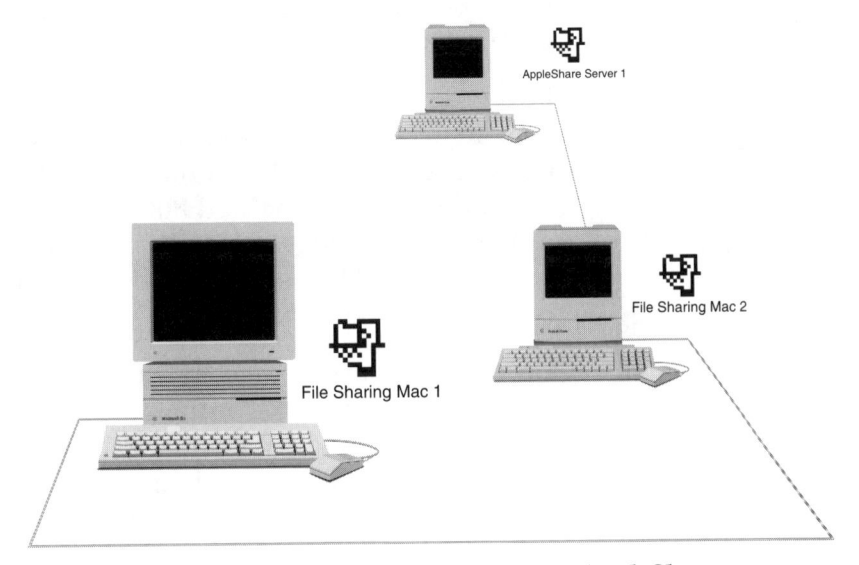

Figure 10-14: A sample network with an AppleShare server and File Sharing Macs.

Edition Manager Tips

Following are several tips you can use when working with the Edition Manager:

- **Republishing an edition.** If you overwrite an edition (by creating a new edition with the same name in the same location as an existing edition), the new edition will be linked to all documents that subscribed to the old edition.

For example, if you wanted to replace an existing edition file named "Corporate Logo" with a new graphic, you could create a new edition named "Corporate Logo," using the Create Publisher command, and save it in the same volume and folder as the old "Corporate Logo" edition. (When you're asked to confirm that you want to overwrite the old file, click the Yes button.) At this point, all documents that subscribed to the old "Corporate Logo" edition file will begin using the new "Corporate Logo" edition file the next time they're updated.

- **Using nested editions.** You can create editions that contain text or graphics subscribed to from other editions. (See Figure 10-15.) After you set appropriate updating options in all associated Publish To and Subscribe To dialog boxes, changes you make to elements in original documents will be correctly updated everywhere they occur.

    For example, if your page layout program subscribed to your "Corporate Logo" for the purpose of using it, along with some text and ornamental graphics, to create a corporate insignia, you could use the Create Publisher command to save an edition file named "Corporate Insignia." This edition could then be subscribed to for use on the first page of all corporate reports created in your word processing programs. If the Corporate Logo edition was updated, this update would appear in the page layout file (where the insignia was created) and extend to the Corporate Insignia edition when the page layout document was opened (assuming the Publisher options and Subscriber options are set correctly). The updated Corporate Insignia edition would then be updated in all documents in which it was used (if you set the appropriate Subscriber option).

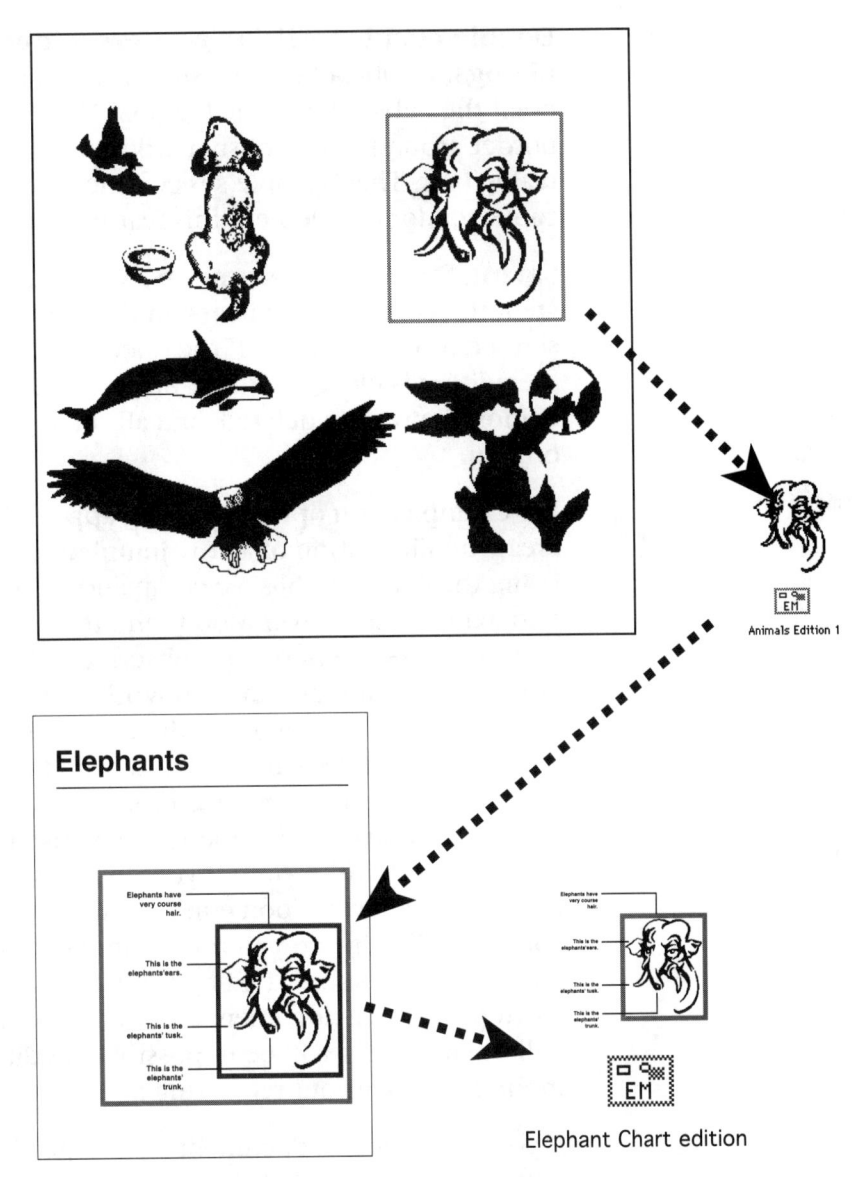

Chapter 10: Inter-Application Communication & OpenDoc   **391**

Figure 10-15: Edition files can contain other editions.

- **Double-clicking edition borders to open option dialogs.** Double-clicking a subscriber in a document will open the Subscriber to dialog box. Double-clicking the border around any publisher will open the Publisher to dialog box. This is Apple's recommended behavior, but some vendors implement this feature and others do not.

- **Saving Publisher documents.** When an edition is created, the edition file appears on disk and can be subscribed to immediately. If the document that published the edition is closed without being saved, however, the edition file will be deleted, and all subscriber links will be broken.

  For example, you open a drawing application and quickly create an illustration of a cow jumping over the moon. Using the Create Publisher command, you create an edition named "Cow Over Moon" and then switch to your word processor where you subscribe to the Cow Over Moon edition and continue to work on your text document. Later, when you're ready to quit for the day, you choose the Shut Down command from the Finder's Special menu, and your drawing application asks whether you want to save the Untitled file you used to create Cow Over Moon. At this point, if you don't name and save this file, the Cow Over Moon edition will be deleted from your disk. The image will remain in the word processing document that subscribed to it, but the link between the word processing document and the deleted edition file will be broken. It will be impossible to edit the graphic in the future without recreating it.

  If you try to close a document with published editions without saving, the dialog box shown in Figure 10-16 will appear.

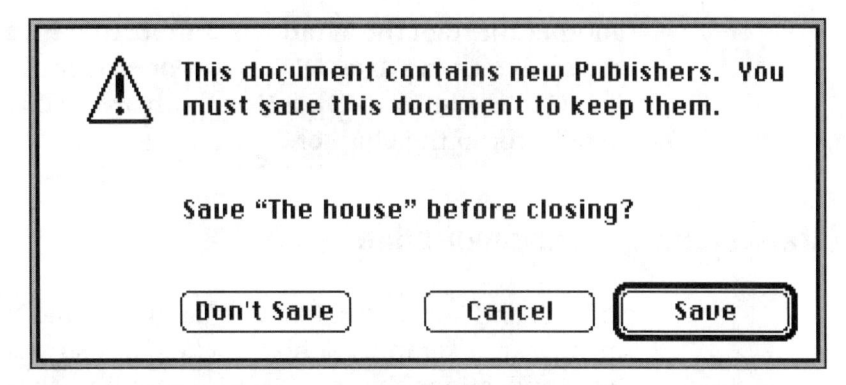

Figure 10-16: This dialog box warns you that quitting the unsaved document will result in the loss of edition files.

- **Using edition aliases.** You can subscribe to edition file aliases just like you subscribe to standard edition files. As always, the alias file will maintain a link to the original file, even if you move or rename the alias or the original. If the alias's original document is on a network server or File Sharing volume, the volume is mounted automatically.

Publish and Subscribe has been available now for over three years, but it gets very little press in Macintosh literature. Apparently, few users make good use of this powerful feature. Perhaps having the data and publisher application available remotely represents a problem for people to conceptualize. That's too bad because Publish and Subscribe is powerful— and it's easy to use.

A similar concept in Microsoft Windows is the linking in Object Linking and Embedding, or OLE. You can link data automatically (hot link) or manually (warm link). When you open a linked document, Windows posts a dialog box asking whether you want the data updated. OLE uses Dynamic Data Exchange, or DDE, (introduced in Windows 3.0) as its messaging system. DDE is similar to AppleEvents, described in the next section. DDE lets one application pass data to and from another through the Windows Clipboard with a reference to the source of the data. DDE is just one layer of OLE's functioning. OLE is similar to OpenDoc; both are discussed in more detail later in the chapter.

Inter-Application Communication

Publish and Subscribe, like the Cut, Copy and Paste commands, are examples of how the Macintosh system software lets applications share data and communicate indirectly with each other. System 7 also provides even broader application-to-application communication, known as Inter-Application Communication (IAC). System 7.5 builds on this system with a continual upgrading of the capabilities of IAC over time.

IAC provides a structural framework within which software applications can send messages and data to other software applications. These capabilities make the Macintosh more powerful in many ways. They reduce the pressure on any one application to "do it all," allowing each application to specialize in what it does best.

Spell-checking is a good example. Almost every Macintosh application allows text to be created, and over the last few years many have added built-in spelling checkers, each with its own version and its own dictionary files. You have to learn and remember how each one works and make room for each data file on your hard drive. And the developers of each program have to spend time and money developing and testing utilities.

Suppose, instead, that one independent spelling checker was the best of them all, offering the biggest dictionaries, the most features and the best user interface. Using IAC, all your software applications could access this one spelling checker, saving you the hassle of learning multiple commands, customizing multiple dictionaries and wasting hard drive space on duplicate files. And your software developers could spend their time and money on other things, such as improving their applications' features.

Understanding AppleEvents

The mechanics of IAC are quite technical, but fortunately you don't need to know anything about them unless you intend to write your own Macintosh programs. You'll be aware of IAC in the future when your updated software versions take advantage of its features; but even then, the entire IAC operation will be translated into friendly Macintosh commands and dialog boxes you're already familiar with. (So you can skip the rest of this section, if you'd like.) However, if you have an interest in AppleScript, Apple's system-wide macro programming language (the subject of the next chapter), AppleEvents is the fundamental messaging system upon which that system is based.

Just in case you're interested, let's take a brief look at the way System 7 provides IAC capabilities to software applications.

IAC is a protocol that defines a new type of communication between applications, and it provides a mechanism for the delivery and implementation of that communication. You can think of IAC as a set of grammatical rules that comprise an acceptable format for messages sent between applications. A message in this format is an AppleEvent.

For example, an application issues an AppleEvent to another application. That AppleEvent is normally a command like Open filename and Copy Data record #, fieldname, followed by the sending application pasting the data somewhere. Using this kind of mechanism it is possible to link a directory with a to-do list, with a calender. In fact, some of the first best implementations of AppleEvents have been in the personal information manager (PIMs) category.

In addition to the AppleEvents format, IAC provides a messenger service, to transmit the properly formatted message from one application to another.

Although IAC defines the communication format, it doesn't specify the message content. The "language" of AppleEvents is being defined by Apple and by the Macintosh software developer community, in cooperation with Apple. This cooperation is very important; a computer language designed to communicate between a variety of software applications developed by different companies must be carefully constructed in order to accomplish its goal of facilitating precise communication.

For an application to send an AppleEvent or to understand an AppleEvent it receives, the program must be specifically programmed to handle that AppleEvent properly. This interoperability is why it's impossible for non-System 7-Savvy applications to use IAC, and why even System 7-Savvy programs will provide only limited IAC support for some time to come. Only when the AppleEvents language is clearly defined can software developers update their programs to engage in an AppleEvents dialog properly.

AppleEvents are described by commands and actions that act on objects. You can think of these constructs as being roughly equivalent to "verbs" and "nouns" in the programming language, as you will see in the next chapter. AppleEvents include nouns and verbs in their definition descriptors, as you can see when you open an application's AppleEvent dictionary. To help software developers implement program support, Apple classified AppleEvents into categories called suites. The suites are as follow:

- **Required suite.** Open Application, Open Document, Print Document, Run Application and Quit Application are the four basic AppleEvents and the only ones required for System 7-Savvy applications. (Think of them as the Hello, Please, Thank You, Start and Goodbye of

AppleEvents.) This suite is the smallest of the standard suites.

- **Core suite.** These AppleEvents are not as universal or fundamental as the Required suite, but they're general enough that almost every Macintosh application should support them. The list of Core AppleEvents, quite large already, is growing as Apple and its software developers work to make sure every type of communication that may be needed is provided for. Using the Core suite applications, you can perform a wide range of tasks.

- **Text suite.** The Text suite supports AppleEvents used by word processors, page layout applications and other applications using text editing functions. The Core suite contains minimal text functions, so the Text suite is for a higher level of support than simple text functions used in dialog boxes.

- **QuickDraw Graphics suite.** QuickDraw events define actions required to draw simple graphics to your monitor, printers or other devices. Most graphics programs adopt this suite. The QuickDraw Graphics Supplemental suite contains additions and extensions to the original suite, such as the ability to rotate objects, and it is yet another level of graphics messaging support.

- **Table suite.** Tables are a fundamental property of spreadsheets, databases and other systems that use two-dimensional data arrays. This suite provides data addressing, retrieval and modification capabilities. Other suites, like the Database suite, and Spreadsheet suites, provide complementary functions.

- **Finder suite.** In System 7.5, a set of 13 Finder commands and actions was added to the Finder. Actions such as copy, trashing and other Finder events are supported. See "The Scriptable Finder" in the next chapter for more information.

The Finder suite contains the following items: open about box, copy to, duplicate, empty trash, make aliases for, move to, sleep, shut down, open, print, put away, restart, and select.

- **Miscellaneous suite.** Apple groups events that don't quite fit into other suites into this grab bag of miscellaneous events. Utilizing this suite allows Apple to extend Inter-Application Communication without having to define large numbers of small suites. There are now many specialized suites in the AppleEvent Registry. Some examples are the Mail, the Personal Information, and the Telephony suites.

- **Custom suites.** A Macintosh software developer might have a need for AppleEvents designed for proprietary or cooperative use by its own applications. If a developer's word processor included a unique feature not controllable with any existing Core or Functional-area AppleEvents, the company could define its own Custom AppleEvent. This AppleEvent could be kept secret and used only by the software developer's applications, or it could be shared with other software developers. Some examples of custom suites are Aladdin System's StuffIt suite, Apple's HyperCard suite and CE Software's QuicKeys suite.

You can see in FileMaker Pro 2.0 a custom suite that is a subset of Core, Table and Database suites. That suite also contains some FileMaker-specific commands. FileMaker Pro also contains a FileMaker suite with two classes: menu and menu items. You can view supported suites using the Open Dictionary command in the File menu of the Script Editor, a standard part of the AppleScript package. Figure 10-17 shows the FileMaker suite in the FileMaker dictionary. Refer to the discussion in the next chapter on application dictionaries.

Chapter 10: Inter-Application Communication & OpenDoc 399

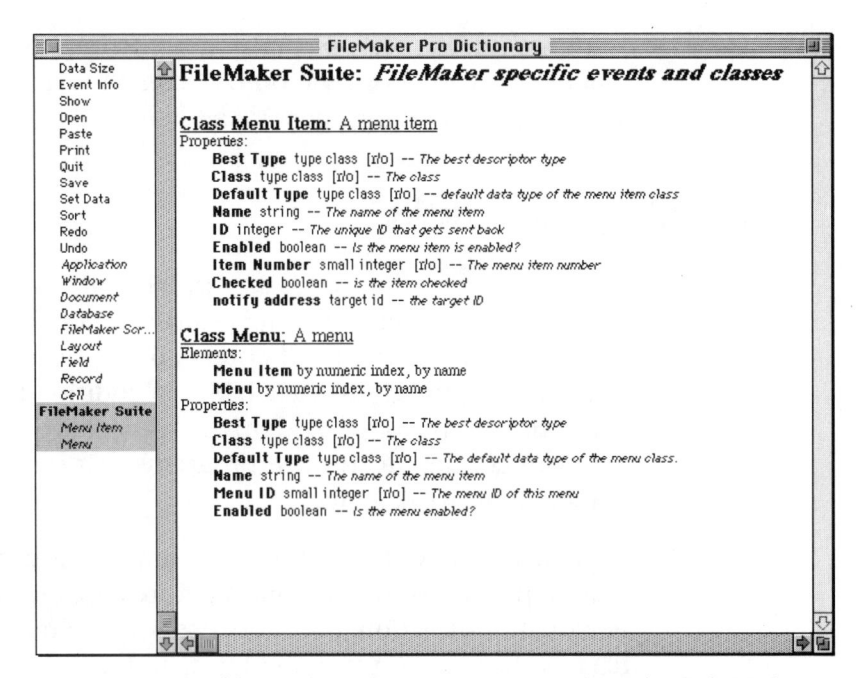

Figure 10-17: The FileMaker suite viewed in the FileMaker Pro dictionary.

The entire current list of AppleEvents, along with detailed descriptions of each, is regularly sent to all Macintosh software developers so they can incorporate these events into their software updates. Apple compiles a standard AppleEvent Registry that developers can refer to.

You can obtain a copy of the current support levels of your favorite applications in a more readable form (and for free) by obtaining the brochure "AppleScript Guide to Scriptable Applications," published by Apple. Request this guide by contacting Apple at the Internet address: APPLESCRIPT@APPLELINK.COM, or by calling 408-996-1010. You can get the "AppleEvent Registry: Standard Suites" ($85) and the "AppleEvent Education Suite v. 1.0" ($25) from the APDA by calling 716-871-6555. AppleEvents have been largely a developer's tool, and not a widely implemented one at that.

With the release of AppleScript and the impending release of OpenDoc, AppleEvents should become more universally adopted and used by a general audience.

AppleEvents & Program Linking

When an application sends an AppleEvent to another program, the receiving program is usually launched and then asked to perform a task. Of course, this process assumes that the receiving program is available. In addition to programs that exist on the same hard drive, AppleShare events, through IAC, can communicate with programs that reside on other parts of a network as well.

AppleEvents have found their first important use linking small related programs together into a more capable system. Several Personal Information Managers use AppleEvents to achieve data exchanges between modules, and make them more powerful and seamless. Other candidates for AppleEvents projects are flat-file databases that require relational capabilities, and application or system macros. In the next chapter, you will learn how to use the Script Editor to record AppleEvent scripts.

Chapter 12, "An Introduction to File Sharing," introduces the System 7 capability that lets any user on the network share data with any other user on the network.

In Chapter 13, "Working on a Network," you'll learn about the Program Linking option, which allows you to access software from other Macintoshes on the network via IAC commands. If you use this option, applications on one Macintosh can use AppleEvents to communicate with applications on other Macs across the network. As with other aspects of IAC, it remains to be seen how this capability will be translated into new Macintosh software features.

OpenDoc

As computers get more powerful and the industry matures, you would expect computers to get easier to use. That has not been the case. There's been a trend in the industry to release ever more feature-filled software packages, as if the quality of a program is measured by the number of check-offs it can achieve on a feature list. Word processors now contain spell checkers, grammar checkers, thesaureses, page layout modules, graphics, charting, outlining, idea processing, table of contents and index generation, databases and mail merges, envelope label printers, telephone and fax machines and e-mail message centers.

What's a user to do? You can hardly find these "features," let alone learn about them. Only "get-a-lifers" can love the current state of the software industry. If there was no penalty to pay, you could safely ignore the stuff you weren't interested in. However, extra features burn up processing power and disk space. Checked your hard drive lately? There are probably half a dozen spell checkers lurking about in there. This trend has probably reached its peak with the release of huge, everything-including-the-kitchen-sink packages such as Microsoft Office, Lotus SmartSuite and Novell's WordPerfect office package.

Vendors have long noted the problem. It's both a resource management opportunity and an industry barrier. Large programs from large software houses crowd out innovative small products from small companies. One solution is to link small programs into a compound document architecture with an object-oriented framework and Inter-Application Communication. Then you can buy and learn just the functions you need—one text editor, one spell checker, one paint module, and so on.

With this goal, Apple, WordPerfect, Novell, Borland and IBM have pursued an industry-wide standard called OpenDoc. OpenDoc is an architecture under which documents are built. OpenDoc is the result of the "Amber" project at Apple, with other technologies added to the mix by the other vendors in the program. OpenDoc should make client/server and multimedia applications easier to create and use.

What Is OpenDoc?

Users viewing demonstrations of OpenDoc have described it as a "bug fix" because it fits into a natural way of working with data objects as parts in a compound document. A compound document is much more natural than an application-centered document: you don't have to do context switching between applications to get the capabilities you need. Just click a part and the menu changes. You don't even notice it. But when you go to the menu, the command you expect to use for that part is there. Need a part? Just add it. OpenDoc supplies the reference to the appropriate part handler.

OpenDoc offers the following user benefits:

- **Easy creation of compound documents.** You use the same Cut and Paste, Drag and Drop, Publish and Subscribe, and other metaphors that you are used to. It looks and feels like a Macintosh. OpenDoc uses the Open Scripting Architecture (OSA), of which AppleEvents and AppleScript are a part, as its messaging medium.

- **In-place editing.** Point at and click what you want to change. Cut and Paste, Drag and Drop, and most other aspects of data handling you've come to know are also supported.

- **Improved multitasking.** You can have several parts "playing" at the same time in the same document. For example, you could have a clock and a video running while you work in a text file. OpenDoc provides a multithreaded, multitasked system time-slicing among all three parts.

- **Central data storage and unified document management.** All your data pieces are in your document; only the services needed to use them are referenced. Therefore, data can't be lost or inaccessible as it can be in the Publish and Subscribe model. You also can track the revision history of your document.

- **Cross-platform support.** OpenDoc is a vendor-neutral, platform-neutral specification supported by major industry players. It will be available on Windows through WordPerfect, and on OS/2 and AIX courtesy of IBM. As yet, Microsoft doesn't directly support OpenDoc. They sell a competing compound document architecture called Object Linking and Embedding (OLE 2.0).

In order to promote OpenDoc and make it an open standard, a nonprofit association called the Component Integration Laboratories (or CI Labs) was formed. CI Labs publishes the OpenDoc standard. It is not only responsible for making OpenDoc available to everybody, but also provides rigorous testing and evaluation procedures to approve software under the program. You can reach CI Labs at their Internet address: cilabs@cil.org or at 415-750-8352.

You'll begin to see the OpenDoc symbol on product boxes over time (see Figure 10-18).

Figure 10-18: The OpenDoc logo.

OpenDoc can work with other compound document architectures such as Microsoft's OLE 2.0 and Taligent's forthcoming operating system, so you can open a document created in those architectures and have access to the services referenced within them. See "Apple's OpenDoc vs. Microsoft's OLE" later in this chapter.

- **Consistency of operation and uniformity of interface.** Use one part editor for each data type. When your needs grow, you can upgrade to a more powerful editor. OpenDoc defines a consistent user interface for documents, parts and part handlers.

OpenDoc has the potential to profoundly impact the way you use your Macintosh. It will make it much easier to customize your environment or for vendors to provide quality vertical market packages (software written for a niche audience) suitable for your line of work. Best yet, you'll see OpenDoc added to system software as an extension (like QuickTime was) in early 1995.

Documents & Parts

OpenDoc adds a few additional words to the vocabulary of the Macintosh user. But these words are based on common ones you use in your everyday speech, so they shouldn't be much of a burden. Documents are the central framework in OpenDoc. A document is no longer tied to a single application but is composed of small pieces of content called parts.

Parts are the fundamental building blocks in OpenDoc. They have the same relationship to documents that atoms do to molecules. Parts come in flavors, which are content containers. Text parts contain characters; graphics parts contain lines and shapes; spreadsheet parts contain cells, formulas and a spreadsheet engine; video parts contain digitized video sequences and a player; and so on. OpenDoc makes its best effort to compartmentalize capabilities within part types, although some mixing occurs. The type of data in each part is known as the part's intrinsic content.

Parts can contain other parts (embedding), so a document has a part hierarchy. That is, a document has a single part at its root level in which other parts are embedded. Developers must decide whether their parts can embed other parts: but if the parts can be embedded, then they can accept any type of part.

Parts are created and modified by part editors. These editors are small programs that are called upon by an OpenDoc document—system routines really. Some part editors will ship with the OpenDoc package so that you will have basic capability right out of the box in system software. This capability is similar to current functions of system software such as TextEdit, QuickDraw, the Communications Toolbox and other routines that let you work with parts of the Macintosh interface in standard ways.

Part handlers are more complex editors that third parties create for OpenDoc. You buy them shrink-wrapped in stores. Part handlers are the equivalent of applications; they are responsible for the following functions under the OpenDoc architecture:

- Displaying the part onscreen and rendering it to a printer.

- Editing the part.

- Storage and management. The part handler reads and writes the part to and from memory and disk. For this reason, part handlers can be of two types: editors and viewers. Many will be both.

- Acting as an interface modifier. The editor part handler is responsible for switching menu commands, adjusting dialog boxes and changing the interface to make available whatever tools a part requires. A viewer part handler is a subset of an editor; it allows users to display and print a part but not edit it. You use viewers to provide security lock-out features for parts in documents.

Another important concept in OpenDoc is that of frames. Whereas parts are areas of one kind of content, frames are the boundaries separating the collection of objects and operations supported by one part from those supported by another. You can embed a button in a part, and that compound construct is a frame that can be manipulated. Frames have properties such as layering (front to back), transparency and so on that will be familiar to users of draw graphics programs. In Figure 10-19, you see a text frame with an embedded button and clock. These elements comprise a frame. Other parts in the document—the table, pie chart and graphic—are not part of the text frame. In this example, they can overlap the text frame, but they are manipulated independently. It may be helpful to think of frames as grouped collections of objects with their own identities.

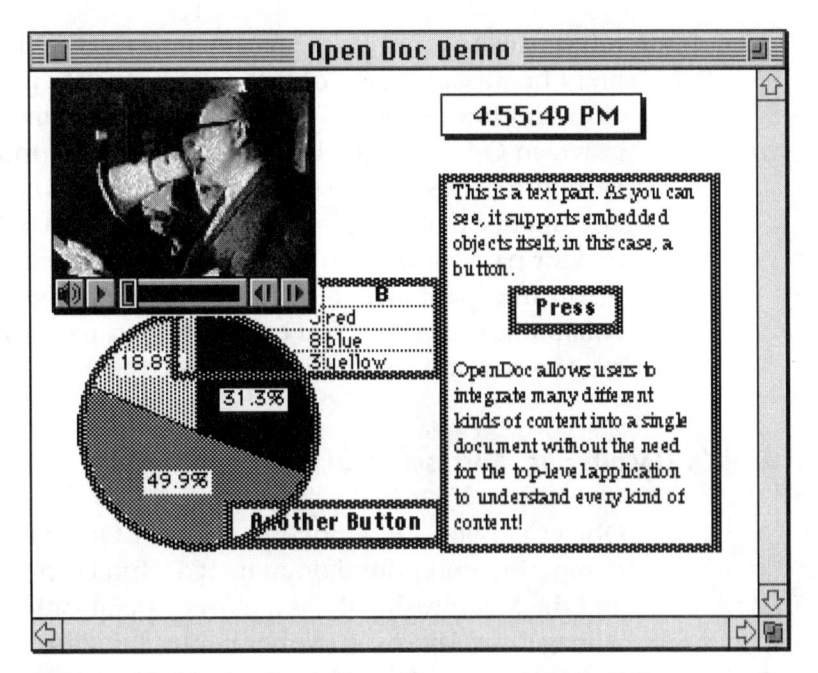

Figure 10-19: An OpenDoc document with a frame and several parts.

Thankfully, it's much harder to explain what a frame is than it is to use one. The notion is almost entirely transparent to the user. Frames are not simply windows that appear or disappear from view; they are persistent. When you open a frame in a window, you see the frame. When you close that window, the part returns to the condition it was in before you opened the window. A frame can show however much of its contents is displayed. That is, if a frame contains a graphic larger than the frame, you would see the cropped part of that graphic within the frame.

Storage of compound documents requires a system of saving the document to disk with each part referenced to its part handler. OpenDoc uses an object-oriented storage model based on Apple's Bento standard. Storing a document to disk compartmentalizes each part as a data object and provides references to appropriate part handlers. Opening that document begins a process of calling appropriate part handlers one after another to "build" the document in memory. When you move an OpenDoc document to another computer or type of computer, these part handler references let the OpenDoc document be opened by other appropriate handlers when the creator part handler isn't available. This system ensures cross-platform capabilities, but it also provides a mechanism for collaborative access. You can write part handlers that are both multiuser- and version history-sensitive.

Apple's OpenDoc vs. Microsoft's OLE

Object Linking and Embedding 2.0, or OLE 2.0, is Microsoft's competing compound document architecture for Windows and the Macintosh. OLE is a closed specification created and managed by Microsoft. Vendors buy a license from Microsoft to implement OLE in their applications. Closed standards have the advantage of being tightly specified but are often less flexible and less quirky. OLE is well established on Windows but not yet a presence on the Macintosh. It is a direct competitor to OpenDoc, and it shares many of the same capabilities and promise.

OLE 2.0's main features are as follow:

- **Visual (or in-place) editing.** This type of editing includes Cut and Paste, Drag and Drop, and so on. Note that the Microsoft implementation of Drag and Drop is somewhat different from Apple's.

- **Client/server metaphor.** OLE server applications create objects; OLE client applications create compound documents.

- **Warm links/hot links.** Links are representations of an object in a client file. They can be updated manually or automatically. Broken links occur when the source document is moved, and you use the Links dialog box in Windows to repair the pointer.

  Publish and Subscribe on the Macintosh uses a Linking metaphor.

- **Embedded objects.** An object is embedded in a client when it is the one and only representation of the object.

  OpenDoc uses an Embedding metaphor.

- **Automation programming.** Using Visual Basic for Applications, you can create compound document automation.

  OLE uses DDE as its messaging service, just as OpenDoc uses AppleEvents. OLE uses Visual Basic, whereas OpenDoc uses AppleScript.

With OLE, the music is similar to OpenDoc, even if the words are different. OLE calls a self-contained unit of information an object. You edit an object using a server application. When you activate the data in an object by selecting the object, you play it. A text object, for example, sits and looks at you when you click on it. The only thing you do is activate the text for editing. With a video object when you click on it it plays. Playing and editing are just two of the actions that a server can perform on objects. As a group, these commands or actions are called verbs; objects are the nouns, just like in "AppleEvents speak."

Linking an object places a representation of the object in your file (the OLE client) with a pointer to the original (source) file. An embedded object places both the native object and presentation for that object into the OLE client (or destination file). OLE uses the registration database file REG.DAT to hold all the information about OLE servers in Windows. You can view this file using the RegEdit utility.

One feature in OLE not found in OpenDoc is the ability to minimize an OLE object in a file down to an icon, which is called a package. Packages are tokenized representations of data objects that can be quite large.

You will often hear people refer to an OLE compound document as a client, although that is not the case. Only a client application can create compound documents. Native data is information stored in the server's format that you can play or edit. Presentation data is read-only; you can't play it.

Clearly, OLE isn't going to ship in Apple system software, anytime ever. If Microsoft wasn't making noise about OLE being cross-platform, then Macintosh users could safely ignore OLE. But the pull of 80 million Windows machines is strong. (OLE also has something of a headstart, although OpenDoc will close the gap quickly.) Some vendors will build OLE into Macintosh products because they need the services of Microsoft applications. Chances are that OLE and OpenDoc will co-exist for some time to come.

The OpenDoc standard works with OLE (and Taligent's operating system, for that matter) by using "wrappers" to map the programming calls from one Application Programming Interface (called an API) to another. The user opens an OLE compound document within an OpenDoc framework, and OpenDoc supplies the translation. You see the menu, toolbar and other interface elements of the OLE document just as it would appear if you were working on a Windows PC. OpenDoc then becomes a superset of OLE. However, you are working on your Macintosh in the usual way within OpenDoc. Initial demonstrations of this capability have been impressive, and it's likely that this capability will be part of the initial release of OpenDoc.

Moving On

Over time the lines between individual applications will blur as the powers of IAC are fully utilized and OpenDoc becomes adopted. As you've seen, the Edition Manager allows you to transfer text and graphics between applications, while maintaining a "live link" to the original data, using just a few simple commands:

- **Create Publisher.** This command saves the selected data to a new edition file on disk.

- **Subscribe to.** This command imports an edition file from disk into the current document.

- **Publish/Subscribe options.** These commands control the way changes to original documents are updated to the edition file and documents subscribing to the edition file.

The OpenDoc architecture provides a framework for creating compound documents using small applications. OpenDoc uses the Open Scripting Architecture, an object model, a portable document format called Bento and other elements of IAC to provide seamless communications among elements or parts of a compound document. OpenDoc holds the promise of changing the way you buy applications, store data—even the way you work with Macintosh computers.

AppleEvents provides a rich object-oriented messaging language that IAC uses to let applications talk to one another. As you will see in Chapter 11, "AppleScript," this system software programming tool uses AppleEvents and a natural programming language to let you automate many actions into easy-to-use programs.

Chapter 11

AppleScript

When the first version of MS-DOS shipped with the IBM PC in 1983, it came bundled with a version of the BASIC programming language. PC users could control their computers and operating systems. With programs called batch files, they could start programs automatically, repeat actions, do timed backups, set the operating environment and more. Over the years, Macintosh owners have gazed longingly upon those capabilities—one of the few areas in which the PC was more gifted, out of the box, than the Macintosh.

Although several third-party developers provide a system-wide macro programming tool—most notably UserLand's Frontier, Affinity Microsystem's Tempo II Plus and CE Software's QuicKeys—none of these were officially blessed by Apple, nor have they achieved broad enough support in the Macintosh community to become a standard. Either they were too hard to learn, or they were too easy to learn but not powerful enough. Apple has finally released its own programming language, AppleScript, to provide these much-needed capabilities, as part of an overall strategy meant to provide automation tools across Macintosh applications and beyond.

AppleScript is expected to have many different kinds of applications:

- Users can use AppleScript to tailor applications and their desktops to their needs.

- AppleScript simplifies the work of developers, systems integrators and Value Added Resellers (VARs), providing custom solutions based upon standard Macintosh applications.

- AppleScript allows you to integrate small components into larger solutions seamlessly. You could write an *applet*, an *intelligent agent* or *a smart document* using AppleScript. This capability is part of Apple's strategy for down-sizing applications, of which Inter-Application Communication, AppleEvents and OpenDoc (described in the preceding chapter) are part.

- New product opportunities are created using AppleScript. You'll see some of these possibilities in Apple Guide and PlainTalk, which incorporate, can be controlled by, and in turn can use AppleScript to control other applications.

AppleScript will become a pervasive part of the Macintosh operating system—one that even if you don't program in, at least you will use routinely.

What Is AppleScript?

AppleScript is a high-level object-oriented natural-language type of programming language. It is a real programming language: it can store variables and lists (records or arrays); repeat through looping; make decisions based on cases; do IF branching; compare; do Boolean logic; and manipulate text, numbers, dates and times, and other values. AppleScript can also declare variables, create user-defined commands or subroutines, and store and manipulate data to return values.

> For information related to this chapter see "Using Scripts for Automation."

AppleScript is object-oriented because it imposes actions on objects that are defined as part of its programming model: objects can be applications (Finder, Scriptable Text Editor, FileMaker and so on), files, resources, interface elements (buttons, windows and so on) and data. In the Finder, objects can be a variety of named Macintoshes, printers, even AppleTalk zones on a network. Objects you can see on your desktop can be manipulated with AppleScript, a capability made even easier with the Scriptable Finder introduced in System 7.5 (described later in this chapter).

Objects have two additional characteristics that are programmatical: *inheritance* and *encapsulation*. Objects, like applications, can contain other objects (encapsulation); objects derived from other objects share common characteristics (inheritance). Third-party applications behave as if they are object-oriented databases to AppleScript because they contain a group of objects. These features impose regularity to objects, making them behave in ways you expect and have come to learn intuitively.

AppleScript uses words and statements to form scripts. Words are nouns (objects), verbs and modifiers. Verbs are common action commands such as open, close, print or delete. Often verbs are derived from standard menu commands. Statements are commands that can be communicated in the form of messages to objects in other applications. Applications themselves are objects because they can be commanded to do actions.

As an example of an AppleScript statement, consider the following:

tell application "Scriptable Text Editor" **to** activate the window **name** "*Untitled.*"

This one-line statement is a complete script that instructs the Scriptable Text Editor to search its list of opened windows, and if an "Untitled" window is open, it makes that the frontmost active window. The formatting of this statement with bolded verbs, plain nouns and italicized variables is traditional but not required. Often you will see AppleScripts written in clegic logic (or display) format, with indentations for each command structure. You can see an example of this formatting in the Add Alias to Apple Menu AppleScript, which is shipped with the collection of Useful Scripts of System 7.5. It is shown in the Script Editor window in Figure 11-1.

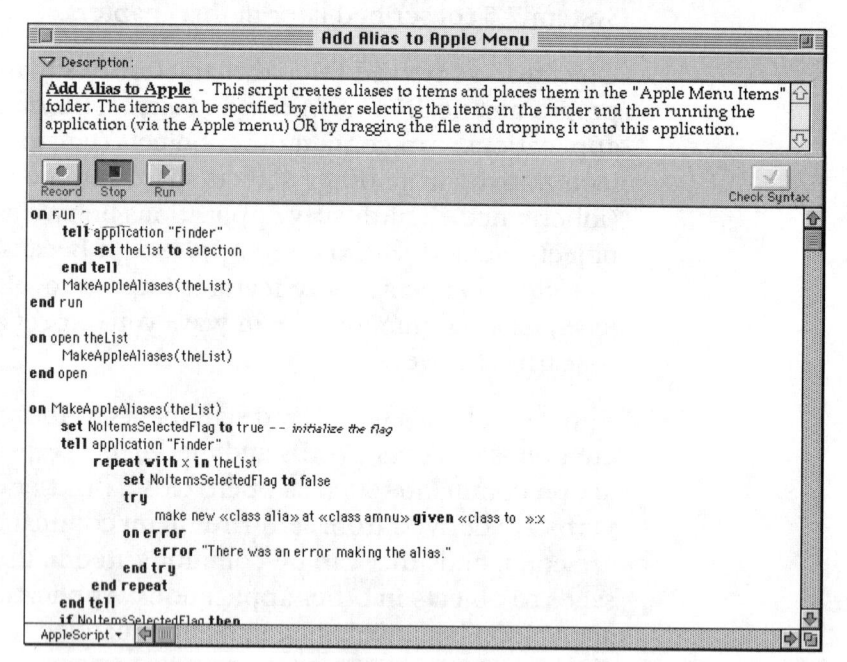

Figure 11-1: The Add Alias to Apple Menu AppleScript shown in the Script Editor window.

As much as possible, AppleScript is written in a manner similar to the way you write and speak. The syntax is much more precise and demanding, to be sure. But the intent is to lower the learning curve for AppleScript by using words, expressions and modifiers that you use in your everyday life in the English language. Other dialects of AppleScript exist for other languages: French, German, Japanese Kanji and so on.

The programs you write in AppleScript, called *scripts*, are like all other high-level programming languages. Scripts must be interpreted and compiled to run on your Macintosh. You can store scripts for interpretation at run time, or you can transform your script into interpreted read-only programs that you can distribute freely to other users. When you compile an AppleScript, it is transformed into a dialect-independent format called "Universal AppleScript." If you open an AppleScript, you will see the script displayed in the default language of the Macintosh you're working on, not necessarily the language that the script was originally written in. A translation from Universal AppleScript has been done.

AppleScript also supports dialects similar to more traditional programming languages such as C. When a programmer writes a script in the C dialect and sends it to you, you would view that script in your own language dialect, such as English. Having that capability makes it easy for programmers to write a driver to retrieve a file on an optical jukebox, for example, but have you call that procedure by using syntax like this:

> **get** *filename* optical jukebox

If you have used the HyperTalk programming language in HyperCard, AppleScript will seem familiar. Unlike HyperCard, AppleScript is extensible by other applications within the language. AppleScript uses a dictionary of commands (verbs), objects (nouns) and modifiers that are defined within each program that has chosen to implement AppleScript. Applications codify their data and functions by defining dictionaries of objects and commands. You can see an application's dictionary by using the Open Dictionary command of the Script Editor. Figure 11-2 shows you FileMaker Pro's dictionary.

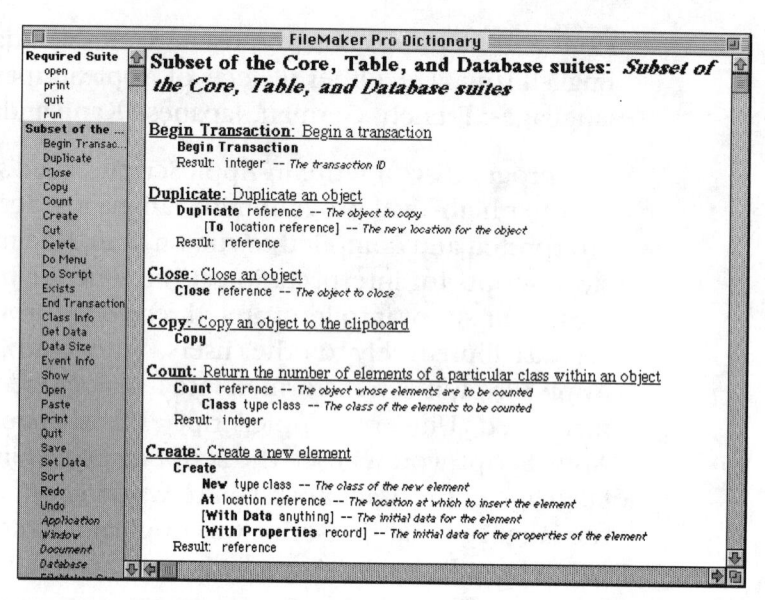

Figure 11-2: The FileMaker Pro AppleScript dictionary.

When AppleScript loads an application's dictionary, external data become objects and external functions become commands, and the language of that application becomes part of AppleScript's syntax.

The AppleScript Architecture

The problem with most programming languages is that they require that you learn a new language, if not a new programming model. To minimize this problem, Apple introduced the Open Scripting Architecture (OSA) as a language standard that others could adopt.

The standards definition phase of OSA began in 1989 and is ongoing. OSA and Apple Event Registry were released concurrent with System 7.0 in 1991. Some key applications that supported AppleScript (such as Excel 4.0, FileMaker Pro 2.0, PageMaker 4.2, and others) were released in 1992.

AppleScript 1.0 followed in 1993 as a separate product. It was bundled with System 7 Pro. Version 1.1 and the Scriptable Finder appeared in System 7.5. Finally, Apple plans to release a cross-platform version of AppleScript at some as yet unspecified time.

AppleScript is one expression of OSA, but other developers could provide their own applications. OSA includes AppleEvents that you learned about in the previous chapter, the Object model, and a reference library of objects and events that are codified by third parties through Apple. These components form the basis for an open standard that Apple hopes others will build upon in the years to come.

As you may remember from the preceding chapter, AppleEvents is a messaging language that makes Inter-Application Communication (IAC) possible in System 7. With AppleEvents, programs communicate with one another, performing inter-application operations. One expression of the power of IAC is Publish and Subscribe. AppleEvents work between applications that are either on the same computer or connected through a network.

AppleScript uses AppleEvents as the messaging medium through which commands are passed and results returned. Scripts are sent to the AppleScript extension, which interprets the statements in a script and sends AppleEvents to the appropriate application. The Apple Event Manager extension serves as the traffic cop that interprets these messages and routes them appropriately. You see the Event Manager in System 7.1; in later systems its function is incorporated into the System file.

To prevent AppleScript from growing in nonstandard ways, Apple imposes a standard language. Objects in AppleScript are identified by compound names, called *references*. The overall naming scheme is called the *Object Model*. With this "dictionary," the language allows you to refer to individual objects in one of several alternate ways, without worrying about how each application prefers to describe an object. Some commands have alternate expressions and so do some objects. It would be a burden to have to learn which application supports which variant, so AppleScript validates both kinds in any application.

A standard syntax is imposed on developers only for common language tasks. Apple has organized events and objects into event suites. These suites are common ways to do tasks based on application categories: text processing, database and spreadsheets, communications, page layout and so on. These suites extend the concept of common menu-command language such as *copy* and *paste* to scripting commands such as *delete, contain, get,* and *set* across the programming language. Event suites were covered in detail in the preceding chapter.

Event suites are evolving, and developers can register their commands, objects and suites in the AppleEvent Registry (available from the Apple Professional Developers Association, or APDA). The event suites in this registry are the standard language for Inter-Application Communication implemented at the machine level, and a standard reference to developers on implementing AppleScript support within their own applications.

Scripting Basics

Upon installation of AppleScript, you will notice that three files are added to your Extensions folder: AppleScript, Record Button and the Apple Event Manager. In System 7.1 you see all three; in System 7.5 only the first two files appear. You may see additional modules depending on your installation:

- **AppleScript extension.** This extension contains the language and the code necessary to interpret the language to your Macintosh. It also passes messages between applications and the Apple Event Manager. AppleScript extension loads at bootup as a 2k handler in system memory when no scripts are running. When scripts are running, the full 330k of the extension are loaded. The icon for AppleScript is shown in Figure 11-3.

Figure 11-3: The AppleScript extension icon.

- **Record Button.** The Record Button enables the "watch me" recorder feature you see in the Script Editor (described later in this section). The Record Button icon is shown in Figure 11-4.

Figure 11-4: The Record Button extension icon.

- **Apple Event Manager.** The Apple Event Manager provides the necessary communications between AppleEvents and AppleScript. The Apple Event Manager is used by other programs for Publish and Subscribe and other features, but it was designed to work hand in hand with AppleScript. The Apple Event Manager extension icon is shown in Figure 11-5.

Figure 11-5: The Apple Event Manager extension icon.

AppleScript can also work with QuickTime Versions 1.5 and later.

- **Scripting additions.** These language extensions can be written in another programming language and added to AppleScript. They are often referred to as user-definable programs. In AppleScript, these scripts are called using simple syntax with the named command or file name.

  As AppleScript develops, you will find scripting additions in third-party books and as shareware or freeware on online services. A scripting addition file icon is shown in Figure 11-6. You can find some sample scripting additions in your Useful Scripts folder of the AppleScript folder (located in the Apple Extras folder on your drive).

  Figure 11-6: An AppleScript Addition file icon.

- **Alternate Scripting components.** OSA provides the capability to exchange messages between OSA-compliant scripting systems, also called *components*. A program's scripting system can send and receive messages from AppleScript, making integration between the two seamless. Each script is tagged with a "creator code" that defines the scripting system from which it originated. Any scripting component required is loaded at the time the script is executed. The icon for an alternative scripting component is the blank extension icon shown in Figure 11-7.

  Figure 11-7: An Alternative Scripting component icon.

In the Apple Extras folder that is part of the System 7.5 installation, you will also notice an AppleScript folder. Additional, nonsystem components of AppleScript are contained there: the Script Editor, a Scriptable Text Editor, AppleScript Guide and a folder of Useful Scripts. These components do the following:

- **Script Editor.** You use this application to write or record, edit, check the syntax of, compile and run scripts. The icon for the Script Editor is shown in Figure 11-8.

Figure 11-8: The Script Editor Application icon.

- **Scriptable Text Editor.** This feature is a completely AppleScript-aware and recordable word processor. As such, it is often used as a teaching aid in AppleScript books and presentations. Figure 11-9 shows the icon for the Scriptable Text Editor.

    The Scriptable Text Editor is *not* part of a standard System 7.5 installation. Depending on how you obtained AppleScript, you may or may not have this application installed in the AppleScript folder.

Figure 11-9: The Scriptable Text Editor Application icon.

- **AppleScript Guide.** This feature is a SimpleText file of the Apple Guide manual that shipped with System 7 Pro.

- **Useful Scripts folder.** Useful Scripts are a series of pre-recorded AppleScripts that you can use in your daily work. An alias of this folder is included in the Apple Menu Items folder. You can initiate the script by selecting its menu command from the Useful Scripts submenu. You will look at some of these scripts later in the chapter.

AppleScript support is added by an application's developer. You should note that three different levels of AppleScript support are recognized:

- **Scriptable.** A scriptable application represents the highest level of AppleScript support. These applications can understand and respond to AppleEvents generated by scripts. A scriptable application can be *controlled* by an AppleScript script.

- **Recordable.** A recordable application is capable of sending itself AppleEvents and reporting user actions to the Apple Event Manager so that a script summarizing these actions can be recorded. When you use the Record button of the Script Editor, recordable applications let you create and compile scripts as applications.

- **Attachable.** This type of application can trigger a script as a response to a user action (such as clicking a button or entering a text string). Apple describes an attachable application as "tinkerable." Attachable applications are useful as a front end to other applications.

Any combination of support is possible, so you can have an application that is both scriptable and recordable, recordable and attachable, scriptable and attachable, or all three. Apple publishes a booklet entitled "AppleScript Guide to Scriptable Applications" with a listing of each application's capabilities. To get this brochure or add an application to the list, you can contact Apple by calling 408-996-1010, or at their AppleLink address APPLESCRIPT, or through Internet at Applescript@applelink.com.

The Script Editor

The Script Editor is the application that Apple provides with AppleScript to open and run scripts, record or write scripts, and save scripts in various forms. The Script Editor illustrates many of the basic principles used in creating and working with AppleScripts, so let's look at this application first.

Recording a Script

The Script Editor comes with a recorder feature that lets you create scripts based on your actions. Other macro programs call this a "watch me" kind of macro programming. As described previously, applications can only be scripted in this way if they are recordable. TeachText is neither scriptable nor recordable, but SimpleText is. The Finder, for example, is only scriptable and recordable in System 7.5 and later.

Start the Script Editor, and in the script window enter the script name. Click the Record button to turn on the recorder. The Script Editor window is shown in Figure 11-10. You will notice that the Apple menu icon flashes as a script is being recorded. Go about switching to the program of your choice and performing other actions as desired. You complete your recorded script by switching back to the Script Editor window and clicking the Stop button. Clicking the Stop button in the Script Editor lets you run that script by name whenever the Script Editor is open. You can also use the commands in the Control menu of the Script Editor in place of the buttons you see in the window.

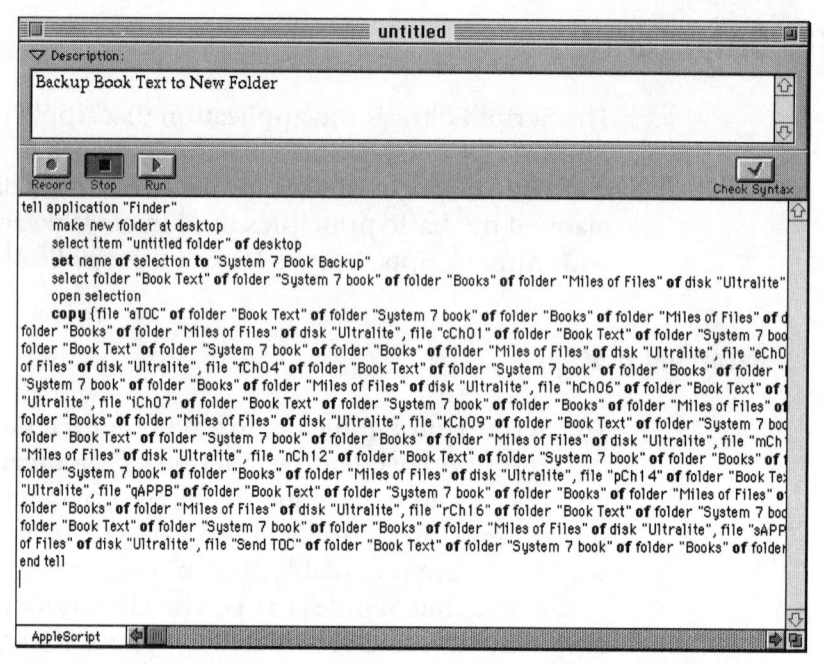

```
┌─────────────────────────────────────────────────────────┐
│                         untitled                        │
│ ▽ Description:                                          │
│ ┌─────────────────────────────────────────────────────┐ │
│ │ Backup Book Text to New Folder                      │ │
│ │                                                     │ │
│ └─────────────────────────────────────────────────────┘ │
│  ●    ■    ▶                                       ✓    │
│ Record Stop Run                                Check Syntax│
│ tell application "Finder"                               │
│     make new folder at desktop                          │
│     select item "untitled folder" of desktop            │
│     set name of selection to "System 7 Book Backup"     │
│     select folder "Book Text" of folder "System 7 book" of folder "Books" of folder "Miles of Files" of disk "Ultralite"│
│     open selection                                      │
│        copy {file "aTOC" of folder "Book Text" of folder "System 7 book" of folder "Books" of folder "Miles of Files" of d│
│ folder "Books" of folder "Miles of Files" of disk "Ultralite", file "cCh01" of folder "Book Text" of folder "System 7 boo│
│ folder "Book Text" of folder "System 7 book" of folder "Books" of folder "Miles of Files" of disk "Ultralite", file "eCh0│
│ of Files" of disk "Ultralite", file "fCh04" of folder "Book Text" of folder "System 7 book" of folder "Books" of folder " │
│ "System 7 book" of folder "Books" of folder "Miles of Files" of disk "Ultralite", file "hCh06" of folder "Book Text" of │
│ "Ultralite", file "iCh07" of folder "Book Text" of folder "System 7 book" of folder "Books" of folder "Miles of Files" o│
│ folder "Books" of folder "Miles of Files" of disk "Ultralite", file "kCh09" of folder "Book Text" of folder "System 7 boo│
│ folder "Book Text" of folder "System 7 book" of folder "Books" of folder "Miles of Files" of disk "Ultralite", file "mCh │
│ "Miles of Files" of disk "Ultralite", file "nCh12" of folder "Book Text" of folder "System 7 book" of folder "Books" of │
│ folder "System 7 book" of folder "Books" of folder "Miles of Files" of disk "Ultralite", file "pCh14" of folder "Book Te│
│ "Ultralite", file "qAPPB" of folder "Book Text" of folder "System 7 book" of folder "Books" of folder "Miles of Files" o│
│ folder "Books" of folder "Miles of Files" of disk "Ultralite", file "rCh16" of folder "Book Text" of folder "System 7 boo│
│ folder "Book Text" of folder "System 7 book" of folder "Books" of folder "Miles of Files" of disk "Ultralite", file "sAPP│
│ of Files" of disk "Ultralite", file "Send TOC" of folder "Book Text" of folder "System 7 book" of folder "Books" of folde│
│ end tell                                                │
│ |                                                       │
│                                                         │
│ AppleScript                                             │
└─────────────────────────────────────────────────────────┘
```

Figure 11-10: The Script Editor window with a sample recorded script.

You will notice that the Script Editor has entered all the commands in stylized clegic logic that correspond to your actions. As with other keystroke macro recorders, only certain actions can be captured by the Script Editor. They are using menu commands, pressing keys, saving files, opening and closing windows and files, and recording the results of clicking the mouse. Drags and clicks are not normally captured because they don't result in any actions or changes. When a click does result in an action, such as activating a button, that action is recorded.

Because the actions were recorded to a script, there is no chance that the syntax requires checking. Therefore, this option (described later) is not available to you using the Check Syntax button in the Script Editor window.

Saving a Script

When you stop the recording of a script in the Script Editor, you save a script within the Script Editor. It's more useful to save the script as a document that you can call up from the Finder. Use the Save command in the Script Editor to bring up the standard Save dialog box shown in Figure 11-11. Scripts are normally compiled when saved. To save a script without compiling it first, hold the Shift key when choosing the Save command from the File menu. The following list describes the three formats of scripts to which the Script Editor can save.

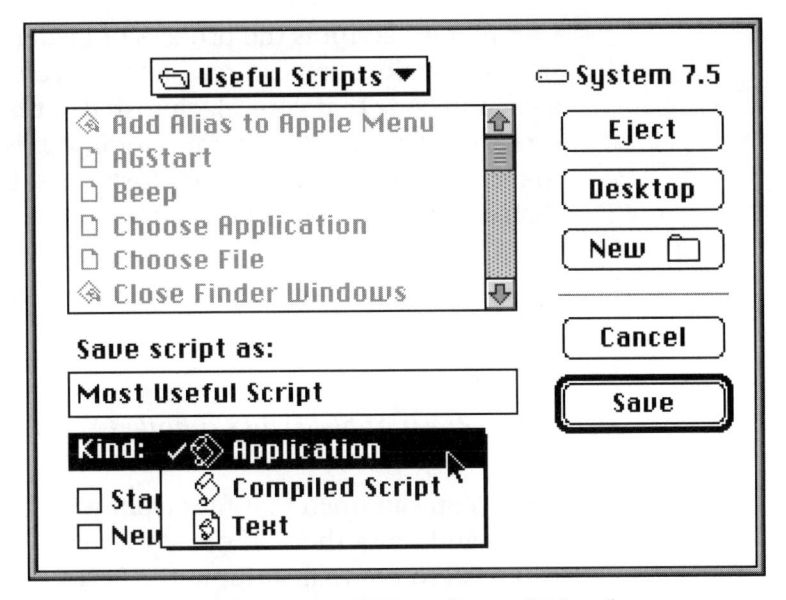

Figure 11-11: The Script Editor Save dialog box.

- **Application.** When you double-click the application icon shown in Figure 11-12, the application runs by itself without the Script Editor open.

  When you select the Application option, you can choose check boxes–to keep applications open after the script is run (Stay Open) or not keep the Script Editor open (Never Show Startup Screen) when the script starts up.

Figure 11-12: An AppleScript Application icon.

- **Compiled Script.** You can use compiled scripts directly or as commands within other scripts. Because run-time and compile engines are separate, scripts execute quickly and with few memory requirements. The icon for a compiled script is shown in Figure 11-13. A compiled script is not double-clickable.

    Compiling a script is the process of changing the script from the dialect you can read into Universal AppleScript, a pseudo-code that your Macintosh can read. A compiled script requires additional translation, but is much closer to the language than the Macintosh's and faster to run than a normal script in a dialect.

Figure 11-13: An AppleScript Compiled Script icon.

- **Text.** You can open text files from within other programs and reuse them. It's best to save as text files when you wish to use that script in the Scriptable Text Editor. The icon for an AppleScript Text file is shown in Figure 11-14.

Figure 11-14: An AppleScript Text file icon.

You can save an application or compiled script as a *run-time*—or as AppleScript calls it *run-only*—version of your script. You cannot save text files as run-only. To save a run-only version of a script, select the Save As Run-Only command from the File menu. The dialog box that appears will ask you to specify its location, name and the format for the script.

As noted previously, you can use the Script Editor to write scripts in other scripting systems or other dialects. If you are using a Macintosh with other scripting systems installed, you can choose from between them in the dialect pop-up menu that appears at the bottom-right corner of the Script Editor window. You can also choose a dialect with the same pop-up menu from within the AppleScript Formatting dialog box shown in Figure 11-17.

Running a Script

There are several ways to run a script depending on how the script was saved. You can select scripts recorded in the Script Editor from the name list by clicking them and then run them using the Run button. You can also double-click a name to run it. You can stop scripts running from within the Script Editor by using the Stop button.

If the script is a Finder file, either an application or a compiled script, you can run it by opening the file. Double-click an application or select that application and give the Open command (as you would any other application) to start the script running. When you launch an AppleScript application, a start-up screen (see Figure 11-15) may appear if you chose that option from within the Save dialog box. Click the Run button or press the Return key to run the script, or click the Quit button or press the Command-Period keystroke to abort the script.

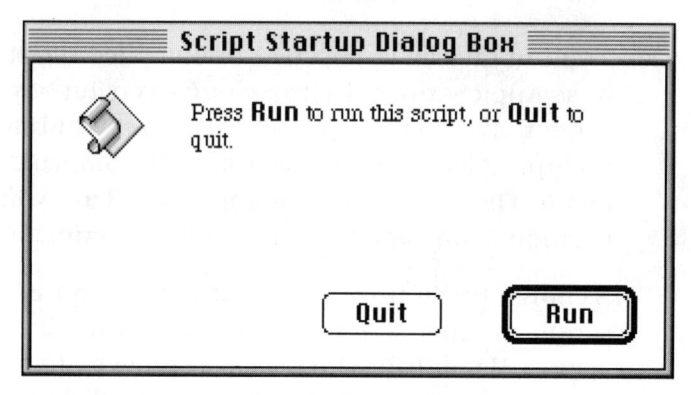

Figure 11-15: An AppleScript application start-up dialog box.

Scripts that are run result in an action. Some scripts return a value or expression based on their results. If you expect an outcome that you wish to see displayed in a window, select the Show Result command from the Script Editor Control menu. The Result window will appear with the result. If there is an error in your script, you may see an error message in the Result window.

Scripts also can be saved in the form of a *droplet*, that is, a drag-and-drop enabled application. Droplets are indicated with a down-facing arrow on their icons, as shown in Figure 11-16. To initiate the action supported by an AppleScript droplet, you simply drag the object you wish the action to take place with over the icon or alias of the droplet. This process is similar to dragging a file icon over a QuickDraw GX printer icon (see Chapter 9, "QuickDraw GX & Fonts") to print the file. If the object is supported by the droplet, action takes place immediately; otherwise, an error message is posted. To make a script a droplet, the object acted upon has to be scripted into the AppleScript program.

Figure 11-16: An AppleScript droplet icon.

Scripts can, of course, be embedded inside other applications or files. In this form as an attached script, there can be many ways to call up that script. Some will be under your control; others will not. You will often see scripts attached to buttons. When you click the button, the script runs. Other scripts will look for a text string in a field, check a condition, or do other tasks for which an action that triggers the script may not be obvious to you. These scripts can often run in the background and escape your detection.

Modifying a Script

Scripts recorded in the Script Editor are fully editable in the script window, as is any text document. To begin modifying a script, you must launch the Script Editor and use the Open Script command from the File menu to open that script by name.

Most of the text editing actions in the Script Editor should be familiar to you from your word processor. Just type in your changes and save the results. In addition to simple clicks and drags, you can use the following shortcuts in the Script Editor window:

- Double-click to select a word; triple-click to select a line.
- Use the arrow keys to move the insertion point.
- Use the Command-left Arrow or Command-right Arrow keystrokes to move to the beginning or end of a line, respectively.

- Use the Command-up Arrow or Command-down Arrow keystroke to move to the beginning or end of the script, respectively.

- Use the Tab key at the beginning of a line to indent it. Tabs typed in the middle of a line are converted to space characters when you apply syntax formatting.

- Use the Return keys at the end of an indented line to apply indenting automatically to the next line.

- Use the Option-Return keystroke to insert a continuation character (¬) and move to the beginning of the next line. This shortcut lets you work with a line that is too long to fit in the view of the active window. AppleScript ignores the continuation character and treats the lines on either side as one line.

- Use the Shift-Return keystroke to move the insertion point from the end of an indented line to the beginning of a new, unindented line.

Notice that the Script Editor has a Check Syntax button for written or modified scripts. This feature will run through a script to check that the syntax of programming steps is correct. Syntax is the collection of the grammar rules for a programming language. That is, if you have a command that required a certain command step (an end to an IF command, for example), that step is in the programming. The Check Syntax button will not correct errors in programming logic, only errors in construction.

When applied, the Check Syntax feature returns the first error as selected text. If there is an error in the text, no formatting is applied to the text in the Script Editor window. When the error is corrected, the Script Editor compiles the script, showing the script with clegic (indented) formatting and other formatting options.

Some Script Editor features let you set the formatting of the script to make it easier to read. Some programs call this "beautifying" the program. You can change fonts, styles, sizes and colors that are used in your scripts. These formatting styles make it easier to read the script and understand it, but they have no effect on the operation of the script. To set formatting options, choose the AppleScript Formatting command from the Edit menu. The dialog box shown in Figure 11-17 appears. Changes you make in this dialog box appear in any script you open from the Script Editor. Other programs that work with scripts, such as the Scriptable Text Editor, have similar features.

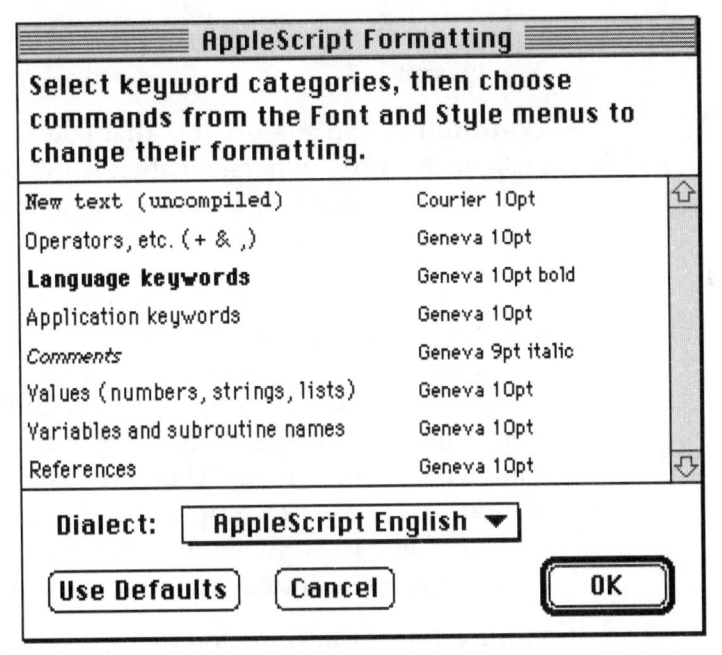

Figure 11-17: The AppleScript Formatting dialog box.

The elements of formatting you can apply based on the AppleScript formatting dialog box are as follow:

- **New text.** Any modifications you make to a script before you check syntax, run or save the results. These modifications let you view your changes easily from a "wall of text."

- **Operators.** Actions (verbs) applied to objects in AppleScript.

- **Language keywords.** Commands available as part of the AppleScript language. They are often also actions and verbs.

- **Application keywords.** Language extensions added to AppleScript by an application called within a script.

- **Operators.** Actions (verbs) applied to objects in AppleScript.

- **Comments.** Explanatory text that you add to a script to make its purpose understandable. Some people add comments to the beginning of a script as a header, to the beginning of a procedure or even after important lines.

    Comments in AppleScript are preceded by a double-hyphen. Anything on a line to the right of the double-hyphen is set in italics when compiled and then ignored at execution time or during a syntax-check. For multiline comments, use an asterisk at the start and end of the comments. Good commenting is the sign of a good programmer. It's an art to supply cogent commenting without overdoing it. For beginners, it is better to over-comment script than under-comment it.

- **Values.** Data or information that AppleScript uses, such as names, words and numbers.

- **Variables.** Containers that you name that can contain values. Values can change based on conditions.

- **References.** A pointer to an object is a reference. When you describe "window 1 of application Scriptable Text Editor," AppleScript knows you are referring to the topmost window open in the application. You see reference formatting in the Result window, not in the script window.

Scripting Applications

Every application has its own set of terms that it can add to the AppleScript vocabulary. Those terms are described in the dictionary within the application. At a script's run time, a called application's vocabulary is added to AppleScript for its use. To view an application's dictionary, choose the Open Dictionary command from the File menu of the Script Editor. Then select the application in the standard file Open dialog box. Items, commands and other verbs are described in the left scroll panel. These items are organized in event suites that the program supports.

When you click an item, you will see the definition of the command in the right panel. Figure 11-18 shows you the dictionary for the Scriptable Text Editor. Items will tell you the kinds of objects they act on, the information or values they require, and the results that are returned. Nearly every AppleScript-aware application supports the required suite and the standard suite of AppleEvents. Refer to Chapter 10, "Inter-Application Communication & OpenDoc," for more information on this topic.

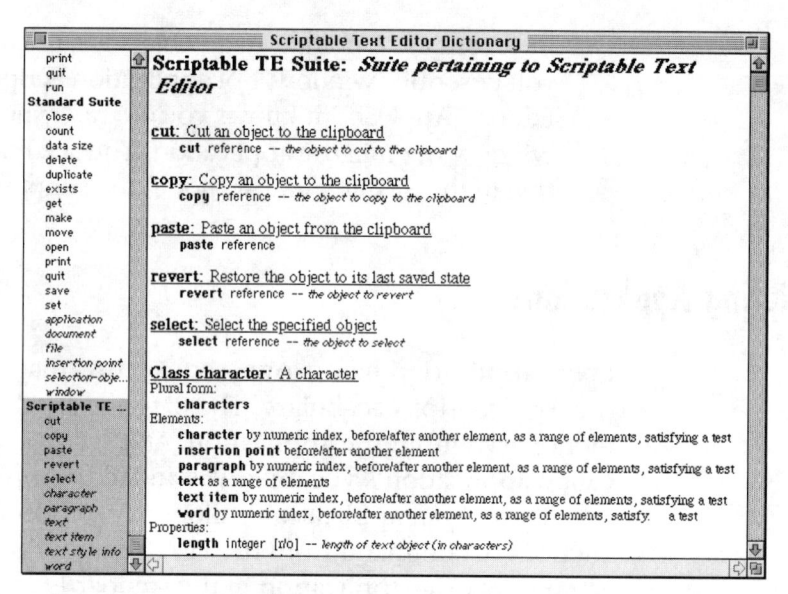

Figure 11-18: The Scriptable Text Editor dictionary.

For applications that support AppleScript, you may find that you can select an object in that application and paste that object's reference into an AppleScript that you are building in the Script Editor. This system is still in its infancy, so this important feature is likely to be extended in the future. For now, you'll have to try out objects based on what you see in an application's dictionary to see what works. An object can be scriptable and recordable without allowing the pasting of object references.

When you can do a paste object, the procedure is simple. Select the object in your application, and use the Copy command from the Edit menu. Then switch to the Script Editor and place the insertion point where you desire. Issue the Paste Reference command from the Edit menu. That reference then appears; for example,

> "word 2 of document 'Untitled'"

The Scriptable Finder

7.5 To use AppleScript to automate tasks of the 7.0 and 7.1 Finder, you needed to use an external library of functions called the finderLib, which was distributed by Apple. These 13 Finder routines, 5 input checking and utility routines and 2 properties checking routines form the basis for the Finder suite that was incorporated into System 7.5's Finder. Now when you open the Finder's dictionary from within the Script Editor, you will see the Finder suite, as shown in Figure 11-19.

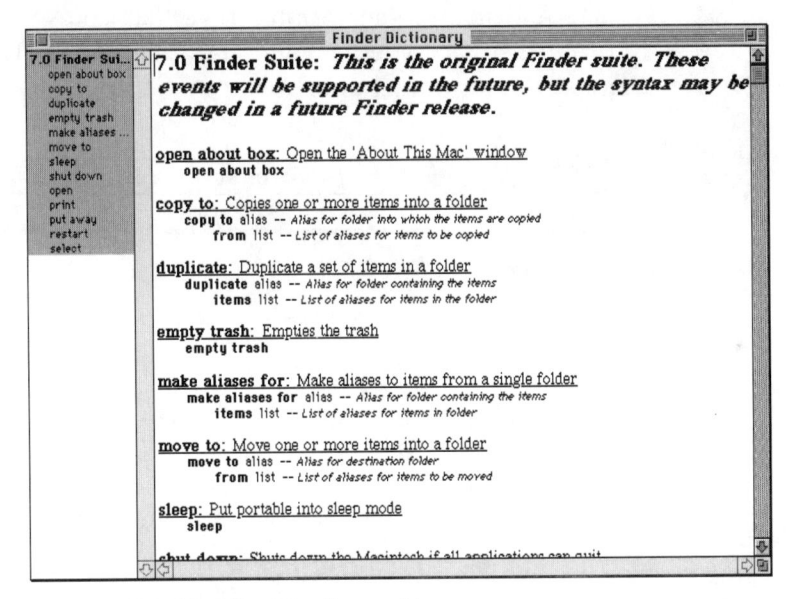

Figure 11-19: The Finder suite.

Scripting the Finder means that these commands can be used directly in scripts that use the Finder, without having to call scripts from this external library. As a matter of convenience, you can record scripts using the recorder function of the Script Editor, using the Finder as one of your applications.

The Useful Scripts Folder

7.5 System 7.5 includes a set of preprogrammed AppleScripts that users can access from a hierarchical submenu of the Apple menu. An alias in the Apple Menu Items folder points to the Useful Scripts folder found in the AppleScript folder.

These scripts are, in fact, very useful because they add additional compound functionality to the Finder. A short SimpleText file, "Useful Scripts Read Me," is included in the Useful Scripts folder describing its contents. Over time you may find many other AppleScripts that you can add to the Useful Scripts folder. Figure 11-20 shows the Useful Scripts folder window in Name view.

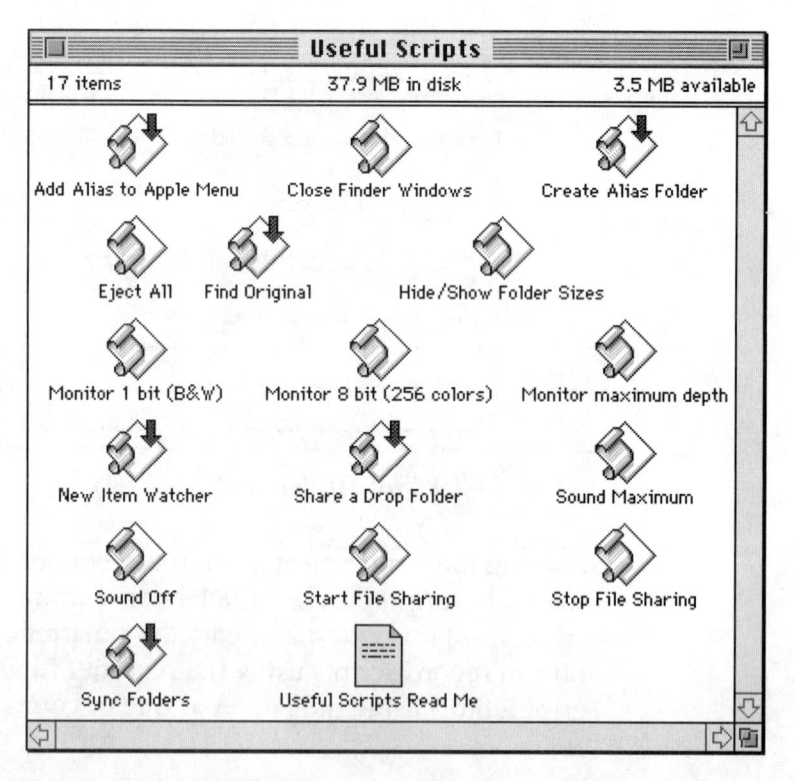

Figure 11-20: The Useful Scripts folder window.

At ship time with System 7.5, the initial set of Useful Scripts were as follows:

- **Add Alias to Apple.** To create an alias to an item in the Apple menu, select the item and choose this command. Because it is a droplet script, you can also drag the item over the AppleScript icon.

- **Close Finder windows.** This script is the equivalent of a Close All windows command, or holding the Option key and clicking a window close box.

- **Create Alias Folder.** This script places files containing the same name as a folder you specify into it. For example, if you select a folder called "Read Me" and choose this command, then aliases to all your files with the text string "read me" in the name will be placed in that folder. Using this script is a handy way to organize all your online documentation. Create Alias Folder is a droplet, so you can drag a folder icon over that script application.

- **Eject All.** This script ejects volumes on your desktop. It closes File Sharing automatically, ejects the disk and restarts File Sharing without first checking whether anyone is using your drive.

- **Find Original.** Select an alias and run this script to find the original file. Using this script is equivalent to using the Find Original button in the Get Info dialog box. It is another droplet AppleScript.

- **Hide/Show Folder Sizes.** This script turns on and off the Calculate folder sizes option in the Views control panel.

- **Monitor 1 bit (B&W), Monitor 8 bit (256 colors), and Monitor Maximum Depth scripts.** These scripts change the color level of your monitor without your having to open the Monitors control panel.

- **New Item Watcher.** When you select a folder and apply this script, AppleScript will watch the folder to see what new items are added to it while the script is running. When a new item is added, you are switched to the Finder, the folder is opened, and the new item is highlighted. This script is useful for monitoring a download or communications folder.

- **Share a Drop Folder.** A Drop folder is one that has full guest-access privileges (as described in Chapter 12, "An Introduction to File Sharing"). Files put there can be copied by another user using File Sharing; others can copy files into that folder. This script creates a Drop folder and turns on File Sharing. If you restart your Macintosh, reapply this command to reactivate the Drop folder.

- **Sound Maximum and Sound Off scripts.** These scripts turn the sound level as far up or down as possible, respectively. If you have the Control Strip active on your PowerBook, its sound level selector is more convenient to use.

- **Start File Sharing/Stop File Sharing.** These two scripts turn File Sharing on and off without your having to open the Sharing Setup control panel. You can also use the Control Strip of a PowerBook for this function.

- **Sync Folders.** With this script, two folders are compared and the contents of both synchronized. That is, both folders are made identical by having missing files added to either and files with more recent modifications replaced by the later version. To use this script, select two folders and apply the command.

Learning More About AppleScript

AppleScript is still fairly new, and there are few good places to go to learn about it. The best beginning introduction to AppleScript is *The Tao of AppleScript* by Derrick Schneider, Hayden Press (1993). This book gives you a feeling for some of the power of the language by scripting some interesting examples. It is also useful for examining the programming processes. You may also want to read *Complete AppleScript*, by Danny Goodman, Random House (1993). This book is more complete and authoritative but less approachable than the one by Derrick Schneider.

For serious "script-heads," there are more powerful applications available for writing scripts. Apple sells the AppleScript Software Kit for $199, a complete package with an interface processor for building projects in AppleScript. You can purchase the AppleScript Scripter's Toolkit, a subset of this product through stores. This toolkit comes with the FaceSpan Interface Processor from Software Designs Unlimited, a Data Access Language scripting addition, development tools, sample code, Finder scripting code and electronic documentation. APDA also sells the Developers's University AppleEvents/AppleScript Tutorial, a $150 course with floppy-based instructions. Call APDA at 716-871-6555 for information.

Other tools for AppleScript will certainly be released over time by third parties.

Moving On

AppleScript fulfills the long-standing promise to provide automation capabilities within the Macintosh operating system. Although still a developing subject, it is thorough and rigorous in its implementation, laying the groundwork for more important and convenient expressions to come.

In this chapter, you've seen how to use AppleScript to

- Record actions with the Script Editor.
- Save scripts as programs that you can run.
- Work with applications that are AppleScript-aware: recordable, scriptable and attachable.

Next, in Chapter 12, "An Introduction to File Sharing," you look at one of the most important features of System 7: support for working together in a workgroup. Using File Sharing, you can exchange data with Macintosh users over a network. It's easy, and it's a powerful feature.

Chapter 12

An Introduction to File Sharing

File Sharing is one area where the Macintosh was ahead of its time in 1984. The first Macintosh also had a built-in AppleTalk port, allowing any number of Macintosh computers to be strung together with inexpensive twisted-pair cable to form a network. Back then, however, there was no compelling reason to create a Macintosh network.

Today, an AppleTalk port remains standard equipment on every Macintosh, and there are many good reasons for putting a Mac on a network. But AppleTalk is no longer the only network available for the Mac; Ethernet and Token Ring networks are available as well.

There are three main reasons why you might want to put your Macintosh on a network:

- **Computer-to-computer communications.** Networked Macintoshes can use electronic mail and messaging systems, and can transfer files directly from one computer to another.

With your Macintosh computer attached to a network, you can now install PowerTalk and AppleMail as part of system software. PowerTalk first appeared in System 7 Pro. PowerTalk provides automatic network connections, workgroup document services (including revision history), encryption and digital signatures. AppleMail is a messaging service with file transfer capability that can be built into any Macintosh application as a pop-up window.

PowerTalk and AppleMail are part of the Apple Open Collaboration Environment (described more fully in Chapter 14, "AOCE–The Apple Open Collaboration Environment"), a suite of system software tools that enables a variety of communication services. AOCE will eventually include in future versions of system software a universal mailbox, intelligent agent searching of your mail and online information, video conferencing and more. And, it all starts with installing your Macintosh on a network.

- **Shared peripherals.** Laser printers, color printers, slide recorders, high-speed modems, fax/modems and scanners are all expensive peripheral devices that can be shared among networked Macintoshes.

- **Centralized or distributed file servers.** Storing large amounts of data on file servers provides an easy way to share information, allows a number of people to participate in workgroup projects and reduces the data storage requirements of individual users. Apple's AppleShare is the dominant file-serving software, but other servers compliant with the AppleShare Filing Protocol (AFP) can also be used.

It's in this last category that System 7 first provided greatly expanded abilities. In System 7 Macintosh users can share files from their hard drives with other computers on the network and access files being shared by these other computers. This new feature is called File Sharing. In this chapter, you'll learn the basics of File Sharing and how to use it to allow others to access your files. Chapter 13, "Working on a Network," discusses additional File Sharing features, including accessing the data shared by other Macs and ways you can connect to your own Macintosh from another computer on your network.

What Is File Sharing?

File Sharing is a System 7 feature that lets you designate up to 10 folders and volumes on your computer to be shared with other computers on your network. For each shared folder or volume, you can assign access privileges, which can limit the use of your shared data to only the computers you specify.

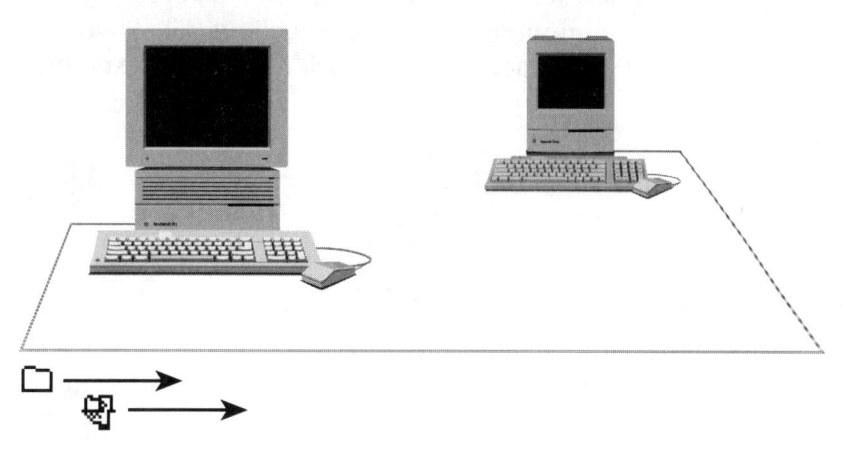

Figure 12-1: File Sharing lets you share your data with others.

File Sharing also lets you access folders and volumes other Macintoshes are sharing, provided you've been granted access privileges. Once accessed, folders and volumes from other Macs appear on your desktop and can be used as if they were your own.

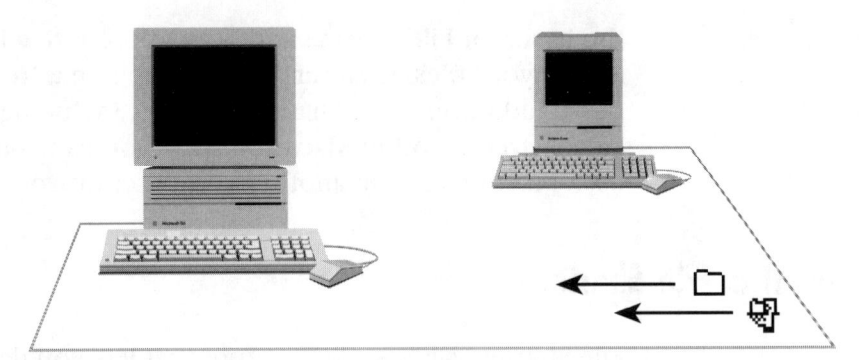

Figure 12-2: File Sharing lets you access data from other computers.

In networking parlance, when your computer is sharing files, it's acting as a server; when it's accessing files from another computer, it's acting as a client. File Sharing allows every user on a Macintosh network to become a server, a client or both.

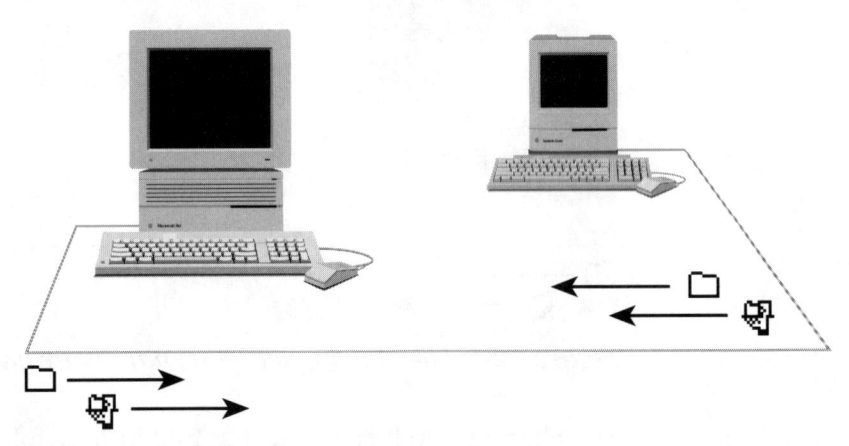

Figure 12-3: Using File Sharing, every Mac on the network can be both server and client.

Sharing data from your Macintosh, and accessing data shared by others on your network, can increase your capabilities and productivity in many ways. Here are some examples of resources that can be shared:

- **Central libraries.** Reference files such as clip art, templates (or Stationery Pads) and historical records can be kept in one location and shared with the entire network.

- **Drop-box folders that send and receive files.** Each network user can define an electronic "In box" and "Out box." By assigning access privileges, you can use an In box to let everyone add files but not look at the folder's contents, and an Out box to let users "pick up" the files they need, but not add any files. System 7.5 has a built-in AppleScript that automatically creates and manages a Drop folder for you, as you will see later in this chapter. (Also see Chapter 11, "AppleScript.")

- **Shared edition files that create living "workgroup" documents.** The Edition Manager features (described in Chapter 10, "Inter-Application Communication & OpenDoc"), together with File Sharing, give network users access to edition files created by many users and stored on several hard drives.

The Limits of File Sharing

Although the capabilities of File Sharing are impressive, it's important to understand that File Sharing is only a "personal" version of AppleShare, Apple's dedicated file-server software. For a small number of Macs, File Sharing is sufficient, while larger or heavily used networks should use a combination of AppleShare and File Sharing. In these situations, File Sharing will supplement AppleShare, not replace it.

There are several reasons why File Sharing in some cases should be limited in this way:

- **Administration requirements.** As you'll see later, the administrative requirements of sharing files are not incidental. When many users need frequent access to numerous files and folders, centralized File Sharing administration, provided by central file servers such as AppleShare, is usually more efficient than distributed administration.

- **Security risks.** To avoid the burden of administrative requirements, users often neglect security issues, leaving confidential or sensitive data unprotected and available to anyone on the network. This is less likely to occur on centralized, professionally managed file servers.

- **Performance degradation.** Even with a very fast Mac and a very fast hard drive, File Sharing takes a noticeable toll on computer performance. Macintoshes or peripherals that aren't particularly speedy to begin with make the problem even worse. The benefits outweigh the inconveniences for the casual or infrequent user, but continually having to deal with long delays can be annoying and counterproductive. A centralized server with resources dedicated to the burdens of serving network users is the practical alternative in these circumstances.

- **Access limitations.** File Sharing can serve only 10 folders or volumes from one Macintosh at a time, and support only 50 logged on users at one time (and that would be pushing it) with perhaps 15–20 concurrent users maximum. These constraints are too restrictive in many cases. Also, the sharing Macintoshes must be left on all the time to ensure files are always available on the network (files on a shut down Mac are not accessible for sharing).

A File Sharing Quick Tour

File Sharing's capabilities are powerful and therefore require more preparation and attention than most other System 7 features. Here are the steps necessary to use File Sharing:

- **Prepare your Macintosh.** This includes physically connecting to a network, installing the File Sharing files and activating AppleTalk.

- **Start File Sharing.** The Sharing Setup control panel provides configuration information and the master switch. In System 7.5 you can start (and stop) File Sharing using one of the AppleScripts found in the Useful Scripts folder under your Apple menu. If you have the Control Strip active on your desktop (for PowerBook users), there is File Sharing switch there as one of the panels.

- **Configure Users & Groups.** Users must be defined, and user preferences and access privileges set in the Users & Groups control panel. In most situations user groups will also need definition. You must also specify access privileges your Macintosh will enforce when network "guests" log on.

- **Specify folders/volumes to share.** To share any folder or volume, the Sharing command must be applied, and sharing options set.

- **Connect with others using File Sharing.** In order to access folders and volumes being shared by others, the Chooser is used to complete a log-on process.

- **Use the File Sharing Monitor to track access to your shared data.** A new control panel, called the File Sharing Monitor, constantly gives you updates on who's accessing what on your computer.

The remainder of this chapter looks in detail at the first four of these steps. The last two are covered in Chapter 13.

Preparing for File Sharing

File Sharing success depends on correctly connecting your Macintosh computers and installing network drivers. The simplest and most common Macintosh networking scheme uses LocalTalk or PhoneNet-style connectors and cabling that plug directly into the AppleTalk port on the back of the Mac.

More sophisticated networks require Ethernet or Token Ring adapters via NuBus or PDS slots (although most newer Macs can be equipped with built-in Ethernet ports). When the network is physically connected, network availability and the presence of network software drivers must be verified by opening the Network control panel, which displays the available network drivers (shown in Figure 12-4).

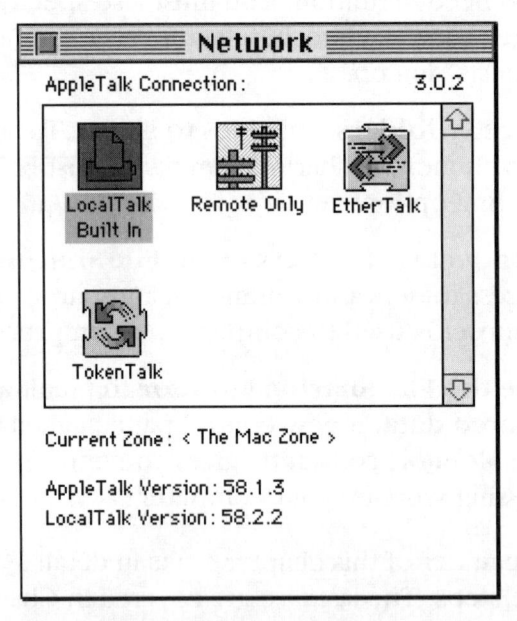

Figure 12-4: The Network control panel displays the icons for available networking systems.

After verifying installation, open the Chooser and call AppleTalk by clicking the "Active" radio button. If your network is divided into zones, the Chooser also displays a list of available AppleTalk zones, as shown in Figure 12-5.

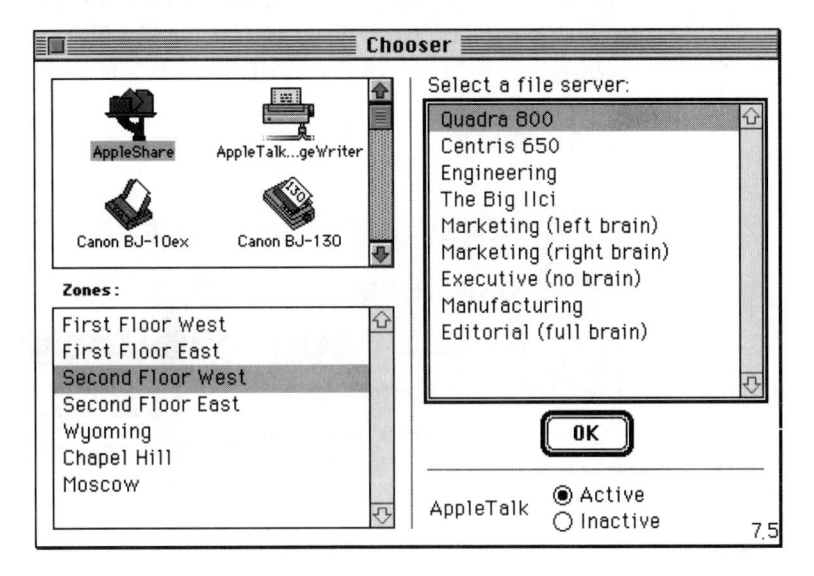

Figure 12-5: The Chooser turns on AppleTalk and selects network zones.

File Sharing also requires, not surprisingly, that the File Sharing software be installed by the Installer application. You can tell that File Sharing software has been installed when the Sharing command appears in the File menu. If it's not there, run the Installer again and choose the "File Sharing" option. (See Appendix A for more information on using the Installer to add File Sharing.)

Starting File Sharing

With your network physically ready and File Sharing installed, you can configure and turn on File Sharing with the Sharing Setup control panel located in your Control Panels folder. The Sharing Setup control panel (shown in Figure 12-6) lets you define your "network identity," turn File Sharing on and off and start and stop Program Linking, using the Network Setup dialog box.

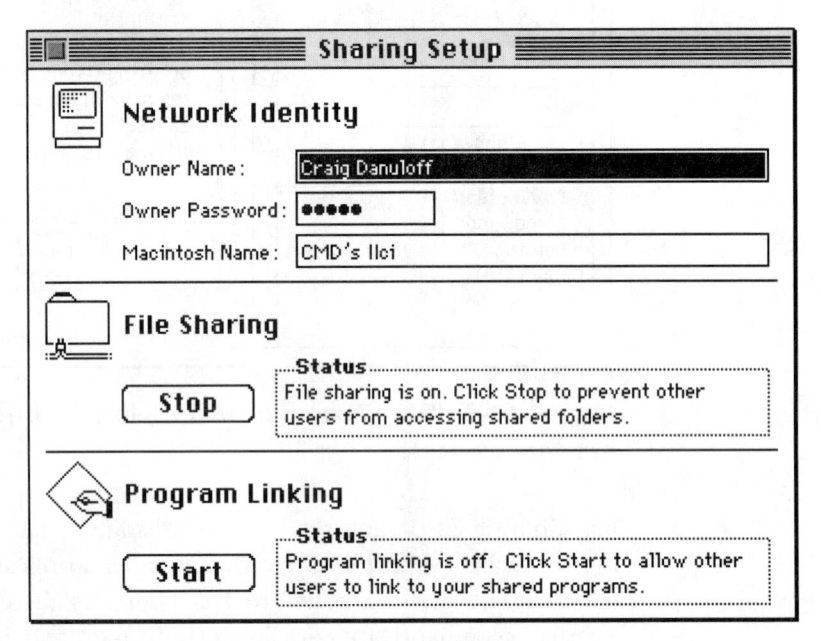

Figure 12-6: The Sharing Setup dialog box.

The options in this dialog box are

- **Owner Name.** The name your Macintosh displays to others when you seek access to their computers via File Sharing. It's also the name you use to access your computer from any other on the network. Any name of up to 32 characters is acceptable, and you can change the Owner Name at any time.

- **Owner Password.** A security gate, allowing you as owner to access this Macintosh's entire hard drive from anywhere on the network when File Sharing is turned on. It also allows you, as an assigned owner, to access any shared folders or volumes. (By default, you're assigned ownership of all folders and volumes shared by your Macintosh. You can then assign this ownership to others, if you wish, as described in "Configuring User Preferences" later in this chapter.)

  Note that this password can be changed at any time, and it's not necessary to know the old password to define a new one. This means you don't have to worry about forgetting your password—which may seem like a breach of security, and it is. But File Sharing controls only remote-user access to your Macintosh. It doesn't apply to anyone who sits down at your Mac's keyboard. Thus, the ability to change the password at any time is consistent with the Mac's total lack of local security.

- **The Macintosh Name.** The name other network users see when looking at your Macintosh from the network. It appears in the Chooser when they click on the AppleShare icon, and when they print to network printers. This Macintosh Name is the equivalent of the Chooser name used in earlier system software versions.

- **File Sharing (Start/Stop).** The master control switch. When the Start button is clicked, File Sharing is turned on and the folders and volumes on your Macintosh are available to the network, based on the access privileges assigned to them. As File Sharing starts, the message in the Status area documents the startup process.

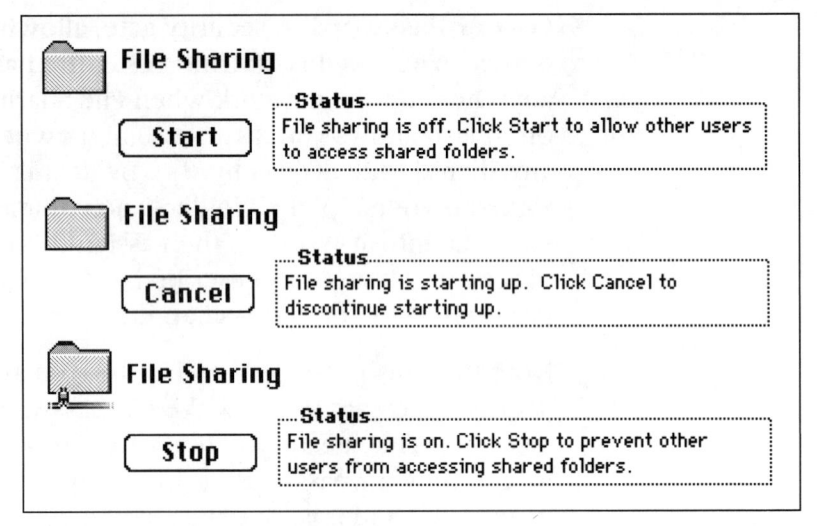

Figure 12-7: After the Start button is pressed, the Status message documents the progress of File Sharing.

Once File Sharing is running, the Start button becomes the Stop button. When the Stop button is clicked, you're asked how many minutes until shutdown. Enter a number between 0 (for immediate shutdown) and 999 (for delayed action).

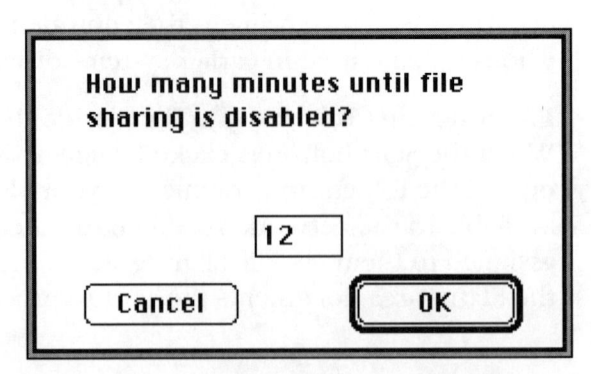

Figure 12-8: The Shut Down dialog box.

After you click OK in this dialog box, the Status message tells you how many minutes remain before File Sharing is turned off. As turn-off time approaches, other users accessing your Macintosh files are warned of impending shutdown, so they can save their work and release any volumes or folders they're using. It's not necessary for users to release your files before the shutdown; contact with your Macintosh is terminated immediately in any case. However, the Mac simply extends the courtesy of warning other users, so they won't lose work or be abruptly interrupted. If you choose the 0 minutes option, cutoff will occur without warning. (To check the number of users connected to your Mac, use the File Sharing Monitor control panel, as described in "Monitoring File Sharing" later in this chapter.)

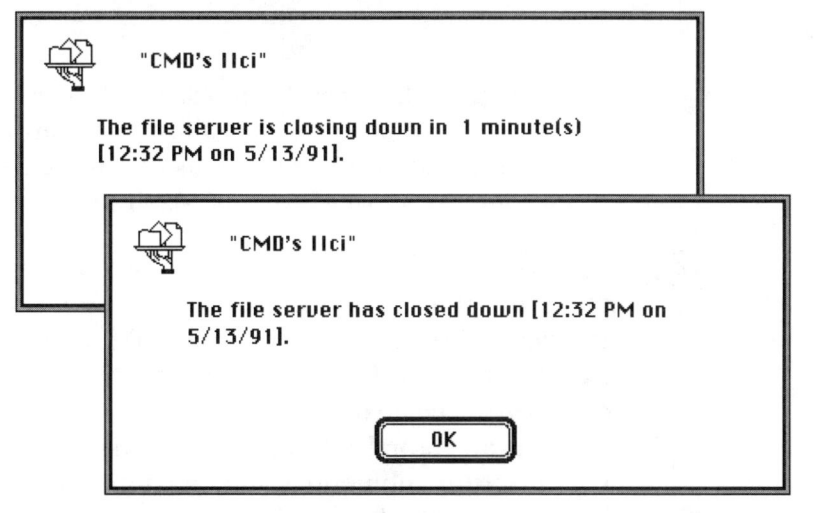

Figure 12-9: Clients are warned before a File Sharing server closes and after it has closed down.

When File Sharing is on and users are connected to your Macintosh, the Shut Down or Restart command brings up the Alert dialog box shown in Figure 12-10. Again, be sure to give your network users enough time to save their work before shutting down. If possible, cancel the Shut Down or Restart and leave your Macintosh running so network use can continue.

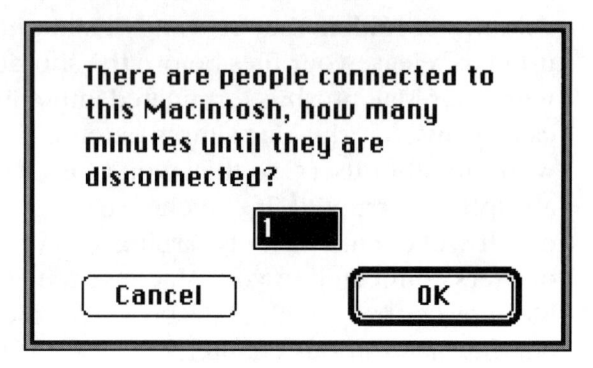

> There are people connected to this Macintosh, how many minutes until they are disconnected?
>
> [1]
>
> [Cancel]   [OK]

Figure 12-10: The alert that appears at Restart or Shut Down.

- **Program Linking (Start/Stop).** Discussed in depth in Chapter 10, this function allows inter-application communication (IAC) commands of remote users to control programs residing on your Macintosh.

7.5 As a convenience, System 7.5 adds two more places where you can turn File Sharing on and off. In the Useful Scripts submenu of the Apple menu you will find two commands (AppleScripts, really): one called Start File Sharing, the other called Stop File Sharing. They do the same thing as clicking the Start and Stop button in the Sharing Setup dialog box. The Useful Scripts submenu is shown later in this chapter. If you have a PowerBook with the Control Strip installed, one of the panels is for controlling File Sharing, as shown in Figure 12-11. It works similarly.

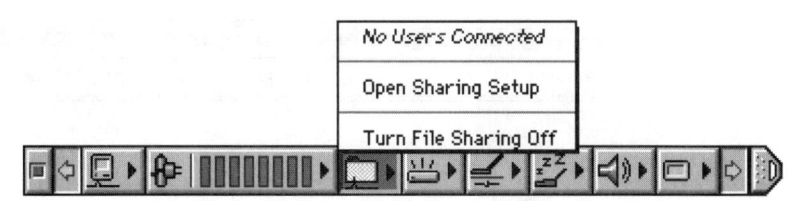

Figure 12-11: The File Sharing section of a PowerBook Control Strip.

Registering Users & Groups

If you plan to use File Sharing to make your Macintosh folders and/or volumes available to other network users, you must decide who may and may not share your files. You may want to share your files with every user on your network, but it is more likely that you will want to restrict access to some or all of your shared files.

To designate access you open the Users & Groups control panel (shown in Figure 12-12), which displays a window containing one icon for each user and one icon for each group registered to access your Macintosh, in addition to a Guest icon and an icon for you, the Macintosh Owner.

Of course, when you open the Users & Groups control panel for the first time, no users or groups are yet defined, so only the Guest and Macintosh Owner icons will appear.

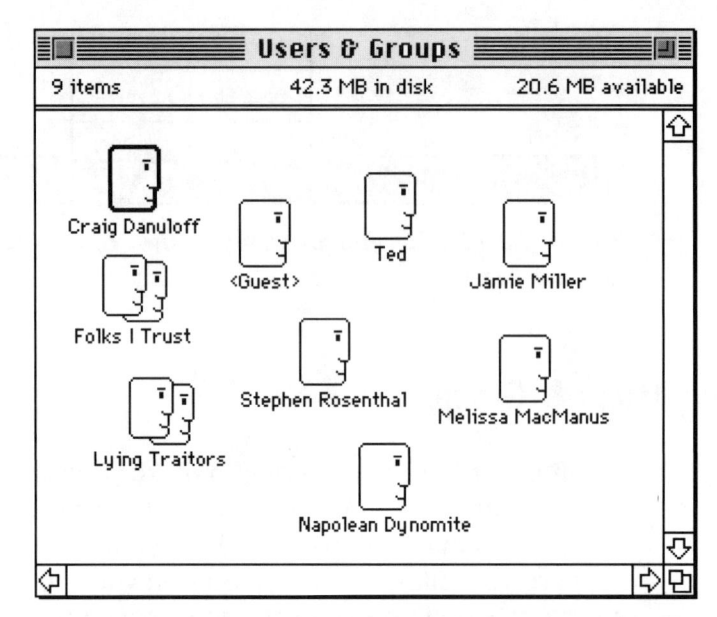

Figure 12-12: The Users & Groups control panel.

Although this control panel looks like a normal Finder window, it's not. You cannot drag-copy user icons or group icons out onto the desktop or to another folder or volume. Nor can you copy other files into this window. If you try to do so, an Alert dialog box will remind you that you can't.

Via the Users & Groups control panel, you can grant access to four user categories:

- **Registered Users.** These are specific people you want to have access to your shared folders or volumes. Registered Users are given access to your data as individuals or as members of a defined Group.

- **Groups.** A Group is a collection of defined Registered Users. Individual Registered Users can be included in any number of groups.

- **Guests.** Any user on your network who has not been defined as a Registered User can attempt to log on to your shared folders or volumes as a Guest. You define whether you want these non-Registered Users to have access to your data.

- **Macintosh Owner.** As the owner, you can give yourself special remote abilities and access privileges to your computer.

In addition to the definitions and privileges mentioned so far, the Sharing dialog box provides additional security safeguards. This dialog box specifies Registered Users and Groups who have access privileges to particular folders and volumes. (More on the Sharing dialog box in "Sharing Folders or Volumes" later in this chapter.)

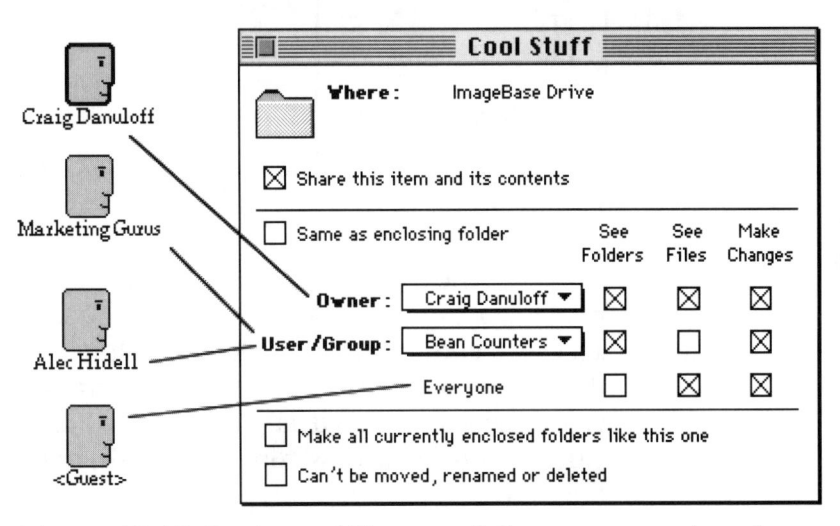

Figure 12-13: Registered Users and Groups are assigned access privileges via the Sharing dialog box.

Creating New Users

To create a new user, open the Users & Groups control panel, and choose the New User command from the File menu. This creates a new "untitled" Registered User icon in the Users & Groups window. Enter the name of the user you want this icon to represent.

It's best to enter the person's actual name, rather than a code name. A code name is more likely to be misspelled when the Registered User logs on.

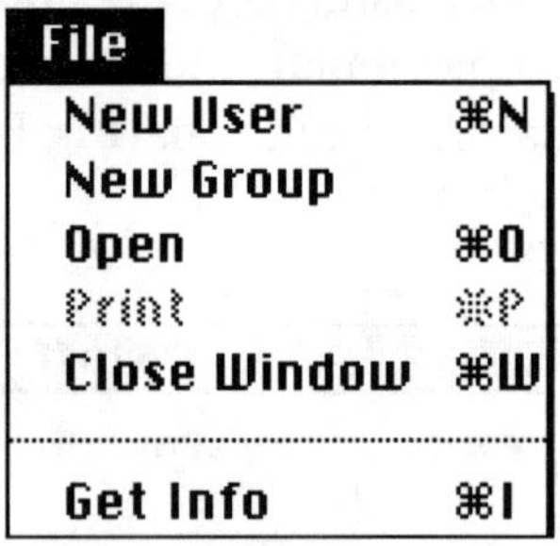

```
┌─────────────────────┐
│ File                │
├─────────────────────┤
│ New User        ⌘N  │
│ New Group           │
│ Open            ⌘O  │
│ Print           ⌘P  │
│ Close Window    ⌘W  │
├─────────────────────┤
│ Get Info        ⌘I  │
└─────────────────────┘
```

Figure 12-14: The File menu provides the New User and New Group commands.

Up to 100 Registered Users can be defined, but Apple recommends staying under 50. If more than 50 people need regular access to certain shared folders or volumes, consider moving that data to a dedicated AppleShare server or allowing all Guests access to that data. (There is no limit to the number of Guests who can access your Macintosh, only to the number of Registered Users.)

You don't need to register users individually unless you want to limit access privileges. If you're going to allow everyone on the network to see and change your data, they can all log on as Guests. If not, you should define Users and Groups.

Configuring User Preferences

After registering a new user, or to alter a user's password or preferences, double-click on the user icon to open the File Sharing options window, as shown in Figure 12-15. This dialog box sets the user's password and allows or disallows the user to connect via File Sharing or Program Linking. This dialog box also displays a list of all groups the user is included in (you can't change or modify group memberships in this dialog box).

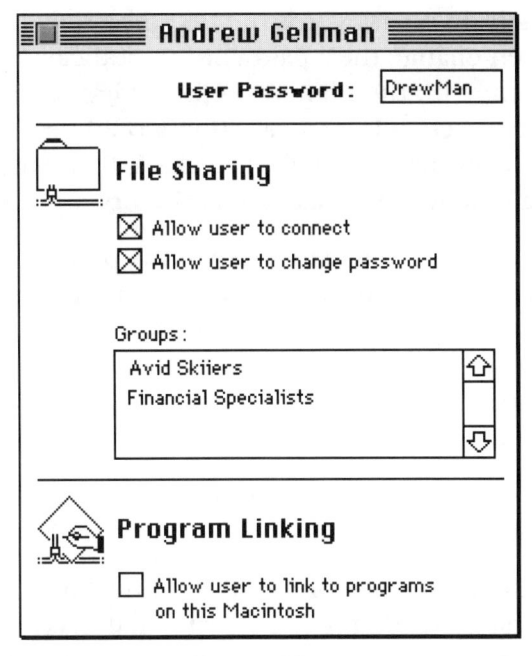

Figure 12-15: The User Preferences dialog box.

Let's look at the options in this dialog box:

- **User Password.** In order to access your data from another Macintosh on the network, a user name and, in most cases, a password must be entered. By default, the user has no password, and logs on by simply entering the user name and leaving the password option blank. (More information on the log-in process later.) This obviously doesn't provide much security assurance that the user logging on is supposed to have network access.

To add a password, type one into the User Password option box. For security, bullets will appear instead of the characters typed.

When you add or change a user password, you must notify the user, for obvious reasons. Another approach is to leave the user without a password, letting them define their own passwords the first time they log on. They can then change their password periodically after that. This is done with the Allow user to change password option, described below. A variation would be to start with an obvious password like the user's first name, then encourage the user to change it at the first opportunity.

You can change any user password at any time. For example, if a user forgets his or her password, there's no way for you to find it; you must "change" it to resolve this problem. Changing a password also lets you bar a particular user's access until you provide a new password.

Avoid using obvious passwords like names, zodiac signs and birthstones, and change passwords regularly.

- **Allow user to connect.** This checkbox is the "personal" master switch for File Sharing that makes it possible or impossible for a user to connect as a Registered User (they still may be able to connect as a Guest). This option is on by default, but occasionally you may want to turn it off. Using this option to revoke access privileges is less drastic than deleting the user, which makes later reinstatement more difficult.

- **Allow user to change password.** This option allows Registered Users to change their passwords using the Change Password button that appears in the Chooser as they log on to your Macintosh. In most cases, this option should be selected, because changing user passwords frequently increases the security of your data. Of course, since you as the Owner can always change passwords directly in this dialog box, you lose no privileges by allowing users this option.
- **Program Linking.** Users can take advantage of this option if the feature is turned on in the Sharing Setup control panel.

Creating & Working With Groups

Since a network comprises many individual users, assigning access privileges to each individual for each item would be a very tedious job. To avoid this, File Sharing lets you define Groups, add Registered Users to these groups, then assign access privileges that apply to all Group members.

New Groups are created by selecting the File menu's New Group command while the Users & Groups control panel is open, which places a new "untitled" Group icon in the Users & Groups window. Enter the name of the group you want this icon to represent (descriptive names are best). Registered Users never see the group names you assign, nor do they need to know which groups they're assigned to.

Groups cannot be combined and you can't make a Guest icon a member of any group; but you can add yourself as the Macintosh Owner to any group. This isn't as useless as it may seem: if you assign ownership of folders or volumes to another user or group, you won't have access to that folder (over the network) if you're not a member of a group that has access privileges (unless you add yourself to that group) or use the Allow user to see entire volume option in your Owner Preferences (described later).

To add Registered Users to the group, drag their icons onto the Group icon and release them. Or you can double-click on the Group icon to open the group's window and then drag user icons directly into this window. Adding a user to a group does not remove the User icon from the main Users & Groups window. You can drag a single user icon into any number of groups. To check which groups a user is part of, double-click the Registered User's icon and see the list in the User Preferences dialog box.

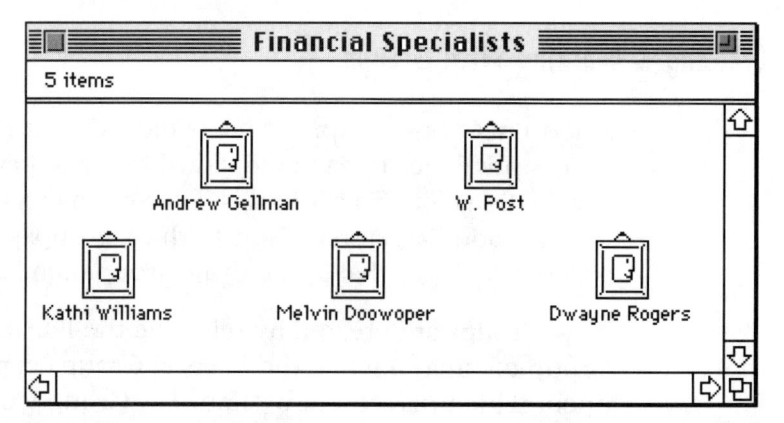

Figure 12-16: A defined Group containing five Registered Users.

To remove a user from a group, open the Group window and drag the user's icon to the Trash. This deletes the user from the group; it does not remove the user entirely, and it doesn't remove the user from any other groups he or she belongs to. Similarly, you can delete an entire group by dragging the group icon to the Trash, which removes the group but does not affect any group member individually.

Configuring Guest Preferences

You may occasionally want to share files with someone on your network who isn't a Registered User. This is made possible by File Sharing's support of guests. A single Guest icon is automatically included in the Users & Groups control panel, and this icon is used to control access to your shared data for all non-Registered Users. The Guest icon cannot be deleted. Double-clicking on the Guest icon brings up the Guest Preferences dialog box.

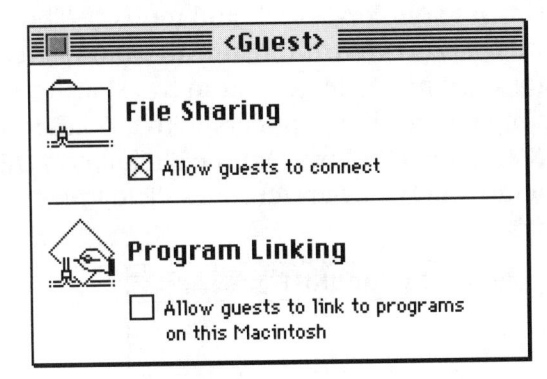

Figure 12-17: The Guest Preferences dialog box.

There are only two options in this window:

- **Allow guests to connect.** This option (the default) is the master switch that lets guests log on to your Macintosh. When this option is deselected, network users can't log on to your Macintosh as guests.

  Allowing guests to log on does not automatically give them access to data. Guests can access folders and volumes based only on the "Everyone" access privileges in the Sharing dialog box, as described later in this chapter. If no folders or volumes are available to Everyone, guests who attempt to log on will find no data available.

- **Allow guests to link to your programs.** Program Linking, as described in Chapter 10, is used by System 7.5's IAC feature. If you select this option, guests can link to your programs; if you deselect it, they can't.

Configuring Owner Preferences

The preferences you set for yourself, the Macintosh Owner, affect the way you can access your Macintosh from elsewhere on the network. They have no affect on what you can do directly from your keyboard (and mouse). The Macintosh Owner icon is created automatically, and named with the Macintosh Owner Name, as set in the Sharing Setup control panel. The Owner icon appears with a bold border in the Users & Groups window. Double-clicking on this icon opens the Macintosh Owner Preferences dialog box.

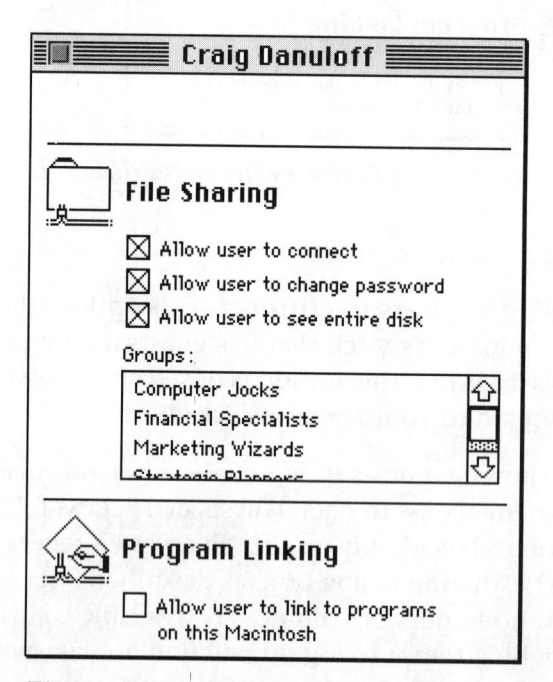

Figure 12-18: The Macintosh Owner Preferences dialog box.

The options in this dialog are the same as those described previously for any Registered User, with the exception of the Allow user to see entire volume option. This option lets you access entire volumes on your Macintosh from anywhere on the network at any time—even when the volumes have not been specifically shared with the Sharing command. When accessing volumes in this way, you have full access privileges to all files, folders and applications.

Caution: This feature is very powerful—and potentially dangerous. It allows you to work on your Macintosh, or access any data stored on your Macintosh, from any Mac on the network just as if you were at your own keyboard. The danger is that anyone else who knows your Owner Name and password could gain the same access.

If you don't need this feature, leave it deselected. If you do use this option, be very discreet with your password, and change it frequently. If you won't need to use this feature over an extended period of time, temporarily deselect it. Of course, there's always the possibility that someone might sit down at your Macintosh keyboard and access your data or change your password, then remotely access your Mac. File Sharing should not lull you into a false sense of security. If you have good reason to believe this could happen, other security measures should be taken.

Sharing Folders or Volumes

For any folder or volume to be shared with others on your network, the Sharing command must initiate sharing and specify access privileges. Any mounted volume, including hard disks, hard disk partitions, removable cartridges, CD-ROMs and any folder on any mounted volume can be shared. Floppy disks and folders on floppy disks cannot.

To initiate sharing, select the folder or volume and choose the Sharing command from the File menu, which brings up the Sharing dialog box (shown in Figure 12-19). This dialog box is used to turn on Sharing and assign access privileges to this item. Access privileges, as you learned earlier, determine who can see the folders and volumes, who can see the files inside those folders and volumes, and who can make changes to existing files or store new files. (More on access privileges later in this chapter.)

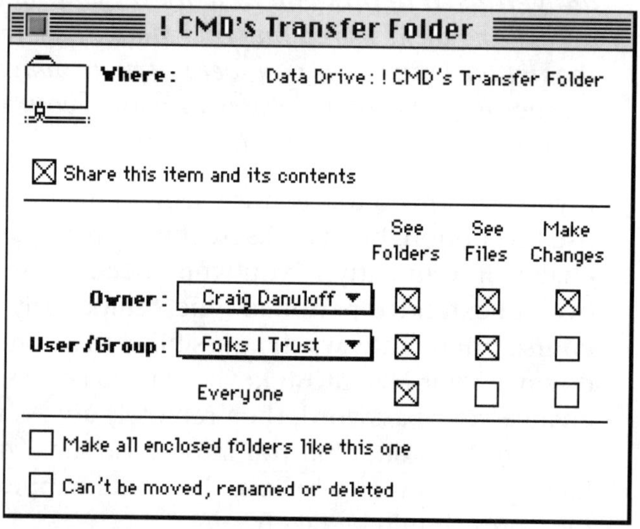

Figure 12-19: A Sharing dialog box.

The Sharing dialog box presents a number of important options:

- **Share this folder and its contents.** This checkbox is the master switch that turns sharing on or off for the selected folder or volume and the contents of that folder or volume. Until this option is selected, all other options in this dialog box are dimmed.

- **Owner.** This option specifies the owner of the selected folder or volume and the owner's access privileges. In most cases, you (as the Macintosh Owner) will remain the owner of shared folders and volumes.

  However, using the pop-up menu, you can designate any other Registered User as the owner of the selected folder or volume. The assignee can then reset access privileges for the item. Your access to the folder or volume from another Macintosh on the network is then dependent on your inclusion in the User/Group option (discussed in the following subsection). Of course, your access to the folder or volume from your own Macintosh will not be affected; these options affect only network access.

  Once an owner has been specified, use the checkboxes to assign access privileges. (More on available access privileges and their use in the next section of this chapter.)

- **User/Group.** This option grants one user or one group access to the selected folder or volume (via the pop-up menu), and defines the access privileges available to this user or group. In many ways, this is the most important Sharing option, because it usually designates the person or group of users that will most frequently access the shared data. (See the "Access Privileges" section of this chapter for the ways this feature can be used, including bulletin boards, drop boxes, read-only filing systems and true workgroup File Sharing and storage systems.)

- **Everyone.** This option specifies access privileges granted to Guest users on your Macintosh. As mentioned before, anyone on your network can log on to your Mac as a Guest, providing you've specified that Guest log-ins are permitted. In that case, the "Everyone" option determines which volumes and folders they can access.

- **Make all enclosed folders like this one.** When you share a folder or volume, all enclosed folders are also automatically accessible to users with access privileges. You cannot "unshare" a folder enclosed in a shared folder or on a shared volume, but you can change the access privileges of an enclosed folder so that they don't match those of the enclosing folder. This option also can reset the access privileges of the enclosed folders so they match those of the currently selected folder or volume.

  For example, a folder called Outbox is shared, with full access privileges by everyone on the network. Inside this folder is a folder called Project A. We want to limit access to Project A so that only members of the Project A group can share it. To do this, after using the Sharing command for the Outbox folder, you'd select the Project A folder and choose the Sharing command again. Now, access privileges are reset, limiting access to group members only. Figure 12-20 displays the Sharing dialog box for the "CMD's Outbox" folder and "Project A" folders.

  Notice that the Share this item and its contents option has been replaced in the "Project A" folder dialog box with a Same as enclosing folder option. This occurs because the "Project A" folder is inside a folder that is already shared. By default, this new option is selected, and the access privileges match those specified for the enclosing "CMD's Outbox" folder. Deselecting this option makes it possible to change the access privileges.

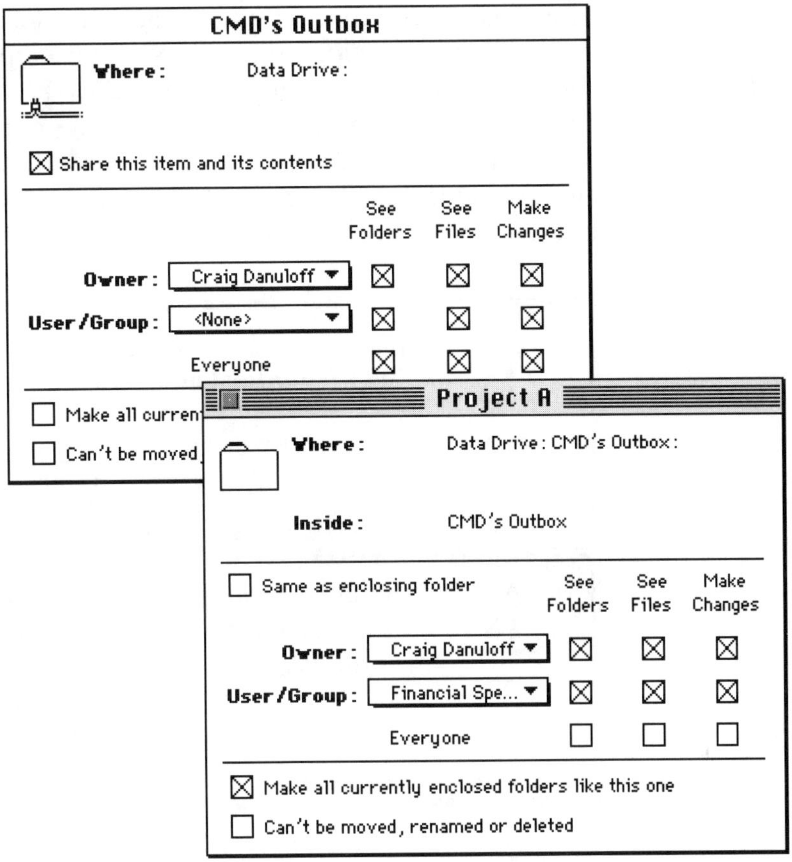

Chapter 12: An Introduction to File Sharing **471**

Figure 12-20: The Sharing dialog box for a parent and child folder.

- **Can't be moved, renamed or deleted.** This option gives you a safety net to ensure that the folder or volume you share is not moved, renamed or deleted by any network user—including the owner. It's a good idea to select this option in all cases, unless you know that repositioning, renaming or deleting the item will be necessary. This will prevent accidental changes with unpleasant results.

After completing these options, click the close box in the title bar to close the dialog box and apply these options to the selected item. If you've made changes to the ownership or access privileges of the item, dialog boxes appear asking you to confirm or cancel the changes requested. A dialog box will also appear if you chose the Make all enclosed folders like this one option. Figure 12-21 displays these warning dialogs.

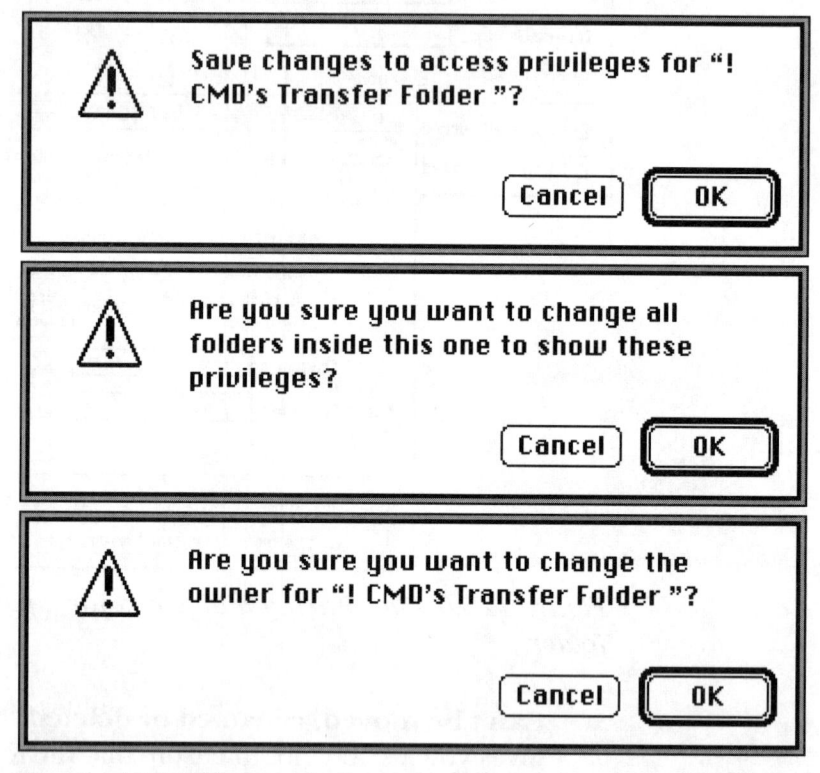

> ⚠ **Save changes to access privileges for "! CMD's Transfer Folder"?**
>
> [Cancel] [OK]

> ⚠ **Are you sure you want to change all folders inside this one to show these privileges?**
>
> [Cancel] [OK]

> ⚠ **Are you sure you want to change the owner for "! CMD's Transfer Folder"?**
>
> [Cancel] [OK]

Figure 12-21: Three confirming dialog boxes appear after changing Sharing options.

Icons of Shared Items

After you have specified and implemented sharing options, icons of the shared folders will modify, confirming their shared status. Figure 12-22 shows a folder icon and its changes.

Figure 12-22: A folder as it appears before Sharing (left), after Sharing (center) and when users are connected (right).

Unsharing

There are two ways to make shared items unavailable to network users: you can turn File Sharing off completely, or you can turn File Sharing off for individual folders and volumes.

To turn File Sharing off completely, open the Sharing Setup control panel and click the File Sharing Stop button, as described earlier. When File Sharing is turned off, the settings and access privileges set with the Sharing command are retained for all shared folders and volumes, and will go back into effect when File Sharing is again turned on.

To turn off the sharing of a particular folder or volume only, select the appropriate folder or volume icon, choose the Sharing command and deselect the Share this item and its contents option. When you close the Sharing dialog box, the selected folder or volume will become unavailable for network access. (An Alert dialog box will appear if users are currently accessing the shared item, as shown in Figure 12-23.) Note that all access privilege settings are lost when sharing is turned off for a particular folder or volume; you'll have to reset them the next time the item is shared.

> ⚠ The shared folder "CMD's Outbox" is in use by users on the network. Are you sure you want to deny these users access to this folder?
>
> [Cancel] [[OK]]

Figure 12-23: Unsharing with users.

As an alternative to turning off File Sharing either completely or for particular folders or volumes, you could also change the Allow user to connect and Allow guest to connect options in the user icons found in the Users & Groups control panel. This method is not generally recommended, but it does allow access privilege settings to remain in force while temporarily making it impossible for some or all users to connect.

Access Privileges

Shared folders, volumes and folders enclosed within those shared folders and volumes are provided to other network users according to access privilege settings you apply in the Sharing dialog box. These privileges, along with users and groups designated in the Users & Groups control panel, are the key to controlling File Sharing.

As shown in Figure 12-24, the three access privilege options are assigned to three different users or groups. Option settings and combinations you apply determine how network users can access and modify your shared data and storage space. Let's look at these access privileges, the users and groups they can be assigned to and the results of applying them in different combinations.

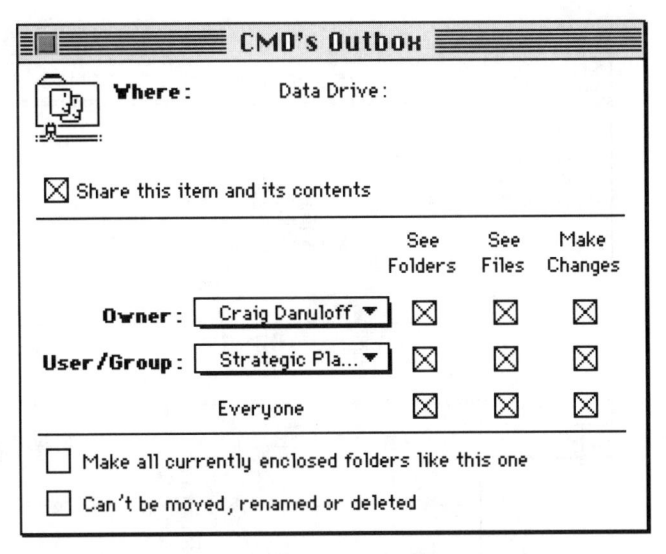

Figure 12-24: The access privilege options.

- **See Folders.** When this option is set, all folders within the selected folder or volume are shown to the specified user or group. Deselecting the See Folders option hides all folders from the specified user or group—users don't even know which folders exist in the selected folder or volume. When the See Folders option is deselected, an icon appears in the upper-left corner of the title bars of all windows accessed via File Sharing, letting the user know that folders are not being displayed.

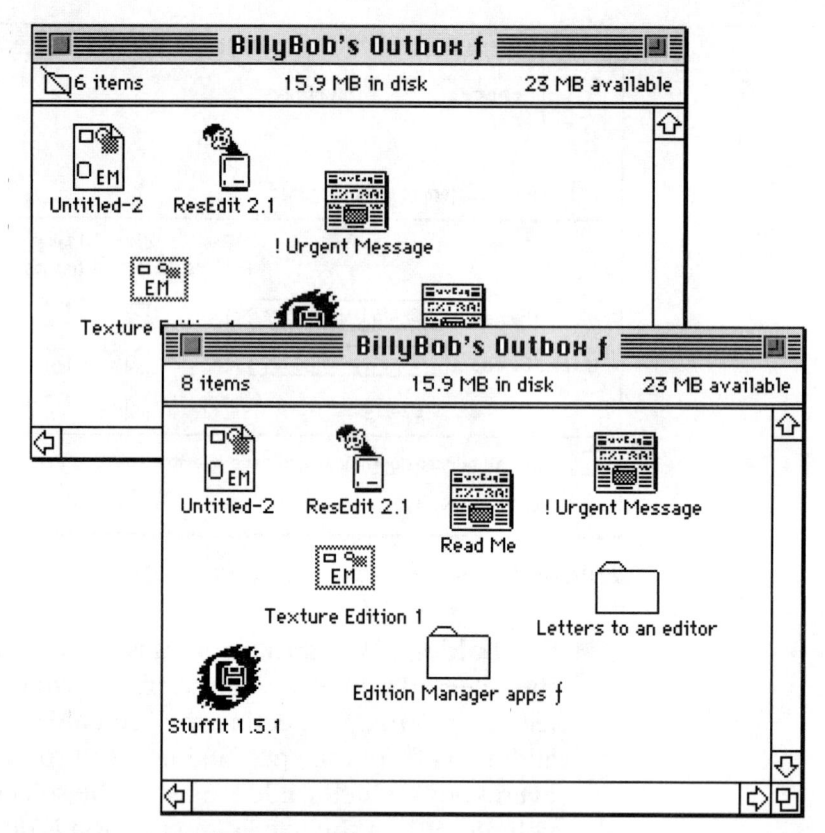

Figure 12-25: A shared folder with and without See Folders privilege.

- **See Files.** All files contained in the selected folder or volume appear normally to the specified user or group. Deselecting this option hides all files from the specified user or group—users don't know which files exist in the selected folder or volume. When the See Files option is deselected, an icon appears in the upper-left corner of the title bars of all windows accessed via File Sharing, letting the user know that files are not being displayed.

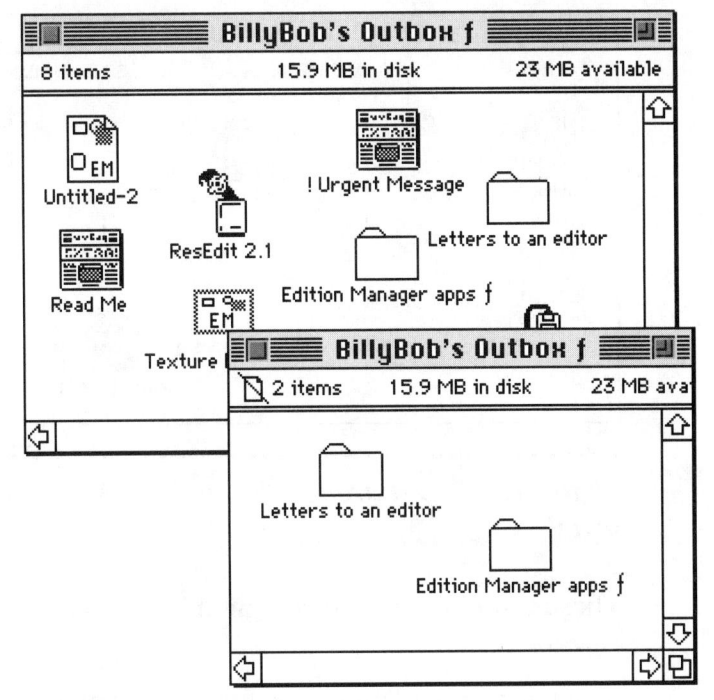

Figure 12-26: A shared folder with and without See Files privilege.

- **Make Changes.** When the Make Changes option is set, the user can save new files, change existing files and create new folders. When the Make Changes option is deselected, the folder or volume is *write protected:* no new files, folders and changed files can be written. When the Make Changes option is deselected, an icon appears in the upper-left corner of the title bars of all windows accessed via File Sharing, letting the user know that the folder or volume is write protected.

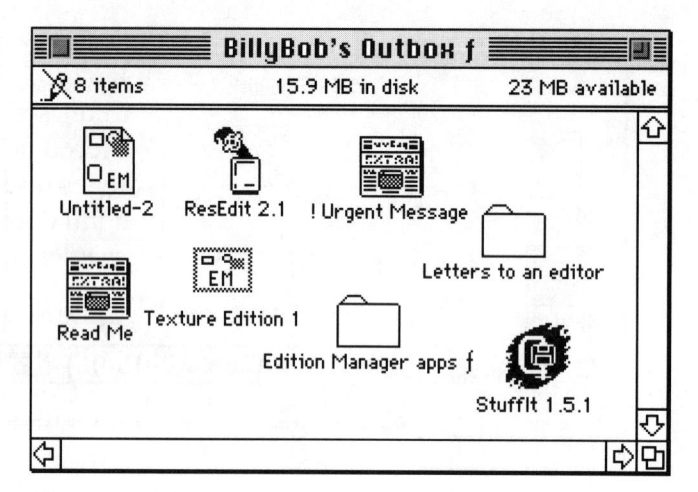

Figure 12-27: A shared folder without Make Changes privilege.

These three options are assigned individually to three user categories:

- **Owner.** The owner of a folder or volume is the person or group who can change the access privileges of that folder or volume while accessing it over the network. The person who creates a folder is automatically the owner of it; therefore, you are default owner of the folders and volumes on your Macintosh. When a user creates new folders in shared folders or volumes, however, that user becomes the owner of the new folders.

    Using the pop-up menu, the owner can be designated as any defined user or group. Or, selecting the <any user> option gives any guest who accesses the folder or volume full owner privileges (including the right to reassign access privileges). When setting access privileges on remote volumes, the "Owner" pop-up menu does not appear and the Owner Name must be entered manually.

- **User/Group.** The User/Group category assigns access privileges to one specific user or group. When sharing folders or volumes, select the desired User/Group from the pop-up menu listing of all registered users and groups. When setting access privileges on remote volumes, the "User/Group" pop-up menu does not appear and the Owner Name must be entered manually.

- **Everyone.** The Everyone category grants access privileges to all Guests who connect to the Macintosh that contains the selected folder or volume. Of course, in order for Guests to log on, the Allow guests to connect option must be set in the Users & Groups control panel.

Access Privilege Strategies

This elaborate matrix of categories and access privilege levels allows precise control over the way shared files can be used. Several common ways of using access privileges are described below:

- **Create an Out box folder.** The key aspect of an Out box is that those who pick up the files can see them but not make changes to them. This is accomplished by providing "See Files" and "See Folders" privileges but withholding "Make Changes," as shown in Figure 12-28. Of course, those who should not have access to the files in the Out box should not even see files or folders.

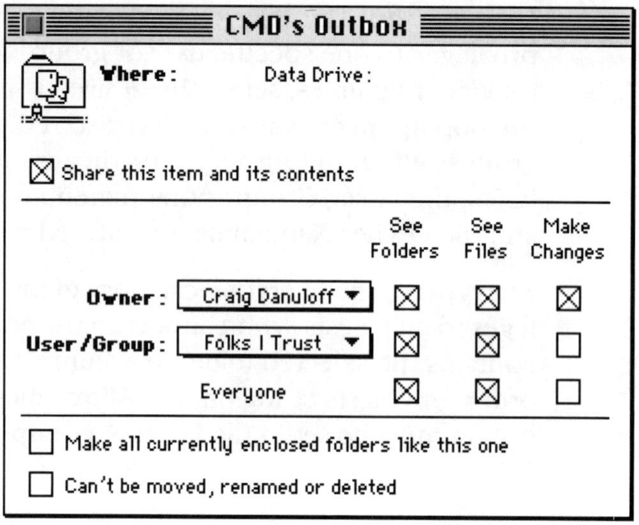

Figure 12-28: A set of access privileges that defines an Out box.

- **Create an In box folder.** The opposite of an Out box, an In box allows users to add files, but not to see anything that's already there—it's like a mail slot. This is defined using the opposite set of access privileges that an Out box has, as shown in Figure 12-29.

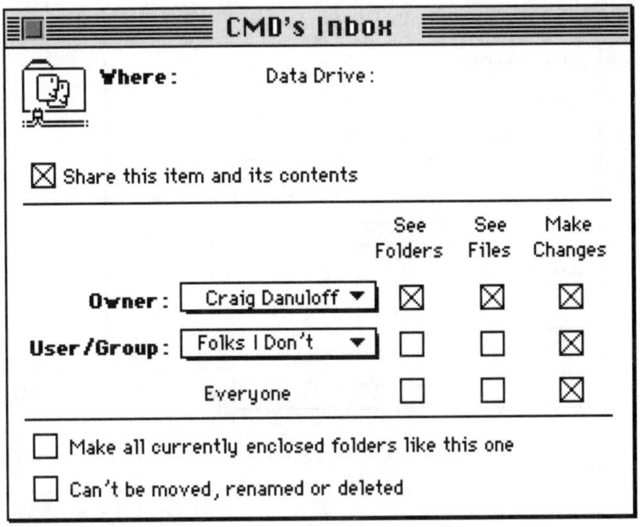

Figure 12-29: A set of access privileges that defines an In box.

- **Create a bulletin board.** Combining the attributes of Out boxes and In boxes in various folders and enclosed folders, you can create a place where people can read and retrieve some files and add and modify others, depending on who they are and which folder they're accessing. Figure 12-30 shows a set of enclosed folders and the privileges that provide such an arrangement.

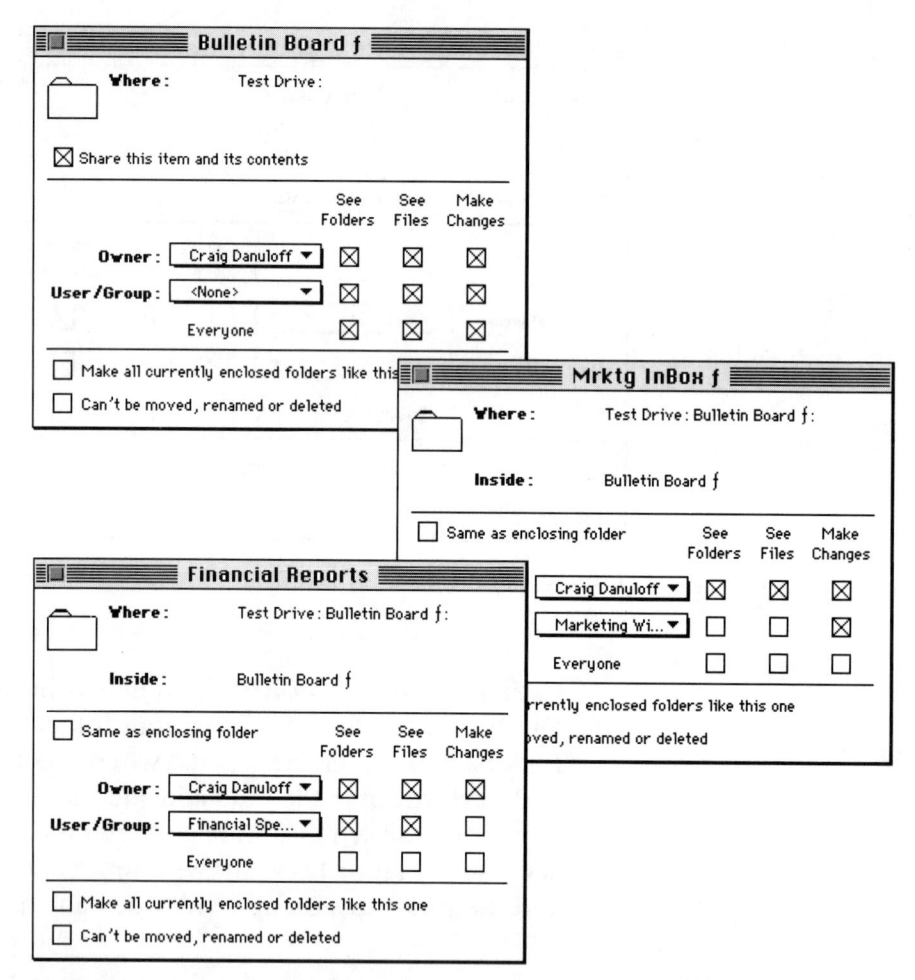

Figure 12-30: Privileges for several folders in a bulletin board.

- **Create a Drop folder.** System 7.5 has script set up to let you create and manage a Drop folder. This folder has the attributes of a bulletin board: everyone can See Folders, See Files, and Make Changes. To create the Drop folder, simply select the Share a Drop Folder command as shown in Figure 12-31. A Drop folder is created in your drive's top level folder, with File Sharing turned on. For your protection, when you restart your Macintosh your Drop folder is left unshared. To share your Drop folder once again, reselect the Share a Drop Folder command from the Useful Scripts submenu of the Apple menu.

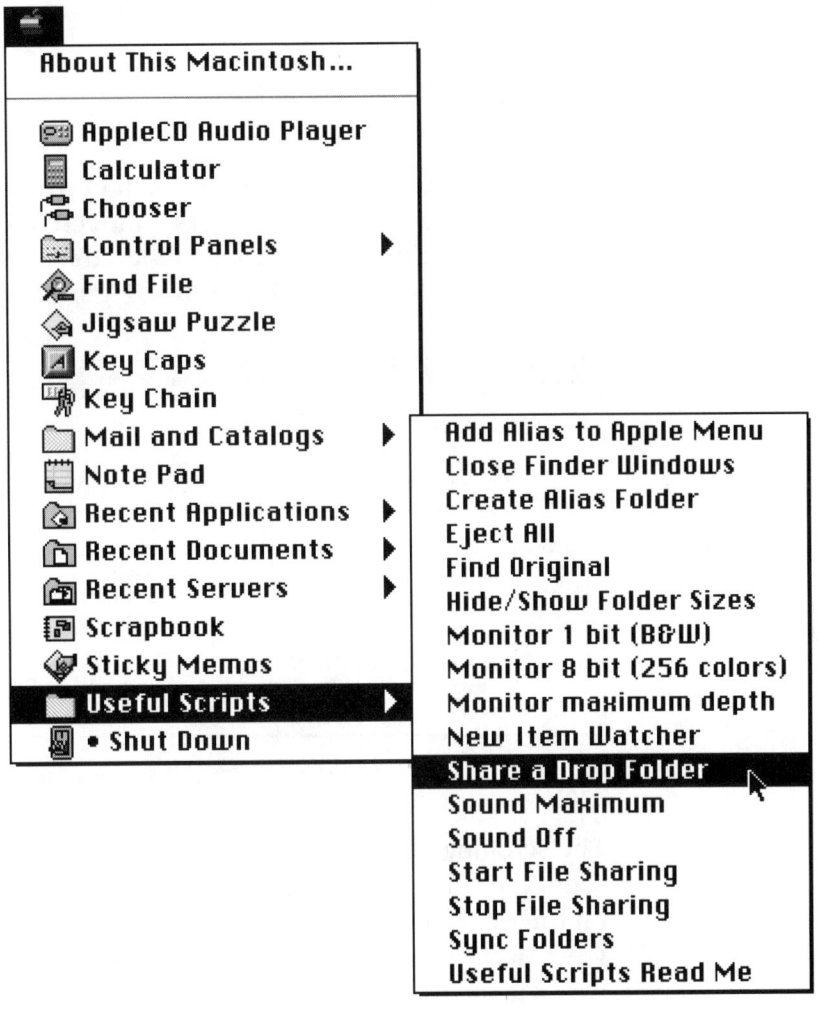

Figure 12-31: The Share a Drop Folder AppleScript.

- **Provide a group work area.** A simpler but more common way to use access privileges is to make a set of files available to specific users and groups. For example, you may have a folder to which the members of the "Engineers" Group have full privileges, while members of the "Sales Reps" team can see the files but not modify them.

Monitoring File Sharing

The File Sharing Monitor control panel gives you information about the items shared, the users connected to your computer and the activities of these users. Open the File Sharing Monitor, and the control panel shown in Figure 12-32 appears.

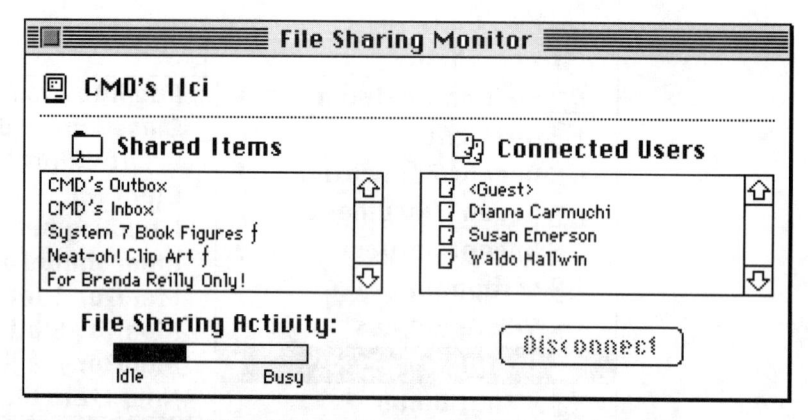

Figure 12-32: The File Sharing Monitor dialog box.

The scrolling window on the left side of this dialog box presents a list of the folders and volumes you've shared. The one on the right side lists network users currently connected to your Macintosh. You can disconnect any user by selecting the user's name from this list and clicking the Disconnect button. A dialog box lets you give the selected user warning by delaying disconnection for the number of minutes you select, or you can use the default 0 minutes and disconnect immediately.

The last item in this control panel is the File Sharing Activity monitor. This gauge fluctuates with the demands on your computer system as connected users access your Macintosh. When the demand is high, the local operation of your Macintosh slows. If slowdowns caused by remote users are a persistent problem, you may need to limit the access of Registered Users and Guests by reducing the amount of shared data you make available. Or you can shift some shared data to dedicated AppleShare file servers.

Moving On

The power and flexibility File Sharing offers will undoubtedly change the way you work on a Macintosh network. File Sharing removes almost all the barriers—physical and psychological—that previously inhibited the flow of data between computers. With File Sharing, you can

- Make any folder or volume on your computer available to anyone connected to your Macintosh network.
- Designate who can access the files and folders you share.
- Specify privileges extended to each regular user and network guest.

In Chapter 13, you'll see the other side of the File Sharing coin—accessing data shared by other Macs and by centralized file servers. You'll also look at other aspects of network life, such as coexistence with Macs running system software 6.0.x.

Chapter 13

Working on a Network

Macintosh users have long known the benefits of computer networking. Shared printers, and other peripheral Mac-to-Mac communications, and remote access to network file servers are commonplace on almost every Mac network. System 7 introduced additional networking capabilities, such as File Sharing, support for aliasing, the Edition Manager and IAC. System 7.5 adds PowerTalk and AppleMail (both described in Chapter 14, "AOCE–The Apple Open Collaboration Environment"), an electronic mail and messaging service and system software networking capabilities.

This chapter focuses on using your Macintosh network to access AppleShare and File Sharing volumes, the effects of access privileges, and how you control files stored on remote volumes. We'll also look at IAC's Program Linking and networks that include Macs still running system software 6.0x.

Accessing Network Volumes

As described in Chapter 12, "An Introduction to File Sharing," every System 7 Macintosh on your network can share up to 10 folders or volumes with other network users, based on user and group access privilege designations for each Mac that shares network data. In addition, dedicated AppleShare file servers can make any number of complete volumes available to all network users, according to specified access privileges.

Connecting to other System 7 Macs for File Sharing and AppleShare file server access is easy. This section describes how to do it and how to manage shared data.

Before beginning to connect to your file server, check that you have the appropriate network services selected. Open the Network control panel and click on either the LocalTalk, Remote Access, Ethernet, TokenTalk (Token Ring), SNA (IBM), DECnet (Digital Equipment Corp.), Novell IPX (NetWare), OSI, or TCP/IP protocols selected. Then proceed with the instructions that follow. For the capabilities of protocols other than LocalTalk, Remote Access, or Ethernet, you may wish to talk to a network administrator.

7.5 ▶ Apple used to sell MacTCP, the TCP/IP (for Transmission Control Protocol/Internet Protocol) protocols, separately. Because of the growing popularity of the Internet it now bundles them in with System 7.5. TCP/IP is used for UNIX networking in the higher education and research communities and has become popular worldwide as a major networking system. It is a universal standard, used for multivendor computers to communicate with one another over a network. For example, you can use TCP/IP to connect a Macintosh to a Sun workstation, a VAX minicomputer or a Cray supercomputer. For a large network installation, you might need TCP/IP to connect to a host computer; more likely you will need TCP/IP to connect via modem to a service providing a gateway onto the Internet.

Connecting With the Chooser

The first step in accessing network data is to open the Chooser (in the Apple menu) and click on the AppleShare icon as shown in the upper-left corner of Figure 13-1. (If this icon does not appear in your Chooser, run the Installer and choose the AppleShare (workstation) option in the Customize dialog box.)

The available network file servers appear on the right side of the window, and if your network is divided into zones, those zones are listed in the lower left corner of the Chooser. If a zone list appears in your Chooser, select the zone in which your Macintosh is registered; available server volumes in that zone will appear.

See the "Network & Telecommunications" and "Troubleshooting" topics for step-by-step help.

The list of file server names that appears includes both dedicated AppleShare file servers and Macs on your network using System 7's File Sharing. There's no easy way to tell from the listing which are AppleShare servers and which are File Sharing Macintoshes. In any case, as a client accessing data over the network, it makes no difference to you whether you're accessing data from a dedicated AppleShare file server or from a File Sharing Macintosh.

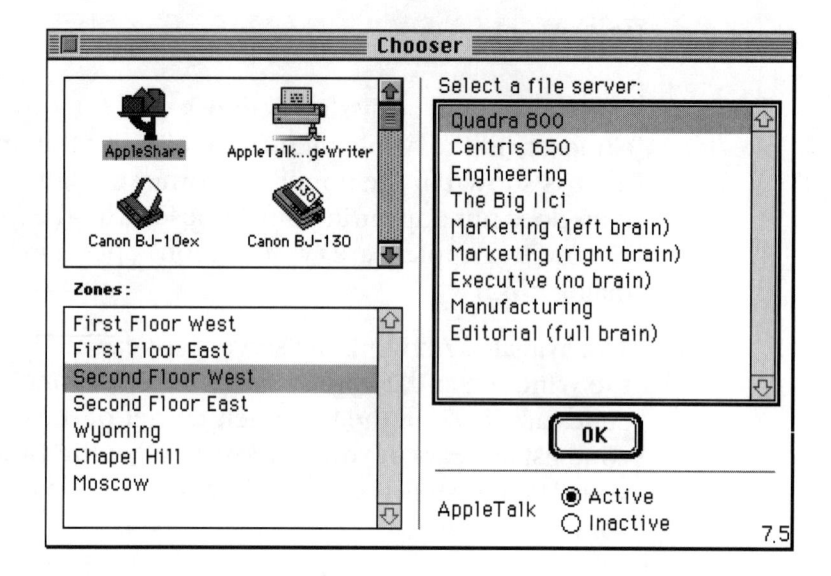

Figure 13-1: The Chooser with zone and file server listings.

When you've located the name of the file server you wish to access, double-click on the file name or click the OK button below the file server list. The Connect dialog box appears (shown in Figure 13-2). This dialog box gives you the option of connecting to the selected file server as a Guest or as a Registered User.

```
┌─────────────────────────────────────────────────┐
│  ┌──┐                                           │
│  │  │   Connect to the file server "Two Old" as:│
│                                                 │
│         ○ Guest                                 │
│         ⦿ Registered User                       │
│                                                 │
│      Name:     │ Jamie Miller              │    │
│      Password: │ ••••   │  (Two-way Scrambled)  │
│                                                 │
│                                                 │
│      ( Cancel )  ( Set Password )  (   OK   )   │
│                                          v7.5   │
└─────────────────────────────────────────────────┘
```

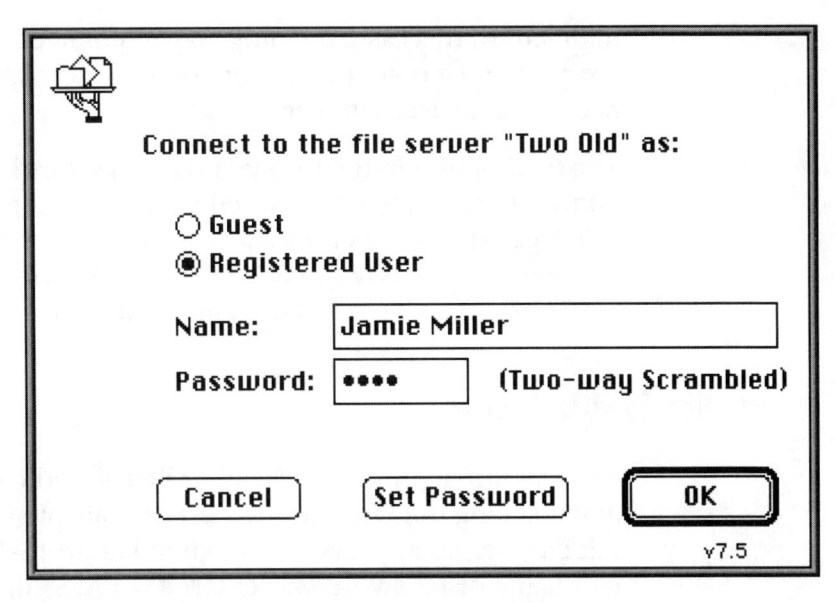

Figure 13-2: The Connect dialog box.

In order to connect as a Registered User, a user icon with your name and password must exist on the AppleShare server or File Sharing Macintosh. This shows that the system administrator or Macintosh owner has created and defined your Macintosh as a Registered User, as described in Chapter 12.

You can now click the Registered User option. The Owner Name specified in your Sharing Setup control panel will appear as the default in the Name option box. If this is not the name under which you're registered, make required changes to the Name option. If a password has been assigned, enter it in the Password option. If none is needed, leave the option blank. Then click the OK button.

Connecting as a Guest is simpler but may restrict your access privileges. Of course, this is your only option if you're not a Registered User. To connect as a Guest, click the Guest option, then click the OK button. If the selected file server does not allow Guests to connect, the Guest option will be dimmed. In this case, the only way to connect is to contact the Macintosh owner or server administrator and ask to become a Registered User.

The final option in the Connect dialog box is the Set Password button which allows Registered Users with appropriate access privileges to reset their passwords for a particular file server. Changing your password affects only the currently selected file server, not all servers on which you're a Registered User.

Selecting Specific Volumes

After identifying yourself as either Registered User or Guest (and clicking the OK button) a list of available volumes on the selected server appears, as shown in Figure 13-3. (If an incorrect name or password was entered, an Alert dialog box appears, and you'll be returned to the Connect dialog box.)

This dialog box lists all volumes that the selected server is sharing with the network. (When accessing File Sharing volumes, it's not possible to differentiate between shared folders and shared volumes, so we'll use the term volumes generically.) The names of any volumes you're not allowed to access will be dimmed. You can mount any one non-dimmed volume by double-clicking on the volume name or selecting the volume name and clicking the OK button. To mount more than one volume, hold down the Shift key while selecting volume names, then click the OK button.

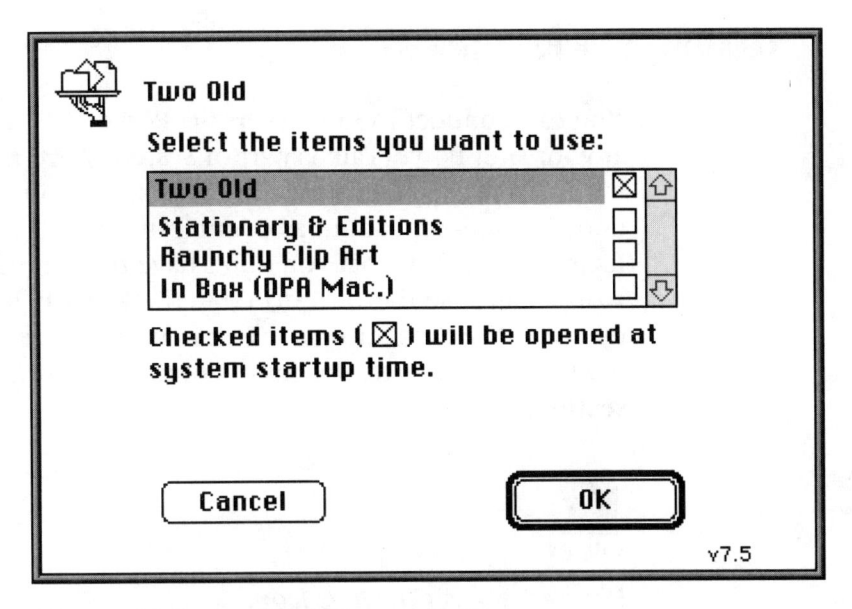

```
┌─────────────────────────────────────────────┐
│  ┌──┐                                       │
│  │📬│  Two Old                              │
│  └──┘                                       │
│        Select the items you want to use:    │
│       ┌─────────────────────────────┬──┐    │
│       │ Two Old                     │⊠ │▲   │
│       │ Stationary & Editions       │☐ │    │
│       │ Raunchy Clip Art            │☐ │    │
│       │ In Box (DPA Mac.)           │☐ │▼   │
│       └─────────────────────────────┴──┘    │
│       Checked items ( ⊠ ) will be opened at │
│       system startup time.                  │
│                                             │
│                                             │
│       ┌──────────┐         ┌──────────┐     │
│       │  Cancel  │         │    OK    │     │
│       └──────────┘         └──────────┘     │
│                                      v7.5   │
└─────────────────────────────────────────────┘
```

Figure 13-3: Available Server listing.

You can also configure the volume to mount automatically each time you start up your Macintosh, by clicking on the check box next to a volume name. But you'll have to enter your password manually each time you start your Macintosh and the volume is mounted, since by default your password is not stored as part of this automatic-mount process. To simplify the automatic mount (but at the same time reduce security), click the "Save My Name and Password" option, then double-click the volume name or click the OK button.

After mounting a volume, you're returned to the Connect dialog box. To mount additional volumes from the selected file server, click the OK button again to return to the volume list, and repeat the mounting process for another volume.

Connecting With PowerTalk

You can connect to file servers via PowerTalk, if it is installed at your site. PowerTalk is part of System 7 Pro and System 7.5. It's about as easy as connecting with the Chooser after you've done it once—and about as counter-intuitive if you've haven't. Its main benefit is that you don't have to remember your passwords, because they are stored in the Key Chain that you set up once. We'll cover PowerTalk in much more detail in the next chapter, but the basics of connecting are covered in this section.

Figure 13-4: A Catalogs icon.

Open your PowerTalk Catalogs by double-clicking on its icon (Figure 13.4) on your desktop; the Catalogs window opens showing you icons for your available services (Figure 13.5). Among your choice may be AppleTalk, AppleShare, Novell NetWare, DECnet, Telephone services, whatever. It's best to think of Catalogs as a folder of communications services, and as server or mail icons as communication settings files. You open a catalog to reveal either more catalogs or services. You launch a service by opening its file.

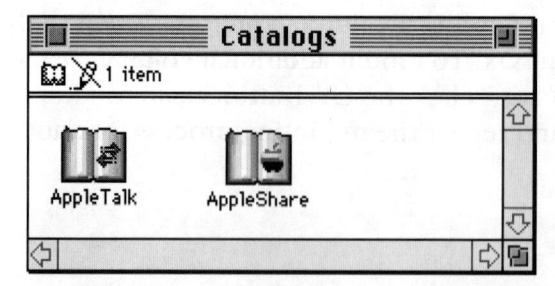

Figure 13-5: The PowerTalk Catalogs window.

Double-click on the icon for the service you wish to connect to, and a window appears showing you the available file servers. Double-clicking on the file server's name to open the file server's information window and then double-clicking on the file server's name in the information window will connect you, mounting it on your desktop. Figure 13.6 shows both an AppleTalk service window and a file server's information window open.

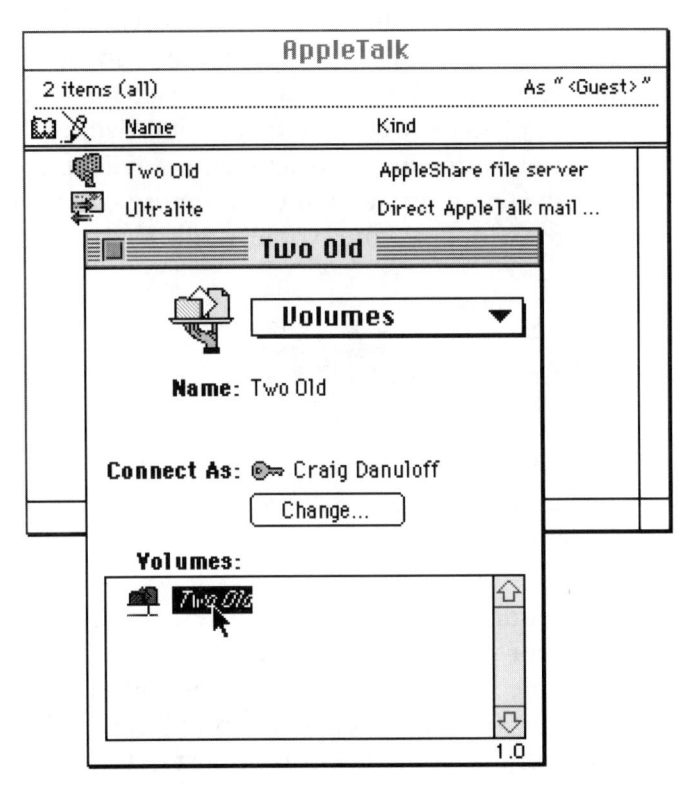

Figure 13-6: An AppleTalk file server and AppleTalk window open. Double-click on the file server as indicated to mount it.

For automatic connection to occur, you must first have registered your personal password in your Key Chain for that service. You can change passwords and preferences from within the Key Chain window, as described in Chapter 14.

Remote Volumes & Access Privileges

Any remote volumes you've mounted appear on your desktop as AppleShare Volume icons, as shown in Figure 13-7. This icon also accompanies these volumes in Open or Save As dialog boxes. These volumes are used just like local volumes (those physically connected to your Mac) except for any restrictions imposed by your access privileges. When your Macintosh is communicating with remote volumes, arrows flash just to the left of your Apple Menu.

Figure 13-7: A volume icon on the desktop (left), and the activity arrows that flash while remote volumes are accessed (right).

As described in Chapter 12, access privileges determine whether you can See Folders, See Files and Make Changes to available volumes. The Finder windows for remotely accessed volumes indicate your access privileges by displaying small icons in the upper-left corner, just below the title bar (shown in Figure 13-8). To see your assigned access privileges, choose the Sharing command from the File menu while the folder is selected or open.

Figure 13-8: The Cannot Write, Cannot See Folders and Cannot See Files icons.

When you don't have Make Changes privileges, you can't save or copy a file to a volume. In Save dialog boxes, the Save button is dimmed when the selected volume is write protected in this way; and, at the Finder, any attempt to copy or create files will bring up the dialog box shown in Figure 13-9.

This same dialog box will appear if you attempt to create a new folder on a volume for which you don't have See Folders privileges.

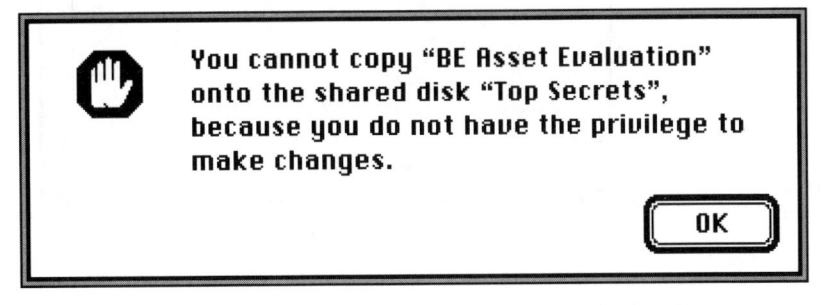

> You cannot copy "BE Asset Evaluation" onto the shared disk "Top Secrets", because you do not have the privilege to make changes.
>
> OK

Figure 13-9: Not Enough Access Privileges dialog box.

Use the Sharing command to see the complete access privileges for any volume you can mount. Select the volume icon and choose the Sharing command from the File menu. If you own the volume, you can change these access privileges. If you create a folder on a shared volume, you're automatically assigned as the folder's owner and allowed to use the File menu's Sharing command to reset the access privileges.

A Volume Access Shortcut

To avoid this lengthy process every time you mount a networked volume, you can create an alias of the volume icon that appears on your desktop and store that icon in a convenient spot on your hard drive. In fact, you can create a folder full of network volume icons (see Figure 13-10).

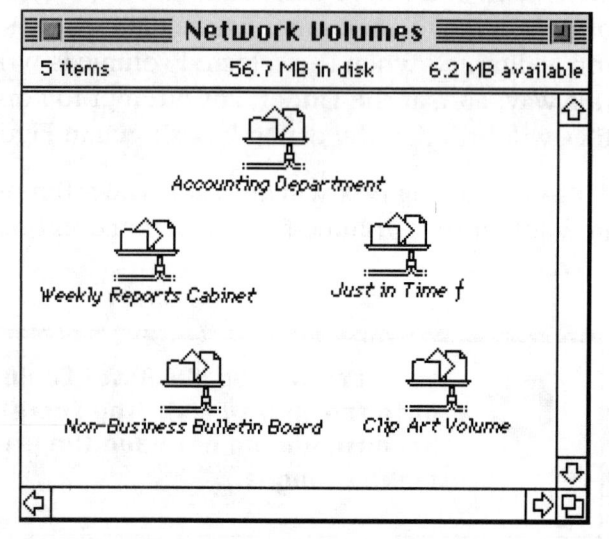

Figure 13-10: Folder of volume aliases.

Double-clicking on the network volume alias icon mounts the volume after you supply any necessary passwords. This shortcut can save lots of time and effort.

You can think of the Catalogs in PowerTalk as a folder containing the alias of different servers and services. It actually is more than that, as your log-on procedure, name, and password are contained in the "alias" when you set it up in your Key Chain. Not having to enter this information into the Connect dialog box (shown in Figure 13-2) is one of the benefits of PowerTalk.

Disconnecting From Remote Volumes

There are three ways to disconnect a mounted network volume:

- **Trash the volume.** Simply drag the volume icon into the Trash. Just as this action ejects removable disks, it releases mounted file server volumes.

- **Shut Down or Restart.** All mounted volumes are also released when you use the Shut Down or Restart command.

- **Put Away.** The File menu's Put Away command, or its keyboard equivalent, Command-Y, dismounts any selected volumes.

Accessing Your Hard Drive Remotely

When File Sharing is on, you can access your entire hard drive and all volumes currently mounted from anywhere on your network—unless you've deselected the Allow user to see entire volume option in the Owner Preferences window of the Users & Groups control panel. This option is accessed by double-clicking on the user icon that displays your Owner name.

To reach your hard drive from another Mac on your network, select the Chooser just as you would to log on to any network volume. Locate the name of your Macintosh in the scrolling file server list, and double-click on it. A new dialog box appears, listing the name of each hard drive connected to your Macintosh. These are not volumes you've shared with the Sharing command; they're complete hard drives as they appear on the Macintosh desktop. To mount your drive, double-click on the drive name, or select the drive name and click the OK button.

Your hard drive then appears on the desktop of the Macintosh you're using, with AppleShare volume icons. You now have complete access to your drive, including all files and folders, with no limitations based on access privileges. You can create files and folders, delete files, redefine Users & Groups, set File Sharing access privileges or do anything else you could do if you were sitting at your own Mac keyboard.

When you're finished using a remotely mounted hard drive, you can release it, just like you would any other volume, by dragging it to the Trash, using the Put Away command, or shutting down and restarting.

Program Linking

As mentioned in Chapter 10, "Inter-Application Communication & OpenDoc," applications specifically programmed to support AppleEvents can communicate with application programs residing on any AppleShare server or File Sharing volume on the network. If you use any programs that can take advantage of Program Linking, and want these programs to communicate with the applications on your hard drive, you must specifically enable Program Linking.

The master control for Program Linking is found in the Sharing Setup control panel, as shown in Figure 13-11. The message in the Status area will document the Program Linking start-up process. Once Program Linking is running, the Start button becomes the Stop button.

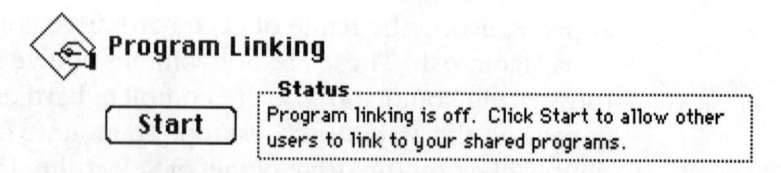

Figure 13-11: The Sharing Setup dialog box provides the master control for Program Linking.

Program Linking must also be enabled in the Macintosh Owner icon found in the Users & Groups control panel. (The Macintosh Owner icon has a dark border around it and displays the name entered in the Sharing Setup dialog box.) Double-clicking on this icon displays the dialog box shown in Figure 13-12. The Program Linking option, in the lower portion of this dialog box, enables Program Linking.

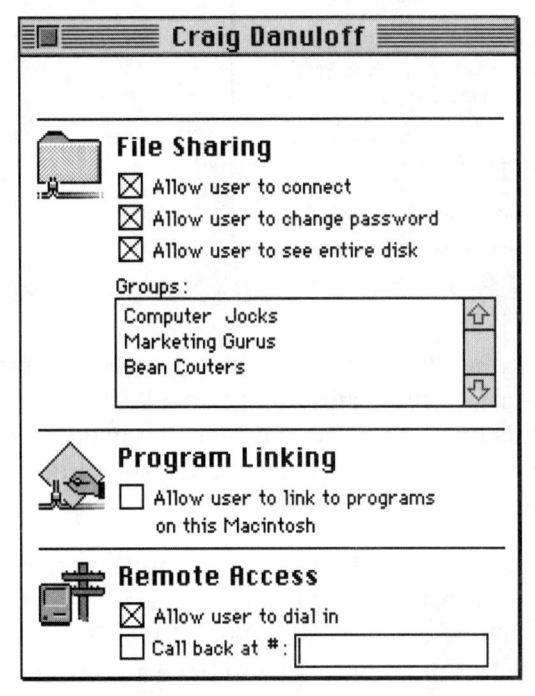

Figure 13-12: The User Options dialog box for the Macintosh owner.

Even when Program Linking has been turned on and enabled in the File Sharing dialog box, it is only available to applications that support it. This remains a very small number of System 7-savvy applications.

To initiate Program Linking for an application that supports it, highlight the application you wish to use, then choose the Sharing command from the File menu. A Sharing dialog box appears.

Figure 13-13: An application's Sharing dialog box.

If the application you selected supports Program Linking, the Allow remote program linking check box is displayed. Otherwise, this option will be dimmed. To make the application available for Program Linking, click the check box, then close the Sharing dialog.

Program Linking is a nice feature, but few people use it today—even most "power users" haven't worked with it much, if at all. There are two main benefits of Program Linking that you should think about. If you have a computationally intensive task, say 3D rendering or visualization studies, you can off-load the assignment to a more powerful computer on your network. The result can then be returned back to you over the network much quicker.

The other important use of Program Linking is to provide you through AppleEvents with additional capabilities that are not resident in your own application. Using Program Linking you can access a remote copy of the application that has the capabilities you need, without having to load the outside program on your own computer. This saves you from additional purchases and reduces the time it takes you to do the task by not having to install it.

Networks With Macs Running System 6.0.x

If some of the Macintoshes on your network aren't upgraded to System 7, you can still run them on the network. It's no problem to run system software 6.0.x and System 7 on the same network, with one small exception. The exception is the LaserWriter driver file that's installed with System 7.

Updating LaserWriter Drivers

In order to allow everyone on your network to share the same laser printers without having to constantly restart them, you'll have to copy the new LaserWriter driver (Version 7.0 or later) into the System Folder of all Macintoshes still using system software 6.0.x. There are three files you will need to copy: the 7.0 LaserWriter driver, LaserPrep and Backgrounder for versions prior to System 7.5. You can either manually copy these files from the System 7 Printing disk or from the System 7 CD-ROM, or run the Printer Update script which will use the Installer to add these files to any existing System Folder.

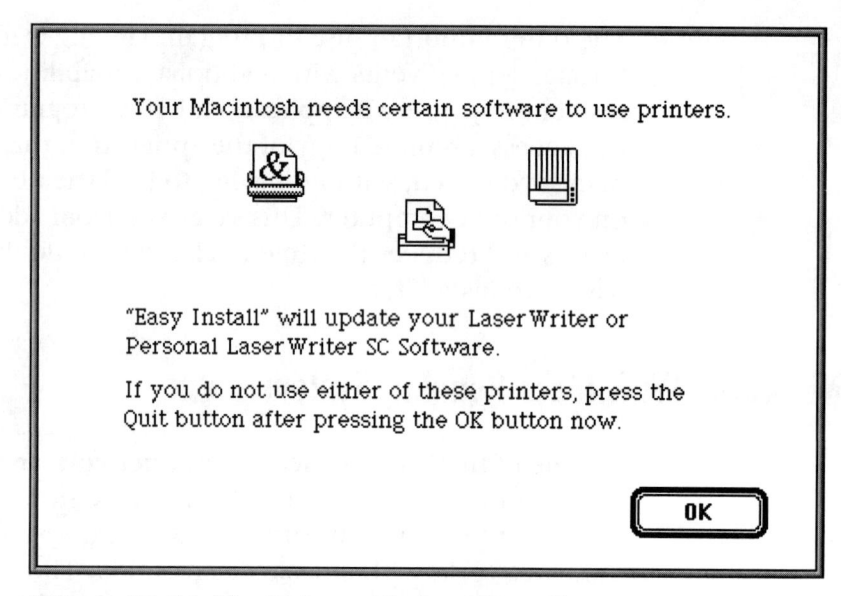

> Your Macintosh needs certain software to use printers.
>
> "Easy Install" will update your LaserWriter or Personal LaserWriter SC Software.
>
> If you do not use either of these printers, press the Quit button after pressing the OK button now.
>
> [OK]

Figure 13-14: The Printer Update Installer screen.

Replacing existing LaserWriter drivers with the LaserWriter driver Version 7.0 will work fine—they won't even notice the difference. It's easy to tell when the LaserWriter driver Version 7.0 is being used because its icon is different from the one used by earlier versions. The icons for LaserWriter driver Version 7.0 and Version 5.2 (which is commonly used with system software 6.0.x) are shown in Figure 13-15.

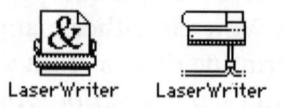

Figure 13-15: The LaserWriter 7.0 (left) and 5.2 (right) icons.

7.5 ▶ System 7.5 introduces the LaserWriter 8.0 (now at Version 8.1.1), and LaserWriter GX printer drivers. If you did an Easy Install, LaserWriter 8.0 and the new print spooling extension Printer Share are installed into your Extensions folder. To install them manually, use the System 7.5 Installer shown in Figure 13-16 to do a Custom Install. LaserWriter 8.0 and Printer Share install as part of the Printing section. Another set of new extensions, LaserWriter GX and PrinterShare GX, install with a QuickDraw GX installation. You can use the Custom Install to update any of your older printer drivers, either locally or over a network. The icon for LaserWriter 8.0 is identical to the one for LaserWriter 7.0 shown in Figure 13-15 (left); the icon for LaserWriter GX is similar, but surrounded by a two-pixel black outline.

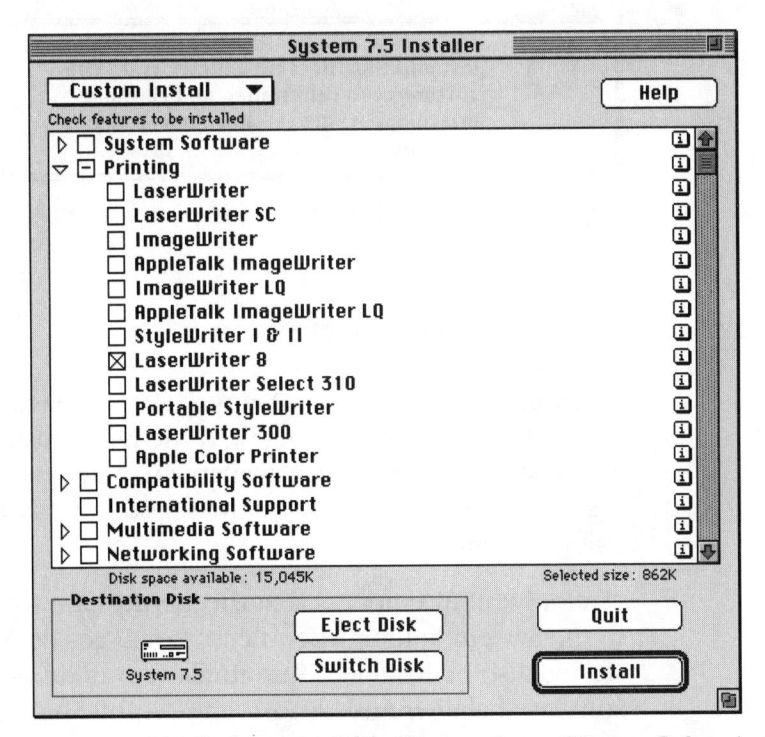

Figure 13-16: Custom Installing a LaserWriter 8.0 printer driver.

It's not impossible to use the older LaserWriter drivers with System 7, which you might be tempted to do if only a few people on your network have upgraded, but this can cause problems with background printing and is not advised.

Caution: If you don't use the same versions of the LaserWriter drivers throughout your network, those who have the different version will be greeted by the Restart Printer dialog box (shown in Figure 13-17) whenever they attempt to print. There's no technical problem with constantly reinitializing your laser printer, but it wastes lots of time. It also causes any downloaded fonts to be removed from the printer's memory at each restart. So, upgrading all LaserWriter drivers to 8.0 (or 7.0) is the practical solution.

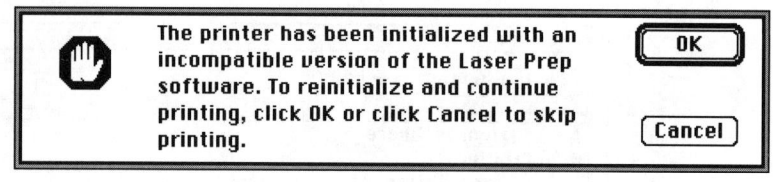

> The printer has been initialized with an incompatible version of the Laser Prep software. To reinitialize and continue printing, click OK or click Cancel to skip printing.
>
> [OK] [Cancel]

Figure 13-17: The Restart Printer dialog box.

Accessing File Sharing Volumes From System 6.0.x

As explained in Chapter 12, any System 7 Macintosh can share up to 10 folders or volumes with the Macintosh network. These shared volumes are available to Macs running earlier system software versions (such as System 6) as well as those using System 7.

The only requirement is that the AppleShare INIT be installed in the System Folder. The Access Privileges desk accessory should also be installed. Running any version of the system software Installer and choosing the AppleShare (workstation software) option will install all the necessary files.

Once these files are installed, volumes shared by a System 7 Mac using File Sharing, as well as volumes from any network AppleShare servers, can be accessed and used by the System 6 Mac exactly as described in this chapter.

Moving On

Most Macintosh users are first interested in connecting to a network in order to share peripheral devices, such as laser printers, or perhaps network modems. But networks also make it possible for computers to communicate with each other, and for data to be shared either between computers or by accessing centralized file servers.

In this chapter you've seen how to make the most of these abilities:

- Using the Chooser to select an available File Sharing Macintosh or AppleShare server.
- Mounting volumes and setting up automatic mounting connections.
- Working with assigned access privileges.

Next, in Chapter 14, we will look at PowerTalk and a number of new services that were introduced with System 7.5. PowerTalk is a mail and messaging service built using AOCE, which is a system software communications framework. Future plans for AOCE call for a "universal mailbox," intelligent active agent searching and filtering of online data, video conferencing, and more.

Chapter 14

AOCE—The Apple Open Collaboration Environment

A substantial percentage of Macintosh users are connected to other Macintosh users on networks of various sizes. For workgroups, AppleTalk and File Sharing covers only a small part of their needs. They need collaborative applications such as messaging, electronic mail, workgroup document revision history, address and service information, authentication and privacy services, encryption and digital signature, to name but a few. Apple has created a suite of integrated system software services called Apple Open Collaboration Environment (AOCE) technology. When you hear AOCE, think "workgroup" software, and you'll be on the mark.

AOCE made its first appearance in System 7 Pro when PowerTalk was released. PowerTalk encompasses all of the features described in the previous paragraph. PowerTalk is the first application running under AOCE services, but other third-party products will undoubtedly follow. In fact, System 7 Pro was primarily released as a vehicle for PowerTalk's introduction. Few users upgraded to System 7 Pro, or were using PowerTalk, but with PowerTalk's inclusion in System 7.5 the number of users should increase significantly.

PowerTalk is a "peer-to-peer" messaging service, just as AppleTalk is peer-to-peer networking. In a peer-to-peer environment computers talk directly to one anther without the intermediacy of a file server. To dramatically expand the number of users and services that can be accommodated by PowerTalk, Apple has released the PowerShare Collaboration Servers. PowerShare extends PowerTalk with store-and-forward AppleTalk-based messaging and file transfer, catalog and privacy services and other team productivity solutions.

In this chapter we'll look at how PowerTalk and PowerShare were implemented in their first versions and at what AOCE portends for future system software releases.

About AOCE & Groupware

Apple has chosen to include group collaborative services in system software to make it easier to implement these features within applications and to provide consistency. When you click the Mail icon in WordPerfect 3.0 you see the same Standard Mail Package that you see in the PowerTalk Mailer described later in "Sending and Receiving Mail." You can access this mailer inside a spreadsheet, database or communication package, which makes it easy to communicate, transfer data or send a file without having to switch out to a dedicated mail package. You learn the service once in its single version, just as you learned to use the Macintosh-standard file dialog boxes.

AOCE system software contains four new collaboration managers: InterProgram Messaging Manager, Catalog Manager, Authentication & Privacy Manager, and Digital Signature Manager. (To this date they have not been translated into native PowerPC code.) These managers provide the following capabilities:

- **Messaging.** You can exchange information between applications asynchronously, that is, at irregular intervals. The InterProgram Messaging (IPM) Manager is similar to System 7's Inter-application Communication architecture you learned about in Chapter 10, "The Edition Manager & IAC," but the IPM Manager also provides store-and-forward capabilities for your messages.

  A message can be received at a later date, sent to multiple users, or through the use of third-party software sent over any type of message transport such as SMPT, MHS, cc:Mail, or X.400. Messages can, for example, be exchanged with Microsoft Mail on Windows-based computers using Microsoft's Enterprise Mail Service (EMS). Gateways are planned to voice mail, pagers, fax devices, QuickMail, CompuServe, the Internet, and AppleLink, among others.

- **Electronic Mail.** Users can exchange letters and documents using the Standard Mail Package mentioned previously that is part of AppleMail. This feature is every bit as much a system software standard as the Open and Save Standard File dialog boxes you've come to know and love.

- **Catalogs.** AOCE stores information in an object database managed by the Catalog Manager. In it you can enter data about users, addresses, passwords, authority, and other data you deem necessary to collaborate. For example, you can store a favored method for a user's information retrieval (which online service, by fax, etc.), and, when you mail out to them, your application uses AOCE services to take care of the details of how you want the message sent.

- **Authentication/Privacy.** The revision history of communications is tracked, so that the environment verifies that persons at both ends of the communications are who they claim to be. Authentication is password-based with the PowerShare catalog server acting as a the verification device. The Authentication and Privacy Manager can encrypt an AppleTalk data stream with a high level RC4 encryption algorithm.

- **Digital Signatures.** This tool allows users to electronically sign documents during routing. The Digital Signature Manager provides positive identification of the signer and can check that the document was not altered after it was signed. It's claimed that this system is more secure than handwritten signatures because it is based on a public-key encryption technique.

The four AOCE collaboration managers are the base of three levels of integrated technologies, as shown in Figure 14.1. The collaboration managers give low-level system services and programming hooks to provide developers options they can build into their application. On top of the collaboration managers are standard mail package and standard catalog package services that provide the interface elements that are used in AOCE applications. (We'll see these standard packages in the PowerTalk sections to come.) Finally, at the desktop level are the elements of the interface that the user interacts with: mailboxes, catalogs, and the key chain.

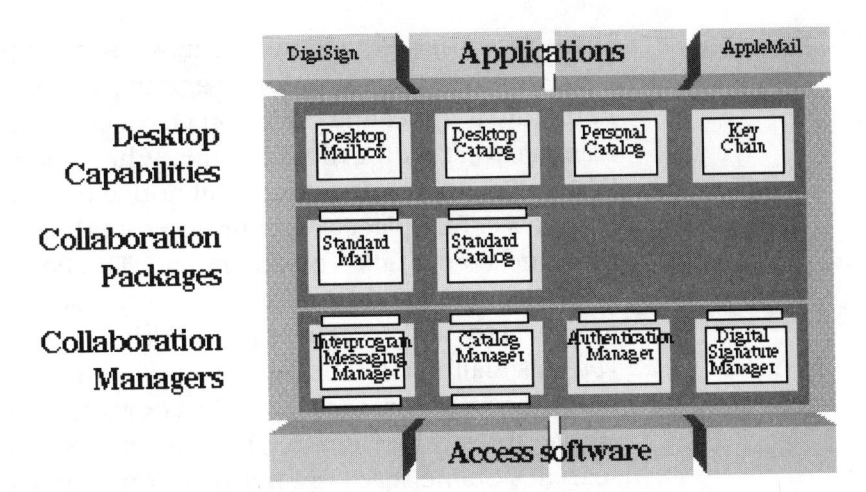

Chapter 14: AOCE—The Apple Open Collaboration Environment 513

Figure 14-1: The AOCE Technology Framework. (Source: Apple Computer.)

AOCE is "middleware," providing services to mainstream Macintosh applications, DigiSign (Apple's digital signature program), and AppleMail. What the user sees and identifies as PowerTalk are primarily the desktop elements of AOCE. PowerShare, the server software for PowerTalk, implements the lower level features found in the collaboration managers' layer of AOCE.

Various messaging software packages: VoiceMail, FAX, Pager, X.400, QuickMail, PROFS, SMPT, Microsoft Mail, and Novell MHS can connect to PowerTalk *without* the use of a server through plug-in modules that these services will provide. For example, Starnine sells a gateway to the Internet, and all of the major online services will have gateways to PowerTalk that will let you send and receive mail through the PowerTalk Mailbox. Similarly, plug-in modules will let users browse and access catalogs through the catalog browser also without the use of server software. You will see developers build private corporate directories, use X.500, DEC DDS, or standard telephone directories accessed on CD-ROM or in a large database and link them to PowerTalk-type catalogs.

Since AOCE and PowerTalk are new, many of their best capabilities are yet to be developed and explored. Some of what's here now is appealing once you get over the learning curve of using PowerTalk for the first time. When you first boot up System 7.5 you undoubtedly will notice the three new icons that PowerTalk places on your desktop: the Catalogs, Mailbox, and PowerTalk Key Chain icon. The PowerTalk Mailbox is an integrated address that can receive electronic documents, faxes and voice messages. Although it isn't here just yet, this Mailbox will become a "universal client" using third-party access software to provide gateway services. For example, the day may come when an active software agent searches online services for articles on your special area of interest, downloads them to your Mailbox and collects all of your electronic mail from the services you subscribe to.

AOCE makes it much easier for developers to include scheduling, calendaring, group authority and other services in their applications. Catalogs provide consistent message storage and routing in a single server. As another example of the kind of problem AOCE is meant to solve, consider the problem posed by forms that require sign-off at various levels within a company. This is the paper equivalent of "phone tag." As requisitions, invoices, purchase orders and check authorizations circulate, they can often take days or weeks to process, resulting in poor efficiency and lost business opportunities. With AOCE, PowerTalk and packages like Shana's Informed Designer, forms can be signed off in a matter of hours by several people. Since PowerTalk clients can utilize remote access capabilities, sign-off can occur at off hours and off site, as well.

PowerTalk

As noted, PowerTalk is messaging and email system software that offers you the following benefits:

- Integration of information from a variety of sources.

- A universal desktop Mailbox that receives correspondence.

- A system for logging onto electronic services automatically through the Key Chain utility.

- A Finder-based file transfer method.

- Digital signatures for documents, and message authentication based on your Key Chain.

- Secure communications and file transfer through robust encryption.

- PowerTalk can access a library of third-party software that will provide security, mail and catalog services, and new messaging options.

7.5 With PowerTalk installed you will notice several new Finder elements. Most prominent will be the three new icons that PowerTalk adds to your desktop: the Catalogs, Mailbox, and PowerTalk Key Chain. The Key Chain appears after you add your first PowerTalk account. You may also notice two new Apple menu items in System 7 Pro: Find In Catalog and Personal Catalog. In System 7.5 you see the new commands: Key Chain and the Mail and Catalogs folder. Inside the Mail and Catalogs submenu on the Apple menu are the AppleMail, Find In Catalogs, and Personal Catalog commands. The PowerTalk folder (found in the Apple Extras folder) contains the AppleMail application and an Untitled Info Card, and the DigiSign utility and a sample Signer file. Figure 14.2 shows you these new Finder elements.

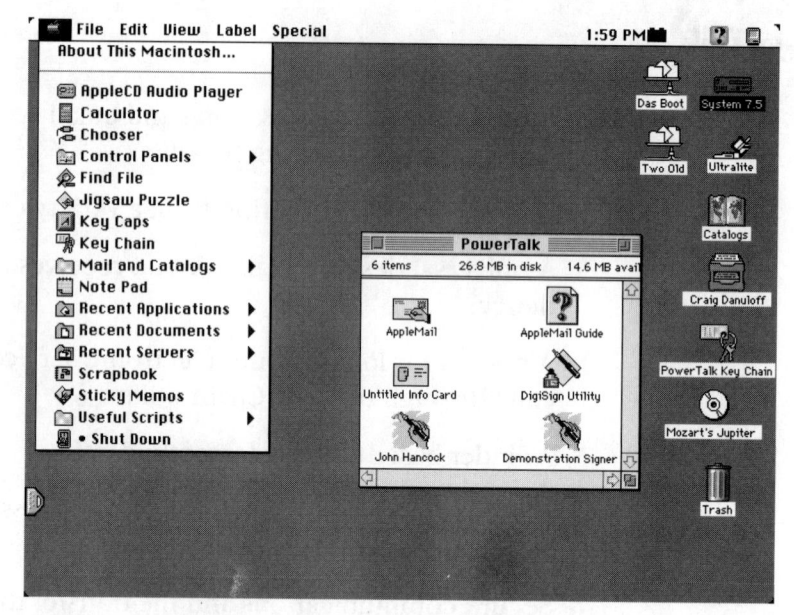

Figure 14-2: PowerTalk Desktop icons, and Apple menu items for System 7.5.

Refer to "PowerTalk Basics" for initial help with PowerTalk.

In System 7 Pro you can use Balloon Help for aspects of PowerTalk, AppleMail, and the DigiSign Utility. System 7.5 adds a PowerTalk Guide help system based on Apple Guide to the Help menu. References to Apple Guide in this chapter refer to the PowerTalk Guide file.

The Mailbox is where correspondence gets sent to you and where you store outgoing messages and files. The name of the icon "Mailbox" changes to your name when you set up PowerTalk for the first time. A mailbox has an "In Tray" for items to be read, and an "Out Tray" for items to be sent. Select these choices from the Mailbox menu when the Mailbox is open. Once you give your Access Code your Mailbox can be opened again in that session without repeating it. Mailboxes are intuitive and should cause you no problems.

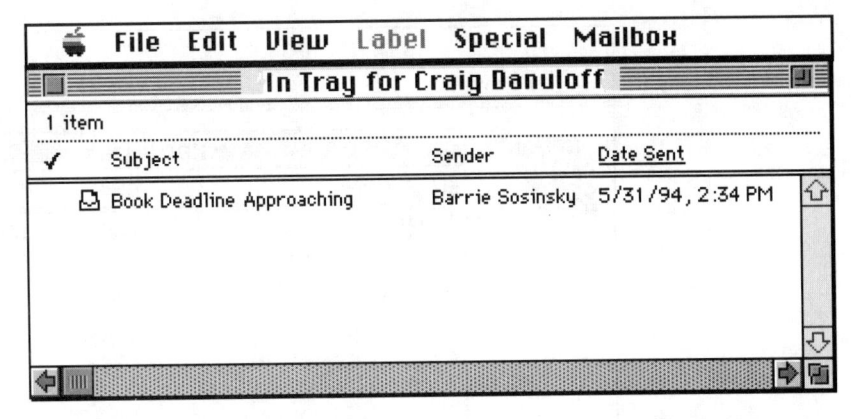

Figure 14-3: The Mailbox In Tray.

Catalogs are folders containing all of the services that you have access to. There are two main types of catalogs: your desktop services catalog and personal catalogs that you can create. During installation a default personal catalog is created for you in the Apple Menu Items folder.

When you open your desktop Catalog you probably will see an AppleTalk service. You may also see AppleShare, DECnet, Novell IPX, and other services if you are connected to them. When you double-click on a service catalog you expose all of the servers and devices that you can automatically connect to based on your settings in the PowerTalk Key Chain. For AppleShare networks with zones you may have to navigate through additional folders to see your connections.

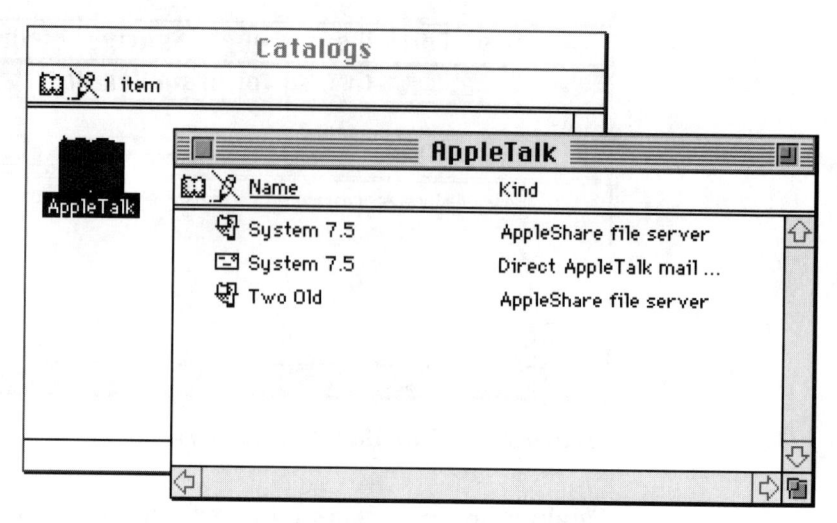

Figure 14-4: An AppleTalk service catalog.

As Figure 14-4 demonstrates, opening an AppleTalk service catalog exposes servers, volumes and other network devices (not shown) that you can connect to. For example, if you could connect to a network printer, that icon would show up in the window. To help you recognize a catalog window you see a catalog in the header. The "no pencil" icon indicates that you cannot modify this catalog. You can't modify a service catalog because the services you see are what you are connected with. You can modify personal catalogs, adding addresses, connections and other objects as you choose. The whole process of working with catalogs has a bit of a learning curve but offers a lot of flexibility once you become comfortable using it.

As described in the previous chapter, "Working on a Network," you can connect to services by double-clicking on them in a Catalog without having to go to the Chooser to select them. This method is preferable to Chooser selection as it stores the path to the service, your name and other information that the service requires, and, most essentially, your password or validation. You don't have to remember any of these details. Only find the service you want in your catalog.

The PowerTalk Key Chain is a password-protected listing of all of your service connections, and the relevant information needed to connect to them. You can think of the Key Chain as a folder containing smart "aliases" to these services. A sample Key Chain window is shown in Figure 14-5. To open a Key Chain you need to choose the Unlock Key Chain command on the Special menu, and provide an Access Code. You can lock the Key Chain by applying the Lock Key Chain command, by shutting down your computer or by setting a preference for a designated period of inactivity for which you want PowerTalk to stay open. These are described below.

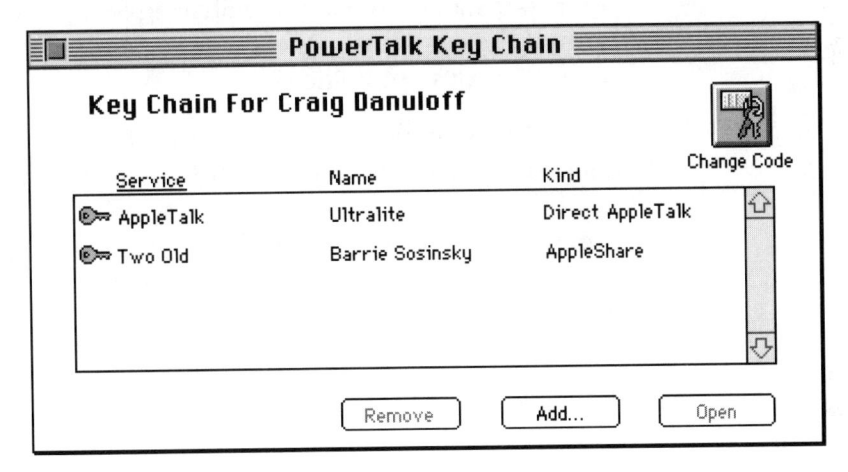

Figure 14-5: A PowerTalk Key Chain window.

Setting Up PowerTalk & PowerShare Servers

PowerTalk is installed automatically as part of an Easy Install of System 7.5 or System 7 Pro. Before choosing to install PowerTalk, keep in mind that for System 7.5 it requires a 68020 or above or PowerPC-based computer. Apple recommends that you install PowerTalk along with QuickDraw GX on 68k computers with at least 8mb of RAM, 16mb of RAM for a Power Macintosh. Also check that your system date and times are correct in the Date & Time control panel, and that each computer is properly named on an AppleTalk network prior to installation using the Sharing Setup control panel. Both of these control panels were described in detail in Chapter 4, "The System Folder."

PowerTalk can be installed with or without a PowerShare collaboration server, which is sold as a separate package by AppleSoft. In a small AppleTalk network of a dozen or so users, peer-to-peer PowerTalk installations are practical. Larger sites should install PowerShare servers so as not to overwhelm the system.

Figure 14-6: The Unlock Key Chain command.

Right after installation you will not see a Key Chain on your desktop. To activate PowerTalk and add the PowerTalk Key Chain to your desktop, you need to initiate PowerTalk. Select the Unlock Key Chain command on the Finder's Special menu (shown in Figure 14-6). The Welcome to PowerTalk screen shown in Figure 14-7 appears. You can also open the Welcome screen by opening the Mailbox. After clicking the Proceed button you are requested to add the key for your PowerShare account. Click Yes to search your volumes for services to add to your Key Chain; No if you aren't connected to a PowerShare service. In either case you will be asked to supply your account information: name and Access Code as in the dialog box shown in Figure 14-8.

Figure 14-7: The Welcome to PowerTalk screen.

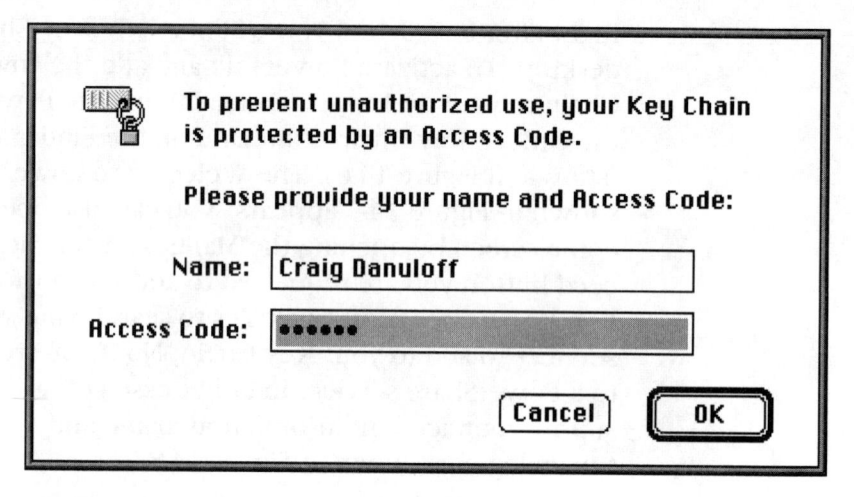

Figure 14-8: The Access Code dialog box.

After you finish adding your Key Chain, it will be available throughout your session. When you restart your Macintosh, you will need again to select the Unlock Key Chain command. With the PowerTalk Key Chain window (Figure 14-5) open on your screen, use the Add button to add additional services or the Remove button to delete ones you've added. You can double-click on a service to open it or click once and press the Open key.

Setting up services and passwords is one of the more confusing aspects of PowerTalk. One other setup chore remains. Using the PowerTalk Setup control panel shown in Figure 14-9, you can turn PowerTalk on or off after restart. This is equivalent to turning off PowerTalk in the System 7.5 Extensions Manager. You can also lock your key chain by selecting the Lock Key Chain command on the Special menu. If you want PowerTalk to lock automatically after a certain period of inactivity, set that option in the PowerTalk Setup control panel. Be sure to always lock your Key Chain when you leave your computer. The Key Chain locks automatically at shut down as a protection. You can also set the control panel to ask for your Key Chain code at startup, which then makes it available during that entire session.

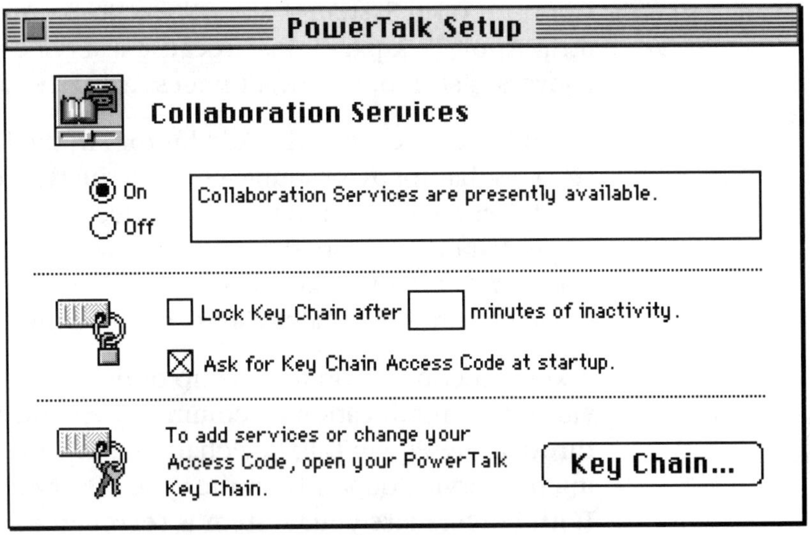

Figure 14-9: The PowerTalk Setup control panel.

Should PowerTalk shut off temporarily due to inactivity, your services will only be available when you open your Mailbox and enter the Access Code. With PowerTalk turned off after restart, you won't even see the Mailbox and Catalogs icons. Should you try to open the Key Chain icon, an alert box appears that tells you PowerTalk is off.

Services & Addresses

Services are added in the PowerTalk Key Chain window as keys in the chain. By double-clicking the Key Chain icon on your desktop when PowerTalk is active, the PowerTalk Key Chain dialog box shown in Figure 14-5 opens. This dialog box contains a listing of all services (keys) that you currently can access. Whether you can connect to these services depends on whether your network connections are correct. For example, to log on to an AppleTalk network service, AppleTalk must be active. That is, you must turn on AppleTalk in the

Chooser, or in System 7.5 on PowerBooks, using the Control Strip AppleTalk panel. Just because a service is listed and the address is stored, you don't necessarily have access to it.

To add a service, click the Add button. In the list of available services that follows, double-click on the type of service desired. Depending on the type of service, you may be further requested to pick a specific service, then it is added to your Key Chain. You remove a key by selecting it and clicking the Remove button. PowerTalk will ask you to confirm the deletion.

A key is a connection to a group of users through some service or communications medium. When you add a service through the PowerTalk key chain, what you see after selecting the service depends on the type of service you added. With PowerShare your system is searched for available services, and you are prompted to select one. Other services may require additional steps. If you want to add an AppleShare server, simply mount it on your desktop with the Chooser. PowerTalk will ask you if you want to add a key for the server to your Key Chain.

Catalogs & Information Cards

Catalogs are collections of information about objects with an electronic address: people and things. The most troublesome point about catalogs to realize is that PowerTalk creates two different types of catalogs. The catalog you see on your desktop lists services and connections. The catalogs you create, called Personal Catalogs, most often contain information cards of people you want to contact with PowerTalk.

Refer to "Catalogs & Information Cards" for further details.

It's obvious what "people" are, but what are "things"? Things can be shared devices on a network—printers or servers, equipment, meeting rooms, and anything else that supports the concept of addressing or queues. People usually think of a Catalog as an object-oriented database, and the information card as a record in that database expressed as a file.

Cards are really the physical expression of a database record, with the object being stored a collection of data about a person, place or thing, or group of people, places and things that you can connect to. So, you can think of a catalog as an object-oriented database of either services or connections.

The service Catalogs you see on your desktop show you whatever service you have logged on to through your network or dial-up connection. Double-click on a built-in service catalog to see a list of people, devices or other connections at that service. Note that a Catalog icon appears in the header of a Catalog window to tell you the window type. The crossed or "no pencil" icon indicates that you can't modify the contents of this window. Double-click on a service to initiate the log-in sequence.

You can also create Personal Catalogs, which are saved anywhere on your hard drive that you like, even on a remote or attached volume. There is no limit to the number of Personal Catalogs you can have. Just to get you started AppleTalk puts a default catalog into your Apple Menu Items folder and onto your Apple menu in System 7 Pro. For System 7.5 this item appears in your Mail and Catalog folder inside the Apple Menu Items folder.

A Personal Catalog icon is shown in Figure 14-10. Note that this one has a bookmark, indicating that it is the *preferred* personal catalog. To find or set a preferred personal catalog, open the Get Info dialog box for a personal catalog and use the Find Preferred and Set Preferred buttons for that purpose. The preferred personal catalog is the one that is opened using the Personal Catalog command on the Mail and Catalogs submenu of the Apple menu in System 7.5.

Personal Catalog

Figure 14-10: A Personal Catalog icon.

You may also see information cards for users in a catalog window. Groups of users are contained in card stack icons that you can open. Any object in a catalog window can be dragged to another catalog. Figure 14-11 shows a Personal Catalog window and the Catalogs menu. To add a new user information card to a catalog, select the New User command from the Catalog menu; for a new group, select the New Group command. After naming the user, you can double-click on the icon to open the information card and supply needed information. You can also open the Group window and drag users into it, or create users. We'll have more to say about information cards in a moment.

There are four main ways to add items to a catalog:

- Drag items from one catalog window to another.
- Create an alias in a PowerTalk service catalog and drag it into a personal catalog.
- Use the Find In Catalog utility and save found items (described below).
- Drag an item from the Mailer's catalog access panel to a catalog, as described in the next section.

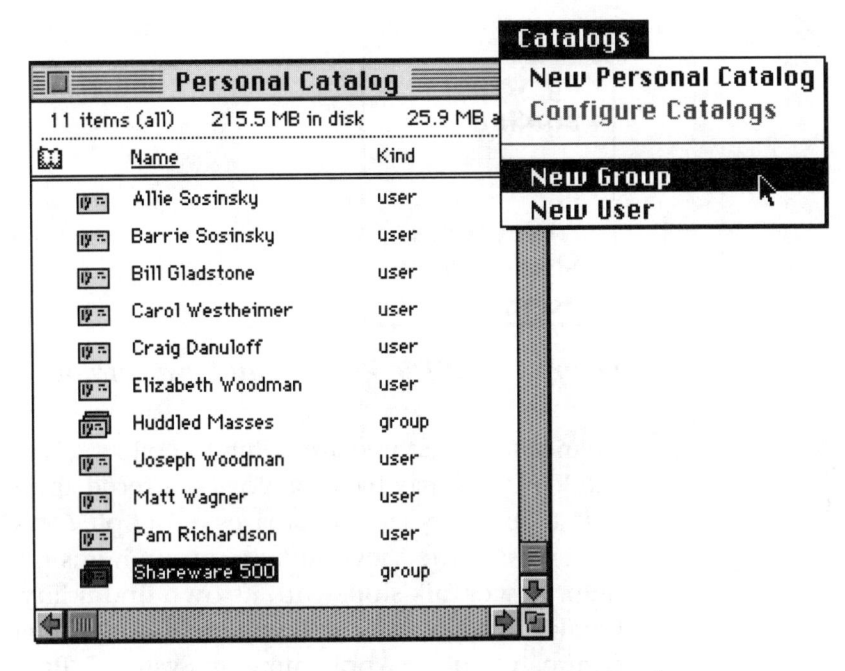

Figure 14-11: A Personal Catalog and the Catalog menu.

When you open a catalog window (an example was shown in Figure 14-11), you see all addresses and connections. Click on the Kind classification in the window header, or select the By Kind command from the View menu of the Finder if you wish to group items that way. Otherwise they are grouped by name. With a catalog open, the View menu changes to reflect other ways of grouping catalog items by Name or Kind: using All, File Servers, Miscellaneous or Users. The View menu with a catalog open is shown in Figure 14-12. You will also note that a Catalogs menu appears whenever a catalog window is open. Use the New Personal Catalog command on the Catalogs menu to create new catalogs.

```
View
✓ by Name
  by Kind

✓ All
  File Servers
  Miscellaneous
  Users
```

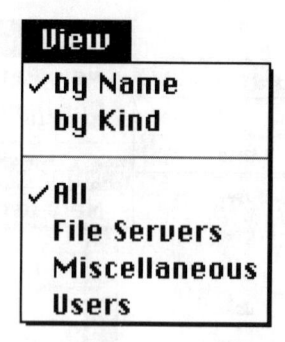

Figure 14-12: The View menu for a catalog.

Chances are that you are going to collect a lot of items in your catalogs, and may have catalogs scattered about. For catalogs that access very large databases of people (on CD-ROM perhaps), using the View menu to group items is not going to help. PowerTalk ships with its own find utility called Find In Catalog. This utility can be opened using the Find In Catalog command on the Apple menu in System 7 Pro; or as shown in Figure 14-13, on the Mail and Catalog submenu in System 7.5. This new submenu (and folders) is a convenient place to store personal catalogs in System 7.5.

```
📁 Mail and Catalogs  ▶   AppleMail alias
📝 Note Pad               Find in Catalog
📁 Recent Applications ▶  Personal Catalog
```

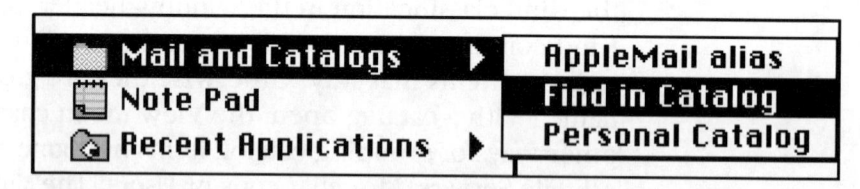

Figure 14-13: The Mail and Catalogs submenu in System 7.5.

The Find In Catalog command opens a Find dialog box that looks and functions similarly to the Find File dialog box used in the Finder. You can search for All, File Servers, Miscellaneous, or User objects in catalogs, and specify on what volumes to search. The match string is not case sensitive. When the find operation returns matching items, you can use the

Save button to save that item to your preferred personal catalog. You can drag an item to your desktop, folder or to another personal catalog, or open it by double-clicking on the name.

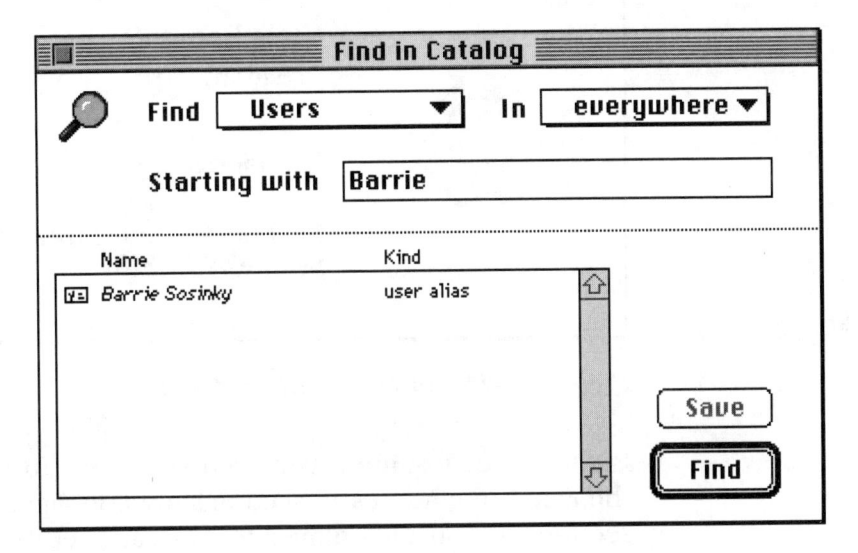

Figure 14-14: The Find In Catalogs dialog box.

Information cards are Finder files or objects that contain information on users. Don't forget that you can use the service catalog on your desktop to find an individual's address and drag copy it to your personal catalog. A sample card is shown in Figure 14-15. Using the pop-up menu, cards can contain a

- Business card. Contains business information.
- Personal Info. Home address and freeform information.
- Phone numbers. Various contact numbers.
- Electronic addresses.

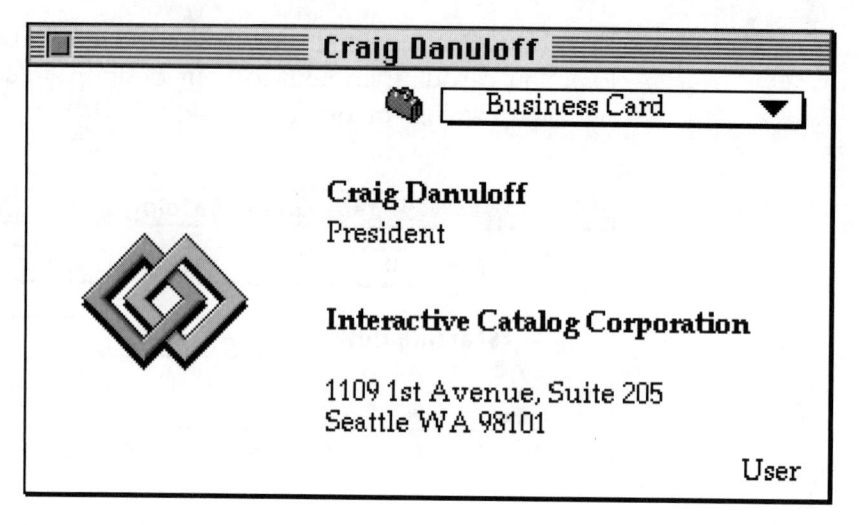

Figure 14-15: An Information Card.

Perhaps the most important section of the information card is the Electronic Addresses section shown in Figure 14-16. This section lets you add online addresses and set the preferred address that mail is sent to. Use the Add button, Remove button or Open button as you learned before for the Key Chain.

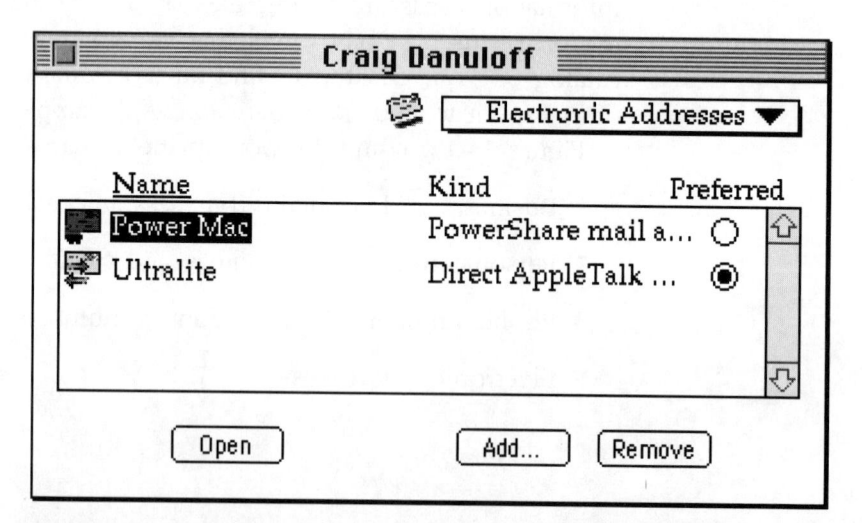

Figure 14-16: The Electronic Addresses section of an Information Card.

Sending & Receiving Mail or Files

With PowerTalk, electronic mail is built into the Finder. You can send files and folders by simply dragging their icons onto the information card of the user(s) or group(s) you want them to go to. Don't drag information cards to groups, because they will be added to the group. To send an information card to a group, first add it to a folder and then drag the folder to a group information icon.

See "Sending & Receiving" for related help.

To check mail you've sent or received open your Mailbox and examine your In Tray and Out Tray. If you want to open a piece of mail, just double-click on the mailing. You can also click once on the mail piece and use the Open command on the File menu. Mail you've looked at receives a check mark. Note that you can sort mail by the categories listed in the header by clicking once on that category (Subject, Sender, Date, etc.). A sample In Tray, and the View menu when the In Tray is active is shown in Figure 14-17.

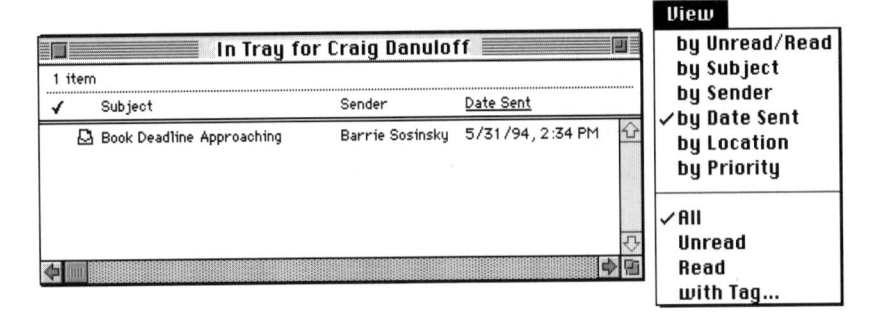

Figure 14-17: A Mailbox In Tray with the View menu also shown.

Mail is categorized by five headings: Subject, Sender, Date Sent, Location, and Priority. The Subject is what gets entered into a letter's subject field, or is the name of the item. Locations can be either remote (on a server), or local (on your hard drive). The Priority is how quickly the mail must be sent and is set by the sender in the Mailer (discussed below). You will also note that tags can be attached to mail. To add a tag, use the Mailbox menu, and attach a tag or label to the mailing. Figure 14-18 shows you the Mailbox menu that appears when the Mailbox is open, and the Tag dialog box. Tags are used to file your mail so that you see only the type of mail you want. Use the With Tag command from the View menu for this option. You can view a mailing's tag by opening the Get Info dialog box for that mail piece. Tags disappear when you drag mail out of the mailbox and copy them somewhere else.

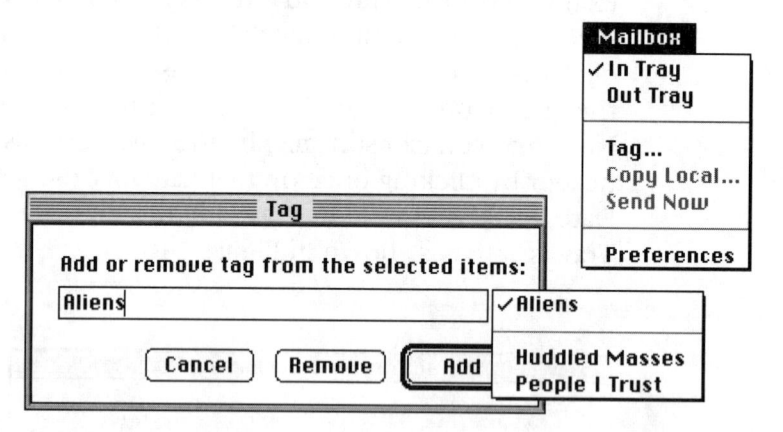

Figure 14-18: The Mailbox menu when the Mailbox is open, and the Tag dialog box.

Remote Connections

With PowerShare installed you can also check your account from another computer somewhere else on the network. If you can't connect to your PowerShare account, you don't see your mail until the connection is reestablished. If you see a Triangle Alert box below the Zoom box of your In Tray, click on it to reconnect immediately to the PowerShare server.

To check your Mailbox from another computer, you need to check the Allow Visitor's Mailbox option in the Preferences dialog box that you access from the Mailbox menu (see Figure 14-18). A Visitor's Mailbox appears on your desktop, and items currently on the PowerShare server will appear in it. When you are on another computer, choose the Visitor's Mailbox from the Special menu, give the service name, your name and your PowerShare password to open the In Tray of the Visitor's mailbox.

You can connect to PowerTalk with a PowerBook from a variety of locations by using the I'm At... command from the Special menu. You can choose the location and the type of service (Direct AppleTalk Mail, PowerShare Server Mail, Direct Dialup Mail, etc.) that you want to use from the dialog box that appears in Figure 14-19. Direct Dialup Mail allows modem connection between two computers, and it is sold separately by AppleSoft. When online mail is sent to remote computers, it is received in your Mailbox's In Tray if you are the receipient. When you send mail off-line, mail is placed in your Out Tray. Once reconnected, use the Send command in the Mail menu when your Out Tray is open to send your mail.

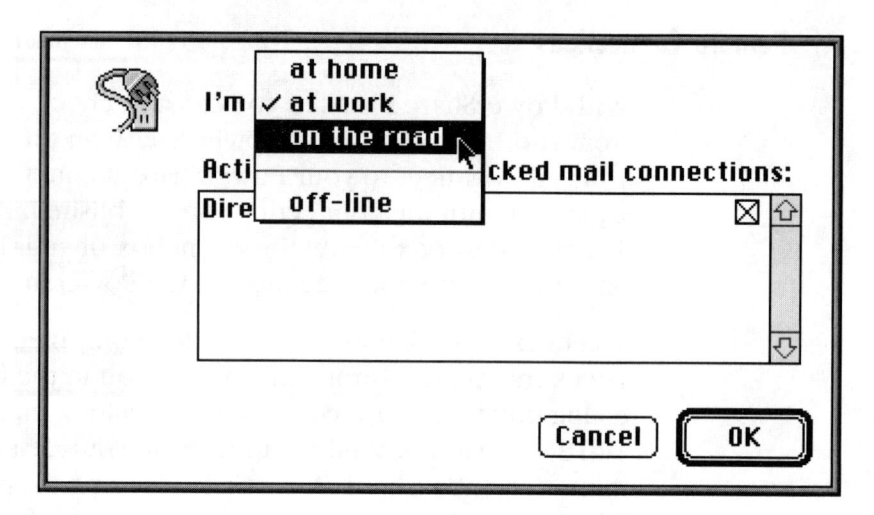

Figure 14-19: The Remote Access dialog box.

AppleMail

You use AppleMail and the Mailer standard package within applications to create, send and reply to letters and enclosures. You will see the mailer in a variety of applications, but it is identical to the mailer in AppleMail. When you write a letter with AppleMail, you can save that letter as a Letter file. To create a new letter, launch AppleMail: an untitled letter with a mailer like the one shown in Figure 14-20 appears. The AppleMail text editor in the bottom panel has the same features as SimpleText. It will accommodate graphics, sound, QuickTime, Drag and Drop, fonts, styles and wordwrap. Use the letter section as you would any word processor window. The top section is the Standard Mail Package or "Mailer."

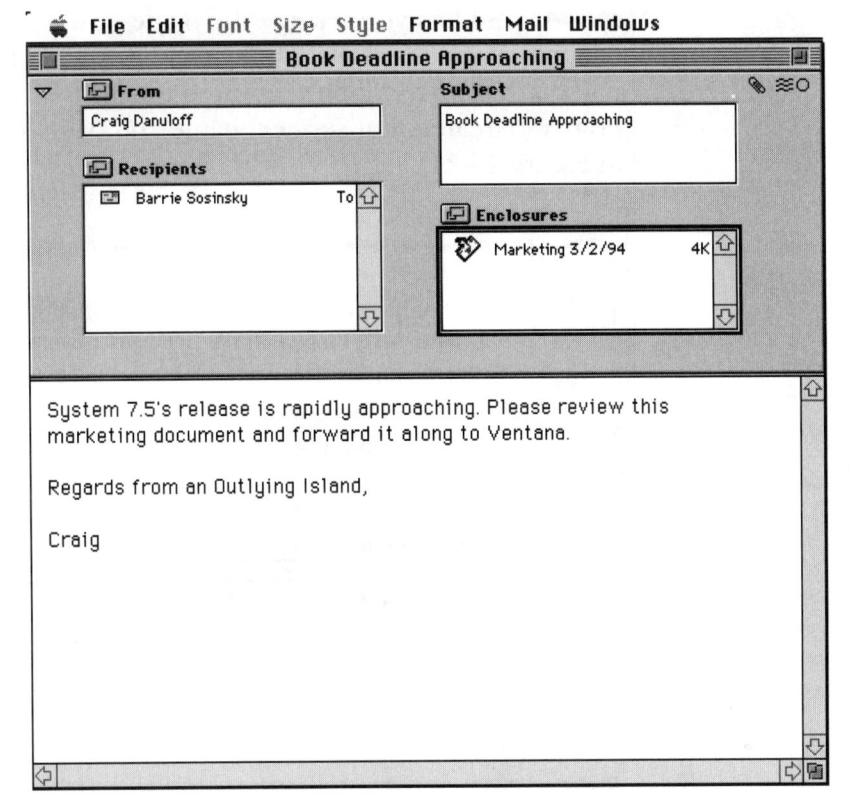

Chapter 14: AOCE—The Apple Open Collaboration Environment

Figure 14-20: An AppleMail letter and Mailer.

The Mailer is the addressing section of a letter. To collapse the letter and just see the Mailer, click the small triangle that appears under the close box of the Mailer (just like using the Outline view of the Finder). There are four distinct areas that you need to fill in: From (the Sender), Recipients, the Subject and Enclosures (attached files and folders). Information you enter here appears in the Mailbox In and Out Trays. When you attach an enclosure, a paper clip appears below and to the right of the Grow box. When a letter is sent, a postmark appears under the Grow box, as well.

The Mailer has some pop-up panels that help you fill in the From, Recipients and Enclosures fields. Clicking the Card icon above From lets you change the name of the sender, which defaults normally to the name of the Key Chain owner. When you do this, you will be requested to supply the new PowerShare account service, name and password, as shown in Figure 14-21.

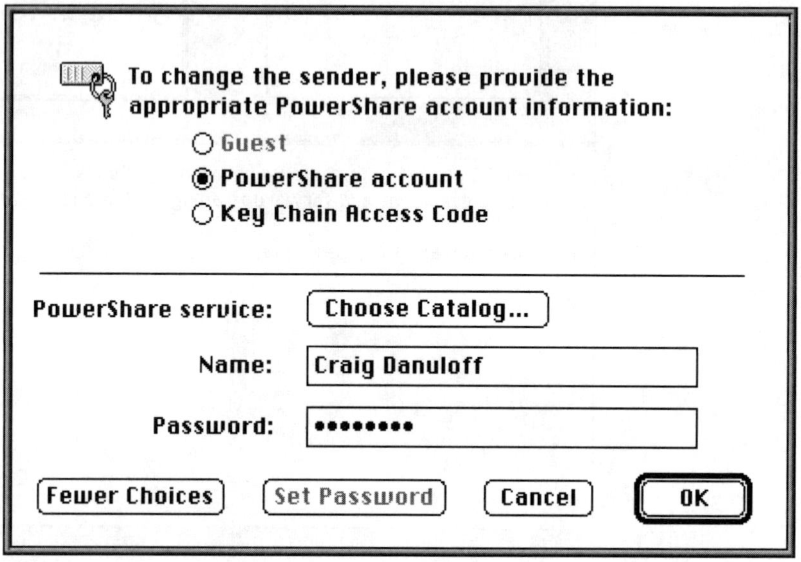

Figure 14-21: The Change the Sender dialog box.

Clicking the Recipients Card icon opens a Catalog Access panel. The four icons are from top to bottom: the Personal Catalog viewer, a Catalog Browser panel, a Find utility based on the Find In Catalog utility discussed earlier and a Type-In Addressing panel. Examples of all four panels are shown in Figure 14-22. Don't forget that you can add recipients by simply dragging their information cards from a catalog into the Recipient sections of a Mailer.

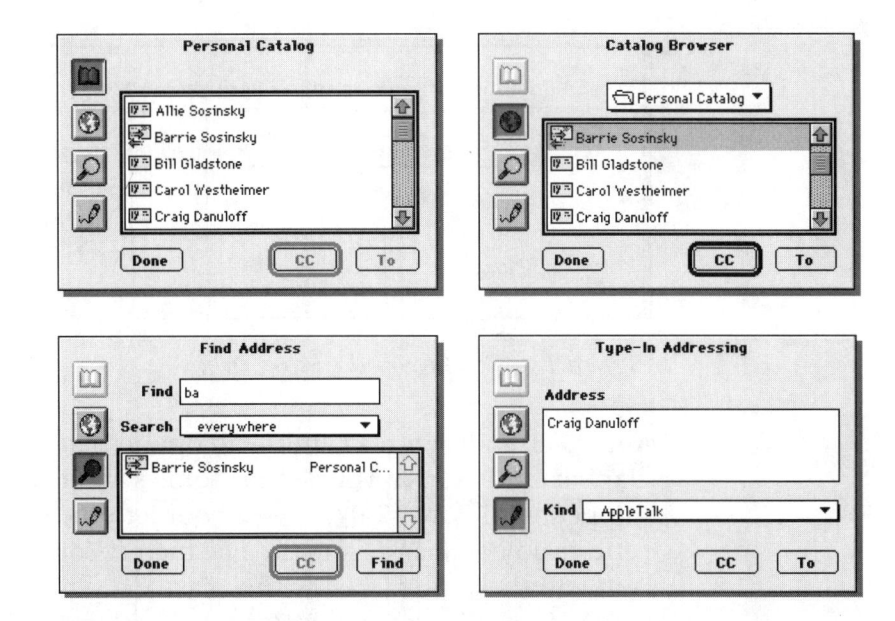

Figure 14-22: The four panels of the Catalog Access Panel.

You add the Subject title of your letter by simply typing it. Finally, to add enclosures you click the Card icon over the Enclosures section of the Mailer. An Open standard file dialog box appears, allowing you to navigate and select the file or folder you wish to enclose.

AppleMail offers you several printing, formatting and handling options. You can print the Mailer as a separate cover page, and the Footer with the From and Subject fields and page number appearing at the bottom of each page. When you are ready to send your letter, choose the Send command from the Mail menu. The Send dialog box shown in Figure 14-23 appears. Options in this dialog box are to send as an AppleMail compatible and editable letter, a bit-mapped graphic or snapshot of the letter or some other format. Additionally you can choose the priority handling of your letter, where it sits in a queue, and whether you want the letter signed using a DigiSign Signer file. Digital signatures are covered in the next section. PowerShare accounts don't need digital signatures for verification.

Figure 14-23: The Send dialog box.

AppleMail ships with a Letterhead option that lets you add a graphic to the top of your letter. Some sample letterheads are shipped with PowerTalk. To see your letterheads, choose the Letterhead command from the File menu. Your current default letterhead is marked with a diamond symbol. To save a new letterhead, create the letterhead within any other application and paste it into the Mailer. Then use the Save As Letterhead option to add it to your list.

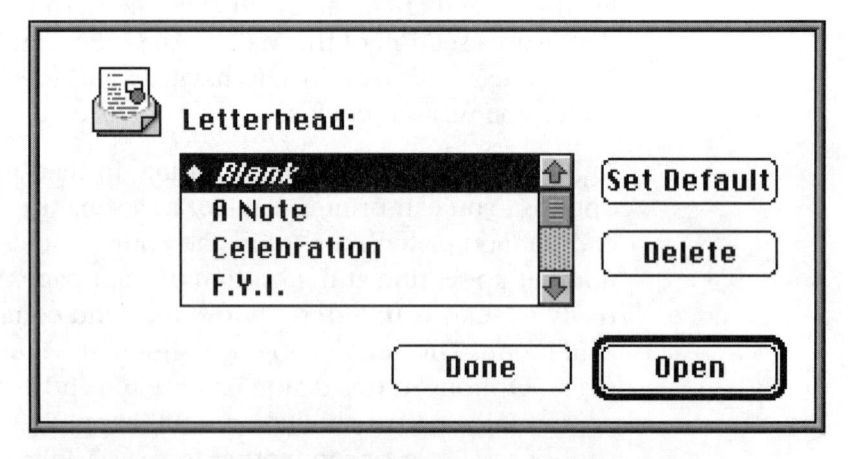

Figure 14-24: The Letterhead selection dialog box.

When you send a letter correctly it appears in your mailbox. When you double-click on the letter, you see it as it was sent. The letter and Mailer are in view. To reply to a letter, select the Reply command in the Mail menu. In the Reply To dialog box you can choose the kind of Letterhead you want to use, if any. Type your reply and choose the Send command also on the Mail menu. You can reply to all of the letter's recipients, or just the sender. You can also forward mail you receive by opening the letter and choosing the Forward command from the Mail menu. Using the Mailer, you then address the letter and send it using the Send command.

DigiSign

To electronically sign files, create a special Signer file with the DigiSign Utility program. Two different files are created, a request form and an unapproved signer. The request form contains personal information, and the unapproved Signer encrypts and encodes the information in a form that will be approved by someone in authority managing your PowerShare site. Once an approval form is received back from the authority, you use the DigiSign Utility to produce an approved Signer. Each of these different file types have unique icons, as shown in Figure 14-25. An approved Signer is what you use to authenticate your document.

Figure 14-25: Various DigiSign Signer file icons.

Caution: *To use the Signer, just drag a file in the Finder to your Signer icon, then enter your DigiSign identification code. Protect your Signer and ID code as you would a credit card, as they can be misused by another party in a similar* *fashion. To check a digital signature, open a document's Get Info dialog box and click on the signature verification button that appears to the right of the Comments section. The name of the signer then appears in a dialog box with confirmation, or DigiSign indicates that it is unable to verify a signature.*

You create a Signer approval request form by first launching DigiSign and then selecting the New Request command from the File menu. In the Signer Request dialog box (Figure 14-26) enter all relevant information. Click OK, then enter an ID code into the Identification Code Creation box that appears. When you dismiss this dialog box, you are requested to save the file to your hard drive. Saving the unapproved Signer will take a few minutes as the files are encrypted and processed. DigiSign will post a dialog box when the process is complete.

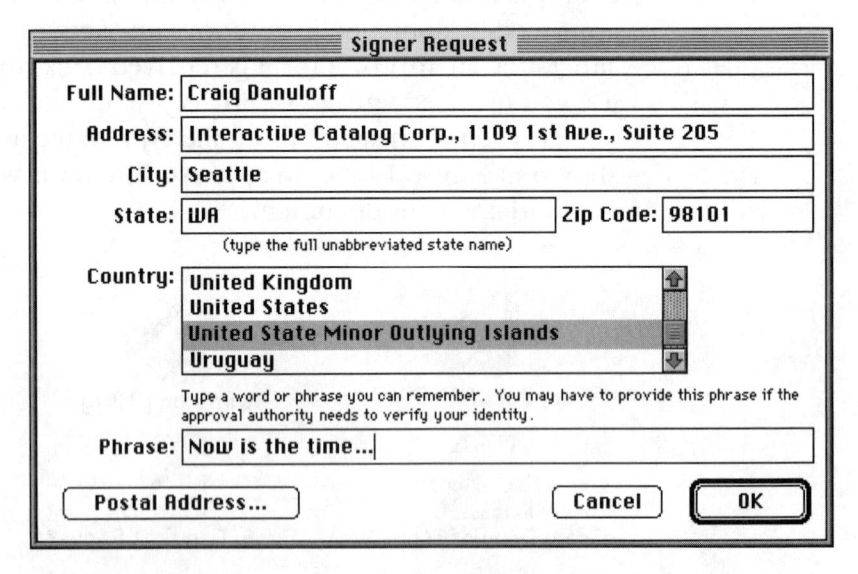

Figure 14-26: A Signer Request approval request form.

When you click OK, you will see a new Signer Approval Request Form with the encoded request information, similar to the one shown in Figure 14-27. Some companies issue approval files to the employees, others request that you send it to the RSA Certification service. Choose Save to save the request form, print the form and send it to the appropriate party along with a disk copy. You will receive a Signer Approval file back from that authority.

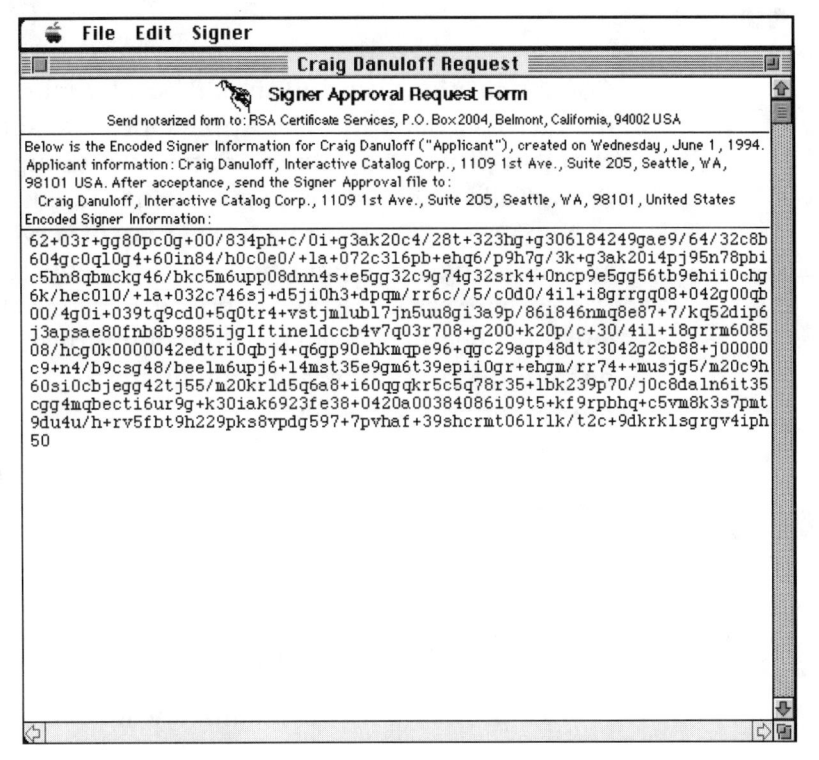

```
                File   Edit   Signer
                           Craig Danuloff Request
                         Signer Approval Request Form
              Send notarized form to: RSA Certificate Services, P.O. Box 2004, Belmont, California, 94002 USA
  Below is the Encoded Signer Information for Craig Danuloff ("Applicant"), created on Wednesday, June 1, 1994.
  Applicant information: Craig Danuloff, Interactive Catalog Corp., 1109 1st Ave., Suite 205, Seattle, WA,
  98101 USA. After acceptance, send the Signer Approval file to:
     Craig Danuloff, Interactive Catalog Corp., 1109 1st Ave., Suite 205, Seattle, WA, 98101, United States
  Encoded Signer Information:
  62+03r+gg80pc0g+00/834ph+c/0i+g3ak20c4/28t+323hg+g306184249gae9/64/32c8b
  604gc0ql0g4+60in84/h0c0e0/+1a+072c316pb+ehq6/p9h7g/3k+g3ak20i4pj95n78pbi
  c5hn8qbmckg46/bkc5m6upp08dnm4s+e5gg32c9g74g32srk4+0ncp9e5gg56tb9ehii0chg
  6k/hec010/+1a+032c746sj+d5ji0h3+dpqm/rr6c//5/c0d0/4il+i8grrgq08+042g00qb
  00/4g0i+039tq9cd0+5q0tr4+vstjmlub17jn5uu8gi3a9p/861846nmq8e87+7/kq52dip6
  j3apsae80fnb8b9885ijglftineldccb4v7q03r708+g200+k20p/c+30/4il+i8grrm6085
  08/hcg0k0000042edtri0qbj4+q6gp90ehkmqpe96+qgc29agp48dtr3042g2cb88+j00000
  c9+n4/b9csg48/beelm6upj6+14mst35e9gm6t39epii0gr+ehgm/rr74++musjg5/m20c9h
  60si0cbjegg42tj55/m20krld5q6a8+i60qgqkr5c5q78r35+1bk239p70/j0c8daln6it35
  cgg4mqbecti6ur9g+k30iak6923fe38+0420a00384086i09t5+kf9rpbhq+c5vm8k3s7pmt
  9du4u/h+rv5fbt9h229pks8vpdg597+7pvhaf+39shcrmt061rlk/t2c+9dkrklsgrgv4iph
  50
```

Figure 14-27: An Approval Request form.

To approve your Signer, copy a duplicate Signer Approval file to your start-up disk. Make a copy of your unapproved Signer file, and open that file (launching DigiSign). Select the Approve/Renew Signer command in the Signer menu. An Open standard file dialog box appears, and once you open the approval file your Signer changes to an approved Signer. You can view your approved Signer by double-clicking on it. Approval is normally for a specified period of two years and contains a unique serial number. From time to time you may want to change your ID code by opening your Signer file and selecting the Change DigiSign ID Code command from the Signer menu.

Moving On

Communications can and should be a lot more than passing files across a network. The Apple Open Collaboration Environment provides a framework for workgroup applications. PowerTalk, a new mail and messaging system software application, uses AOCE to provide a variety of services for sending and receiving communications. Using PowerTalk and PowerShare servers, you can create an electronic post office and intelligently manage the flow of information to a mailbox on your desktop. PowerTalk integrates these capabilities into the Finder.

In this chapter you've seen how to make the most of these abilities:

- Using PowerTalk to set up directories of electronic services and users.

- Send mail and files easily to other people.

- To protect, verify and authenticate communications.

Next, in Chapter 15, "Apple's System 7 Extensions," we will cover a number of advanced technologies that Apple is building into system software. The extension of today is the ROM code of tomorrow. Among the subjects being covered are QuickTime Movies, cross-platform computing issues , file translation with Macintosh PC Exchange and with Macintosh Easy Open, text-to-speech, PlainTalk voice recognition, telephony and the At Ease interface for novice users. Some of the most interesting and exciting additions to System 7.5 will be covered in the next chapter.

Chapter 15

Apple's System 7 Extensions

INITs, control panels and extensions have been an important part of the Macintosh system software for years, but only since the release of System 7 has Apple itself chosen to deliver significant new features in the form of extensions. QuickTime, PC Exchange, At Ease, Macintosh Easy Open, ColorSync, AppleScript, QuickDraw GX and ATM are all extensions that Apple has made available as part of the System 7 release.

This modular approach to system software features has several benefits for both Apple and Mac users. It makes new capabilities optional so that those who don't need a particular new feature don't have to waste the hard drive space and RAM it requires; it also allows new capabilities to be offered very quickly, without waiting for the next major system software update; and finally, it makes it possible for Apple to charge for separate features individually. Obviously, this last point may not be considered a benefit by everyone!

You've learned about some of these new extensions in other chapters, where they could be discussed in context. You'll find the following extensions discussed elsewhere:

- **Apple Guide.** The new System 7.5 help system is covered in Chapter 2, "The Finder."

- **Extension Manger.** Another new System 7.5 extension turns other extensions on and off at startup. It is described in Chapter 4, "The System Folder."

- **QuickDraw GX.** Apple's advanced graphics routines are the subject of Chapter 9, "QuickDraw GX & Fonts."

- **ATM.** Adobe Type Manager improves the display and print quality of PostScript typefaces on any Mac. It is also described in Chapter 9 as part of the discussion of fonts.

- **ColorSync.** This extension compensates for the differences between various input, viewing and output devices when you're working with color files. As part of QuickDraw GX, it is also described in Chapter 9.

- **AppleScript.** System 7's macro programming language is the subject of Chapter 11, "AppleScript."

- **AppleTalk Remote Access.** This extension for connecting by modem to an AppleTalk network is described in Chapter 13, "Working on a Network."

- **PowerTalk.** The mail and messaging system part of AOCE is described in Chapter 14, "AOCE–The Apple Open Collaboration Environment."

In this chapter, you learn about extensions that don't fit into neat categories.

Apple's extensions range from bug fixes (MODE 32) to hardware enablers (PC Exchange) to radical new technologies (QuickTime). In the following sections, you'll look at each Apple offering, with an especially detailed look at the revolutionary QuickTime extension.

MODE 32

As described in Chapter 8, "Memory Management," a number of Macintosh models contain ROM chips that render them incompatible with the 32-bit addressing capabilities in System 7. MODE 32 is an extension, developed by the Connectix Corporation, that corrects this incompatibility for the Macintosh IIx, IIcx, SE/30 and Mac II (with optional PMMU chip installed) when using System 7 Version 7.0 or Version 7.01. MODE 32 is available without charge from Apple dealers, online services and user groups.

Because Version 1.2 of MODE 32 is incompatible with virtual memory under Version 7.1, Apple has released a new *system enabler*—a special kind of extension—that will allow certain older Macs without 32-bit clean ROMs to become 32-bit compatible with System 7 Version 7.1. MODE 32 has not been updated for System 7 Pro or System 7.5, and there are no further plans at Apple for continuing support for this enabler.

PC Exchange

Mac hardware has had the capability to read PC disks for more than five years. But in that time, Apple's only software support for this capability was Apple File Exchange, a Font/DA Mover-like utility that made it possible to copy files from PC disks onto Mac disks or hard drives.

But while everyone else was wondering why PC disks wouldn't just mount at the desktop so files can be dragged to and from disks directly, Apple ignored the issue in release after release of the system software. With PC Exchange, a $79 extension, AppleSoft finally provided this capability around the time that System 7.1 was released. PC Exchange is compatible with any version of System 7.

7.5 ▶ The PC Exchange was also shipped as part of the Macintosh PowerBook/DOS Companion package. The Macintosh File Assistant, used for synchronizing files between drives, was also part of the Companion package, and it is discussed in Chapter 6, "Power Macintosh & PowerBook System Software." In System 7.5, PC Exchange was bundled in as part of the standard system software.

When PC Exchange is installed, a PC disk inserted into a 1.44mb SuperDrive floppy drive appears on the Mac desktop just like other Mac disks. A PC disk icon is shown in Figure 15-1. Via the control panel, you can specify which Macintosh application you want to use to open files from PC disks when you double-click the file icon. When you open a PC file from within an application using the Open command from the File menu, you can apply the translators that are part of that program without using the PC Exchange in the conversion.

Figure 15-1: A PC disk icon.

Files dragged to PC disks will automatically have their names changed to comply with PC file-naming conventions (eight characters and a three-character extension). Figure 15-2 shows the PC Exchange control panel.

Chapter 15: Apple's System 7 Extensions

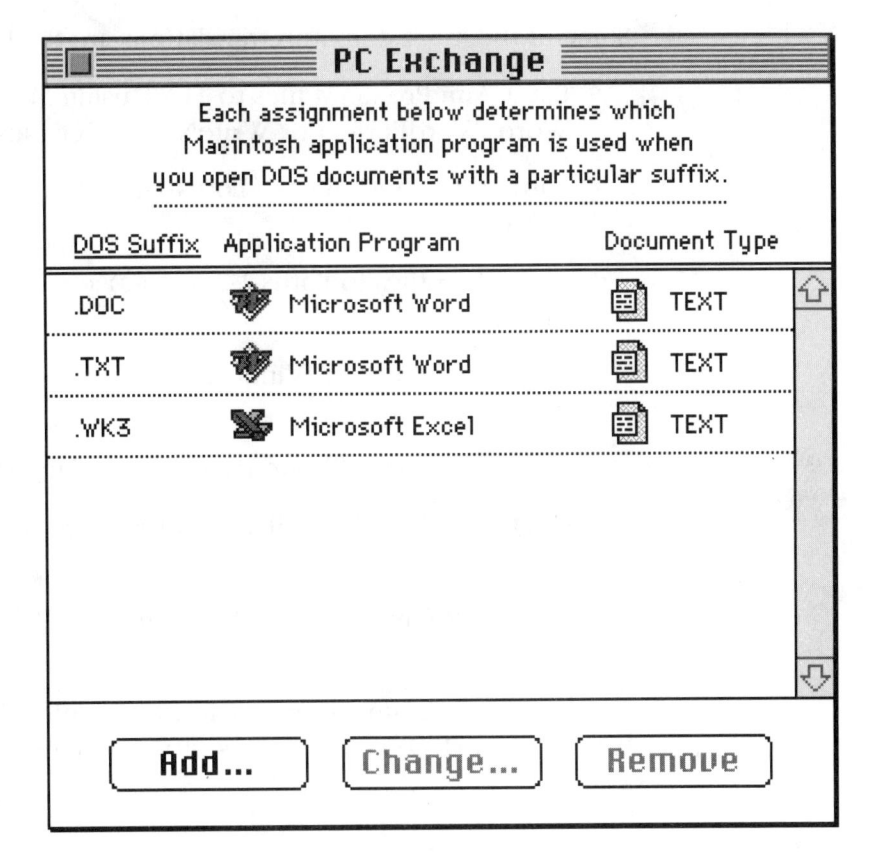

```
┌─────────────────────────────────────────┐
│▀▀▀▀▀▀▀▀▀▀▀▀ PC Exchange ▀▀▀▀▀▀▀▀▀▀▀▀▀│
│       Each assignment below determines which │
│       Macintosh application program is used when │
│       you open DOS documents with a particular suffix. │
│                                         │
│  DOS Suffix   Application Program    Document Type │
│                                         │
│   .DOC        Microsoft Word         TEXT │
│                                         │
│   .TXT        Microsoft Word         TEXT │
│                                         │
│   .WK3        Microsoft Excel        TEXT │
│                                         │
│                                         │
│       ( Add... )  ( Change... )  ( Remove ) │
└─────────────────────────────────────────┘
```

Figure 15-2: PC Exchange control panel.

Setting up the PC Exchange control panel requires only a few steps. You can add conversions of DOS files to the list in the control panel by clicking the Add button. Enter the three-letter extension, select a Macintosh application that you would like to open when that file is used, and then select the type of document you want that application to translate the DOS file into. Any translators are shown in the pop-up menu for the Document type. Figure 15-3 shows an example of a .WK3 (Lotus 1-2-3) file being converted to an Excel TEXT file.

Some of the more common translations are the following:

- Lotus Ami Pro .SAM files to TEXT using MacWrite, MS Word, WordPerfect or WriteNow TEXT files

- Lotus 1-2-3 .WKS files to Lotus 1-2-3 (Mac) and MS Excel TEXT files

- Excel .XLS files to Lotus 1-2-3 (Mac) and Excel (Mac) TEXT files

- Microsoft Word for Windows .DOC files to Word (Mac) WDBN files

- PageMaker .PM4 files to PageMaker (Mac) ALB4 files

- Quattro (DOS) .WK1 files to Lotus 1-2-3 (Mac) and Excel TEXT files

- Ventura Publisher .CHP files to Ventura Publisher VCHP files

Use the Open command from within an application to open WordPerfect (DOS) files, as no suffix is assigned to those files.

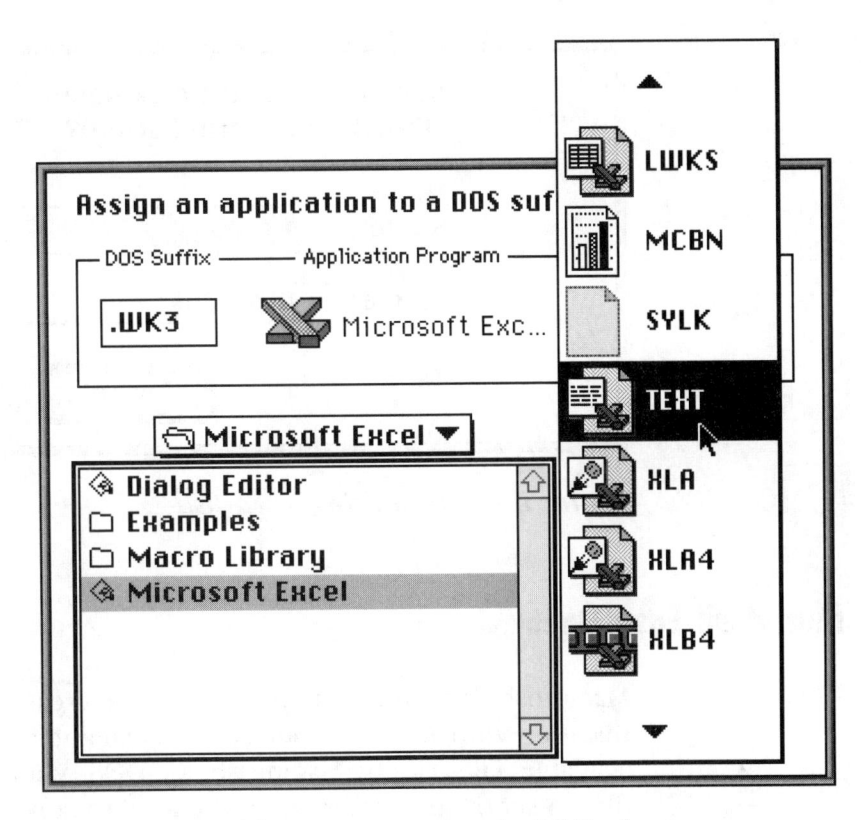

Figure 15-3: Adding a conversion in PC Exchange.

PC Exchange enables you to format a floppy disk as a PC disk using the same Erase Disk command on the Special menu that you use to format a floppy disk as a Macintosh disk. The Erase Disk dialog box is shown in Figure 15-4.

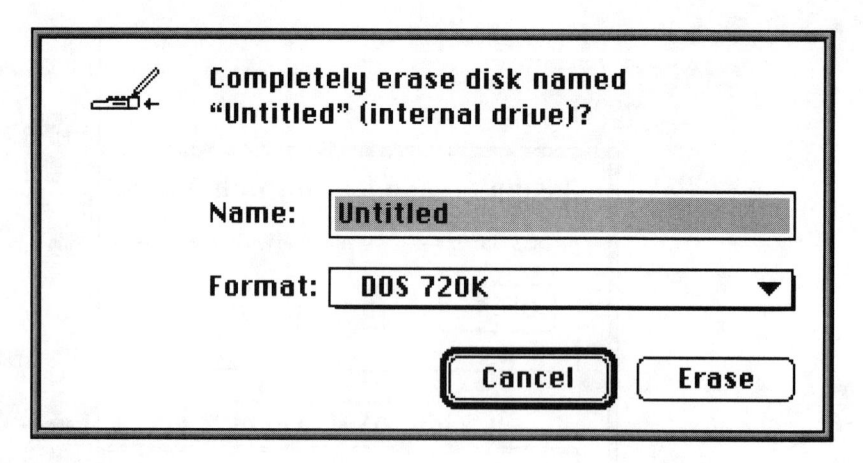

Figure 15-4: Formatting a PC disk.

Macintosh Easy Open

Macintosh Easy Open lets you open a file created by one application with another when the original application is not available. Files can be Macintosh, MS-DOS, Windows or OS/2 files. A set of "translators" files are used to convert the file, and you are prompted to select an appropriate application from a list of possible choices. If you have DataViz translators installed (part of the MacLinkPlus PC package), then Easy Open will work with these translators.

For example, when someone sends you a PICT file, you can open that file in SimpleText. Easy Open works together with PC Exchange to make opening files on your Macintosh easy.

Some Power Macintosh configurations ship with System 7.5 and Insignia Solutions' SoftWindows. SoftWindows is a native PowerPC application that emulates an Intel 80x86 microprocessor with Microsoft's Windows library. Insignia Solutions licensed the Windows Toolbox directly from Microsoft. Using Easy Open and SoftWindows, you can set up documents to open inside other Windows applications, instead of opening in Macintosh applications.

To turn Easy Open on or off, open the control panel shown in Figure 15-5. You can select the Always Show Choices check box to display the list of compatible applications; otherwise, Easy Open will make a selection for you. When you set the Include Choices from Servers check box, Easy Open will use applications on other Macintosh computers to open your file. An example of the Easy Open selection dialog box is shown in Figure 15-6.

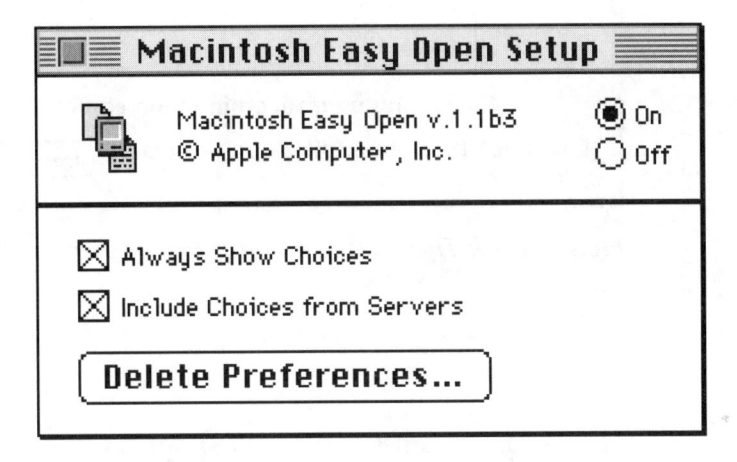

Figure 15-5: The Macintosh Easy Open control panel.

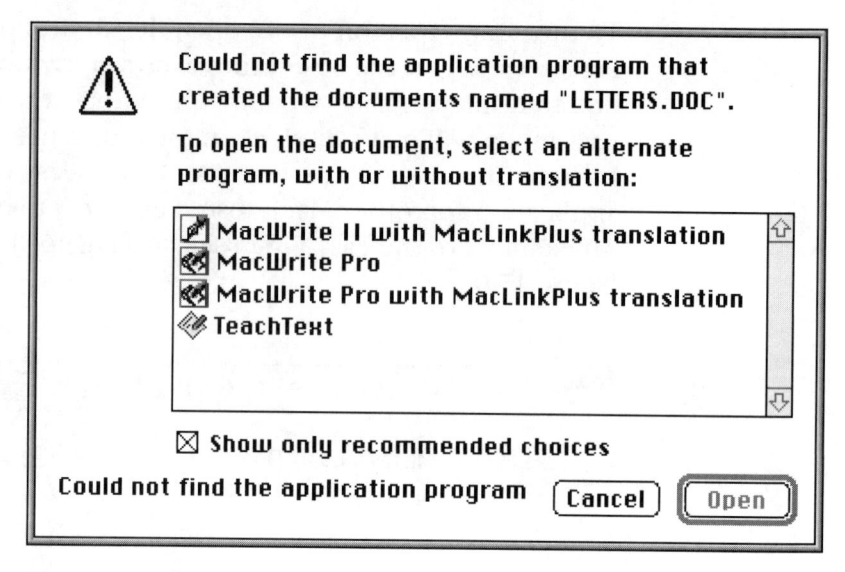

Figure 15-6: The Easy Open application selection dialog box.

At Ease

The At Ease extension is a very simple application launcher, which also provides basic security by limiting access to the Finder and control panels. At Ease is bundled with system software Version 7.01P and Version 7.1P, which ship with Macintosh Performa models. It is also available separately for $59 and can be used along with any version of System 7. A multiuser version of At Ease called At Ease for Workgroups is also sold.

When you launch At Ease, it scans your hard drive(s) for applications. You can add those applications or documents to the At Ease launcher windows using the Setup dialog box shown in Figure 15-7. When At Ease is running, tabbed index cards appear onscreen, looking a lot like HyperCard stack. Clicking (not double-clicking, as is usually the case) any application or document icon from one of these cards launches the application or document.

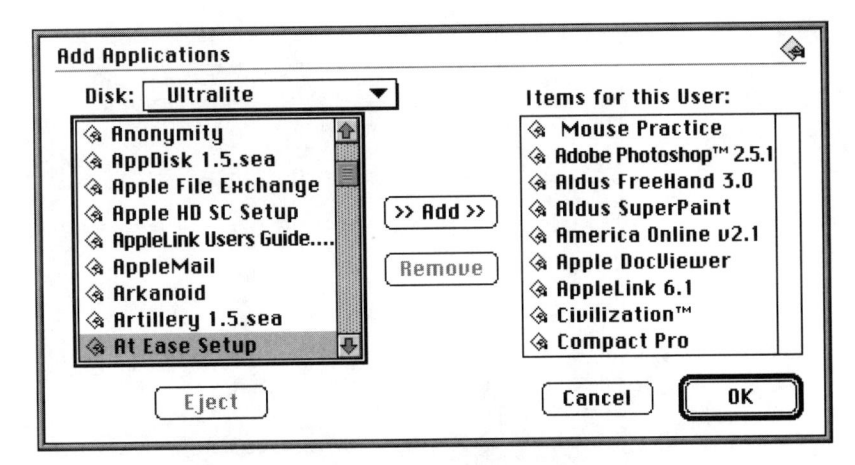

Figure 15-7: The At Ease setup dialog box.

At Ease runs on top of the Finder, and the Finder is hidden from view. Finder Hiding was added to System 7.5 in the General Controls control panel (see Chapter 4, "The System Folder"). When At Ease is running, launching any application immediately hides all other applications. The Control Panels folder is also removed from the Apple menu. To access the Finder or the Control Panels folder, choose the Go To Finder command from At Ease's File menu.

If a password was specified, you must enter it to gain Finder access. Because At Ease is password protected, an administrator can assign users to At Ease setups, and each user must supply his or her own password.

As part of the registration process, you add applications, files and other items to At Ease. You can select options that show a minimal menu, full menus and an option to speak button names. Other options let you assign a location for opening and saving files, and they allow access to the Finder. Items appear as tiles on a file folder that you can click to launch. You can switch to another "file folder" that contains additional items by clicking the tab of the folder you are interested in. In this way, you can create a hierarchy of several levels of folders. An example of an At Ease setup is shown in Figure 15-8.

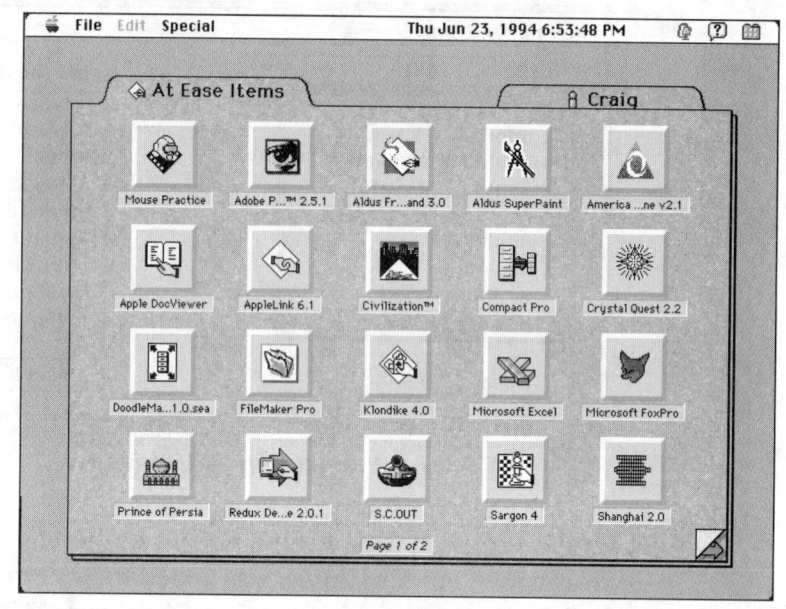

Figure 15-8: An At Ease installation.

The intent of At Ease is to provide a limited interface that novice users can work with on their Macintoshes. At Ease could be valuable to you in a home environment with young children around, in a classroom with students, in a business training environment, or when you want to provide limited access to other users and protect your Macintosh applications and files.

At Ease is a very nice utility to simplify Macintosh operations so that children can use two or three Mac programs unattended without causing their parents any computer-related grief. But as a utility for older, more experienced users, At Ease is far too limiting and much less powerful than many other launcher-style Finder replacement utilities. It's easy to see why the application has proved so successful in classroom and home settings.

QuickTime

The Macintosh has led the way for personal computers in typography, graphics, sound and high-resolution color. With the introduction of QuickTime, the Macintosh continues this tradition by leading the way in video and multimedia.

QuickTime is an extension that gives your Macintosh the ability to play and record moving video images, animation and sound in ways never before possible. It makes moving images and sounds a basic type of Macintosh data. All types of applications—word processors, databases, presentation graphics packages, page-layout programs—can now incorporate these moving images as easily as they now use standard graphics.

Any Macintosh model containing a 68020 or later processor that uses System 6.07 or later (including Systems 7.0 and above) can use QuickTime—all you need is the QuickTime extension. QuickTime Version 1.0 has been available since January 1992, and an improved version, QuickTime 1.5, was released in November 1992. The current version of QuickTime is 1.6.2. A major upgrade called Version 2.0 is scheduled for release late in 1994 and will be slipstreamed into System 7.5 after introduction. A QuickTime player for Microsoft Windows has also been released by Apple.

There is no charge for the QuickTime extension, although in typical Apple fashion that doesn't mean you will be able to get it easily or without cost. QuickTime is being distributed in a number of different formats and channels

- QuickTime is included as part of the System 7 Personal Upgrade Kit and the System 7 Network Upgrade Kit.

- The QuickTime Starter Kit features the QuickTime extension, a player utility, a few sample movies and more and can be purchased from any Apple reseller, or most mail-order software dealers, for around $160.

- QuickTime can be downloaded from online services or obtained from most Macintosh user groups.
- You can legally copy QuickTime from another Macintosh user who has it.
- Many QuickTime-dependent applications include the QuickTime extension on their distribution disks.
- QuickTime is included with all Macintosh Performa systems (but not with any other Macintosh models).

QuickTime Movies

The QuickTime extension adds support to your Macintosh for a new file format, called Movie (file type MooV.) Like other file formats, such as PICT, EPS or TIFF, the Movie file format saves a certain kind of data—in this case moving video, animation or sound (or all of these)—in a way that can be viewed at a specified rate and quality. By defining this new file format at the system software level, Apple makes it easy for application developers to support this kind of data, which encourages them to develop sophisticated ways to create and use data that changes or reacts over time (such as moving images or sounds) on the Macintosh.

A QuickTime movie acts much like any other text or graphic element—you can select it, cut, copy or paste it either within or between QuickTime-savvy applications, and store it in the latest version of the Scrapbook. In some cases, you can't even tell that an object is a movie until you select it; before that, it looks just like any other graphic element. When you select a movie, however, it displays an identifying set of controls that allow you to adjust the volume and play the movie, as well as fast-forward, reverse or randomly adjust the movie. (See Figure 15-9.)

Figure 15-9: A QuickTime movie with its controls.

The image you see in a movie element when the movie isn't playing is called its *poster*. The poster is a selected image from the movie. Because it's often not the first frame of the movie, you'll see the image of the poster jump to another image when the movie begins.

If the poster is a still-frame from the movie, a *preview* is a moving representative of the movie. Not all movies have previews, but most longer ones do. A preview gives you a quick look at the movie highlights. Many standard file dialog boxes let you see the poster or a preview before you open a movie.

QuickTime & Data Compression

One of QuickTime's most important technological breakthroughs is the real-time compression and decompression it provides to video, animation, photographs and other graphics. QuickTime supports several built-in compression schemes and can easily support others as necessary. The built-in compression is a software-only solution, capable of achieving ratios as great as 25:1 without any visible loss in image quality.

With specialized hardware, compression ratios as high as 160:1 are possible. (See Figure 15-10.)

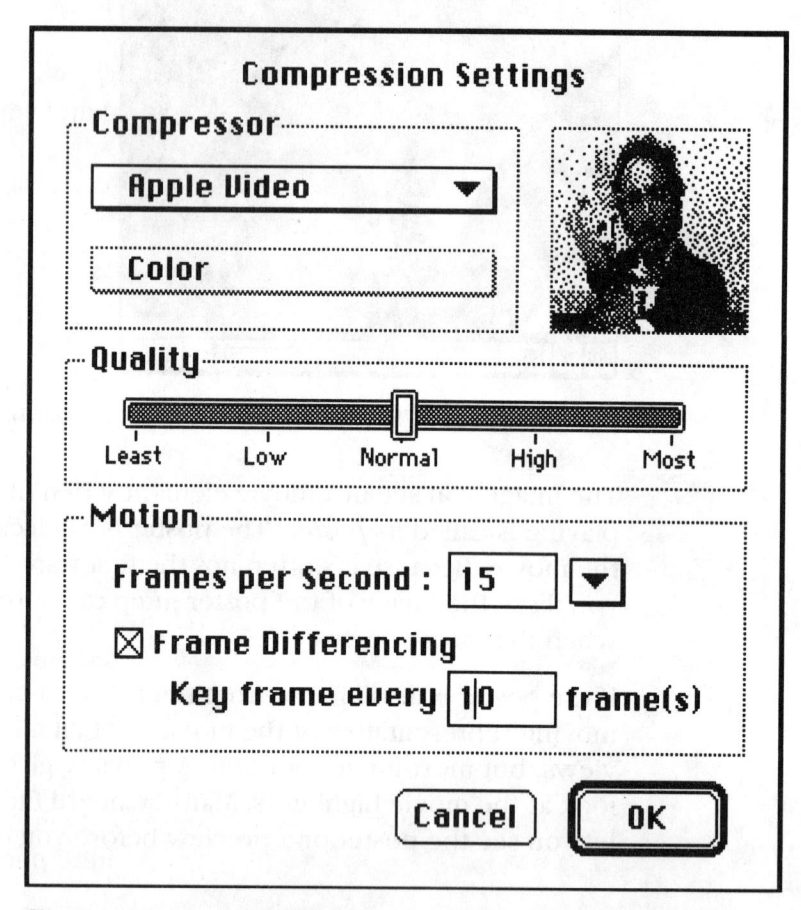

Figure 15-10: A QuickTime Compression Options dialog box.

Compression is particularly important because of all the data needed to generate moving images and accompanying sounds. A good rule of thumb for estimating movie size is that every minute of motion consumes 10mb of disk space. As another example, a seven-minute, full-size, full-resolution video movie could consume 200mb in its uncompressed form. Compressed, that same movie might need only 45mb.

Of course, most movies are significantly shorter (lasting between 5 and 30 seconds), so files in the 200k to 1mb range are common.

The actual size of a QuickTime movie depends on the following:

- **Image size.** Measured in horizontal and vertical pixels, the image size determines how large the movie will appear onscreen. The larger the image, the larger the movie file. Movies defaulted to 160 x 120 pixels in QuickTime 1.0, but Version 1.5 expands this default to 240 x 180 pixels.

- **Resolution.** QuickTime supports all the Mac's resolutions—or depths of color—including 1, 2, 4, 8, 16, 24 and 32-bit. The higher the resolution, the larger the movie file.

- **Frames per second.** Most QuickTime movies are recorded using 10, 12, 15 or 30 frames per second (fps). Without additional hardware, 15 fps is the QuickTime standard, although 30 fps, which is the standard for commercial-quality video, is supported by QuickTime 1.5. The higher the frame rate, the larger the resulting movie file.

- **Audio sampling rate.** This rate can be thought of as the "resolution" of the sound. The Macintosh supports 8, 11, 22 or 44 KHz audio sampling, although anything higher than 22 KHz requires additional hardware. The higher the sampling rate, the larger the sound portion of a movie file.

- **Compression.** As mentioned earlier, QuickTime supports a number of compression schemes; and for each you can select the degree of compression used. Increasing compression reduces movie size but sometimes affects playback quality. New compression schemes introduced with QuickTime 1.5 should reduce or eliminate these kinds of problems.

- **Content.** Beyond the above-mentioned technical factors, the actual set of sounds and images contained in a movie is what will finally determine its size. This factor makes it difficult to estimate the size of a QuickTime move solely based on its length or technical characteristics.

Using QuickTime

You can use QuickTime to watch movies (which may be included on CD-ROM disks, obtained from user groups or online services, or come embedded in documents you get from other Mac users); or you can create your own QuickTime movies. It's easy for almost anyone with a Mac to view a QuickTime movie, but creating one requires a fairly substantial investment in hardware, software and the development of what may be brand-new skills.

Most QuickTime movies now being delivered are part of CD-ROM-based information discs, providing education or information on music, history, sports, news, entertainment or computer-related topics. CD-ROM is the perfect media for QuickTime because it has huge storage capabilities (650mb), can be inexpensively reproduced and has access times sufficient to deliver good-quality playback of QuickTime movies. CD-ROM support for QuickTime has recently been enhanced by faster CD drives (such as the Apple CD 300) and performance improvements included in QuickTime 1.5.

Most movies delivered as part of these CD-ROM discs are viewed using some controlling application, such as HyperCard or a MacroMedia Director player, that is included on the CD. Movies included as part of other documents can be viewed from within their applications, such as Microsoft Word, Aldus Persuasion and others. To watch movies which exist only as stand-alone Movie files, you'll need a player application.

Several movie-player applications are available as shareware or freeware. One from Apple is called Simple Player, and another is called Movie Player. Aladdin Systems, makers of the StuffIt line of compression utilities, offers a player called Popcorn (the perfect movie companion), which is available online and from most user groups. If you ever need to view a movie but you don't have one of these movie-player utilities handy, just create a document using any QuickTime-compatible application, import the movie and play it from within the document.

QuickTime 2.0

Shortly after System 7.5 is released, QuickTime 2.0 will appear. QuickTime 2.0 has many new features, most of which are performance-related and "under the hood." You will notice improved performance, especially on Power Macintosh computers. Movies can now vary from 240 x 180 pixels at 1 fps to up to 320 x 240 pixels at 30 fps depending on your Macintosh type. The MoviePlayer 2.0 application replaces the Simple Player application that shipped previously with QuickTime.

The following aspects of QuickTime have undergone improvement in Version 2.0:

- **QuickTime DataPipe.** The DataPipe improves performance on all types of CD-ROM drives. Tracks can be preloaded into memory prior to playback.

- **Music.** Movies can now contain music tracks. Data is stored as a series of note commands like MIDI.

- **MPEG.** When you install an MPEG board in your Macintosh, you can use MPEG compression with QuickTime. These routines further improve performance of video playback.

- **TimeCode.** QuickTime 2.0 can store a timecode (SMPTE or otherwise) in a movie. Timecodes point to the source tape.

- **Burnt Text.** QuickTime 1.6 introduced anti-aliasing text. Version 2.0 adds the capability to store prerendered text in a compressed image for faster redraw.

- **Drag and Drop.** With version 2.0, you can drag one movie to another to perform a paste operation. You can also pull a movie from the Finder when you are in MoviePlayer to drag it into a sequence. When you drag a text movie into a SimpleText document, the text is extracted into the document.

- **Power Macintosh.** All compressors and decompressors are now native on the PowerPC. Cinepak compression is two and a half to three times faster on a model 8100 than on a Quadra 950.

- **Copyright Dialog.** You can now add copyright information directly to a movie. You use the Set Movie Information command in the MoviePlayer 2.0 application to add the information in the authoring mode. View the information with the Show Copyright command.

- **Miscellaneous.** A number of other small changes have been added. They include the ability to play AIFF sound files directly, a standard export dialog box and an improved grayscale slider bar.

PlainTalk

Many system extensions are specific to particular models of Macintosh computers. Some of these extensions install directly in an installation. Others are released on disk when you purchase those computers. The Macintosh Telephony Architecture, which lets an AV Mac interface to a telephone, is an example. PlainTalk is another notable extension that comes with your computer purchase.

Power Macintosh and AudioVisual (AV) Macintosh computers support Apple's PlainTalk voice-recognition technology. Using PlainTalk, you can speak to a computer with DSP capabilities and have your spoken words translated to Finder or application action or menu commands. PlainTalk works well and is a boon to impaired users.

PlainTalk uses a trainable system in which you speak words into the computer to make them recognized. The system trades some accuracy for general recognition by any user using your language.

Turn PlainTalk on using the Speech Setup control panel shown in Figure 15-11. PlainTalk uses about 2mb of RAM. A slider bar lets you set how tolerant speech recognition is. PlainTalk responds initially to the name "computer." You also can switch your computer to other cute personalities.

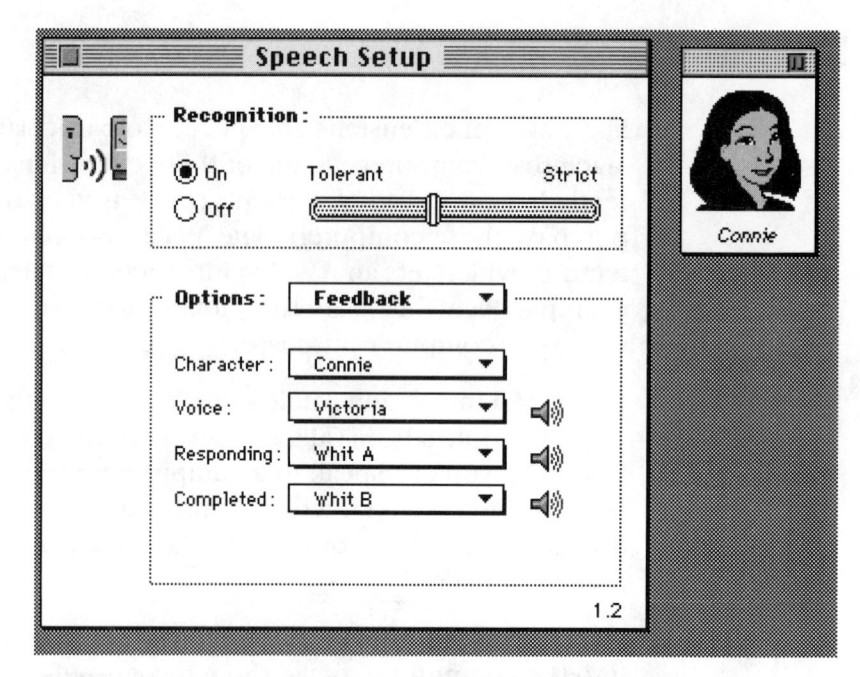

Figure 15-11: PlainTalk's Speech Setup control panel.

When PlainTalk is on, a speech recognition feedback window appears on your screen. This window floats above all others. The condition of speech recognition is shown iconically. States include sleeping, listening, hearing, working and confused. Figure 15-12 shows how the character Pat shows these states in the feedback window.

	Sleeping: Speech recognition is inactive. To make it active, press the attention key you chose in the Speech Setup control panel.
	Listening: The computer is ready to hear you speak a command.
	Hearing: The computer is hearing you speak a command.
	Confused: The computer doesn't understand what you said. You may have used words it doesn't know.
	Working: The computer is performing the command you spoke.

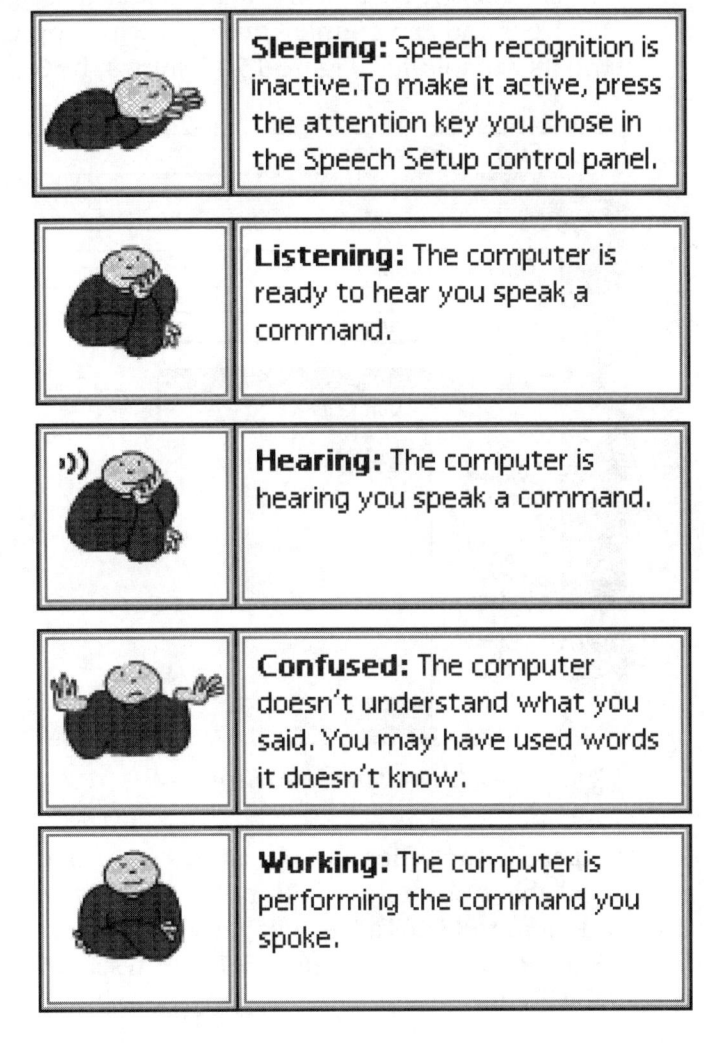

Figure 15-12: Speech recognition's five states.

PlainTalk uses AppleScripts to create speakable macros. The process of recording macros is similar to what you learned in Chapter 11, "AppleScript." PlainTalk ships with the Speech Editor, a macro recorder similar to the Script Editor. The syntax of a speech macro and the programming language uses the AppleScript vocabulary. PlainTalk also uses a version of QuicKeys and can couple QuicKeys with AppleScript to extend its capabilities. Figure 15-13 shows the Speech Editor.

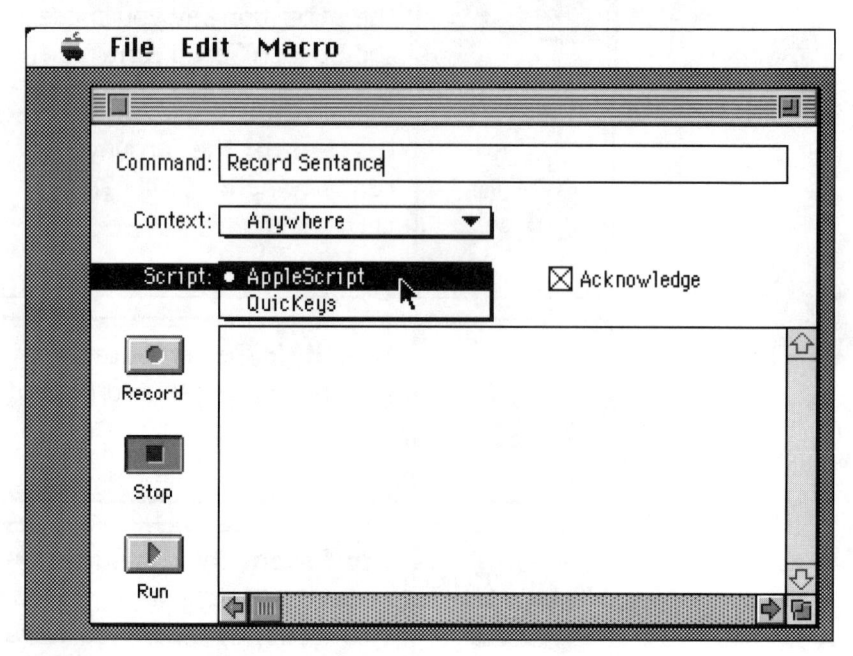

Figure 15-13: The Speech Editor.

You can launch files and put aliases or named scripts into a Speakable Items folder within the Apple Menu Items folder to add them to PlainTalk's vocabulary. Any menu resource can be chosen by name. Figure 15-14 shows a typical Speakable Items folder.

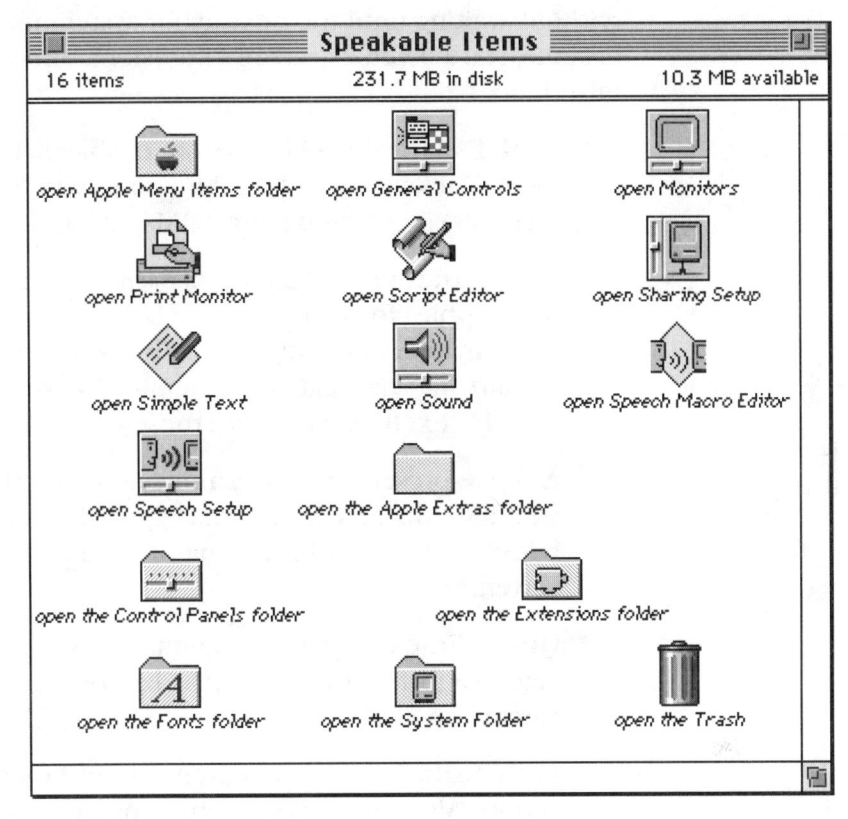

Figure 15-14: A Speakable Items folder.

Moving On

With the advent of System 7 and the use of extensions, Apple has embarked on an innovative new method of delivering improvements and corrections to its system software. Extensions allow Apple and other developers to deliver specialized capabilities and enhancements only to those users who want and need them, without forcing uninterested users to waste drive space and memory working with an unwanted extension. Extensions also allow Apple to deliver new features without waiting until the next major system upgrade. Apple has released a diverse array of extensions since System 7 was introduced.

- **MODE32** (or the 32-bit system enabler) allows certain older Macs to use 32-bit addressing (and therefore, more memory) by making their ROMs 32-bit clean.

- **PC Exchange** lets Mac users easily mount on the desktop floppies formatted for the DOS environment. It also helps map documents created by DOS applications to certain Mac applications. Macintosh Easy Open works with PC Exchange to make these translations.

- **At Ease** presents a less complicated interface to children and first-time Mac users. It also guards against the possibility of important files being deleted or changed inadvertently.

- **QuickTime** brings video, animation and sound to the Mac in a format that is standard across the entire Macintosh line.

- **PlainTalk.** This system extension for Power Macintosh and AV Macs enables speech recognition. It uses AppleScript and QuicKeys to create speakable macros.

But despite Apple's continuing efforts to enhance the Mac's operating system through the release of new extensions, many users are still wishing for everything except what they already have. As has often been the case in the development of the Macintosh, a host of third parties have filled the gaps left by Apple by releasing special utilities that pick up where System 7 leaves off. In the next chapter, we'll take a look at some of the best shareware and commercial utilities available for System 7.

Chapter 16

Third-Party Utilities

Apple isn't the only company that has released utilities to augment System 7. Dozens of programmers—from small firms to large corporations—have found ways to improve Apple's system software. These modifications affect nearly every aspect of the system, including the Apple menu, Balloon Help, dialog boxes, fonts, the Finder, icons, File Sharing and more.

In this chapter, you'll look at dozens of the best utilities available for System 7. Some of these utilities are available without charge from online services or user groups, some are shareware (which means you can try them out for free but must send in a specified payment to their author(s) if you decide to keep them), and others are commercial packages available from your favorite software reseller.

Apple Menu Utilities

Some of the first utilities for System 7 overcame a shortcoming most people found immediately obvious: folders in the Apple menu should hierarchically display their contents. (Although System 7.5 addresses this problem from within the Apple Menu Options control panel, previous versions of System 7 do not.) Most of these early programs were public domain or shareware programs that allowed displays of up to five levels of subfolders. Since their origination, these utilities have matured, offering a range of options at a range of prices. (See an example in Figure 16-1.)

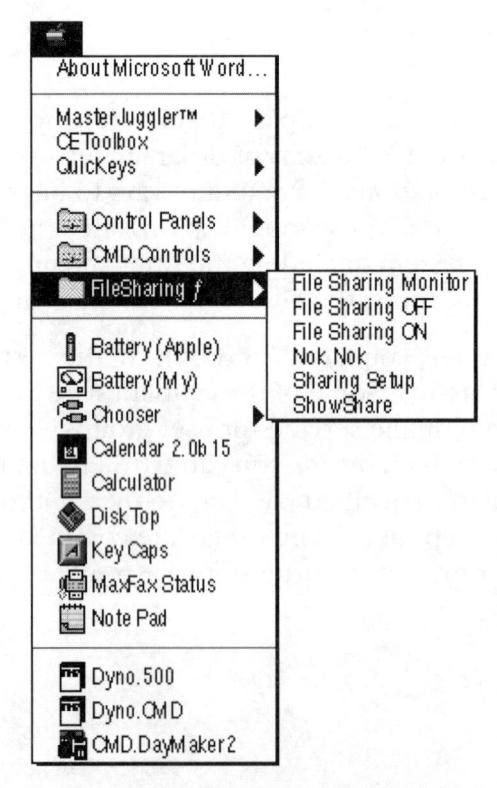

Figure 16-1: NowMenus provides a wide range of options for creating hierarchical menus.

HAM 1.0
Inline Design; $99

HAM is the only stand-alone commercial hierarchical menu utility reviewed here; the others I discuss are part of some larger utility package. As such, it's no surprise that HAM offers the widest range of menu control options, or that it is the largest utility of its kind—more than 100k for the control panel plus up to 100k for its preferences file—and the most expensive.

In addition to enabling hierarchical display, HAM lets you sort Apple menu items by name, size, kind or label, or reorder the items in a custom order. This ability to customize the order of items is unique and really improves the functionality of the Apple menu. HAM also adds its own item to your Apple menu, the Recent Items folder. This folder lets you quickly access the applications, files, folders and servers you have opened most recently. Finally, HAM offers the ability to launch a group of applications and documents with a single selection by grouping them into a single Apple menu item.

NowMenus 4.01 (part of Now Utilities)
Now Software; $85.95

NowMenus is a descendant of HierDA, the first utility that ever presented hierarchical Apple menus. HierDA, which was later renamed DA Menuz, provided hierarchical access to control panels, the Chooser and other desk accessories under System 6. This extensively redesigned version is a part of the great Now Utilities package.

NowMenus lets you do almost anything you could ever dream of doing with the Apple menu. You can freely reorder items, add separator bars and even include special hierarchical menus listing the most recent applications or documents you have used. Or you can include an Other... command that lets you launch any program you have not added to your Apple menu.

Beyond these Apple menu customizations, NowMenus also supports two other drop-down menus from your menu bar—one at the far right and one at the far left—both of which you can customize as application launchers. Finally, it provides a great memory map that can help you track how your RAM is being used, and a utility for changing the RAM requirements of your applications.

MenuExtend (part of Alsoft Power Utilities)
Alsoft; $65

This straightforward utility adds hierarchical support to the Apple menu and provides an option that sorts each submenu so that files and folders are listed separately. Not much flash, but a solid utility that doesn't hog much memory. It is perfect for PowerBooks, or whenever memory and disk space are limited.

PowerMenus (sold separately or bundled with PowerWindows)
Kiwi Software; $39.95

Another small and fast program, PowerMenus offers several very nice options including control over the font used in your Apple menu and the ability to show more than five levels of hierarchical menus. It also allows you to specify if menu changes should be updated manually or automatically, which makes it possible to access Apple menus on the PowerBook without causing the hard drive to spin up.

MenuChoice
Kerry Clendinning; shareware $15

Its shareware status makes this hierarchical menu utility a good low-cost offering. Hierarchical menus are provided for all Apple Menu Items folders, and a Recent Items folder is added automatically, but no control over the order of Apple menu items is provided.

Trash Utilities

There's room for improvement everywhere, even in the Trash. Although Apple made some Trash-related improvements in System 7, the following utilities take waste management to entirely new levels.

TrashMaster 1.1
Utilitron; $69.95

This utility adds just about every function you can imagine to the Trash. Most noticeably, it adds a hierarchical menu to your Empty Trash command that lists the name of each mounted volume separately and then the names of files from each of those volumes that are currently in the Trash. By selecting volumes or file names, you can selectively delete items from the Trash, leaving unselected items alone. A progress dialog box lists the name of each file or folder as the Trash is emptied.

The TrashMaster control panel lets you take further control of the way trash is treated, allowing you to define filters that can specify when your trash will be emptied based on the length of time files have been in the Trash, the size of trashed files, the type of trashed files, or the applications that created these files. You could, for example, specify that files over 100k be emptied from the Trash every day, that files created by Microsoft Excel be emptied every hour, and that all files be emptied once they've been in the Trash for a week. The Incinerator option allows you to actually overwrite the space a file occupies on a hard disk when it is emptied from the Trash. You can use this option for any or all files emptied from the Trash as specified by your filters.

TrashPicker 1.0

Bill Johnson & Ron Duritsch; shareware $10

TrashPicker is slightly less extensive than TrashMaster but does a great job of adding the kind of intelligence to the Trash that Apple probably should have added. You can specify if and when the Trash should be emptied (for instance, it can be emptied as soon as items are thrown away), and you can also instruct TrashPicker to empty the Trash on startup or shutdown, at any timed intervals or only when available disk space falls below a certain level. (See Figure 16-2.)

Figure 16-2: The TrashPicker control panel.

TrashMan

Dan Walkowski; shareware $10

An even less extensive trash dumper, TrashMan lets you specify the number of days and hours a file should be in the Trash before it is automatically deleted. Small, efficient, and to the point.

Trash Chute 2.0
Melissa Rogers; freeware

This little System 7 utility is basically an icon for the Empty Trash command. If you place it into your Startup Items folder, the Trash is emptied each time you start up. If you put an icon of it on the desktop, you can drop files onto it just like you drag them into the Trash, but they will be trashed and emptied immediately. Watch out when using this capability for aliases, however, because the alias icon *and* the original file the alias refers to will both be deleted.

Alias Utilities

Aliases are one of the important new features introduced by System 7, but exploiting their full power requires a number of capabilities beyond those provided by Apple. The utilities in this section offer lots of powerful features, helping you keep track of aliases, make sure they are connected to their original files, create new aliases more easily and even make sure aliases get deleted when they are no longer useful.

Alias Stylist
Bill Monk/Ziff Davis Publishing; freeware, available only via Ziffnet/Mac

This simple program lets you change the default type style for new aliases, from italic to any combination of bold, italic, outline, shadow, condensed or whatever you'd like.

AliasBOSS
Scott Johnson; shareware $20

This program makes it easy to both create new aliases for groups of files and to manage the aliases that you have already created. It allows you to search for files by name, type or creator and then create new aliases of just a few or all the found files. You can even have the aliases created onto any location you specify, not just within the same folder, as is normally the case. You can search for existing aliases and verify that they are still linked to their original files. If they are not, you can relink them to old, new or different files. This capability is one that Apple definitely forgot! (See Figure 16-3.)

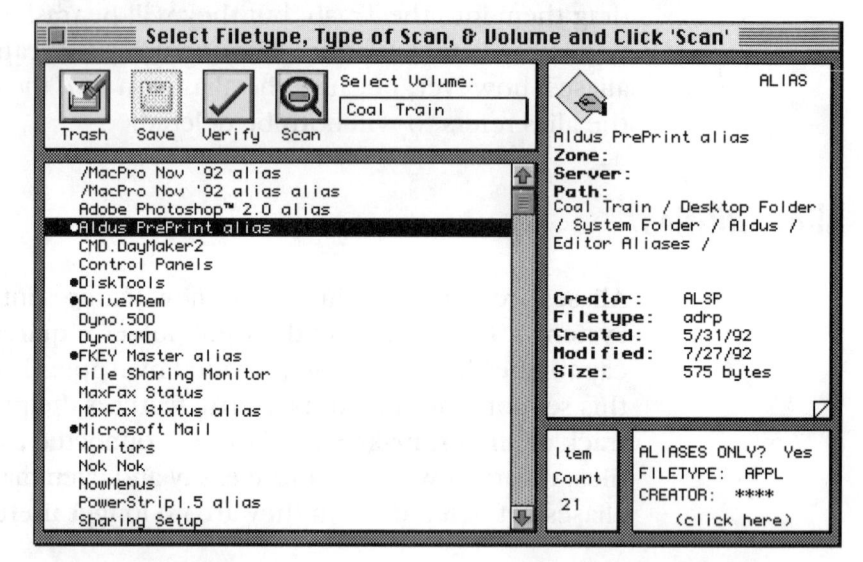

Figure 16-3: AliasBOSS offers many options for controlling your aliases.

AliasZoo

Blue Globe Software; shareware $15

This program could be called "Alias Killer" because it searches a drive for aliases, lists all that are found and allows you to delete any aliases that you no longer want. Orphaned aliases—those that are no longer linked to their original files—are listed in bold, as shown in Figure 16-4.

Figure 16-4: AliasZoo lists orphaned aliases in bold.

Mount Alias

Jeff Miller; freeware

This little control panel automates one of the tips from Chapter 3, "Managing Your Hard Drive." It automatically aliases any AppleShare or File Sharing volumes that you mount, so you can remount those volumes easily in the future by just clicking the aliases. Via the control panel, you can specify which folder these aliases are stored in and how the aliases are named.

ZMakeAlias

Mike Throckmorton/Ziff Davis Publishing; freeware

Installing this extension adds a button to your Save dialog boxes, allowing you to create and position aliases of the current file without returning to the Finder and doing it manually. This is another utility that shows Apple how it should have been done!

TrashAlias 1.1.1
Maurice Volaski; freeware

One of the little annoyances of the way aliases are implemented in System 7 is that when you delete a file that has been aliased, the alias(es) remains on your hard drive even though it is no longer functional. This extension eliminates that problem, automatically deleting aliases when the files they point to are deleted.

Is this capability really worth a stand-alone utility? Probably not, unless you work with aliases extensively. It is a nice idea though, and we hope Apple builds this functionality into future versions of the system software.

Font Managers

With the introduction of System 7's capability to add fonts without the Font/DA Mover, and Version 7.1's Fonts folder, some people thought that the need for third-party font-management utilities was going to subside. Nothing could be further from the truth. Unless you seldom add or delete fonts, you need one of the font utilities described here.

These programs allow you to access and use fonts that are not actually loaded in your System file or located in the Fonts folder. The fonts stay in their font suitcases, located anywhere on any mounted volume, but act as if they were in the System file or Fonts folder. The programs also let you add or remove fonts very quickly and easily, and because they don't really copy fonts in and out of the System file, there is no chance of harming the System file itself. They also let you add and remove desk accessories, and provide a number of other enhancements to your Macintosh.

Suitcase II
Fifth Generation Software; $55

This is the utility that introduced the idea of font management to the Macintosh, and it remains the most popular font utility. Beyond the basic capability of adding and removing fonts, Suitcase lets you

- **Work with font sets.** You can name and save groups of font suitcases—which you might need to use for different projects—and then load or unload all the fonts in a set with a single mouse click.

- **Resolve name/ID conflicts.** Suitcase alerts you to any conflicts between fonts you try to open and provides a dialog box that allows you to rename one of the fonts or cancel the font opening.

- **Create empty suitcases.** System 7 users soon discover that there is no way to create new empty suitcases without Font/DA Mover Version 4.2, and because Apple does not provide it with System 7, Suitcase provides a handy command to solve the problem.

- **Share fonts for networks.** Many large font users store their fonts on network file servers that are shared by many users. Suitcase specifically supports network font use, allowing you to open shared fonts so other Macs can use them simultaneously.

MasterJuggler
Alsoft; $25

MasterJuggler has always been the upstart competitor to Suitcase, and it offers a user interface I prefer over Suitcase. All the basic functions are the same—it can remember where font suitcases are located, show you samples of any selected fonts, compress fonts to save hard drive space, work with FKEYs and DAs, automatically resolve font ID conflicts, and it lets downloadable fonts work from any folder on your hard drive.

In addition, MasterJuggler lets you attach sound files and assign different sounds to nine different system activities (disk eject, shutdown, launch and so on). It also features the FontShow utility (that can provide extensive font samples), methods of launching applications from either a dialog box or pop-up program list, and a utility to locate and correct any name or ID number conflicts in your font, DA, FKEY or sound files. (See Figure 16-5.)

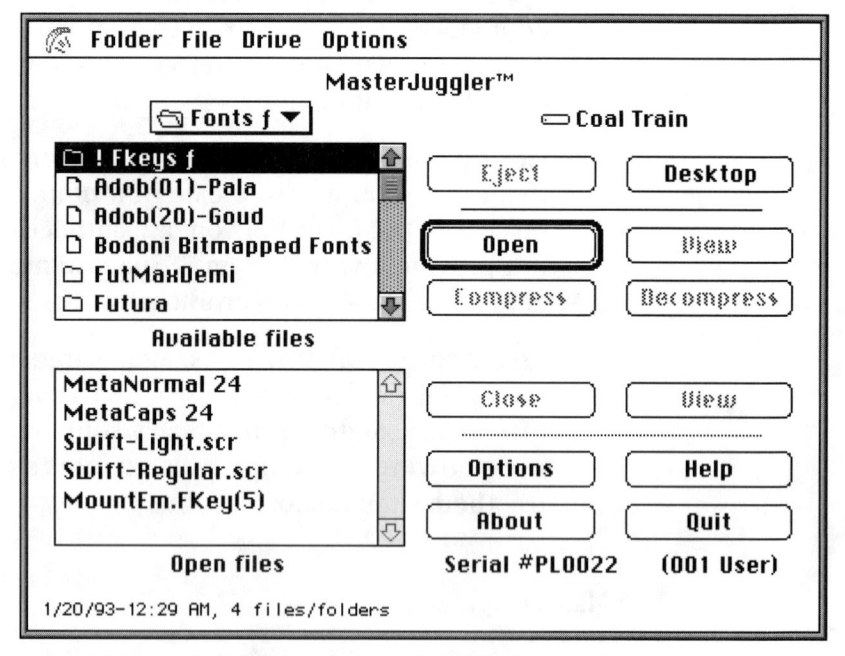

Figure 16-5: MasterJuggler has some features Suitcase can't match.

Carpetbag

James Walker; shareware $5

Another shareware alternative offering basic functionality at a very low price, Carpetbag lets you specify folders that contain your fonts, and it will either automatically open fonts in those folders at startup, or you can use the control panel to open or close fonts at any time. If you use fonts extensively, one of the commercial programs is probably more appropriate, but for the marginal font fanatic, CarpetBag is a nice (and cheap) alternative.

System Software Selectors

Although the recommended procedure for moving to System 7 is to have it replace System 6 entirely, some people prefer to keep both system software versions installed, or must do so in order to keep using applications that are incompatible with System 7. It is possible to have both system software versions installed on one hard drive, and alternate between them without problems, using one of the utilities described here.

Installing System 7 without removing System 6 is relatively easy: simply move the Finder out of the System 6 System Folder to some other location (but don't trash it) and then install System 7. Following these easy steps will create a new System 7 System Folder. Then copy the System 6 Finder back into the System 6 System Folder. Use one of the utilities described here to "bless" one of these folders as the one you want used at startup.

System Switcher
Canon Sales; freeware

A list of available volumes is presented by System Switcher, and clicking the Open button for any selected volumes lists available System Folders. To select the folder you want to designate as the System Folder when you next restart, highlight the folder and click the Switch button. (See Figure 16-6.)

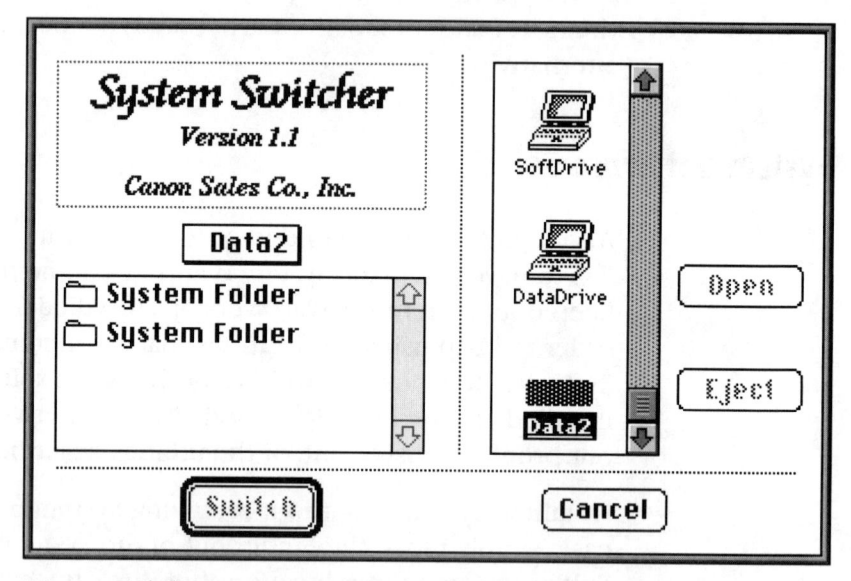

Figure 16-6: System Switcher lets you "bless" one of many System Folders.

System Picker
Kevin Aitkin; freeware

System Picker performs the same function as System Switcher, but it works a little differently. When you launch System Picker, it automatically searches for all System Folders on all mounted volumes, and presents a pull-down menu that you can use to select the one you want to use. (See Figure 16-7.)

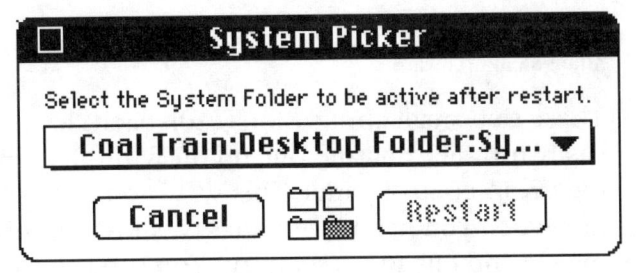

Figure 16-7: System Picker scans for System Folders and lets you pick one as the active folder.

File Sharing Utilities

One of the first items to appear on the wish list of any File Sharing user is a better way to know who is connected to your Mac (and when they are connected). Another frequent wish is for a quicker way to turn File Sharing on and off. These and other capabilities are added by the utilities described here.

Nok Nok
Trik; $49.95 (AppleShare 3.0 version, $295)

When this control panel is installed, you can choose to be informed of users logging onto your Mac with a dialog box, a flashing icon in the menu bar, a sound, the opening of the File Sharing Monitor or some combination of these options. A special version is available for use on AppleShare 3.0 networks.

ShowShare
Robert Hess; freeware

This rather comprehensive utility adds to your menu bar a File Sharing icon that shows you the status of File Sharing (starting up, on, off, shutting down or error) and provides a drop-down menu with commands that let you set user preferences, check user information and even send messages to logged-on users via the network.

File Sharing Toggle
Adam Stein; freeware

These two small applications (10k each) let you quickly and easily turn File Sharing on and off without going to the Sharing Setup control panel. This way, you can use File Sharing just when you need it, which saves RAM, improves performance and enhances security. You can leave these apps on your desktop, alias them to the Apple menu or use them with your favorite launching or macro utility to make them easily accessible.

Extension Managers

You know you've arrived as a Mac user when your extensions get out of control. There are so many great extensions and control panels available (and not-great-but-interesting ones) that it's easy to find that you have installed too many, which leads to conflicts, slowdowns and general confusion. In System 7.5, as you saw in Chapter 3, "Managing Your Hard Drive," you can use the Extension Manager to turn extensions on and off. For other versions of System 7, you may want to use one of these other products.

Each of the utilities described here lets you take control over the chaos of your start-up documents, selectively turning them on or off without having to move them in or out of their respective folders. Most also let you build sets of extensions, so you can load the group of extensions relevant to the work you intend to do. You can also use an extension manager to avoid memory-intensive extensions (and thus, possible conflicts) when you know you won't need them. For example, you could use one group when you're going to use all your telecommunications programs, another when you want to use File Sharing, another when you want just the minimum number loaded and so on.

Init Picker
MicroSeeds; $59.95

The best of the first-generation extension managers, Init Picker remains a powerful tool, although it is no longer the most powerful program available. In addition to the basic extension manager features described above, it allows you to select one of your extension groups by holding down a key at startup, and to configure a key that temporarily disables all extensions. Another nice feature of Init Picker is that—unlike other extension managers—it does not change the file type of the extension it disables.

Startup Manager (part of Now Utilities)
Now Software; $149

My current favorite extension manager, Startup Manager boasts all the basic capabilities an extension manager needs plus several powerful enhancements: icon wrapping is included (taking care of the problem of having more extensions than can fit along the bottom of your screen at startup); you can force the display of icons for extensions that don't normally display icons; extension conflicts can be controlled using a very handy linking feature, which prevents conflicting extensions from running simultaneously or loading in the wrong order; and any extension that crashes at startup is automatically temporarily disabled. (See Figure 16-8.)

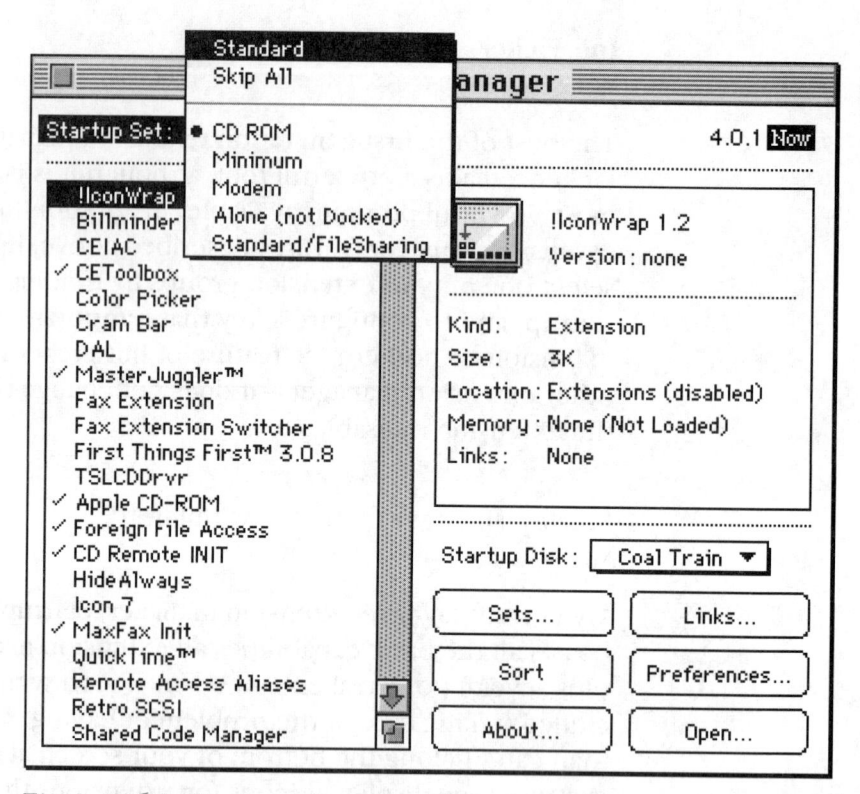

Figure 16-8: Startup Manager packs lots of features into an extension manager.

On Startup
Icom Simulations (On Cue II); $99.95

This extension manager provides all the basic capabilities you'll need, including start-up access and extension groups. It can automatically turn off extensions that cause crashes at startup, and it provides a handy way to select from extension groups at startup (just hold down the mouse button after the Welcome to Macintosh dialog box appears).

Extension Manager
Apple Computer; freeware

Even if Apple has officially ignored the Mac's need for an extension manager, at least one of their employees hasn't. Richard Batista's Extension Manager is a nice freeware program, offering all the basic capabilities, including reordering items, creating and choosing extension groups, and the ability to configure extension loading at startup.

Init Loader
Ian Hendry; freeware

This System 7 utility isn't really an extension manager, but it adds the capability of loading extensions that are stored in folders other than the Extensions folder, Control Panels folder or the System Folder itself. It allows you to designate any other folders that hold extensions and have those extensions load, even if those folders are on other volumes—even remote network volumes.

Printer Extensions

As discussed in Chapter 9, QuickDraw GX introduces a new class of system extensions called printer extensions. Printer extensions can customize your printer, controlling a wide variety of printer functions. You can limit access to printers, do custom print jobs, enable different kinds of print modes and much more. It will be some time before all the possibilities of printer extensions are mined by developers.

Pierce Print Tools

Pierce Software, Inc.; $95

Pierce Print Tools (PPT) is a collection of print extensions and utilities that offers a whole new range of printer options for any Macintosh application. You can manage shared output devices, personalize printout and save money by ganging print jobs together. Figure 16-9 shows a Print dialog box with Pierce Print Tools installed.

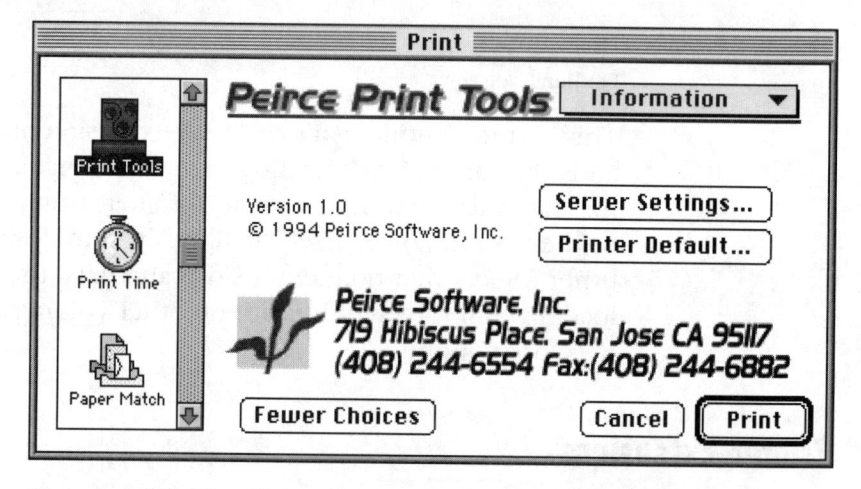

Figure 16-9: The Print dialog box of Pierce Print Tools.

PPT contains the following extension elements:

- **PrintLogger.** This extension lets you monitor the usage of your printer so that you can bill customers or clients for your materials. You can log custom data for your print jobs: P.O. numbers, job numbers, or comments. Then you can view the log by categories: user, date, page count and so on, and export the data as a file to Excel or FileMaker Pro.

- **WaterMarker.** This extension can print text or pictures on the background of a page in a specified shade of gray. These watermarks can be a company logo, the word *confidential*, *draft*, *shred* or whatever you'd like.

- **BorderMaker.** You can frame pages with a variety of border types.

- **Pamphleteer.** Using Pamphleteer, you can gang print 2, 3, 4, 6, 9 or 16 pages on each printed page. This option is useful for drafts, summaries or presentation handouts.

- **DoubleSider.** This printer extension helps you print documents on both sides of a page.

- **BackToFront.** This extension will print your pages in reverse order.

- **CoverPage.** Using this extension, you can create a cover page for each print job. You can add messages or pictures, user names, page counts, dates and other useful information.

Finder Performance Boosters

The utilities in this grouping provide a whole range of minor Finder modifications, each of which is helpful and, when taken together, should not to be missed.

System 7 Pack
Adam Stein; demoware $29.95

This great utility, written by a young man who was in high school when it was first introduced, has continued to evolve and improve. (Version 3.5 is current as of this writing.) Here are just some of the Finder enhancements provided:

- **File copying speed improvement.** By allowing the Finder to use more RAM when copying files, the time it takes to copy files from one volume to another is reduced dramatically.

- **Remove zooming rectangles.** A simple check box turns off the Finder's zooming animation which appears when folders are open, saving a few fractions of a second during folder display.

- **Quit Finder menu.** You can add this Quit menu to your Finder, making it possible to quit the Finder just like any other application, thereby freeing the memory the Finder normally uses for other purposes.

- **Set Rename Delay.** Modify the delay after a file or folder has been selected before you can rename it.

- **Change alias suffix.** I'm not sure what else besides "alias" you would like to call your aliases, but here's your chance.

- **Application linking.** Specify which application will open different document types when you don't have the creating application on your hard drive. Set Microsoft Word to open MacWrite files, for example.

- **Finder command keys.** You can modify or assign command keys to any command in any Finder menu.

- **Rename Finder commands.** For certain commands in the Finder, you can completely rename them to amuse yourself or confuse your friends.

Figure 16-10 shows a window in the System 7 Pack.

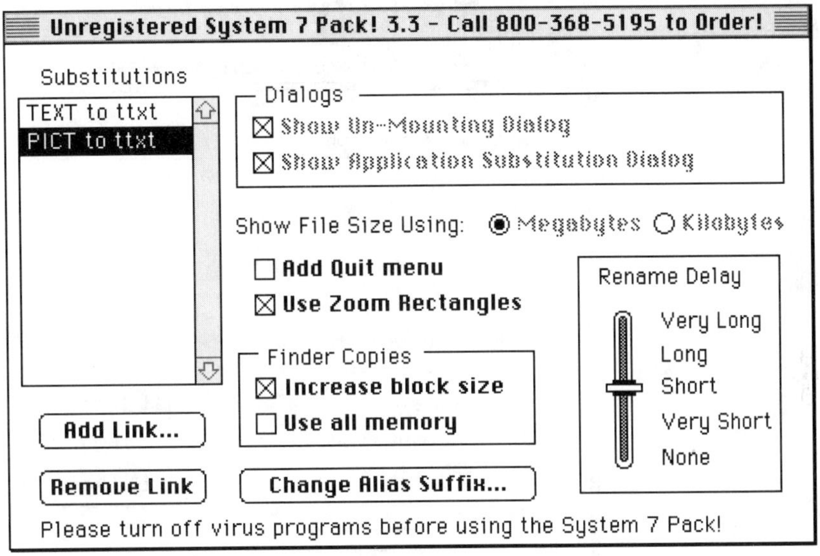

Figure 16-10: The System 7 Pack grants users the ability to change several aspects of their Finder.

SpeedyFinder7
Victor Tan; shareware $20

Another great Finder utility written by a college student, this one lets you make a number of modifications: speed up Finder copying and Trash emptying (which can be painfully slow in System 7), remove zoom rectangles, remove the rename delay and set links between stranded documents and your application programs. It can also add menu commands to certain Finder commands, add nice icons for your floppy disks, resolve "lost" aliases, change alias names and hide the Balloon Help menu while still allowing instant access to help balloons. This is a great utility with a nice user interface. (See Figure 16-11.)

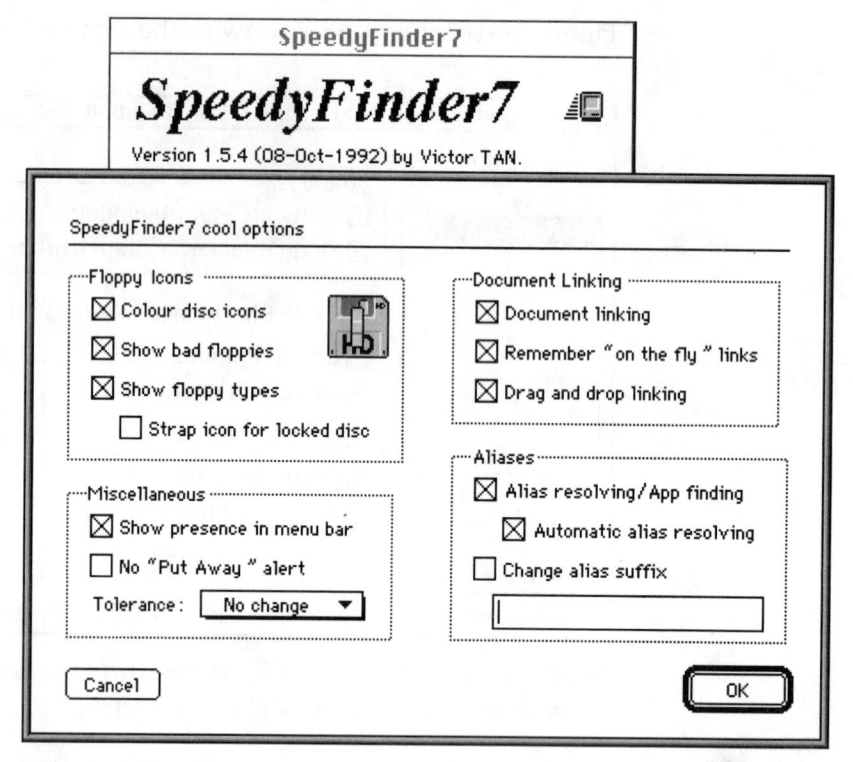

Figure 16-11: SpeedyFinder7 dialogs feature an attractive interface.

SuperBoomerang

Now Utilities, $129

The jewel of the Now Utilities package, SuperBoomerang puts hierarchical menus of recently used files, applications and folders in your menus and Open and Save dialog box. SuperBoomerang also places a search function, new folder option and other configuration options in your dialog boxes. A Macintosh is not complete without this essential utility. SuperBoomerang is a tremendous time saver.

PopupFolder
Inline Software, $59.95

Another small essential utility for navigating the Finder. With PopupFolder you click and drag on any folder to view its contents and the content of anything it contains. With one click and drag you can open a folder nested any number of layers deep. You can also use this system within Open and Save dialog boxes to view the contents of folders in the scroll box.

Utility Collections

Many System 7 utilities offer only a single function or feature and, when viewed individually, may seem rather minor. Lately, it has become popular to put together a collection of programs that all enhance System 7 in some way. Following are some of the best of these collections.

7 for Seven
Peter Kaplan; freeware

This package includes seven handy modifications for the System 7 Finder:

- **Set Rename Delay.** This option allows you to change the number of seconds you must wait after selecting a file name before the I-beam cursor appears. It is intended to undo a change in System 7 that annoys many people.

- **Change Alias Style.** By default, aliases have their file names set in italics. This option lets you pick any other type style (or type style combination) for your aliases.

- **Balloon Help Size.** If you find the 9-point size of text in Balloon Help too small, this option lets you pick a larger point size instead.

- **Application Linker.** This option lets you build links between certain document types and the application programs you would like to use to open those documents. If you use Microsoft Word as your word processor, for example, you can use this option to have MacWrite documents open in Word when double-clicked.

- **Add Quit to Finder.** The fact that the Finder is always open in System 7 means that it is also always using some RAM (about 200k). Adding a Quit command to the Finder lets you reclaim this RAM for use by other applications in memory-tight situations.

- **Show/Hide Command Key.** This option adds a command key equivalent to the Hide Others and Show All commands in the Application menu.

- **Remove ZoomRects.** When you open a window in the Finder, a slight animation effect called zooming rectangles occurs. This option lets you disable that animation, which improves Finder speed slightly.

7.0 PLUS Utilities
Robert Gibson; shareware $29.95

This series of utilities—they aren't usually packaged together but are instead available individually from online services and user groups—provides a wide variety of new and enhanced functions for System 7. Most take advantage of System 7's drag-and-drop (or drop-launching) capabilities. With drop-launching, you can, for instance, drag a document file icon onto the icon of an application, and the application will launch and open the document. In the case of these utilities, the drop-launching performs a specific function other than simply opening a file. The 7.0 PLUS Utilities include

- **Blindfold.** This program makes files or folders visible or invisible at the Finder. This capability allows you to hide files from others who may use your Mac.

- **Catapult.** Drag a document icon onto Catapult and you can then choose which application you want to use to open it. This form of on-the-fly application linking is useful for occasions when you get a file created by an application you don't have.

- **Custom Killer.** System 7 allows custom icons to be applied to files, folders or disks. This utility removes them, restoring original icons.

- **DeIcon.** If you like to leave a lot of files on your Finder desktop, you may sometimes wish there were a way to limit the amount of desktop space these files consume. With DeIcon, your files appear on the desktop with names only—no icons appear. This capability allows you to fit more files on the desktop in less space.

- **Deflate.** For the extremely space conscious, this utility will remove the help resources from application files, thereby making them slightly smaller without compromising functionality (except help capabilities).

- **Desktop Deleter.** The invisible desktop file that System 6 created on your hard drive (assuming you previously used System 6 and have not reformatted your hard drive since) is sitting uselessly around wasting disk space, until you use this utility to remove it.

- **GetInfo.** Not to be confused with the Finder's Get Info command, this utility lets you view and change technical information about a file, such as its creator, Finder flags and locked bit.

- **Locksmith.** Locksmith allows you to lock or unlock files, folders and disks quickly and easily without the trouble of the Finder's Get Info windows. Locked files and disks cannot be modified until they are unlocked. No locked item can be renamed or deleted until it is unlocked. When you used this extension with System 7's drop-launching capabilities, you can modify entire groups of items.

- **Obliterate.** This great utility provides an alternate Trash that automatically empties as soon as any files or folders are put in it. This capability saves you the trouble of using the Empty Trash command when you throw things away that you want deleted immediately. Obliterate does not, however, actually remove files from your disk, as its name might suggest. Obliterated files can still be retrieved with undelete utilities, so it should not be used for security purposes.

- **Pesticide.** Empty folders, files without data and aliases whose original items have been deleted can clutter your hard disk. Pesticide deletes these types of files, so you don't have to worry about them.

- **Recoverup.** This utility is designed to help fix the "missing files" bug that affected some people using System 7 Version 7.0 and Version 7.0.1. Tune-Up Version 1.1.1 fixed the problem, however.

- **Scale.** This utility could be called "Group Get Info" because its main use is to find the combined size of a group of files and/or folders. Normally, you must accomplish this task by either dumping all the items into a single folder and checking its size or selecting the items and Getting Info on each of them and manually adding up their sizes.

- **SCSI Startup.** Rather than using the Startup Disk control panel to specify a start-up drive, you can use this program to drag and drop a drive icon to designate your intended start-up disk. Unless you change start-up drives constantly, SCSI Startup may be the least useful utility in this set.

- **Sound Roundup.** A scavenger for beep sounds, this program makes a copy of sounds contained in any files or applications you drag onto it, and it puts them in a new folder or suitcase. You can then use these sounds in your System file or with any sound utility.

- **Stationer.** When you drag a file's icon onto this utilities icon, it toggles the Stationery Pad check box normally found in the Get Info window. This capability makes it easier to turn groups of files into Stationery Pads.

- **Pink Slip.** A control panel that adds a Quit command to the Finder, allowing you to recover the memory that the Finder uses while open.

- **Wait!** This utility is a control panel for changing the delay when renaming files and folders.

- **Zap!** This utility is a control panel for resetting the parameter RAM of your Mac, which holds information set by other control panels, such as the start-up disk, time, date, keyboard preferences, mouse preferences, screen bit-depth, volume and port configurations. Without this utility, the only way to reset the parameter RAM is to hold down Command-Shift-Option-P-R during startup.

7th Heaven
Logical Solutions; $99.95

A commercial package of utilities, 7th Heaven focuses on adding functionality to the Finder and making System 7 a little more fun. The utilities in 7th Heaven are

- **FinderExpress.** A utility to improve the allocation of memory to the Finder during file copies, thereby speeding up file copying dramatically.

- **FileMapper.** Another utility to define which application should be used to open documents whose creating applications are not available. FileMapper has a better user interface than either Catapult or the Application Linker option of Seven for 7, and it allows linking lists to be imported and exported so that once a list has been created, it can be shared among different Macs. (See Figure 16-12.)

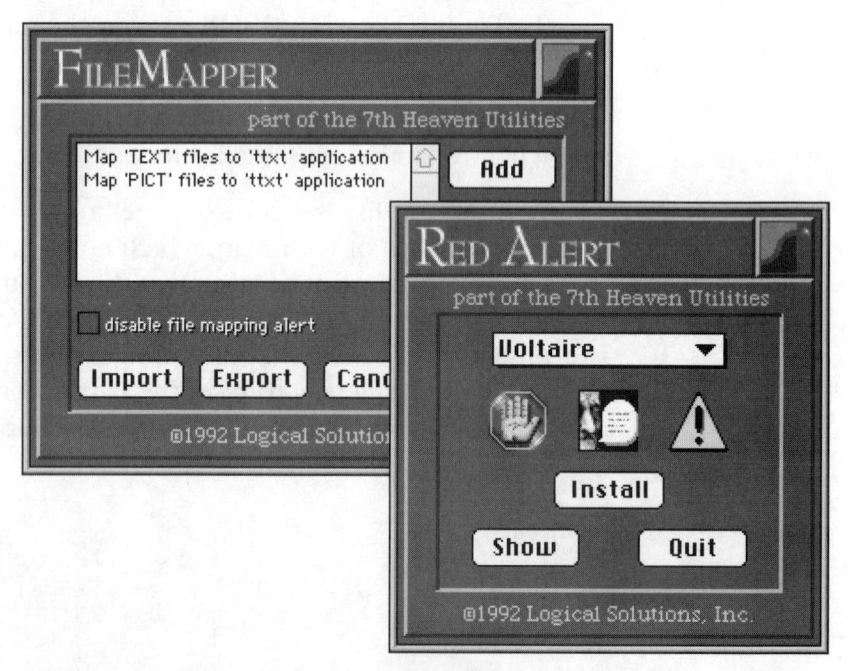

Figure 16-12: FileMapper and Red Alert.

- **Red Alert.** The Alert, Info and Warning icons in System 7 get updated to your choice of new, more dramatic color icons with this utility. (See Figure 16-12.)

- **Informant.** Providing all the info Apple left out of the About This Macintosh... dialog box, this program tells you just about everything about your Mac, extensions, SCSI drives and NuBus cards. (See Figure 16-13.)

- **Calendar.** The desk accessory Apple forgot—a 10,000 year calendar that can show one or three months, as well as the current time. It can even function as a decorative calendar, with a new image or graphic every month. (See Figure 16-13.)

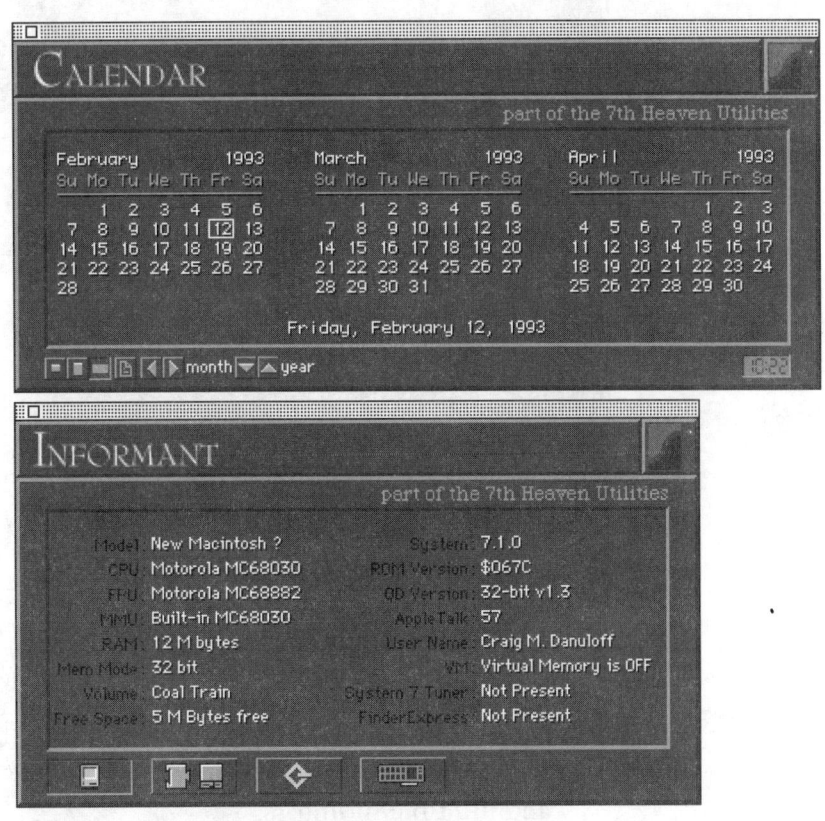

Figure 16-13: Calendar and Informant.

- **Chameleon.** Desktop patterns go high resolution and beautiful with this utility, which lets you install one of dozens of predesigned patterns to replace your normal desktop. You can also import other patterns from professional designers or create your own. (See Figure 16-14.)

Figure 16-14: Chameleon is a nice change of pace from the normal desktop.

- **Vector Plasma.** A rather low-tech screen saver, offering just one display (a constantly moving and changing object), no automatic launching options, no security options and no waking options. It does, however, use very little memory or processing power, and it supports color and multiple monitors.

Super Seven Utilities

Atticus Software; $69

Another commercial package (but one focusing more on core system software enhancements and adding the little niceties that Apple forgot), the Super Seven Utilities offer a number of unique control panels:

- **Alias Assistant.** While aliases are one of the handier features of System 7, they can also be one of the most annoying. Large collections of aliases can become outdated as you rename removable or remote volumes, throw away old files or applications and move files from disk to disk. Alias Assistant helps you master the situation by deleting "orphaned" aliases (those whose original item cannot be found), and allowing you to relink your aliases to originals that have been moved.

- **Helium Pro.** This upgraded version of the shareware utility Helium 2.1.1 adds functionality to Balloon Help, by allowing you to access help balloons anytime, without using the Balloon Help menu (just hold down a Command key combination and all balloons appear until you release the keys). You can also use Helium Pro to customize the font and size of help balloons and remove the balloon icon from your menu bar altogether.

- **Mighty Menus.** One of several features Apple talked about for System 7 that didn't make the final release was tear-off menus (like in HyperCard) for the Finder and all other applications. This utility provides tear-off menus, turning any menu into a floating palette you can access easily at any time.

- **Desktop Extras.** The new Finder menu provided by this utility includes commands to copy, move, alias and trash selected files. Using this menu, you can perform these operations without having to open the destination windows on the desktop.

- **Speed Beep Pro.** Sound is one of those capabilities that Apple touts as a Macintosh strength but barely supports with its system software. This control panel lets you control the volume of individual sounds, set random sound selection for system events, group different sounds for different applications, and play sounds without tying up your Mac, so you don't have to wait for long sounds to finish before continuing to work.

- **Super Comments.** Another early System 7 promise that Apple failed to keep is the survivability of Get Info comments when the Desktop file is rebuilt. This control panel makes comments more useful in System 7, letting you add them when you save a file, see them when you open files and preserve them when the Desktop file is rebuilt.

And so we conclude our look at System 7. Through the course of this book, we've examined nearly every aspect of the system software and, I hope, provided the explanations, information, tips, tricks and suggestions you were looking for when you first grabbed this book off the bookstore shelf.

As with so many aspects of the Mac, exploiting the operating system is a talent that has as many different approaches as there are Macintosh users. I welcome your comments, suggestions and discoveries; see the Introduction for information on how to reach me.

Appendix A

Installing or Updating System 7.5

When you decide to install System 7 for the first time, or to update from one version of System 7 to another, it is important that you carefully perform a number of steps in order to ensure that all your hardware and software will be compatible with your new system software.

This appendix looks at everything you should know, before and during system software upgrades or updates. (Generally speaking, an upgrade involves moving up a whole number–like from System 6 to System 7–whereas an update means moving up a decimal place–like from Version 7.1 to 7.5.) We'll cover preparing your hard drive, using the Apple Compatibility Checker program, tips for using the Installer application and strategies for arranging files on your hard drive after the installation.

Hardware Requirements

Before even starting the installation process, you should be sure your hardware is System 7-compatible. Fortunately, satisfying this requirement is easy: any Macintosh with at least 2mb of memory (although 4mb or more is highly advised) and a hard drive is fine for versions System 7.0 through 7.1.2. You'll need between 3 and 5mb of free hard drive space (depending on the installation options you choose) to hold System 7 and all its related files.

7.5 With System 7.5, the minimum requirements for a 68k Mac are 4mb of RAM; 8mb of RAM if you want to install PowerTalk and QuickDraw GX. If you wish to install System 7.5 on a Power Macintosh, you need to double these amounts. The System 7.5 Safe Install utility will check your system configuration for available RAM and free disk space, and let you know whether any or all of these components can be installed. A complete System 7.5 installation will require between 18 and 20mb of hard disk space.

Although all Macs can use System 7, some models cannot use the virtual memory or 32-bit addressing features. These limitations are fully explained in Chapter 8, "Memory Management."

System 7 is compatible with all existing Macintosh SCSI peripherals, although some of the INITs or control panels these peripherals use may be incompatible. In most cases, you'll be able to get new System 7-compatible software from hardware vendors. Most third-party video monitors and display adapters should also be compatible, although software driver updates may be required for these, too. Any printers you currently use with your Macintosh will continue to be compatible.

Replacing System 6.x With System 7

Caution: If you've upgraded or updated your system software before, you may be tempted to add System 7 by simply running the Installer application. This shortcut is not a good idea. Some of the fundamental changes made in System 7 make it necessary to first prepare your hard drive, and the Installer application doesn't always remove and replace the correct files when System 7 is installed over System 6, so manually removing certain files is recommended.

Following is a list of the installation steps I recommend. Each of these steps is described in detail in the following sections of this appendix. Please read through all the steps before starting your installation.

- Back up your entire hard drive
- Update your hard disk driver
- Run the Apple Disk First Aid utility
- Run the Apple Compatibility Checker
- Delete certain existing system software files
- Run the System 7 Installer
- Install QuickDraw GX and PowerTalk
- Configure your new System Folder

Back Up Your Hard Drive

As you prepare for the installation of System 7, your first step should be a complete backup of all data on your hard drive. There's always the remote possibility that the installation process could leave your hard drive inaccessible. It would be foolish to install System 7 without first backing up your data!

In fact, you should always back up your data before performing any major modification to your hard drive or system software. If you have a regular backup scheme in place, the effort required to do a backup should be minimal. If you don't have a regular backup scheme in place, then the effort required will be worth it, and if you're smart, you'll use this opportunity to start a new habit of complete and regular backups.

If your hard drive is partitioned, be sure to back up each partition. Although the System 7 installation will be targeted as a single partition only, it will affect the hard drive in ways that could put all your data at risk. Again, this risk is highly unlikely but worth the effort of taking precautions.

So, have you backed up your data yet? **Do not continue** until you've done a complete backup!

Prepare Your Hard Drive

After you've backed up your data, it is important to verify the integrity of your hard disk and to make sure its hard disk driver is current. To check your hard disk, you'll need the Apple Disk First Aid utility, which is included on the Disk Tools disk, and the software program that was used to format your hard disk.

To use Disk First Aid, restart your computer using the Disk Tools disk as a start-up disk. Launch Disk First Aid, and from the resulting dialog box, select the name of the disk onto which you intend to install System 7. Select the Repair Automatically command from the Options menu, and then click the Start button.

Disk First Aid will then verify your disk and should report: No Repair Necessary. If it indeed finds some problem with your disk, it will attempt to repair it and will notify you if it cannot repair the problem. In this case, you will need to either reformat your hard drive or attempt repairs using Norton Utilities, MacTools or some other commercial repair utility. In any case, you should not install System 7 until Disk First Aid gives your drive a clean bill of health.

Next, you need to make sure that a System 7-compatible hard disk driver is installed on your hard drive. If your hard drive has not been reformatted with a current formatting utility in the last two years, you will probably have to update your driver. An incompatible hard disk driver will probably not make it impossible for you to use System 7, although it may make virtual memory unusable. In any case, installing a current driver is a good idea—it will probably improve the performance of your hard drive.

You can update your hard disk driver without reformatting your drive by using your formatting utility. If you purchased a hard drive that was preformatted by Apple, the Apple HD Setup utility was probably used to format your drive. A copy is included on the System 7 Disk Tools disk. If you purchased your hard drive from your Apple dealer, or from a mail-order reseller, you should have received a copy of the hard disk formatting software. Whichever software was used, launch the utility and choose the Update Drivers or Install New Drivers option.

Note: If you are not certain which utility was used to format your drive, you should be very careful when updating drivers, and under no circumstances should you perform the update without first backing up your hard drive. The drivers from one formatting utility may work properly on a drive formatted with another utility, but they may not. In this situation, the best advice is to actually reformat your drive, install new drivers and then restore all your data from your backup.

If you are using the Apple HD Setup utility, you may want to take advantage of this opportunity to instead use one of the commercially available formatting utilities, such as Drive7, SilverLining or Hard Disk Toolkit. Although it may seem unusual to purchase a utility program to replace one that Apple provides without charge, each of these programs provides better drive performance, compatibility with a wider range of devices (including removable cartridges such as Syquest or Bernoulli), and better drive repair, salvage and troubleshooting support. Reformatting your drive with one of these utilities is a good investment in your Mac system.

Caution: System 7.5 installations can be very sensitive to the health of your hard drive. Problems that aren't readily apparent during everyday operation may show up when you're using the Safe Install utility. Follow the procedures in this section before doing a System 7.5 install.

Run Apple's Compatibility Checker or Safe Install

To help you discover which pieces of software you're currently using that are compatible with System 7, Apple developed the Compatibility Checker 2.0, which provides a very good, although not comprehensive, survey of the files on your hard drive and a summary of the way these files will react once System 7 is installed. This utility, now called Safe Install, has been upgraded for System 7.5 and is more intelligent in action.

The program has a handy tool for moving all your System Folder files known to be incompatible, or untested by Apple for compatibility, to a special folder where they will not conflict with System 7. You can then test each of these files individually or replace them with newer System 7-Savvy versions.

Earlier versions of the Compatibility Checker required HyperCard, but Version 2.0 is a stand-alone application. After you launch the Compatibility Checker, you select the drives you want to check. In most cases, you should select all the volumes you'll use on your new system. (See Figure A-1.)

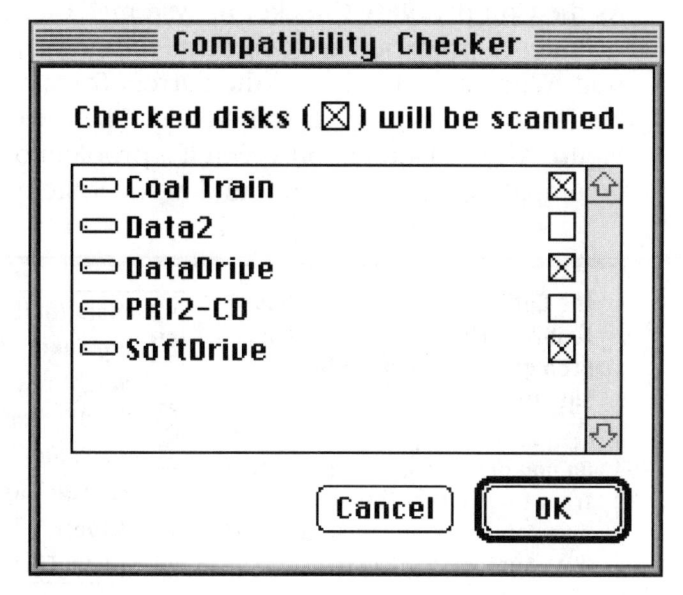

Figure A-1: The Compatibility Checker's Select Drives dialog box.

7.5 ▸ In System 7.5, the Safe Install utility comes on a separate disk called The Safe Install Utility for System 7.5. This utility checks system software extensions on your hard drive for System 7.5 compatibility, and it automatically moves items out of the Extension folder into a new folder called May Not Work with System 7.5. Applications are not checked with Safe Install.

You have two options with the Safe Install: Quick or Detailed. Quick issues a short report of items that may not work with System 7.5. A Detailed report provides version numbers, vendor names and a vendor telephone number for each application. Safe Install can scan any attached disks.

Caution: *If you are using At Ease on your computer, it is very important that you disable it before you use the Safe Install utility. Drag the At Ease components out of the Extension folder. You can restore them to the Extension folder after you are done with Safe Install.*

As the Compatibility Checker in System 7.1 examines your volumes, a progress bar documents the percentage of completion. When all volumes and the current System Folder have been checked, an incompatibility list, like the one shown in Figure A-2, will appear onscreen if a problem or a suspected incompatible file has been found in the System Folder.

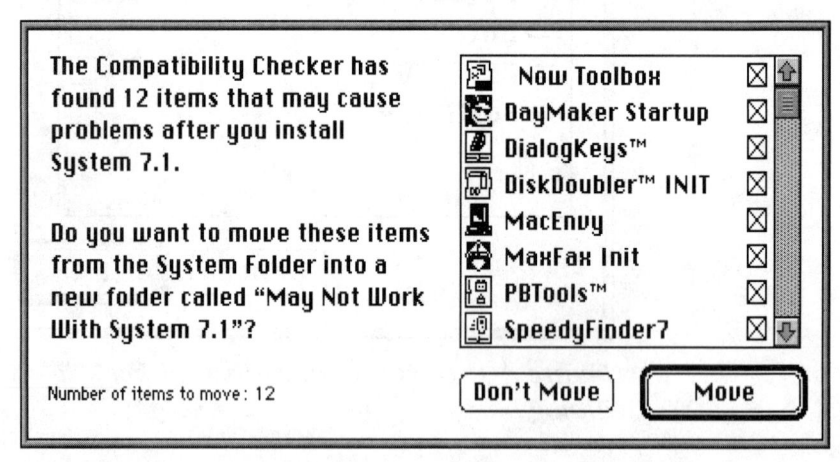

```
The Compatibility Checker has          Now Toolbox
found 12 items that may cause          DayMaker Startup
problems after you install             DialogKeys™
System 7.1.                            DiskDoubler™ INIT
                                       MacEnvy
Do you want to move these items        MaxFax Init
from the System Folder into a          PBTools™
new folder called "May Not Work        SpeedyFinder7
With System 7.1"?

Number of items to move: 12       [ Don't Move ]   [[ Move ]]
```

Figure A-2: Incompatibility Warning list.

The Compatibility Checker can move these files to a safe location—the May Not Work with System 7.5 folder—where they can't cause problems. Move the files by clicking the Move button. You can later replace those that are incompatible with newer System 7-compatible versions and test those that Apple has not tested.

Next, the complete Compatibility Report (shown in Figure A-3) appears. It lists each executable file found on the selected volumes, plus each INIT or Control Panel device, and documents its status as identified by Apple.

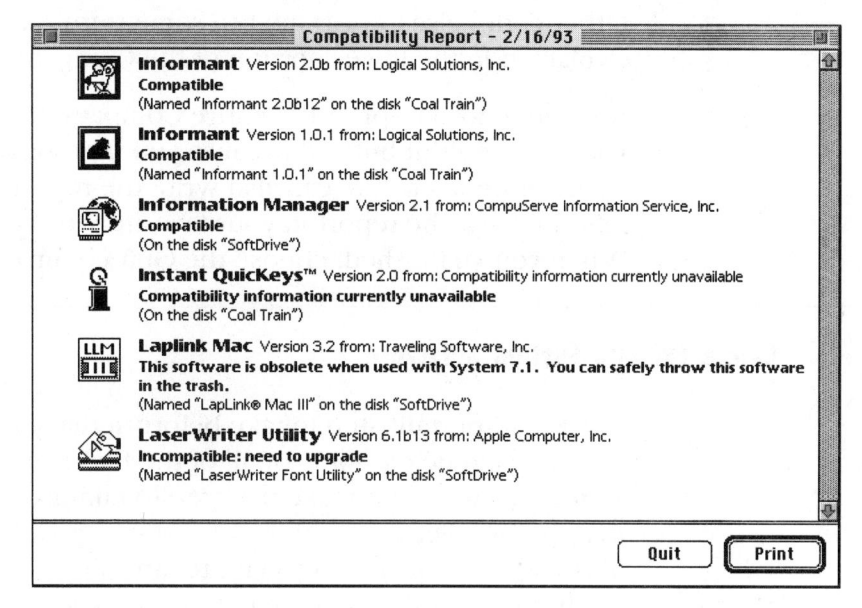

```
┌─────────────── Compatibility Report – 2/16/93 ───────────────┐
  Informant  Version 2.0b from: Logical Solutions, Inc.
  Compatible
  (Named "Informant 2.0b12" on the disk "Coal Train")

  Informant  Version 1.0.1 from: Logical Solutions, Inc.
  Compatible
  (Named "Informant 1.0.1" on the disk "Coal Train")

  Information Manager  Version 2.1 from: CompuServe Information Service, Inc.
  Compatible
  (On the disk "SoftDrive")

  Instant QuicKeys™  Version 2.0 from: Compatibility information currently unavailable
  Compatibility information currently unavailable
  (On the disk "Coal Train")

  Laplink Mac  Version 3.2 from: Traveling Software, Inc.
  This software is obsolete when used with System 7.1. You can safely throw this software
  in the trash.
  (Named "LapLink® Mac III" on the disk "SoftDrive")

  LaserWriter Utility  Version 6.1b13 from: Apple Computer, Inc.
  Incompatible: need to upgrade
  (Named "LaserWriter Font Utility" on the disk "SoftDrive")

                                                    [ Quit ]  [ Print ]
```

Figure A-3: Compatibility Report as it appears onscreen.

There are four main status categories in this report:

- **Compatible.** An application is either System 7-compatible or System 7-Savvy, and you'll have no problems using it with System 7.

- **Upgrade available.** Although your version is System 7-compatible, the software developer recommends using a more recent version with System 7.

- **Must upgrade.** The software is incompatible with System 7. You must use a newer version with your new system software.

- **Unknown.** The software has not been tested for compatibility. Most of these items will prove compatible with System 7, but you'll have to make that determination yourself, as you'll learn later in this appendix.

Other codes also appear next to some status names. They're explained in the lower portion of the Compatibility Report.

It's a good idea to print the entire Compatibility Report, by clicking the Print button, because you'll probably need this information later. You can also write the report to disk, which lets you view the report in your favorite word processor. When you've finished, choose the Quit command to exit.

Delete Existing System Software

The last important step to take before actually running the installer is to delete some or all of the files from your existing system software. You take this step to eliminate the possibility that the Installer application will not completely replace these files with new ones. (Although, technically, you can just run the Installer without deleting old files, experience has shown that these installations are not very stable.)

Before you begin trashing files, you may want to run your Font/DA Mover for one last time, and transfer any non-standard fonts (anything except Chicago, Geneva, New York, Monaco, Times, Helvetica, Courier and Symbol) that are in your System file into a suitcase file elsewhere on your hard disk so that you can reinstall them after your System 7 installation. You should also save copies of any non-standard desk accessories from your System file, as well as any FKEYs that have been installed.

To delete your existing system software, just drag the Finder, System file and other Apple system software files to the trash. You won't be able to empty the trash because many of these files are in use, but that isn't a problem. Be careful not to trash any non-Apple files, such as third-party INITs, Control Panel devices or other files that you may need once System 7 is installed. If you're not sure what a file is, just leave it. As long as you delete the Finder and/or System file, the installation will occur properly.

After you have dragged the system software files to the trash, rename your existing System Folder to something like "OLD System Folder" so that its name will not conflict with the new System Folder added by the Installer.

You're now ready to use the System 7 Installer to install System 7. A new System Folder will be created on your hard disk. (Complete details on using the System 7 Installer, how to reinstall the fonts, DAs and other files you removed from your old System Folder are included in the "Configure the System 7 System Folder" section later in this appendix.)

Run the Installer

You can run the System 7 Installer from the System 7 CD-ROM, from floppy disk or from a mounted AppleShare file server. Because the System 7 Installer is unlike earlier versions, you can actually install System 7 onto the hard drive that's your current start-up disk (the one containing the system software the Mac is currently using).

If you are going to install over existing system software (which I don't recommend), you should disable any virus-checking utilities you regularly use because they would likely be triggered repeatedly by the actions of the Installer, making it difficult or impossible for the Installer to complete its tasks successfully.

If you are going to install from an AppleShare volume containing the System 7 Installer, mount that volume normally, using the Chooser. If you're installing from a System 7 CD-ROM, insert the CD so that it appears on your Finder desktop. To install from the System 7 floppy disk set, restart your Mac using Install Disk 1 as a start-up disk.

7.5 ▶ Launch the Installer application by double-clicking its icon. You're now ready to install System 7.5. The first screen of the Installer lets you do an Easy Install, a Custom Install or a Custom Remove (for the first time) by selecting the pop-up menu, as shown in Figure A-4. It also displays the name of the drive on which the system software will be installed. If the selected disk is not the one you want, click the Switch Disk button until the name of the desired hard drive appears. System 7.5's installer is a redesigned grayscale dialog box.

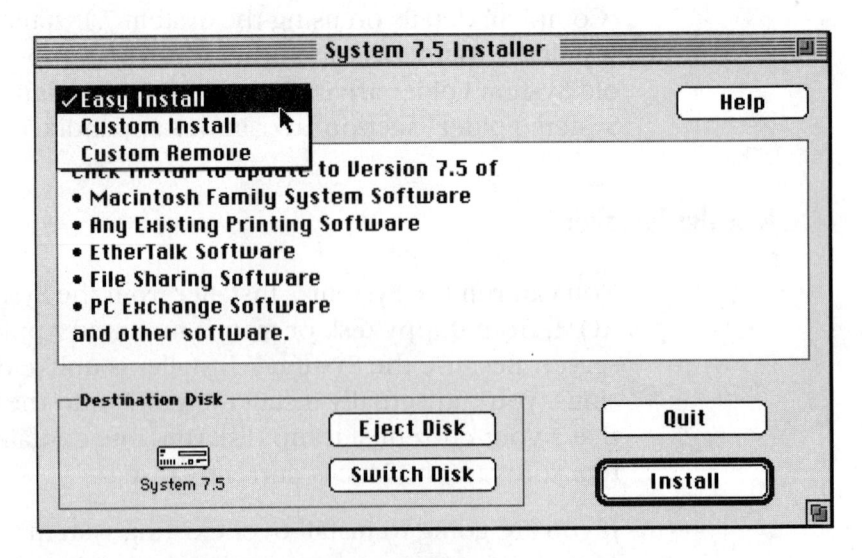

Figure A-4: The System 7.5 Installer.

Following are the options from the Installer menu:

- **Easy Install.** If you want to perform a default installation, select Easy Install from the menu, and click the Install button to install the listed software onto the named hard disk or volume. Use this option if you're sure you want the recommended options or if you're not sure which options you want installed. (The discussion later in this appendix should help you avoid that situation.)

    Note that for System 7.5 an Easy Install installs all system software components except for PowerTalk and QuickDraw GX. Before the installation is over, if the installer determines that your Macintosh has enough RAM, it posts a dialog box telling you not to forget to install PowerTalk and QuickDraw GX. They are separate installations using their own Installer scripts.

- **Custom Install.** Selecting the Custom Install option lets you choose the specific drivers and other files you want installed along with your system software by clicking on each item while holding the Shift key. Then click the Install button to install just those components. These files are organized by topics, as shown in Figure A-5.

- **Custom Remove.** If you've previously installed System 7.5 and wish to remove it (or certain elements of it), use the Custom Remove option and select the various files you want to delete.

- **Quit**. Click this button to forget this whole thing; let's go back to System Software 6.0x! This option will leave your original system software untouched and exit the Installer.

The scrolling window in the Custom Install dialog box provides options covering the system software, printing software, File Sharing software and network driver software. Click the check boxes next to the options you want. Categories like Printing and Control Panels have several options, indicated by a triangle next to the category. Click the triangle to display the category's contents—select those you wish to install by clicking their check boxes (the main category box will display a dash), or select them all by clicking the box next to the category heading.

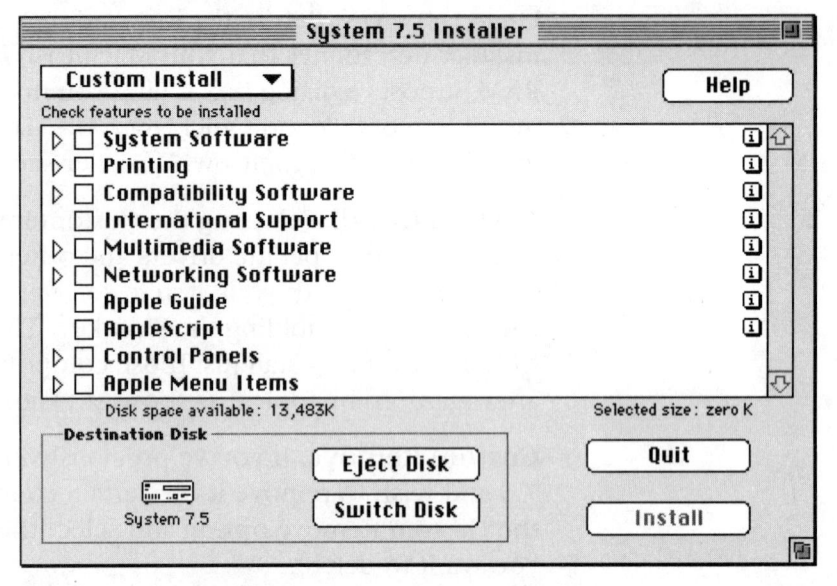

Figure A-5: The System 7.5 Custom Install.

The Customize dialog box options include the following:

- **System Software.** These options include System for any Macintosh, System for this Macintosh only, Minimal System for any Macintosh and Minimal System for this Macintosh only. You can choose only one of these options.

Choose System for any Macintosh if the destination drive will be connected to different Macintosh computers at different times. If you were to choose one of the system software options specific to one Macintosh model, that hard disk would not be able to support some Macintosh models. This option might add a few more files than you really need for your Macintosh, but these files consume only a small amount of disk space and will cause no problems for you.

Choose System for this Macintosh only if you're sure the hard drive you're installing on will be used with one specific Macintosh model only.

Choose Minimal System for any Macintosh if you're installing on a hard drive that will be used on more than one Macintosh model, but you have limited free space on that hard drive.

You also can use this option to create a 1.44mb floppy disk of System 7.

Choose Minimal System for this Macintosh if you're sure that the hard drive you're installing on will be used with one specific Macintosh model only, and there's limited free space on that hard drive.

- **Printing.** The options for printer drivers include LaserWriter, LaserWriter 8, LaserWriter 300, Personal LaserWriter SC, Portable StyleWriter, StyleWriter I and II, ImageWriter and AppleTalk ImageWriter, ImageWriter LQ and AppleTalk ImageWriter LQ, and the Apple Color Printer. Choose according to the printers you'll use with your Macintosh. There's no limit to how many of these options you can select for installation at one time.

- **Compatibility Software.** This option installs PC Exchange and Macintosh Easy Open for opening and translating files.

- **International Support.** This option installs date, time, number, string and other support for foreign languages and character sets.

- **Multimedia Software.** QuickTime, AV Mac software and CD-ROM files are installed with this option.

- **Networking Software.** If you will be operating System 7 on a network and want to share folders or volumes with other Macintoshes or access your hard drive from another network Macintosh, select this option. If your Mac is EtherTalk or TokenTalk capable, select the appropriate network driver option. You can install both of these drivers, but you'll likely need only one of them. If you're using an AppleTalk network, you don't have to select either option.

  Files supporting File Sharing, EtherTalk, TokenTalk and MacTCP are installed with this option. In versions of the Installer prior to System 7.5, this group was called File Sharing Software and Network Drivers. MacTCP is not installed as part of an Easy Install, unless a previous version of the file exists on your hard drive.

- **Apple Guide.** The Apple Guide help system in System 7.5 is installed with this option.

- **AppleScript.** This option installs AppleScript files.

- **Control Panels.** You can install any single file or combination of files in the Control Panel folder using this option.

- **Apple Menu Items.** You can install any single file or combination of files in the Apple Menu Items folder using this option.

When you run a Custom Install, you can install one or all of the files in any one or all of these options. A Custom Install can override the preferences that an Easy Install provides. For example, you can install AV files on a PowerBook using a Custom Install.

After selecting the appropriate options, click the button to begin the installation. You can also use the Easy Install menu option to return to the previous dialog box or the Quit button to cancel the entire installation.

Once the installation begins, its progress is displayed. If you're installing from floppy disks, you'll be prompted for disks as required. When the installation is complete, the Installation Successful dialog box appears. Click the Continue button if you need to return to the Easy Install dialog box, or click the Quit button to return to the Finder.

After quitting the Installer, you should restart your Macintosh to confirm that installation was successful and that System 7.5 will launch properly. Welcome to System 7.5!

Install QuickDraw GX & PowerTalk

If you have 8mb of RAM in a 68k Mac or 16mb of RAM in a Power Macintosh, you can install QuickDraw GX and PowerTalk in your computer. Put the first QuickDraw GX installation disk into your floppy disk drive, or find the Installer utility in the QuickDraw GX folder and double-click the QuickDraw GX installer. You run the Installer as you did in the previous section.

Note that certain QuickDraw GX utilities require a Custom Install. The Type 1 Enabler utility that converts PostScript Type 1 fonts to the QuickDraw GX format is one of these components. The Type 1 Enabler was described in Chapter 9, "QuickDraw GX & Fonts."

When QuickDraw GX is installed, PostScript Type 1 fonts in your System folder are modified to work with GX. Your fonts in their original Type 1 format are copied to a folder called "•Archived Type 1 Fonts•" so that you can use them again on other systems. You must modify fonts in this folder using the Type 1 Enabler to use them with QuickDraw GX.

To install PowerTalk, you go through an additional installation. Insert the first PowerTalk installation disk, or find the PowerTalk folder on a CD-ROM and double-click the Installer icon to begin your installation of PowerTalk. The installation proceeds as before.

With PowerTalk, it is important that you make sure that your system clock is properly set for your time zone. Also, check that your computer is named correctly for identification on an AppleTalk network. Refer to Chapter 14, "AOCE—The Apple Open Collaboration Environment," for additional information on PowerTalk and PowerShare servers.

Configure the System 7 System Folder

Now you can customize your system software by adding fonts, additional extensions, control panels and other files to the System Folder. If you created the OLD System Folder as described previously, carefully move all files from this folder into your new System Folder. Make sure you don't move any files that are part of your old system software. You should drag files in small groups, and cancel the copying if a dialog box appears telling you that files with the same names as the files you are moving already exist. Getting this dialog box message probably means you are trying to move a file from System 6 that already exists in a System 7 version. (See "Installing Fonts" in Chapter 9, "QuickDraw GX & Fonts," for details on the font installation process.)

You install extensions (formerly called INITs) and control panels into the System Folder by dragging their icons onto the System Folder icon. The Macintosh will then automatically place them in the Extensions or Control Panels folder. Alternatively, you can manually drag them into the Extensions or Control Panels folder yourself. (See "Adding Files to the System Folder" in Chapter 4, "The System Folder," for more information on installing extensions and control panels.)

Because extensions and control panels can contain special code that is executed at startup and that modifies the System file as it's loaded into memory, it's important to avoid those that are incompatible with System 7. The report you created with the Compatibility Checker (System 7.0 through System 7 Pro) or the Safe Install (in System 7.5) will identify extensions and control panels that are compatible and those that require an upgrade before you can use them with System 7.

Copy all files the Compatibility Checker or Safe Install utility listed as compatible to the System Folder. Don't install those requiring an upgrade; contact the software developer at the address listed in the Compatibility Report to obtain a compatible version.

Many of your files will be listed by the Compatibility Checker or Safe Install utility as "Unknown," which leaves it up to you to test their compatibility. The only way to do this is to add these files one at a time to your System Folder and then restart your Macintosh and test for compatibility.

It's easy to tell that a file is incompatible—your Mac crashes on startup. If this happens, press the reset switch on your Macintosh or turn its power off and on; then hold down the Shift key during startup. This shortcut will disable all extensions, allowing you to open the System Folder and remove the problem file.

If the Macintosh starts up without incident, test the extension by using it in one or two different situations. In most cases, if incompatibilities didn't show up during startup, they'll become apparent as soon as the extension or control panel is used. If you find an incompatible file, remove it from your System Folder. Continue this testing process for each new control panel and extension until you have added all the ones you want to use.

Next, move all the miscellaneous files from your previous System Folder (things such as dictionaries, help files, preferences files or even entire folders) into the newly installed System Folder. Most of these files should go into the System Folder itself, although preferences files should be moved into the Preferences folder.

To install your desk accessories, you can either drag them to the System Folder, which will place them into the Apple Menu Items folder automatically, or convert them into stand-alone applications that you can launch by double-clicking. To do so, double-click any DA Suitcase, and all enclosed DAs will appear with individual application icons. Dragging them out of the DA window and into any other folder or volume converts them into double-clickable applications. (See Chapter 5, "System 7.5 & Your Software," for a more complete discussion of converting DAs.)

After you have converted a DA into an application, you can use it just like any application. You can store the converted DA in any folder; you can usually launch it by double-clicking its icon; and you can install the DA or its alias in the Apple Menu Items folder so it can be launched from the Apple menu.

Updating System 7

Moving from one version of System 7 to another is far easier than moving from System 6 to System 7, although there are a few special recommended steps:

- Run Apple Disk First Aid before updating. This utility can find problems with your hard drive before they cause real problems with new system software.

- Run Safe Install before updating. This utility can find problems with system software extensions on your hard drive that may cause problems. It moves these questionable extensions to a folder called May Not Work with System 7.5 in your System Folder so that your system can safely boot after installation.

- Drag the Finder to the Trash and rename your old System Folder before booting from the Install 1 disk to run the Installer. Following these steps will cause the new system software to be installed in a new System Folder. If you don't take this approach, the new system software will be installed over the old system software, and although Apple intends for updates to be handled this way, it has not proven very reliable.

- After the installation, carefully drag all non-Apple system software files from your old System Folder to the new System Folder. Be especially careful not to overwrite any new system software files with old ones or to move old system software files that are no longer needed.

Appendix B

A Brief History of System 7

Since its initial release, System 7 has been enhanced, extended and updated several times. At the time of this writing, there are five main System 7 versions (7.0, 7.0.1, 7.1, 7 Pro and 7.5), three bug-fix/performance improvement extensions (Tune-Up 1.0, 1.11 and Macintosh Hardware System Updates 1.0 and 3.0), two special versions (7.0.1P and 7.1P, for the Macintosh Performa line) and a slew of system enablers resulting finally in one universal enabler.

The Many Faces of System 7

This book covers all these versions of System 7. Any time the reference "System 7" is used, the features being described are common to all versions listed above. Whenever a feature unique to one version is described, the software is referred to by its specific version name, such as "Version 7.0.1" or "Version 7.1P."

Details about each version of System 7, the Tune-Ups and enablers are provided in this appendix.

System 7.0

System 7.0 was the original "golden master" release of Apple's new system software. It is the foundation on which all subsequent versions are based, and the overwhelming majority of its features are common throughout all versions of System 7.

System 7.0.1

System 7.0.1 was released to support the Mac Classic II, Quadra 700, Quadra 900 and the PowerBooks (models 100, 140, 145 and 170). While it is compatible with any Macintosh, only users of the models listed above, or the IIci, IIfx or IIsi, would benefit from upgrading from Version 7.0 to Version 7.0.1.

Beyond the changes made to support the Classic II, Quadra 700, Quadra 900 and PowerBooks, Version 7.0.1 updates the ROM-based Standard Apple Numeric Environment (SANE), which improves computational speed on Mac's equipped with math coprocessors.

Version 7.0.1 was shipped with the Classic II, Quadra 700, Quadra 900 and PowerBooks. It was not offered for sale because Apple did not recommend users of all Mac models upgrade from Version 7.0 to Version 7.0.1. Version 7.0.1 is available, however, without charge from many user groups and online services. In addition, you may legally install someone else's copy of Version 7.0.1 on your Macintosh.

System 7 Tune-Up

Tune-Up is a System 7 bug-fix and performance improvement, which installs an extension called System 7 Tuner, as well as new versions of the Chooser, File Sharing extension, LaserWriter and StyleWriter files into your System 7 System Folder. Installing the Tune-Up files improves the performance of System 7.0 or 7.0.1, and fixes a number of bugs in the first two releases of System 7.

There are two versions of Tune-Up, Version 1.0 and Version 1.1.1. Both are compatible with System 7 Version 7.0 and Version 7.0.1. Fixes and improvements in Tune-Up 1.0 include faster Finder copying, better printing speeds (50 to 200 percent), enhanced memory management (especially in low-memory situations), savings of 100k when AppleTalk is turned off in the Chooser and correction of several file sharing problems. Tune-Up 1.1.1 corrects a bug that causes folders to disappear from the Finder, and provides a new LaserWriter driver (Version 7.1.1) that improves performance on the LaserWriter Plus, LaserWriter NTR and LaserWriter IIf and IIg.

When Tune-Up is installed, a dot appears next to the System Software version number in the About This Macintosh dialog box. You cannot tell by looking at this dot whether Version 1.0 or Version 1.1.1 of the Tune-Up file is installed. Neither version of Tune-Up is required when using Version 7.1 or later (all Tune-Up features have been built into these versions).

Anyone using System 7 Version 7.0 or Version 7.0.1 should obtain and install Tune-Up. The System 7 Tune-Up disk is free and is available from Apple, Apple dealers, user groups, online services and bulletin boards.

System 7.1

System 7.1 has been positioned as the first major update to System 7.0, but for most users it isn't very significant. It does, however, have some underlying technological changes that will become more important in the future.

The biggest new feature of Version 7.1, from Apple's point-of-view, is called *WorldScript*, a technology that allows System 7 to be customized more easily for foreign languages, including Japanese, Chinese and other languages with large character sets. This may be important to Apple, but it is hardly significant to most Macintosh users in the United States.

The change every Mac user will notice is the new Fonts folder inside the System Folder. The new Fonts folder becomes the official home of all fonts—screen, printer, bitmapped, PostScript and TrueType—in Version 7.1. This new folder means fonts are no longer stored in the System file or loose in the System Folder. Use of the new Fonts folder is fully described in Chapter 9, "QuickDraw GX & Fonts."

One of the changes in Version 7.1 that users will eventually notice is that new Macintosh models will no longer require new versions of the system software, as they frequently have in the past. Instead, special files called system *enablers* will be shipped with future Macintoshes, allowing these new machines to be used with Version 7.1. Most existing Macintoshes use Version 7.1 without system enablers (which function much like extensions), although the Macintosh Performa line is already using enablers.

The features found in the Tune-Up releases described above have been built-into Version 7.1, so neither release of Tune-Up is needed. QuickTime 1.5, an extension that allows a number of multimedia capabilities to become part of the Macintosh system software, is bundled with Version 7.1 (see Chapter 15, "Apple's System 7 Extensions" for a complete discussion of QuickTime), and the DAL extension that was provided with Version 7.0 and Version 7.0.1 is no longer included with Version 7.1. DAL is used for database server access, and will be available with other software products requiring it.

System 7 Version 7.1 differs from previous system software releases in one important way—it is not available as a free-of-charge update. Apple's upgrade policy and pricing is as follows:

- If you do not receive Version 7.1 along with your Macintosh when you purchase it, you must purchase a System 7.1 Upgrade Kit in order to legally obtain Version 7.1.

- Upgrade kits containing only the Version 7.1 disks are available directly from Apple for $34.95 at 800-769-2775.

- A complete System 7.1 Personal Upgrade Kit, including manuals, is available at most Apple dealers for $99. A System 7.1 10-user MultiPack Upgrade Kit is available through dealers for $499.

- Customers who purchased Version 7.0 of the System 7 Personal Upgrade Kit or the System 7 Group Upgrade Kit after September 1, 1992, will receive the Version 7.1 product free of charge by providing proof of purchase. For more information, call 800-769-2775.

Additional minor versions of System 7.1 were released that were meant for hardware support. Version 7.1.1 supported certain AV models, while version 7.1.2 supported the Power Macintosh series of computers. Unless you have one of these Macintosh computers, there is no reason to upgrade to these incremental releases. Version 7.1.1 also appeared in System 7 Pro. System 7.1.2 hid a major upgrade of native PowerPC code and emulation software that the Power Macintosh series needs. As such it is a smart installer, installing only the software that a Power Macintosh needs, or the more familiar 68k code for previous Macintosh computers.

System 7.1 Hardware System Update 1.0

To prove that it is working tirelessly to continually improve System 7, Apple released Macintosh Hardware System Update 1.0, which is like a tune-up extension for Version 7.1. It is shipped along with Version 7.1.1 of the Memory control panel. Using these two files improves high speed serial communications, system clock accuracy, floppy ejection during shutdown and system performance in low memory situations. The extension is recommended for all Mac II, LC, PowerBook and Quadra models, as well as the Classic II. Performa users should not use this extension, as these features are built into the current system enablers for Performas. (See the last section of this appendix for details on enablers.)

Several other versions of the Hardware System Updates have appeared. They are detailed in the section "Hardware System Update 3.0," later in this appendix.

System 7.0.1P, System 7.1P

The introduction of the Macintosh Performa series brought with it two new variants of System 7, Version 7.0.1P and Version 7.1P. These versions are identical to Versions 7.0.1 and 7.1 as described above, and throughout this book, with a few exceptions:

- **Application Launcher.** An application launcher control panel is included, which provides a window at the Finder displaying large icons for frequently used software. This makes it easier for users to launch these programs. Application icons can be added to the launcher window by placing aliases of the applications in the Launcher folder inside the System Folder.

- **Default Folders.** When using the standard Open or Save dialog boxes, default folders named "document folder" and "application folder" are located automatically. This is intended to make it easier for new users to find files they want to open and to save files in the correct location. Of course, users are still free to navigate to any other folder or volume if the default locations are not correct.

- **Application Hiding.** When any application is launched, all other applications, including the Finder, are hidden. This has the same effect as automatically using the Hide Others command in the Application Menu. This change makes the screen less cluttered and confusing for new Macintosh users.

- **Desktop Patterns.** The General control panel has been modified to make selection of a desktop pattern easier.

- **Backup and Restore.** A very simple backup program is included, allowing the entire hard disk, or just the System Folder, to be backed up or restored.

- **8-Bit Default.** When using a Performa 400 or 600, the Monitors control panel is automatically set to 8-bit color (instead of 2-bit black and white) by default.

- **At Ease.** This Apple extension is bundled with all "P" versions (and is also sold separately for anyone else who may want it). It provides a simpler interface for the Finder, making it easier to launch applications, find and save files, and limit access to the standard Finder and the Trash. Restricting access to the Finder is designed to prevent unsophisticated users (such as children) from accidentally deleting or moving files. Chapter 15, "Apple's System 7 Extensions," provides more details on At Ease.

System 7 Pro

System 7 Pro was a vehicle for releasing a number of new system extensions in a bundled package. It is really Version System 7.1.1 plus goodies. In System 7 Pro you got the additional components of AppleScript, PowerTalk and an update for QuickTime. These components and more appeared as part of the universal release of System 7.5. System 7 Pro also installs the Hardware System Update Version 2.0.1.

Hardware System Update 3.0

Hardware System Update 3.0 is a set of enhancements for users running System 7.1, 7.1.1 (System 7 Pro), or 7.1.2 (Power Macintosh). System Update 3.0 consolidates all the enhancements that were part of Hardware System Updates 2.1, 2.0 and 1.0. The number of enhancements are numerous, making this a valuable update for users of these versions of system software.

There are really too many enhancements in Hardware System 3.0 to detail. Some highlights are performance improvements, updates to the standard file package, replacement of TeachText with SimpleText, updates to the Memory, PowerBook and Easy Access control panels, and updates to all of the enablers. By all means run the Update if you are a candidate.

Hardware System Updates 2.0.1 and 2.0 provided some relief to reliability problems with modems and clock accuracy of several Macintosh models; addressed floppy disk ejection problems; updated enablers; and installed the Sound Manger Update, Autoremounter and Disk First Aid 7.2.

System 7.5

System 7.5 adds numerous changes. Some of them are performance and bug fixes, others are totally new components. Making their first appearance in system software were Apple Guide, Macintosh Drag and Drop, Finder enhancements like desktop notes, submenus for the Apple menu, menu-bar clocks, and desktop patterns. Other changes are the Scriptable Finder, PowerBook utility enhancements like the Control Strip, energy saving features, audio CD controls, the hideable Finder, additional networking support and support for disks larger than four gigabytes.

Just how compelling will System 7.5 be to most users? Typically about 25 to 33 percent of Macintosh users will upgrade for a substantial, but nonversion number upgrade.

Which Version Should I Use ?

It's not hard to understand why many people are confused about which version of System 7 they should be using:

- The many well-known problems with past releases of new system software made some users wary of the first release of System 7—simply because it was the first release. "I never use any software whose version number ends in a zero," was the familiar refrain from some skeptics, who sat and waited for some sort of update, regardless of the reason for it.

- Those who did make the move to System 7 were just settling into Version 7.0 when Version 7.0.1 came along, accompanied by conflicting reports about who should use it. Distribution limitations and uncertainty about Apple's policy regarding this release further inhibited its use.

- The Tune-Up extensions were fairly well publicized, (if you read *Macworld* or *MacUser*), but details on who needed them and why were scarce. Word quickly spread that Tune-Up 1.0 didn't fix all the initial problems, and Tune-Up 1.1 was quickly released and then discontinued. Understandably, people were a bit queasy about Tune-Up 1.1.1. Distribution of Tune-Up disks was better than that for 7.0.1, but for folks without easy access to online services or user groups, it was still a little hard to come by. Tune-Ups 2.0, 2.0.1 and 3.0 have now appeared without much fanfare.

- The release of Version 7.1, with all the significance of that first decimal place and the valiant but ineffectual attempt by Apple to suggest that this release was technically significant, actually did convince many holdouts that it was time to move to System 7, and provided Version 7.0 users with hope that the comedy of 7.0.1 and the Tune-Ups was over. This ground swell of support was quickly dashed, however, when Apple announced that their long-rumored plan to charge for system software updates would be implemented beginning with those updating to Version 7.0.1. In other words, users who supported Apple's System 7 from the start were asked to pay $30 (or more) for WorldScript and the Fonts folder. Many have understandably opted to stick with 7.0.1 and Tune-Up 1.1.1 instead.

- The release of the Macintosh Performa series—based on the supposition that anyone who shops at Sears won't actually visit a computer store—brought the "P" variants of System 7: Version 7.0.1P and Version 7.1P. Most Mac users haven't heard of these versions, and when they do, they will probably be confused. Most Performa users do not realize they have a special version of the system software, and will therefore be very confused when the next update comes out and they install it and find their training wheels missing.

- The somewhat mysterious "system enablers" introduced along with System 7.1 are needed for Macs released after System 7.1. The Performas, Duos and Centrises have them, as does the Quadra 800 and PowerBook 160, 165c and 180. Enablers are discussed in greater detail later in this appendix.

Given all this, what system software version should you use? Ideally, you should always use the latest version of the system software that is appropriate for your machine. At the time of this writing, that means Version 7.5 or 7.1.1 (System 7 Pro), or 7.1P, if you have a Performa and need or want the modifications. Even as time passes, and the version numbers and incidents described here become distant memories, new version numbers and new incidents will almost certainly replace them.

But a few general rules can help keep you out of trouble when upgrading or updating your system software:

- New versions of system software are released to provide more features, and generally make things better. There are exceptions to this rule, but it is the rule. This is why you should always use the latest version.

- Don't use a new version of system software for at least one month after it is released. Let the daredevils and the press figure out if it has any bugs first. If there are bugs, read the articles in the trade magazines carefully to determine how serious and widespread they are. While the press does a good job in making these kinds of problems known, it generally overstates and exaggerates them. (No one said this was going to be easy.)

- The primary factor behind needing to change your system software (beyond basic hardware compatibility and overall performance) is the applications and utilities you use. In other words, if you don't regularly update your software or use new programs or utilities, there is less reason to continually update your system software. In this case, your Mac is a closed environment, so if it ain't broke, don't fix it. Of course, to get the most from your Mac, you will inevitably have to update your applications, try new ones and add utilities. When you do (or better yet, before you do) move to the latest version of the system software as well.

Enablers

Historically, each time Apple releases a new Macintosh model, it has had to release a new version of their system software. These new hardware-specific releases changed the second decimal place of the current version number when they occurred with System 6 (Versions 6.0.5, 6.0.6, 6.0.7, etc.), and usually included a few bug fixes and performance improvements in addition to the additional hardware support.

For System 7, Apple has decided to avoid releasing new versions of the system software for each new Macintosh model, turning instead to a new form of system file, called a *system enabler*. These files work much like extensions—they reside in the System Folder and are loaded at startup.

Enablers are not required for Macintosh models released before the introduction of Version 7.1, but are required by all subsequent models. Enablers were first released in October 1992. The chart below lists the current system enabler version for each Mac model.

System Enablers are required for the Macintosh models indicated below with System 7.1 or later. Macintosh computers that require System Enablers will not operate properly with System 7.0.1 or earlier. This chart shows the appropriate System Enabler for the indicated Macintosh computer.

The following Macintosh computers do *not* need a System Enabler:

- Macintosh Plus, SE, SE/30, Classic and Classic II
- Macintosh LC and LC II
- Macintosh II, IIx, IIcx, IIsi, IIci and IIfx
- Macintosh Quadra 700, 900 and 950
- PowerBook 100, 140, 145 and 170
- Performa 200, 400, 405, 410 and 430

System Enabler Table

Macintosh	System Enabler	Version	Note
Macintosh Color Classic	401	1.0.5	
Macintosh LC III	003	1.0	
Macintosh LC 475	065	1.1	
Macintosh LC 520	403	1.0.2	
Macintosh LC 550	403	1.0.2	
Macintosh LC 575	065	1.1	
Macintosh TV	404	1.0	
Macintosh PowerBook 160	131	1.0.3	A
Macintosh PowerBook 165c	131	1.0.3	A
Macintosh PowerBook 180	131	1.0.3	A
Macintosh PowerBook 180c	131	1.0.3	A
Macintosh PowerBook Duo 210	PowerBook Duo Enabler	1.0	B
Macintosh PowerBook Duo 230	PowerBook Duo Enabler	1.0	B
Macintosh PowerBook Duo 250	PowerBook Duo Enabler	1.0	B
Macintosh PowerBook Duo 270c	PowerBook Duo Enabler	1.0	
Macintosh IIvi	001	1.0.1	
Macintosh IIvx	001	1.0.1	
Macintosh Centris 610	040	1.1	
Macintosh Centris 650	040	1.1	
Macintosh Centris 660AV	088	1.1	
Macintosh Quadra 605	065	1.1	
Macintosh Quadra 610	040	1.1	
Macintosh Quadra 650	040	1.1	
Macintosh Quadra 660AV	088	1.1	
Macintosh Quadra 800	040	1.1	
Macintosh Quadra 840AV	088	1.1	
Performa 600	304	1.0.1	
Performa 450, 460, 466, 467	308	1.0	
Performa 475, 476	364	1.1	
Performa 550	332	1.1	

Notes:

A   System Enabler 131 replaces System Enabler 111 and System Enabler 121.

B   Express Modem users should also install the Duo Battery Patch (Extension).

Changes:

1) PowerBook Duo Enabler
    - 1.0 First release. Replaces System Enabler 201.
2) System Enabler 001
    - 1.0 First release.
    - 1.0.1 Improved support for high speed serial communications and improved accuracy of the system clock. Also addressed a rare problem where floppies may not be ejected properly at shutdown.
3) System Enabler 003
    - 1.0 First release.
4) System Enabler 040
    - 1.0 First release.
    - 1.1 Added support for Quadra 610 and Quadra 650.
5) System Enabler 065
    - 1.0 First release for Macintosh LC 475 and Macintosh Quadra 605.
    - 1.1 Added support for Macintosh LC 575.
6) System Enabler 088
    - 1.0 First release.
    - 1.0.1 Required for System 7 Pro 7.1.1 support.
    - 1.1 Added support for Quadra 660AV.
7) System Enabler 131
    - 1.0 First release to support the PowerBook 180c. Replaced System Enabler 121 (supporting 165c) as well as System Enabler 111 (supporting 160 & 180).
    - 1.0.2 Corrected a problem involving the serial driver. If a user has the serial driver open, but is not transmitting, and then puts the PowerBook to sleep, any attempt to transmit upon waking, would cause the system to hang.
    - 1.0.3 Added support for the PowerBook 165.

8) System Enabler 401
   - 1.0.4 First release.
   - 1.0.5 Fixed a problem involving erratic mouse movement with Apple II mouse based applications running on the Apple IIe card installed in the PDS slot.

9) System Enabler 403
   - 1.0   First release.
   - 1.0.1 Manufacturing release only.

10) System Enabler 404
   - 1.0   First release.

Source: Apple Computer, Inc.

Appendix B: A Brief History of System 7

System enablers have been a major sore spot in the Apple system software distribution scheme. Their logistical implications are incredible. Requiring different enablers for different Macs might make theoretical sense, but a much simpler solution would be to have a single enabler that can be used on all Macs released once a specific system software version is released. Using the new Apple System Enabler Collection 1.0, network managers can administer a group of Macintosh computers, and install the needed enablers on the appropriate computers.

Building emergency startup floppies that can be quickly used to boot any Mac has become almost impossible. Already overwhelmed Mac users and system administrators now have another set of files (with crystal clear names like "system enabler Version 1.2.1") to keep track of, each with their own functions and version numbers. So now you must know the version number of your system software, the tune-up number and version (when applicable), and the system enabler number and version (when applicable). What could be easier?

Enablers are included with all models that require them, but at the time of this writing, Apple does not allow them to be freely distributed via online services, user groups or dealers. Because several specific enablers have already been updated themselves, there appears no clear way for a Mac user without either an AppleLink account or Apple Internet FTP to keep their enablers current.

Starting with System 7.5, Apple went to a universal enabler that included the entire current, updated suite of enablers. While this adds a little extra overhead to a system folder, it does away with the Russian Roulette that we have all been playing with enablers.

System Software/Hardware Compatibility Table

Use the following chart to determine which version of system software you should be using on your Macintosh computer.

Macintosh	7.5	7 Pro	7.1	7.0.1	7.0	6.0.8	6.0.7	6.0.5	6.0.4	6.0.3	6.0.2	3.2
128K	!	!	!	!	!	!	!	!	!	!	!	OK
512K	!	!	!	!	!	!	!	!	!	!	!	OK
512KE	!	!	!	!	!	!	!	!	!	!	!	OK
XL/Lisa	!	!	!	!	!	!	!	!	!	!	!	OK
Plus	!	!	OK	OK	OK	OK	OK	OK	OK	OK	OK	!
SE	OK	OK	OK	OK	OK	OK	OK	OK	OK	OK	OK	!
SE/30	OK	OK	OK	OK	OK	OK	OK	OK	OK	OK	OK	OK
Classic	OK	OK	OK	OK	OK	OK	OK	!	!	!	!	!
Classic II	OK	OK	OK	OK	!	!	!	!	!	!	!	!
Color Classic	OK	OK	OK	!	!	!	!	!	!	!	!	!
Portable	OK	OK	OK	OK	OK	OK	OK	OK	OK	!	!	!
II	OK	OK	OK	OK	OK	OK	OK	OK	OK	OK	OK	!
IIx	OK	OK	OK	OK	OK	OK	OK	OK	OK	OK	OK	!
IIcx	OK	OK	OK	OK	OK	OK	OK	OK	OK	OK	!	!
IIci	OK	OK	OK	OK	OK	OK	OK	OK	OK	!	!	!
IIfx	OK	OK	OK	OK	OK	OK	OK	OK	!	!	!	!
IIsi	OK	OK	OK	OK	OK	OK	OK	!	!	!	!	!
IIvi,IIvx	*	*	*	!	!	!	!	!	!	!	!	!
LC	OK	OK	OK	OK	OK	OK	OK	!	!	!	!	!
LC II	OK	OK	OK	OK	OK	OK	!	!	!	!	!	!
LC III	*	*	*	!	!	!	!	!	!	!	!	!
LC 475	*	*	*	!	!	!	!	!	!	!	!	!
LC 520	*	*	*	!	!	!	!	!	!	!	!	!
Macintosh TV					!	!	!	!	!	!	!	!
Centris 610	*	*	*	!	!	!	!	!	!	!	!	!
Centris 650	*	*	*	!	!	!	!	!	!	!	!	!
Centris 660AV	*	*	*	!	!	!	!	!	!	!	!	!
Quadra 605	*	*	*	!	!	!	!	!	!	!	!	!
Quadra 610	*	*	*	!	!	!	!	!	!	!	!	!
Quadra 650	*	*	*	!	!	!	!	!	!	!	!	!
Quadra 660AV	*	*	*	!	!	!	!	!	!	!	!	!
Quadra 700	OK	OK	OK	OK	!	!	!	!	!	!	!	!
Quadra 800	*	*	*	!	!	!	!	!	!	!	!	!

Macintosh	7.5	7 Pro	7.1	7.0.1	7.0	6.0.8	6.0.7	6.0.5	6.0.4	6.0.3	6.0.2	3.2
Quadra 840AV	*	*	*	!	!	!	!	!	!	!	!	!
Quadra 900,950	OK	OK	OK	OK	!	!	!	!	!	!	!	!
PowerBook 100	OK	OK	OK	OK	!	!	!	!	!	!	!	!
PB 140, 145	OK	OK	OK	OK	!	!	!	!	!	!	!	!
PB 145B, 170	OK	OK	OK	OK	!	!	!	!	!	!	!	!
PB 160, 180	*	*	*	!	!	!	!	!	!	!	!	!
PB Duo 210, 230	*	*	*	!	!	!	!	!	!	!	!	!
PB 250, 270c	*	*	*	!	!	!	!	!	!	!	!	!
PB 165c, 180c	*	*	*	!	!	!	!	!	!	!	!	!

Notes:

- !   Not supported.
- OK   Works with this version of system software.
- *   Works with this version of system software, but requires a Macintosh System Enabler (see below).
- PB   PowerBook.

System 3.2 is included because early Macintosh computers will not operate with System 6.

Source: Apple Computer, Inc.

Macintosh Memory Configurations

Use the following chart to determine how much memory you can install in your Macintosh computer.

System	RAM Soldered on Board	Number of SIMM Slots	Possible SIMM Sizes (mb)
128*	128K	0	N/A
512K/512KE*	512K	0	N/A
Plus*	0	4	256K, 1
SE*	0	4	256K, 1
SE/30*	0	8	256K, 1, 4
Classic*	1	2	256K, 1
Classic II*	2	2	1, 2, 4
Color Classic	4	2	1, 2, 4
LC*	2	2	1, 2, 4
LC II*	4	2	1, 2, 4
LC III	4	1	1, 2, 4, 8, 16, 32
LC 475	4	1	1, 2, 4, 8, 16, 32
LC 520	4	1	1, 2, 4, 8, 16, 32
LC 550	4	1	1, 2, 4, 8, 16, 32
LC 575	4	1	1, 2, 4, 8, 16, 32
Performa 200	2	2	1, 2, 4
Performa 400, 405, 410, 430	4	2	1, 2, 4
Performa 450	4	1	1, 2, 4, 8, 16, 32
Performa 460, 466, 467	4	1	1, 2, 4, 8, 16, 32
Performa 475, 476	4	1	1, 2, 4, 8, 16, 32
Performa 550	4	1	1,2,4, 8, 16, 32
Performa 660	4	4	256K, 1, 2, 4, 16
Macintosh TV	4	1	1, 4
II*	0	8	256K, 1, 4
IIx*	0	8	256K, 1, 4
IIcx*	0	8	256K, 1, 4
IIci*	0	8	256K, 512K, 1, 2, 4
IIfx*	0	8	1, 4
IIsi*	1	4	256K, 512K, 1, 2, 4
IIvi*	4	4	256K, 12, 4, 16
IIvx*	4	4	256K, 12, 4, 16

Appendix B: A Brief History of System 7

System	Physical RAM Configs(mb)	Speed (ns)	Notes
128*	128K	N/A	
512K/512KE*	512K	N/A	
Plus*	1, 2.5, 4	150	1, 4
SE*	1, 2, 2.5, 4	150	1, 4
SE/30*	1, 2, 4, 5, 8, 16, 17, 20, 32	120	4
Classic*	1, 2, 2.5, 4	150	1, 2
Classic II*	2, 4, 6, 10	100	3
Color Classic	4, 6, 8, 10	100	3
LC*	2, 4, 6, 10	100	3
LC II*	2, 6, 8, 10	100	3, 8
LC III	4, 5, 6, 8, 12, 20, 36	80	3, 11, 14
LC 475	4, 5, 6, 8, 12, 20, 36	80	3, 11, 15
LC 520	4, 5, 6, 8, 12, 20, 36	80	3, 11
LC 550	4, 5, 6, 8, 12, 20, 36	80	3, 11
LC 575	4, 5, 6, 8, 12, 20, 36	80	3, 11
Performa 200	2, 4, 6, 10	100	3
Performa 400, 405, 410, 430	2, 6, 8, 10	100	3, 8
Performa 450	4, 5, 6, 8, 12, 20, 36	80	3, 11, 14
Performa 460, 466, 467	4, 5, 6, 8, 12, 20, 36	80	3, 11
Performa 475, 476	4, 5, 6, 8, 12, 20, 36	80	3, 11, 15
Performa 550	4,5,6,8,12, 20, 36	80	3,1 1
Performa 660	4, 5, 8, 12, 20, 68	80	3, 10
Macintosh TV	5, 8	80	3, 11
II*	1, 2, 4, 5, 8, 17, 20	120	1, 4, 5, 6, 7
IIx*	1, 2, 4, 5, 8, 16, 17, 20, 32	20	1, 4, 5
IIcx*	1, 2, 4, 5, 8, 16, 17, 20, 32	120	4
IIci*	1, 2, 3, 4, 5, 6, 8, 9, 10, 12, 16, 17, 18, 20, 24, 32	80	3
IIfx*	4, 8, 16, 20, 32	80	3, 9
IIsi*	1, 2, 3, 5, 9, 17	100	3
IIvi*	4, 5, 8, 12, 20, 68	80	3, 10
IIvx*	4, 5, 8, 12, 20, 68	80	3, 10

System	RAM Soldered on Board	Number of SIMM Slots	Possible SIMM Sizes (mb)
Centris 610*	4	2	4, 8, 16, 32
Centris 650*	4 or 8	4	4, 8, 16, 32
Centris 660AV*	4	2	4, 8, 16, 32
Quadra 605	4	1	1, 2, 4, 8, 16, 32
Quadra 610	4	2	4, 8, 16, 32
Quadra 650	8	4	4, 8, 16, 32
Quadra 660AV	4	2	4, 8, 16, 32
Quadra 700*	4	4	1, 4
Quadra 900*	0	16	1, 4
Quadra 950	0	16	1, 4
Quadra 800	8	4	4, 8, 16, 32
Quadra 840AV	0	4	4, 8, 16, 32
Power Macintosh 6100/60	8	2	4, 8, 16, 32
Power Macintosh 7100/66	8	4	4, 8, 16, 32
Power Macintosh 8100/80	8	8	4, 8, 16, 32
Apple Workgroup Server 60	4	2	4, 8, 16, 32
Apple Workgroup Server 80	8	4	4, 8, 16, 32
Apple Workgroup Server 95	0	16	1, 4

System	Physical RAM Configs(mb)	Speed (ns)	Notes
Centris 610*	4, 8, 12, 20, 36, 68	80	3, 11, 13
Centris 650*	4, 8, 12, 16, 20, 24, 28, 32, 36, 40, 44, 48, 52, 56, 60, 64, 68, 72, 76, 80, 84, 88, 92, 100, 104, 108, 116, 132	80	3, 11, 12, 13
Centris 660AV*	4, 8, 12, 20, 36, 68	70	3, 11
Quadra 605	4, 5, 6, 8, 12, 20, 36	80	3, 11, 15
Quadra 610	4, 8, 12, 20, 36, 68	80	3, 11, 13
Quadra 650	4, 8, 12, 16, 20, 24, 28, 32, 36, 40, 44, 48, 52, 56, 60, 64, 68, 72, 76, 80, 84, 88, 92, 100, 104, 108, 116, 132	80	3, 11, 12, 13
Quadra 660AV	4, 8, 12, 20, 36, 68	70	3, 11
Quadra 700*	4, 8, 20	80	3
Quadra 900*	4, 8, 12, 16, 20, 24, 28, 32, 36, 40, 48, 52, 64	80	3
Quadra 950	4, 8, 12, 16, 20, 24, 28, 32, 36, 40, 48, 52, 64	80	3
Quadra 800	4, 8, 12, 16, 20, 24, 28, 32, 36, 40, 44, 48, 52, 56, 60, 64, 68, 72, 76, 80, 84, 88, 92, 100, 104, 108, 116, 132	60	3, 11, 12, 13
Quadra 840AV	8, 16, 32, 64, 128	60	3, 11
Power Macintosh 6100/60	8, 16, 24, 40, 72	80	3, 11, 16
Power Macintosh 7100/66	8, 16, 24, 32, 40, 48, 72, 80, 136	80	3, 11, 16
Power Macintosh 8100/80	8, 16, 24, 32, 40, 48, 56, 64, 72, 80, 96, 104, 120, 136, 168, 200, 216, 264	80	3, 11, 16
Apple Workgroup Server 60	4, 8, 12, 20, 36, 40, 44, 52, 68	80	3, 11
Apple Workgroup Server 80	8, 12, 16, 20, 24, 28, 32, 36, 40, 44, 48, 52, 56, 60, 64, 68, 72, 76, 80, 84, 88, 92, 96, 104, 108, 112, 120, 136	60	3, 11, 12
Apple Workgroup Server 95	4, 8, 12, 16, 20, 24, 28, 32, 48, 52, 64	80	3

Notes:

* Product no longer being produced by Apple.

1) Third-party 1mb SIMMs that have only two 1mbx4 memory chips soldered on the SIMM PCB are incompatible with these computers. These computers continue to support 1mb SIMMs with eight 1mbx1 DRAM chips soldered on the SIMM PCB. All Apple labeled upgrade kits provide compatible SIMMs for all CPU systems. These two 1mbx4 1mb SIMMs may be found, however, in Apple Finished Goods System bundles of the Macintosh SE/30, Macintosh IIci, IIsi, LC and Quadra 950.

2) The Macintosh Classic has 1mb of RAM soldered to the main logic board. Additional RAM can be added using an expansion card. Apple's Macintosh Classic 1mb Memory Expansion Card has 1mb of additional RAM and two SIMM connectors.

3) These systems have 32-bit-clean ROMs. Computers with 32-bit-clean ROMs can take advantage of more than 8mb of physical RAM under System 7.

4) The ROMs in these systems are not 32-bit-clean, but with the 32-Bit System Enabler under System 7.1 or MODE32 with versions of System 7 prior to 7.1, they can run in 32-bit mode and can take advantage of more than 8mb of physical RAM.

5) The Macintosh II and Macintosh IIx require special 4mb SIMMs. Be sure to specify your Macintosh model when ordering these SIMMs and ensure that the vendor is aware of the difference. The Macintosh II requires the Macintosh II FDHD Upgrade to use 4mb SIMMs.

6) To take advantage of more than 8mb of physical RAM, the Macintosh II must have a PMMU installed, so that the 32-Bit System Enabler (or MODE32 with versions of System 7 prior to 7.1) can expand the system's memory map.

7) The Macintosh II won't start up if you install 4mb SIMMs in bank A. You'll hear musical chimes at startup, indicating a hardware failure. Install 4mb SIMMs in bank B, and use 256K or 1mb SIMMs in bank A.

8) These systems can address a maximum of 10mb of RAM. When the SIMM slots are filled with 4mb SIMMs, the lower 2mb of DRAM on the logic board can't be addressed. For more information on configurations and limitations, search on "Macintosh LC II and RAM."

9) The Macintosh IIfx requires 64-pin SIMMs.

10) Only the eight chip 16mbx1 SIMMs have been tested on the Macintosh IIvi and Macintosh IIvx.

11) These systems use 32-bit wide, 72-pin SIMMs (fast-paged mode) not previously used in Macintosh computers.

12) The Centris 650 and Quadra 800 use "memory interleaving," which occurs when SIMM pairs are used (for example: two 8mb SIMMs). This allows the memory subsystem to perform certain operations faster. Basically, it allows the memory subsystem to write to the same memory address in different banks of memory before incrementing the address. Depending on how memory intensive the application, this can improve performance 5 to 10 percent.

13) The Centris/Quadra 610, Centris/Quadra 650 and Quadra 800 have flexible memory systems, meaning that any supported SIMM size can go into any SIMM socket in any order, and they can run with partially populated banks. They don't support 1mb, 2mb or 64mb 72-pin SIMMs.

14) The Macintosh LC III and Performa 450 are functionally similar and have the same RAM specifications.

15) The Macintosh LC 475, Performa 475/476 and Quadra 605 are functionally similar and have the same RAM specifications.

16) SIMMs must be installed in pairs of the same size and same speed.

General Notes:

- At this writing, Apple does not manufacture 16 or 32mb SIMMs. The use of these SIMMs requires a third-party product.

- The binary attachment (ex. utility/application/file/extension) mentioned is currently undergoing revision. It will be reposted as quickly as it can be revised.

Source: Apple Computer, Inc.

Glossary

Adobe Type Manger ATM is a PostScript Type 1 font rasterizer. It smoothes type on your screen and printer. Ships with System 7.5 as ATM GX.

Alias An alias is a duplicate icon for any file, folder or volume. The alias icon is linked to the original icon used to create it, and opening the alias opens the original file. Even if an alias is moved or renamed, the link to the original file remains.

AOCE The Apple Open Collaboration Environment is a set of messaging protocols for workgroup software.

AppleEvents A set of system software messages that can be passed between applications.

Apple Guide An active context sensitive help system that is part of system software.

AppleMail A messaging system that can add a standard message component or mailer to any Macintosh application.

Apple Menu folder A folder inside the System Folder used to hold all applications, documents, folders, volumes and desk accessories that you want to appear in the Apple Menu. Up to 50 files or aliases can be stored in this folder.

AppleScript A high level macro language that is part of system software.

At Ease A simplified Finder application sold with Performas and also separately. A workgroup edition also exists.

Balloon Help A context sensitive help system that explains elements of your screen that you point to with information in a balloon.

Catalog An object database in PowerTalk that lists services, users, passwords and addresses.

CISC Complex Instruction Set Computer. Microprocessors that use a larger instruction set for ease of programming. The 68k Macintosh series of computers uses a CISC chip.

Comments Short descriptive notes attached to any file, folder or volume. Comments are entered into the Get Info dialog box by choosing the Get Info command. To display comments in Finder windows, use the Views control panel to select the "Show Comments" option. You can search for a file by text contained in its comment using the Find command.

ColorSync A color matching system that is part of QuickDraw GX.

Control Panels folder A folder inside the System Folder which contains all control panel files used on a Macintosh. Control panels must reside in this folder so that they are properly loaded at startup, although you can create aliases of them and store those aliases in other locations.

Copeland The project name for a future version of system software due out in late 1995 or 1996.

Desktop (level) The top of the Mac's disk and file hierarchy, equivalent to the display seen at the Finder desktop. The desktop level includes all mounted hard disks and volumes, mounted floppy disks and any files or folders that have been placed on the Finder desktop.

Digital Signature A system for "signing" and authenticating an electronic file.

Drag and Drop A technique for direct manipulation of data in documents, files, and applications.

Edition files Edition files are normal Macintosh files that contain text or graphic elements saved by the Create Publisher command. Edition files are imported into other documents using the Subscribe To command.

Edition Manager A feature that allows software applications to exchange data using the Publish and Subscribe commands. This umbrella term covers both the specific commands associated with data exchange and the underlying technology that manages edition files after they have been created.

Extension A small program that modifies or extends the capabilities of the system software. This includes startup programs (INITS), printer drivers, network drivers and other types of files. All extensions must be kept in the Extensions folder inside the System Folder in order to load properly at startup.

Font scaler A small program that is automatically sent to PostScript printers when documents containing TrueType fonts are printed.

File Sharing A feature that allows any Macintosh running System 7 to make folders and volumes available to other network users, and to access shared data from other File Sharing Macs, or from AppleShare file servers.

Frame A boundary of a collection of parts in an OpenDoc document.

Gershwin The project name for the next version of system software due out in 1995.

Help balloons Small information windows that pop-up to provide simple explanations of commands, dialog box options and on-screen icons. Help balloons only appear when the Show Balloons command is selected, and can be removed by choosing the Hide Balloons command.

Hiding Removing the windows of an open application from the screen without quitting the application. This is done with the Hide commands found in the Applications Menu. To see windows after they are hidden, the Show commands are used.

Hierarchical view The ability of a Finder window to display a folder and the files inside that folder in a single window.

IAC An abbreviation for Inter-Application Communication. This is a set of protocols that make it possible for Macintosh applications to communicate and control each other. IAC is used by Apple Events, which are commands issued and understood by some software applications that have been specifically upgraded for System 7.

INITS See Extensions.

Information Card A user's electronic address in a catalog.

Ink A QuickDraw GX term for shape colors.

Installer A Macintosh application that installs software based on a script file. System software uses an installer.

Labels A set of user-defined categories that can be applied to any file, folder or volume as a means of classification. Labels are defined with a title and color using the Labels control panel, and applied by selecting an icon, or group of icons, and choosing the appropriate label from the Labels menu.

Launcher A control panel that puts a window with items on your Desktop. Click an item to launch or open it.

Localization The process of converting software from one language or culture to another.

Memory Allocation The amount of RAM assigned to an application when it is open.

Modern Memory Manager A rewritten set of memory access routines that are used for the Power Macintosh series of computers.

Movie A QuickTime video file.

Mozart The System 7.5 project name.

Multitasking Running more than one program at the same time. Both foreground and background applications are processing information concurrently.

OpenDoc A compound document architecture that lets you mix and match parts managed by small applications within a document.

OLE Microsoft's Object Linking and Embedding is a system of interapplication communication similar to OpenDoc.

Part A small piece of content in an OpenDoc document. When you click on a part, the part handler or part editor (a small application) that manages that data type is activated.

PlainTalk A speech recognition system that lets you manipulate a Power Macintosh or AV Macintosh computer.

Portable Digital Document A PDD file can be opened by any user who has QuickDraw GX installed on their computer, whether they have the creator application and fonts or not.

PostScript Adobe's graphics programming language for handling type, shapes, colors, and other elements of a page. A page description language. PostScript printers contains a rasterizer for printing PostScript files.

PowerTalk Apple's mail and messaging application for System 7.5 and 7 Pro. Works with PowerShare servers, or as a peer-to-peer system.

Printer Extension Small program extensions that modify the behavior of output devices. Part of QuickDraw GX.

Print Spooler A program for printing documents in the background. Spooled files are placed in a print queue.

Publish/Subscribe See the Edition Manager.

QuickDraw GX A set of advanced graphics routines that are part of the Macintosh Toolbox. GX draws fonts, shapes, anything you see in a window. It also renders documents to printers, and manages printers and output devices. QuickDraw GX is a page description language, as well.

QuickTime A video storage and playback system. Enabled by a system software extension of the same name.

RISC Reduced Instruction Set Computer. Microprocessors that use a smaller instruction set for improved performance. The Power Macintosh series of computers uses a RISC chip.

68k Macintosh The series of Macintosh computers based on the 680x0 Motorola microprocessors.

Safe Install The System 7.5 version of the Compatibility Checker. A program that checks your system for out-of-date or suspect files prior to an installation.

Script A program written in the language of AppleScript. An AppleScript macro.

Startup Items folder A folder inside the System Folder used to store applications, folders or documents that you want opened automatically at startup.

Stationery Pads Any document in System 7 can be designated a Stationery Pad, or template. Stationery Pads are automatically duplicated when opened, providing their content as the starting elements that make it easier to create other documents.

Style A QuickDraw GX term for line and text attributes.

System 7-Savvy Software applications that pass Apple's checklist for compatibility and compliance with System 7. This checklist includes support for MultiFinder, the Edition Manager, IAC, Balloon Help, File Sharing, 32-bit addressing, Stationery Pads and more.

Glossary

32-bit addressing A method of addressing memory which makes it possible for users of certain Macs to use up to 128 Mb of actual memory, and up to 4 gigabyte of virtual memory. Some software is incompatible with 32-bit addressing. The current standard is 24-bit addressing, which is still used on all other Macs, and with software that is not compatible with 32-bit addressing.

Transform An algorithm that is applied to a shape by QuickDraw GX to modify it.

TrueType An outline font format created by Apple for System 7. TrueType fonts are scaled on-screen to provide smooth high-resolution display, and print at the resolution of the output device on either PostScript or QuickDraw printers. TrueType GX are fonts that can use QuickDraw GX's advanced graphics routines.

View A way of looking at and organizing a Macintosh window. You can change views using the View menu, View control panel, or clicking on headings in a window.

Virtual memory A scheme which allows hard drive space to act like RAM, providing applications with additional memory. Because it uses hard drive space in place of SIMMs, virtual memory comes as close to providing something for nothing as anything you're likely to find on the Macintosh.

Unicode A standard character set containing all other character sets.

WorldScript Apple system software that lets you easily change programs from one language or culture to another, a process called localization.

Index

A

About the Finder 297-98
About This Macintosh
   command 45
   dialog box, managing memory
    with 294-97, 303-6
Access privileges.
   See File Sharing; Networks
Adobe Type Manager
   choosing correct version 328-29
   overview 325-27
   using 327
Alert dialog boxes 14.
   See also specific function
Alert sounds 30
AliasBOSS 575-76
Aliases 102-20
   aliases for 109
   command for making 44, 47-48
   creating 106
   deleting 110
   Find command and 134
   for folders or volumes 113-15, 119
   Get Info dialog box for 98
   launching applications via 177, 180
   managing 106-8, 439
   multiple 109
   on networks 498
   original files
     deleting 111
     finding 111-12
   moving 110-11
   overview 102-3
   replacing icons for 112
   for Stationery Pads 191
   third-party utilities for managing 575-78, 593, 601
   for Trash 119
   uses for 104-6, 115-19
Alias Stylist 575
AliasZoo 576-77
Always snap to grid option 59
Apple Disk First Aid 606-7, 623
AppleEvents
   AppleScript and 419, 421
   application support of 396, 399
   categories 396-98
   overview 395-96
   program linking and 400
   System 7 compatibility and 172
Apple Guide 50-51, 83-86, 175
Apple HD Setup 7.3 206, 608
AppleMail
   overview 534
   printing, formatting and handling 537
   using 535-36, 538-39
Apple Menu
   adding aliases to 439
   illustrated 44
   launching applications via 179, 180, 181
   managing contents of 147-50
   Options control panel 46
   third-party utilities for 570-72

Apple Open Collaboration Environment
　　capabilities　510-14
　　overview　509-10
　　PowerTalk.
　　See PowerTalk
Apple Remote Access　237-38
AppleScript
　　applications and　424, 435-36
　　architecture for　418-20
　　books and kit for　441
　　development of　413
　　overview　414-18
　　scripting components　420-24
　　scripts
　　　　embedding　431
　　　　formatting　433-35
　　　　modifying　431
　　　　navigating　431-32
　　　　preprogrammed　438-40
　　　　recording　425-26
　　　　running　429-31
　　　　saving, 427-29, 430
　　　　syntax　432
　　System 7.5 compatibility and　173-74
　　uses for　414
　　using with AppleEvents　395
　　using with Apple Guide　86
　　using with Finder　437
AppleShare
　　connecting to　489-92
　　File Sharing vs.　447
　　INIT for　506
　　System 7 compatibility and　173
AppleTalk
　　accessing　494-95
　　controlling privileges for　47
Applets　32, 414

AppleWindow control panel　54
Application Not Found dialog box　177, 178
Applications
　　AppleScript and　424, 431, 435-36
　　closing　80
　　compatibility with System 7.
　　　　See Compatibility with applications
　　controlling, menu for　44, 51-52
　　extensions. See Extensions
　　finding files by　134
　　hiding　267-70, 274, 631
　　launching. See Launching applications
　　linking. See Inter-Application Communication; OpenDoc
　　list of last-used　46
　　PostScript font problems and　320-22
　　sharing data between. See Apple Open Collaboration Environment; Publish/Subscribe
　　support of AppleEvents　396, 399
　　third-party utilities. See Third-party utilities
　　32-bit addressing and　291-92
　　using labels with　137
　　using on PowerBook. See PowerBook
　　using on Power Macintosh. See Power Macintosh
　　version numbers. See Version numbers
　　working with multiple. See Multitasking
　　See also specific application
Application script format　427
ASCII　350
Assistant toolbox　228
At Ease　552-54, 632
ATM. See Adobe Type Manager
Audio. See Sound
AutoRemounter　236-37
A/UX　256

B

Background applications, vs. foreground   258-60
Backup
   before upgrade to System 7   605-6
   Find command in   135
   introduction of utility for   631
   labels in   137
Balloon Help   50-51, 86-88, 147
Batteries, PowerBook   226, 229-30, 240
Behavior (in Text control panel)   29
Bento   407, 411
Big endian instructions   215
Bitmapped fonts   315
Blinking control   23-24
Borders, in edition files   382-83, 392
Bug fix   627
Bulletin boards   481-82

C

Cache, disk   283-84, 292-93
Cache Switch   223-26
Calculator   207
Carpetbag   581
Catalogs
   adding items to   526
   creating   527
   information cards, described   524, 529-30
   overview   511, 517, 524-25
   Personal Catalogs   525
   viewing items in   494, 528-29
   See also PowerTalk
Cdevs   56

CD-ROM   560, 561
Check boxes   14
Chooser
   described   21-22
   networks and   451, 489-92
   background printing and   262
   QuickDraw GX and   353
   See also Printers; Printing
CISC microprocessor   209-14
Clean Up All command   81
Clean Up By command   81
Clean Up command   44, 49-50
Clean Up Desktop command   80
Clean Up Selection command   82
Clean Up Window command   81
Clear command   33
Clicking   18, 28
Clients, network   446. *See also* Networks
Clip (Publish/Subscribe)   375, 377, 378
Clipboard   32-34
Clippings   31, 38
Clock, in menu bar   44, 50
Closing
   applications   80
   Finder windows   80, 439
   folders   80
Coach marks   83
Code Fragment Manager   218
Color
   controlling display of   26-27
   ensuring consistency in   362-64
   in labels. *See* Labels
   overview   361-62
   System 7.5 compatibility and   174
ColorSync   362-64
Commands
   blinking, controlled   23

choosing 18
menus. *See* Menus
oral 563-67
PowerBook Control Strip 239-41
third-party utilities for 602
types 16
See also specific command
Comments
 basic use 139-40
 finding files by 126-31, 139
 in Get Info dialog box 95
 listing files by 68-69
 loss of, in desktop rebuilding 140
Compatibility
 with applications
  limitations of 175-76
  overview 170-72
  requirements for System 7
   compatibility 146-47, 173-76
 between System versions 608-12
Compiled Script format 427, 428
Complete AppleScript 441
Compressing files, QuickTime and 557-60
Context-sensitive help 50-51, 86-88, 147.
 See also Help
Control panels 22-30
 folder for 151-52
 system software and 8
 unknown, automatic placement of 145
 See also specific panel or function
Control Strip 239-41
Cooperative multitasking 248
Copy command 32. *See also* Clipboard;
 Scrapbook
Core events 172, 397. *See also* AppleEvents
Create Publisher command 373-74
Currency, control panel for 31

Cursors 17. *See also* Mouse
Customizing installation 616-19. *See also*
 Installation and updating
Cut and paste 32-36

D

DAs. *See* Desk Accessories
Dates
 control panel for 23-24
 in Finder windows 62, 67
 finding files by 126-31
 in Publish/Subscribe 376, 380-81
 stamping files with 241-44
Deleting
 aliases 109, 111
 data 33
Desk accessories
 converting to System 7-compatible
  applications 199-200
 opening 200-201
 overview 198-199
 system software and 8
Desktop
 cleaning up 80
 clippings 31, 38
 overview 193
 pattern control panel 24-25, 631
 using
  basic procedures 194-96
  keyboard equivalents for 196-98
 See also Finder
Dialog boxes
 alias appearance in 107
 overview 13-14
 system software and 10

Dictionaries, application   435
DigiSign   539-42
Disk cache   283-84, 292-93
Diskettes. *See* Floppy disks
Disk First Aid   606-7, 623
Disks
   aliases for   114-15, 119
   CD-ROM, QuickTime and   560, 561
   Find command and   134
   floppy. *See* Floppy disks
   management, as system function   3
   storage, vs. memory   270-71
Display. *See* Screen
Document (OpenDoc component)   405. *See also* OpenDoc
Documents. *See* Files
Dot matrix printers. *See* Printers; Printing
Double-clicking   18, 28
Drag and Drop
   basic procedure   36-40
   QuickTime movies and   562
   scripts and   430-31
   System 7 compatibility and   148
Dragging   18, 28
Drawing. *See* QuickDraw
Drivers   6, 360-61, 501-4
Drop folders (File Sharing)   482-83, 440
Droplets   430

E

Easy Open   182-83, 550-52
Edition Manager. *See* Publish/Subscribe
Edit menu   44
Email
   AppleMail. *See* AppleMail

   built-in PowerTalk utility   510, 514, 531-32
   using other programs with PowerTalk   513
Empty Trash command. *See* Trash
Enablers
   drawbacks   640-41
   overview   637
   required for startup   9
   for specific Mac models   638-40
Encapsulation   415
Endian, big vs. little   215
Energy saving   206, 229-33
Erasing disks   20-21
Events. *See* AppleEvents
Extension Manager   587
Extensions
   control panels vs.   8
   managing   155-56
   overview   6-7, 152-53, 543
   for printing   6, 358-59
   problems with   154-55
   third-party utilities for managing   584-87
   unknown, automatic placement of   145
   See also specific extension

F

Fat binary applications   225
Fewer Choices button   130
File Assistant   241-44
FileMaker Pro   398, 399
File mapping   218
File menu   44
Files
   aliases for. *See* Aliases

compressing, QuickTime and 557-60
electronically signing 539-42
finding. *See* Find command; Find Original button
list of last-used 46
locked 95-96, 596
managing
   background copying 266-67
   deleting 111
   via Find command 133
   in Finder windows. *See* Finder windows, files in
   by label. *See* Labels
   moving 110-11
   naming 74, 94
   opening 74, 133
   as system function 3, 9
moving data between 34-35
overview 18-19
portable digital documents 312-13, 359-61
printing. *See* Printing
sending 531-32
sharing. *See* File Sharing
synchronizing, on different computers 231-34, 440
templates for. *See* Stationery Pads
translating between PC and Mac. *See* PC Exchange
See also Finder windows
File servers. *See* Networks
File Sharing
   accessing remote hard drive 499-500
   access privileges
      options for 475-79
      overview 474
      remote volumes and 496-97

   strategies for controlling 479-84
   basic procedure 448-9
   connections and software installation 450-51
   IAC and. *See* Inter-Application Communication
   icons for shared items 473
   limitations of 447-8
   monitoring 484-85
   options for 468-72
   overview and benefits 445-7
   passwords. *See* Passwords
   protecting files under 471, 477. *See also* Passwords
   restricting 473-75. *See also* File Sharing, access privileges
   running and stopping 454-57, 467-68
   setup for 452-53
   third-party utilities for 583-84
   unsharing 473-74
   user and group registration
      guest preferences 465-66
      managing groups 463-64
      managing users 460, 464
      overview and categories 457-59
      owner preferences 466-67
      user preferences 461-63
   using System 6 with 506-7
   See also Networks
File Sharing Toggle 584
Find command
   overview 121-22
   under System 7.5 48-49
   using
      basic use 122-23
      finding by file name 123-25
      finding by other criteria 125-30

new features under System 7.5   131-33
    tips and limitations   134-35
See also Find Original button
Finder
    AppleEvents for   397-98
    automating tasks of   437
    edition files in   384-85
    Get Info command. *See* Get Info command
    Help. *See* Help
    hiding   271-72
    navigating from keyboard   73-75
    overview   41-43
    switching to, accidentally   183, 271
    system software and   5
    third-party utilities for   589-94, 598-600
    Trash. *See* Trash
    windows. *See* Finder windows
    See also Desktop; MultiFinder
Finder windows
    arranging icons in   80-82
    closing   80, 439
    controlling appearance of. *See* View menu; Views control panel
    files in
        dragging between windows   75-76, 77
        viewing and moving   69-72, 73-78, 195-99
        working with multiple   76-78
    keeping track of   54-55
    managing multiple   76-78
    navigating from keyboard   73-75, 170-73
    overview   53-54
    scrolling   78

See also Windows
Find In Catalog command   528-29
Find Original button   98, 111-12, 439
Floppy disks   20-21
    for or from PCs. *See* PC Exchange
    See also Disks
Folders
    aliases for   113-14
    calculating size of   60-61, 439
    closing   80, 173
    finding   134
    opening   198
    overview   18-19
    size of   60-61
    for Stationery Pads   191-92
    synchronizing   442
    See also Files
Fonts
    Adobe Type Manager. *See* Adobe Type Manager
    books on typography   350
    in Finder windows   57-58
    folder for   156-57
    foreign languages and   346, 349, 350-51
    getting information about   330-32
    glyphs   345-47
    installing   330-36
    NFNT font resource   321, 323
    overview and evolution   307-8, 314-16
    PostScript. *See* PostScript fonts
    printer fonts   163, 335-36
    removing   336
    substituting   320
    System 7 compatibility and   173
    system software and   10
    text effects   346-47
    third-party utilities for managing   578-81

TrueType. *See* TrueType fonts
using both TrueType and
PostScript 342-45. *See also*
PostScript fonts; TrueType fonts
See also Text
Foreground applications, vs. background 258-60
Foreign languages
control panel for 29
fonts and 346, 349, 350-51
Formatting disks 20-21
Found Items dialog box 133
Fragmented memory, 296
Frames 404-5. *See also* OpenDoc

G

General Controls control panel 22-23
Get Info command
for aliases 98
dialog box, managing memory with 298-303
overview and options 93-96
for Trash 96-97
Glyphs 345-47
Graphical user interface
icons 11-12
menus 15-16
mouse operations 17-18
overview 11
windows 12-15
Graphics
sharing between files. *See* Publish/Subscribe
working with. *See* QuickDraw
Graphing Calculator 207-8

Grid options, for icons 59
Guests, on networks. *See* File Sharing; Networks

H

HAM 571
Hard disks
battery conservation and 233
freeing space via Trash 92
info about, in header 61-62
mounting PowerBook as external drive 236
preparing, for upgrade to System 7 605-6
remote access of 499-500
virtual memory and 274-75
See also Disks
Hardware System Updates 630, 632-33
Help
additional, provided by applications 88-90
context-sensitive (Balloon Help) 50-51, 86-88, 147
for Finder 88-90
menu for 44, 50-51
overview 82-83
searching, with Apple Guide 83-86
System 7 compatibility and 173
third-party utilities for 593
Helping Hand 164-65
Hiding
applications 267-70, 274, 631
Finder 53, 245
windows 52
Hierarchy, file 69-72

Index

I

IAC. *See* Inter-Application Communication
IBM-compatible computers. *See* PCs
Icons
   appearance of 59-60
   arranging 80-82
   described 11-12
   in Get Info dialog box 94, 112
   replacing, for aliases 114
In box folders (File Sharing) 480
Information cards 524-25. *See also* Catalogs
Inheritance 415
Init Loader 587
Init Picker 585
INITs 6. *See also* Extensions
Ink jet printers. *See* Printers; Printing
Installation and updating
   hardware requirements 604
   System 6.x to System 7
      checking compatibility 608-12
      configuring System Folder 620-22
      deleting existing system 612-13
      hard disk preparation 605-8
      installing PowerTalk and QuickDraw GX 619-20
      insufficiency of Installer 605
      running and customizing Installer 613-19
   System 7 updates 629, 636, 623
Installer
   adding files to System Folder via 163
   insufficiency of, for upgrade to System 7 605
   See also Installation and updating
Instruction sets 212

Inter-Application Communication
   limitations 502
   overview 367, 394-95
   running 502-3
   setup 500-501
   See also AppleEvents
Italics, alias names in 107

K

Keyboard
   control panel for 27-28
   keystroke combinations. *See specific command or function*
   navigating Finder from 73-75
Key Chain 519. *See also* PowerTalk

L

Labels
   configuring 136-37, 138
   finding files by 126-30
   listing files by 66-67
   overview 44, 49, 136
   uses for 137-38
LaserWriter. *See* Printers; Printing
Launching applications
   aliases in 104, 115-16
   by double-clicking 176
   with Launcher control panel 183-85, 631
   with Macintosh Easy Open translator 182-83, 552-54
   memory use and 275-76
   multiple applications 256-57

668 The System 7.5 Book

options, under System 7.5   175-78
tips on   180-82
as system function   9
LineLayout Manager   312
Links
   between aliases. *See* Aliases
   between applications. *See* Inter-Application Communication; OpenDoc
   for Publish/Subscribe. *See* Publish/Subscribe
Little endian instructions   215
Localization   312, 350-51
Locked files   95-96, 126

M

Macintosh
   enablers for specific models   637-41
   memory configurations for specific models   644-50
   system compatibility for specific models   642-43
Macintosh Easy Open   182-83, 550-52
Macintosh Telephony Architecture   563
Macros. *See* AppleScript; PlainTalk
MacTCP   488
Mail. *See* Email
Mailbox   516, 531-32. *See also* PowerTalk
Mailer. *See* AppleMail
Make Alias command. *See* Aliases
Marquee   76-77
MasterJuggler   579-80
Math coprocessors   223
May Not Work with 7.5 folder   145
Memory
   amounts recommended   288-89, 293-94, 303
   configurations, for specific Mac models   644-50
   conserving, by data compression   557-58
   control panel for   205, 281-82, 292-94
   disk cache   283-84, 292-93
   fragmented   296
   getting information about   45, 96
   managing
      with About This Macintosh dialog box   294-97, 303-6
      with Get Info dialog box   298-303, 304-5
      Modern Memory Manager   205, 292
   multitasking and   252, 275-77
   overview   279-81
   requirements for updates   604, 619
   ROM   5, 264
   shortage, alerts of   296
   32-bit addressing   289-92, 294, 545
   virtual. *See* Virtual memory
Memos, Sticky   31, 38-39
Menu Bar Clock   44, 50
MenuChoice   572
MenuExtend   572
Menus
   overview   14, 15-16
   third-party utilities for   570-72, 601
   See also specific menu or function
Microprocessors
   basic functions and properties   210-13
   CISC   209-14
   math coprocessors   223
   PowerPC   214-18. *See also* Power Macintosh
   RISC. *See* RISC microprocessor

Index

Mixed Mode Manager 221-22
MODE 32 545
Modern Memory Manager 205, 292
Monitors control panel 25-26
More Choices button 123, 125-30
Mouse
   basic operations 17-18
   control panel for 26-27
   Mouse Tracks 27
Mount Alias 577
Movies. *See* QuickTime
MultiFinder 199, 248, 251-53
Multitasking
   background file copying 266-67
   background printing 261-66
   background processing 260-61
   basic use 256-58
   benefits of 249-51
   foreground vs. background applications 258-60
   hiding applications 267-71
   hiding Finder 271-72
   memory and 252, 275-77
   with MultiFinder 199, 248, 251-53
   new features, under System 7.5 253-56
   OpenDoc and 402-403
   overview and types 247-49
   tips for using 272-74
   System 7 compatibility and 172

N

Native code. *See* Power Macintosh, emulation vs. native applications
Network drivers 6. *See also* Chooser
Networks

accessing volumes
   access privileges and 496-97.
   See also File Sharing,
   access privileges
   aliases in 498
   connecting to servers 489-92, 494-96
   overview 487-88
   remote hard disks 499-500
   specific volumes 492-93
aliases and 106, 119
clients vs. servers 446
disconnecting from remote volumes 499
edition files on 388-89
IAC and. *See* Inter-Application Communication
list of last-used servers 46
reasons for using 443-44
with System 6 Macs 503-7
system software and 10
See also Apple Open Collaboration Environment; File Sharing
NFNT font resource 321, 323
Nok Nok 583
Note Pad 39-40
NowMenus 570, 571-72
Numbers, control panel for 29-30

O

Object Linking and Embedding (OLE) 404, 408-10
Object Model 419
On Startup 586
OpenDoc
   documents and parts 405-6

frames   406-7
as multitasking example   255
need for   401-2
OLE vs.   408-10
overview and benefits   368, 402-4
Opening
application dictionaries   435
applications. *See* Launching applications
desk accessories   200-201
Desktop management while   196-98
files   74, 133
folders   198
scripts   431
Open Publisher button   385
Open Script command   431
Open Scripting Architecture (OSA)   418-20
Operating system. *See* System software
Option boxes   14
Out box folders (File Sharing)   479
Outline fonts. *See* PostScript fonts; TrueType fonts
Owner, on networks. *See* File Sharing; Networks

P

Palettes   14
Parts   405-8. *See also* OpenDoc
Passwords
careful selection of   467
for File Sharing   453, 461-62, 463
PowerShare and   512
Paste command   32. *See also* Clipboard; Scrapbook
Patterns, desktop   25-26
PC Exchange
overview   545-46
setup   547-48
using   546, 549-50
PCs
handling disks from   205. *See also* Power Macintosh; PowerPC microprocessor
utility for sharing files with. *See* PC Exchange
PDDs   312-13, 352, 359-61
Pentium microprocessor   213, 214, 216. *See also* CISC microprocessor
Pierce Print Tools   588
Pipelining   210-11
PlainTalk   563-67
Pointing   17
PopupFolder   593
Pop-up menus   14, 78-80
Portable digital documents   312-13, 352, 359-61
PostScript fonts
development of   309, 310
drawbacks   319-24
overview   316-18
printer fonts, under System 7   335-36
printing and   324-25
TrueType vs.   339-40, 342-45
using with non-PostScript printers. *See* Adobe Type Manager
using with QuickDraw GX   318-19
See also Fonts
PowerBook
automatic remounting   236-37
battery conservation   226, 229-33
books on using   228-29
connections and remounting   236-37
Control Strip   229-31
display management   234-35

Index

features 226-29
file synchronization 231-34
overview 203-4, 226
remote access 237-38
Setup control panel 227
Power Macintosh
    emulation vs. native applications
        improving application performance 223-24
        Mixed Mode Manager 221-22
        overview 218-21
    interface 204-6
    overview 202-3
    PowerPC chip 214-18
    QuickTime and 562
    RISC vs. CISC chips 209-14
    software written for 204, 224-26
PowerMenus 572
PowerOff control panel 206-7
PowerOpen 215
PowerPC microprocessor 214-18.
    See also RISC microprocessors
PowerShare 520.
    See also PowerTalk
PowerTalk
    accessing file servers with 494-96
    activating 521
    adding services and addresses 523-24
    AppleMail. *See* AppleMail
    benefits 515
    built-in mail utility 531-33
    Catalogs. *See* Catalogs
    components 515-19
    electronically signing files 539-42
    information cards 529-30
    installation 520
    overview 510

remote connections 532-33
setup 520-23
System 7 upgrade and 619-20
System 7.5 compatibility and 175
See also Apple Open Collaboration Environment
Preemptive multitasking 248
Preferences folder 157-58
Printer fonts 163, 316-18, 335-36.
    See also PostScript fonts
Printers
    drivers 6, 358-59, 501-4
    updating drivers for networks 503-6
    using TrueType fonts with 341-42
    See also Chooser
Printing
    background 261-66, 352
    with Drag and Drop 38
    from Find command 133
    options for 352-53
    overview 352-53
    PostScript fonts and 324-25
    QuickDraw GX and 264-66, 351-52, 356
    spooling. *See* Spooling, print
    system software and 10
    third-party utilities for managing 587-89
    See also Fonts
PrintLogger 588-89
PrintMonitor 262-64
Processor cycling 232
Program linking. *See* Inter-Application Communication
Protect System Folder option 162
Publish/Subscribe
    borders 382-83
    commands, overview 373-83

edition aliases   393
files
   copying to documents   374-75
   creating   373-74
   on networks   388-89
   unavailable   387-88
   using in Finder   384-85
limitations in editing subscribers   383-84
links, maintaining, breaking, and
   recreating   385-86
nested editions   390, 391
operation explained   370-72
overview and benefits   367, 368-69
publishing options   375-79
republishing editions   389-90
saving publisher documents   392
subscribe options   379-82
Pull-down menus   13-14
Put Away command   499

Q

Queue, print. See Spooling, print
QuickDraw
   AppleEvents for   397
   GX
      application compatibility and   174
      features of   311-13
      graphics primitives under   313-14
      installation and requirements   313
      portable digital documents
         312-13, 352, 359-61
      printing under   264-66, 351-52,
         356
      System 7 upgrade and   619-20
   overview and evolution   308-9

System 7.5 compatibility and   174-75
QuickTime
   data compression and   557-60
   movie playing applications   561
   new features, under version 2.0   560-62
   overview   555-56
   using   556-57, 560-61
Quitting, forcing   272, 273

R

Radio button   14
Read Me files   38
Recent Applications and Recent Documents
   commands   44, 46
   submenus   179, 180, 181
Recent Servers command   44, 46
Record button   421, 425
Registered users. See File Sharing; Networks
Restarting, multitasking and   273
RISC microprocessor
   CISC chips vs.   209-14
   described   3
   PowerPC chip   214-18
ROM (Read-Only Memory)   5, 290
Run-only scripts   429

S

Safe Install   608-12, 623
Saving
   documents
      Desktop management while
         196-98
      multitasking and   272

Index

Publisher documents   392, 393
    scripts   427-29, 430
Scrapbook   34-36
Screen
    control panel for   26-27
    desktop pattern control   25-26
    display as system function   10
    PowerBook   234-35
Screen fonts   316-18.
    See also PostScript fonts
Script (in Text control panel)   29
Scripts   417. *See also* AppleScript
SCSI disk mode   236
Searching for files. *See* Find command
Security
    electronically signing files   539-42
    labels in   138, 139
    passwords. *See* Passwords
Servers, network   446. *See also* Networks
7.0 PLUS Utilities   594-97
7 for Seven   593
Shared Library Manager   218
Sharing command   45, 47
Shortcuts command   89-90
Show All command   269-70
Show Balloons command. *See* Balloon Help
Show Borders command   380-81
Show date option   62
Show label option   62
ShowShare   583
Shut Down, multitasking and   273, 274
Signer files   539-42
SimpleText   30, 37-38, 180
Sizing windows   80
Sleep mode   231, 232-33, 235
Snap (Publish/Subscribe)   376, 377, 378
Software

applications. *See* Applications
    system. *See* System software
SoftWindows   219, 550
Sound
    alert sounds   30
    control panel for   28-29
    in QuickTime movies   559, 561, 562
    third-party utilities for   597, 602
    voice recognition   563-67
Special menu   44
Speech recognition   563-67
SpeedyFinder   591-92
Spooling, print
    background printing and   262-64
    PowerBook and   227
    QuickDraw GX and   356-58
    See also Printing
Staggered grid option   59
Standard Apple Numeric Environment
    (SANE)   223
Startup
    folder for   158-59
    launching applications at   179
    system software and   9
    See also Extensions
Startup Manager   585-86
Stationery Pads
    creating   186-90
    overview   96, 186
    System 7 compatibility and   173
    using   178, 191-93
Sticky Memos   31, 38-39
Storage, memory vs.   270-71
Straight grid option   59
Subscribe. *See* Publish & Subscribe
Suitcase II   579
Suites (AppleEvents)   396-98

SuperBoomerang   592
System File
   accessing and modifying   160–61
   immunity to File command   134
   overview   159
   system software and   5
System Folder
   adding files to
      procedures   163–65
      reasons for   161–63
   Apple Menu folder   147–50
   Control Panels folder   151–52
   deleting files from   166
   Extensions folder   152–56
   files stored automatically by
      applications   162, 163–64
   Fonts folder   156–57
   locking   162
   overview   143–45
   Preferences folder   157–58
   Startup folder   158–59
   under System 7.5   145–46
   third-party utilities for managing   581–83
   See also System File; System software
System Picker   582–83
System 7
   choosing appropriate version   634–36
   compatibility of System 7.5 with
      applications. *See* Compatibility with
      applications
   enablers   637–41
   installation and updating. *See* Installation
      and updating
   upgrading   629, 636, 623
   version compatibility with
      hardware   642–43
   version overview

   Hardware System Update 1.0   630
   Hardware System Update 3.0
      632–33
   7.0   626
   7.0.1   626
   7.0.1P   631–32
   7.1   628–30
   7.1P   631–32
   7.5   633
   System 7 Pro   632
   Tune-Up   627
   See also System software
System 7 Pack   589–91
System 6
   networks and   503–7
   upgrading to System 7. *See* Installation
      and updating
System software
   basic functions   9–11
   components of   4–8
   overview   2–4
   See also System 7
System Switcher   582

T

Tables, AppleEvents for   397
Tao of AppleScript   441
TCP/IP protocol   488
Text
   AppleEvents for   397
   control panel for   29
   effects, with QuickDraw GX   351–52
   fonts. *See* Fonts
   saving scripts as   427, 428–29
   sharing between files. *See* Publish/

Subscribe
  standards for 350–51
  See also Labels
Third-party utilities
  for alias management 575–78
  for Apple Menu 570–72
  for File Sharing 583–84
  for Finder 589–94, 598–600
  for font management 578–81
  for managing extensions 584–87
  packages 593–602
  for print management 587–89
  for system software management 581–83
  for Trash 573–75
32-bit addressing 289–92, 294, 545
Thread Manager 254
Time
  control panel for 23–24
  menu bar clock 44, 50
  in Publish/Subscribe 375, 380–81
  stamping files with 241–44
Title bar
  described 12–13
  pop-up menu from 78–80
Transferring data
  cut and paste 32–36
  Drag and Drop. *See* Drag and Drop
  overview 30–32
  See also File Sharing; Networks
Trash
  alias for 119
  emptying 44, 50, 91, 93
  Get Info dialog box for 96–97
  overview 90
  positioning 92–93
  retrieving items from 92
  third-party utilities for 573–75
  warnings concerning 91–92, 97
TrashAlias 578
Trash Chute 575
TrashMan 574
TrashMaster 573
TrashPicker 574
TrueType fonts
  development of 310
  overview 336–37
  PostScript vs. 339–40, 342–45
  technology behind 340
  TrueType GX 337–39
  use, with various printers 341–42
  See also Fonts
Tune-Up 627, 634

U

Unicode 346, 350–51
UNIX 215, 256
Upgrades. *See* Installation and updating
Useful Scripts folder 438–40
Users, network. *See* File Sharing; Networks

V

Version numbers
  finding files by 126–30
  in Get Info dialog box 95
  listing files by 68
  for System 7. *See* System 7
Video Monitor 1.0.1 206
View menu
  overview 44, 64

viewing by comment 68-69
viewing by date 67
viewing by icon 64-65
viewing by kind 65-66
viewing by label 66-67
viewing by size 65
viewing by version 68
See also Views control panel
Views, hierarchical 69-72
Views control panel
   calculating folder sizes 60-61
   command and column display 62-64
   disk info in header 61-62
   font control 57-58
   icon control 59-60
   overview 55-57
   See also View menu
Virtual memory
   determining right amount 288-89
   disabling 289
   enabling 286-87
   overview 284-86
   performance and 288, 294
   32-bit addressing and 290-92
Voice recognition 563-67
Volumes. *See* Disks

W

Windows
   Finder windows. *See* Finder windows
   hiding 52
   overview and types 12-15
   recognizing active 258-59
   sizing 80
   switching between 259-60

   See also specific window or function
WindowShade control panel 54-55
Workgroup software. *See* Apple Open Collaboration Environment
WorldScript 350, 628

Z

ZMakeAlias 577
Zooming windows 80

Colophon

The System 7.5 Book was produced using PageMaker 5.0 on a Macintosh Quadra 700 computer with 20mb of RAM and a Pentium PC-compatible with 32mb of RAM. The video system used by the PC is a Cornerstone Dual-Page 120 grayscale monitor driven by an Image-Excel controller. The body copy is set in Garamond and headlines are Kabel and Bernhard Fashion, all from the Digital Typeface Corporation collection.

Pages were proofed on a Hewlett Packard LaserJet 4M Plus. Final output was produced on film using a Linotronic 330.

MACINTOSH

MAC BOOKS—MAGIC & MASTERY

Explore Cyberspace!
The Mac Internet Tour Guide
$27.95
290 pages, illustrated
ISBN: 1-56604-062-0

Mac users can now navigate the Internet the easy way: by pointing and clicking, dragging and dropping. In easy-to-read, entertaining prose, Internet expert Michael Fraase leads you through installing and using the software enclosed in the book to send and receive email, transfer files, search the Internet's vast resources and more! BONUS: Free trial access and two free electronic updates.

Handy 3-in-1 Guide!
Mac, Word & Excel Desktop Companion, Second Edition
$24.95
308 pages, illustrated
ISBN: 1-56604-130-9

Why clutter your desk with three guides? This money saver gets you up and running with Apple's System 7.1 software and the latest versions of Microsoft Word and Excel for the Mac. A complete overview, examples of each program's commands, tools and features and step-by-step tutorials guide you easily along the learning curve for maximum Macintosh productivity!

Software $avings!
The Mac Shareware 500, Second Edition
$34.95
504 pages, illustrated
ISBN: 1-56604-076-0

This book is a fantastic reference for any designer or desktop publisher interested in saving money by using the vast resources shareware offers. Literally thousands of fonts, graphics, clip-art files and utilities are available for downloading via dozens of online services. To get you started, this book includes two disks of shareware.

Join 1,000,000 Friends Online!

The Official America Online Membership Kit & Tour Guide, Second Edition
$27.95
406 pages, illustrated
ISBN: 1-56604-127-9
This book takes Mac users on a lively romp through the friendly AOL cyberscape. Bestselling author Tom Lichty, a.k.a. MajorTom, shows you how to make friends, find your way around, and save time and money online. Complete with software to get you started. BONUS: 20 free hours of online time for new and current members and a free month's membership.

Cruise the World Wide Web!

The Mosaic Quick Tour for Mac
$12.00
208 pages, illustrated
ISBN: 1-56604-195-3
The Mosaic Quick Tour introduces the how-to's of hypertext travel in a simple, picturesque guide, allowing you to view linked text, audio and video resources thousands of miles apart. You can use Mosaic to do all of your information hunting and gathering, including Gopher searches, newsgroup reading and file transfers through FTP.

Become a Voodoo Guru!

Voodoo Mac, Second Edition
$24.95
400 pages, illustrated
ISBN: 1-56604-177-5
Whether you're a power user looking for new shortcuts or a beginner trying to make sense of it all, *Voodoo Mac* has something for everyone! Computer veteran Kay Nelson has compiled hundreds of invaluable tips, tricks, hints and shortcuts that simplify your Macintosh tasks and save time, including disk and drive magic, font and printing tips, alias alchemy and more!

DESIGN AND CONQUER!

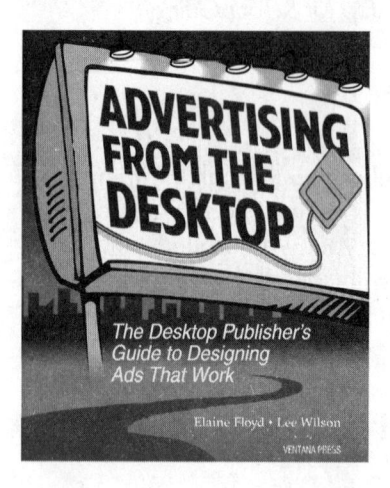

Advertising From the Desktop
$24.95
427 pages, illustrated
ISBN: 1-56604-064-7
Advertising From the Desktop offers unmatched design advice and helpful how-to instructions for creating persuasive ads. With tips on how to choose fonts, select illustrations, apply special effects and more, this book is an idea-packed resource for improving the looks and effects of your ads.

The Presentation Design Book, Second Edition
$24.95
320 pages, illustrated
ISBN: 1-56604-014-0
The Presentation Design Book is filled with thoughtful advice and instructive examples for creating business presentation visuals, including charts, overheads, type, etc., that help you communicate and persuade. The *Second Edition* adds advice on the use of multimedia. For use with any software or hardware.

The Gray Book, Second Edition
$24.95
262 pages, illustrated
ISBN: 1-56604-073-6
This "idea gallery" for desktop publishers offers a lavish variety of the most interesting black, white and gray graphic effects that can be achieved with laser printers, scanners and high-resolution output devices. The *Second Edition* features new illustrations, synopses and steps, added tips and an updated appendix.

Looking Good in Print, Third Edition
$24.95
412 pages, illustrated
ISBN: 1-56604-047-7
For use with any software or hardware, this desktop design bible has become the standard among novice and experienced desktop publishers alike. With over 200,000 copies in print, *Looking Good in Print* is even better, with new sections on photography and scanning.

Newsletters From the Desktop, Second Edition
$24.95
306 pages, illustrated
ISBN: 1-56604-133-3
Now the millions of desktop publishers who produce newsletters can learn how to improve the design of their publications. Filled with helpful design tips and illustrations, as well as hands-on tips for building a great looking publication. Includes an all-new color gallery of professionally designed newsletters, offering publishers at all levels a wealth of ideas and inspiration.

Can't wait? Call toll-free:
800/743-5369 (U.S. only)

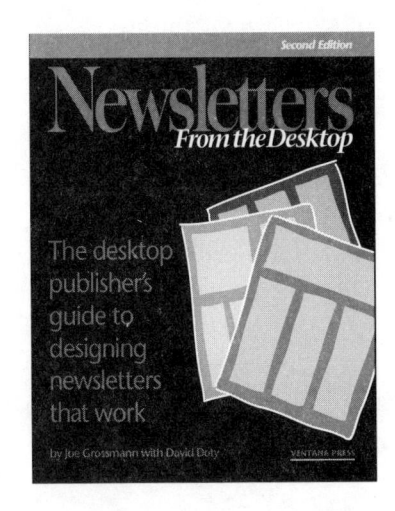

INTERNET. HERE. NOW.

1-800-209-3342

Ventana Media is proud to announce the **INTERNET MEMBERSHIP KIT**, *your easy-access on-ramp to the information superhighway. Both* **MACINTOSH** *and* **WINDOWS** *versions put you in control of a sleek* **GRAPHICAL INTERFACE**, *allowing you to skip frustrating command-line gibberish and take advantage of the Internet's vast information resources with point-and-click convenience. The Kit includes two national bestsellers,* The Internet Tour Guide *and* The Internet Yellow Pages, *plus a one-month* **FREE MEMBERSHIP** *with CERFnet and* **SIX FREE HOURS** *online. Also included are step-by-step instructions for using* **MOSAIC**, *one of the most powerful tools available to information surfers, as well as all the software you'll need to get up and running in no time! Suggested retail price $69.95.*

To order any Ventana Press title, fill out this order form and mail it to us with payment for quick shipment.

	Quantity	Price	Total
The Mac Internet Tour Guide	_____ x	$27.95 =	$ _____
Mac, Word & Excel Desktop Companion, 2nd Edition	_____ x	$24.95 =	$ _____
The Mac Shareware 500, 2nd Edition	_____ x	$34.95 =	$ _____
The Official America Online Membership Kit & Tour Guide for Macintosh, 2nd Edition	_____ x	$27.95 =	$ _____
The Mosaic Quick Tour for Mac	_____ x	$12.00 =	$ _____
Voodoo Mac, 2nd Edition	_____ x	$24.95 =	$ _____
Advertising From the Desktop	_____ x	$24.95 =	$ _____
The Presentation Design Book, 2nd Edition	_____ x	$24.95 =	$ _____
The Gray Book, 2nd Edition	_____ x	$24.95 =	$ _____
Looking Good in Print, 3rd Edition	_____ x	$24.95 =	$ _____
Newsletters From the Desktop, 2nd Edition	_____ x	$24.95 =	$ _____
Internet Membership Kit, Macintosh Version	_____ x	$69.95 =	$ _____
Internet Membership Kit, Windows Version	_____ x	$69.95 =	$ _____
		Subtotal =	$ _____

SHIPPING:
For all regular orders, please add $4.50/first book, $1.35/each additional.   = $ _____
For Internet Membership Kit orders, add $6.50/first kit, $2.00/each additional.   = $ _____
For "two-day air," add $8.25/first book, $2.25/each additional.   = $ _____
For "two-day air" on the IMK, add $10.50/first kit, $4.00/each additional.   = $ _____
For orders to Canada, add $6.50/book.   = $ _____
For orders sent C.O.D., add $4.50 to your shipping rate.   = $ _____
North Carolina residents must add 6% sales tax.   = $ _____
TOTAL = $ _____

Name _____ Company _____

Address (No PO Box) _____

City _____ State _____ Zip _____

Daytime Telephone _____

___ Payment enclosed ___ VISA ___ MC # _____ Exp. Date _____

Signature _____

Mail or fax to: Ventana Press, PO Box 2468, Chapel Hill, NC 27515 ☎ 919/942-0220 Fax 919/942-1140

CAN'T WAIT? CALL OR FAX TOLL-FREE
☎ 800/743-5369 FAX 800/877-7955 (U.S. only)

Notes

Notes

Notes

Notes

Notes

Notes

Notes

Notes